The Pennsylvania Magazine of History and Biography

by Historical Society of Pennsylvania

CONTENTS OF VOLUME XVII.

iv			*Contents of Volume XVII.*

No. 65.

PENNSYLVANIA

MAGAZINE

OF

HISTORY AND BIOGRAPHY.

PUBLISHED QUARTERLY.

No. 1 OF VOL. XVII.

April, 1893.

"I entertain an high idea of the utility of periodical publications: insomuch
that I could heartily desire copies of the Museum and Magazines, as well as
common Gazettes, might be spread through every city, town, and village in
America. I consider such easy vehicles of knowledge more happily calculated
than any other to preserve the liberty, stimulate the industry, and meliorate the
morals of an enlightened and free people."—*Washington to Mathew Carey*,
June 25, 1788.

PUBLISHED BY
THE HISTORICAL SOCIETY OF PENNSYLVANIA,
FOR SUBSCRIBERS.
PHILADELPHIA:
1893.

BOUND VOLUMES OF THE MAGAZINE.

Copies of all the volumes of this MAGAZINE can be obtained at the Hall of the Historical Society, bound by Messrs. Pawson and Nicholson, in the very best manner, in the style known as Roxburgh, half cloth, uncut edges, gilt top, for $3.75 each and the postage. They will be furnished to subscribers in exchange for unbound numbers, in good condition, on the receipt of 75 cents per volume and the postage.

Address F. D. STONE, 1300 Locust St.

PRINTED BY J. B. LIPPINCOTT COMPANY.

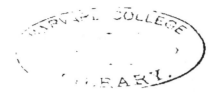

THE

PENNSYLVANIA MAGAZINE

OF

HISTORY AND BIOGRAPHY.

| Vol. XVII. | 1893. | No. 1. |

PENNSYLVANIA POETS OF THE PROVINCIAL PERIOD.

BY FRANCIS HOWARD WILLIAMS. READ BEFORE THE HISTORICAL SOCIETY OF PENNSYLVANIA, NOVEMBER 14, 1892.

In inviting attention to the Pennsylvania poets of the Provincial period, I am conscious of the danger involved in the title. That I incur the risk of being reminded that there were no poets in the Provincial period, I am well aware.

But I am fortified to endure this criticism when I reflect that there are those who go so far as strenuously to deny the existence of any American literature, and who, even at this day, brush aside the achievements in American letters as unworthy the consideration of students of universal art in its several manifestations. Extremists are unsafe guides, and for a mind not judicially constituted I know of no course more likely to lead to a just estimate than to study extreme assertions on both sides, and then, disregarding both, to adopt a point of view midway between the two.

Let us, then, assume that there is an American literature

to-day, and that there was a germ which properly may be termed national, and which flourished on Pennsylvania soil as early as the first decade of the eighteenth century. If I presume to speak of this germ as a literature, it will be understood that certain allowances must be made for the necessary limitations of language; and if I venture to apply so august a name as poetry to a portion of the verse-writing of the period, the term must be accepted in its most elastic significance.

Especially should we bear in mind the conditions which of necessity surround the creative faculties and hem in artistic impulse in a new country, where men are brought face to face with a scarcely tamed nature, and where the daily pressure of material needs leaves scant margin for the cultivation of those nobler capabilities which, because they are finer, are assumed to be less essential.

Whatever of art is to be found in the Pennsylvania of the early Colonial days exists in virtue of its inherent forces. It lives only because it is in principle immortal. If imagination had been capable of death, the conditions in Pennsylvania one hundred and fifty years ago assuredly would have killed it.

But imagination lived; there was not only beauty, but the perception of it; not only the perception, but the expression of it; here, then, are the elements of poetry, and if I can but show that the expression was adequate, I shall have proved my right to speak of the *poets* of the Provincial period.

That nearly all the work of the time was based upon accepted European models is a matter of course. The fact counts for nothing in forming an estimate of the writers at whom we are about to glance.

The spirit and feeling may be national, but art in its essence is universal. And we are to remember that Pope and Dryden being then the literary dictators of Europe, their influence upon cisatlantic letters was paramount by a law of necessity.

But there are yet other limitations. With regard to much

of the early Provincial literature it is hard to say whether it properly belongs to Pennsylvania, or is to be accounted an English flower temporarily growing in our soil.

We do indeed find, in the earliest examples coming under our notice, that the subjects are American, though the treatment be not so. This is notably the case in what is probably the first metrical composition written in Pennsylvania,—namely, "A True Relation of the Flourishing State of Pennsylvania," by John Holme.[1]

The original MS. of this poem was presented to the Historical Society by Rufus W. Griswold. It was printed in the Bulletin of the Society for 1845–47, and from a leaf of manuscript inserted in the volume I learn that Holme came to America about 1684, and that the poem was written—probably—in 1689.

The composition begins sedately, with an Introduction :

> "Good people all, who dwell far off or near,
> And do desire the truth from hence to hear,
> Mark well the things which to you I relate,
> They will inform you of our happy state."

After which he dwells upon the excellence of the soil, the fruits, the fields, the sugar, the beasts, the fowl, the fish, the saw-mills, the schools, and even the inhabitants. Of himself he says,—

> "If those who know me not by name
> Do say : What fellow is this same ?
> Where doth he dwell, is he a Friend ?
> Or is it safe for to depend
> On this report he doth indite ?
> This answer unto such I write :
> In Philadelphia I do dwell
> And it is truth which I do tell."

[1] From a carefully-prepared biographical notice of Holme, shown to me by Horatio Gates Jones, Esq., I learn that he came hither by way of Barbadoes, where he had been a sugar planter ; that he was a man of wealth and social standing ; that he was appointed Justice of the County Court in 1690, and represented the city in the Assembly in 1692. Holme appears to have been a man of more than ordinary culture, and possessed a library which, in his day, was remarkably large and well selected.

And so on through a dozen more complacent lines.

But if Holme's poem was the first composition in Pennsylvania, it holds that honor by only a narrow margin of time.

In the Philadelphia Library there is a unique copy of one of the earliest books printed by William Bradford.

This is Richard Frame's "Short Description of Pennsilvania," 1692.

Very little seems to be known concerning Frame. He is not mentioned in Proud's "History of Pennsylvania," and neither Mr. Wharton's Essay on our Provincial literature, nor Mr. Fisher's biographical notices contain his name.

As a curiosity of literature the volume in the Philadelphia Library is of deep interest. As verse the effort is beneath contempt. There are about one hundred and thirty lines of it, but I abstain from quotation.

I mention Holme and Frame at the outset because I desire to dismiss them. They were not poets; yet a review of Provincial verse hardly can ignore them, because they were in a measure the pioneers in a movement of much import. That any one should express a thought in a couplet was *something*, but it cannot be claimed that the general body of the literary work of the time was of sufficient fibre to be worthy of serious criticism. Then, too, as already remarked, the nationality of the verse was dubious.

There, for example, was James Ralph, the friend of Franklin, who went to England in 1724, and between 1730 and 1745 published a series of plays almost wholly English in atmosphere, and nearly all of which failed dismally at Drury Lane. Among them may be mentioned "The Fashionable Lady," "The Fall of the Earl of Essex," "The Lawyer's Feast," "The Astrologer," etc.

His poems include "Clarinda," "Zeuma," "The Muses' Address," and one of much more note, that bitter attack upon Pope, induced by "The Dunciad," and entitled "Sawney," which the little nightingale of Twickenham honored with notice in the oft-quoted couplet,—

"Silence ye wolves, whilst Ralph to Cynthia howls,
Making night hideous; answer him, ye owls."

Again, the chronicler sometimes is puzzled as to proper classification of the writers of this period. Satire, and that of the most virulent type, is so interwoven with the out-pourings of the muse as to make it doubtful whether the versifiers of the time have any claim to consideration in an essay on Provincial poetry.

It is not easy, for example, to know where to bestow a writer like James Taylor, at one time Surveyor-General of the Province, and who resided in Chester County. His longest poem, published in 1728, and entitled "Pennsylvania," has certain merits considered as verse, but his "Story of Whackum," ridiculing quack doctors, puts him in the list of satirists who are more pungent than poetical; and there is another poem, published anonymously in the *Mercury* in April, 1731, and called "The Wits and Poets of Pennsylvania," which entitles the author to a like classification.

Franklin himself aspired to verse, and his *jeu d'esprit* called "Paper" is likely to survive, but he was hardly a poet. Neither can we consider him altogether sound as a critical judge of poetry. Nevertheless, he sometimes pointed with unerring finger. Thus, when he spoke of Aquila Rose as "a very tolerable poet," he delivered himself of a just and well-balanced criticism; first, because Aquila Rose *is* a poet, and secondly, because—having adjudged him worthy of this noble appellation—we must in honesty confess that he is only tolerable. That he is something more than a mere rhymester is shown not only by his mastery of the English heroic couplet, but by sudden gleams of imagination which bespeak true insight and inspiration. He was by birth an Englishman, but emigrated to this Province at an early age, and found employment in Bradford's printing-office. It is quite within the bounds of possibility that his talent might have developed into something really worthy, had he not been cut off at the early age of twenty-eight. He produced at least one fine lyric, which I shall quote by and by, and in the thin volume of his work which is preserved to us there are evidences of an appreciation of the beautiful, all too rare in our Colonial writers.

The title-page of Aquila Rose's volume bears the following inscription:

Poems | On Several Occasions | By | Aquila Rose: | *To which are prefixed* | Some other Pieces writ to him, and to his Memory after his Decease. | Collected and published by his Son *Joseph Rose*, of *Philadelphia.* | Philadelphia: | Printed at the *New Printing Office*, near the *Market*, 1740.

And we are reminded of the singular persistence of human frailty, from one generation to another, when we read in Joseph Rose's advertisement or introduction to the volume these words:

"But many of his [Aquila's] best pieces were lent out, after his Decease, by my mother, to Persons who have forgot to return them: And, perhaps the publishing these few, will put them in mind of sending them to me."

After some three hundred lines of eulogy, we come to the collection proper, beginning with a translation of Ovid (Book I. of the second Elegy), followed by a rather more satisfactory rendering of the first book of the third Elegy. That the versification is fluent, and that it comes from a hand well practised in the mechanism of the art, is immediately evident. The opening of the third Elegy invites quotation,—

> "When the sad Image of the Night came on,
> The last to me in Rome's delightful town;
> When I recount my Joys and Pleasures there,
> Then slides along my Cheeks a briny Tear.
> The fatal Day had almost lost its Light,
> Vail'd by the Curtains of the Sable Night:
> Cæsar's allotted Hour was nigh at Hand,
> When I must leave the Sweet Ausonian Land.
> How short the Space! Myself too unprepar'd,
> To be from all my Joys at once debar'd."

This is quite in the manner of the best English verse of the time, and Rose reaches a yet higher level in describing the parting scene,—

> "I must resign, 'tis Death to stop my Flight,
> This last sad Hour must tear me from your Sight,
> I left my Words imperfect on my Tongue,
> And on each Friend with close Embraces hung.
> But whilst we speak and weep, the Morning Star
> Aloft in Heaven, scarce peep'd thro' twilight Air.
> How grievous was the first Approach of Day,
> That forced Wife, Children, Friends and all away!
> Such searching Pain, my Friends, I felt for you,
> This last sad Time I bad you all adieu,
> As if my Limbs in adverse Halves were torn,
> One part to Stay, and One to Exile borne.
> So Priam look'd, When *Greeks* in Arms came down
> From out the monstrous Horse, and fir'd the Town."

The thought of being cut off from the pleasures of life seems to have been a recurrent one. We find it cropping out in the creative, as well as in the translated, work. The line which I have quoted above from the third Elegy—

> "To be from all my Joys at once debar'd"—

repeats itself in the musical song

> "To his Companion at Sea."

I cannot forbear quoting this entire:

> "Debarr'd, my Friend, of all the Joys
> The Land and charming Sex can give,
> Nor Wind, nor Wave, our Peace destroys;
> We'll laugh, and drink, and nobly live.

> "The gen'rous Wine imparts a Heat
> To raise and quicken every Sense.
> No Thoughts of Death or Bliss defeat,
> Nor Steal away our Innocence.

> "Secure, should Earth in Ruins lie,
> Should Seas and Skies in Rage combine;
> Unmov'd, all Dangers we'll defie,
> And feast our Souls with gen'rous Wine.

> " For, should a Fear each sense possess,
>   Of chilly Death and Endless Fate,
> Our sorrow ne'er can make it less ;
>   But Wine alone can dissipate.
>
> "Then fill the Glass ; nay, fill a Bowl,
>   And fill it up with sparkling Wine ;
> It shall the strongest Grief controul,
>   And make soft Wit with Pleasure join."

The call to fill the glass, followed immediately by the afterthought, " nay, fill a *Bowl*," and the further adjuration to fill it *up*, lead one to suspect that Aquila was a bit of a *bonvivant*, but such suspicion has no right to intrude itself upon an inquiry which seeks to be purely critical.

The important fact for us to note is that this little piece has a lyrical quality not often surpassed among poems of its kind. It fairly sings itself and trips from the tongue with the agile movement of a cadence. The rhyme is perfect, for we must remember that the " wine" and "join" of the last stanza not only have the indisputable authority of Pope, but that in the middle of the last century they were of precisely similar sound. From beginning to end there are none of those technical slips which the critics of that time so readily condoned, and which those of our day are so quick to condemn.

The inscriptions to Richard Hill and to Sir William Keith are in the stock phraseology of works of that order, and scarcely call for comment. The lines " On the Death of his Friend's much lov'd Child" are in a higher strain, and show imagination and originality. The versification is correct pentameter throughout. The same is true of the lines, " To the Memory of his Sister, who died on his Birthday."

I do not know how well his praise of that lady was merited, but certainly it was well expressed,—

> " Her Virgin Youth was past unknown to Strife,
> Each fleeting hour as if the last in life :
> No word from her e'er stole upon the Ear
> But what an Angel might delight to hear :

Actions received a tincture from her Heart,
Unmix'd with Fraud, and unimproved by Art.
* * * * * *
"Sweet as the op'ning Roses' infant Bloom
Who their own Lives in Fragrancy Consume."

The three following pieces were written for the boys who carried the weekly newspapers, and were used as appeals for the Christmas and New Year generosity of their patrons. They were composed respectively in 1720, 1721, and 1722, and doubtless subserved their purpose well. After some unimportant lines on the gift of a boat, there follow six verses written extempore, and the fact that they were so written is their sole excuse for being.

Bound along with the thin volume of Aquila Rose's poems, from which I have made the foregoing extracts (a volume, by the way, which is, I believe, quite rare, and to which I have had access through the courtesy of the librarian of this Society), is an elegy by Elias Bockett, of London. This poem was originally printed in the *Mercury*, June 25, 1724. It is a dialogue between *Damon* and *Marino*, wherein the latter recounts to his friend the happenings in the Western world, and especially dwells upon the untimely death of *Amintas* (under which musical appellation Aquila Rose is mentioned). *Marino* tells how

"Merit like his cou'd ne'er be long unknown,
His native *Britain* saw it not alone;
Where e'er he came, distinguish'd it appear'd,
At every Port *Amintas* was rever'd,
Scarce was our *Philadelphia* in his View,
Before his Fame o'er all the Province flew;
His Virtues *Pennsylvania* soon confest,
They shone conspicuous, tho' by Fate oppres't;
Fate, even there, frown'd on the Bard awhile,
But smooth'd her Brow at length and cast a flatt'ring smile."

I pause to remark that Fate has been kept busy frowning upon the bard in Pennsylvania ever since.

Mr. Bockett's tribute is fairly well done. It is in accord with the classicism of the day, and is rigidly hedged in with rhymed couplets, broken here and there by a triplet, after the Dryden and Pope manner.

Another elegy, anonymously contributed, celebrates Rose under the name of *Myris*, but is inferior, I think, to Bockett's. This also is bound with the poems. But the third, and much the best known of these tributes, does not appear in this volume. I refer to the elegy of Samuel Keimer, a name familiar to the readers of Franklin's autobiography, and one to which the subject now naturally leads me. He arrived in Philadelphia probably late in 1731, and set up as a moral reformer. He proposed to teach the negroes to read the Holy Scriptures, and wrote in regard to this enterprise,—

> " Let none condemn this undertaking
> By silent thoughts, or noisy speaking;
> They're fools whose bolt's soon shot upon
> The mark they've looked but little on."

Which would seem to be an insinuation that the hasty critic's shafts often prove to be boomerangs.

It is of Keimer that Franklin relates the droll incident touching upon his appetite for roast pig. Keimer came to Franklin and asked him to let his beard grow, because Moses had commanded that men should not "mar the corners of their beards." Franklin agreed, provided Keimer would bind himself to abstain from animal food. Keimer assented, but soon broke down and invited his friends to sup with him upon roast pig. They accepted, but before they could arrive Keimer, whose appetite had been whetted by his unwonted fast, devoured the pig himself. It may be presumed that Franklin thereafter felt at liberty to follow the bent of his own inclinations in the matter of his beard.

It is to be remarked that, up to this point, the imitation of accepted English forms is almost servile.

This imitation, as I have already said, is inevitable, and constitutes one of the special restrictions of any art in a new land. An eminent critic[1] has said of the American

---

[1] Edmund Clarence Stedman, " Poets of America."

poet that " he represents the music and ardor of a new country . . . a new nation, yet not forced, like those which have progressed from barbarism to a sense of art, to create a language and literature of their own ; a new land with an old language, a new nation with all the literature and traditions behind it of the country from whose colonies it has sprung." And again : " The thought and learning of this people began in America just where it had arrived in the motherland at the dates of the Jamestown and Plymouth settlements."

It is well that these facts should be pointed out to us, for we are apt to forget how largely they enter into a proper critical estimate of the literary product of the period under review.

But we must pass on to greet a writer of larger calibre than those whom we have been considering.

In 1758 a little poem called " The Invitation" was sent anonymously to the editor of *The American Magazine*, and was seized upon with avidity and published, with the following note : " This little poem was sent to us by an unknown hand, and seems dated as an original ; if it be so, we think it does honour to our city." Shortly afterwards an " Ode on Friendship" and one on " Wine" came from the same source, and a " Night-Piece" made its appearance. All were published promptly, and received commendatory notices from the editor, who seems especially to have been delighted with the " Ode on Wine," concerning which he said, " It is wrote with much poetic warmth," and then continues, " These pieces, and some others of his, fell into our hands by accident, soon after the appearance of ' The Invitation,' which was found among the rest ; and we reckon it one of the highest instances of good fortune that has befallen us, during the period of our magazine ; that we have had an opportunity of making known to the world so much merit, we mean in consideration of his circumstances and means of improvement."

These are strong words. If the MS. of a poetical aspirant of this our day were to receive such treatment at the hands of an editor, I hardly know what would happen.   I am not sure but that the shock would prove too much for the nervous system of the bard.

But it is time to give the name of the author of these inspiring pieces.   It is Thomas Godfrey, the son of a glazier who lived in Philadelphia, who was noted as a mathematician, and who was probably the inventor of the quadrant which has been called Hadley's.

Godfrey appears to have possessed a talent for music and painting but little below that which he had for poetry.   He rose quickly in the public esteem, and was patronized by the principal *literati* of the Province.   His poems were collected in 1765 and published in a quarto volume at Philadelphia, under the title, "Juvenile Poems on Various Subjects, with the *Prince of Parthia*, a Tragedy."   From a copy of this volume in possession of the Historical Society I make the following extract from "The Invitation."

DAMON.
"Haste! Sylvia! haste, my charming maid!
    Let's leave these fashionable toys;
Let's seek the shelter of some shade,
    And revel in ne'er fading joys.
See spring in liv'ry gay appears,
    And winter's chilly blasts are fled;
Each grove its leafy honours rears,
    And meads their lovely verdure spread!"

Damon goes on to make love to *Sylvia* in approved fashion, and the latter, after an amiable return of his sentiments, confesses that she is quite ready to quit the unreal diversions of town life for the bucolic pleasures which he so eloquently portrays.   She closes the poem with these words:

"How sweet thy words! but, Damon cease,
    Nor strive to fix me ever here;
Too well you know these accents please,
    That oft have filled my ravish'd ear.
Come, lead me to these promis'd joys,
    That dwelt so lately on thy tongue;
Direct me by thy well known voice,
    And calm my transports with thy song!"

Perhaps the first thing which strikes one in this versification is its extreme correctness. Its mechanism is nearly without a flaw, and this very fact militates against the satisfaction derivable from it as poetry. It is certainly less lyrical than the song of Aquila Rose which I quoted a few moments ago. It lacks the "first fine careless rapture" which should show itself in the work of a young man of twenty-two, if it shows itself at all. We feel that *Damon* and *Sylvia* are very lovable young people, and we cannot deny that they give musical utterance to their mutual admiration; but we are conscious all the while that somebody is pulling the wires which cause *Damon's* eyes to roll and *Sylvia's* gentle breast to heave. The poet has not quite enough art to conceal his art, and the stage effect is spoiled by an unfortunate glimpse of the *deus ex machina*.

The same defect mars the "Verses Occasioned by a Young Lady's asking the author *What* was *a Cure for Love?*" published also in 1758.

> " From me, my Dear, O seek not to receive
> What e'en deep-read Experience cannot give.
> We may, indeed, from the Physician's skill
> Some medicine find to cure the body's ill.
> But who e'er found the physic for the soul,
> Or made the affections bend to his controul?"

We here inevitably are reminded of *Macbeth's*

> " Canst thou not minister to a mind diseased?"

though the universality of the sentiment in its application is sufficient to acquit Godfrey of a charge of plagiarism.

The "Ode on Friendship," owing to the fact of its being written in the irregular versification usual to this form, moves more freely and we see less of the wires. It reaches well up towards the heroic at its climax. I can afford room only for a single stanza, the sixth :

> " Round the field Achilles flies,
>   For Hector he cries,
>   At length the Trojan chief espies,
>   Horribly glorious midst the war,
>   Upon his bloody shield the God of day
>   Darts pendant rays;
>   The crimson mirror far
>   Reflects the blaze;
>   And all around him glories play.
>   Patroclus' mantle loosely flung,
>   The pledge of brave Achilles' love,
>   And by the fair Ægina wove;
>   Upon his manly shoulder hung."

The " Epistle to a Friend, from Fort Henry" brings us back from classic fields to our own beloved soil. It was written when the author was a lieutenant in the Pennsylvania forces garrisoned at Fort Henry, and contains a picture (one of the very few preserved) of the distress of our frontier settlers, and of their sufferings at the hands of the savages who laid waste their homes.

It is regrettable, however, that there is more of historic truth than of poetry in these lines:

> " If in this wild a pleasing spot we meet,
>   In happier times some humble swain's retreat;
>   Where once with joy he saw the grateful soil
>   Yield a luxuriant harvest to his toil,
>   (Blest with content, enjoyed his solitude,
>   And knew his pleasures, tho' of manners rude);
>   The lowly prospect strikes a secret dread,
>   While round the ravag'd cott we silent tread,
>   Whose owner fell beneath the savage hand,
>   Or roves a captive on some hostile land,
>   While the rich fields, with Ceres' blessings stor'd,
>   Grieve for their slaughtered, or their absent lord."

I pass over some pastorals and other pieces to direct your attention to " The Court of Fancy," which is, perhaps, Godfrey's chief title to fame. There is here a sense of the picturesque rarely discoverable among versemen of the Colonial period. Moreover, Godfrey provides us with an atmosphere for his picture,—an attention to one's artistic needs which one learns to appreciate after a few weeks' work among the early Pennsylvania writers.

> " Methought I pensive unattended stood,
> Wrapt in the horrors of a desert wood;
> Old night and silence spread their sway around,
> And not a breeze disturb'd the dread profound."

After describing the temple, he gives us this description of the goddess herself,—

> " High in the midst, rais'd on her rolling throne,
> Sublimely eminent bright Fancy shone.
> A glitt'ring Tiara her temples bound,
> Rich set with sparkling Rubies all around;
> Her azure eyes roll'd with majestic grace,
> And youth eternal bloom'd upon her face,
> A radiant bough, ensign of her Command,
> Of polish'd gold wav'd in her lily hand;
> The same the Sibyl to Æneas gave,
> When the bold Trojan cross'd the Stygian wave."

Contrast this with the description of *Delusion*,—

> " Now swiftly forward false Delusion came,
> Wrapt in a fulvid Cloud appear'd the Dame.
> Thin was her form, in airy garments drest,
> And grotesque figures flamed upon her vest;
> In her right hand she held a magic glass,
> From whence around reflected glories pass.
> Blind by the subtle rays, the giddy crowd
> Rush'd wildly from the Dome and shouted loud.
> The few remain'd whom Fancy did inspire
> Yet undeceiv'd by vain Delusion's fire."

It is clear that the author got his idea of the transition from the Court of *Fancy* to that of *Delusion* from Chaucer's " House of Fame," wherein the change is from the House of *Fame* to that of *Rumour*. We know, indeed, that he was a student of Chaucer, from his paraphrase of part of the poem, " The Assembly of Foules," and from the internal evidence of other portions of his work.

There is also an echo of Pope in " The Court of Fancy," which is a poem that ought to be read in its entirety, and which I shall mar by only one further quotation.   It is but just, however, to direct attention to the propriety and elegance of the allegory.   The offspring of the muses, *Poetry*, *Painting*, and *Music*, are the attendants upon *Fancy*, in the character of the three masters, Homer, Apelles, and Timotheus, and the scheme is worked out with a fidelity and consistency much to be commended.

That our poet had a becoming sense of modesty is shown in the humble position assigned to himself among the attendants upon the goddess *Fancy*,—

> " Close at her feet, a Bard, in raptures lost,
>   Was plac'd, and wildly round his eyeballs tost.
>   Great *Fancy* was his theme! the soothing strain,
>   In floods of pleasure, thrill'd thro' ev'ry vein."

The year following the publication of "The Court of Fancy," the remarkable song called "Victory" made its appearance in the *Pennsylvania Gazette.*   It is a pæan of triumph, filled with loyalty to Britain, and exhibits to a degree too pronounced for our present taste the machinery of the classic school of English verse.

The piece opens with a picture of *Britannia* reclining

> " On a soft bank, wrapt in the gloomy groves,
>   (Thro' which Ohio's ever rolling wave,
>   Unaw'd by moons, meandring wildly roves,
>   And sweetly murm'ring seems to mourn the brave).
>
> " Her spear and laurel wreath aside were thrown,
>   The big round pearly drops each other trace
>   From her bright eyes in gushing torrents down,
>   And wash'd the roses from her beauteous face."

The construction here leads me to call attention to the singular want of perception which characterized all the early versifiers in the matter of tenses.   It seems strange that one familiar with classical models could speak of the pearly drops that *trace* each other from *Britannia's* eyes and *wash'd* the roses from her face.   Yet similar slips are of frequent occurrence, and probably have made themselves uncomfortably felt in some of the quotations already given. This, however, merely as parenthesis; I must not delay *Britannia* in her quest,—

> " ' And why, (then cry'd the bright angelic maid)
>   Why is my breast a prey to foul despair?
>   It is but folly thus to mourn the dead,
>   No longer then I'll idly loiter here.
>
> " ' I'll seek where Victory her seat doth rear,
>   And all around her pow'rful influence spread,
>   She yet perhaps may listen to my pray'r,
>   And grant revenge for ev'ry gallant shade.' "

And so the bright angelic maid spreads her sunny wings (a proceeding which leads one to fear a mixing of metaphors, and causes surprise that *Britannia* was not represented as a full-fledged goddess) and flies to the palace of *Victory.* The massy gates standing ajar disclose the celestial beauty within, but the gates are guarded by the porter, whose name is *Horror;* and at his side stand grim *Death* and shivering *Fear.* There, too, are *Pain* and *Sorrow;* but I cannot describe the scene half so well as does our poet,—

> " Clad in deep sables *Sorrow* did appear,
>   All wan and ghastly with dejected eye,
>   Eager she treasur'd ev'ry Widow's tear,
>   And murmur'd ev'ry helpless Orphan's sigh.
>
> " High on her shining seat was *Victory* plac'd,
>   Sweet were her smiles, but dreadful was her frown,
>   Her left hand with the spreading palm was grac'd,
>   And in her right she held the Victor's crown."

And now come four lines of unusual brilliancy and color,—

> " One perfect Ruby was her glitt'ring throne,
>   Gold were th' ascending steps, but smear'd with blood,
>   Close by her side bright laurel'd *Glory* shone,
>   And *Fame* with her loud sounding Trumpet stood."

There is a haunting cadence here which somehow makes one think of Thomas Gray. Apart from the sense, the verses just read might be slipped in between two stanzas of the "Elegy written in a Country Church-yard" without injury to the perfect unity of that well-nigh perfect poem.

It is one of those coincidences which occur so often in literature, and about which criticism so often wanders off into idle conjecture.

Britannia makes her obeisance to *Victory* in the great hall

> " Around (whose) wall, in curious niches plac'd,
>   The imag'd Heroes sternly frown'd in gold,"

and enters complaint that the goddess once smiled upon her arms,—

> " ' But now in vain, forsook by heav'n and Thee,
>   In vain they strive, their courage all is vain ;
> Tho' the dear prize is Fame and Liberty,
>   They see triumphant slaves and dread the chain.' "

The goddess promises much glory for the future, and with a tribute to Britain's fleet and a touching allusion to General Wolfe, who is compared to the noble *Decius*, the poem comes to an end.

I have spoken of this production as a remarkable one, because it is so different from the prevailing manner of the time, and because it contains certain stanzas and single lines of real felicity. It cannot be said that the imagination displayed is of a particularly high quality, but the handling of the theme is respectable, and in places skilful. Of the structure the extracts offered furnish a sufficient notion.

I can pause only to mention a " Paraphrase on the First Psalm," quite a commonplace piece of work; and a " Cantata on Peace," addressed to " Mr. N. E." (presumably Rev. Nathaniel Evans). The scene of the last-named poem is the banks of the Schuylkill, and the verse is fairly musical. There are also songs, addressed, in true classic style, to the *Celias* and *Sylvias* of the poet's acquaintance, but which have lost their interest with the passing of the occasions which inspired them.

We come now to a work of unusual significance, from

the fact that it was probably the first attempt made in Pennsylvania at dramatic composition. I refer to " The Prince of Parthia," a tragedy composed by Godfrey in 1759, and which he finished somewhat hurriedly during a temporary residence in North Carolina, in order that it might be in season to be performed by the company of players at Philadelphia.

This haste is quite evident in the later scenes, and some of the elisions and false quantities are very trying to a delicately-attuned ear; nevertheless, we should go far astray did we brush aside the piece as unworthy of consideration. It has passages of great nobility, and is an essential element in the literary product of the period under review.

" The Prince of Parthia" does not strictly observe the " unities" of the classic drama, and while it actually is improved by its departures from the rigid limitations of its class, we are forced to note these departures as a defect when we come to pass critical judgment upon the piece as a work of art.

Otherwise the tragedy is wrought out on correct lines, and the management of the action combines good taste with a nice attention to the exigencies of stage presentation. I should say that " The Prince of Parthia" is one of the very few examples of a closet drama which is at the same time a practicable acting play. No one who has not tried knows how much cleverness is necessary to effect this combination, and the writers of our own time might take a valuable leaf from Godfrey's experience in this regard.

The scene of the tragedy (which consists of the canonical five acts) is laid at Ctesiphon, the story being the old one of a good king, a false queen, a noble son, and a wicked son, and the complications thence arising being similar to those with which we are familiar in Shakespeare and the French tragic writers. The love-story is delicate and tender, and Godfrey, in his arrangement of the sequence of his scenes, has displayed a sense of the law of contrast,—a quality in which the Colonial poets were strangely deficient. There is some strong writing in the sixth scene of Act

II., where *Arsaces* visits *Bethas* in prison. Greater poets than Godfrey would have no cause to be ashamed of blank verse such as this,—

BETHAS.

"Away, away.
Mock with your jester to divert the court,
Fit scene for sportive joys and frolic mirth ;
Think'st thou I lack that manly constancy
Which braves misfortune, and remains unshaken?
Are these, are these the emblems of thy friendship,
These rankling chains, say, does it gall like these?
No, let me taste the bitterness of sorrow,
For I am reconcil'd to wretchedness.
The Gods have empty'd all their mighty store
Of hoarded ills upon my whitened age;
Now death—but oh! I court coy death in vain,
Like a cold maid, he scorns my fond complaining."

Or again, note these almost Shakespearian lines spoken by *Arsaces* in Act IV., Scene 4.

ARSACES.

"Why should I linger out my joyless days,
When length of hope is length of misery?
Hope is a coz'ner, and beguiles our cares,
Cheats us with empty shows of happiness,
Swift fleeting joys which mock the faint embrace ;
We wade thro' ills pursuing of the meteor,
Yet are distanc'd still."

But for the false accent of the last line this passage would be technically perfect. Written by a youth of Godfrey's years and under the conditions of his environment, it is remarkable.

The fifth scene of this act is almost a paraphrase of "Hamlet." Just as *Hamlet* visits *Gertrude* to upbraid her, and is reinforced in his purpose by the appearance of the late king's ghost, so, by a slight alteration in the situation, *Thermusa*, the queen, visits her son *Arsaces*, and is struck with terror by the apparition of the ghost of the murdered king, her husband.

Note the similarity running like a thread through the dialogue,—

ARSACES.

" What means the proud Thermusa by this visit?
Stoops heav'n-born pity to a breast like thine?

* * * * * *

Why gaze you on me thus?   Why hesitate?"

QUEEN.

" This, with the many tears I've shed, receive."
                                    (*Offers to stab him.*)

ARSACES.

" Nay, do not mock me with the show of death
And yet deny the blessing.

* * * * * * *

Why drops the dagger from thy trembling hand?

* * * * * * *

Why this pause?"

QUEEN.

" It surely was the echo to my fears,
The whistling wind, perhaps, which mimick'd voice;
But thrice methought it loudly cry'd, ' forbear !'
                              (*Ghost of Artabanus rises.*)

" Save me, oh, save me, ye Eternal pow'rs!
See, see, it comes surrounded with dread terrors,
Hence, hence! nor blast me——"

And even as Shakespeare shows that the ghost is an hallucination existent only in the mind of *Gertrude*, so Godfrey makes his ghost apparent only to *Thermusa*. And he does this in precisely the same way and in almost identical language,—

ARSACES.

" Your eyes seem fix'd upon some dreadful object,
Horror and anguish cloath your whiten'd face."

* * * * * * *

QUEEN.

" What!   Saw'st thou nothing?"

ARSACES.

" Nothing."

QUEEN.
" Nor heard ?"

ARSACES.
" Nor beard."

The plagiarism here is so magnificent that we almost applaud its boldness. The ghost does not appear as a character at all, but is merely shown upon the stage so that the audience may understand the vision in the queen's disordered brain. But Godfrey does not stop here. He deliberately slashes a line from "Macbeth" to fill out his scene from "Hamlet," and rechristens the whole as "The Prince of Parthia"—

QUEEN (*addressing ghost*).
" Ah, frown not on me—
Why dost thou shake thy horrid locks at me ?
Can I give immortality ?"

I note these appropriations rather for the purpose of showing Godfrey's close study of the universal poet than with a view to finding fault with his tragedy. There is enough in it of original thought to carry it through bravely.

But it is time to leave this work. Before I do so, however, I must quote the charming song—almost in the manner of Waller—which enriches the otherwise sterile fifth act,—

" Tell me, Phillis, tell me why
    You appear so wondrous coy,
When that glow, and sparkling eye,
    Speak you want to taste the joy ?
Prithee give this fooling o'er,
Nor torment your lover more.

" While youth is warm within our veins,
    And nature tempts us to be gay,
Give to pleasure loose the reins,
    Love and youth fly swift away.
Youth in pleasure should be spent,
Age will come, we'll then repent."

" The Prince of Parthia" may be regarded as an historical tragedy, though the author has not hesitated to depart quite widely from history. According to Tacitus, Strabo, and Josephus, Queen Thermusa was the wife, not of Artabanus, but of Phraates, Artabanus being the fourth king of Parthia after him. In other ways also he has deviated, but he amply has atoned for these lapses in the artistic truth of his characterizations.

In taking leave of Godfrey, I naturally am led to speak of one who was his close friend, and who wrote the appreciative memoir prefixed to the volume just noticed.

I refer to the Rev. Nathaniel Evans, born in Philadelphia in 1742, and sent as missionary to New Jersey by the Society for Propagating the Gospel. This writer seems to have been fired with that enthusiasm for the muse which, in his day, was too often but an affectation, and in our day is nearly always a theme for jest. At the opening of his preface he says,—

" Poetry has been accounted the most peculiar of all the liberal arts, and it is the only one in the circle of literature which a man of common capacity cannot, by mere dint of constant application, become master of."

And again,—

" The prose writer may indeed warm his reader with a serene and steady fire; he may keep up his attention with the energetic, the flowing period. But the poet's it is to wrap him in a flame,—to dissolve him, as it were, in his own rapturous blaze."

One who speaks thus must be a man of sentiment, susceptible to outward impressions and strongly guided by the artistic impulse and the poetic view of nature and life. And there are indications in his work that these tendencies were developed by the accidents of his career. Having gone to England upon the taking of his degree at the Philadelphia Academy, he returned thence in December, 1765, having had for his fellow-passenger (among others) the lady who figures in our Colonial literature under the pseudonyme of *Laura.* This lady was Miss Elizabeth Graeme, a daughter of Dr. Graeme and granddaughter of Sir W. Keith, a woman of unusual gifts, who afterwards became the wife of a Scotchman named Hugh Ferguson, and at whom it will be convenient for us to glance at this time.

I am unable to state how far the acquaintanceship between *Laura* and Evans was of a romantic origin and character. But certainly it influenced his verse, if not his life, and many of the best pieces in the poems (published in duodecimo in 1772) are the addresses and replies of these congenial friends.

The volume opens with an elegy upon Evans, written by *Laura*, and conceived in a spirit of fervor and devotion. To turn from this production to the parody on Pope's lines, "Eloisa to Abelard," is immediately to become aware of *Laura's* versatility and wit. This parody, by the way, was the occasion of much pleasant raillery between *Laura* and Evans. The latter accepts the lines as good-humored banter, and writes in reply,—

> " I lately saw, no matter where,
> A parody by Laura fair;
> In which, beyond dispute, 'tis clear
> She means her country friend to jeer;
> For well she knows her pleasing lays
> (Whether they banter me or praise,
> Whatever merry mood they take)
> Are welcome for their author's sake."

To which *Laura* replies,—

> " *Laura* to *Damon* health doth send,
> And thus salutes her saucy friend."

And after laughing at him for supposing himself to have been in her thoughts, she exclaims,—

> "Unhappy me! who ne'er could dream
> That you should think yourself the theme,"

and proceeds to make very fine mince-meat of him, thus:

> "You want to prove, in wondrous haste,
> That *Laura*, too, has Stella's taste;
> As if it must directly follow,
> Since you are favored by Apollo,

> That he his choicest gifts must send
> To every scribbling female friend.
> I thank you, sir—you're wondrous kind !
> But think me not so vain or blind
> As to believe the pretty things
> Your muse, with ease, at Laura flings."

And so the carte-and-tierce goes on apace pleasantly enough, and with no little brilliancy in sally and repartee.

But Evans's mood was serious at times, and he seems also to have been moved by love of his native land and desire to celebrate in song her glories.

> "Shall fam'd Arcadia own the tuneful choir,
> And fair Sicilia boast the matchless lyre?
> Shall Gallia's groves resound with heav'nly lays
> And Albion's poets claim immortal bays?
> And this new world ne'er feel the muse's fire;
> No beauties charm us, or no deeds inspire?
> O Pennsylvania! shall no son of thine
> Glow with the raptures of the sacred nine?"

This extract is from the " Daphnis and Menalcas," a pastoral eclogue written in 1758, when the poet was but *sixteen !*

Of the epistolary odes to various friends I think silence the kindest criticism. The *"Panegyric"* to the memory of General Wolfe is in a higher key. There is a fine heroic swing in this, for example :

> " Where great St. Lawrence rolls its awful flood,
> He, daring, led Britannia's warrior-band,
> Scal'd its proud banks, and pierc'd the desert wood,
> That veils the horrors of the hostile land.
>   *   *   *   *   *   *
> " Now lights his vengeance on the dastard foe—
> So once Pelides, on the Trojan field
> (Whilst death stood glaring on his crimson'd shield),
> Fill'd every trembling Dardan heart with woe."

The " Elegy to the Memory of Theophilus Grew, Professor of Mathematics in the College of Philadelphia," is rather commonplace, and the same confession must be made in regard to the remaining pieces in this form.

There is an " Anacreontic Ode," beginning

> " Hence with sorrow, spleen, and care !
> Muse, awake the jocund air ;
> Wreathe thy brows in myrtle twine,
> And assist the gay design ;
> Strike the trembling string with pleasure,
> Till it sound the enchanting measure,"

which has a free movement and some beauty, and there are occasional songs that linger affectionately in the ear, but Evans does not appear to have had the lyrical gift of his friend Godfrey. There is nothing in him like the song in " The Prince of Parthia," or the pretty lyric of Aquila Rose, both of which I have quoted. As to his imitations of Horace, they do not imitate, and hence fail at the point where they make their appeal to our judgment. Writers are apt to think that what they do least well is precisely their main excellence, and it is one of the thankless offices of criticism to point out these errors, and try to show wherein merit really resides. And so, in Evans, we seem to find his best work where he has laid the least stress.

I have time only to mention the pieces in Latin, of which the " Carmen Pastorale," beginning

> " *Urbs colitur priscis quondam celeberrima Scotis,*"

is probably the best.

I may take advantage of this opportunity to enumerate certain minor versifiers, whom the chronicler has no right wholly to ignore. John Solomon, a professor of French, established himself in Philadelphia, and, seemingly with a view to obtaining pupils, sent a communication to Franklin which was without signature, and which duly appeared in the *Pennsylvania Gazette* for August 2, 1736. It was accompanied by a sonnet written (as was also the letter) in French, wherein Mr. Solomon scouts the notion of riches being essential to happiness :

" Oui, je l'ai dit cent fois, ce n'est que fiction
De croire le répos attache à l'opulence."

Nevertheless, Mr. Solomon appears to have appreciated the necessity of obtaining an income.

Of more interest to us is a German paraphrase of several portions of Scripture from the pen of the hermit John Kelpius. These may be found in the *Pennsylvania Gazette* of March 31, 1742.

Kelpius also composed a Book of Hymns, which were done into English verse by Christopher Witt, and more especial reference to which may be found in Watson's "Notes on the Early History of Germantown."

These references to the *Pennsylvania Gazette* bring to mind a group of writers, who, though perhaps of minor note individually, composed a body of prose and verse of no little importance in estimating the value of the literary output of the Provincial period. There was William Lowry, the author of several Latin odes and other pieces, a good sample of whose powers may be found in a *Carmen Gratularium* to Governor Thomas, which appeared in Franklin's *Universal Magazine* in 1741, though I believe the authorship is not undisputed.

There, also, was John Beveridge, a Scotchman, who, in 1758, was appointed professor of languages in the College of Philadelphia, and an interesting obituary notice of whom appears in the *Gazette* for July 2, 1767. In 1765 he put forth a small collection under the title, *"Epistolæ et alia quædam miscellanea,"* which contains some lyrical work of merit. Beveridge was accounted the best writer of Latin verse in the Province.

Nor must we forget Francis Daniel Pastorius, who composed sundry acrostics and other pieces addressed to the daughters of his friend Thomas Lloyd, with whom Pastorius came to America in 1683; nor David James Dove, whom Mr. Graydon mentions as a popular satirical poet about 1750. Dove was the first master of the Germantown Academy, coming to that position in 1762. His composi-

tions are largely political and personal satires.   His attack
upon William Moore, of Moore Hall, is very bitter, and
its title, " Washing the Black-a-moor White," furnishes a
clue to its quality.

We are reminded also of William Rakestraw, who, in
1707, was charged with writing " several scurrilous libels
and rhymes against the proprietor."

Also of David French, who presented certain poetic
translations of some of Anacreon's odes and two of the
elegies of Ovid.

I must mention, too, in passing, Susanna Wright, who lived
near Philadelphia, removing later to the banks of the Susquehanna.   Her muse was religious, and she displayed more
piety than poetry; nevertheless, she had a certain noble
quality of utterance which we may not judiciously despise.

The same remarks apply to Hannah Griffitts, daughter of
Thomas Griffitts and granddaughter of Isaac Norris, senior,
who composed some religious verses of merit, and was
rated highly by her contemporaries.

It is sufficient here merely to catalogue the names of John
Wilcocks, who produced pastorals, epigrams, and fables of
considerable wit and elegance; Joseph Brientnall, a member of the Society of Friends, and the first secretary of the
City Library Company, who was one of the earliest members of the *Junto ;* and James Logan, who, though a finished
scholar, was not distinctively a poet.   The latter translated
the Distichs of Cato into English verse for the use of his
daughters.   He also wrote Latin verses, and produced a
Greek ode of some distinction.

Reference to James Logan induces mention of Thomas
Makin, who, in 1728–29, dedicated to Logan two Latin
poems which are still, I believe, in the collection of manuscripts preserved at Stenton.   One is entitled " Encomium
Pennsylvaniæ," and the other " In Laudeþ Pennsylvaniæ,"
from which one may infer that Makin was possessed of a
due share of State pride.   I find a copy of the latter piece,
together with an English rendering, in Proud's " History
of Pennsylvania" (Vol. II. pp. 360, 361).   It opens thus :

" First, Pennsylvania's memorable name
    From Penn, the founder of the country, came;
    Sprung from a worthy and illustrious race,
    But more ennobled by his virtuous ways."

Which reminds one of those adolescent excursions into the realms of the muses, wherein we are taught the order of the alphabet through the medium of a jingle. Even now my ears are ringing with the theme,—

"*A* was an apple-pie," etc.

And these reflections lead me to speak of " Kawanio Che Keeteru; a True Relation of a Bloody Battle fought between George and Lewis, in the Year 1755," [1] said to be by one Nicholas Scull, and beginning

"There liv'd a man not long ago——"

Ah! who can hear that line without thinking of the immortal gentleman who leaped into a bramble-bush and discovered a homœopathic cure for lost eyesight?

Lack of imagination seems to be the prevailing difficulty in these productions, and we find the same conditions in the work of William Satterthwaite, an Englishman, and a person of some learning, who is chiefly memorable as the author of a poem written in 1738, and entitled " Mysterious Nothing." Of this piece I would say that the title precisely describes the contents. Mr. Satterthwaite wrote also an " Elegy on Jeremiah Langhorne," and a poem called " Providence;" but Mr. Satterthwaite was not a poet.

This stigma, however, does not apply to John Dommett, whom Mr. Joshua Francis Fisher (in his admirable paper on Provincial literature) styles the first " *professional* poet" that our country produced.

We may, without much reluctance, dismiss the works of John Parke, a native of Delaware, who became interested in verse-writing while a student in the college at Philadel-

[1] The title is in the Indian language, and is expressive of a hero relying upon God to bless his endeavors.

phia, and who made a fair translation of the Odes of Horace. He produced also " Virginia; a Pastoral Drama," which is sufficiently pastoral, but not very dramatic.

I can stop only to mention the names of Charles Osborne and Joseph Watson, who were clerks in the office of Charles Brockden, and who made some pretension to literature, and can only refer to Henry Brooke as the author of "A Discourse on Jests."

These writers exhibit some descriptive power, but usually fail to rise to anything approaching fervor. And this recalls to my mind that one of the most remarkable descriptions which Colonial literature affords is that contained in the Rev. Dr. Smith's poem on visiting the Academy in Philadelphia in June, 1753. In this folio of some three hundred lines he speaks of Penn, whose form he sees in the clouds, where he,—

" With sky-tinged mantle clad, and lifted hands,
In act to touch the string, majestic stands."

Considering how fundamental is the injunction of Friends to "plainness of speech, behavior, and apparel," it is rather startling to think of William Penn dressed in a sky-blue mantle and playing the harp. Nevertheless, we must make due allowance for the poetic license.

Dr. Smith's funeral sermon upon W. T. Martin was perhaps his ablest production, and it has for us an added interest on account of the elegies of the Rev. Jacob Duché, assistant minister of Saint Peter's, and of Paul Jackson, which appeared in the same volume. Still more by reason of the elegy written by Francis Hopkinson, and prefixed to Dr. Smith's sermon.

Hopkinson was a profound lawyer and a man of varied talents and wide scholarship. He excelled in music and poetry, and had some knowledge of painting. As a humorist and satirist he ranked very high. His first poem appeared in the first number of the *American Magazine*, being an "Ode on Music." This was followed by two poems, after Milton, and by an "Ode on the Morning," and other verses. In 1758 appeared a poem " On the Invention of Letters and the Art of Printing," which Professor Smyth, in his very interesting volume on the " Philadelphia Magazines," attributes to Hopkinson.

It may be noted, however, that this writer's fame rests chiefly upon his occasional pieces. " The Battle of the Kegs;" " Treaty, a Poem," written on the banks of the Lehigh in 1761; " Science, a Poem," written in the year following, and other like works, attest his powers. He died in 1791.

From " Science" I make the following extract :

> " Goddess sublime ! on whose advent'rous wing,
> Like the sweet lark, fleet fancy mounts to sing ;
> Whether it chance to please thee, youthful queen,
> With airy step to grace the rural scene ;
> Or softly languish thro' the breezy grove,
> In all the dying tenderness of love:
> Whether thro' some untrodden flow'ry way
> With contemplation mild, thou lov'st to stray ;
> Or on a tempest's rapid fury rise,
> And dip thy plumage in the wat'ry skies ;
> Or moonlight wand'ring by the wave-worn shore,
> Wait on old ocean's melancholy roar :
> Where'er thou art, once more my prayer attend,
> Once more, celestial muse, thy influence lend."

The opening stanza of " The Battle of the Kegs" jingles musically, but is very like doggerel :

> " Gallants attend and hear a friend
> Trill forth harmonious ditty ;
> Strange things I'll tell which late befel
> In Philadelphia City."

There are several songs and other lyrics which I should like to quote, did space permit, but I must content myself with referring the student to the volume of the " Miscellaneous Essays and Occasional Writings of Francis Hopkinson, Esq., printed by J. Dobson at Philadelphia, 1792," which I have examined with some care.

Among the best pieces of book-making which came from

the press of William Bradford were the "Familiar Epis-
tles of Beveridge," some of which were done into English by Stephen Watts, Alexander Alexander, and Thomas
Coombe, Jr.

The latter gentleman also wrote a poem called "Edwin,
or the Emigrant," which he dedicated to Goldsmith, and
which is a continuation of the story of the "Deserted Village." It is said to have been written with a view to dis-
couraging emigration to this country, and by its unattractive
pictures of the condition of the people here was certainly
calculated to produce that effect. Along with "Edwin" are
printed some small pieces, including "The Unfortunate
Lovers," etc., but the quality of the work is mediocre.

The same criticism must be passed upon much of the
anonymous verse contributed to the *American Magazine* about
this time. Side by side with the poetry of Godfrey, Hopkinson, and others, we find such pieces as "The Squabble,
a Pastoral Eclogue," "The Manners of the Times, a Satire
by Philadelphiensis," "A Panegyric, by Strephon," which
appears to be a reply to the "Satire," and many odes on
"Liberty," "Oppression," and kindred themes, inspired,
doubtless, by the resistance of the Colonies to Great Britain,
none of which command our attention as poetry.

Occasionally, however, the investigator is rewarded by
finding work of a higher order, such as that of George
Webbe, the author of "Bachelor's Hall," who, in addition
to that rather creditable performance, published a short
piece in praise of Pennsylvania, and other minor poems.
Webbe, it will be remembered, was engaged with Keimer
in the publication of the *Pennsylvania Gazette*, and was in
some measure a patron as well as a devotee of the muse.

Indeed, an examination of the columns of the periodical
press of the time reveals a large body of verse, much of
which is creditable, some of which is very bad, and a little
of which deserves to be called by the noble name of poetry.

It has been my endeavor, in reviewing the verse-makers
of the Provincial period, to arrive at a fair notion of the
poetic feeling and of the general culture which prevailed.

That the proportion of wheat to chaff is distressingly small may as well frankly be conceded; but when the conditions are fully considered, I think the fair-minded critic must admit the creditable character of the literary product of the time; and I believe that the literary student of Pennsylvania letters who has heretofore passed over, as utterly sterile, the first three-quarters of the eighteenth century, will modify his opinion so soon as he devotes to the study of this period the care and attention without which no just estimate is possible.

THREE CRITICAL PERIODS IN OUR DIPLOMATIC RELATIONS WITH ENGLAND DURING THE LATE WAR.

PERSONAL RECOLLECTIONS OF THOMAS H. DUDLEY, LATE UNITED STATES CONSUL AT LIVERPOOL.

In the various conflicts which take place in the world diplomacy often performs an important part, second only to that performed by the men in arms upon the bloody field. The war of the Rebellion in the United States was no exception to this rule, and diplomacy on several occasions played its part, and a very important part, in the struggle.

England, at the commencement of the war, outside of her trade with us, had no particular regard for the people of the United States. She looked with a jealous eye on our growth and prosperity as a nation; and the fact that the people in the Northern States generally were in favor of developing the resources of their own country by a protective tariff, which the English regarded as interfering with their trade and limiting their market for their manufactured commodities, created anything but respect for the people of the North.

The English system of a duty for revenue only, or what they termed free trade, at the time it was introduced by Sir Robert Peel and adopted by Parliament, was supposed, by its advocates, would be followed by all other governments and become the universal economic principle among all civilized nations. If this had proven true England would then have been, what she desired to be, the great workshop of the world for manufactured commodities; but, unfortunately for her hopes, the other nations did not all see it as she did, and some of them refused to follow her example; among them was the United States.

England soon had to learn another unpleasant lesson, that

the United States were disposed to manufacture some things for themselves rather than buy everything from her. Then, too, the energy which we displayed in commercial matters, in building ships and pushing our commerce with all parts of the world, was distasteful, if not injurious to her trade. She did not like our sharp competition upon the ocean. Our republican form of government, too, did not inspire her aristocracy or the other monarchial nations of Europe with regard. The republic of the United States had been looked upon as a constant menace to England and all other monarchial governments, and will continue to be so long as we remain a united country. These were some of the reasons which had an effect in moulding public opinion in England unfavorably towards our country before the war commenced.

The great mass of their people, therefore, had no love for us at the time when the war broke out. They were quite willing, if not desirous, to see us disrupted and our prosperity checked. There is not much doubt that England thought it was her true interest that our power as a nation should be broken. The only thing that troubled her was the fear that the war might cut off or interrupt her supply of cotton. This alone disturbed her.

Soon after the election of Mr. Lincoln the leaders of the Confederacy in the South sent over two ambassadors in an unofficial capacity to apprise the English and French governments what the South contemplated in inaugurating the Rebellion. They were to secure the co-operation of these governments if it were possible to do so. If they could not obtain this co-operation at once, they were to pave the way for friendly intercourse and recognition at an early day, after the Rebellion should have been commenced. These envoys were Thomas King, of Georgia, and Dudley Mann, of North Carolina. On their arrival in England they had an interview with Lord Palmerston and Earl Russell, the one the Premier and the other the Secretary of Foreign Affairs. What took place at these interviews is not known, other than unofficially, and from reports which were given out at the time. These reports informed us that they had been well received, and had obtained assurances that if the Rebellion was a success, and assumed the proportions which it afterwards did assume, that then the Confederacy would be recognized by England, and commercial relations established. These ambassadors were equally successful in their conference with the Emperor Napoleon, and obtained similar promises from him. He, too, did not like a republican form of government any more than England did, and was quite willing to see the great republic broken. The promises received from these two nations, though in an unofficial form, gave great encouragement to the South, and had much to do with the inauguration of the Rebellion. They looked upon these promises as making success almost certain.

The States in the South, one by one, passed the ordinances of secession, and the so-called Confederacy was formed. Beauregard opened his batteries on Fort Sumter and the war began. It was very evident from the commencement that the South not only had the sympathy of the people of England, but that the English stood ready to assist them in every way they could. I speak now of the great mass of the English people. One war-vessel, the " Oreto," afterwards known as the " Florida," had been built in Liverpool for the rebels by William C. Miller & Sons, the senior member of which firm was, during the time of her construction, an officer in the employ of Her Majesty's government, with an office in the Custom-House in Liverpool. This vessel was in the river Mersey, being fitted out as a war-steamer, at the time when the " Trent" difficulty occurred. Even before this period, however, many blockade-runners had been chartered, and were then actively engaged in carrying supplies and munitions of war from England to the rebels in the South.

Such was the condition of affairs in England at the time when Mason and Slidell were seized and removed from the English steamer "Trent" by Captain Wilkes, commanding the United States steamer "San Jacinto." Although Mr. Seward wrote a most friendly and conciliatory despatch to the English government as soon as he had been informed of the seizure, even before he had received any complaint or even notice from England, the English, on their part, at once seized upon the occasion as a proper time for them to carry out their promises made to the Confederate ambassadors, King and Mann, to recognize the South and take up arms in their behalf.

Public sentiment became very strong and bitter against the United States. The feeling ran all one way. The cry was for war, even before they knew whether the act of Captain Wilkes would be approved or condemned by our government. The great mass of the people did not seem to care what we said or did. We had insulted their flag and they wanted to fight us. They desired their government to strike, and at once.

As a matter of form, in order to justify themselves before the world in the course they intended to take, the question of the right to make the seizure on the " Trent" was referred to the law officers of the crown. These officers gave an opinion that the United States had no right to make it. The strange thing about this opinion and the action of the government was the fact that England had always claimed the right of search as against the United States, and had actually exercised this right in some hundreds of cases, by boarding United States vessels sailing under our flag and taking from them not only English subjects whenever found on board, in the same manner that Captain Wilkes had done in taking Mason and Slidell from the steamer " Trent," but in many instances taking American citizens as well from our ships and impressing them as seamen into the English service. England had carried the doctrine of the right of search so far as to go to war with the United States in 1812 to maintain this principle. She had fought this war out rather than yield this right, and peace had been concluded between the two countries, leaving it an unsettled question. Up to the time of the " Trent" difficulty England had never relinquished this right, which her own law officers now pronounced illegal, and for exercising which in this one instance she was now ready to declare war against the United States. No more strange and inconsistent conduct than that of England on this occasion can be found in history. It is a singular fact that the treaty of peace between England and the United States, made in December, 1814, and known as the Treaty of Ghent, does not so much as mention the right of search, or refer to it in any way.

Earl Russell framed an offensive despatch, addressed to our government, complaining of the seizure, and demanding the surrender of Mason and Slidell. This despatch was written as an excuse for the war which they intended to declare, and was couched in such language as to bring it about. If this despatch had been sent in the way it was written it would undoubtedly have precipitated a war between the two countries. We could never have afforded to surrender Mason and Slidell at the dictation of such a despatch. Our government would never have done it. Our dignity and self-respect as a nation would not have permitted us to do so. That England at that time intended war with us cannot be doubted. Everything indicated this. *Punch*, the great English cartoonist, published its celebrated cartoon of Britannia resting her elbow on a loaded cannon, pointing towards the United States, with this inscription under it,—"Waiting for an answer."

Preparations for war, and war at once, on an extensive scale were commenced by the English government. It issued an order to fit out and prepare immediately all its war-vessels for sea, and hired steamers and merchant-ships as transports to carry troops, munitions of war, and supplies to Canada and Halifax. These vessels were taken up and loaded and despatched as fast as possible with troops and war-materials; and thousands of troops and tons of ammunition and war-supplies of every kind were landed upon our continent, ready for the conflict. A proclamation was issued by the government, prohibiting the export of salt-petre, powder, cannon, arms, lead, and munitions of war. It was said at the time that orders were also issued for the construction of six more iron-clads as soon as it was possible to complete them. One thing is very certain, no steps were left undone by the English government to prepare for immediate war. And all this, as has been stated, was done before the United States had time to explain, justify, or disavow the seizure of Mason and Slidell. It did not seem as if England was willing even to give time for an answer to be made.

It is the custom of the English government that important despatches from the Foreign Office, addressed to other governments, shall be submitted to the Queen for her approval, before being forwarded. The offensive despatch prepared by Earl Russell in this case, addressed to our government, was taken to the Queen. It was placed in her hands while she was sitting at the bedside of her sick husband, the Prince Consort. She betrayed emotion while reading it, which was observed by the Prince. He turned and asked her what it was that so disturbed her. She told him, and expressed her displeasure at the language and tone of the despatch. He asked to see it. It was handed to him, and after he had read it over he remarked, " This will never do ; it must not be sent in this form ; it is couched in offensive language, such as will irritate and provoke a war between the two nations." He asked for a pencil, and they propped him up in bed ; he took the pencil and went through the despatch, striking out the offensive and harsh language, and interlined it so as to modify and tone it down. After he had gone through it and made these alterations, he requested the Queen to have it sent in the form as he had changed it. This was done. The despatch as modified was respectful in language and tone, and the United States government acceded to the demand and surrendered Mason and Slidell, and thus put an end to the intended war ; and, by so doing, at the same time settled the question of the right of search among the nations of the world once and forever, and in accordance with what we as a nation had claimed and contended for almost from the formation of our government up to that time. The despatch written by Mr. Seward on this occasion was probably the most able state paper he ever wrote.

During the "Trent" difficulty John Bright, of Rochdale, played a very important part, which should not be forgotten. It is due to history no less than to his memory that it should be mentioned.

Mr. Bright was friendly to the United States, and had not permitted his feelings to be distorted or his judgment perverted. He knew the Rebellion had been inaugurated to extend and perpetuate human slavery. He knew, too, that the success of the South would fasten and rivet more firmly the shackles upon the slave. He did not desire this. He was opposed to human slavery and opposed to war; but among his countrymen at that time he stood almost alone.

His neighbors and friends at Rochdale tendered him a banquet, to be given on the 4th day of December, 1861, for the purpose of enabling him to express his views upon this question, which was then agitating all England. It was when the excitement ran the highest. The "Trent" incident was the only topic of conversation, and the opinions were all one way,—in condemnation of the United States. There was not a newspaper of any consequence in the kingdom that excused the act or said one word in extenuation, and scarcely a voice was raised in our favor. It was at such a time as this that Mr. Bright was invited by his neighbors to attend this banquet. A mutual friend asked me if I would like to be present. I told him I would. I had never seen John Bright. On the afternoon of the day we took the cars for Rochdale, and reached there about seven o'clock in the evening. It was a murky, cold, dark night, such as one often experiences in England. My friend said it would be unfair to Mr. Bright to call on him at his house at that time, as he would most likely be thinking over what he intended to say. I agreed with him, and we went directly to the hall where the banquet was to be held. The room was large; my friend found a seat had been assigned to me on the raised platform at one end of the hall, and he suggested that I should take it, whilst he would take one immediately below the platform. No persons were in the room except ourselves, but it soon began to fill, and all the seats were occupied. Just before the time set for the banquet a side door was opened and several gentlemen entered and took their seats on the raised platform where I was seated. A stout gentleman took a seat by my side. Very soon after taking it he turned and said, "I presume this is Mr. Dudley, the United States consul at Liverpool?" I answered that it was, and he replied, "My name is John Bright." This was my introduction to Mr. Bright, and the commencement of a friendship which continued until his death. He commenced to converse, and told me that he felt the weight of the responsibility resting upon him that night heavier than he had ever felt it before. He seemed exceedingly depressed. I said to him in reply as many cheery words as I could, but I did not know at that time what I learned afterwards, that he had a letter in his pocket from his friend, Richard Cobden, declining to come out and sustain him (Bright) in the stand which he had resolved to take; not that he differed from him in sentiment, but he did not think it was necessary for him and Bright to make the sacrifice; that they were not called upon to do so. I was informed about this letter some time after the banquet had been given, and of Mr. Bright's answer to it, telling Mr. Cobden that he was wrong in the position he had marked out; that they each had a duty to perform; that they should stand up for the right without regard to the consequences or what others might say or do; that neither had a right to shirk this duty.

As soon as the banquet had been partaken of, Mr. Bright arose and made that memorable speech which stands forth to-day as one of the finest specimens of forensic eloquence in the English language. He spoke for nearly two hours, and concluded with these words,—

"Now, whether the Union will be restored or not, or the South achieve an unhonored independence or not, I know not, and I predict not. But this I think I know, that in a few years, a very few years, the twenty millions of freemen in the North will be thirty or even fifty millions,—a population equal to or exceeding that of this kingdom. When that time comes I pray that it may not be said among them that, in the darkest hour of their country's trials, England, the land of their fathers, looked on with icy coldness, and saw unmoved the perils and calamities of their children.   As for me, I have but this to say.   I am but one in this audience, and but one in the citizenship of this country; but if all other tongues are silent mine shall speak for that policy which gives hope to the bondsmen of the South, and which tends to generous thoughts, and generous words, and generous deeds between the two great nations who speak the English language, and from their origin alike are entitled to the English name."

This speech made a profound impression both in England and the United States.   It was published in all the leading newspapers of the kingdom, and read generally by all the people.

It required a degree of moral courage and patriotism such as you rarely see in these times, for a man to stand up as John Bright did on such an occasion as this, in the face of an almost infuriated people, and make the speech he made.   To my mind it was one of the grandest spectacles I ever witnessed.   To me it seemed almost like another Curtius, who was willing to plunge into the chasm to save Rome.   Bright stood alone in England when he arose to make this speech, but when he sat down there were hundreds, including such men as Richard Cobden, William E. Foster, the Duke of Argyle, Professor Cairns, Professor Beasley, and Charles Edward Rawlins, who were ready to gather around and stand by him.   These men did come forward and raise their voices for the right in the mighty struggle with slavery and the slave power which was then going on in the United States, and their influence was afterwards felt throughout England and continued to be felt so long as the war lasted.

I must digress for a moment and note an incident that should be remembered.   Some years after this James Bains, an Englishman, residing at Manchester, a friend of John Bright, and a great admirer of Abraham Lincoln, conceived the idea of presenting Mr. Lincoln with a marble bust of John Bright. I was asked if I would send this gift to Mr. Lincoln when it was completed, and I promised to do so. The bust arrived at my office in Liverpool on the day we received the sad intelligence of Mr. Lincoln's assassination. I wrote to Mr. Bains, and asked him, now that Lincoln was dead, what I should do with the bust. He replied, " Give it to the people of the United States." And I forwarded it to Washington; and this bust now stands somewhere in the White House, probably without a history or so much as a name attached to it to tell who it is.

The history of the despatch prepared by Earl Russell, demanding the surrender of Mason and Slidell, was not known until some time after the " Trent" difficulty had been settled. It came out in this way: Lady Cowley, the wife of Lord Cowley, the British minister at Paris at that time, was a very intimate friend of Queen Victoria's before either were married. They were young girls together, and the friendship formed in youth continued, and was kept up until after Victoria came to the throne. Lady Cowley was in the habit of visiting the Queen quite frequently. While on a visit to her at Windsor Castle the Queen told her all about the despatch, and how the Prince Consort had altered it whilst lying on his death-bed. The Queen remarked that this was the last official act of his life, and went on to say that she was rejoiced to think that this act was in the interest of peace between the two nations.

I became acquainted with these facts in relation to this despatch at the legation in Paris. I was on a visit to Judge William L. Dayton, our minister. One morning Mr. Dayton received a letter from Lord Cowley, requesting him to call on Lady Cowley during the day, stating that she was anxious to see him. He showed me the letter, expressing curiosity as to the cause of its being written. He ordered his carriage during the forenoon and drove to the British legation and saw Lady Cowley. She told him that she had just returned from a visit to the Queen, and that while there the Queen had informed her about the despatch and the changes made in it by the Prince Consort, with the request that she (Lady Cowley) should communicate the facts to Judge Dayton with the view of their being made known to the people of the United States; that this was the reason for her sending for him. The judge informed me during the evening of what Lady Cowley had told him, and wrote the same to the State Department at Washington.

Up to the time of the "Trent" difficulty the North had not made much progress in putting down the Rebellion, or displayed very much skill in conducting the war. The fight at Bull Run had not redounded much to our credit; Vicksburg had not been taken, and the bloody battles which afterwards took place had not been fought. England had not formed a very high opinion of our soldiers, or of our military skill or ability to carry on a war. The London *Times* and other leading newspapers of Great Britain had said over and over that a people educated as ours were, and brought up with republican ideas such as we had, would never do for soldiers; that they would not submit to the military discipline necessary to make soldiers. They might be drafted into the army, but when the army was formed it would be nothing more than a mob of men, and would break into pieces like a rope of sand when the first strain should be put upon it. This was the opinion generally entertained by their people. The English at that time regarded a war with the United States as a very small matter; they believed if it took place we would be an easy conquest for them. They changed this opinion before the war was over, and learned that an educated people, brought up under a republic, with republican ideas, submitted to military discipline, and made as good soldiers as any the world has ever seen, quite equal to those brought up under a monarchial government.

I was dining with Sir William Brown, of Liverpool. The dinner had been given to the judges of the Court of Assizes. My seat was next to an English admiral. During the dinner he turned in a condescending manner and asked me if we had any news from the war. I answered, yes, that there had been a naval engagement, a fight between the "Monitor" and the "Merrimac." He made a remark in effect asking me if I regarded such an insignificant affair as worthy of much consideration. I told him that I did; that I regarded it as the most extraordinary naval fight that had taken place during the century. I shall never forget the contemptuous look he gave as he turned from me. I said nothing more to him, or he to me. It took time for the English mind to grasp and take in the importance of this engagement. Two weeks afterwards the London *Times* came out with a long editorial, commenting upon this fight and its importance in naval warfare, and winding up with the startling statement that England had no navy; all she had, the paper went on to say, was a parcel of old tubs that would not stand up for an hour before the "Monitors" which were being constructed in the United States. England had come at last to realize the effect and consequences of this battle. I wrote home to the State Department that there was now no longer danger of intervention on the part of England in behalf of the South. And I would say here that this fight between the "Monitor" and the "Merrimac" did more to preserve the peace between England and the United States than any other event that took place during the war. England was quite willing to strike at us if she could do so without getting hurt herself. It was fear rather than love that prevented a conflict between the two nations.

The next critical period in our diplomatic relations was when the French Emperor, Napoleon the Third, conceived the idea of recognizing the Confederacy and taking the risk of a war with the United States, provided England would join him. I obtained early information of what was going on at the French court. I learned that the Emperor had made up his mind that the time had come to redeem the promises made to the Confederate envoys, King and Mann, to recognize the Confederacy. To ascertain whether England would join him he sent over a special ambassador to London to interview the government and, if possible, obtain its co-operation. His plan was for both governments to recognize it simultaneously and then join forces, raise the blockade, and establish the Confederacy. As soon as I learned of the arrival of the ambassador in London I sent for a member of the English Parliament who resided in Liverpool, and who held the closest relations with Mr. Gladstone, the then Chancellor of the English Exchequer. I knew that any communication that I might make to this person would be carried to Mr. Gladstone, who would inform the government, and this was what I wanted. I told him of the arrival in London of this ambassador from the French court. He had not heard of it, and was incredulous at first. I convinced him of its truth, and told him that while I had no expectation that any information I might give him would result in anything, yet I wished him to know what was going on, and the effect it would have if the French ambassador succeeded in his mission. I said to him, " You must understand that a recognition of the Southern Confederacy at this time would be followed by war with the United States ; it means mediation on the part of the French and English governments, and mediation means war." I then told him that there was a very considerable element among the people in the Northern States, belonging mostly to the Democratic party, composed largely of foreigners, who had not entered heartily into the war; that many of them had gone so far as even to oppose the war, and that these men were ready and willing to take up arms in behalf of the government if England should attempt to take part in it. I informed him that a war with England would be popular with these men, and if it took place I would go home myself and undertake to raise an army of five hundred thousand men in the North, without one cent of bounty, for the purpose of invading Canada; and just as certain as the sun would rise, if England should take this step she would lose Canada and all her other British possessions in North America. I admitted to him that they might succeed in establishing the Confederacy, but, if they did, it would be at a great sacrifice on their part as well as ours. I told him to strike at us if they wished to do so, but I wanted them to fully understand what the consequences would be. I said, "Your treasury will be emptied, your business at home and abroad injured, your commerce swept from the ocean by our cruisers, and you will lose forever your possessions on the North American continent." I told him this was certain to follow. I then called his attention to the injury England had already done us in the war; how she had raised a loan for the Confederates to enable them to carry on the war; how our commerce had been swept from the sea by the cruisers which England had built and sent out to make war upon us; how they had sustained the rebels by the arms, munitions of war, and supplies they had sent them; and how it would have been impossible for the South to have carried on the conflict for one year if it had not been for the aid and assistance which they had received from England.[1] I knew the man I was talking with, and I knew what I said would be communicated to Mr. Gladstone as soon as it was possible for him to do it. I had the pleasure to learn that he took the next train for London and went directly to Mr. Gladstone's house. I followed him in a later train and went to the legation, where I had a conference with Mr. Adams, and told him what I had done. Mr. Adams approved of my action, and in an interview with Earl Russell the next day confirmed the statement that I had made. What took place in the English Cabinet, in their discussions upon this question, we have never been informed; the only thing we know is this, that the proposal made by the French Emperor was declined by England, and a bloody war thus averted.

The third incident where diplomacy played an important part during the war was in relation to the building of the two war-vessels for the Confederate government by the

[1] I reported no less than one hundred and thirty steamers sent out from England to run the blockade and carry war-material and supplies for the rebel army. These were in addition to the sailing-vessels engaged in the same business. The sailing-vessels generally landed the supplies at Bermuda or Nassau, and then they were loaded on the steamers and run through the blockade into some of the Southern ports.

Laird Brothers, of Birkenhead. They were called the
"rams," because of the projection built on the stem of the
ships for butting and sinking vessels they might come in
contact with. They were called and known as Laird's
"rams." John Laird, the senior member of this firm, was
a member of the English Parliament at the time they were
being built. I was early informed of their construction,—in
fact, almost as soon as the keels were laid,—and communicated the matter to our government, and sent duplicates of
my despatches to Mr. Adams, our minister in London. One
was christened at the time of the launching as "El Tous-
soun," and the other as "El Monassir." After the vessels
were launched it was given out that they were intended for
the Egyptian government. The collector of the port at Liverpool told me this. I informed him that he was mistaken;
that I knew they were being built for the Confederacy; that
Captain Bullock, the Confederate naval officer in England
at that time, had made the contract with the Lairds for
their construction. They then gave out that they belonged
to M. Bravay, a Frenchman residing in Paris. We applied
to the French government, and were enabled to show the
untruthfulness of this pretence.

Mr. Adams made complaint to the English government,
and asked it to take steps to stop their sailing. Earl Russell replied that it was necessary for the English government to be furnished with evidence proving that they were
being built for the Confederates before it could take any
action in the matter, and requested that the United States
consul at Liverpool, if he had any evidence, should submit
it to the collector at that port. I took the ground that
when the representatives of a foreign government gave
notice to the government to which they were accredited
that they had reason to believe that the laws of neutrality
were being violated by any of the subjects belonging to that
government, and pointed out the particulars wherein they
were being violated and the parties who were doing it, that
then it was the duty of the government which had the courts
and all the legal machinery for doing it to make the inves-

tigation and ascertain if the charges were true or false ; and if true, take the necessary steps to prevent their violation, and not throw it upon the foreign government to do this. The action of the United States towards England had always been right the reverse of what England was now doing. During the Crimean war in 1855, Mr. Barclay, the English consul at New York, wrote Mr. Crampton, the English minister at Washington, that he had reason to believe that the barque "Maury" was being fitted out in New York as a cruiser for Russia against England. Mr. Crampton wrote to the Secretary of State, Mr. Marcy, and he communicated with Mr. Cushing, the Attorney-General, who directed the United States district attorney at New York to take immediate steps for the detention of the vessel, and this was done. In 1838, during the Canadian rebellion, the United States, at the instance of England, passed a special act of Congress to prevent our people from aiding the rebellion. I prepared a pamphlet containing the correspondence in the case of the "Alabama" and the barque "Maury" and the special act of Congress just referred to, to show the difference between the United States and England in the enforcement of neutrality.

I sent a copy of this pamphlet to all the members of the House of Commons, the leading members of the House of Lords, and many of the prominent people in the kingdom. The English government, in a despatch dated September 25, 1863, addressed to Mr. Adams, refused to pass a new law to preserve its neutrality.

It seemed to me to be a great hardship for the English government to throw the burden of vindicating its laws upon the United States, especially when we had no power to compel any one to give evidence or testify. But inasmuch as it refused to do anything until we should furnish the evidence, I undertook the task, and employed counsel to prepare such affidavits as we could procure to make out the case. The great difficulty we had to contend with was to get any one to testify ; we had no means to compel them to do so, and those who knew the most were the least willing to give evidence; indeed, they generally were directly interested in concealing from us the facts which they knew.   Even those who were not interested and had knowledge, as a rule, would not testify or aid us, because it would injure them in a business point of view in a hostile community such as Liverpool was at that time.   It seemed to me to be worse for us than the task which was imposed upon the Israelites of old to make bricks without straw, because we had not only to make the bricks without the straw, if we could do so, but had in addition all the people arrayed against us, doing what they could to thwart us.   In many instances persons who gave us information were turned out of employment, and were unable afterwards to obtain work in Liverpool, because they had aided us.   To this extent was public feeling carried.   One can therefore understand how hard the task must have been to procure any evidence.   We did our best, and had such affidavits as we could obtain served on the collector at Liverpool, in conformity with Earl Russell's directions.   At the same time we sent duplicates of the affidavits to Mr. Adams, our minister in London, who laid them directly before the government at the Foreign Office.   We did this in order to preclude any question being raised as to the sufficiency of the notice we gave.   We deemed this all the more necessary from the fact that it was evident from the first that the English government did not intend to assist us in any manner.   Mr. Adams and myself were satisfied that it intended to throw every obstacle it could in our way, and permit the vessels to sail if it were possible to do so.   In answer to the demand made by Mr. Adams to detain these vessels, Earl Russell, after he had taken time to consider the matter, wrote that the English government did not regard the evidence which we had put in as sufficient to warrant it in stopping the vessels.   After writing this despatch, Earl Russell started for Scotland, and whilst there delivered his celebrated speech at Blair-Gowrie.   In this speech, which was published in all the leading newspapers, he went over the matter and gave an explanation of the action of the government in refusing to detain the vessels. He claimed that it was the duty of the American government not only to procure actual and positive proof that the vessels were being built for the Confederate government, in contravention of the English laws of neutrality, before it could take action, but that the evidence itself, so furnished, must be credible evidence. He used this term "credible evidence" because among the affidavits that had been sent to the English government there was one made by Clarence Randolph Young, who had been purser on board the steamer "Alabama," and who was conversant with all the doings of the Confederate government in Europe with regard to the construction of war-vessels. He had left the "Alabama" and was in Liverpool. He knew, what everybody in Liverpool knew, except the officers of Her Majesty's government, that these vessels were being built for the Confederates. I obtained Young's affidavit, proving the fact that they were being built for the rebels. With this affidavit the proof was complete. It brought home the construction directly for the Confederate government, and hence the necessity of either ignoring the affidavit or stopping the vessels from sailing. Earl Russell took it upon himself to ignore the affidavit. He threw it out on the ground that it was not credible. He did this in a preliminary proceeding, contrary to all practice and all precedent under the English law as practised in England or the United States. The difficulty about Mr. Young, to whom Earl Russell objected, was this : On one of the voyages of the "Alabama" to the West Indies, Young, while purser, had married a quadroon girl, a native of the West Indies. It was this act of marrying a quadroon girl that had tainted him in the estimation of Earl Russell, and justified the rejection of the evidence on the ground that it was not credible. His affidavit was not even to be considered, much less regarded. To this extent was the English government driven to shield the Confederates and enable them to get their war-vessels out. Mr. Gladstone had said in his Newcastle speech that Jefferson Davis had organized an army and was then building a navy. I wrote home in reply to this speech, and said yes, it was true that the rebels were having a navy built; but it was being built by Englishmen in Great Britain and not in the South. At that time there were no less than five war-vessels being constructed in Great Britain for the rebels. These did not include the "Florida" and the "Alabama," which were already on the sea, burning and destroying all vessels they met sailing under the United States flag.

To this despatch of Earl Russell's, refusing on the part of the English government to stop these vessels, Mr. Adams wrote that if they were permitted to sail, the United States would construe it as a belligerent act on the part of England; in other words, that the United States would regard it as war. I was aware of the serious turn matters had taken, and went up to London. I found Mr. Adams in a very depressed state of mind; he regarded war with England as inevitable. I shall never forget how he walked up and down his drawing-room, discussing the gravity of the situation. He said, "We would have only nineteen days more in England; that he would have to leave as soon as he heard from Washington, which would be in about nineteen days; he could see no alternative but war. The Rebellion had been kept alive by the aid and assistance it had received from England. There were hundreds of English steamers and vessels then engaged in carrying munitions of war and supplies from England for the rebel army, besides the war-vessels which had been built and were then in the course of construction in the kingdom. They had their financial department, their commissary department, their ordnance department, and their naval department in England; and it had come almost to this, that the war was being actually conducted and carried on against us by Englishmen, and from England. The matter had been fully considered by our government, and it was prepared to take action. It could not permit matters to go further than they had gone. Our government could not do otherwise than it had done, and there was no way out of it but war. The English navy was superior to ours, and it was quite likely that they would defeat us on the ocean, and might inflict much damage, perhaps burn some of the cities on the sea-coast; but we would have the advantage on the land, and could march our forces into Canada and capture those provinces; but no one could compute the consequences,—the human lives that would be taken, or the damages that would be done, or the treasure that would be spent in the prosecution of such a war." At this time, whilst we were speculating, it was fortunate that our people at home did not know the perilous condition of affairs in England. It is sometimes best that we should remain ignorant of the dangers that surround us; that we should not have seen the hidden pitfalls beneath our feet that we have passed over in safety. They had enough at home to bear in the conduct of the war without having this added; and, fortunately, before they were apprised of the peril the danger had passed. Whilst we were still walking up and down the drawing-room I observed through a side window a Queen's messenger approaching the house. The bell rang, and soon Mr. Adams's servant delivered to him a despatch which the messenger had brought. He opened it and read it aloud. It was to this effect: " That Her Majesty's government still had the subject of the detention of the ' rams,' which were being built by the Lairds at Birkenhead, under consideration." I said, " This is a back-down on the part of the English government." He replied, " It looks that way." And in a moment we were both breathing more freely; the crisis had passed.

The history of the occurrence is this: After Earl Russell had sent his despatch to Mr. Adams he started for Scotland, as has been mentioned, regarding the matter as settled, so far as the English government was concerned. It had decided not to stop the vessels, but permit them to sail. Lord Palmerston, who was at that time at Tunbridge Wells, came up to London and went to the Foreign Office, and asked how matters stood with the American government about the " rams." He was told of the correspondence that had taken place, and that if the vessels were permitted to sail the American government would regard it as war on the part of England.

Lord Palmerston asked to see the correspondence; after reading it he said that the matter had gone far enough; that England did not want war with the United States at that time, and directed the despatch to be prepared, telling Mr. Adams that Her Majesty's government still had the subject of the stoppage of these vessels under consideration. After this steps were soon taken by the government to prevent these vessels from sailing. All that took place between the Lairds, the government, and Captain Bullock, the rebel agent, is not known to the public. What we know is this, that the English government finally bought the vessels. This was done after the Lairds had been informed of the condition of affairs, and of the intention on the part of the government to prevent their sailing as Confederate vessels. After the "rams" had been purchased by the government they became a part of the English navy, and if afloat are now sailing under the English flag.

There are events in the lives of most persons that make a profound impression; those here recorded are of that nature, and will not be forgotten, but remain so long as memory lasts. The lines thus made do not grow dim with years, but deepen as the shadows pass.

GENEALOGICAL GLEANINGS, CONTRIBUTORY TO A HISTORY OF THE FAMILY OF PENN.

BY J. HENRY LEA, FAIRHAVEN, MASSACHUSETTS.

(Continued from Vol. XVI. p. 842.)

PREROGATIVE COURT OF CANTERBURY.

[The list of Penn Wills in this important court, which was printed in the PENNA. MAGAZINE for April, 1890, and subsequent numbers, was the result of a general gathering by several hands, and, as a natural result, many wills were overlooked, which would not have been the case had a regular and systematic search of the Calendars been undertaken. This search the writer was about to undertake, waiting only till the time could be found for the tedious task, when his friend, Mr. H. W. F. Harwood, who had just completed the same search for the name of Penny (taking incidentally all Penns), very kindly placed his note-book at his disposal, giving an exhaustive list of the name by which the following wills have been checked and may be relied upon as giving all Penns in this court to the year 1700.]

1592—William Penne of Minety, Glouc.
[Following this will, given in the first part of these Gleanings,[1] occur the names of " Wm : Legard, Pet : St. Eloy, Hen : Stevens Deputy Registers." These names are not in the original register and are those of officials in the Probate Court a century later, and were probably appended to an official transcript made for some of the family at that time.]

1655—Thomas Penn—Jan. 29, 1655–6 Letters of Admon. issued to Richard Stratton, principal Creditor of Thomas Penn late of Stratford in parish of Passenham, co. Northton., but intestate dec'd., to admr. &c.—Act Book, fo. 11.

1659—Katherine Penne of Hagley, co. Worc., widow, sick in bodie. Dated 18 March 1658. To dau. Rebecca Titterre £10; dau. Sibell James £10; Sarah Lench, dau. to

[1] PENNA. MAG., April, 1890, Vol. XIV. pp. 58–61.

my son-in-law Thomas Lench £30 a bedd chest, Trunk &c in 2 years; eldest son of my son Joseph Browne £5; eldest son of my son Gabriel Browne £5; cos. Humphrey Penne of Romesley in parish of Hales Owen, co Salop, gent. 10s; Margaret Goodier of Hagley, widow, £1; Margaret Cardale of Hagley, spinster, £1; Mary wife of William Cardale £1; Ffrances wife of Richard Allchurch of Stourbridge, co. afsd., Chandler, £1–4–0; dau. Sibill James all rest of household goods; master John Addenbrook of Bewdley, gent., £1; Wm. Bardale of Hagley £1; Thomas Lane 2s.; Thomas Watkis 1s.; to poor widows of Hagley 12d. each; son-in-law Thomas Lench £5; Residuary Legatees the son of my dau. Sibill James, dau. of my dau. Rebecca Tetterie, ch. of my son Joseph Browne & ch. of my son Gabriel Browne; Executors Mr. John Addenbrook of Bewdley, co. worc., gent., & William Cardale of Hagley, yeoman; Witness Ellenor Price & Margaret Goodier; Signs by mark; Codicil 19 Mar 1658, nuncupative, has no new names; Pro. 27 June 1659 by Exrs.—Pell, 245.[1]

1661—John Penn of Kilkewydd in psh. of fforden, Co. of Mountgomery & Dioc. of Hereford; dated 2 Mar. 13 Chas. II, 1660; To be bur. in psh. Church of Chirbury; to my now wife Margarett £13–13–4; to kinsman James Alderson £20; to nephew Robert Davis the like sum of £30 (*sic*); to nephew Richard Roberts £20; to my sister Elizabeth Davis £10 if alive, otherwise to her dau. Katherine H. Humphreys; to neece Katherine Lloyd, wife of Richard Lloyd £5; to children of my kinsman John Roberts of Willmington £5; to my nephew Cessar Roberts £10 he oweth to 4 of his children, Cessar, Richard, Thomas & Mary; to cosin Richard Penne 40s.; to kinsw. Mrs. Hanna Harris £5; to Anne, dau. of Thos. Lloyd £8–13–4; to Johane, dau. of Richard Griffithes of Wallope 40s.; to Elizabeth, wife of Oliver Watters 40s.; to zachews Jones & Elizabeth Jones each

---

[1] The above will was omitted in former paper (see PENNA. MAG., Vol. XIV., No. 2, July, 1890, folio 170), the abstract having been received too late for incorporation.

50s.; to Nicholas and Peter Jones each 20s.; to servant Wynefred Purcell 40s.; & a Wainscot Bed & furniture after decease of my wife; to servt. Reynald Kerver 40s. & all apparell; to Nicholas Wyne, gent. £5; to Richard Jones, gent., 20s. for a ring; to brother law Thomas Edwards, gent. 10s. for ring; to Jane wife of Thos. Lloyd the same; to Magdalen Rogers 30s.; to George sonn of George Purcell 10s.; to Thomas sonn of Thomas Jenkes 10 groates; to children of my 2 Nephews Robert Davis and Richard Roberts £10; to poor of fforden & Chirbury £4; to Mrs. Anne Griffithes & Mrs. Mary Griffithes my best feather Bed &c.; to wife Margarett my best kine & all household goods that were hers before marriage; to Robt. Davis, Rich. Roberts & Katherine Lloyde all brass & pewter; to Jane wife of Thos. Lloyd a Truckle bed; to nephew Robt. Davis all bills, bonds &c & he Res Leg & Exor.; Wit. Thomas Lloyd, Thomas Lloyd the younger & Richard Jones; bequest to James Alderson changed to £20 before signing; Wit. William Draper, RLL, Richard Jones.   Pro. 15 ffeb. 1661 by Exor. named in will.—Laud, 24.

1670—Sir William Penn of London, Knt.   Will dated 20 Jan. 1669; To be buried in Parish Church of Redcliffe in the City of Bristol "as nere vnto the body of my dear mother deceased as the same conveniently may be"; To have erected a handsome and decent tomb for my mother & myself to be erected by Exr.; Wife Dame Margaret Penn £300 & all jewells not otherwise bequeathed & use for life of one moiety of plate, hou. stuff, coaches & coach horses & all cows; To younger son Richard Penn £4000, my fawcett dyamond ring & all swords, guns & pistols to be paid at 21 years of age & until then £120 per ann.; To granddau. Margaret Lowther £100; Nephews James Bradshaw & William Markeham each £10; Nephews John Bradshaw & George Markeham each £5; Cozen William Penn, son of George Penn, late of the Forest of Brayden in the Co. of Wilts., Gent., deceased, £10; To Cousin Eleanor Keene £6 per ann. for life; To late servant William Bradshaw 40s.

for ring; To servant John Wrenn £5; To poor of Redcliffe & St. Thomas parishes, Bristol, each £20; To eldest son William Penn my gold chain & medall with all residue of plate, hou. stuff & personal estate unbequeathed & remainder goods to wife at her decease; son William Executor; Mourning to wife, son Richard, dau. Margaret Lowther & son-in-law Anthony Lowther & Dr. Whistler & his wife &c; Any differences between Executor & wife to be referred to final judgement of my worthy friend Sir William Coventry of St. Martin-in-the-Fields, co. Middlx Wit. R. Langhorne, John Radford & William Markham. Pro. 6 Oct. 1670 by Executor named in will.

Marginal Note:—Quinto Aprilis 1671° Recepi Testum orile dñi Willimi Penn defti e Reg^{ro} Curiae Praerogativae Cantuar *p* me Wm Penn. Testibus Car Tuckyr Ri: Edes.—Penn, 130.[1]

1672—Robert Pen. Mar. 12 Commission issued to Michael Pen, brother of Robert Pen late of St. Michaels Cornhill, London, bachelor, but intestate decd. &c.—Act Book, fo. 26.

1673—Thomas Penn of Barner Gardner, co. Surry, Gardner, sicke in body dated 18 May 24 Chas. II, 1672; To my sonns Thomas, John and Joseph Penne & daus. Mary & Elizabeth Penn all my Coppyhold & all goods &c. for the bringe of them upp according to discretion of my Exors & goods to be divided between Thomas, John, Mary & Elizabeth; to sonn Joseph all said Copyhold lands, he paying his sister Mary & Elizabeth each £10; to Ellen Stephens 10s. for ring; friends John Smith & Thomas Singould to see will fulfilled; brother William Blind & sister Mary Watson, widdow & Cittizen of London, to be Exors.; Wit. Matt: Preston, John Farmare, Thomas Singnell & Moses Burnham; Pro. 7 May 1673 by Exors.—Pye, 63.

---

[1] An abstract of this important will (not taken by the writer) has been already printed (see PENNA. MAG., Vol. XIV., No. 2, July, 1890, folio 171), but as several omissions of importance occur in the former, it has seemed best to reproduce it here in full.

1673—William Penn of Brodford in psh. of Bellbroughton, co. Worcester, Gent., in bodily health; dated 6 Aug., 20 Chas. II, 1668; To my dau. Margarett Penn all lands in Bellbroughton & Kingsnorton or elsewhere in co. Worc., & she Res. Leg. & Extrx.; to wife Mary Penn a rent charge of £15 yearly for her life; Wit. Humfrey Perrott, Elizabeth Barcroft, her mark, & William Perrott. Pro. 27 Nov. 1673 by Margarett Harris *alias* Penn the Extrx. named in the will.—Pye, 149.

1676—Richard Pen of St. Paul Shadwell in co. Middx., marriner, outward bound on a voyage to sea; dated 5 May 1675, 27 Chas. II; I appoint kinsman Richard Pen of same place, waterman, to be my lawful attorney to demand all debts, wages, &c. & he to be my Res Leg & Exor.; Wit. Tho : Somerby, Not. Pub. & Theop : Haydock his servant; Pro. 3 ffeb. 1676 by Exor.—Hale, 23.

1677—Bartholomew Penn. Sept. 24 Com. issued to John Penn, father of Bartholomew Penn late in partibus transmarinus, Bachelor, dec'd to administer &c.—Act Book, fo. 111.

1679—Elizabeth Pen. Dec. 22 Com. issued to William Carver Grandfather (*Avo ex filia*) & Curator assigned to Elizabeth Pen junior, the daughter of Elizabeth Pen late of Petersfeild, co. Southton., widow, to admr. during minority of said Elizabeth Pen junior.—Act Book, fo. 173.

1680—Edward Penn. June 2 Com. issued to Dorothy Pen, neece of Edward Penn late of Affrica, in Guinea a Bachelor deceased intestate, to admr. &c.—Act Book, fo. 93.

1683—Robert Penne. June 14. Com. issued to Dorathy Penne widow, relict of Robert Penne late of St. Botholph Aldgate, co. Middx., to admr. &c.—Act Book, fo. 86.

1683—John Penne of Bodicote, co. Oxon., yeoman, weake in body; dated (*blank*) Mar. 1682; To Aunt Grant of Bodicote £5 & to her 7 children £5 apeece, that is to say, to my couzins William & Samuel Grant, Bridgett Judd of Adderbury, Alice Dodivell of Banbury & Jane & Elizabeth Grant of Hornton; to couzin Leonard Bradford of Sutton & his sonn & dau. £5 apeece; to coz. Thomas Heynes of Sibbord £5; to coz. Thomas Penne of Cittie of Oxford £5; to coz. Joanna Richeson of Pillerton £5; to coz. Askill of Geden £5; to coz. Elizabeth Penne £4 per ann. for life by hands of my bro. Thomas Penne; to poor of Bodicott £5; brother Thomas Penne sole Exor.; Wit. Elizabeth wrighton, Richard Smith & Samuel Huckell; Pro. 5 Dec. 1683 by Exor.—Drax, 143.

1683—Rachel Penn. Dec. 18. Com. issued to Hanna Luested (wife of John Luested) sister of Rachel Penn late of psh. of St. Olaves Southwark, co. Surry, Spinster, (*solute*) dec'd., to admr. &c. Inv. ex. xxxv[u].—Act Book, fo. 181.

1684—Thomas Penn. Mar. 22. Com. issued to Samuel Penn, brother of Thomas Penn late of Bodicote, co. Oxon., Bachelor, decd., to admr. &c.—Act Book, fo. 43.

1686—Susanna Penn. Dec. 6. Com. issued to Thomas Penn husband of Susanna Penn late of Kenver (?) in co. Stafford., to admr. &c.—Act Book, fo. 184.

1686—Anthonie Penne. Dec. 6. Com. issued to Dorathe Penne widow, the relict of Anthonie Penne late of psh. of St. James in Liberty of Westminster (*infra Litatem Westm*) in co. Middx., decd to admr.—Act Book, fo. 186.

1686—Samuel Pen, Merchant, sometime of Bodicott, co. Oxon.; dated 5 Dec. 1686, 2 Jas. II; The house &c in Bodicott which was my fathers (subject to trust for my sister Ann Penn) to my neece Mary Askell (or whatsoever her Christian name may be), wife of Mr. Michaell Askell of Geydon in co. Warwick, for life, remainder to my friends Capt. Robert Smith & John Broome of London, Hosier, in trust for her sonnes &c; The farme at Bodicott called

Knights, purchased by my brother John Penn, to said Michael Askell & my friend William Barnes the elder of Bodicott, yeoman, for life of my sister Ann Penn on trust for said sister for life, rem. to neece Mary Askell; House & land near Long Marston, co. Glouc., to my cozen John Penn of Oxford, Shoomaker, for 99 years, rem. to his heirs, rem. to neece Mary Askell; to coz. John Penn of Oxford £200; to Thomas Haines sonn of Charles Haines of Sibford, co. Oxon., £100; to kinswoman Mary ffrogley and her 3 ch. Richard, Jane & Mary £10 apeece; to kinswoman Joane, dau. of Michaell Penn decd., £10; to Aunt Jane Grant, widow, £5 & to her 6 ch. William Grant, Jane Lyornes, Elizabeth Trusse, Alice Aldington, Bridget Judd & Susanna Grant £10 apeece; to kinswoman Elizabeth White of Dodington £5; to 2 children of Leonard Bradford decd., Elizabeth & her brother, £5 apeece; to servt. Richard Smith £10 & to servt. Jane Aris £3; £100 to be divided by my Exor. among such of my Mothers relations whose names are or have been Herne (of the same family of the Hernes of which my Mother was one) who shall be found in low condition or want; to Elizabeth Righton, widdow, 20s.; to Wm. Barnes afsd. £10; to Capt. Robert Smith 50 guineas; to John Broome £100; to James Wallis of London, Merchant, 50 guineas; to poor of Bodicott £5; to dau. of my neece Mary Askell £1000 at 21 or marr.; neece Mary Askell & her ch. Res Legs; Michaell Askell Exor.; James Wallis & John Broome Overseers; Wit. Charlis Beswick, George Young, Jeremy Mount Att'ney in King street nere Guildhall; Pro. 14 Dec. 1686 by Exor.—Lloyd, 169.

1690—James Penn of Herst, co. Berks, Butcher, very sick & weake; dated 17 June 1 Wm. & Mary, 1689; To sonn in law Thomas Chanler one shilling; sonn in law Henry Creed the same; to grandchild James Chanler £6 & to his bro. & sist., 2 other of my grch., 40s. apeece; to Joane Creed, wife of Robert Creed decd., & her 2 ch. 1s. apeece; to my brother Thomas Penn's widdow & all her ch. 1s. apeece; to bro. George Penn's widdow & her ch. the same; to Simon Wincleoll & his wife & ch. the same; to Thomas Harbert & his wife & ch. the same; to soun in law Joseph Geats the same; to dau. in law Mary Geats same; sonn in law Benjamin Geats same; wife Isabell Res Leg & Extrx; Wit. Thomas Draper, his mark, Thomas Simonds & Robert Brant; Pro. 23 July 1690 by Extrx.—Dyke, 118.

1697—William Penn of City of London, Marriner, now in Petuxant River in Maryland, sick & weak; dated 20 Sept. 1696; to my 3 sisters £50 sterling apeece; my wife Res. Leg. & Extrx.; Wit. Robert Marsham, Jn° Wight & Tho: Greenfeild; Pro. 18 Nov. 1697 by Elizabeth Penn the relict & Extrx named in the will.—Pyne, 249.

[The three wills which follow have been already printed in Mr. H. F. Waters's invaluable "Gleanings," [1] but may well be reproduced here as in continuity with the history of the Founder's family, as also the will of Mary Pennington, from a later number of the same collection. [2]]

1726—Hanna Penn, widow, Relict of William Penn late of Ruscombe in co. of Berks., Esq.; Dated 11 Sept. 1718; Refers to will of husband dated 27 May 1712 & to Trust under said will as to disposal of all lands &c in Pennsylvania &c, legacies to his dau. Aubrey & the 3 children of his son William & the conveyance of the rest of said lands &c in America amongst his children by the now Testatrix his second wife; All said lands, tenements & personal estate to be divided as near as may be into 6 equal parts whereof to my eldest son John Penn & his heirs three sixths or one full half he to pay his sister Margaret £2000 at her marriage or age of 21 years & remaining half unto my 3 other sons Thomas, Richard & Dennis Penn respectively, each one sixth part of the whole divided as aforesaid, with remainder of deceased children to the survivors; Wit. Susanna Perrin,

[1] New Eng. Hist. and Gen. Reg., April, 1890, Vol. XLIV. pp. 190–192.

[2] Ibid., July, 1892, Vol. XLVI. p. 305.

Mary Chandler, Hannah Hoskin, Thomas Grove & S. Clement.

Admon. with will annexed issued 16 Feb. 1726 to John Penn, Esq., natural & lawful son & principal legatee named in the Will of Hanna Penn late of the Parish of St. Botolph Aldersgate, London, widow, deceased &c to administer according to tenor of Will.—Farrant, 49.

1746—John Penn of Hitcham, co. Bucks., Esq.; Dated 24 Oct. 1746; Personal estate in England to William Vigor of Lond., merchant, Joseph Freame, citizen & banker of same, & Lascelles Metcalfe of Westminster, Esq., as Exrs. in trust & also all moneys and effects in America which, before my death shall be heard of in the City of Philadelphia, shall have been collected or remitted by agents there to any part of Europe on own acct. or jointly with my bros., all which to be part of English personal estate; To afsd Exrs all lands &c in & near the City of Bristol & the co. of Gloucester to be applied to charges of trust, debts, funeral & legacies; Sister Margaret Freame annuity; Servant John Travers £100; each of English Exrs one hund. guineas; old servants Thomas Penn & Hannah Roberts; Jane wife of Henry Aldridge of White Walthan, Berks.; nephew John Penn to be educated; nephews & nieces Hannah Penn, Richard Penn & Philadelphia Hannah Freame; bro. Thomas Penn; nephew John Penn my share of mannor of Perkassie, tract of Liberty land & High Street Lot (claimed under deed by late father or will of late grfather Thos. Callowhill); brother Richard Penn all property in New Jersey in America & sd bro. Exr. for New Jersey; My moiety of inheritance of Pennsylvania & the 3 lower Cos. of Newcastle, Kent & Sussex upon Delaware in America to bro. Thomas Penn for life, rem. to his sons in order of age, rem. to bro. Richard with rem. to his sons John & Richard, rem. to latter & his male issue, rem. to neice Hannah only dau. of sd brother Richard & her male issue, next in entail to be sister Margaret Freame & her issue & niece Philadelphia Hannah Freame, next nephew (of the half blood) William

Penn of Cork in Kingdom of Ireland, Esq., then to Springett Penn his eldest son & his male issue, rem. to Christiana
Gulielma Penn, only dau. of said William Penn, next to
grand nephew (of the half blood) Robert Edward Fell, only
son now living of Gulielma Maria Fell, dec'd, then great
niece Mary Margaretta Fell, eld. dau. of sd Gulielma Maria,
then another great niece Gulielma Maria Frances Fell only
other living dau. of said Gulielma Maria Fell, dec'd. &c;
Bro. Thomas Penn to be Exr. for Province of Pennsylvania
& the 3 lower Counties of Newcastle, Kent & Sussex upon
Delaware.   Proved 18 Nov. 1746.—Edmunds, 332.

1775—Thomas Penn of Stokehouse, co. Bucks., Esq.;
Dated 18 Nov. 1771; Wife Lady Juliana Penn & son-in-
law William Baker of Bayford Bury, Herts., Exrs for personal estate except in America; Recites an Indenture tripartite dated 15 Aug. 1751 in consideration of then intended
marriage; James Hamilton, Esq., Revd. Richard Peters &
Richard Hockley, Esq., all of City of Philadelphia, certain
lands in Pennsylvania in trust; Mr. Duffield Williams of
Swansea, co. Glamorgan, £20 per ann.; sons John & Granville Penn; daus. Sophia & Juliana; Recites Agreement
entered into with late brother dated 8 May 1732, 31 Jan.
1750 & 20 Mar. 1750; Nephew Richard Penn, Lieut. Gov.
of Pennsylvania, & Richard Hockley, Esq., Exrs for Province of Pennsylvania; Codicil dated 11 July 1772, names
dau. Juliana as advanced in marriage; 2nd. Codicil dated
18 July 1772 to Mrs Harriott Gordon of Silver Street
Golden Square £20 per ann. & Grace Armagh & Mary Clarke
each £10 per ann.; 3rd Codicill 28 June 1774; Pro. 8 Apr.
1775.—Alexander, 166.

1682—Mary Pennington, dated "att my house att Woodside in Amersham psh. & co. of Bucks this Tenth day of the
third moneth called May One thousand six hundred eighty,"
but signed & sealed 5 July 1680; Refers to personal estate
"which I had before marriage to my deare husband Isaac
Pennington which he made over for my use by a deed be-

The

Pennsylvania

Magazine

OF

HISTORY AND BIOGRAPHY.

Vol. XVII.

PHILADELPHIA:
PUBLICATION FUND OF
THE HISTORICAL SOCIETY OF PENNSYLVANIA,
No. 1300 LOCUST STREET.
1893.

fore marriage to my cousin Elizabeth Dallison." I have taken unto me the debts of my husband by administering after his death. As for my daughter Penn though she be very near to me and hath deserved well of me in her own particular and upon her worthy father's account, yet she hath a large proportion of this world's substance and these my latter children have not anything but what I give them, the Lord having seen it good to strip their dear and pretious father and left him without a capacity to do anything for them, and if so my estate not being great I can only signify my naturalness to my dear daughter Penn and hers by some little things for them to remember me by, and I do believe the witness of God in her will answer to the righteousness of it. To my son William Pennington £500 sterling, £100 to bind him to some handsome trade that hath not much of labor, because he is but weakly, & the other £400 to be paid him at the age of 22 years; to son Edward Pennington the like sums upon the like conditions; to my daughter Mary Pennington £30 a year till she marr & then £300; to my dear son William Penn £50 & to my friend Thomas Elwood the like sum; to my cousin Mary, wife of William Smith £50; I give £20 towards a meeting house when friends of Chalfont meeting think it convenient to build one; to Martha Sampson £2 a year for life; To Martha Cooper *als* Heywood £3 a year for life; to my daughter Gulielma Maria Penn her choice of a suit of damask except that suit marked I $\frac{P}{M}$; to her son Springett Penn my great platt with the Springett's and my coat of arms upon it and the silver two eared cup made in the fashion of his mother's golden one; to her daughter Letitia Penn my silver chafin dish & skimmer with a brasile handle & that large nun's work box & a little basket of nun's work & a purse & a girdle of black plush & a black straw basket which her father brought me out of Holland &c &c; to my son William Pennington my dear husband's watch; Other bequests to son Edward Pennington & dau. Mary, to cousin Mary Smith the elder & her daughter Mary; to son John Pennington my house & land at Woodside & all my husbands houses in Kent (upon conditions); Reference to will of my mother the Lady Prewed "that is annext to my fathers Sir John Prewed," also to "my mother's sister the Lady Oxenden"; I would have my son John Pennington lay mee in friends burying ground at Jordans very neare my deare and pretious husband Isaac Pennington" My son John to be executor and my dear son William Penn and my loving friend Thomas Ellwood to be overseers; Proved 11 October 1682. —Cottle, 121.

[The testatrix was daughter and heir of Sir John Proude and wife of Sir William Springett, who died in 1643, having had issue by her a son, John Springett, who died young, and a daughter, Gulielma Maria Springett, the first wife of the Founder and the legatee named in the will of her mother, who had remarried to Isaac Pennington.

The following Pennington Admon is interesting as showing a member of that family dying in America five years before the founding of Pennsylvania, whether connected or not with William Penn's step-father-in-law the writer is ignorant.]

1679—James Pennington. Feb. the last day. Com. issued to Mathew Travers, principal Creditor of James Pennington late of the psh. of St. Bartholomew Royal Exchange, London, but in Maryland in partibus transmarinus decd. intestate, to admr. &c, Sara Pennington, the relict, having renounced.—Act Book, fo. 20.]

[The wills which follow, of Dennis Hollister and Thomas Callowhill, are most valuable as confirming and extending the knowledge of the ancestry of Hannah Callowhill, the second wife of the Founder, which was obtained from the deeds printed by the writer in the last number of these Gleanings.[1]]

1676—Will of Dennis Hollister of Bristol, Grocer, in perfect health. Dated 1 Sept. 1675; To only sonn Dennis all

[1] PENNA. MAG., Vol. XVI., No. 3, October, 1892.

corner house & shopp in Mary Part in Bristoll aforesaid where I now dwell & certain furniture, linnen, " best silver belly pott with its cover," all shopp Jmplements &c, £600 & a caudle cupp with leggs & a cover; To dau. Hannah, wife of Thomas Callowhill new house late built in ffryers Orchard in parish of Jamesses in suburbs of Bristol & stable & houses in same lately purchased in which one Hannah Hollister & Jeane Partridge, Widdow, now dwell, & Warehouses in Peters parish with remainder, as to the last, to my granddau. Sarah, eldest dau. of my said dau. Hannah Callowhill, remainder, if she die without heirs, to my granddau., Hannah Callowhill, after said dau's decease remainder of houses in ffryers bought of Henry Lloyd to granddau. Bridgett Callowhill, remainder as to new house in ffryers to sonn-in-lawe Thomas Callowhill for his life with remainder to my grandsonn Dennis Callowhill eldest sonn of my said dau., remainder to grandsonn Thomas Callowhill second sonn of same, & to said dau. certain linnen, silver, &c &c and £200 over her marriage portion & to Thomas Callowhill, her husband, £10; To dau. Lydia Jordan wife of Thomas Jordan new house late builded at fframton Cotterill, co. Glouc., late bought of Humphrey Hooke, Knt., with remainder to her husband for life, remainder at his death or marriage to my granddau. Bridgett Jordan, eldest dau. of my said dau. remainder to grdu. Lidia Jordan, second dau. of same, and to my said dau. Lydia Jordan certain furniture &c, & £200 & to her husband £10; To dau. Mary Hollister new house in Mary part Streete in Bristol & outlet or pavement over Kitchen of house wch I now dwell in & wch was devised to sonn Dennis, & certain furniture &c & £500, silver beare bowle & a little silver bottle; To dau. Phebe Hollister moyety of Jnn called White Hart in Broadstreet in Bristol, one fourth of which was my Wives inheritance & one fourth late bought of Ann Yeomans decd., & other fourth late bought of Edmond ffrench sonn & heire of Elizabeth ffrench also decd., & other fourth late bought of Henry Rowe & Judith his wife, which said Judith, Elizabeth, Ann & my wife were the daus. & coheires of Edmond

Popley, Merchant, dec'd., also to my said dau. Phebe certain furniture &c and "lesser belly pott," and £500; To grandchildren Dennis, Thomas & Hannah Callowhill £20 apeece; To granddaus. Sarah & Bridgett Callowhill £15 apeece; To grchil. Bridgett & Lidia Jordan £20 apeece; To kinswoman Lydia that late served me & is now become the wife of Edward Hackett £100 over what I have given her towards her marriage; To Beloved ffriends George ffox, William Dewsbery, Alexander Parker, George Whitehead & John Storye £10 a peice and to Thomas Briggs, John Wilkinson of Westmerland, James Pooke, Steeven Crispe & John Wilkinson of Cumberland £5 a peece as a toaken of my love to them & the service they have done for the Lord & for his people & to be paid only to the above named who hath often lodged at my House & eaten bread at my table & are well known to my Executors; To Mary Goulding, Wife of Tho: Goulding of Bristol, Grocer, and to Magdalene Love, Wife of John Love of same £20 & to said Tho: Goulding & John Love £10 for certain poor people; To each of my Brothers a peece of old gold of 20s. value; To each of Brothers' & Sisters' children the same except Samuell sonn of my brother Thomas Hollister and Nathaniel Tovie, only sonn of my sister Margery Tovie, dec'd., who because they are ill husbands & like to misspend it, nothing, but to Samuell Hollister's wife for benefitt of his children & to Nathaniel Tovie's children that are in England at my decease; To Nem Dawson, Widdow, 40s. p. ann. for life; To Joanne Pillerne, Widdow, £3; To Margaret Price, Widdow, 40s.; To Mary Evans, Widdow, 20s.; To servant Joseph Smith £5; To all other domestick Servants 20s. apeece; To dau. Phebe house & lands called Old feilds at Vrcott in parish of Almesbury in co. Glouc' for rest of tearme of yeares; friend Alexander Parker, Geo: Whitehead, Walter Clements & John Story to be Overseers & to each 40s.; Only sonn Dennis Hollister & two sonns-in-lawe Tho: Callowhill & Tho: Jordan Executors;—"in testimony that this is my absolute Will contayned in these 5 sides & this little peece of paper written every word with my owne hand & subscribed in the margent of every side with my owne name." Wit: J. Chauncey, John Eckly & Rich: Hawkesworth.

Codicil dated 6 July 1676, being sicke & weake, considering that since making my will it hath pleased God to take out of this World my sonn Dennis & severall others, I revoke all Legacies to all who are now dead; To daus. Hannah, Lydia & Mary my house at corner of Mary Port Street where I now dwell & keepe shop; I do confirm to dau. Phebe the Jnn called White Hart in Bristol and revoake house & lands called Oldfeild in parish of Almondsbury & give same to my four daus. for tearme; To dau. Hannah Callowhill's three children, Hannah, Thomas & Elizabeth messuage & lands at Westerleigh held of Dean & Chapter of Wells; My grandchild Lydia Jordan being dead her £20 to grandchild Bridgett Jordan; To sonn-in-lawe Thomas Jordan £150 towards the purchase of the fee simple of house & lands at fframpton Cottrell given to my dau. Lydia Jordan; Revoake such part of bequest of 20s. each to the children of brother & sister as refers to Cosen Lydia, now wife of Edward Hackett, having otherwise provided for her, & to cos. Samuell Hollister, sone of my bro. William Hollister £10; To servt. Joseph Smith £5 more; To servt. Dorcas (*blank*) £5; To Dennis sonn of Abel Hollister £10 to bind him an Apprentice; To Samuell Hollister, grandsonn of brother William & sonn of Jacob Hollister £5; To Mary Hollester dau. of Jacob Hollester aforesd £10 more than what I have bestowed in placeing her; To sonn-in-lawe Thomas Jordan best bay gelding; To sonn-in-lawe Thomas Callowhill best horse beast & to both of them £50 apeece; To my four daus. all overplus of estate; Thomas Speed to be an Overseer in place of John Story; To servt. ffrances (*blank*) £5; Wit: J. Chauncey,[1] John Eckley & Rich:

[1] Ichabod Chauncey, the second son of Rev. Charles Chauncey, President of Harvard College from 1654 to 1671. He graduated at Harvard, was chaplain in the regiment of Sir Edward Harley, at Dunkirk, and had some clerical function in England, but, being persecuted for his non-conformity, became a physician and settled at Bristol, where he

Hawksworth. Proved 21 July 1676 by Exors named in will.—Bence, 91.

1712—Will of Thomas Callowhill of City of Bristoll, Linnen Draper, in health of Body; Dated 28 November 1711; I am possessed of the residue of term of 1000 years in certain garden whereon I have erected certain buildings adjoyning my now dwelling in parish commonly called St. James granted me by Edward Baugh, Whitetawer, since dec'd., & residue of 1000 years granted by Edward Baugh, Jr., of tenmts, garden, malt house, &c, erected on same garden & other term of 1000 years lately granted me by my dau. Hanna of all messuage &c on South side of Quaker's Meeting house in place called the ffryers now or late in occupation of Simon Barnes, Daniell Kindall & William Timbrell, I bequeath all same to kinsmen Brice Webb of said City, Linnen Draper, & Charles Harford of same, Merchant, on trust for wife Hanna *als* Anna for her life with remainder to my granddau. Margarett Penn, dau. of Hannah Penn; my daughter, by William Penn, Esq., her husband, for her life, remainder to grandson John Penn, son of said dau., for rest of term; By an indenture 27 instant month between me and Brice Webb & Charles Harford, Linnen Drapers, & Richard Champion, Merchant, I have conveyed to them lands in said City, in Co. of Somerset, & other places in England & in Pennsylvania, to uses therein menconed, confirm said deed save that said Trustees may sell any part of a Close called Barrs Leaze *als* Brick Leaze adjoining my now dwelling, & said trustees to grant to said dau. Margaret Penn or John Penn afsd 4 messuages in street called Broad Meade in parish of St. James, being part of wives Joynture, wherein Richard Hooper, John Hide & Edward Cullimore now dwell; And whereas I have an In-

died July 25, 1691, aged fifty-six, and was buried at St. Phillip's Church in the same city. His will, which is dated March 19, 1688, with codicil September 26, 1690, was probated February 17, 1691/2, at P. C. C. (Savage I., 368; Pedigree of Fam. of Chauncey by Stephen Tucker, Somst. Herald, Lond., 1884, p. 7.)

terest in the province of Pennsylvania as a security for
£1000 due to me from said William Penn & am interested
in lands in Caldecott in co. Monmouth as security for £160
due from Mary Herbert, spinster, sole heir of ffrancis Herbert, Esq., dec'd., & am possessed of residue of 90 years
granted by Samuell Price & others of Society of Merchants
of said City of the tenth part of the whole of several messuages &c neare the hot well in parish of Clifton, co. Glouc.,
& am interested in one sixteenth part of Brass works in
ptnershipp with James Peters, Jeoffry Pinnell & others,
now carried on about Terren, co. Salop, & am also interested in a twentieth part of Copperworks with same partners at Colebrooke Dale, co. Salop, & also one sixteenth of
certain Packett Boats now Trading for the port of Bristoll
to New York & other places in America, in partnership
with Brice Webb, Richard Champion & others, I give to
said Brice Webb & James Peters all right in lands &c given
me by said William Penn of lands in Pennsylvania afsd. &
in Caldecott by said Mary Herbert, & lands at Hot Well,
Brass & Copper Works & Packett Boats in trust for uses
hereafter menconed, to dispose of same & settle moneys so
raised on my dau. Hanna & her children. In the first place
to pay to said William Penn & Hanna his wife £26 yearly
in satisfaction of Rents of Estate at ffrenchan & Hambrooke
which I promised them, & residue to paymt. of £800 & Interest due to said Brice Webb & others by Deed dated 5
July last past between me & said Brice Webb, Charles Harford & Richard Champion, residue to said John Penn of
houses at Hot Well &c, & residue of Brass & Copper Works
& Packett Boats to Thomas Penn, another sone of said
Hanna Penn & all remainder to said Margaret Penn; My
brother Walter Duffield is bound by two obligations, viz.,
one dated 12 Jan. 1694 for paymt. of £25, & other dated 13
Aug. 1674 for £14–10–0, he to pay Executrix £25 only; If
sister Elizabeth Iaveling pay to Executrix in one year what
she owes her bonds to be discharged; To neices Elizabeth
Iaveling, Duffield Iavelin, Sara Gurman & Mary Gurman a
peice of gold apeece of 23s. 6d.; To late servt. Elizabeth

Weekes a peice of like value; To housemaids a guiney apeice; To tenant Simon Barnes 10s.; To Ancient friend George Whitehead of London & Benjamin Coole, Paul Moon & John Pope, my friends in Bristoll, 2 broad peices of gold of 23s. 6d.; To old servt. & friend John Isgar best suit of Clothe & Beaver Hatt; To poor of parish where I dwell £5 in hands of Charles Weeks, Gardiner there, for Coles; To bind sonn of any poor friend an Apprentice £10; Wife Hanna *als* Anna Res. Legatee & Executrix; Brice Webb & Charles Harford Overseers & to them 2 broad peices of gold apeice; Will written on 2 peices of parchment, the greater containing 63 lines & the lesser 9 lines. Wit: Nicholas Taylor, Ben: Bisse & Jon Gregory. Proved 24 Dec, 1712 by Hanna Penn (wife of William Penn) dau. of dec'd., the Executrix, Hanna *als* Anna Callowhill having died before Executing. On 19 Oct 1738 Com. issued to John Penn, Esq., son & Admrr. with Will annexed of Hanna Penn, widow, dec'd., while living dau. & only child (*sic*) & administratrix with will annexed of Thomas Callowhill, to administer goods &c left unadministered by said Hanna Penn &c.—Barnes, 232.

[In this connection the following extracts, for calling my attention to which I have to thank Mr. Henry Gray, the genealogical bookseller of Leicester Square, may be of interest. The name of Callowhill is a very uncommon one, and it may well be that the earlier members of this family were among the progenitors of Thomas Callowhill, of Bristol. At the least it may serve as a clue to the origin of the Bristol family.]

PARISH REGISTER OF KNIGHTWICK,
Co. Worcester.[1]

1620—Charles sonn of Thomas Callowhill & Alice his wyfe was baptized the vij day of Maie anno suprascript.

[1] "Parish Registers of Knightwick and Doddenham, County of Worcester, from 1538 to 1812." Edited by Joseph Bonstead Wilson. London, 1891.

the same buryed the xiiijth daye of June anno supra-scripto.

Katherine the Daughter of William Callowhill & (Margerie) his wyfe was buryed the xxvjth day of October anno suprescripto.

Gulielmus Callowhill sepel iebatur quinto die Novembris Anno superscripto. (*From Bishop's Transcripts.*)

1615—Margerie the daughter of William Callowhill & Margerie his wyfe was baptized the xviij of October Anno p. dicto.

1618—Thomas the sonn of William Callowhill & Margery his wyfe was baptized the twenty nynth of March Anno p. dicto.

1634—James the sonn of Richard Callowhill & Anne his wife was baptized the xxviijth day of Julye anno praedicto.

1637—Thomas Callowhill & Allice Brooke were married October the Third Anno praedicto.

1638—Mary the daughter of Thomas Callowhill & Allice his wife was baptized June the third : Anno p. dict.

Mary the daughter of Thomas Callowhill ye younger & Allice his wife was buryed June ye Twenty.

1640—ffravncis Callowhill & Bridgett Perry were married the 7th day of february Anno supra dicto.

1641—Thomas the sonn of ffravncis Callowhill & Bridgett his wife was baptized the 7th day of November 1641.

Allice the wife of Thomas Callowhill the younger was buried Aprill 26th.

1642—William the sonn of William Callowhill was baptised ffebruary the 20th Anno supra dicto.

1644—John the sonn of William Callowhill was baptised Aprill 7th.

1662—Elijah y° son of Wm: Callowhill (and Dorathy his wife) was bapt. June the tenth Anno p. dicto.

1663—Anne ye daughter of James Callowhill & Margery his wife was bapt. December y° 22ᵈ. (*Transcripts.*)

1674—Tho: Callowhill, Churchwarden.

1675—Thomas Callowhill was buried March y° 10ᵗʰ anno pr. dicto. (*Transcripts.*)

PARISH REGISTER OF DODDENHAM.

1713—Hannah Gulielmi & Mariae Callowhill εβαπτισθιν.

1718—Dec. 21—Gulielmus Gulielmi et Mariae Callowhill 'ΕΒΑΠΤΙΣΘΙΝ.

1702—John Jones of City of Bristoll, Linnendraper, in health of body; dated 13 Dec. 1699; To ffather Cha: Jones, 2 Jacobus, & to mother Ann Jones the same; to that brother or sister whom parents may think most worthy in one years time 100 guineas; to ffatherlaw William & motherlaw Ann Smith each 2 guineas; to use & benefit of people called Quakers inhabiting the City of Bristoll £200 to be disposed by father Chas. Jones, William Smith, Charles Harford Senior, Benjamin Cool & Cornelius Sarjant; to ffather & mother Jones each 4 Jacobuses more; to meeting people that are poore that belong to Congregation where Andrew Gifford doth preach, at disposal of sd. And. Gifford & John Bowman Cooper or Henry Parsons Grocer in Thomas St.; to parish of Thomas, the place of my nativity £20 to be given to poor in bread & apparell by Henry Parsons in Thomas St. & Richard Taylor Jronmonger in Ratcliffe St.; to parish of Nicholas wherein I now live £20 to be distributed by William Bush Draper & Alderman Wallis to poor as before; to (*blank*) Read, he that preaches in the publick place of worship of sd. psh. £10; to late erected Hospitalls Boys & Maides but most especially to the ancient thereof £100 at discretion of Major Wade, Thomas Callowhill, Edward Martindale and my father Chas. Jones; to William ffallowfield that commonly lyes at Charles Harfords & often hath preached very well in our meeting house one guinea & £50 sterling; to Jeremy Hignell Cooper in Temple St. £50; to John Pope Senior that lives over against the Glass hous without Lowfords Gate £25; to Benjamin Coole Senr, that lives on Michael hill in this City £50; to Uncle Char: Harford one guinea; to bro. Charles Jones, bro. Michael Jones & bro. Mathias Jones each £100; to sister Sarah that is married to ffrancis Roach £200; to sister Elizabeth that is married to Edward Harford £200; to Peter Young my brother law £50; to ffrancis Roach my brother law the same; to Peter & Ann Young children of my sister Young each £500; to brother Charles Jones more £600 if he agree with Exors. on the account of the late brigantine Expedition; to bro. Michael Jones £600; to sister Roach the same; to sister Elizabeth married to Edward Harford the same; to kinsman Mathias Jones Senr of London £100; to John Keinton that was my apprentice £60; to servant Jane Persevell £10; to servant Martha Gifford £5; to John Horwoods wife £5; to 6 or 12 bearers who carry me to the grave each 20s.; to Arthur Thomas Pewterer £5; to cousin Thomas Dickson £3; to Charles Harford Jr. £3; to Elias Osborne, Richard Yeomans, Robert Priest & Arthur Taylor each one guinea; to Arthur Sawyer same; to aunt Smith £5; to William Pope my porter £10; to sister Roach my part of ship called Susannah; to cousin Widow Low of this City £5; to cousin Martha married to William Stafford £100; to cousin Mary married to William Penn £100;[1] cousins Peter & Ann, children of sister, & Rachell daughter of my brother Michaell, & 2 youngest children of sister Harford to be Res. Legs. & these 5 Exors.; Wit. William Rushton, Richard Hawkesworth & Richard Vickris, Jr.; Pro. 4 Aug. 1702.—P. C. C. Herne, 136.

[1] William Penn, eldest son of the Proprietor of Pennsylvania, by his first wife, Gulielma Maria Springett, and from whom the Penns of Shanagary, Ireland (now represented by the Gaskell-Halls), were descended, married Mary Jones. This valuable will gives, as far as the writer is aware, the first clue to her identification.

AN ACCOUNT OF A VISIT MADE TO WASHINGTON AT MOUNT VERNON, BY AN ENGLISH GENTLE-MAN, IN 1785.

FROM THE DIARY OF JOHN HUNTER.

[Through the courtesy of Evan Powell, Esq., of Llandiloes, Wales, and Dr. James J. Levick, of this city, we are enabled to publish the following account of a visit made to Washington at Mount Vernon, by Mr. John Hunter, an English gentleman, who was making a tour in 1785–86 through Canada and the United States. The diary is now in the possession of his grandson, Major W. C. Hunter, of the British army.]

ALEXANDRIA, VIRGINIA.

Wednesday 16th. of Nov'r. 1785.—After breakfast I waited on Colonel Fitzgerald. A fire that had broke out in the town hindered us from getting off so soon as we intended. However, after some trouble it was extinguished and at half past eleven we left Alexandria with Mr. Lee, the President of Congress, his son and the servants. You have a fine view of the Potomac till you enter a wood. A small Rivulet here divides the General's Estate from the neighbouring farmers. His seat breaks out beautifully upon you when you little expect, being situated upon a most elegant rising ground on the banks of the Potomac, ten miles from Alexandria. We arrived at Mount Vernon by one o'clock—so-called by the General's eldest brother, who lived there before him, after the Admiral of that name. When Colonel Fitzgerald introduced me to the General I was struck with his noble and venerable appearance. It immediately brought to my mind the great part he had acted in the late war. The General is about six feet high, perfectly straight and well made; rather inclined to be lusty. His eyes are full and blue and seem to express an air of gravity. His nose inclines to the aquiline; his mouth small; his teeth are yet good and his cheeks indicate perfect health. His forehead is a noble one and he wears his hair turned back, without curls and quite in the officer's style, and tyed in a long queue behind. Altogether he makes a most noble, respectable appearance, and I really think him the first man in the world. After having had the management and care of the whole Continental army, he has now retired without receiving any pay for his trouble, and though solicited by the King of France and some of the first characters in the world to visit Europe, he has denied them all and knows how to prefer solid happiness in his retirement to all the luxuries and flattering speeches of European Courts. The General was born and educated near Fredericksburg on the Rappahannock. He must be a man of great abilities and a strong natural genius, as his master never taught him anything but writing and arithmetic. People come to see him here from all parts of the world—hardly a day passes without; but the General seldom makes his appearance before dinner; employing the morning to write his letters and superintend his farm, and allotting the afternoon to company; but even then he generally retires for two hours between tea and supper to his study to write.

He is one of the most regular men in the world. When no particular Company is at his house, he goes to bed always at nine and gets up with the sun. It's astonishing the packets of letters that daily come for him, from all parts of the world, which employ him most of the morning to answer, and his Secretary Mr. Shaw (an acquaintance of mine) to copy and arrange. The General has all the accounts of the war yet to settle. Shaw tells me he keeps as regular Books as any Merchant whatever, and a daily Journal of all his transactions. It's amazing the number of letters he wrote during the war : there are thirty large folio volumes of them upstairs, as big as common Ledgers, all neatly copied. The General is remarked for writing a most elegant letter. Like the famous Addison, his writing excels his speaking. But to finish this long digression. When I was first introduced to him he was neatly dressed in a plain blue coat, white cassimir waistcoat, and black

breeches and Boots, as he came from his farm. After
having sat with us some time he retired and sent in his lady,
a most agreeable woman about 50, and Major Washington
his nephew, married about three weeks ago to a Miss Bes-
sot : She is Mrs. Washington's niece and a most charming
young woman.   She is about 19.   After chatting with them
for half an hour, the General came in again, with his hair
neatly powdered, a clean shirt on, a new plain drab coat,
white waistcoat and white silk stockings.   At three, dinner
was on table, and we were shewn by the General into another room, where everything was set off with a peculiar
taste, and at the same time very neat and plain.   The
General sent the bottle about pretty freely after dinner, and
gave success to the navigation of the Potomac for his toasts,
which he has very much at heart, and when finished will I
suppose be the first river in the world.   He never under-
takes anything without having first well considered of it
and consulted different people, but when once he has begun
anything, no obstacle or difficulty can come in his way, but
what he is determined to surmount.   The General's character seems to be a prudent, but a very persevering one.
He is quite pleased at the idea of the Baltimore Merchants
laughing at him, and saying it was a ridiculous plan and
would never succeed.   They begin now, says the General,
to look a little serious about the matter, as they know it
must hurt their commerce amazingly.

    The Colonel and I had our horses ready after dinner to
return to Alexandria, and notwithstanding all we could do,
the General absolutely insisted upon our staying on account
of the bad afternoon.   We therefore complyed, (although
it was fully my intention to have set off either to Fredericksburg in my way to Mr. McCall's, in the stage, if the
morning was fine, and if not, most certainly back again to
Baltimore) as I could not refuse the pressing and kind invitation of so great a General, tho' our greatest enemy, I
admire him as superior even to the Roman heroes themselves.

    After tea General Washington retired to his study and

left us with the President, his lady and the rest of the Company. If he had not been anxious to hear the news of Congress from Mr. Lee, most probably he would not have returned to supper, but gone to bed at his usual hour, nine o'clock, for he seldom makes any ceremony. We had a very elegant supper about that time. The General with a few glasses of champagne got quite merry, and being with his intimate friends laughed and talked a good deal. Before strangers he is generally very reserved, and seldom says a word. I was fortunate in being in his company with his particular acquaintances. I am told during the war he was never seen to smile. The care indeed of such an army was almost enough to make anybody thoughtful and grave. No man but the General could have kept the army together without victuals or clothes; they placed a confidence in him that they would have had in no other person. His being a man of great fortune and having no children shewed them it was quite a disinterested part that he was acting with regard to money making and that he had only the good of his country at heart. The soldiers, tho' starving at times, in a manner adored him.

We had a great deal of conversation about the slippery ground (as the General said) that Franklin was on, and also about Congress, the Potomac, improving their roads, etc. At 12 I had the honor of being lighted up to my bedroom by the General himself.

Thursday 17th. November.—I rose early and took a walk about the General's grounds—which are really beautifully laid out. He has about 4000 acres well cultivated and superintends the whole himself. Indeed his greatest pride now is, to be thought the first farmer in America. He is quite a Cincinnatus, and often works with his men himself —strips off his coat and labors like a common man. The General has a great turn for mechanics. It's astonishing with what niceness he directs everything in the building way, condescending even to measure the things himself, that all may be perfectly uniform. The style of his house is very elegant, something like the Prince de Condé's at Chantille,

near Paris, only not quite so large : but it's a pity he did
not build a new one at once, as it has cost him nearly as much
repairing his old one.   His improvements I'm told are very
great within the last year.   He is making a most delightful
bowling green before the house and cutting a new road
thro' the woods to Alexandria.   It would be endless to attempt describing his house and grounds—I must content
myself with having seen them.   The situation is a heavenly
one, upon one of the finest rivers in the world.   I suppose
I saw thousands of wild ducks upon it, all within gun shot.
There are also plenty of blackbirds and wild geese and
turkies.   After breakfast I went with Shaw to see his
famous race-horse Magnolia—a most beautiful creature.   A
whole length of him was taken a little while ago, (mounted
on Magnolia) by a famous man from Europe in copper—
and his bust in marble—one by order of Congress to be
kept wherever they sit, and the other by the State of Virginia, to stand in the House of Assembly.   They will cost
about 6000 sterling Shaw says.   He also showed me an
elegant State Carriage, with beautiful emblematical figures
on it, made him a present of by the State of Pennsylvania.
I afterwards went into his stables, where among an amazing
number of horses, I saw old Nelson, now 22 years of age,
that carried the General almost always during the war :
Blueskin, another fine old horse next to him, now and then
had that honor.   Shaw also shewed me his old servant,
that was reported to have been taken, with a number of the
General's papers about him.   They have heard the roaring
of many a cannon in their time.   Blueskin was not the
favourite, on account of his not standing fire so well as
venerable old Nelson.   The General makes no manner of
use of them now ; he keeps them in a nice stable where
they feed away at their ease for their past services.   There
is a horse of Major Washington's there that was reckoned
the finest figure in the American Army.   It's astonishing
what a number of small houses the General has upon his
Estate for his different Workmen and Negroes to live in.
He has everything within himself—Carpenters, Bricklayers,

Brewers, Blacksmiths, Bakers, etc., etc. and even has a well assorted Store for the use of his family and servants.

When the General takes his coach out he always drives six horses; to his chariot he only puts four.   The General has some fine deer, which he is going to enclose a park for —also some remarkable large fox hounds, made him a present of from England, as he is fond of hunting, and there are great plenty of foxes in this country.   I forgot to mention Mrs. Washington's sweet little Grand-children, who I imagine, will come in for a share of the General's fortune with the Major.   I fancy he is worth 100,000 Pounds sterling and lives at the rate of 3 or 4000 a year; always keeping a genteel table for strangers, that almost daily visit him, as a thing of course.   There is a fine family picture in the Drawing room of the Marquis de La Fayette, his lady and three children—another of the General with his marching orders, when he was Colonel Washington in the British Army against the French in the last war; and two of Mrs. Washington's children: Her son was reckoned one of the handsomest men living; also a picture of Mrs. Washington when a young woman.

The General has some hundreds of Negroes on his plantations.   He chiefly grows Indian corn, wheat and tobacco.

It's astonishing with what raptures Mrs. Washington spoke about the discipline of the army, the excellent order they were in, superior to any troops she said upon the face of the earth towards the close of the war; even the English acknowledged it, she said.   What pleasure she took in the sound of the fifes and drums, preferring it to any music that was ever heard; and then to see them reviewed a week or two before the men were disbanded, when they were all well clothed was she said a most heavenly sight; almost every soldier shed tears at parting with the General when the army was disbanded: Mrs. Washington said it was a most melancholy sight.   The situation of Mount Vernon is by nature one of the sweetest in the world, and what makes it still more pleasing is the amazing number of sloops that are constantly sailing up and down the River.

Indeed, all the ships that come to Alexandria or George Town must sail by the General's house.

At eleven we took leave of him. I shook him heartily by the hand and wished him all happiness. Mr. Lee and his son left us soon after to go to their seat on this side of the Rappahannock about 16 miles from Mr. McCall's at Hobb's Hole. In our way to Alexandria we fell in with Mr. Lunn Washington, the gentleman who managed the General's estate during the war.

We were soon after joined by a gentleman with a pack of fine hounds in search of a fox. They had had a fine hunt this morning and killed one. We arrived at Alexandria, by one.

SWEDISH SETTLERS IN GLOUCESTER COUNTY, NEW JERSEY, PREVIOUS TO 1684.

BY JOHN CLEMENT.

It is only within the last half-century that any inquiry has been made in regard to the emigrant settlers who made their homes along the eastern side of the river Delaware, in New Jersey. They were of different nationalities,—Swedes, Finns, and Dutch,—much the larger number being Swedes. They had a common object, which was to procure furs from the Indians in exchange for articles of home manufacture, and which brought them valuable returns.

Much effort has been made to trace the title to the land they occupied, but has generally failed for want of reliable documents in the shape of deeds, wills, Bible records, and family traditions.

Many tracts of land known to have been occupied by these early comers to New Jersey show no evidence of legal title until the English arrived and exercised their rights under the Proprietors.

Indirectly, however, something may be gathered from the ancient records in the office of the Supreme Court in Trenton, New Jersey, in charge of Benjamin F. Lee, Esq., who observes a jealous care of the old documents, and who is always seeking for hidden treasures among the musty tomes in his custody. One volume there, known as the record of the proceedings of the several courts of Burlington County, commencing in 1681, throws considerable light upon this subject.

It must not be forgotten that the jurisdiction of Burlington County at that time extended from Oldman's Creek up and along the river front to the most northerly point of the colony near where is now the city of Port Jervis, including all of West New Jersey except Salem County, for Gloucester County was not established until May 26, 1686.

The government under the Proprietors was in full force, and persons desirous of locating lands naturally began to inquire how the Swedes and their neighbors became the owners of the soil they occupied.

The attention of the court, which, at that sitting, consisted of Thomas Olive, governor; Robert Stacy, William Biddle, Elias Farr, Robert Dimsdale, Daniel Wills, Robert Turner, Thomas Gardiner, and Francis Collins, justices, was called to this subject, and their honors directed Hanse Hopman, a constable and an officer of that court, to summons all persons settled on lands from the third tenth (Great Timber Creek) to Oldman's Creek, to report the quantity of land each one occupied and by what right they claimed title to the same.

The records show that the third day of the Fourth month, 1684, was the time fixed for the appearance of these settlers, and they very generally responded.

Mons Jonson, Hanse Hopman, and Peter Jonson claimed a large tract, about one mile in front, from Oldman's Creek to a small run upward. They said they held it by permit from Governor Philip Carteret, dated June 25, 1668, but did not produce the permit, neither did they know the quantity of land, not having had it surveyed.

Claus Jonson, Hanse Woolson, and David Livezey claimed four hundred and fifty acres by permit of Governor Carteret; did not produce the paper, nor have the land surveyed.

Jannes Ealason, *alias* Illman, Lansing Coleman, Noels Matson, *alias* Lawson, by John Anderson in possession, held three hundred acres by permit from Governor Carteret.

Israel Holmes claimed six hundred acres by permit of Governor Carteret, but did not produce his deed.

Philip Carteret was appointed governor of the whole territory by Lord John Berkeley and Sir George Carteret, with power to grant lands, and hence the title of the Swedes and Finns and Dutch to the soil occupied by them and by permit from Governor Carteret was of a kind which the Proprietors were slow to question, and discloses a fact so long sought for by inquirers in that direction.

Peter Errickson and Wooley Derrickson had one hundred acres they purchased of Thomas Budd, but did not produce their deeds.

James Sanderland had two hundred acres conveyed to him by Samuel Jenings and Thomas Budd. Said his deed was recorded.

Hanse Hopman claimed two hundred acres bought of Richard Basnett.

Paule Curwen guessed he had one hundred acres " without any face of title."

Peter Rambo showed that he owned six hundred and fifty acres by deed from Thomas Bowman ; deed recorded.

Peter Dalboe and Wooley Dalboe bought two hundred acres of Thomas Budd and Samuel Jenings ; deed recorded.

Anthony Nealson had one hundred and eighty acres he purchased of Budd and Jenings.

Andrew Homan bought one hundred and fifty acres of Thomas Budd, and Hanse Peterson had fifty acres conveyed to him by the same person.

Benjamin Bramma had one hundred acres bought of Thomas Mathews.

Neale Mattson did not appear, and Neale Lawson and John Anderson had been before the court at a previous session.

This was a proper inquiry to be made by the members of the court, for they were *ex officio* commissioners to direct the disposal of lands in the province. This regulation existed until 6th day of 7th month, 1688, when the Council of Proprietors was established and relieved the court of this duty. It is to be regretted that the permits were not produced and the boundaries of each tract put on record so as to show their character, and particularly locate the place of each resident. It is known, however, that not all had land on the river front, but many settled on the several creeks that ran inland, and gradually utilized the upland for agriculture, and improved the marshes for meadow.

Their dwellings were built of logs, but made comfortable against the rigors of the cold, long winters, without any fear of starvation where the forest and streams were so prolific of food.   They were a quiet, inoffensive people, and submitted to the government, be it Swedish, English, or Dutch, and were seldom involved in disputes among themselves.

There were other settlements along the river on the easterly side, the largest of which was near and above the mouth of Penisaukin Creek, where the town of Palmyra now stands, and in that neighborhood.   In some of the original locations made by the English settlers reference is made to the " Swedish land," yet every effort to trace these titles has so far failed.   Tradition had it that this particular colony was the remnant of Sir Edmund Ployden's followers who erected Fort Eriwonick on the river near that place, and were left to their fate after Sir Edmund's idea of founding a great nation in the wilds of America had vanished.   They were not alone, for the settlements at Wiccaco and Tinicum were of easy access by boats, and from whence intercourse was maintained with their friends at home.

The home government was careful to give them spiritual advisers, and the little church at the mouth of Raccoon Creek or that on Tinicum Island were the resorts when matrimony was contemplated, where their children were christened and their dead buried.

There was no desire on the part of the English owners to antagonize the people they found occupying the lands coming within their purchase, but rather to offer inducements for their remaining, and therefore neighborly relations were soon established between them.   William Penn saw at once the benefit of having his grant occupied by settlers, and was careful that nothing should be done to make these pioneers discontented.

In one of his letters he writes as follows : " They are a plain, strong, industrious people, yet have made no great progress in the culture or propagation of fruit-trees, as if they desired rather to have enough than plenty, or for traffick; but I presume the Indians make them the more careless, by furnishing them with the means of profit, to wit: skins and furs in exchange for rum and such strong liquors. They kindly received me as well as the English who were but few, before the people concerned with me came among them, I must needs commend their respect to authority and kind behaviour to the English."

This had reference to those on the western shore of the river, yet applied to those on the eastern shore as well.

In another noticeable case this same fact crops out and shows that the people who preceded the English settlers had just claim to the land they occupied, and made no hesitancy in producing their title.

This was an issue heard in the Upland Court in 1679, between Peter Jegou, plaintiff, and Thomas Wright and Godfrey Hancock, defendants, regarding the ownership and possession of a tract of land at Burlington, New Jersey.

Jegou produced to the court a permit and grant from Philip Carteret, governor, and proved his occupancy of the land by living there and keeping a house of entertainment for travellers. Thomas Wright and Godfrey Hancock claimed title from the Proprietors, and had planted corn, cut timber, mowed hay, and exercised other acts of ownership thereon.

The court, after hearing both parties and examining the papers, decided that the title was in Peter Jegou, to the exclusion of Thomas Wright and Godfrey Hancock, holders under the Proprietors' estate.

Gradually these facts are being developed, and it is to be hoped that in the near future some of these permits or deeds or the record of the same may come to light, and settle a long-mooted question touching this subject.

EXTRACTS FROM THE RECORDS OF THIRD HAVEN MONTHLY MEETING OF FRIENDS, EASTON, TALBOT COUNTY, MARYLAND, 1680.

CONTRIBUTED BY HELEN HOPKINS JONES.

[Winlock Christison (as he spelled it) was a conspicuous figure in the persecutions of the Quakers at Boston, and has become more widely known as the hero of one of Longfellow's New England tragedies. After his banishment from Boston, the death penalty having been remitted, he went by way of Barbadoes to the Eastern Shore of Maryland, and there settled and died. Some of the monthly meetings were held at his house while living, as appears from the records before me.— H. H. J.]

Att our Man Meeting at John Pitts the 14th of the 3rd m° 1680

William Dixon and Eliz^a Christerson appeared before the meeting and declared the Jntentions of comeing together as husband and wife it being the Second time of their laying it before the meeting Jnquiry being made by Stephen Keddy and Bryon Omealia who were appointed by the Meeting to Jnquire into Wm Dixons cleerness. Likewise Sarah Edmondson and Mary Sockwell being made Choice of by the womens meeting to Enquire concerning Eliz^a Christersons being cleer and upon Jnquiry of the meeting the afd friends informs the meeting that they find nothing to the contrary but that they are cleere. the meeting having nothing against their comeing together but for the truths Sake and their sakes did make Jnquiry of Eliz^a, wheather her former husbands will were pformed or not and wheather she had or would sett out anything for her Children and she not being in a Capacity to answer without further advice the meeting appointed Wm Berry Jn° Edmondson Wm Southebee & John Pitts with the Executors Tho: Taylor and Wm Sharpe to meete the next 3rd day att the widdows house to prufe the will and to see that it may be answered and to settle the estate as neere as may be agreeable to the same and if it should so happen that any of the aforesaid friends should not be there then the rest that meet have power from the meeting to make choyce of others in their stead and friends give an account to Our next mans meeting at Howell Powells—after which time things being cleered, the meeting hath allowed of their in marriage according to the Order of Truth they appointing a time for that end and making it Publick.

The next monthly mtg was held 4. 11. 1680 at the house of Howell Powell—but this matter was referred to the next monthly mtg—when *it* was held at Kings Creek at the house of Tho. Taylor 5. 19. 1680 it was thought best that the account of Winlock Christersons will, then brought in by the Friends appointed, be referred to the next Quarterly Meeting—hence we find the account in full under the following date—

Att Our Quarterly mans Meeting at Tho : Hutchinsons The 23ʳᵈ of the fifth month 1680.

Those friends concerned by the meeting to Inspect into the Estate of Winlock Christerson Deceased so as to see that his will might be answered as nere as might be, have therein Acted, and given an accompt thereof to this Meeting and the Meeting is Well Satisfied therewith and doe advice that the Jnventory be entered and also the bond of the executrix past by her to Wᵐ Sharp and Tho : Taylor for their security they being Jointly concerned with her as Executors by the will she being wholly possessed with the estate and neere altering her condition by marriage.

An Jnventory of the estate of Winlock Christerson of Talbott county deceased given in by yᵉ Relict the executrix and Wᵐ Sharp and Tho : Taylor who were Left as her assistance and valued by the Request of the afd. Elizᵃ Christerson widdow and by her assistants By John Edmondson Bryon Omealia and Wᵐ Southebee as follows—

Jmpʳ One Large Standing Table, eight pewter porringers five large pewter dishes two pewter Basons one Turned Brass candle Stick one warming pan one brass ladle one bell mettle pott one Jron pott about 7 or 8 gallons two great brass kettels one great Jron pott one small skillitt one old feather bed feather bed for Eliz^a Harwood one Chest of Drawers one Trunk m: c: the two best feather beds and furniture according to will, two pair of Sheets halfe worne ye one p^r of holland the other of Canvas Two pillow cases those things above mentioned are given by will as Legacyes so not valued.

2nd Two paire of sheeting cloth sheetes Seaven napkins one pillow case one table cloth two towells one bolster case these forementioned Linen belongs to Mary Christerson being her third part according to will so not valued.

	£	s.	d.
a pcell of pewter	01	05	00
a pcell of Brass	01	14	00
a pcell of Earthen ware	00	04	00
2 brashes and 1 grater	00	01	00
a pcell of Tinnory ware	00	04	00
a small Jron pott	00	02	00
one spitt and one Clever	00	02	00
a pcell of old bedding for servants	01	00	00
1 pr. pottracks, one gridiron one fire } shovell and tongs 2 frying panns }	00	06	00
a pcell of Lumber	00	01	06
one bible & a pockett booke	00	03	00
One Clocke	00	14	00
one case bottle 5^s & 5 chairs 8^s	00	13	00
2 old boxis and an old baskett	00	02	06
2½ yds of hair camblett	00	08	00
4 yds parragan	00	16	00
3½ yds Diaper	00	03	00
3 gunns and pcell old Jron	01	16	06
one feather bedd bolster and pillows & Rugg & 1 pr } blanketts one old couch bedd and one old pillow one } old blankett & 2 old coverleads and old bedstead }	04	00	00
one cross cutt saw and a sett } of wedges and hammer }	00	08	00
3 yds Kersey	00	04	00
1½ yds Cotton	00	01	00
2 yds Kersey	00	03	00
3½ yds Dowlace	00	03	00
3 yds Jermaine holland	00	08	00

	£	s.	d.
one flock bedd	00	10	00
one hand-mill	00	12	00
one old Boate	01	00	00
2 Chests	00	08	00
one table & fourm	00	08	00
4 pr : of Sheets	01	05	00
one pillow case	00	02	00
one table cloth	00	01	00
12 napkins	00	10	00
3 towells	00	01	06
one cubbard	00	12	00
one old Couch	00	04	00
	20	11	06

This above valued goods to be divided betwixt yͬ widdow Elizᵃ Christerson and her Daughter Elizᵃ Christerson as by will,—The servants and yͤ horses and yͤ remaining part of yͤ cattle and yͤ Debts due to the estate to goe and be to & for the paying of the Debts and yͤ maintenance of the widdow and her children so not valued—

This being our Judgments according to the best of our knowledg with the aprobation also of the executors we have subscribed this 18ᵗʰ day of the third month called May 1680.

> ELIZABETH CHRISTERSON }
> THOMAS TAYLOR } *Executors*
> WILLIAM SHARP }

> JOHN EDMONDSON }
> BRYON OMEALIA } *assistants*
> WILLᴹ SOUTHEBEE }

Maryland ss

Know all men by these p̃sents that J Elizabeth Christerson executrix to yͤ estate of Winlock Christerson deceased am bound and firmly obleddg-d and doe by these presents acknowledge to owe and stand truly Jndebted unto Tho : Taylor and Wᵐ Sharp both of the County of Talbott and executors to yͤ abovsd Christersons estate in the full and just sum of one hundred pounds sterling money of England to be well and truly paid unto them their heirs

executors adm⁽ᵐ⁾ or assigns in witness whereof J bind my
selfe my heirs executors adm⁽ᵐ⁾ or assigns to the True pform-
ance of the abovsaid prmissess   in witness whereof J hereunto sett my hand and fix my seale this 18ᵗʰ day of the 3ʳᵈ
m° 1680.

The Condicon of this Obligation is Such that if the above
bounden Elizabeth Christerson her heirs, executors and
adm⁽ᵐ⁾ still from time to time and att all times pforme all
and Singular the points and Clawes of the above mentioned
Winlock Christersons will in paying of all the Debts and
Legacyes in the within mentioned will and to the Cleering
Releasing indemnifieing and Bareing harmless the abovsd
executors Tho : Taylor and W⁽ᵐ⁾ Sharp and their heirs executors adm⁽ᵐ⁾ and assigues from all and singular the points and
Clawes of the abovsd will and that none of the Creditors or
Legatees nor no other pson nor psons mentioned in the said
will or otherwise may not at any time hereafter Challing
trouble or demand anything of the above mentioned Taylor
and Sharp and that the abousaid Christerson her heirs and
assignes shall att all times cleere, Release indamnify and bear
harmless the abovesd Taylor and Sharp their heirs executors
adm⁽ᵐ⁾ and assignes that they may att no time be brought
into any trouble by the neglect of the abovsaid Elizabeth
Christerson or her heirs or assignes by not pforming the
said Winlock Christersons will so that then this abovsaid
obligation to be void and of none Effect or otherwise to
stand in full force power and vertue in Ju wittness whereof
J have hereunto sett my hand & fixt my seale the day and
year above mentioned.

Signed and sealed in
the presents of us
                his
Robert R Braslington
            mark
W⁽ᵐ⁾ Southebee

} John Edmondson
  Bryon Omealia
    his B-O : mark

                        her
        Elizabeth EC Christerson
                       mark

CORRESPONDENCE OF GEORGE AND SARAH DILLWYN.

PHILADA. 10 mo: 27, 1771—9 oclock
1ˢᵗ Day mornˢ.

MY DEAR SALLY:

Notwithstanding we came down Time enough to see our dear Aunt Morris alive, yet we are not much too soon here to pay the last office of Respect to her Remains. She died at about 11 OClock of 6 Day Night nothing very remarkable attending her Departure, unless it was a Continuance of the sweet Peace which had been the Companion of her Spirit for some Time before, & wᶜʰ indeed did not forsake in the awful approach of Death, but was with her "always to the End." . . . . . It is proposed to bury her Tomorrow afternoon, & to meet at the House at 2 oclock. It wᵈ be well if there is Time to send a general Note to the few particular Friends of the Family if it is not already done by way of Invitation; not forgetting Jonathan Guest's & Thoˢ Powell's Families who are Relations. . . . .

GEORGE DILLWYN.

RAHWAY 8 mo: 17ᵗʰ 1777.

MY DEAREST CREATURE:

Thro' a desolated Country we arrived here Yesterday to dinner, without any Interruption. The first Night we lodged a mile or two on this side Bordentown, at Marmaduke Watson's, where our Number made 47, in addition to 43 Soldiers quartered upon them for about a Week past, & the time of their continuance unknown. We stop'd at Isaac Clark's to breakfast, the next day spent an Hour or two at Benjamin's & Samˡ Worth's, dined in Prince Town at Joseph Horner's & passing over a Bridge a little above Brunswick, reached a Friend's (who has suffer'd much from the Armys) at about 9 at night & were rec'd with much

Kindness. Hence we came here (about 14 miles) thro' open Fields & here & there ruined Houses, affording a melancholy Contrast to the Appearance of Opulence & Plenty which this part of the Country was remarkable for, when I was in it before. Rahway (having been many times in the Hands of both Parties) has the fewest marks of Ruin in it of any Place on this side Burlington; but it has been often violently threatened with Destruction. They are at present very quiet, tho' only 4 or 5 miles from Staten Island, where the King's Troops are encamped.

I left my Buckles at home, & have been obliged to borrow. Please to put them in my Chest. We have been much favor'd in respect to our Horses. We overtook Cornell Stevenson 4 miles from Burlington, with Wm Jones, in the Waggon, & they eased us of our Saddlebags, which they brought all the way to this Place. I suppose this will go by their Return. I propose to send back one Shirt by them as unnecessary, & burthensome to my Horse, tho' he has performed very well, & is much approved of by my Fellow-travellers.

20th We are now about setting out for Planefield Monthly Meeting. Thence, intend for Mendem, & so on thro' the Great Meadows & drown'd Lands, towards New Windsor, (or Peek's Kill) at the North River. Our Minds are preserved in Stilness . . . . The Comp^a of our dear Friends Saml Emlen, Wm Jones, Henry Drinker, Cornwel, his Wife & Daughter, all from our own Neighbourhood, has been very pleasant to Benj^a & me. . . . . Tell my dear Brother & Sister Moore, Aunt Rachel, Brother C. & M. Moore, Brother Wells, Sister Wells & Sister Morris (when you write to Philad^a) & Father Worrall, Mother & our own Nancy & Sukey & Children at home, they are now present in a lively manner to my Remembrance. . . . Don't forget me to dear Edward Cathrall, Neighbour Harris, Neighbour Smith, Ann Hume, Widow Ferguson's afflicted Daughter, & Jenny Burling, with whom I sympathize. . . . . . . I have altered my mind & keep the Shirt.

GEORGE DILLWYN.

LONDON 1ˢᵗ m° 3ʳᵈ 1785.

[To HANNAH MOORE, Philadelphia.]

. . . . . I made my home at our dear W. D's till the 11ᵗʰ m° 29ᵗʰ last, when, receiving a note from my G. D. in London informing that S. E. and himself had a prospect of being in & abᵗ the City . . . . and that he had taken lodgings for us at a worthy friend's house (Adey & Martha Bellamy's) No. 10 in the Poultry, I accordingly came to Town that even'g in Bʳ W. D's charriot. The house is 4 stories high with conveniencies of water &ᶜ upstairs. . . . They are a kind good spirited couple. . . . S. Fisher can tell thee all abᵗ them. . . . . They are a happy couple without children, . . . with one niece abᵗ 15, a modest handy girl, whom they call my waiting maid, one woman servant, & 2 obliging lads being an apprentice & clerk. . . . We have a lodging room, & under it a handsome parlor with a fire lighted in it every day, & a kitchen on the same floor . . . . with a fine large cistern of water. . . . . I'm so incog. that I can rub out Caps & nobody the wiser. It's true London is a most sad dirty smutty place to live in, but . . . the inexpressible satisfaction of havᵍ my poor G. D. with me of an evnᵍ & often accompanying him to meetings makes up for all that's disagreeable. . . . . . . While I was writing this mornᵍ Jos. Norris paid me a little visit, I think it's the 4ᵗʰ time he has been here. . . . . I told him my dear Sisʳ Moore used to call him her boy & that I should claim a share of him on that accᵗ & hopᵈ he wᵈ come to see us freely. I bantered him aboᵗ his appearance as a friend. He smiling said he hoped to be much plainer by the time he returned to Philadᵃ hinting as if he tho't S. Griffits was not the worse friend for his travails, but I shᵈ not like his mother to tell him what I say. One of the Barclays told my G. D. he had received a letter from him ending with " yʳ very humble servᵗ." . . . . . I treat him just as I used to do my Dick or Gideon, & gave him some Philadᵃ Bisquits. Abᵗ a fortnight ago Bʳ W. D. invited us to dine at Clapton. . . . they put me under Josey's care & we went in Larkins regular stage coach, which passes W. D's door several times in a day. I being like the "monkey that had seen most of the world," could not help laughing in my sleeve at his surprise, and at the remarks that he made at the new sights & pretty places we passed.   When we got out of the carriage (the coachman ringing the bell at the gate) J. N. said, how different they live here, from what we do in America !   I broke off writing to receive M. & H. Bisset, they came in Br. Lamar's coach which waited at the door ab^t an hour & half while they staid. . . . . they said they never dined till 4, & were going a shopping. . . . . The dear creatures seemed very affectionate & chatty, bidding me to be sure to give their love & a kiss to Nunks, which is the name they call B^r Lamar by too. . . . . my very heart was drawn to poor Henrietta, who looked pale, has a cough & is short breath^d.   She says she can't dance for it. . . . . They have been in town but a day or 2, so they've not seen J. N., they intend to have us there when he is invited. . . . . Sist^r Lamar lately heard from Sist^r Scott, who had her health much better than for a long time past.   I'm afraid I shall find it difficult to send her one of the gammons, but will try.   Thee can't imagine the difficulties attending things going thro the Custom house.   Tho the Commerce & Willet have been so long arrived we did not receive the things till ab^t a week ago, & for want of proper care, poor dear sister Morris's Keg of Cranberries were stole off the Keys . . . . . 5th of the 1st m^o 1785.   I fancy we were misinformed ab^t the loss of the cranberries, for 2 barrels & 2 kegs were sent to our lodgings just now. . . . . . . I sent Jo^s Stansberry's letters to him & he called on me the next day, I read him what concerned him, and the poor fellow's eyes filled with tears.   He said that B^r Wells & thyself were such friends as were seldom to be met with. . . . . I went to see Sally at her grandfather Ogeers, who is since dead, he was then ill . . . . . her little heart was full.   Oh, Mrs. D., said she, I hope S. D. will never come over here, unless she can expect more indulgence than I do, it's very, very hard.   The old lady twisted her ab^t to shew how she had got her slip alter^d to a habit—"did ever any body see so great a girl in a frock, hold up your head." She told me that S. had come over in a very bad time. How? said I. "Because her grandfather is so ill." The eldest daughter is an accomplished girl, is kept at a boarding school & comes home once a week. . . . . John Lindoe's niece of Norwich—her name was Marg[t] Hopson, now Fincham—call'd to see me this morn[s], enquired kindly after & sent her love to Henry Drinker, Benj[a] Swett & Sam[l] Sansom. She's well married. . . . . . John Lister, of Lotherbury, London, desires that enquiry may be made concerning one Jane Moreland, who was recommended to —— Harding a Roman Catholic Priest belonging to the Chapel of Philad[a] ab[t] the years 1751 or 52 . . . . . that being the time she went to America, & we have been informed of her being in Philad[a] in the years 1759 & 60, we also were informed she was employed in the service of a Farmer, who was a Dissenter, ab[t] 80 miles up the country & she desired her sister to direct to her at some place like the name of Newcastle Bridge. Now John Lister . . . . . can inform her of something to her advantage. . . . . A letter from Ireland of the 28rd from Rich[d] Shackleton of Ballytone mentions that Tho[s] Ross . . . . . . was minded to unite with John Pemberton in his line of service, which is much among people of other persuasions. John P. has been lying by at Barclay Clibborns in Moat County Westmeath with a sore on the back of his right hand, which some have tho't cancerous. . . . . . . I sh[d] be much obliged to my dear sister Morris if she would write a few lines to W[m] Mathew's wife at York Town . . . . letting her know that her husband's grown fat, & writes my G. D. that he finds good wages in his service. . . . . . Tell our dear Father Worrall & sister A. D. that this great dirty noisey city often turns our minds to our much loved Burlington, which is as great a contrast to it as one can well conceive, & the pavements are so different from the soft Turf there, that my poor feet & petticoat tails pay for it. . . . . . D[r] Fothergill's . . . sis[t] Ann & myself are hand & glove. She has given me the yo ( ) . . . . she also gave me a handy little Desk top that was the Doct[rs]. In the room where I lodged, when at her house, are 2 nice small pieces of shell work, one of them a small Temple, made by Bʳ Well's mother & presented to the Doctʳ.   We see a little curiosity of one sort or other stuck abᵗ the house. . . . . I was pleased with a little green bug, cased, with a magnifying glass at one end, the back of the insect appeared to be set with shining green stones . . . . my G. G. is more sweetly tender & affectionate to me than ever, his heart seems to overflow with gratitude for my attachment to him—our dear sistʳ L. & the girls seem fond of him, but they've not been to one meeting yet that I know of.   I fancy they are afraid of being caught.   Quakerism & Freedom is the same thing, to my thinking—this I tell them, but the dear creatures can't understand me. . . . . . Don't send any preserves, my love —they have fruits of all the kinds we have, & by art bring them to great perfection. . . . . . I don't know what my dear sister Moore will think of me for not going to see Kitty Mead.   Bobby Barclay's wife told me that she had had bad fits some time ago, which greatly distressed Parson Duchee's wife, & that she had been removed from there a good while, & it was reported was got better of the fits. . . . . . When thou sees Betsey Roberts & Nancy Emlen give my love to .them, and to our good neighbours in 3ʳᵈ Street & M. Craig. . . . . . My dear A. D. remarks that there's no such thing as writing long letters without saying silly things (or to that purpose).   Is not this letter a full proof. . . . . . .

SARAH DILLWYN.

RECORDS OF CHRIST CHURCH, PHILADELPHIA.
BAPTISMS, 1709–1760.

BY CHARLES R. HILDEBURN.

(Continued from Vol. XVI. p. 456.)

1759 Aug.	23	Knowles Margaret d. John and —— May 13 1758
1734 Jan.	2	Knowlman Susannah d. Robert and Dorothy 5 wks.
1734 July	17	Kollock Jane d. Jacob and Margaret 6 mos.
1741 Aug.	19	Jacob s. Jacob and Mary 1 mo.
1746 Mch.	4	John s. Jacob and Mary baptised by Mr. Aneas Ross Dec. 9 1745
1748 Nov.	6	Phillip s. Jacob and Mary Sept. 26 1748
1751 July	25	Margret d. Jacob and Mary Nov. 4 1750
1754 June	24	Jacob s. Jacob and Mary July 29 1753
1751 Nov.	6	Kooly George s. George and Priscilla Oct. 16 1751
1734 Dec.	26	Krameren Jacobina Margareta d. John Matthias and Margaret 6 mos.
1755 Nov.	14	Kuhl Mary d. Samuel and Susannah Oct. 21 1755
1736 May	29	Lacey William s. Thomas and Mary 9 mos.
1738 Dec.	20	Mary d. Thomas and Mary 2 wks.
1726 Oct.	31	Lacy Joanna d. Thomas and Mary Oct. 26
1733 Jan.	1	John s. Thomas and Mary 4½ yrs.
1733 Jan.	1	Thomas s. Thomas and Mary 6 mos.
1734 Oct.	27	James s. Thomas and Mary 1 mo. 3 dys.
1740 Aug.	14	Elizabeth d. Thomas and Mary 1 mo.
1734 Feb.	6	Lamborth Oliver s. Oliver and Ruth 5 wks.
1744 June	10	Lane John s. John and Ann 3 mos.
1746 May	17	Mary d. Joseph and Anne Dec. 23 1745
1747 April	12	Anne d. Edward and Mary March 31 1747
1748 Jan.	1	William s. William and Ruth Nov. 21 1747
1754 Jan.	7	Langdon Peter s. Peter and Anne March 2 1751
1754 Jan.	7	Agnis d. Peter and Anne Nov. 3 1752
1754 Jan.	7	Newel s. Peter and Anne Nov. 11 1753
1735 Sept.	28	Langley Jane d. Samuel and Penelope 2 wks.
1737 Nov.	28	Thomas s. Thomas and Penelope 2 wks.
1752 May	6	Lardner John s. Lyndford and Elizabeth Sept. 6 1751
1745 July	26	Larrance Elizabeth d. Thomas and Mary July 6 1744
1747 Feb.	17	Thomas s. Thomas and Mary Jan. 19 1747
1749 Dec.	8	Lewis Morris s. Thomas and Mary Oct. 26 1749

1751 April	7	Larrance George s. Thomas and Mary July 25 1750
1753 Jan.	20	Catherine d. William and Charity May 20 1741
1786 Jan.	6	Lathbury Elizabeth d. William and Hannah 4 yrs.
1756 Sept.	27	Laur Magdalenah d. Hartman and Barbary Aug. 28 1756
1723 Jan.	2	Lawrence John s. Thomas and Rachel ——
1728 Aug.	11	Longfield s. Thomas and Rachel 1 yr. 2 mos.
1728 Dec.	25	Catherine d. Thomas and Rachel 7 wks.
1731 June	18	Longfield s. Thomas and Rachel 1 mo.
1744 April	14	Catherine d. Thomas and Mary Junr. 2 mos. 9 dys.
1746 April	27	Thomas s. Thomas and Mary Oct. 6 1745
1751 Oct.	24	John s. Thomas and Mary Sept. 15 1751
1754 Sept.	5	Robert Hunter s. Thomas and Mary Aug. 28 1754
1755 Nov.	14	Mary d. Thomas and Mary Sept. 22 1755
1758 Mch.	8	Morris s. Thomas and Mary Dec. 16 1757
1758 Aug.	30	Mary d. Thomas and Elizabeth June 8 1758
1760 Oct.	25	Staats s. Thomas and Mary Feb. 15 1760
1727 April	7	Laycock Samuel s. John and Mary 3 wks.
1755 July	2	Samuel s. John and Hannah Sept. 24 1754
1755 Nov.	19	Susannah d. Richard and Katherine July 27 1755
1758 Jan.	22	Catherine d. Richard and Catherine Jan. 26 1756
1757 Nov.	29	Lea Thomas s. Thomas and Elenor July 26 1757
1720 Oct.	21	Leacock Mary d. John and Mary Sept. 20
1722 Oct.	6	Susannah d. John and Mary ——
1730 Jan.	9	John s. John and Mary 19 dys.
1732 Feb.	11	Sarah d. John and Mary 2 wks.
1734 Feb.	5	Joseph s. John and Elizabeth 1 mo.
1786 Oct.	20	Rebecca d. John and Mary 1 mo.
1739 Aug.	5	Thomas 6 mos. Sp.
1731 July	15	Leaden Abraham s. Benjamin and Susannah 4 mos.
1732 Dec.	27	Ledra Herman s. Noel and Elizabeth 3 mos. 1 wk. -
1738 Mch.	8	Le Drew Solomon s. Noel and Elizabeth 2 wks.
1740 Mch.	14	Joseph s. Neel and Elizabeth 7 mos.
1734 Aug.	17	Le Dru Elizabeth d. Noll and Elizabeth 12 dys.
1736 Dec.	27	Ledrew John s. Noal and Elizabeth 7 mos.
1743 Sept.	6	Samuel s. Noel and Elizabeth 26 dys.
1756 Oct.	8	Rebecca d. Noel and Elizabeth July 11 1752
1716 July	21	Lee Catherine d. William and Sarah 12 dys.
1745 Oct.	18	Leeanan William s. William and Ruth April 14 1745
1720 Sept.	2	Leech Hester d. John and Mary Aug. 29
1723 Feb.	27	Mary d. John and Mary
1728 Aug.	25	Rebecca d. John and Mary 1 yr. 4 mos.
1729 June	27	Joseph s. John and Mary 7 wks. 5 dys.
1729 Mch.	15	John s. Ephraim and Jane 3 wks.
1732 May	28	James s. John and Mary 1 mo.
1736 May	9	Benjamin s. John and Mary 3 wks.

1737 Jan.   6 Leech Hester d. Thomas and Ann April 28 1723
1737 Jan.   6   John s. Thomas and Ann June 3 1725
1737 Jan.   6   Thomas s. Thomas and Ann Feb. 18 1727
1737 Aug.   2   Benjamin s. John and Mary 1 dy.
1756 April 11   Thomas s. William and Elizabeth Feb. 29 1756
1759 June   7   Mary d. Thomas and Mary Sept. 2 1758
1728 Aug.   18 Leek Sarah d. James and Patience 4 mos.
1734 Feb.   21 Lees Anne d. Ralph and Mary 16 dys.
1735 April   1   John s. Ralph and Mary 9 wks
1736 May   21   William s. Ralph and Mary 1 mo.
1758 Sept. 25 Leet Ann d. John and Mary Sept. 11 1758
1744 Jan.   5 Le Gay Jacob s. Jacob and Mary 23 dys.
1748 May   25 Legay Benjamin s. Jacob and Mary Nov. 26 1746
1741 Nov.   29 Leigh Thomas s. Ralph and Mary 3 yrs. 2 mos. 12 dys.
1755 Oct.   16 Lender Mary d. William and Sarah Oct. 5 1755
1721 July   30 Lennington Samuel s. Samuel and Katherine June 23
1725 Aug.   18   John s. Samuel and Katherine Jan. 1
1731 Sept. 26   James s. Samuel and Katherine 1 wk.
1731 Sept. 26   Mary d. Samuel and Katherine 4 yrs.
1740 June   29 Lennox Richard s. William and Margaret 6 dys.
1745 Oct.   13 Lester Phillip s. Adam and Anne March 15 1743
1758 Sept. 17   Margaret d. John and Mary April 17 1758
1760 Dec.   17   John s. John and Mary Oct. 5 1760
1712 June   22 Letort Judith d. James and Elizabeth ——
1712 June   8 Levens Letitia d. William and Rebeckah
1720 Oct.   9 Levering John s. Abraham and Anne Sept. 29
1722 Oct.   19   Randle John s. Abraham and Anne ——
1757 Oct.   1 Levers Mary d. Robert and Mary Dec. 21 1756
1754 Sept. 18 Lewersage Elizabeth d. William and Elizabeth July 4 1754
1729 Feb.   23 Lewis John s. John and Elizabeth 9 dys.
1730 Aug.   16   Joseph s. Phillip and Catherine 4 mos.
1733 July   18   Benjamin s. Phillip and Catherine 6 mos.
1735 April 10   Jane d. Phillip and Catherine 10 wks.
1754 June   30   Mary d. Henry and Rebecca Oct. 10 1753
1735 Aug.   3 Lincoln Mordecai s. Abraham and Rebecca 15 mos.
1750 Feb.   11   John s. John and Catherine Dec. 17 1749
1731 July   18 Lindsey Sarah d. Alexander and Sarah 19 yrs.
1731 July   18   Mary d. Alexander and Sarah 16 yrs.
1752 June   21   Mary d. William and Sarah April 14 1752
1733 April 29 Linney Joseph s. Peter and Frances 5 wks. 3 dys.
1734 Dec.   15   William s. Peter and Frances 2 wks. 7 dys.
1737 July   10   Joseph s. Peter and Frances 3 wks.
1738 Dec.   27   Samuel s. Peter and Frances 17 dys.
1747 Mch.   8 Linning William s. William and Ruth Jan. 26 1747
1734 Aug.   17 Lions Robert s. John and Catherine 7 mos.

1739 Nov. 21 Lisby Mary Catherine d. Zachariah and Septima 11 mos.
1757 Mch. 14 Littleboy Mary d. Robert and Honour Feb. 15 1757
1731 Dec. 25 Lloyd John s. William and Rebecca 10 mos. 3 wks.
1735 Sept. 20   Susannah d. Charles and Elizabeth 13 mos.
1735 Nov. 5   Mary d. Charles and Elizabeth 4 yrs.
1736 Aug. 8   Susannah d. Charles and Elizabeth 3 wks.
1749 Nov. 5 Lock Catherine d. William and Jane Oct. 11 1749
1753 Feb. 4   William Okley s. William and Jane Jan. 4 1753
1744 Oct. 8 Lodwigspigle Ann Catherine d. John and Eve Mary 6 dys.
1732 Jan. 19 Loftes Frances d. Charles and Mary 1 mo.
1714 Nov. 21 Loftis James s. Lester and Anne 3 wks.
1710 Feb. 24 Loftus Thomas s. Leason and Ann ——
1749 Feb. 26 Long Elizabeth d. Robert and Jane Feb. 17 1749
1742 June 2 Longcomb Ann d. Richard and Grace 13 yrs. 6 mos.
1710   Lord Gregory was born ye 1st and baptised ye 8th of March
1711 May 18   Gregory s. Theodorus and Mary 2 dys.
1714 Aug. 29   Mary d. Theodorus and Mary ——
1748 Dec. 23 Lorte Mary d. John and Susannah June 9 1747
1744 Sept. 8 Loure Hermon s. Edmund and Barbara Dec. 25 1743
1714 Oct. 20 Lovegrove Mary d. John and Dorothy 2 wks.
1715 Dec. 28   John s. John and Dorothy 1 dy.
1737 Aug. 14 Lovelespe Robert s. George and Susannah 14 dys.
1734 Oct. 30 Low Robert s. Robert and Margaret 9 mos.
1738 Mch. 14   James Bullar s. Robert 1 yr.
1738 Dec. 29 Lowder Samuel s. Ralph and Catherine 3 yrs.
1738 Dec. 29   Susannah d. Ralph and Catherine 7 mos.
1748 Aug. 21   Mary Catherine d. Hartman and Barbara July 15 1748
1751 Mch. 8 Lower Mary d. Hartman and Barbara Aug. 18 1750
1732 Oct. 1 Lownes George 24 yrs.
1734 June 6 Lowry Hugh s. Richard and Mary 5 dys.
1746 April 2   Martha d. Robert and Mary Nov. 4 1745
1760 Oct. 13   Mary d. Robert and Mary Feb. 13 1760
1721 Mch. 10 Lowther Robert s. Ralph and Catherine March 3 1721
1726 Mch. 9   Mary d. Ralph and Catherine 4 mos.
1740 April 8   Mary d. Edward and Elizabeth 18 mos.
1748 Nov. 6 Ludgate Elizabeth d. John and Jane Sept. 18 1748
1731 Mch. 7 Lunn John s. Samuel and Sarah 4 mos.
1740 Jan. 20 Lushwood Anne Margaret d. John and Anne Margaret
                 5 wks.
1730 Feb. 22 Lybert Henry s. Michael and Barbary 2 wks.
1753 June 30 Lyndal Mary d. Thomas and Judith April 5 1751
1753 June 30   —— s. Thomas and Judith March 18 1753
1748 Mch. 16 Lyneal Samuel s. Richard and Dorcas 5 dys.
1738 April 8 Lynn John s. John and Elizabeth 13 dys.
1726 Sept. 11 Lyons John s. John and Elizabeth July 20

1748 Oct.	23	Lyons Elizabeth d. James and Grace March 17 1747
1758 April	19	McAfee William s. Daniel and Honour April 4 1758
1723 May	1	McCall William s. George and ———
1729 Aug.	20	Margaret d. George and Anne 1 mo.
1731 Sept.	20	Margaret d. George and Ann 5 mos.
1732 July	19	Elinor d. George and Ann 5 wks.
1733 Dec.	26	William s. George and Anne 14 dys.
1737 May	28	Jane d. George and Anne 4 mos.
1739 Feb.	10	William s. George and Anne 6 mos.
1740 May	3	Anne d. Samuel and Anne 16 mos.
1740 May	3	Samuel s. Samuel and Ann 7 wks.
1742 April	7	John s. Samuel and Ann 18 mos. 15 dys.
1744 Feb.	2	John Serl s. Samuel and Ann 2 mos. 3 wks.
1744 June	22	Isabella d. Samuel and Ann May 24 1743
1745 June	5	Mary d. Samuel and Anne Sept. 8 1744
1745 July	20	Jasper s. George and Lydia
1746 Mch.	6	Anne d. Samuel Junr. and Anne ———
1747 April	8	Margret d. Charles and Mary March 7 1747
1747 July	23	Samuel s. Samuel Sr.
1748 Jan.	5	Mary d. Samuel and Anne March 13 1747
1748 Oct.	13	Catherine d. George and Lydia Nov. 20 1748
1749 Oct.	26	Mary d. George and Lydia June 2 1749
1749 Oct.	26	Catherine d. Samuel Senr. and Anne Aug. 9 1749
1750 Jan.	1	George s. Samuel and Anne Sept. 21 1749
1753 Feb.	9	Elinor d. Samuel and Anne Jan. 14 1753
1754 June	11	Lidia d. George and Magdalen Sept. 29 1753
1742 Nov.	10	McCleian Elizabeth d. John and Deborah 2 wks.
1731 July	18	McCollister John s. John and Mary 2 mos.
1733 Aug.	5	Mary d. John and Mary 5 wks.
1735 July	28	John s. John and Mary 3 mos.
1721 Jan.	9	McCoomb Rebecca d. John and Elizabeth Jan. 9 1721
1721 Feb.	10	John s. John and Elizabeth Dec. 22 1696 and Rebecca his wife d. Joseph Redman March 3 1703
1723 Aug.	21	John s. John and Rebecca
1734 Jan.	13	McCoy Francis s. Francis and Elizabeth 2 wks.
1740 Mch.	2	Margaret d. Francis and Margaret 6 wks.
1740 Sept.	24	McCuah Patrick s. Patrick and Hannah 9 dys.
1742 Aug.	8	McDaniel Charles s. James and Mary 6 wks. 2 dys.
1742 Aug.	8	James s. James and Martha 5 yrs. 10 mos. 3 wks.
1748 July	10	Mary d. James and Mary April 6 1748
1756 May	20	James s. Hugh and Mary Feb. 24 1752
1759 Oct.	14	Sarah d. John and Bridget Aug. 24 1757
1749 May	1	McDonald Sarah d. William and Jane Feb. 5 1749
1738 Oct.	17	McDowell William s. Robert and Ann 12 dys.
1789 Oct.	15	Robert s. Robert and Ann 5 wks.

1746 Oct.   6 McFarling Simiah d. Neal and Anne Sept. 20 1746
1758 Oct.   23 McFunn Mary d. William and Lydia June 5 1758
1740 Dec.   27 McGaugh William s. William and Elizabeth 5 mos.
1752 May   5 McGlaughlin Mary d. Phillip and Hannah Feb. 27 1752
1751 July   28 McGloghlin William s. William and Mary June 13 1751
1757 Dec.   9 McKane Thomas s. Daniel and Elinor Dec. 10 1757
1759 July   8 McKenny Rebecca d. William and Hannah Feb. 23 1759
1736 Jan.   16 McKinnen Charles William s. Samuel and Sarah 2 mos.
1755 Sept. 28 McKinsey Temperance d. Kennath and Mary Sept. 15 1755
1758 Aug.   23 McKinsie William s. Kenneth and Mary July 30 1758
1738 Mch.   4 McKnight Martha d. William and Martha 3 wks.
1789 Oct.   30   William s. William and Martha 1 dy.
1744 Feb.   24   George s. William and Martha 1 dy.
1731 May   18 McLoughlin William s. Edward and Anne 7 wks.
1736 Nov.   8 McLoughlin Oliver s. Dennis and Alice 1 mo.
1740 June   22 McMahone John s. William and Elizabeth 10 wks.
1738 Sept.   9 McMekin Agnes d. Robert and Sarah 9 dys.
1741 Jan.   5 McMekins John s. Robert and Sarah 7 wks.
1741 Dec.   24 McNorton Mary d. Phillip and Sarah ——
1757 Feb.   3 McOleton Jane d. William and Sarah Feb. 11 1757
1727 Aug.   18 McVeagh William s. Neal and Margaret 1 wk.
1738 Jan.   26 Maack Catherine d. Jacob and Anne 6 dys.
1715 May   15 Mackarty Abigail d. Daniel and Sarah 8 yrs. 6 mos.
1728 April 25 Mackchall Archibald s. George and Anne 10 mos.
1735 Aug.   7 Mackrill Anne d. John and Margaret 16 mos.
1749 June   7   Thomas s. Mary widow Nov. 3 1736
1721 Aug.   22 Macomb Elizabeth d. John and Thomasin Aug. 14
1729 Aug.   6 Maddox Mary d. Joshua and Mary 3 wks. 5 dys.
1732 Feb.   4   Mary d. Joshua and Mary 3 wks.
1739 Sept. 21   Alexander s. Joshua and Elizabeth 6 yrs. 11 mos.
1760 Sept.   7   Francis s. Francis and Judith Sept. 1 1760
1760 Sept.   7   David s. Francis and Judith Sept. 1 1760
1742 Feb.   14 Made John s. John and Ann 16 dys.
1755 July   27 Magee William s. Thomas and Elizabeth June 29 1755
1780 Nov.   13 Maggee John s. George and Elizabeth 2 wks.
1749 Dec.   24 Malcolm Margret d. John and Margret Nov. 24 1749
1751 Jan.   20   William s. John and Margret Nov. 28 1750
1752 July   21   John s. John and Margret April 18 1752
1755 May   12   Mary d. John and Margaret March 8 1755
1757 Jan.   16 Malcomb Henry s. John and Margaret Dec. 12 1756
1735 July   15 Mallaby Elizabeth d. Thomas and Anne 5 wks.
1715 May   29 Mallard James s. Robert and Sarah 3 mos.
1739 Nov.   11 Manaville Richard s. William and Mary 4 yrs. 6 mos.
1751 April 14 Manaway Henry s. Henry and Dorothy Feb. 22 1747
1759 Feb.   25 Manlove George adult 1758

1748 Aug. 20 Manney Francis s. Francis and Margret July 21 1748
1751 Dec. 28   Margret d. Francis and Margret Nov. 26 1751
1737 April 24 Many Anne d. Francis and Mary 3 wks.
1738 Sept. 10   Mary d. Francis and Mary 3 wks.
1741 Dec. 25   James s. Francis and Mary 6 wks.
1750 June 15   Anne d. Francis and Margret May 17 1750
1754 April 11   John s. Francis and Margaret March 11 1754
1760 Jan. 24   Mary d. Francis and Margaret Dec. 31 1759
1728 Dec. 26 Marcomb Mary d. John and Thomasine
1756 July 18 Mark Ruth d. John and Rachel July 4 1755
1757 Jan. 6   Margaret d. John and Rachel Nov. 26 1756
1755 Sept. 10 Markland John s. Thomas and Anne Aug. 8 1755
1741 Mch. 13 Markley Elenor d. Theodore 8 wks.
1760 Dec. 20 Marks John s. John and Rachel Sept. 24 1760
1750 June 24 Marr Sarah d. Garret and Mary May 25 1750
1754 Aug. 18 Marsden Humphry s. Humphry and Mary Oct. 4 1752
1754 Aug. 18   Mary d. Humphry and Mary Aug. 11 1754
1737 April 19 Marshall Mary d. James and Margaret 5 wks.
1742 Jan. 14 Marshel John s. James and Margaret 6 wks.
1757 Oct. 23 Martindall Elizabeth d. Joseph and Margaret Oct. 10 1757
1726 July 27 Mason Ann d. Thomas and Mary
1729 July 16   Thomas s. Thomas and Mary 1 mo.
1756 June 7   James s. Abraham and Catherine Feb. 3 1756
1759 Mch. 19   James s. Abraham and Catherine Sept. 21 1757
1760 Oct. 6   Catherine d. Abraham and Catherine April 12 1760
1725 Nov. 24 Mathias William s. John and Elizabeth Oct. 16
1725 Nov. 24   William s. John and Elizabeth Oct. 16
1785 July 10 Matthews Henry s. Henry and Martha 1 dy.
1786 Nov. 15   Joseph s. Christopher and Elizabeth 3 yrs. 10 mos.
1786 Nov. 15   John s. Christopher and Elizabeth 1 yr. 10 mos.
1748 Feb. 5   Elizabeth d. James and Elizabeth Dec. 5 1747
1741 Aug. 19 Mattucks Sarah d. Henry and Rebecca 2 yrs. 6 mos.
1740 July 24 Maugridge George s. William and Anne 7 wks.
1743 Dec. 18   Ann d. John and Elizabeth 25 dys.
1743 May 15 Maxey Mary d. Joseph and Dorothy 21 dys.
1711 Sept. 7 May Moses s. Jacob and Susannah ——
1756 Sept. 22   John s. Robert and Susannah April 22 1756
1758 Dec. 6   Rebecca d. Anthony and Mary Aug. 27 1758
1729 Aug. 13 Maynyard Samuel Guy s. Samuel and Catherine 1 wk.
1782 April 21 Mayor Mary d. Robert and Elizabeth 4 mos.
1757 Oct. 8 Mays Ann d. John and Ann April 27 1757
1734 Aug. 12 Mekins Elizabeth d. Robert and Sarah 1 dy.
1739 May 5 Melcher Susannah d. John and Mary 5 wks.
1750 May 8 Meredith Hugh s. Hugh and Margaret April 3 1750
1760 Oct. 11   Hannah d. Charles and Mary March 8 1760

1712 Mch. | 30 | Meridith Joan d. Owin and Susannah 6 dys. |
1725 Dec. | 19 | Sarah d. John and Margaret Oct. 18 |
1726 Sept. | 9 | Thomas s. Owin and Hannah Sept. 4 |
1730 Oct. | 24 | Mary d. John and Margaret 10 yrs. 10 mos. |
1741 Aug. | 26 | Jane d. Hugh and Mary Dec. 5 |
1742 Mch. | 7 | Hannah d. John and Margaret 11 yrs. |
1742 Mch. | 7 | Rachel d. John and Margaret 8 yrs. |
1745 Aug. | 6 | John s. John and Margaret June 18 1745 |
1746 May | 22 | Thomas s. Hugh and Mary Jan. 10 1745 |
1748 June | 26 | Benjamin s. Hugh and Mary Aug. 12 1747 |
1758 Jan. | 22 | Mary d. Charles and Mary Dec. 22 1757 |
1760 Nov. | 13 | Merritt John s. John and Mary 6 mos. |
1714 Feb. | 24 | Middleton Mary d. John and Elizabeth —— |
1741 June | 9 | Edward s. Edward and Ann 5 yrs. 6 mos. |
1741 June | 9 | Thomas s. Edward and Ann 3 yrs. 6 mos. |
1741 June | 9 | Ann d. Edward and Ann 7 mos. |
1745 May | 19 | John s. Edward and Ann April 20 1745 |
1782 Nov. | 12 | Miles John 23 years |
1749 Sept. | 24 | Milington John s. Thomas and Jane Aug. 25 1749 |
1712 July | 25 | Miller Benjamin s. Stephen 1 yr. 2 mos. |
1720 July | 6 | Nathaniell s. Jonathan and Blandina June 29 |
1742 Nov. | 14 | Mathias s. Michael and Margaret 1 wk. |
1742 Nov. | 14 | Michael s. Michael and Margaret 1 wk. |
1745 June | 7 | Elizabeth d. Nathaniell and —— |
1745 Nov. | 2 | Jonathan s. Nathaniell and Elizabeth Sept. 18 1745 |
1751 Mch. | 17 | Anne d. William and Margret Feb. 19 1750 |
1754 Jan. | 20 | Frances d. John and Frances Dec. 22 1753 |
1754 Feb. | 24 | Mary d. William and Margret Aug. 6 1753 |
1756 Sept. | 16 | John s. Henry and Catherine Sept. 4 1756 |
1758 June | 25 | John s. William and Margret Sept. 20 1755 |
1758 June | 25 | Elizabeth d. William and Margret April 5 1758 |
1759 Feb. | 1 | Henry s. Henry Sept. 11 1758 |
1760 Nov. | 18 | Ann d. Henry and Catherine Nov. 4 1760 |
1752 Feb. | 12 | Millington Thomas s. Thomas and Jane Jan. 15 1750 |
1738 June | 18 | Miranda Joseph s. George and Ann Magdalen 1 mo. |
1739 Sept. | 13 | Isaac s. Samuel and Mary 3 yrs. |
1740 June | 4 | Mary d. George and Ann Magdalen 8 dys. |
1741 Dec. | 25 | Mirander Jeremiah s. George and Anne Magdalen 4 mos. |
1786 June | 11 | Mirick Henrietta d. Richard and Sarah 4 mos. 2 wks. |
1727 Dec. | 27 | Mitchel Elizabeth d. Nehemiah and Rachel 13 wks. |
1720 Sept. | 4 | Mixell Johannes s. Andreas and Anna Maria —— |
1729 Oct. | 1 | Mockridge Mary d. William and Ann —— |
1725 Oct. | 18 | Mois James s. James and Sarah —— |
1726 Nov. | 11 | Rebecca d. James and Sarah Nov. 4 |
1734 Oct. | 6 | Moite Daniel s. John and Sarah 4 mos. 2 wks. |

1748 Dec. 4 Molineux Francis s. Francis and Elinor March 14 1748
1712 June 15 Mollart John s. William and Catherine 1 mo.
1747 July 26 Monemaker Sarah d. Henry and Alice June 10 1747
1746 July 13 Monroe Roland s. Roland and Rebecca June 14 1746
1747 July 21   Rebecca wife of Rowland
1733 Oct. 7 Montaune John s. Peter and Margaret (Indians) 3 yrs.
1731 Mch. 14 Montgomery Anthony s. Thomas and Elizabeth 1 wk.
1733 Aug. 6   Elizabeth d. Thomas and Elizabeth 5 wks.
1735 June 8   Thomas s. Thomas and Elizabeth 3 wks.
1738 April 12   Thomas s. John and Elizabeth 2 wks.
1720 Aug. 17 Moon Elizabeth d. Jasper ——
1720 Jan. 12 Moone Elizabeth d. Thomas and Elizabeth
1711 July 19 Moor Somerset s. John 5 dys.
1729 Jan. 5   Sarah d. Francis and Susannah 8 wks.
1729 Oct. 22   William Lock s. William and Wilhelmina 3 yrs. 2 wks.
1729 Oct. 22   Wilhelmina d. William and Wilhelmina 2 yrs. 5 mos.
1729 Oct. 22   John s. William and Wilhelmina 3 wks. 2 dys.
1730 April 30   Elizabeth d. Robert and Elizabeth 13 mos. 3 wks.
1733 Feb. 28   Rebecca d. William and Wilhelmina 7 dys.
1734 Feb. 6   Mary d. Francis and Susannah 8 yrs.
1735 Nov. 5   Charles s. Robert and Elizabeth 2 yrs. 9 mos.
1736 Aug. 27   Elizabeth d. Robert and Elizabeth 4 mos.
1737 Jan. 31   Sarah d. John and Mary 6 mos.
1737 Jan. 31   Ann d. John and Mary 6 yrs.
1716 April 30 Moore Catherine d. William and Phœbe 3 dys.
1728 Sept. 22   John s. Robert and Elizabeth 8 mos.
1731 June 1   John s. William and Wilhelmina 4 mos.
1733 July 25   Isaac s. James and Anne 5 mos.
1739 May 24   Elizabeth d. Charles and Mary 1 dy.
1740 Oct. 7   Charles s. Robert and Elizabeth 10 mos.
1742 Oct. 11   John s. Charles and Mary July 3 1742
1744 Oct. 11   Margaret d. Charles and Mary 8 dys.
1759 Aug. 11   Thomas s. Thomas and Mary Sept. 6 1758
1760 Aug. 16 More Jane d. Robert —— 3 wks.
1710 Jan. 1 Morgan Blandina 17 yrs.
1713 June 14   Cadwallader s. John and Winifred 6 yrs. 6 mos.
1713 June 14   Ann d. John and Winifred 7 yrs. 6 mos.
1713 June 14   Catherini d. John and Winifred 3 yrs.
1713 June 14   Elizabeth d. John and Winifred 1 yr.
1721 Feb. 22   John s. Benjamin and Sarah Jan. 25 1721
1725 Dec. 27   Ann d. Phillip and Margaret ——
1726 Oct. 18   Samuel s. Benjamin and Sarah Oct. 7
1730 Mch. 30   Sarah d. Benjamin and Sarah 3 wks.
1737 Nov. 27   Mary d. Evan and Mary 3 wks.
1739 Nov. 22   Sarah d. Evan and Mary 1 mo.

1741 Aug. 30 Morgan Elizabeth d. Evan and Mary 6 wks. 4 dys.
1744 Nov.   2   Ann d. Evan and Mary 1 mo.
1753 Sept. 24 Morgatroid Mary d. James and Mary April 6 1751
1730 Oct. 25 Morgrage William s. William and Ann 1 mo. 3 dys.
1732 June 17 Morphew Owen s. Owen and Elizabeth 2 mos.
1735 June 14   John s. Anne 5 dys.
1711 Oct. 18 Morris Jane wife Israell 29 yrs.
1722 Jan. 22   Branscom ——
1728 July 10   James s. James
1729 Oct.   5   John s. David and Bridget 4 dys.
1738 July   9   Sarah d. James and Elizabeth 5 yrs.
1738 July   9   Hannah d. James and Elizabeth 1 mo.
1739 Mch. 28   Kesia d. Thomas and Lydia 8 mos.
1741 Aug. 13   Thomas s. Thomas and Abigail 2 mos. 11 dys.
1754 May   7   Robert s. Francis and Catherine April 21 1754
1754 Aug. 15   Samuel s. John and Hannah March 4 1754
1757 Oct.   1   John adult
1757 Oct.   1   John s. John and Hannah June 18 1757
1743 April 30 Morriss Miriam d. Thomas and Lydia 6 mos.
1745 June 14   Lydia d. Thomas and Lydia
1737 Mch. 25 Morrow Hannah d. Patrick and Abigail 5 mos.
1744 April 1 Morton Catherine d. William and Esther 7 wks. 4 dys.
1746 Jan. 19   William s. William and Hester Jan. 7 1745
1760 July 12   George s. George and Sarah Oct. 29 1759
1760 Oct. 11   Hannah d. Benjamin and Catherine March 7 1760
1730 May   31 Moss Ann d. Matthew and Elizabeth 1 mo.
1735 Oct. 26   Thomas s. Thomas and Sarah 1 mo.
1721 Jan. 28 Mountague Elizabeth d. John and Elizabeth Jan. 27 1721
1736 Sept. 27 Moyer George Henry s. George and Parvenor 14 dys.
1752 Nov. 16 Moyes James s. John and Anne Oct. 20 1752
1737 Nov. 13 Moyte John s. John and Sarah 1 yr.
1714 April 25 Mullard Ann d. Robert and Catherine ——
1740 Nov.   2   Sarah d. John and Christian 5 wks.
1740 May   25 Mullen Robert s. Thomas and Anne 1 yr. 10 mos.
1740 May   25   John s. Thomas and Anne 1 yr. 1 mo.
1756 June   3   Elizabeth d. Thomas and Margaret July 21 1755
1743 May   30 Mulleneux Elenor d. Francis and Elenor 1 yr. 9 dys.
1741 July 12 Mullin Thomas s. Thomas and Ann 3 wks. 4 dys.
1742 Aug. 24   Ann Magdalene d. Thomas and Ann 3 wks. 3 dys.
1743 Nov. 20   Mary d. Thomas and Ann 18 dys.
1745 Aug.   6   Elizabeth d. Thomas and Ann July 14 1745
1745 Feb. 17 Mullinox James s. Francis and Elenor 17 dys.
1750 Dec.   5 Mullock Mary d. Joshua and Elinor Nov. 2 1750
1727 Aug.   9 Mullord Willmot s. Robert and Katherine 6 yrs.
1752 April 3 Mulock Thomas s. Joshua and Elizabeth March 25 1752

1734 Sept. 5 Multy Joseph Pratt s. Robert and Frances 8 dys.
1740 Sept. 10 Munroe John s. Patrick and Abigail 14 mos.
1737 Aug. 7 Murdock Susannah d. William and Mary 2 wks.
1739 July 15   William s. William and Mary 3 wks.
1741 Oct. 19   Samuel s. William and Mary 5 wks.
1744 Mch. 7   Thomas s. William and Mary 19 dys.
1746 Jan. 28   Hannah d. William and Mary Jan. 5 1745
1748 July 21   John s. William and Mary June 27 1748
1750 Aug. 8   Margret d. William and Mary July 15 1750
1752 Feb. 27   Sarah d. William and Mary Feb. 1 1752
1753 Dec. 20   James s. William and Mary Nov. 27 1753
1753 Aug. 5 Murray —— d. James and Christiana July 21 1753
1756 Oct. 8 Murrey George s. James and Christiana Sept. 19 1756
1759 June 3 Murry James s. James and Catherine Feb. 26 1759
1734 May 19 Myter Jacob s. John and Anne Margaret 4 wks.
1751 April 23 Naglee Catherine d. John and Elizabeth Dec. 31 1750
1717 May 29 Nailor Benjamin s. Robert and Dorothy 1 mo.
1731 Nov. 7 Nawden Henry s. Henry and Elizabeth 26 wks.
1723 June 16 Naylor James —— P. B.
1734 Dec. 10 Neal James s. Tobias and Alice 2 mos.
1737 Dec. 28   William s. Tobias and Alice 3 mos.
1739 May 27   Elizabeth d. Thomas and Nabella 4 mos. 3 wks.
1748 Jan. 30   Susannah Catherine d. John and Catherine 9 mos.
1758 Nov. 14   Mary d. James and Mary Nov. 1 1758
1738 June 25 Neesham William s. John and Elizabeth 2 mos.
1740 Nov. 14 Neeson Margaret d. John and Mary 3 wks. 2 dys.
1743 July 10   George s. John and Elizabeth 1 mo.
1739 July 9 Neeve Barnabas s. Thomas and Dina 3 yrs. 6 mos.
1739 July 9   Sarah d. Thomas and Dina 6 yrs. ——
1735 Mch. 3 Nellson Nelse Newble s. Nelse Newble and Alice 1 dy.
1735 Mch. 3   Daniel s. Nelse Newble and Alice 1 dy.
1711 Nov. 3 Nelty Rebekah d. Matthew and Ann 4 yrs. 9 mos.
1729 Aug. 19 Newberry William s. John and Elizabeth 3 wks. 3 dys.
1743 Sept. 11 Newman John s. Andrew and Catherine 9 mos. 1 dy.
1746 Aug. 7 Newton Robert s. Robert and Elizabeth
1751 July 21   Mary d. Richard and Rebeca Aug. 6 1750
1758 Dec. 1   John s. Robert and Rebecca March 29 1758
1731 Dec. 27 Nicholas William s. William and Elizabeth 2 dys.
1728 Feb. 11 Nicholds Dianah d. Edward and Eliza 2 yrs.
1733 Aug. 19 Nicholls Sarah d. Richard and Anne 6 mos.
1733 Aug. 2 Nichols Elizabeth d. William and Mary 8 dys.
1758 Oct. 6 Nicholson Abraham s. William and Grace Aug. 15 1757
1760 Nov. 2   John s. George and Sophia July 3 1760
1746 Oct. 9 Nickelson Mary d. William and Mary Oct. 11 1742
1746 Oct. 9   Sarah d. William and Mary Sept. 26 1746

1718 Sept.	3	Nickolson Daniel s. John 1 yr. 9 mos.
1709 Oct.	28	Night Mary d. William and Elizabeth 7 mos.
1747 June	10	Nigley John s. John and Elizabeth March 2 1747
1728 Dec.	5	Nixon Boell s. Richard and Sarah 2 wks.
1730 Dec.	11	Thomas s. Richard and Sarah 6 mos.
1735 April	19	John s. Richard and Sarah 2 yrs.
1735 April	19	Sarah d. Richard and Sarah 3 wks.
1739 Sept.	12	John s. John and Mary 9 wks.
1742 Nov.	21	Joseph s. James and Mary 3 mos.
1740 June	30	Noble Anthony s. Anthony and Flower 10 wks.
1744 July	5	Thomas s. Anthony and Flower 18 mos.
1714 June	6	Norris ——— d. Thomas and Rebecca 16 yrs.
1759 July	15	Elizabeth d. John and Mary June 6 1759
1759 July	15	Sarah d. John and Mary 175–
1725 Aug.	13	North Sarah d. John and Sarah ———
1726 Mch.	7	John s. John and Sarah 5 yrs.
1742 Oct.	19	Hannah d. George and Ruth 6 mos. 2 wks.
1751 July	30	Mary d. George and Ruth Sept. 12 1746
1751 July	30	George s. George and Ruth Oct. 16 1750
1755 June	12	William s. John and Susannah April 20 1755
1727 July	2	Norton Jacob s. William and Mary 5 wks. 3 dys.
1730 Oct.	29	Norton s. John 6 dys.
1748 Feb.	21	James s. Jonathan and Dorothy Feb. 16 1748
1749 Aug.	13	William s. Jonathan and Dorothy July 1 1749
1725 Oct.	24	Norwood Elizabeth d. Henry and Elizabeth
1726 Dec.	26	Matthew s. Henry and Elizabeth 2 wks.
1728 Dec.	26	Henry s. Andrew and Sarah 3 mos. 2 wks.
1730 Jan.	2	Mary d. Henry and Elizabeth 4 mos. 3 wks.
1730 Nov.	5	Charles s. Andrew and Sarah 2 wks.
1731 Sept.	24	Elizabeth d. Henry and Elizabeth 8 wks.
1733 Nov.	27	Susannah d. Henry and Elizabeth 9 wks.
1734 Aug.	1	Sarah d. Andrew and Sarah 19 mos.
1738 July	4	Ann d. Henry and Elizabeth 16 dys.
1740 Mch.	30	Anne d. Henry and Elizabeth 5 mos.
1741 Aug.	30	William s. John and Mary 10 dys.
1747 May	13	Joseph s. John and Mary June 18 1745
1753 Dec.	24	Nuttle Samuel s. Samuel and Mary Dec. 8 1753
1757 April	27	James s. Samuel and Mary Dec. 31 1756
1759 Mch.	4	John s. Samuel and Mary Jan. 18 1759
1710 Feb.	10	Oakly Ann d. Thomas and Mary 2 mos.
1728 May	12	Mary d. Thomas and Susannah 11 wks.
1730 Aug.	4	Jane d. Thomas and Susannah 8 mos.
1738 Dec.	19	O'Brian Margaret d. Timothy and Honor 2 mos.
1758 April	16	John s. William and Catherine April 15 1758
1731 Mch.	9	Oburn Mary d. William and Anne 3 yrs. 3 mos.

1782 Nov. 19 Oburn William s. James and Mary 7 wks.
1752 Oct. 5 Okil Anne d. George and Anne Aug. 25 1752
1745 Jan. 10 Okill John s. George and Ann 20 dys.
1747 July 31 Jane d. George and Anne July 3 1747
1744 May 26 Oliphant Benjamin s. Thomas and Mary 7 mos. 20 dys.
1721 July 5 Oliver Elizabeth d. John and Elizabeth born ye first day
of June at sea on board ye London Hope
1747 Dec. 25 William s. Thomas and Elizabeth Nov. 11 1747
1750 Sept. 29 Thomas s. Thomas and Elizabeth Feb. 22 1749
1731 Nov. 27 O'Neal Susannah d. Terrance and Mary 1 mo.
1735 Sept. 30 Alice d. Bryan and Margaret 12 mos.
1738 Oct. 27 Margaret d. Bryan and Margaret 2 yrs. 8 mos. 3 wks.
1747 June 10 Ord John s. John and Anne March 9 1747
1748 Aug. 10 Martha d. John and Anne April 16 1748
1749 Nov. 8 William s. John and Anne Oct. 11 1749
1752 Mch. 20 Thomas s. John and Anne Dec. 20 1751
1729 Aug. 24 Osborn Sarah d. Robert and Mary 6 wks.
1751 June 2 Peter James s. George Lewis and Jane April 6 1751
1740 July 21 Osborne Jeremiah s. Robert and Mary 5 mos.
1725 Mch. 2 Osburn Jeremia s. Robert and Mary
1731 May 22 Robert s. Robert and Mary 4½ mos.
1734 May 30 Samuel s. Robert Jonathan and Maria 6 dys.
1735 July 16 James s. William and Mary 2 wks
1735 Oct. 5 George Ellwood s. William and Jane 3 wks.
1752 Oct. 31 Isabella d. George Lewis and Jane Sept. 2 1752
1735 Oct. 6 Oswald Mary d. James and Mary 3 yrs. 5 mos.
1735 Oct. 6 Elizabeth d. James and Mary 14 mos.
1736 May 9 Margaret d. James and Mary 9 dys.
1742 April 11 Oswell Jacob s. John and Dorathea 11 dys.
1740 April 21 Overthrow George s. William and Martha 16 wks.
1716 May 13 Owen Mark s. Peter and Mary 1 mo.
1728 July 28 Mary d. James and Susannah 3 wks.
1737 July 31 Owner James s. James and Margaret 2 wks.
1786 Oct. 24 Ozburn George s. George Lucas and Jane 1 mo.
1737 Jan. 1 Robert s. Robert and Sarah 2 wks.
1712 Aug. 16 Paddison Ann d. Robert and Sarah 2 wks.
1711 Oct. 14 Page John s. George and Mary 2 wks.
1715 May 1 Amey d. George and Mary 1 mo.
1742 Feb. 14 Painder John Jacob s. Jacob and Margaret 4 dys.
1756 Jan. 16 Paine Sarah d. Thomas and Mary Jan. 6 1756
1756 Jan. 16 Ann d. Thomas and Mary April 6 1755
1717 Aug. 1 Pairtree —— d. James and Ann 8 dys.
1751 Aug. 18 Pall James s. William and Elizabeth Nov. 6 1750
1714 Mch. 14 Palmer Daniel s. Jonathan and Ruth 4 yrs. 6 mos
1714 Mch. 14 Ruth d. Jonathan and Ruth 2 wks.

1714 Mch. 14 Palmer Sarah d. Jonathan and Ruth 2 wks.
1721 Jan.   6   Mary d. George and Mary Dec. 10 1720
1721 Sept. 21   John s. Robert and Elizabeth Aug. 24
1731 Jan.   10   Israel s. Jonathan and Ruth 6 yrs.
1744 June 20   Lethea d. John and Elizabeth June 23 1743
1747 May   2   Elizabeth d. Samuel and Jane April 30 1747
1748 Mch. 19   Margret d. John and Deborah Feb. 11 1748
1750 Jan.   20   Deborah d. John and Deborah Jan. 3 1749
1751 April 23   Hester d. Samuel and Catherine April 24 1750
1753 Feb.   10   Mary d. John and Deborah Jan. 15 1753
1753 Sept. 26   Samuel Alexander Jenkins s. Samuel and Catherine
                      Aug. 27 1753
1755 Sept.   6   Thomas s. Samuel and Catherine July 30 1755
1751 Dec.   8 Pane Rachel d. James and Mary Dec. — 1751

(To be continued.)

NOTES AND QUERIES.

Notes.

HALL—BRADING—CARMICKE.—The following entries are copied from an old Breeches Bible in the possession of Captain P. G. Watmough, Chestnut Hill, Philadelphia:

W⁰ Hall the first sun of William Hall and Sarah his wife wass borne one the 22 day of October in 1701 it being betweene 3 & 4 aclock in thee morning and one the 4ᵗʰ called Wednes Day

Sarah Hall thee Eldest Daughter of William Hall & Elizabeth his first wife wass borne thee 18 day of Aprall in thee year 1689 ☉ in ♌ die ol hoe 4 and Departed this Life on Thursday the 27ᵗʰ Oct abt 11 aclock at night 1748

Hanna Hall thee 3 daughter of William and Elizabeth wass borne one the 20 day of March in the yr 1692

Elizabeth Hall thee 4 daughter of William & Elizabeth wass born one thee 31 day of Desember 1694 of a monday about 3 aclock in thee after noone

Elizabeth Hall died the day before —— day in ye year *1699*

Ann Hall the 5 daughter of William Hall and Elizabeth wass born one y⁰ 9 day of Desember in the yeare of our lord *1699* it being one a tuesday a boute 4 in the morning & departed this life one ye 15 day of Feborray 170½, on a fasst day

¹ Sarah Hall Borne the 18ᵗʰ Day of Aapʳˡ 1689 and Departed this Life on Thursday 27ᵗʰ Octobʳ abᵗ 11 aclock at night in the year *1748*

¹ Hanna Hall the 3 Daughter of William Hall and Elizabeth his wife was Borne on y⁰ 20 day of March in 1692

¹ Elizabeth Hall y⁰ forth Daughter of William Hall and Elizabeth wife was Borned Desamber y⁰ 31d in y⁰ yeare *1694* of a Monday a bout three aclock in y⁰ after noone

Nathaneill Brading Aidged aboute Thirtysix: years of age Died y⁰ ninth Day of January aboute Three or four a Clock In y⁰ morning In y⁰ year of our Lord 1712–13

Laus Deo In Salem

On the 16ᵗʰ Day of 8ᵇʳ Anno Domine 1713 Peter Carmicke and Sarah Brading Daughter of Wm Hall of Salem towne wear Maried together By ye Revᵈ Mr Boise

On Tuesday the 17ᵗʰ day of Augt. in the forenoon at eleven John Carmicke eldest son of Peter & Sarah his wife was Borne Anno yʳ *1714* on the 25ᵗʰ 9ᵗʰ our Son John recd Baptism by ye revᵈ Mr Mansell who was his Godfather 1715 & Departed the 27 May 1754

On Thursday 14ᵗʰ Feby: Eliz: eldest Daughter of Peter & Sarah was borne about a quarter of eight at night 1716 & Apll 14ᵗʰ 1719 she was Baptised by ye Revᵈ Mr Gerard who was her Godfather

On Saturday Stephen Second son of Peter and Sarah was Borne abt. twelve at noon 1718–9 Jan 31ˢᵗ and Apll. 14ᵗʰ 1719 he was Baptized by ye Revᵈ Mr Gerard & my Son Joⁿ was his Godfather

On Monday 15ᵗʰ day of Jan. 1721–2 abt. 10 at night Sarah second

¹ These appear to be duplicate entries, in another part of the Bible.

Daughter of Peter & Sarah was Borne & on the 11ᵗʰ day of March was Baptizᵈ by ye Revᵈ Mr Hodgson & Doc. Reily & Mary Saill stood for her 1721–2

On Monday ye 26 of 8ᵗʰ 1724 abt. 3 in yᵉ morning Clementina ye third Daughter of P. & Sarah was borne and on ye 24ᵗʰ of 9ᵗʰ she was Babtizᵈ & Mr Hodgson who was her Godfather. On ye 15ᵗʰ Jany 1724–5 she Departed this Life & on May 24 1728 my wife Sarah was Delivrd of a Dead Girl by Doctors Graham & Griffeth Owen after a terrible Labour of 3 days &c.

AN INCIDENT IN THE SIEGE OF BOSTON, MASSACHUSETTS, 1775.— We are indebted to Captain P. G. Watmough, Chestnut Hill, for the following extracts of a letter from E. E. Watmough, an officer on the British man-of-war "Glasgow," Captain Teringham How, to his brother James Horatio Watmough, Esq., in Rotterdam, and dated at Boston, June 4, 1775:

"I have just retr'd after spending a very agreeable 4 months with my friends at Halifax, on leave from the Admiral. It is a favour that is Rarely obtained. I wrote you from Halifax and gave you an account of a skirmish between the Yankees and Regulars—The Regulars met with a almost total Defeat. Superiority of numbers on the side of the Provincials in a great measure contributed to it. But last Saturday 27th. May, the signal for landing the Marines from the fleet was made. I was ordered to go in our Long boat to cover the Landing, which we did. I then had the command of 8 men and 2 swivels. After the soldiers were landed we went 3 miles up Chelsea River to bring down a schooner of arms. We began to tow her at 8 o'clock at night. At 9 o'clock the Provincials began their fire on us at about 100 yards distance and kept it up 'till 4 in the morning. The schooner was burnt tho. we defended her 'till the last. She had four 4 pounders continually firing on them; there was likewise 2 field pieces on boats besides swivels. I had one man shot in my boat, one wounded and my self, but I can assure you I came off with more honour than hurt—a small scratch in the side was all I suffered. We lost in all 15 killed and wounded—their loss is uncertain. We are all in a very melancholy situation at present, under a breastwork or fortification thrown up by the Yankees. The Continental Congress has voted 100,000 men for the ensueing Campaign, which at present are within 2 miles of our advance works. God only knows what will be the end of all this, I hope it will end well."

AMERICAN JEWISH HISTORICAL SOCIETY.—The first meeting of this Society was held on December 15, 1892, at the Stratford Hotel, Philadelphia, and was opened by an address from the President, Hon. Oscar S. Straus, outlining the scope of the work of the Society. The following papers were submitted: Dr. Cyrus Adler, Smithsonian Institution, Washington, "Jews in the American Plantations between 1600 and 1700," "Americana at the Anglo-Jewish Exhibition," "A Political Document of the Year 1800;" Rev. Henry Cohen, Galveston, Texas, "Historical Notes on the Jews of Jamaica;" Dr. S. Solis-Cohen, Philadelphia, "Note on David Hays, a Patriot of the Revolution;" Moses A. Dropsie, Esq., Philadelphia, "Reminiscences concerning the Jews of Philadelphia;" Herbert Friedenwald, Philadelphia, "Notes on Jews mentioned in the Journals of the Continental Congress;" J. H. Hollander, Baltimore, "Dr. Jacob Lumbrozo, of Maryland;" Prof. Morris Jastrow, Jr., University of Pennsylvania, Philadelphia, "Notes on Jews of Philadelphia from published Annals;" Col. Charles C. Jones, Jr., Augusta, Georgia, "Settlement of the Jews in Georgia;" Max J. Kohler, New York, "Beginnings of New York Jewish History;" Prof. J. B. McMaster, University of Pennsylvania, Philadelphia, "On Methods of Historical Research;" Rev. Dr. S. Morais, Philadelphia, "The First Jewish Congregation in Philadelphia;" Lucien Moss, Philadelphia, "John Moss;" Barnet Phillips, New York, "Note on Jews in the U. S. Navy;" N. Taylor Phillips, Esq., New York, "A Landmark;" Hon. Simon W. Rosendale, Albany, New York, "A Pennsylvania Document concerning the Franks Family;" David Sulzberger, Philadelphia, "Notes on the Jewish Burial-Grounds of Philadelphia."

ROSTER OF THE OFFICERS OF "THE LEGION OF THE UNITED STATES" (PENNA. MAG., Vol. XVI. p. 423).—For "Thomas Butter" (p. 427), Major of the Fourth Sub Legion, read Thomas Butler. He was the officer who refused to obey the order of General Wilkinson, directing the cutting off of queues, and was court-martialled. When he died he was buried with his queue. Ensign William Pitt Gassaway (p. 428), of the same Sub Legion, and noted "deceased," was killed in a duel at Legionville by Lieutenant Daniel St. Thomas Jenifer (p. 428). I. C.

A JOURNEY TO PITTSBURGH, PA., BY STAGE, IN 1808 (PENNA. MAG., Vol. XVI. p. 458).—The "Mrs. Butler and her daughter, Mrs. Mason" (for "Mason" read Meason), were the widow and daughter of General Richard Butler. Mrs. Butler resided on what was then called Marbury Street, a short distance from the magazine bastion of Fort Pitt. The house is still standing. Mary Butler was born in Carlisle, Penna., April 10, 1785; in April of 1805 married Colonel Isaac Meason. She died November 30, 1878, at Uniontown. I. C.

DATES OF BIRTH AND DEATH OF CHARLES THOMSON AND HIS WIFE.—Joseph Parker Norris, writing to John Jay Smith, under date November 6, 1838, states:
"Agreable to promise I now furnish you with the date of the birth and decease of Mr. and Mrs. Thomson.
"Charles Thomson was born in the Village of Gortede, County of Derry, in the North of Ireland, in November, 1729. Died at Harriton, Merion Township, Montgomery County, August 16th, 1824. Aged 94 Years 9 months & — days.
"Mrs. Thomson was born December 1st, 1731, and died September 6th, 1807.
"Of Charles Thomson it may be said,
"Homo amantissimus patriæ, maximi animi, summi consilii, singularis constantiæ.

"A Patriot's even course he steered,
'Mid Faction's wildest form unmoved,
By all who marked his course, revered,
By all who knew his heart, beloved."

DANIEL HUMPHREY, OF HAVERFORD.—On page 471 of Dr. George Smith's "History of Delaware County," in the biographical notices there is what purports to be a list of the children of Daniel Humphrey. This list is both incomplete and incorrect, as will be seen on an examination of his will at the office of the register of wills, Philadelphia. The following is a short abstract of that document. Will of Daniel Humphrey, No. 402 of 1735, Book E, page 327:
"Daniel Humphrey of Haverford wife Hannah, Sons Samuel, Joshua,

Charles, Edward, Jonathan, Solomon, Benjamin [the latter deceased, leaving a widow, Esther, and two children, Hannah and Anne], daughters, Hannah, Elizabeth Martha, Rebecca,—Executrix, wife Hannah and daughter Hannah, Trustees—cousins John Humphrey and David Humphrey and sons Samuel, Joshua and Edward, Dated the 26th day of 9th month 1734 proved April 7 1735." HOWARD WILLIAMS LLOYD.

A LIST OF PERSONS BELONGING TO BURLINGTON PARTICULAR MEETING, 1776. I enclose a copy of "A List of Persons belonging to Burlington particular Meeting; taken in the 9th mo: 1776," in the handwriting of George Dillwyn, with marginal note, "113 men & women of Age to be active Members." The first column of figures is headed "The Families number'd," the second "Whole Number of Men Women & Children," the third "The number of Persons who are independent in each Family." The list of names is headed "The Names of the independent Members in each Family."

1	{	Thomas Rodman		1	{	2		
	{	John Barker's Wife		4	}			
2		John Rodman's Wife		4		1		
3		Rich'd Smith's Wife		4		1		
4		Daniel Smith		7		1		
5		James Craft		4		1		
6	{	Peter Worrall		2	}			
	{	William Dillwyn		2	}	4		
	{	Ann Dillwyn		1	}			
	{	Hannah Smith		1	}			
7	{	Martha Noble		1	}			
	{	Edward Cathrall		1	}	4		
	{	Jane Burling		1	}			
	{	John Smith		1	}			
8		Catherine Callender		1		1		
9		Joseph Smith		3		1		
10		Thomas Gardiner		1		1		
11	{	Robert Smith		2	}			
	{	Robert Smith jun'r		1	}	4		
	{	Catherine Smith		1	}			
	{	Sarah Smith		1	}			
12		Samuel Allinson		6		1		
13		John Watson		4		1		
14		Daniel Bacon, Sen'r		2		1		
15		Richard Smith Merch't		3		1		
16	{	George Dillwyn		3	}	3		
	{	Margaret Morris		5	}			
17	{	James Verree		1	}			
	{	Mary Harris		1	}	3		
	{	Rebecca Harris		1	}			
18	{	Hannah Hartshorne		1	}	2		
	{	Hutt Hartshorne jun'r		1	}			
19		Jane Smith		1		1		
20		Samuel Eyre's Wife		1		1		
21	{	Sam'l Fowe's Wife		1	}	2		
	{	Rebecca Watson		1	}			
22	{	George Hulme		3	}	2		
	{	Faith Butler		4	}			
23	{	William Hewlings		5	}	2		
	{	James Smith jun'r		3	}			
24		Thomas Weatherill		2		1		
25		Ann Carlisle		1		1		
26		Joseph Weatherill		1		1		
27		Grace Buchanan		1		1		
28	{	Elizabeth Johnson		1	}	2		
	{	Abigail Bishop		1	}			
29		Pearson Rodman		7		1	
30		Christopher Weatherill		1		1	
31		James Smith Sen'r		3		1	
32		Isaac Collins		6		1	
33		Hannah Decou		1		1	
34	{	Elizabeth Barker		1	}		
	{	Abigail Martin		2	}	3	
	{	Mary Barker		1	}		
35	{	John Hoskins		11	}	2	
	{	Sarah, his Daughter		1	}		
36		Benjamin Clark		1		1	
37		Jonathan Guest		6		1	
38		Mary Quest		1		1	
39		James Kinsey		8		1	
40		Elizabeth Haines		2		1	
41		William Burradaill		4		1	
42		William Elton		8		1	
43		Thomas Pryor		8		1	
44		Ralph Smith's Wife		1		1	
45		Sangston Carlisle's Wife		1		1	
46		David Overton		1		1	

	{ Persons living at a Distance } from Town.				
47	{ Robert Grubb		4	}	1
	{ Elizabeth Miller		1	}	1
48	Abraham Scott		7		1
49	James Rinear's Wife		1		1
50	Isaac Weatherill's Wife		1		1
51	William Hullings jun'r		1		1
52	Zachary Antrim		7		1
53	{ Tho'r Rodgers Sen'r		4	}	2
	{ John, his son		1	}	
54	Tho'r Rodgers jun'r		4		1
55	{ William Jones		2	}	2
	{ Mary Gaskill		1	}	
56	Joseph Antrim		1		1
57	Samuel Deacon's Wife		1		1
58	William Deacon		1		1
59	Rich'd Fennamore's Wife		1		1
60	George Deacon		6		1
61	Barzillai Deacon		1		1
			218		85
	Jon'a Jones		3		2
	Rich'd Smith Moores Town		3		2

T. S.

LETTER FROM ELIAS HICKS TO SAMUEL PARSONS, OF NEW YORK.—

"PROVIDENCE, 8th of 3d mo. 1816.

" . . . I noticed thy remark on the increase of rents, and the cause from which it most likely doth proceed, Covetousness . . . it seems to

be a time and a case similar to one the Apostle makes mention of, that
blindness in part has happened to Israel. . . . And when my mind is
brought to an enquiry what is the cause of this blindness, and turning
away from the truth & seeking after this world's Glory and riches, the
answer is, that the principal first cause is an undue thirst after human
learning and science, as this kind of knowledge always puffeth up young
minds, and the time spent in obtaining it introduces idleness and Idleness generates a desire to obtain riches by their wit and their learning,
in opposition to Honest and frugal Industry. I therefore am brought
to believe that the striveing after and obtaining much human science,
by our young friends, will prove (I fear) the most baneful of any thing
that can happen to them, as I am persuaded that in the same proportion as they give up their precious time, in the pursuit of unecessary
earthly studies and creaturely science, in the same proportion (as a
general rule) will such grow more and more blind and ignorant, in
divine knowledge. And I think every observing mind will assent to
this truth, if they will let the multitude of facts speak and be witness
in the case.

"I have made my observations as I have passed along in this Country,
and it is clear to my observation that human learning and science is a
means of producing more suffering and oppression on the inhabitants
than any other cause, and yet the poor creatures are too blind to see it;
their taxes I believe are generally treble to what they are in our State,
and I see nothing else to create the excess but their abundant Schools,
Colleges, and learned men, who are to be supported without labour, by
the industry of a few, and these are so stript with taxes, I do not know
how they get along as well as they do, but my pitty is often excited as
I pass from place to place under a sense of their great ignorance and
superstition, by which they are burthened and borne down. . . . With
love to Self Wife and Mother in which my companion joins, I rest
thy affectionate Friend

"ELIAS HICKS."

THE WELSH TRACT.—The following is a copy of an original paper
endorsed "D. Powels Acc' of y° Welch Purchasers in Gen¹," but unfortunately lacks any date.

"An account of the purchasers concerned in the Welsh Tract granted
by the Generall war' by wich the said tract was Laid out and such
Lands as hath bin Laid out by war" Dulie Executed within the same
and ist of y° ould England Parishes.

"Charles Lloyd and Margaret Davis, 5000 acres; Richard Davis,
5000; William Jenkins, 1000; John Poy, 750; John Burge, 750; William Mordant, 500; William Powell, 1250; Lewis David, 3000; Morris
Llewlin, 500; Thomas Simons, 500; John Bevan, 2000; Edward Prichard, 2500; John Ap John and Thomas Wyn, 5000; Edward Joanes
and John Thomas, 5000; Richard Davis, 1250; Richard ap Thomas,
5000; Mordicia Moore, in Right of ——, 500; John Millinton, 500;
Henry Right, 500; Daniell Med——, 200; Thomas Ellis, 1000; Thomas
Ellis for B. Roules, 250; Thomas Ellis, on acc' Humphrey Thomas,
100; David Powell, 1000; John Kinsy, 200; David Meredith, 250;
David Davis, 200; Thomas John Evan, 250; John Evans, 100; John
Jormon, 50; David Kinsy, 200; Evan Oliver, 100; Samuell Mills,
100; Thomas Joanes, 50; David Joanes, 100; John Kinsy, 100;
Daniell Hurry, 300; Henry Joanes, 400; John Ffish, 300; John Day,
300; Burke and Simson, 1000; The whole Complⁿᵗ 50000 acres."

Queries.

BRISTOL AND LLOYD FAMILIES.—The first Bristol of whom I have found any record is Thomas, whose name is in the Philadelphia tax-list for 1693. There is one assessment for £80, and farther on in the list a second for £40. Were there two of the name, father and son, or but one? Is anything known of ancestry and marriage of Thomas Bristol? August 16, 1762, Dan. Bristol took out letters of administration on the estate of Thomas Bristol, deceased. Was Dan. a son of Thomas, and was the latter the Bristol of the tax-list? The administrator filed no account, so that the papers give but little information.

A Margaret Bristol married Robert Gerrard June 9, 1711. Was she a sister of Dan.? Date of death, etc.?

Dan. Bristol, who lived in Oxford Township, and was a farmer, married Hannah ——? Should like to know something of her, date of marriage, etc.

The children of Dan. and Hannah,—1, Thomas; 2, Hezekiah; 3, Isaac; 4, Jacob; 5, Margaret; 6, Rebecca; 7, Elizabeth; 8, Hannah.

Dan. Bristol's will was written March 1, 1768, and proved April 11, 1770. The bequests are,—To Thomas, 5 shillings; to Hezekiah, £25. and 5 acres of land at s. e. corner of plantation I now live on, adjoining land of Richard Finny and Tacony lane [where is that on the present city plan?]; to Dan, £40; to Jacob, £5; to Sarah, £5; these are children of Hezekiah,—to son-in-law William Busby, £5; to son-in-law George Keen, 5 shillings; to daughter Margaret, wife of George Keen, £40; to daughters Rebecca and Hannah, £55; to sons Jacob and Isaac, the remainder of money from sale of house. [This house at corner of Fourth and Race Streets, and the above bequests were paid from proceeds of sale of house.] The remainder of property went to Mrs. Bristol, whose will was proved September 7, 1778; she left everything to her son Thomas.

1. Thomas Bristol lived at 403 N. Second Street, old numbering, and owned other property, and he was a flour- and grain-dealer. Will executed August 3, 1802, and proved November, 1802. Bequests,—403 N. Second Street to sister Hannah, also other property;—to nephew Robert Wells;—to sister Margaret Arden;—to Mary dau. of his brother Isaac Bristol;—residue to Thomas L. Bristol, Rebecca, dau. of William Busby, Elizabeth Wells, wife of Samuel Wells, to Sarah McGrady widow, and to Thomas Keen, son of Elijah Keen.

2. I have seen no notice of Hezekiah Bristol, except in his father's will. A Sarah Bristol married Chas. McGrady June 6, 1790. Was she a daughter of Hezekiah?

3. Isaac married Mary Jenkins May 10, 1774. They had a daughter Mary, mentioned in will of Thomas Bristol. A Mary Bristol died August 11, 1833, aged fifty-six years, in Second Street above Green, also another Mary Bristol, February 25, 1828, aged seventy-nine years (see Friends' Records, Northern District). I suppose they were the widow and daughter of Isaac. An Elizabeth Bristol married William Sammons May 15, 1800. Was she a daughter of Isaac or Hezekiah?

4. Jacob Bristol married Sarah Lloyd, license dated September 25, 1769, St. Paul's Church Record. Children,—Thomas Lloyd, died January 9, 1809, aged thirty-three; Tacy, said to have died of yellow fever, 1804—there is some dispute about the existence of this daughter; Elizabeth, married to Hugh Maxwell, November 15, 1800, the ceremony

performed by Rev. Ezekiel Cooper. Mrs. M. died in Lancaster, March 26, 1826, in her forty-fifth year.

5. Margaret married, first, George Keen, July 31, 1755. Was Elias or Elijah Keen, mentioned in wills of Thomas and Hannah Bristol, a son of George and Margaret (Bristol) Keen? Mr. Keen was still alive in 1768. His widow married, secondly, Arden, of New Jersey.

6. Rebecca ; was she wife to William Busby, mentioned in will of Dan. Bristol as his son-in-law?

7. Elizabeth Bristol married, February 26, 1776, James Landy. Was she the Elizabeth Wells, wife of Samuel Wells, mentioned in will of Thomas Bristol, and twice married, first to James Landy, and secondly to Samuel Wells?

8. Hannah Bristol died 1834. Will executed December 13, 1833. Bequests were,—

   1. To Thomas, son of Elijah Keen.
   2. To each of the seven children of Thomas Keen.
   3. To John, son of Elias Keen.
   4. To Rebecca Caroline Busby. [Was she a daughter of William Busby?]
   5. To Rebecca Folwell. [A friend.]
   6. To Hannah, wife of William Comly, and daughter of Samuel Wells.
   7. To Betsy, or Patsy, daughter of Samuel Wells.
   8. To Mary Narr, daughter of Sarah McGrady.
   9. To John Landy. [Was he son to Elizabeth and James Landy?]
   10. To each of the children of " my niece" Elizabeth Maxwell.
   11. To Isaac Eliot, a friend.
   12. To Catherine Hilbourn, her nurse.
   13. Residue to above legatees, share and share alike.

Ruth Lloyd, in her marriage certificate, is said to be the daughter of Thomas Lloyd "late of the County of Bucks and Province aforesaid Deceased and Sarah his wife." I should like to know something of the ancestry of Thomas Lloyd and wife. Rebecca Folwell, mentioned in the will of Hannah Bristol, was a friend of the two families, and the Folwells being early settlers in Southampton Township, Bucks County, it may be that these Lloyds were from the same district.

I do not know of more than three children of Thomas and Sarah Lloyd, though I think there were sons.

1. Sarah married Jacob Bristol. Mr. Bristol's name is in the directory for 1791, and his widow's name appears for 1793. Mrs. Bristol died in the home of her son-in-law, Hugh Maxwell, at Lancaster, July 15, 1831. One MS. obituary states that she was one hundred and eight at her death ; another statement places her birth in 1732. She was buried in Friends' Ground at Lancaster. Family tradition bears that her daughter was disowned by Fourth and Arch Streets Meeting on account of her "disorderly" marriage.

2. Ruth Lloyd married in Philadelphia Meeting William Cox, of Philadelphia, son of John and Martha Cox, deceased, of Newcastle, Delaware. Date of marriage January 14, 1773, Friends' Records, Book B, p. 233. In what meeting-house were they married?

The bride's mother was a resident of Philadelphia at this time, apparently. They had, I think, but one child, John G., who was living in the latter part of 1801, but was dead when his father's will was made in 1810. William Cox's property, after death of all annuitants, reverted to Philadelphia Friends for the education of poor children; he died April 30, 1811. Mrs. Cox died February 21, 1822, aged eighty-five.

Her will made January, 1818. Bequests to John C. Maxwell, her grand-nephew; to Margaret Williams; to James Lloyd, of Darby, son of Isaac Lloyd [was there any relationship between Mrs. Cox and these Lloyds?]; to Sarah Kite, wife of Isaac; income of residuary estate to niece Elizabeth Maxwell, principal to be divided among the latter's children on the death of their mother.

3. Priscilla Lloyd, daughter of Thomas and Sarah, died in Philadelphia, February 3, 1826, aged seventy-five.

Was there any relationship between these Lloyds and Jonathan Worrill, of Philadelphia, son of Robert and Elizabeth Worrill? May 11, 1784, he married Sarah, daughter of Robert and Katherine Lloyd, deceased. In his will, proved August 8, 1819, he makes bequests to Catherine Shepherd, wife's niece; to Rebecca Simmons, sister of Catherine Shepherd; to Margaret Williams; to Catherine, wife of Richard Johnson, an annuity, to go, at her death, to children of her brother Robert Lloyd; to Susannah, wife of Nathaniel Chamberlain; to Lydia, wife of Robert Lloyd, son of Levi and Hannah.

Thomas Kennedy and Daniel Niles were witnesses to this will, and also to Mrs. Cox's.

I should like to have dates and place of birth, marriage, death and burial, and any other facts concerning the two families.

E. C. M.

THE ANCESTRY AND EARLIER LIFE OF GEORGE WASHINGTON (PENNA. MAG., Vol. XVI. p. 261).—In this interesting paper Dr. E. D. Neill quotes (pp. 267, 278) as historical, Colonel J. L. Peyton's delightful romance, "The Adventures of my Grandfather," a work published at London in 1867, edition one hundred copies. On page 278 Dr. Neill erroneously makes the living author instead of his ancestor, John Peyton, dine with Braddock and Washington in 1755. Dr. Neill has also used "The Adventures" as historical in other papers, since Dr. J. M. Toner, in his address, April 10, 1891, on "George Washington as an Inventor," etc., page 17, quotes the same extract as to Washington (p. 278) from Neill's "Washington adapted to a Crisis," etc. Dr. Neill is an accepted authority on Virginia history, and his reputation and accuracy justify reliance on his statements. Will he kindly give in the PENNSYLVANIA MAGAZINE the grounds on which he bases his acceptance of Peyton's romance as historical authority? Justin Winsor, in his "History of America," pronounces the work as "not above suspicion." No Virginia writer quotes from it as historical. Neither the hero, John R. Peyton, nor his father, John Peyton, the supposed friend of Dinwiddie and Washington, appear on any page of Virginia history. They were evidently quiet, retiring Virginia gentlemen. In the voluminous correspondence of Dinwiddie and of Washington their names are not found. Very few, if any, of the statements in "The Adventures" are susceptible of historic proof. If the work is historical, much is lost to the student of history by the limited edition of the book, and it should be reprinted. If it is a romance, it were best recognized as such. Dr. Neill is too excellent an historian to allow himself to be misled.

W. H. E.

HOUSTON, HEUSTON, OR HEUSON.—Information wanted of —— Houston, who settled in Philadelphia. His brother was Dr. Clarke Houston, who had a large Presbyterian congregation at Ballymena, in the north of Ireland. His sister, Mary Houston, married Thomas McKee, and went to Albany, New York, to settle.

C.

GRIFFITH MILES.—Information is requested as to the descendants of Griffith and Bridget Miles, who were married in Radnor, June 20, 1692, and whose names also appear in the records of the Pennypack Church in 1693?

Washington, D.C.

M. MILES.

A PICTURE OF THE OLD FRIENDS' MEETING-HOUSE IN BURLINGTON, NEW JERSEY.—I have a painting by Doughty (*b.* 1793, *d.* 1856) of the Friends' Meeting-House in Burlington, New Jersey, that was replaced, in the latter part of the last century, by the present building. Doughty, who, of course, had never seen the original structure,—the latest date that has been given for its demolition being the year before his birth,—was carefully instructed by good authorities in making his drawing, and had also the advantage of a sketch already existing, so that his representation is probably a fairly accurate one. It is said on page 168, Vol. VIII. of the PENNA. MAG., that the old house "was not demolished until 1792." Was it not a back building, attached to the "hexagonal one" (page 167), represented in my picture and in prints, that was taken down in this year, and had not the latter disappeared some years before? My reason for supposing this to be the case is to be found in a letter from Daniel Smith, dated "Burlington, 11 mo. 17th, 1786," in which he says, "Our Meeting House is now finished except the Steps to the out Doors which have temporary Ones of ruff Boards ; at our last Quarter the House was Crowded ; the Building is thought by most to be convenient, for the most part well executed and looks well. . . . a Wall in Front and at the sides of the Lot with stables we wish to have done, but a Way to accomplish it for want of Cash does not at present open. *The Six Square Building* is taken down, the back part is yet standing but not with the full Consent of the Committees. . . . it is intended at our next Quarter or after to get Liberty to convert it to the use of the School house, and presuming on that Meeting's consent we have already moved the School Forms into it, and purpose to open the School there next Week, under the Tuition of my son Benjamin whose Mind of late seems turned again to that Employment."

The article above referred to (Vol. VIII.) says that the new building was completed in 1784, and that the original document giving names of subscribers and sums donated for the building still exists. At the close of the year 1786, according to Daniel Smith's letter, "about £260" of the total subscriptions (some £1700) "remains unpaid being mostly in the Hands of some tardy subscribers." There may still be some "Friends in Burlington" who might be interested in Smith's report of the state of the congregation at the time he wrote. "Our Meeting," he says, "on the first Day of the Week in the Forenoon remains much as heretofore in respect to Number, the Seats below Stairs of one Half of the House (the two Gallery Seats excepted) are often nearly filled, sometimes rather crowded, but in the Afternoon on First Day, and on fifth Days our Company is much smaller, and we do not a little miss those who have been of late by Death removed."

Doughty's picture is painted upon the face of a tall clock that once belonged to George Dillwyn.

S.

TRADITIONS OF "HOPE LODGE" WANTED.—"A Journey from Philadelphia to Bethlehem, June, 1753," is the title of some MS. verses before me. Germantown is thus described :

"Cheerful we mount, and while the sun ascends,
Reach the high Hills where Germantown extends ;

> Here various tasks, mechanic Arts assume,
> And growing Stockings twirl along the loom;
> Here Beauty shelter'd in umbrageous Seats,
> Eludes the Dog-star's prejudicial heats;
> Here the sly quack, by astrologic rules,
> Restores lost Goods to poor believing Fools."

It would be interesting to learn something more of this astrologer, but my query is more particularly concerned with the mystery of the "lofty structures" presently brought to view. It may be observed that the mention of Whitemarsh and the Morris house (not to be confounded with the one near the Morris road, which was not built until some time after 1790) does not preclude the possibility of Chestnut Hill being the location of the castle of this "hapless owner," with its "rooms of state" and "lofty chambers." It was certainly, according to the bard, on this side of the Wissahickon. The name "White-marsh" is sufficiently indefinite to permit the supposition that in "coming" to it the poet meant only that the party had reached the descent from Chestnut Hill to the Valley.

> "Hence our way to fair White-marsh we came,
> White-marsh, the mansion of the Morris name."

But this, I confess, does look as if this Morris house, wherever it was, was "White-marsh" itself, at least in the poet's conception, or misconception. Is its location known? There is still standing a fine mansion built by John Morris, in the first half of the last century (or perhaps by Anthony Morris for his son John), near Spring Mill, but this would be too far away for the course of our journey.

The next lines immediately follow those last quoted above:

> "Where the high Hill its humble Temple shows,
> And thro' the Vale where Wissahickon flows."

This would apply well enough to the Whitemarsh church, which has been described as "a goodly stone building" in 1718, with a congregation of about fifteen members.

Now for the enchanted castle and its disenchanted lord. Who was he, and where was his remarkable dwelling?

> "But lo! what lofty structures yonder rise,
> O'erlook the plain, and tower to the skies,
> Yet why's there such a solitude profound,
> Why hangs a hov'ring melancholy round?
> Fair Amaryllis, fairest of the plain,
> The grave Amyntor lov'd, but loved in vain,
> Yet still fond hope, th' unhappy Swain deceives,
> Still flattering Love the fairest prospect gives,
> For her the Spring its earliest bloom prepares,
> For her the Bark inscriptive Letters wears,
> For her alone, these lofty Structures rise,
> And Art with Nature, to attract her, vies.
> Mistaken Swain! too late, alas, you'll prove
> That Groves and fountains are the Seats of love,
> For thee, tho' Nature lavish all her stores,
> And Peace and plenty smile around thy doors,

Ah, what avail thy rural wide domains,
Thy flow'ry meadows, and thy fertile plains?
What all the plenty that thy harvest boasts,
What all the treasures of Peruvian coasts,
While restless Woe usurps these happy Seats,
And disappointed Love each joy defeats?
These scenes but serve each torment to renew,
The hapless Owner sickens at the view,
In rooms of State his cruel lot bemoans,
And lofty chambers echo to his groans,
Or, lonesome, stalks in a deserted Hall,
While sighs repentant whisper round the wall.
Touch'd with such woe, we the sad scene forsook,
And, Wissahickon, cross thy chrystal brook."

The only ancient building of importance still standing near White-marsh village is that formerly occupied by the Watmough family, and known as Hope Lodge. It certainly has lofty chambers and a spacious hall, and might once have had ornamental gardens, besides other "structures" which have been taken down. I learn from a grandson of James Horatio Watmough, that Hope Lodge was a gift to the latter from his friend and cousin, Henry Hope, one of the famous bankers of Amsterdam. The conveyance is said to have been made some years before 1782. Montgomery, I believe, was detached from Philadelphia County in 1784, but I can find no grantee of the property in question, of the name of Hope, in the books at the recorder's office in Philadelphia. The identity of the founder and occupant of Hope Lodge (*circa* 1750) remains, therefore, uncertain, supposing, of course, that our "Amyntor" was known of men as Mr. Hope. My informant tells me that Mr. Watmough was born in 1756, and Henry Hope about 1740. It is probable that among the well-known descendants of the former in this city, some one will be found able to tell the story of Hope Lodge, a spot unaccountably neglected by the historians of Montgomery County.

T. S.

PENNSYLVANIA VIEWS ON CHINA-WARE.—Information is desired as to whether there are Pennsylvania views, in dark blue, on china, other than the following: old Philadelphia Library, the Philadelphia Water-Works in Centre Square, Fairmount Park views, Staughton's Church, the United States Bank, Hamilton's Woodlands, Girard's Bank, United States Hotel, the bridge at Columbia, Pa., Mendenhall's Ferry, Penn's treaty with the Indians, Arms of Pennsylvania, Pennsylvania Hospital, views of Philadelphia, and Franklin's tomb.
West Chester, Pa.   E. A. BARBER.

WHITELOCK.—Information is requested of Thomas Whitelock, who was buried in Christ Church in October of 1758,—his parentage, when and where born.
Baltimore.   W. W.

BRYAN MCDONALD is supposed to have emigrated from Scotland and landed at New Castle, Delaware, in 1690 or 1691. He had several sons, among them John, Richard, James, and Bryan, Jr. In what part of Scotland did he reside?
Forest Grove, Oregon.   W. H. M. D.

BYERS.—Dr. John Byers presented a claim for "Compensation for services as Revolutionary surgeon" to the Second United States Congress, first session, 1792–93. The claim was referred to a select committee, which appears never to have made any report. The claim will be found on page 464 of the House Journal.

Who was this Dr. John Byers? Was he from Cumberland County, Pennsylvania, or Sussex County, Delaware? I will be grateful for a reply.

Wilkes-Barre, Pa. REV. HORACE EDWIN HAYDEN.

WEBB, MAULE, AND WAY, OF DELAWARE. —— Webb, of Delaware, had :

I. James, of Lewes.
II. Mary Louisa, *m.* Maule, and had :
    i. Louisa, ii. Charles, iii. William, iv. John, v. Harriet, vi. Deborah, *m.* Theodore Parker.
III. Ann Bond, *m.*, September 6, 1797, Joseph Way, and had :
    i. Harriet, ii. Anne, iii. Joseph Albert, iv. William.
IV. Harriet, *m.* 1ˢᵗ, 1803–4, John Byers, of Lewes, son of Dr. John Byers, of Delaware; *m.* 2ᵈ ——? Had, i. Charles, *b.* 1804; ii. John Alphonse, *b.* 1806; iii. Joseph, *b.* October, 1808; the latter two civil engineers in charge of divisions of the James River and Kanawha Canal, Virginia.

Information of the above families desired by

Wilkes-Barre, Pa. REV. HORACE EDWIN HAYDEN.

Replies.

GARRETT—KNOWLES (PENNA. MAG., Vol. XVI. p. 128).—The following minutes are from the Records of Darby Monthly Meeting :

7th mo. 5th, 1789, "Nathan Garrett Requesting a Certificate in order for marriage with Ann Knowls belonging to Abington Monthly Meeting, John Griffith and John Davis are appointed to Inquire of his Clearness and Draw a Certificate thereof and produce them at our next meeting for aprobation."

8th mo. 3d, 1739, "The ffr'ds appointed to Draw a Certificate for Nathan Garrett produced one which was read aproved of and Signed."

M. B.

MIS CAMPBELL (PENNA. MAG., Vol. XVI. p. 469).—Captain Robert Mis Campbell, of the "Legion of the United States," was named after Mr. Robert Mis, a connection of the Campbells. He was killed in the action of August 20, 1794.

I. C.

ANCESTORS OF CALEB GRIFFITH.—Refer to History of York County, Pennsylvania, and examine the article on the settlement of Warrington Township for account of a Griffith family settled there prior to French and Indian war. The family, I believe, came from Chester County. An examination of the records at York will determine whether Caleb Griffith was connected with this family.

Hughesville, Penna. REV. A. STAPLETON.

PRINCIPIO FURNACE (PENNA. MAG., Vol. XVI. p. 470).—In the query of "S" the name of Barnabas Hughes is mentioned. It is supposed that he was born in Donegal, Ireland, where he married Elizabeth Waters, about the year 1745 or '46. In 1748 they settled in the borough of Lancaster, where he bought some lots, and three years later rented the Black Bear tavern and farm of two hundred and thirty acres, on Conoy Creek, where the Paxtang and Conestoga road crossed, from Lazarus Lowry, the Indian trader. The tavern was built in 1732 by Captain Thomas Harris, who removed to Harford County, Maryland, and was purchased by Mr. Lowry in June of 1751. On June 30, 1753, Mr. Hughes became the owner, and established an Indian trading-post, which became the starting-point of many Indian traders of Donegal and vicinity, with their pack-trains for the Indian country. The merchants of Philadelphia who supplied the traders with supplies forwarded them to the Black Bear for distribution among the consignees. Mr. Hughes also became an Indian trader, and made frequent trips to the Ohio country. During the French and Indian war, the tavern was the first stopping-place after Lancaster, made by the military, as the journals of Colonel Burd, Wilkins, and Chaplain Charles Clinton Beatty attest. In 1753 Mr. Hughes laid out a town, which, in honor of his wife, he named Elizabethtown. In the summer of 1758 he was appointed commissary to supply Fort Hunter, and he also supplied camp equipage to Raystown for nine companies. He was present at the battle of "Loyal Hanna," in the autumn of 1758, and was one of the first messengers to bring the news to Carlisle. He erected a furnace in Washington County, Maryland, about six miles east of Hagerstown. After the Pontiac war, Mr. Hughes removed to Baltimore, where he died January 2, 1765. He left surviving him his wife Elizabeth and four sons and one daughter.

1. *Daniel* became the owner of the furnace at Black Creek, South Mountain, Maryland, and also of Mount Etna furnace, one mile farther down the creek. He owned a third furnace on Antietam Creek, near Hagerstown. During the Revolution he manufactured cannon, and was commissioned a colonel in the service. He married, first, Rebecca Lux, the daughter of a prominent merchant of Baltimore; second, Susanna, daughter of the Rev. Michael Schlatter; and third, Mrs. Anne Elliot, of Carlisle, Penna., the mother of Commodore Jesse P. Elliot. Colonel Hughes left a large family, who intermarried with prominent families in Maryland and Virginia.

2. *John* became a captain in the Revolutionary army. He married Miss Chamberlain, of Kent County, Maryland, and by her had three sons and three daughters.

3. *Samuel* moved to Harford County about the year 1764. His three brothers transferred their interest in the Black Bear farm and lots in Elizabethtown to him, which he sold in 1791 to Captain Alexander Boggs. He built a fine residence in Havre de Grace, and also erected a furnace near that place, and was interested in the Principio furnace. During the Revolution he made cannon, some of which a few years ago were stored in the Navy-Yard at Boston. In October of 1813 the British burned and destroyed his furnace and other property. He married Sarah ——, who died prior to 1790, and had by her several daughters, but no sons.

4. *Barnabas* was a posthumous son. He married Miss Beltzhoover, of Hagerstown, and died in his twenty-third year.

5. *Elizabeth* died unmarried.

The descendants of Barnabas Hughes are widely scattered through the Southern and Western States.

Columbia, Pa.   SAMUEL EVANS.

DORSEY—GALE—DENWOOD—HILL (PENNA. MAG., Vol. XVI. p. 127).—A valued correspondent, who permits me to quote from his letter, writes, "If you will turn to the Dillwyn pedigree, given in Burke's

Landed Gentry, Vol. I. p. 461, ed. of 1882, you will see it stated that both the father and grandfather of the Dillwyns you mention lived in America, the grandfather (William Dilwyn) coming to Pennsylvania . . . in the time of William Penn. As I remember having seen the name ' Dilwyn' on some of the Lancaster County Tax-Lists of the last century, I feel sure that George Dillwyn referred to *his* relatives and not to his wife's." My correspondent's conclusion has been confirmed by other evidence.   T. STEWARDSON.

HOWELL—MONTGOMERY—WHEELER (PENNA. MAG., Vol. XVI. p. 382).—If " G." will call at 3246 Chestnut Street he can hear in reference to the Howell, Montgomery, and Wheeler families; also of Mrs. C. A. Thurney, daughter of Major-General Howell, of the Revolutionary army.   MISS M. W. CLARKSON.

Book Notices.

SWEDISH HOLSTEINS IN AMERICA FROM 1644 TO 1892. COMPRISING MANY LETTERS AND BIOGRAPHICAL MATTER RELATING TO JOHN HUGHES, THE "STAMP OFFICER" AND FRIEND OF FRANKLIN, WITH PAPERS NOT BEFORE PUBLISHED, RELATING TO HIS BROTHER OF REVOLUTIONARY FAME, COLONEL HUGHES, OF NEW YORK. THE FAMILIES OF DEHAVEN, RITTENHOUSE, CLAY, POTTS, BLAKISTON, ATLEE, COATES, AND OTHER DESCENDANTS OF MATTHIAS HOLSTEIN, OF WICACO, PHILADELPHIA, ARE INCLUDED. THIRTY-FIVE FAMILY PICTURES AND FAC-SIMILES OF LETTERS OF BENJAMIN FRANKLIN AND REV. NICHOLAS COLLIN, D.D., ARE GIVEN. By Anna M. Holstein, Upper Merion, Montgomery County, Pennsylvania. Norristown, Pennsylvania, 1892. 8vo, 307 pp., including indices. Price, $4.00.

The title correctly explains the contents of this well-printed book, and the author's portrait, placed at the head of the " Introduction," is that of one who has led a useful life in the service of her country, in the hospitals, on the battle-field, and as the well-known Regent of the Valley Forge Association, with an energy in nowise abated. This old Swedish-American family of Holstein is well represented in portraits and biographical sketches, which show a patriotic and respectable class of citizens through nine generations. The fac-simile of the Rev. Dr. Collin's letter is a quaint and curious autograph, and the thirty-eight portraits (three were added after the title-page was printed) are well done, and are all fine-looking men and women, with barely an exception. The charming pictures of several children are a pleasant and unusual feature in books of this kind. Worthy of special mention are the Hughes portraits and the valuable historical material of general interest, here printed for the first time, connected with the Welsh-American family, of whom was John Hughes, the "Stamp Officer," Lieutenant-Colonel Isaac Hughes, Colonel Hugh Hughes, General James Miles Hughes, Major Peter Hughes, the late Hon. Francis W. Hughes, Attorney-General of Pennsylvania, Isaac Wayne Hughes, M.D., and the Hughes of North Carolina. There are some remarkable letters of Anthony Wayne to John Hughes, dated 1765. Wayne, then nineteen years and a half old, managed the affairs of sixteen land companies in Nova Scotia, looking after the interests of Benjamin Franklin, Hughes, Galloway, and others. His letter on Colonel McNutt vindicates the charges against Hughes of deceiving the settlers. A most interesting and useful letter in the history of Presbyterianism in this vicinity is that of John Hughes to the Archbishop of Canterbury. The gem of this collection (pp. 53 and 252, where a photograph copy is given) is the letter of Benjamin Franklin to John Hughes, dated London, August 9, 1765, which has never been in print, in which Franklin expresses his dissatisfaction with the rebellious opposition to the Stamp Act, advises Mr. Hughes to hold on to his stamp office until the people get used to him, pays his fees, sends him his commission, and shows his genius as an able "trimmer" in this transaction, against which the tocsin of revolt sounded from Boston to South Carolina. Hughes bore the odium. It is not too much to say that this letter, published in the lifetime of Franklin, would have ruined his political career forever.   P.

THE GERMAN ALLIED TROOPS IN THE NORTH AMERICAN WAR FOR INDEPENDENCE, 1776–1783. Translated and abridged from the German of Max von Eelking, by J. G. Rosengarten. Albany, New York, Joel Munsell's Sons. 360 pp. Price, $5.00
Captain von Eelking, who is an officer in the army of Saxe-Meiningen, originally published his valuable book in 1863, in two volumes of six hundred and seventy pages. It has been his aim to give a general view, from original documents, of the part taken by the German auxiliaries of Great Britain during our war for independence, and he has also sought to protect and restore their good name and credit, which has so often been attacked for their taking part in a foreign war. To the translator, who has omitted all that relates to the general history of the Revolution, and has confined himself to the services of these troops, we are indebted for this additional contribution to our history. He has also added many valuable annotations to the roster of officers of the Hessian corps. A portrait of General Knyphausen and an index of names are included in this attractive volume.

THROUGH COLONIAL DOORWAYS. By Anne H. Wharton. Philadelphia, 1893. J. B. Lippincott Company. Illustrated. Price, $1.25.
Miss Wharton's new book, which is now going through the press, will contain the following chapters: "The Meschianza," "New York Balls and Receptions," "The American Philosophical Society," "The Wistar Parties," "A Bundle of Old Love-Letters," and "The Philadelphia Dancing Assemblies." It will be attractively printed.

THE FIRST ANNUAL REPORT OF THE GENEALOGICAL SOCIETY OF PENNSYLVANIA, TOGETHER WITH THE SEVERAL ADDRESSES DELIVERED AT THE MEETING HELD ON WEDNESDAY EVENING, NOVEMBER 30, 1892. Philadelphia, 1893. Printed for the Society by J. B. Lippincott Company. 55 pp.
The collecting of genealogical information has long been recognized as an essential part of the work of the Historical Society of Pennsylvania, which has expended large sums in the acquisition of its now extensive and valuable collection of books and manuscripts pertaining to this subject. But the immense amount of material yet to be gathered from fast-perishing manuscripts greatly overtaxed the resources of that Society applicable to this department, and many members felt the rapid growth of interest in genealogy, which has developed of late years, rendered the moment an auspicious one for the formation of an auxiliary society, which should make the transcribing of records its special object. This was effected in February of last year. From the first annual report of the Society we find that its object is the promotion of genealogical

research; the collection and preservation of registers of births, marriages, and deaths kept by religious societies or individuals, or making transcripts thereof; as well as transcripts or abstracts of all kinds of official records affording genealogical information. Its membership is restricted to members in good standing of the Historical Society, and all the material collected becomes the property of that institution. Some of the results accomplished are: the records of St. George's Methodist Episcopal Church, Philadelphia, and the German Reformed (now Market Square Presbyterian) Church, Germantown. The following records are in the course of preparation: Trinity Protestant Episcopal Church, Oxford, Philadelphia; St. Thomas's Protestant Episcopal Church, Whitemarsh; Pennypack Baptist Church; Third Reformed Dutch Church, Philadelphia; St. Michael's Evangelical Lutheran Church, Germantown; the Swedish Lutheran Churches at Swedesborough and Penn's Neck, New Jersey; German Reformed Church, Alexandria, New Jersey; Baptisms in Christ Church and St. Peter's; and an abstract of the wills recorded in Philadelphia, 1683–1800. In all, thirty-five thousand entries from church records and two thousand abstracts of wills have been made. This is an exceedingly creditable showing for the first year's work of the Society, and with a largely-increased membership still greater results may be confidently expected. The Society will be glad to receive and preserve the work of individuals relating to their own or other family history, whether printed or in manuscript, and we are pleased to note that a large number of valuable gifts of this kind have been received. In addition to the annual report and addresses, the report of the treasurer and a roster of officers and members are given. Printed on heavy linen paper, with wide margins, in clear black type, with a rubricated title-page heavily panelled, this veritable *édition de luxe* has been published through the generosity of a few public-spirited members of the Society. The dues of the Society are five dollars annually.

THE CONSTITUTION OF THE SOCIETY OF SONS OF THE REVOLUTION, AND BY-LAWS AND REGISTER OF THE NEW JERSEY SOCIETY. Trenton, 1892. 40 pp.

We have received the first register of the officers and members of this Society, compiled by their Registrar, Foster C. Griffiths, Esq. It is printed on heavy linen paper and embellished with rubricated headpieces and initial letters. An interesting feature, which we can commend to other State Societies, is the list of persons represented in the New Jersey Society, including the names of persons representing them in the Societies in the States of New York, New Jersey, and Pennsylvania.

WANTED.—The annual catalogues of the College or Arts Department of the University of Pennsylvania for the years 1830, 1836–37, and 1838–39, to complete a collection.

[... are some of the Historical and Genealogical serials to be found on the tables in the Library:

FOREIGN.

Collections of the Powys-Land Club	London.
Gloucestershire Notes and Queries	London.
Miscellanea Genealogica et Heraldica	London.
Northamptonshire Notes and Queries	Northampton.
Notes and Queries	London.
Northern Notes and Queries	Edinburgh.
The East Anglian, or Notes and Queries on subjects connected with the Counties of Suffolk, Cambridge, Essex, and Norfolk	Ipswich.
The Genealogist	London.
The Index Library	London.
The Western Antiquary or Note Book for Devon, Cornwall, and Somerset	Plymouth.
Yorkshire Notes and Queries : with Yorkshire Genealogist, Yorkshire Bibliographer, and Yorkshire Folk-Lore Journal	Bradford.

DOMESTIC.

American Journal of Numismatics and Bulletin of American Numismatic and Archæological Societies	Boston.
American Notes and Queries	Philadelphia.
Essex Institute Historical Collections	Salem, Mass.
Magazine of American History	New York.
Magazine of Western History	Cleveland.
New York Genealogical and Biographical Record	New York.
Notes and Queries, Historical and Genealogical	Harrisburg, Pa.
Proceedings and Collections of the Wyoming Historical and Geological Society	Wilkesbarre, Pa.
Proceedings of the Academy of Natural Sciences	Philadelphia.
Southern Historical Society Papers	Richmond, Va.
The American Journal of Philology	Baltimore, Md.
The American Catholic Historical Researches	Philadelphia.
The Book Mart	Pittsburg, Pa.
The Cambrian	Cincinnati.
The Granite Monthly	New Hampshire.
The Historical Record, with Notes and Queries	Wilkesbarre, Pa.
The Iowa Historical Record	Iowa City.
The Journal of the Military Service Institution	New York.
The ... Journal	New York.
...	New York.
... and Historical and Genealogical Register	Boston.
... and Magazine and Bay State Monthly	Boston.
...	Philadelphia.
... Magazine	Newport.

[... of other serials will please forward prospectus.]

CONTENTS

BOUND VOLUMES OF THE MAGAZINE.

Copies of all the volumes of this MAGAZINE can be obtained at the Hall of the Historical Society, bound by Messrs. Pawson and Nicholson, in the very best manner, in the style known as Roxburgh, half cloth, uncut edges, gilt top, for $3.75 each and the postage. They will be furnished to subscribers in exchange for unbound numbers, in good condition, on the receipt of 75 cents per volume and the postage.

Address F. D. STONE, 1300 Locust St.

PRINTED BY J. B. LIPPINCOTT COMPANY.

MAJOR ISAAC ROACH.

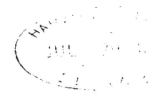

THE

PENNSYLVANIA MAGAZINE

OF

HISTORY AND BIOGRAPHY.

| VOL. XVII. | 1893. | No. 2. |

JOURNAL OF MAJOR ISAAC ROACH, 1812–1824.

CONTRIBUTED BY MARY ROACH ARCHER.

[Major Isaac Roach served throughout the war of 1812 and until April 1, 1824, when he retired to civil life. His father, Captain Isaac Roach, had distinguished himself during the War of the Revolution, in the operations in the Delaware River and lower bay, in command of the gunboat "Congress" and other vessels, being severely wounded several times in a very active series of operations against the enemy's vessels in the defence of the approaches to the city. Major Roach was elected mayor of Philadelphia in 1838. He also served as guardian of the poor, commissioner on the Almshouse purchase, vestryman of St. Peter's Church, Third and Pine Streets, manager of Christ Church Hospital, member of the Select Council of the city and Board of Health, and treasurer of the United States Mint at Philadelphia. He died December 30, 1848.]

My grandfather was a Scotchman and a sailing master in a British Fleet which was sent to ascertain the boundary between Maryland and Delaware, about 1740. He left the service and settled in Delaware near Rehoboth Bay, where my father was born in 1748, and where he continued until apprenticed to Mr. Fisher of Lewestown, Delaware, a pilot of the Bay and River Delaware. He became a skilful pilot

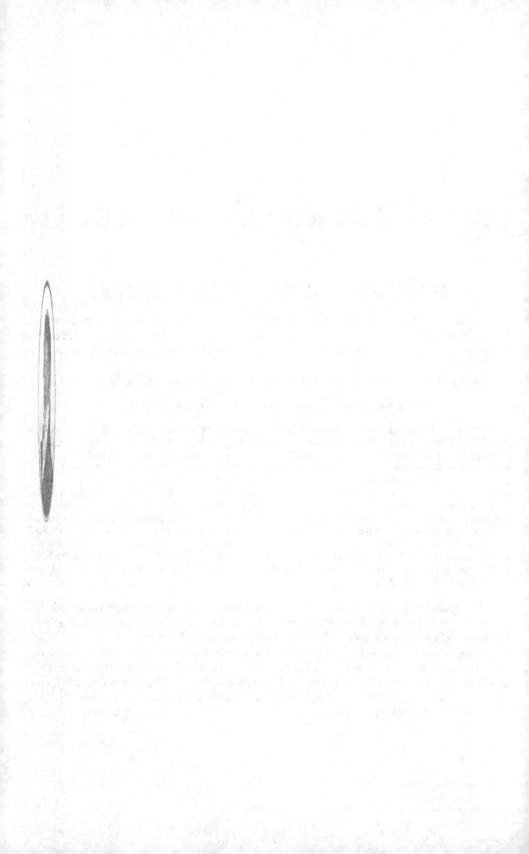

THE

PENNSYLVANIA MAGAZINE

OF

HISTORY AND BIOGRAPHY.

| VOL. XVII. | 1893. | No. 2. |

JOURNAL OF MAJOR ISAAC ROACH, 1812–1824.

CONTRIBUTED BY MARY ROACH ARCHER.

[Major Isaac Roach served throughout the war of 1812 and until April 1, 1824, when he retired to civil life. His father, Captain Isaac Roach, had distinguished himself during the War of the Revolution, in the operations in the Delaware River and lower bay, in command of the gunboat "Congress" and other vessels, being severely wounded several times in a very active series of operations against the enemy's vessels in the defence of the approaches to the city. Major Roach was elected mayor of Philadelphia in 1838. He also served as guardian of the poor, commissioner on the Almshouse purchase, vestryman of St. Peter's Church, Third and Pine Streets, manager of Christ Church Hospital, member of the Select Council of the city and Board of Health, and treasurer of the United States Mint at Philadelphia. He died December 30, 1848.]

My grandfather was a Scotchman and a sailing master in a British Fleet which was sent to ascertain the boundary between Maryland and Delaware, about 1740. He left the service and settled in Delaware near Rehoboth Bay, where my father was born in 1748, and where he continued until apprenticed to Mr. Fisher of Lewestown, Delaware, a pilot of the Bay and River Delaware. He became a skilful pilot and much respected by the mercantile community. He was married in 1774, and at the commencement of the war between this and the mother country he promptly decided for his Country's Liberty, took up arms and fought till his country was free. He commanded the armed vessel or gun boat "Congress" which was actively engaged in the defence of the Delaware River and Bay. He was also an officer on board the brig "Charming Sally" which was in company with the "Hyder Ali" when she captured the British ship "General Monk." The "Charming Sally" was captured by the British, but my father succeeded in retaking her, and was badly wounded. He was put on shore and the brig went to sea.

He held commissions successively under the Proprietary of Pennsylvania, from Franklin, Washington, John Adams, Jefferson and Madison, and with the exception of a few years he continued in government service until his death in 1817. He was much respected as a brave and zealous officer.

I had from my infancy listened to my father's recitals of the injuries sustained by this country and the violation of every principle of justice by Great Britain, and now [1812] it had become a jest and byword in England that the country "could not be kicked into a war;" but we were kicked into it, and totally unprepared for such a contest. After a peace of thirty years, and entirely engrossed in trade, every means had been neglected to prepare for war. Our treasury poor, our arsenals empty, fortifications in ruin, our Navy neglected, Military Science unknown, our Army nominally about 6000 men, the country divided in opinion, one-half advocating British measures, the other French, and no national feeling or true patriotism until the Declaration of War, which was carried by that party called "Democrats," and opposed by those called "Federalist." Indeed with few exceptions the war was carried on to its termination by the "Democrats," and violently opposed by their own citizens who advocated the conduct of the British, even during the struggle.

I had some doubts of the propriety of leaving my aged parents, but I had heard my father's opinion relative to the duty of defending our beloved country, and I did not long hesitate but without any delay applied for a commission in the army as soon as the Bill for War passed Congress, and obtained the appointment of second lieutenant in the 2nd Regiment U. S. Artillery. As I had requested to be assigned to this Regiment of Artillery, I was obliged to accept of the lowest rank. This regiment was 2000 strong, and commanded by Col. George Izard, and Lt. Col. Winfield Scott, so long my immediate commanding officer and highly valued friend. On coming home to dinner one day my father said,—"Here is a package for you from the War Department"—which I opened, and taking from it my letter of appointment handed it to him to read. He said,—" why did you not consult me ?" I replied, because I knew his opinion of the propriety of my conduct and wished to surprize him. He was well satisfied, and my beloved mother who seemed to hang on me as her last stay, said : " my dear son, you know your mother cannot spare you, but I trust the Almighty will protect you, and I hope you will always do your duty."

In July, 1812, I joined my regiment then forming on the east bank of the Schuylkill, under command of Lt. Col. Scott,—who applied to Col. Izard and I was appointed Adjutant. This to a young officer without family, friends or influence, was a good beginning. It introduced me more intimately to both those valuable officers, to whom I was subsequently indebted for many proofs of their regard, and I can truly say I endeavored faithfully to do my duty on all occasions as well towards them as to my country.

Early in September 1812, Col. Scott applied for orders to proceed to the Canadian frontier with the Companies of Capt. N. Towson and Capt. James N. Barker. Our Troops were very much disheartened at this period by the very disgraceful surrender which had been made by Genl. Hull of his Troops at Detroit, yet every officer and man in our little detachment seemed desirous to be in the field, and proceeding through New Jersey to headquarters, then at Green Bush, near Albany, where we halted a few days and obtained Gen. Dearborn's orders for Buffalo, where we arrived with our field Artillery and about 160 men on the 5th October, and reported to Genl. Smyth who was subsequently famous for Proclamations threatening the British Army. From the best information obtained it was not likely the British would act offensively and from the tardy movements of several regiments we had passed on our route, we had not much to expect from our own Troops that season.

Not wishing to be idle I requested Col. Scott to offer my services to Lt. Elliott, of our Navy, who was fitting out a small vessel at Black Rock, for services on Lake Erie. When the Col. returned to our encampment, our Battalion was ordered down to Black Rock to protect our vessels, and I was informed that my desire to smell gunpowder was soon to be gratified. Lieut. Elliott thinking his outfit too tedious in movement, took a fancy to two of the Enemies vessels already equipped and riding at anchor in apparent Security close under the cannon of Fort Erie at the outlet of Lake Erie and directly in sight of us.

Lt. Elliott informed me that he intended to embark at night in two Row boats and cut out the Two Brigs,—both of them were armed. But we must have them, as they would add to our intended force on Lake Erie. He was much pleased with my offer to take 50 men from our Regiment. It was arranged that I was to go in the boat with him and to attack the largest vessel. She was called the "Detroit" and was well manned with small arms and Pikers and carrying 4 Iron 6 Pounder cannon, the other Brig was the "Caledonian" not so well armed. An incident occurred previous to embarkation very flattering to a young and untried officer but exemplifying the attachment of officers and men to an Adjutant who is zealous to do his duty. When Col. Scott paraded the Battalion and I read the order directing the detail of 50 men to be placed under the command of Adjt. Roach for the purpose of attacking the Enemy's vessels that were in sight and moored for safety under their batteries—the Colonel informed the Battalion that no one could go without expecting a hard fight and advised that none but brave and discreet men should go, as so much depended on their coolness.   He was disposed to give some of our lads an opportunity of tilting with our enemy and directed that the Volunteers at the word "march" should step four paces to the front of the line : When I ordered Volunteers to the front, "March!" I believe every man, officers and all rushed forward.   This was a proud moment to me and I could not but feel that some of this burst of zeal arose as well from confidence in myself as patriotism.   Turning round to Col. Scott I found him delighted with this evidence of spirit and said :—" drop your line, Sir, and select your volunteers"—and this was not easily done, for while going down the line with my Sergeant Major every face was pushed forward with " can I go, Sir?"   " I'm a Philadelphia boy ;" " don't forget McGee ;" " take me Mr. Adjutant," and a great variety of such expressions, making it difficult to select where all deserved to go, and I was compelled to take 60 men.

The battalion was dismissed ; volunteers to remain ; then a new feeling was to be produced.   My gallant friends, the officers, all gathered around me, Captain Towson and Barker, Lieutenants McDonough, Davis, Stewart, and Hook, and even our little surgeon Dr. Near,—one and all insisted on going under my command.   Was not this enough to flatter one?   Would not this make any one proud?   Towson and Barker were so determined on going, I began to think our tea party would be broken up, as Col. Scott and Lt. Elliott both declared no one should go to rank me.   Towson went to his tent and wrote his resignation, sent it to the Colonel, and volunteered as a citizen.   This would not do. I begged for one of the Captains to go.   The Colonel consented.   Mr. Elliott said they should not go in the boat with him.   Towson won the chance to go, and went with the Sailing Master, George Watts, in the 2nd boat, who had orders to board the smaller vessel.—Night came—every man ready,—arms in order,—and the boats prepared, oars muffled and grappling irons at hand,—sailors skipping about as merry as crickets.   A parcel of tars who had been marched from Albany, had just arrived, and were glad to see a vessel again.   About 8 o'clock we hauled out of Skin-gaucite Creek and tracked our boats silently up against the rapid current of the Niagara to the mouth of Buffalo Creek. Here we were to embark, to row up into Lake Erie, where there was no current, and descend to the attack on the British side where we would be least expected.   A detach-ment of the 5th Infantry here joined us under Ensign Pres-ton, and the tide on the bar being low, we were obliged to wade up to our shoulders, and push the boats over the bar of Buffalo Creek.   This was one of our cold sleety even-ings in October, when the water of Lake Erie is too cool to bathe in, and we were obliged to sit in our wet clothes for three hours in a small boat, and not allowed to even laugh to keep ourselves warm.

We rowed very quietly up the Lake several miles before we crossed, and then came down upon friend "John Bull" in hopes to catch him napping; but when we neared him we found him wide awake.   There was a fire on board the "Detroit" in the caboose which light we steered by.   Our boats were steered like the whaleboat with a long oar. When within a half mile of the brig Lt. Elliott directed our men not to fire but to be silent.   I told the sailor who was steering to give me the helm, and get ready his grapple. We were now within musket range when I headed for her fore foot and rounded too, so as to board her head to tide. They now hailed from the brig, and immediately fired all their musketry, and we received a second volley before we were alongside,—as I preferred laying alongside securely, and not to miss our game as the Sailing Master did in the other boat, which swung under the enemy's stern, lost sev-eral men, and undoubtedly would have sheered off, if Cap-tain Towson had not ordered the men to haul up alongside, boarded and carried her.

In our boat we were no sooner alongside than well secured, and every one mounted on board.   Lt. Elliott and myself boarded in the main rigging, which brought us directly into conflict with the officers of the brig on the quarter-deck. The Captain aimed a severe blow at Elliott's head, but in the dark he struck on one side and knocked his hat overboard. In five minutes we were in possession, and our prisoners driven below, and the hatchways secured. Some hands were sent aloft to loose the topsails, whilst I examined the brig's guns and found them loaded; but we had surprised the crew and they had not had time to fire them. I ordered them all hauled over to the starboard side next Fort Erie, to be ready for an attack from the shore. But upon bringing up the Second Mate he denied having any ammunition on board, and not until he was brought to by some hard threats did he agree to show us where his chest was with 42 rounds of cartridges in.

Until this period the British on shore knew not which party had conquered, and they now hailed to know. Lt. Elliott ordered the fire on deck extinguished, and the topsails loosed, and when we were hailed again, said they would fire if we got under way; and I told Mr. Elliott my guns were all ready when they opened the ball; and all the quick match I had was a bundle of candles held by my guard in the companion way. Whiz! comes a shot over our heads;—"John Bull" always aims too high;—this went about 20 feet over us, ricochetted and as our shore was lined with friends anxiously waiting our movements, this first shot fired from Fort Erie after the Declaration of War, killed Major Cuyler of the New York militia whilst sitting on horseback. Bang! went my battery of 6-pounders;— "up helm, boys! Stand by that cable with the axe! Cut away!"—and now we get the battery guns on us;—our neighbors Watts and Towson in the other brig were under way, and this served to distract the enemy's fire; The day dawned, and with it came a light breeze of wind, and we had hopes of getting up against the current into Lake Erie. All my cartridges were expended, and now we had quietly to take the penetrating "arguments" of the Fort to stop us, every shot telling as we had to come nearer the shore.

These guns I fired were the first directed against the enemy on the Niagara. The wind became lighter, and in place of getting up into the Lake, out of the current and gun-shot, we were compelled to sheer over to our shore, and in our attempt to get into the harbor, both our prizes grounded.

The prisoners were all sent on shore, the "Caledonian" which was full of furs was unloaded; and as every preparation was making by the enemy to burn her [the "Detroit"] that night, the General commanding ordered Major Chambers to set fire to her in the evening,—the policy of which I could not admire. The "Caledonian" was saved and added to our fleet and aided the gallant Perry in his victory on the Lake.

On mustering our forces we found two officers wounded, and about ten men killed and wounded. Our brother officers on shore praised us extravagantly, and we were well satisfied to have brought ourselves back with a whole skin. Now when it is remembered that our country had been at peace 30 years, and all her old soldiers dead or very aged, and scarcely a man in our expedition had ever faced an enemy, and that this was the attack of raw recruits on veterans; without flattery it may be said to have been a handsome affair. It had another good effect of giving to our men a little confidence, and inspiring the whole brigade with life and ardour.[1]

We now had at Buffalo a brigade of U. S. Infantry and volunteers, and at Queenstown 25 miles below, Major General Van Rensselaer had a large brigade of the neighboring Militia stationed.

At Fort Niagara there were stationed two companies of Artillery, and Captain Gibson's company of Light Artillery had just arrived at Lewistown.

It appears General Van Rensselaer contemplated an attack on the British 49th Infantry and part of the 41st, stationed at

[1] "The capture of the 'Detroit' and the 'Caledonia' (whether placed to our maritime or land account), for judgment, skill, and courage has never been surpassed."—Henry Clay, in Debate on Army Bill. Annals of Congress, 1813, p. 674.

Queenstown directly opposite to Lewistown. But the General did not sufficiently estimate either the strength of his enemy or the inefficiency of his own undisciplined corps, and he appeared desirous to prevent the Regulars from engaging in the expedition. Our gallant Colonel had gained permission to descend the river to join the General, tho' it would seem as if he was not expected to get down, as the new roads were then so cut up that empty wagons were seen sticking in the road; therefore it was impossible to get on with Artillery, and baggage and ammunition wagons. The Colonel would not leave his cannon. I was the Adjutant and acting Quarter Master, and suggested to the Colonel that I could dismount our guns and take them and the battalion down by water. He was much pleased, and I went to work in a tremendous heavy rain, and taking the same boats with which we had just captured the "Detroit" and "Caledonian," I rigged a platform from the shore, and embarked our guns and ammunition, and reported to Col. Scott, who soon marched down his men; and off we pushed for Lewistown, halted that night above Schlosser, and next morning landed at Schlosser, 7 miles above Lewistown; and whilst my brother officers were breakfasting at the tavern, I went to work and had my guns remounted and ready for a march. Col. Scott then galloped over to head-quarters to obtain further orders; and in the evening we moved down the road, and arrived at General Van Rensselaer's camp about two hours before his troops embarked to the attack of Queenstown. But the General's jealousy would not permit any more Regulars to join him, and we were ordered to the bank of the Niagara to cover the boats in crossing; and as soon as daylight appeared we commenced firing on the British Artillery at a distance of 600 yards. Col. Scott and myself rode down to the shore to witness the embarkation; when Lt. Col. Christy who had been on the British side and returned to hasten the movements, told the Colonel he wanted a Lieutenant of Artillery to go with him; when I dismounted, left my horse tied to a fence, and jumped into a boat with Col. Christy and in a few minutes I was on

British ground for the first time, and climbing up the preci-
pice, joined our troops, then under the command of Col.
Christy.   Our troops were now attacked by a reinforcement
of British from Fort George under command of Col. Brock,
of the 41st Infantry,—a very gallant officer who had served
with distinction under Abercrombie in Egypt, and who had
captured our troops under Hull at Detroit.   This brave man
was killed by our advance and his aid Major McDonald also.
The enemy again retreated from the Heights, and in about
an hour I was pleased to see Col. Scott, who had also succeeded in volunteering to cross the river without his battalion, but before he could make any movement of the
troops, the " Old Patroon"—as General Van was called—
sent over Brigadier General Wadsworth to take the command from Col. Scott, determined to keep the Militia officers in command.

The enemy again returned to the attack, and, aided by
their Indians drove in our Albany volunteers, (who had
fought very bravely,) and were received by Col. Scott with
the 13th Infantry and repulsed.

In the attack I was severely wounded thro' the left arm
whilst commanding a detachment of the 13th Infantry,—
which formed our right,—and having for a week previous
undergone much fatigue, and being half starved also, I was
compelled to leave the line, and retire to the rear.   At the
moment I was wounded I was directing a soldier to take
aim at an Indian hid under a small bush, and the same Indian was taking a good aim at me.   Col. Scott and myself
were in full dress Chapeau and plume, which made us a
good mark.   This is imprudent at all times, more especially
when opposed to Savages, who always endeavor to kill officers, as well, to aid in the defeat as in expectation of plunder, and being able to boast in the number of their scalps,
that of a chief warrior.

In an hour or two the surgeon who had the care of Captain John E. Wool of the 13th Infantry and myself, determined to take us over to our side of the river, as he had no
means of dressing some of the wounds; and by crossing

to our own side, I escaped being made prisoner, as all our detachment was captured :—occasioned, no doubt, by the ignorance and obstinacy of our Militia General, in sending so small a detachment to retain possession of the post—so cut off from reinforcements and supplies by a deep and very rapid river—at that place full of whirlpools and rapids requiring much skill to cross it. As an evidence of the folly of placing any dependence on the Militia, I will relate what occurred after our defeat. On recrossing to Lewistown I found my horse where I had left him early in the morning, and being lifted on him I was enabled to find the 2nd Artillery, and right glad were my comrades to see me alive again. I found the troops all withdrawn a mile from the shore, and that night when it was reported the British and Indians had crossed at Five Mile Meadow, below, our gallant Militia began to think they had seen service enough, and walked off to the rear by companies; one Colonel whose name I never heard, recommending to his men "to make the best of their way into the Interior,"—and sure enough they did.

The day following General Van Rensselaer sent for Captain Towson, and gave him command of his camp, directing Majors, Colonels &c. all to obey his instructions.[1]

My wound, and fatigue of being up every night, bro't on a fever which confined me for two months, and I did not entirely recover for five months. Indeed, very few who were attacked with those fevers, ever recovered. It was called Typhus and Lake fever and was accompanied in my case by dysentery, and trying to the strength of my body, I was removed during illness five times in wagons and boats a distance of 80 miles, and suffering constantly for want of nourishment, and those kind attentions so requisite in sickness. In all my changes I found Captain Towson the same kind friend.

Col. Scott being kept a prisoner, and our battalion much weakened by deaths, and the campaign soon closing, I applied for orders to join Col. Izard in Philadelphia; and in

---

[1] See "Thompson's History of the War" for particulars of this affair.

the beginning of December I was able to be removed from Buffalo by placing my buffalo skin in the bottom of a Pennsylvania wagon, and the first day rode seven miles.   By degrees I reached Batavia, when, the snows commencing, I obtained a sleigh and with three other officers, was enabled to travel comfortably,—strengthened with the reflection that I was travelling homeward, soon to meet my parents, who would be delighted to see me, and not less so for being informed that I had done my duty to my country.

I arrived at Philadelphia, December 26th, 1812, and found my parents in tolerable health, and all my friends delighted to see me again, and I not a little gratified to find all my brother officers disposed to do me more than justice for my exertions.

On my arrival in Philadelphia I joined Col. Izard, who was organizing his regiment for the ensuing campaign; and my friend Scott who had been carried a prisoner to Quebec, was paroled and arrived in Philadelphia in the Winter.   In February, 1813, Col. Izard was promoted to the rank of Brigadier General, and ordered to the command of New York and the defences near it, and I was ordered to accompany him.   On our arrival in New York, we found the British fleet were off Sandy Hook, and the inhabitants of the city in the expectation of an attack.   They were much pleased with the exchange of the command from old General Burbeck to General Izard.

The General visited all the posts down to Sandy Hook, where we found a 6 gun battery.   There were large batteries on both sides of the Narrows, and works on the Heights on Long Island, on Governor's, Bedlow, and Ellis's Islands, and in the city circular batteries,—Forts Clinton, Gansevoort and North Batteries on the North River side.

The British fleet often threatened to enter the harbor, but as often declined, as our forces were too numerous.   As the Spring advanced I began to look towards the frontier, where we expected the most active operations, and tho' I could have remained with General Izard in all the luxury of the city, I felt as if I was not doing my duty; and so stated to the General, who ordered me on duty to the War Department with dispatches, and introducing me to General Armstrong, then Secretary, who received me very flatteringly. Having dined with him in company with my friend Wm. Jones, then Secretary of the Navy, I was next morning told by General Armstrong he had given me a Captain's commission in the 23rd Infantry, in which regiment he said he had two sons. This compliment I thanked him for but hesitated to accept it, as I could not think of leaving the 2nd Artillery where I had so many friends; but when I reflected I was jumping from a 2nd Lieutenancy to a Captaincy over all the Lieutenants in service, I soon determined to accept and posted off for the Niagara River to join my regiment in time for the attack on Fort George opposite Fort Niagara, which the Secretary said I would just have time enough to do, after remaining a week in Philadelphia with my parents, and changing my uniform from Artillery to Infantry.

I left Philadelphia the latter end of April, 1813, for the army, and without delay of an hour, hastened again to the field, passing in my route many officers who expressed much desire to get to the frontier, forgetting they had not applied for orders, which were seldom refused to those who asked for them.

In my memorandum of the movement of our battalion,— 2nd Artillery, from Albany to Buffalo, N. Y. in September, 1812, it might possibly benefit some to know the many disadvantages to be incurred in going into a war so totally unprepared as we were in 1812.

The army was to be organized at Green Bush opposite Albany, N. Y. Major General Dearborn, who had served in the Revolution was to command.

When the 2nd Artillery arrived at Head-quarters we found about 1500 men, including the 3rd regiment Artillery, commanded by Col. Macomb (now [1836] Major General commanding the army). Col. A. Smyth, Adjutant and Inspector General was drilling the troops. He was standing *cross legged* reading the words of command from a book, he said he had compiled from the French, and this book with "Toupard" for the Artillery was all the instruction we had to aid us in our discipline. Col. Scott, thinking he had not much to learn at head-quarters, preferred taking some practical lessons from the enemy, and urged General Dearborn to order him to the Niagara; and we moved off in a day or two, leaving Col. Macomb to prepare his regiment for the next spring.

From the arsenal of the state near Albany, we received two iron 6 pounders, guns and implements, and from the Quarter Master 20 horses and harness. These horses had been purchased in the neighborhood, and sold by the owners —not for their many good qualities. They had not been tried at work; the harness had been made by contract,— which in those days meant that the Government was to be cheated by the agent and contractor together, as General Pike said to the Secretary of War, of Tench Coxe, the Purveyor; when to exhibit the gross impositions on the soldier, the General folded up very neatly one of Coxe's blankets in an envelope addressed to the War Department, to show in a stronger manner than language could, the covering 4 feet by three, intended for a Canadian winter. As to stockings, they would fit any sized foot; for if too short, the soldier had only to push his toes between the threads.

As I have said, our horses and harness were alike untried, and when ordered forward some pulled back, others jumped entirely out of their harness,—away went girths and traces and away went horses and thus every day several times was our line of march disordered in breaking horses and in breaking harness too. In a few days half our horses were galled and lamed by bad made harness, and by the time we came to the bad roads and swamps, our horses were broken down; and we had sometimes to take a double team to drag one 6 pounder out of the mire.

As to funds—"the sinews of war"—there was but one Pay Master in New York, Mr. Aiken, and he as usual without funds; and with a positive order from General Dearborn I was enabled to get 2 months' pay. As we had left

Philadelphia at 48 hours' notice, there was a plentiful scarcity of cash among the officers, and before we had marched 8 days, there were not $10 in the mess except my late acquisition of pay, which was to pay all the bills to the last shilling, and that shilling also.   But none of us cared for money. We were as good to be shot at, poor as rich, and as merry as crickets.   But seriously, it must be madness in the extreme in any Government to push an army into the field, without being in some degree prepared with the munitions of war, of which in 1812 we were entirely destitute; and when I now passed over the same route again in 1813, things looked no better as to the materials.   There were more troops on the road, but no better supplied, no better disciplined.   But I had to obey orders, and as I told General Armstrong I would be at Fort Niagara before the first spring fight, I arrived there May 9th, and reported to Col. Scott now Adjutant General of the army and also commanding the 2nd Artillery.   My old comrades said they did not know whether to congratulate me on my promotion or not, as they did not like to see me in " pewter."—a nickname for Infantry uniform.

The 23rd regiment, to which I belonged, arrived in a few days, and I began to regret my promotion when I began to make comparisons with officers and men ; for I sincerely think there could not be a nobler collection of warm hearts and willing hands than the officers of the 2nd Artillery then at head-quarters,—say Col. Scott, Captains N. Towson—J. Hindman—J. N. Barker—Thos. Biddle—Sam'l Archer— Spotswood Henry—Wm. Nicholas, and Lieutenants—Zant- zinger—Kearsley—Tyler—McDonough—Fontaine—Davis —Hook and Stewart—not one individual of whom but is borne on the reports as having been distinguished ;—Scott, Towson, Biddle and McDonough in every battle that was fought, and McDonough only was killed.   I believe all the others were wounded, except Hindman.

Previous to this period an attack had been made on the British at Little York, U. C.   The place was taken, but with much loss on both sides.   Many of the enemy were killed by our riflemen, and we lost several hundred, killed and wounded, by the treachery of the British blowing up their magazine after the white flag was hoisted by them and our troops marching into the battery. Brigadier General Pike was killed here. All the wounded were brought in Commodore Chauncey's fleet up to Fort Niagara.

We had now assembled about 6000 men, aided by Commodore Chauncey's fleet, and they were about 3000, and their fleet not on the Lake. We now had the experiment to repeat, of sending superannuated men of the Revolution to command. As the failure of the aged Patroon, General Van Rensselaer, lost us everything in 1812, so was the age and infirmity of General Dearborn the cause of many errors.

About the 10th May, a council of general officers was called, when it was asked by General Dearborn : " is it expedient that we attack the enemy ?" " Yes," was the unanimous reply from Generals Lewis, Chandler, Boyd and Winder, and Quarter Master General Swartwout. " Then we do attack," said General Dearborn ; and the council dismissed. *Nothing was done on our part for two weeks*, except the issuing of orders and counter-orders ; at one time resigning the command to Genl. Lewis and the same hour ordering the internal arrangement of the Division, until confidence in our Commander was very much diminished. Not wishing to go into action with the raw recruits of the 23rd Infty. I volunteered as an aid to my old friend Col. M. Potter, in command of the Artillery and was offered the appointment of Aid to Brig. Genl. Winder. But I preferred going to the attack of Fort George with Col. Scott, who was appointed to command the advance, and although the 2nd Artly to compose the advance was to do duty as Infantry I as Captain of Inf'ty was permitted to join it with a light Field Piece. This was quite a compliment from the Col. commanding and it was followed by Towson and Biddle, Hindman and others, saying, " take what men you want for your gun from our Companies." On the night of the 24th, whilst I was yet remaining with Col. Porter on the right bank of Niagara, where his command having in Fort

Niagara 6 12 prs., 2 nines, some 6s and a mortar; Battery No. 2 at the Graveyard one 12 pr. and a Mortar; No. 3 Lt. Murdoch 2 6 prs.; No. 4 or salt Battery named from furnishing it with barrels of salt covered with earth, 2 beautiful 18 prs. called rifles, 2 6 prs., 2 8 in. French Howitzers and 2 8 inch mortars, here we had Col. Porter, Capt. Totten, 11 Engineers, Capt. Archer and myself; No. 5 Lt. Davis 2 12 prs.; No. 6, or Fox point, Captain Gates, 2 12 prs.;— these batteries forming a crescent to the enemy's works, distant about 700 yards.

On the night of the 24th, when some of our boats were sent down from 5 Mile Meadow by Major Van DeVenter, Directing Quarter Master General, the enemy fired on them; when Col. Porter opened his battery on Fort George for about two hours. The British were now certain we were coming; but no orders for embarkation yet,—no enquiry from head-quarters, 4 miles off, to know why we fired. Next morning May 25th, Col. Porter again opened all his batteries with hot shot, and in one hour we had burnt the enemy's large block-house in Fort George, and by 8 A. M. we had burnt four large block-houses inside and three storehouses outside their works. But one building remained, and Col. Porter directed me to proceed to head-quarters and report to General Dearborn our operations. It was said the old General had not been seen to smile for a week previous, but he was delighted to hear what we had done. I returned to Col. Porter with instructions for him to use his own discretion in burning the remaining buildings in Fort George.

Now the venerable Col. Porter had from the first persisted, and even swore we could not burn a building at that distance; because when he was at Fort Mifflin, in the Revolution, the British fired heated shot for a week but could burn nothing. Our officers persuaded the Colonel, and he said to the officers of the batteries near him:—"Load all the guns, and I will give you one hour to burn the blockhouse." He gave the signal with his gold-headed cane. Bang! went the shot; and in less than ten minutes by my watch, the blockhouse was on fire. The old Colonel, leaning on his cane with both hands, jumped off the ground, swearing he could set the world on fire, and said to me—" Stop the firing, and let us go in to breakfast."

I would here remark that altho' the British engineers and Artillery officers should have been so much our superiors, our shot and shell, did double the execution. Not one of their shells burst in our battery, whilst in Fort George we could see our shells burst in the most desirable places, and the weather boards of the buildings frequently flying when they burst.

On the 27th May, 1813, before daylight, we embarked to attack Fort George, and I was attached to Col. Scott's advance with a light piece of Artillery. I was shot in the right arm, and before night we were in quiet possession of Fort George.[1]

In the landing of our advance, 650 strong, after ascending the bank, which was a soft sandy soil, we formed in good order with my " grasshopper Artillery" on the left. The enemy now charged and drove us off the bank, where the officers of the old Second succeeded in making a stand, and with the bank for a cover, opened a severe fire on the enemy. They lost in killed and wounded nearly 300, and we only one-third the number. This shews the advantage which troops of inferior numbers may find in taking a position such as the above or covered by the edge of a ravine. Brush wood, a wall, or even a post and rail fence, affords shelter, gives confidence to undisciplined men, and disguises your actual number from a stronger enemy. When we took possession of Fort George, I had evidence enough of the effect of heated shot and shells. Every building had been burnt, and even the fire engine entirely destroyed; indeed, everything seemed destroyed or scattered in fragments. Every few yards was the mark of a shell, and the ploughing up of our heavy shot. Nothing was saved but those articles placed in detached magazines in the ramparts. I would suggest several small magazines in a garrison, to

[1] See a correct account in " Thompson's History of the War."

divide the risk of explosion, as well as to facilitate the serving of batteries in action.

I took up my quarters in Fort George with my veteran friend Porter, who was promoted to a Brigadier General; and being wounded I did not join my regiment for several weeks, but remained with my Artillery friends in Fort George.

From the confusion in crossing, marching and counter-marching there was some difficulty in obtaining my company, owing to my promotion and some others. Many of the First Lieutenants of Infantry resigned and left the army, but an order from General Armstrong accepting all their resignations soon stopped the affair, and about the 20th I obtained a full company in the 23rd Infantry, and tho' unable to do duty, proceeded to clothe and discipline my men, who altho' now in the enemy's country, were destitute of both.

From the day of taking Fort George there had been a constant marching and counter-marching of our troops, and either owing to the ill health or age of General Dearborn it must have been evident to the enemy we wanted discipline. Almost every night we were kept under arms, and for weeks it rained very hard, until more than half our men were on the sick list. Indeed for several nights I have known the officers generally to have to turn out with muskets at night to patrol. General Dearborn was sick and unable to command, and yet he would not permit General Lewis to do so,—who was in everything his superior.

It was the practice to send every day or two some of the battalions into the country to reconnoitre the enemy, who had taken a very strong position at Burlington Heights; and amongst the applicants for command was a Col. Boerstler, commanding the 14th Infantry, who had served the year before on the Niagara with but little credit.

On the afternoon of June 23rd, 1813, I was engaged in issuing clothing to my men, which I had obtained by the friendship of Col. Christie of the 13th Infantry. Captain Horatio Armstrong, son of my good friend the General, had been relieved from guard and was sleeping in my tent, when the Adjutant, Lieutenant Burr came in saying Captain Armstrong was detailed for command.   Knowing the hard duty of our Captains at that time, I volunteered to go in his place tho' I could scarcely draw my sword.   In less than an hour I marched my company to the 2nd brigade. My friend Captain McChesney of the 6th, who had been with me in 1812, at the battle of Queenstown joined at this moment, and Captain McDowell of the Light Artillery.   In a few minutes the 14th Infantry appeared, and then their Colonel Boerstler, who mounted and took command.   My old friends,—General Porter, Towson, Hindman, Doctor Near, and Captain Totten—were standing in the rear of my company to see us move off, and who all knew we had no confidence in the Colonel of the 14th.

I stepped to the rear, and handing my pocket-book to Major Hindman, said:—" I have no doubt we shall get broken heads before we return, and if so, send my trunk and pocket-book to my family."   My opinion of Col. Boerstler was verified.   He was totally unfit to command.   We moved off to Queenstown, where we halted that night, and next morning took the road through St. Davids, and to the Beaver Dams.   The road now became bad, and our men were much fatigued.

The column was in files,—Chapin's 40 volunteers in front; next 14th Infantry; and then Captain McDowell's Light Artillery Company; then Captain McChesney's 6th Infantry; then Roach's 23rd Infantry; and sixteen men of Burn's Light Dragoons under Cornet Burd, forming a rear guard.

The column was halted to bring in a few men of the Canadian Embodied Militia, and the Dragoons were close to my company.   A soldier said; " The Indians," and on turning to the rear, I observed a large and close body of Indians moving rapidly across the road.   I instantly wheeled my company into platoons, and moved on the enemy, the Dragoons charging them.   As soon as the Dragoons were close up with them, the Indians fired a smart volley.   The

Cavalry horses wheeled round, and came plunging thro' the right of my platoons, knocking down and breaking about one-third of each platoon. I quickly formed in line and fired on the enemy, who broke from the road and took to the woods on each side. On the left of our line of march were four cultivated fields and a farm house, but in front and rear and right a close woods. At the moment the Indians broke Col. Boerstler rode up and ordered me to file my company into the open field; which bro't me into a close fire with that part of the Indians which had taken post in the woods. Captain McDowell now opened a 12 pounder down the road on which we had advanced. I pulled out my watch, and it wanted 15 minutes of nine A. M. Captain McChesney now took post on my right, and the main body of Indians, about 800, commenced a destructive fire on our two companies; a smaller part attacking the troops which continued in the road. I noticed how useless the fire of Artillery was, and requested Major Taylor to have the pieces depressed, showing him how Captain McDowell was cutting off the upper limbs of the trees.

All this time I saw but one Red Coat, but the Indians behaved with uncommon bravery, several times dashing out of the woods to within 30 or 40 yards, as tho' confident of their numbers, they would close on us, and old McChesney and myself were left to take care of ourselves. My men behaved very well. They had nearly emptied their cartridge boxes. Ammunition was bro't up, and while they were firing, my Lieutenant, Griswold, assisted me in filling up the boxes; the musicians being engaged in carrying the wounded to the rear, to prevent their falling into the hands of the Indians when we should move. It is also an advantage to remove from the line the wounded, to prevent making an impression on the others. Not one of my men, I believe, had ever been in a fight; my Lieutenant was direct from West Point Academy, yet he was cool and attentive.

From the division of the enemy into two parties, our detachment became divided for more than an hour. Several movements were now made by Col. Boerstler to draw the Indians from the woods, but ineffectually. The enemy were now reinforcing, as we could observe, and now was the moment to have made a retreat. But the Colonel said that would never do, as we had beaten the enemy, and his orders were positive to proceed to De Con's house, which was yet 8 miles in advance.

The fire of the enemy was slackened, but he was busy in getting his Indians on our rear. Another attempt was made to draw him from cover, and we moved to a by-road near the farm house. Not being able to draw him out, our sapient Colonel now thought of looking towards retreat. A column of platoons was formed in a road perpendicular to the main road, and placing the 14th in front, next Artillery, then the wagons with wounded, then McChesney, and last, in the post of honor, my company. Now no doubt it was Col. Boerstler's object to retain his own regiment without loss, but it was decided injustice to compel my company to remain in the Rear-guard so long as he did; and Captain McChesney who ranked all of us, was remonstrating against the injustice done him, and as he was badly wounded in the wrist, we both were cross enough. We encouraged our men for a charge thro' the woods, and a retreating fight; and at the moment we expected the order to move on the enemy, Major Taylor whispered me, that he feared our Colonel was frightened, as a flag was received from the enemy, and in another half hour Col. Boerstler agreed to surrender his command, reporting to the Government that he held a council of his officers; which was not true, as Major Taylor, McChesney, and myself knew nothing of it.

It was now five minutes past twelve o'clock M., and a few of Dr Chapin's Forty Thieves, having deserted in the early part of the action, reported to General Dearborn, that Col. Boerstler had surrendered without firing a musket, and this the General reported to the Government. We were engaged three hours; twice my cartridge boxes were filled and expended. But fighting is not the hardest part of a soldier's life. Now came the tug of war.—We were sur÷

rendered without discretion to a detachment of about 80 British Regulars under Lieutenant Fitzgibbon,—about 200 Embodied Militia under Lieutenant Colonel De Ham, who were equal to Regulars,—and a body of North Western Indians, about 550 in number, who had that morning arrived from the upper country under the direction of Ker the Indian agent. Lieutenant Colonel Bishop with 120 men joined them at the moment of surrender, and took the command. But instead of being received by the British, we were surrounded by the Indians, who commenced their business of plundering the officers. I slipped my sword under my coat, in hopes to save it; but one Indian demanded it, while another very significantly made a flourish of his gun over my head and took my sword.

I believe our wise Colonel now saw the snare he was in when too late, and how little dependence can at any time be placed on the promises of a British army officer. Col. Boerstler surrendered on condition that his wounded should be protected; his officers retain their side arms, and be paroled to return to Fort George immediately. Not one item of this was ever complied with. Nearly all our wounded were killed by the Indians that night. The officers were marched 7 miles to Col. Bishop's quarters, thro' various parties of Indians, and protected by 2 officers and 2 men, who were more afraid and less accustomed to the Indians than ourselves; my time was occupied in attending to my friend McChesney whose wound was very painful, as the ball passed through the wrist joint and cut off the blood vessel, when he was shot being near me. I had placed my field Tourniquet on his arm but he continued to bleed all that night and when quartered for the night we were surrounded by savages intoxicated by the Liquor found in our wagons. I barricaded the door and armed with McChesney's sword I watched him all night, at one time I expected the Indians to break into our room, as they were in the house and not thinking my comrade would live till morning as his arm continued bleeding and he did not expect to live but in the morning the bleeding stopped and his arm was saved as the British were to have taken it off in the morning. Next day the 25th we were taken to Head Quarters at Burlington Heights and were again marched through several parties of Indians and insulted and plundered. The officers having us in charge not daring to oppose them. On our arrival at Head Quarters in the evening the officers signed a Parole except myself, who refused. We were then embarked on board the British Fleet, myself and two others went on board the Brig "Earl Moira," Capt. Dobbs, who was a kind gentlemanly officer. We were now told we could not be sent to Fort George as agreed upon but Sir James Yeo would run up to the Niagara and obtain our baggage and as I had intended when I refused to sign the Parole, if we run near the shore to take leave of them if possible; but about one o'clock next morning when within three miles of the river the wind headed us off and not wishing to meet our Fleet which had gone towards Sackett Harbor, we bore away for Kingston, where we arrived June 28th. Captain Dobbs was a well educated gentlemanly officer, but there was nothing like Man O' War regularity on board. There was much severity and roughness of conduct between the different grades without discipline; and tho' there appeared to me no want of personal bravery, there was wanting a confidence in and a respect for, the abilities of others, exhibited in every grade of officers on board *a la milice*, which I think must give our Regulars the advantage in a fight. I have known Captain Dobbs lecture his Lieutenant, McGee, in my presence, in terms not suited to a warrant officer for some trifling neglect.—McGee was afterwards killed.

On our arrival at Kingston, U. C., we were escorted to head-quarters and paroled by Lieutenant Colonel Drummond (subsequently of bayonet memory), and tho' paroled we were confined to our quarters, and occasionally visited by the loyal inhabitants, and insulted by the Indians, some of whom threatened to "skin our heads."

Kingston is situated at the head of the St. Lawrence River, on the left bank or north side, and opposite to Wolfe

Island. It occupies the site of our old Fort Frontinac. It has a barrack for troops; quarters,—hospital,—storehouses,—an Episcopal church,—courthouse and gaol. The cove affords a good harbor for shipping.

The town is defended by a blockhouse in front, and on Wolfe Island by a blockhouse and a water battery of 10 guns; and on the right of the town is a strong battery, and in the rear another blockhouse. The navy yard is on Wolfe Island. Large vessels seldom go below Kingston, tho' it is navigable 70 miles downward.

July 1, 1813, the American officers, prisoners on parole, departed for Quebec under escort of Lieutenant Colonel Boucherville, of the militia, aid to Sir George Prevost, and from whom we received many kind attentions,—and whose treatment, like that of nearly all the Canadian officers, was kind, and very different from the abusive and unfeeling conduct of the British officers generally. Colonel Drummond knew we were to have been paroled and sent back to our army by the terms of the capitulation,—not one article of which was ever complied with; and we were not allowed to remain even for our baggage, to obtain a change of clothing for which we were suffering.

The passage from Kingston to La Chine in boats was very pleasant, and served to amuse us in our trouble, and having been placed under the care of Canadians who were disposed to feel for us, we now began to shake off some of the melancholy and moroseness consequent on our capture, as we most of us felt it a disgraceful surrender on the part of our Bobadil Colonel. We now began to look pleasantly on the scenery around us, and occasionally jested with each other on our appearance, and the smart looks of some one who had obtained the sight of a mirror on shore and beautified his appearance by turning out the least dirty part of his cravat for the seventh time;—or some one remarked on the comforts of clean linen, who said he had just turned his shirt and would do for another week.

The passage down the St. Lawrence is very pleasant and in many places very interesting. The current is generally.

six miles an hour, and the rapidity with which the traveller passes from one scene to another cannot fail to amuse. On the afternoon of the first of July we passed an immense number of islands, called "Mille Isle," and truly of a thousand different shapes and sizes. It is here one begins to feel and observe the rapidity of the current, when, passing so swiftly from one view of the scenery to another, it appeared as if the scenery was truly being changed, instead of our moving past it; and it was as pleasing as varied. Our boatmen (who knew no will but their master's) rowed all night singing their Canadian boat songs, and by sunrise next morning (the second) we were at Prescot, 60 miles from Kingston. Prescot is a place of military importance, well defended, and with works to contain a thousand men; and commanding the passage down the river, and the main road. It is opposite Ogdensburg on the American side, where Messrs. Parrish & Ogden have extensive iron works, and which was protected by the British during the war, as Mr. Parrish was a British subject and had made a declaration that he had not loaned money to the U. S. Government but as an agent for others.

On the 2nd Instant we passed "the Cedars" where the passage is very dangerous. The best channel is on the Canadian side, and close to the shore. We passed over a fall about 6 feet high, which is not perceived in descending the fall until directly on it, and requires much skill in steering thro' it. In the early conquest of Canada, forty bateaux filled with soldiers were lost in passing over this fall. Here is a lock for upward navigation and some remains of field fortification.

In a few minutes after passing "the Cedars" we come to "the Long Sault" or Rapids, the length of which is three miles.

The passage thro' the Rapids, tho' somewhat dangerous, is indeed beautiful,—the rocks in many places appearing above the surface, against which the rapid current threatens to dash the boat, and must alarm the passenger, until, when within a few feet of them by the pilot's skilful hand, the boat is turned in another direction, and one could almost step on the rock. At every turn the scene varies; becomes more beautiful and less dangerous; until having passed the Rapids in safety, the Canadian boatman crosses himself, returns thanks to his Heavenly Preserver, and again resumes his song, the subject of which is some brunette, whom he extols in even more extravagant terms than Don Quixotte did his Dulcinea Del Tobosa,—and perhaps they were equally deserving of praise.

This day—July 2nd—we reached Coté Du Sac, a village situate on a small stream, both sides of which are fortified. The principal works are on the north side, and consist of three blockhouses and a field work of masonry,—a heptagon with a large ditch. Here is also a lock in the passage.

July 3rd at 12 M., we arrived at La Chine, about 9 miles above Montreal, and the nearest navigable point, owing to rocks and falls. Opposite to La Chine is a very fine Indian village, probably the best in the country, of about 150 houses and a large church. The tribe is called Cockinawa, and are Catholics.

It is here that the great Council Fire of all the northern tribes is lighted. There is another tribe, whose village joins the Cockinawa's and tho' they have lived thus neighbors for many years, not one instance of intermarriage has occurred, nor do they speak the same language.

At 2 P. M. we arrived at Montreal, and were quartered in Dillon's Hotel Place Des Armes and ordered not to leave the house. Indeed we were not desirous of appearing abroad, as we were without our baggage and destitute of even a change of linen until we sent to a store and purchased it on the evening of our arrival.

Montreal is situated on an island of this name, and was formerly enclosed by a wall. But this has been taken down and the city extended. The houses are of stone, well built, and mostly with iron covered shutters. The inhabitants are mostly natives of Scotland and the United States.

July 4, 1818. I had the honor to be born under a free Republican Government, and from my earliest youth I had been taught and accustomed to welcome the anniversary of my country's freedom with thankfulness for this blessing which was purchased so dearly.   This was a sad reverse to all of us, smarting as we were from our recent capture. But the most of us were young, and looking at the fair side of things, we were enabled to spend this day with some satisfaction, remembering that some of our comrades were in arms, and we might ere long be enabled to join them.

July 6th.   Left Montreal for Quebec.   One observes nothing interesting on the passage.   The river is generally about 1½ miles wide passing thro' Lake St. Peter.   The banks are low and regular until one arrives near Quebec, when they become very high and rough.   About 30 miles above Quebec are considerable falls, which are dangerous to pass in the night.   The channel is in the middle of the river—the current rapid and cannot be ascended but with a fair wind or steam.   The River Chaudine empties into the St. Lawrence about 3 miles above Quebec on the south side.

July 7th.   At daybreak arrived at Quebec, when our amiable and attentive escort—Colonel Boucherville—waited on Major General Glasgow, Commanding, to report our arrival, and about 8 A. M. an officer in naval dress came alongside and ordered us on board the prison ship to be paroled.   On our arrival here we were paraded in the presence of about 480 of our men, who had been taken previously to ourselves.

We were now examined as to age, height, &c. &c. by a clerk, and paroled by Captain Kempt of His Majesty's Royal Navy, who was very offensive in his enquiries; but from further acquaintance it was found to proceed from weakness of intellect.   Our parole enjoined on us not to do any violence, to conform to the laws, &c., not to leave our quarters after sunset, and to keep within two miles of the church of Beauport, 5 miles north of Quebec, on the left bank of the St. Lawrence.

About noon we landed at Beauport, and were turned loose among a people with whose language we were unacquainted (except Col. Boerstler, who spoke French).   The inhabitants received us very kindly. We had no other guide than to keep within 2 miles of the church steeple. Here we found on parole Brigadier Generals—Winchester of Tennessee, Chandler of Massachusetts, and Winder of Maryland, Colonel Lewis and Major Madison of Kentucky, and Major Van de Venter, Directing Quarter Master General, and Lieutenant S. Smith of the U. S. Navy, and about a dozen others, which with our addition of about twenty, made a sad collection of long faces. The village extends along the road about 8 miles, and from its commencement at the southern limit 8 miles from Quebec, the ground gradually ascends to the northern boundary at the falls of Montmorency. The inhabitants or "habiton," as it is pronounced in French, are native Canadians, with the exception of a few families, who at this time, 1813, were Col. Du Bon, Col. Lewis, Col. Lewis De Sallibury, and Col. Du Chesney of the militia, Col. Touch a retired Colonel of the army, and S. Ryland Secretary of State for the L. Province, and who was active in the affair of Henry's conspiracy to gull the U. S. Government in 1810.

From Colonels Touch, De Sallibury, and Du Chesney, most of our officers received continued kindness, and to those of us who properly appreciated such attentions, their kindness was unremitting and continued to the last day of our sojourn among them. But to Colonel De Sallibury and family I cannot do justice for the delicacy with which the Colonel evinced his sympathy for our misfortune. Having taken a fancy that Van De Venter, Randall of the 14th, and myself either could speak French or would soon learn to do so, not many days passed without an invitation of some kind being received from the family.

The Colonel was of the "anciene Régime," born in France. His father had been a Colonel in the army of Louis XVI, and our Colonel entered the French army before or about the period of the conquest, and came to Canada. He served many years in the Canadian Militia, and now has two sons, who are very gallant officers in the Embodied Militia.

Some of our officers messed together, others boarded with the "habiton," and some who were disposed to be dissipated went to a tavern. Every one took his own course for amusement.

From the elevated part of the village one has a beautiful view of the north side of Quebec, abruptly arising from the margin of the point where the River St. Charles enters the St. Lawrence. The city rises to a great height, the houses at a little distance appearing to stand on each other, and as most of them are covered with tin, they look very gay. I could not learn whether this tin was in manner prepared for roofing, but it did not corrode any. The air is remarkably pure, and nothing seems to rust, for even the old men and women did not seem to fall off their hinges. As a humorsome midshipman of our Navy used to say—they had shelves near the stoves where they laid old people during the winter, and in the spring they became animated and sallied forth again. The appearance of these old Canadians at their church on Sunday was interesting. For here everybody who is able to leave home goes to church in the morning, but as in all Catholic countries, each one seeks his own amusement in the afternoon and even thinks it no sin to take down his violin; and the family soon begin to foot it away, but with sobriety and apparently with "pious mirth." And such is the force of example, good or bad, that I have known some persons from the land of steady habits, after looking on this picture of domestic happiness for a while, at length stand up, and after a few awkward looks and turns of the man, begin to shuffle away as if they were Canadians born.

(To be continued.)

BRITISH AND AMERICAN PRISONERS OF WAR, 1778.

CONTRIBUTED BY WORTHINGTON C. FORD.

Among a collection of Revolutionary papers—a very small part of the correspondence of Colonel Samuel Blachley Webb, of the Connecticut line—I found two lists of officers, prisoners of war, one prepared at the request of the commissary-general of prisoners in the Royal army. Colonel Webb, after serving at Bunker Hill in Colonel Chester's regiment, became an aide to Major-General Putnam, and later entered the military family of Washington. He was an aide to the Commander-in-chief for six months, and received an appointment to command one of the " additional regiments" authorized in 1777. For a year he was occupied in raising his regiment, and in active service in the Highlands under Putnam, George Clinton, and Parsons; but had the misfortune to be taken prisoner while making a descent upon the British outposts at Setauket, on Long Island. He at once sought to secure his exchange, but unfortunately political questions prevented its consummation. The British general would not enter into a formal cartel, of binding force, as such an act would compromise the claims of Great Britain over the rebellious colonies. He was willing to make an exchange as a personal act, but was forbidden by his instructions from pledging the faith of the King or of Parliament to such a measure. Partial exchanges were discountenanced by the commanders of both armies, and so there was nothing for the Colonel to do but keep alive the question of a cartel, until some agreement could be reached, and a regular course of exchanges entered into.

In this his connections greatly assisted him. His brother, Joseph Webb, was the Connecticut commissary of prisoners, and passed freely to and from the island. He had thus established relations with many British prisoners in Connecticut, who remembered his courteous indulgence on their release on parole, and returned it by kindness to Samuel B. Webb. Samuel lived with Miles Sherbrooke, of no little repute in the city, and he appears to have had many privileges not accorded to other prisoners,—such as hunting in the country,—obtained by his connections with the British officers. It is noteworthy, too, that he made the comfort of his fellow-prisoners his care, and was easily the most prominent among them. Through him did the British make known their orders and regulations for controlling the prisoners; and through him did the prisoners seek for new privileges, or for redress of insult or injury. He drafted their petitions, and pleaded their cause before the Continental Congress. Hence much of his correspondence relates to the subject of prisoners of war, and these tables were prepared to govern the exchanges, as the following letters prove.[1]

From Major Beatty to Colonel Webb.

PRINCETON July 30th 1778.

MY DEAR COLLONELL:

I have but a Moment to write you, as an Exchange of a Number of the Fort Washington Officers will in a few days take place. I must request you to furnish me with a return of the whole of the officers on the Island—beginning with those oldest in Captivity—ascertaining their Rank & the time of their Captivity—I am obliged to take this Step—both to do Justice to the Prisoners—& to prevent any reflections upon my Character—the utmost Impartiality is meant to take place & if I err in any respect, it must be attributed to the gentlemen there, who do not do Justice to themselves. I have no list to proceed upon, except an Inaccurate one from New York—I must beg the gentlemen will rectify this Matter —& if any dispute arises, with those of the same rank & who were taken at the same time, it is Genl Washington's Opinion, that they either draw Lotts, or it shall be determined by Precedency of Rank. Whatever return they make me, it shall regulate all future Exchanges—I must request a report from you as speedily as possible.

[1] There are in press three volumes of the " Correspondence and Journals of Samuel Blachley Webb," published under the direction of his grandson, William Seward Webb, of New York. These tables will not appear in them.

I enclose you two of our latest Papers—it contains as much as I am at Liberty to write. Peruse it & lend it to your Neighbours. Remember me very affectionately to the good Family you live in. My Comp⁵ to M⁵ Clarkson's & M⁵ Van horne's Family—tell them I saw their Friends very lately—Particularly *Matt* [Clarkson ?]—who are all well—Tell *Tommy* at the Dominy's, to keep up his Spirits—another Twelve month will put him on the List for an Exchange. I dare say, he Enjoys the Sweets of Confinement as fully as any of you—I flatter myself some times with seeing you—but fear I shall not be able to accomplish it.

I am w⁵ Comp⁵ to all the gentlemen
D⁵ Sir, your most Obed⁵ Hum. Serv⁵
JN⁵ BEATTY.

George Tudor begs to write his name & to say he expected to hear from Col⁵ Webb & Col. Antle [Antill] before this in answer to two letters wrote to them some time past. Adieu & believe him sincerely yours.

To Major Beatty.

FLAT BUSH ON LONG ISLAND,
August 15ᵗʰ 1778.

DEAR SIR:

We have met and made out a return of the officers and other Prisoners upon this Island, we have taken up the mode settled in our army with regard to their respective ranks, as the General rule of our conduct in the arrangement, we have signed and sent you, by which means you will be possessed of the situation we are in here and enabled the better to do justice and give satisfaction to all parties If you should be acquainted with any circumstances relative to the prisoners that have not come to our knowledge you will make such alterations (*in the roster of exchange*) as you shall think proper We have put down the third Lieutenants by themselves tho' we suppose they will rank as Ensigns and be exchanged accordingly. We are further to inform you that we have taken no notice of those in the Provost Guard nor the Marine or Sea officers

We remain with Respect you Hbb⁵ Serv⁵⁵
JAMES IRWINE B. Gen⁵ P. S.
S. B. WEBB, Col⁵ Amer⁵ Army
EDD ANTILL L. Col⁵ D⁵
JN⁵ BRUYNE L⁵ Col⁵ D⁵
JOHN SMOCK L⁵ Col⁵ Jersey Mili.
ANDREW GILBRITH Maj⁵ Pen⁵ Flying Camp
EDWARD TILLARD Maj⁵ Conn⁵ Army
TARLTON WOODSON Maj⁵ Conn⁵ A⁵
LEVIN JOYNES Maj⁵ 9ᵗʰ Virg⁵ Reg⁵
SAM LOGAN Maj⁵ Conn⁵ Army

RETURN OF THE OFFICERS ON PAROLE IN THE DISTRICT OF
NEW EUTRECHT, THIS 11TH DAY OF AUGUST, 1778.

WILLIAM ALLISON, Colonel N. Y. militia. Commissioned, 15 September, 1775. Taken at Fort Clinton, 6 October, 1777.

ANDREW GAILBRAITH, Major in Col. Watts' Pennsylvania regiment (Flying Camp). Commissioned, 18 September, 1776. Taken at Fort Washington, 16 November, 1776.

EDWARD TILLARD, Major in Col. Williams' Maryland regiment. Commissioned, 10 April, 1777. Taken on Staten Island, 22 August, 1777.

SAMUEL LOGAN, Major in Col. Dubois' New York regiment. Commissioned, 21 November, 1776. Taken at Fort Montgomery, 6 October, 1777.

JOHN SMOCK, Lieut.-Col. in New Jersey militia. Commissioned, 27 March, 1778. Taken in Monmouth County, 27 May, 1778.

STEPHEN FLEMING, Captain in third regiment, New Jersey militia. Commissioned, 12 February, 1778. Taken in Monmouth County, 27 January, 1777 (*sic*).

ELIJAH SMITH, Captain in the fourth Connecticut regiment. Commissioned, 2 December, 1776. Taken at Norwalk, 15 March, 1777.

JOHN MERCER, First Lieutenant in the first New Jersey regiment. Commissioned, 14 November, 1775. Taken near Bound Brook, 7 March, 1777.

EPHRAIM FENNO, of Massachusetts, Capt.-Lieut. in Col. Lamb's artillery. Commissioned, 1 January, 1777. Taken at Fort Montgomery, 6 October, 1777.

JACOB COVENHOVEN, Captain of Light Horse in 1st New Jersey militia. Commissioned, 18 May, 1778. Taken in Monmouth County, 27 May, 1778.

THOMAS LITTLE, Second Lieutenant in 3d New Jersey militia. Commissioned, 13 February, 1778. Taken in Monmouth County, 27 January, 1777 (*sic*).

THEOPHILUS LITTLE, First Lieutenant in 3d New Jersey militia. Commissioned, 26 September, 1777. Taken in Monmouth County, 27 May, 1778.

JOHN GALE, First Lieutenant in Col. Price's Maryland regiment. Commissioned, 10 April, 1777. Taken on Staten Island, 22 August, 1777.

ROBERT CHESLEY, First Lieutenant in Col. Price's Maryland regiment. Commissioned, 10 April, 1777. Taken on Staten Island, 22 August, 1777.

WILLIAM ROBERSON, adjutant in Col. Matthew's Virginia regiment. Commissioned, 22 May, 1777. Taken at Germantown, 4 October, 1777.

TOBIAS PARHAMAS, Second Lieutenant in 1st New Jersey militia.

Commissioned, 30 May, 1777. Taken in Monmouth County, 13 February, 1777 (*sic*).

SOLOMON PENDLETON, First Lieutenant in Col. Dubois' New York regiment. Commissioned, 21 November, 1776. Taken at Fort Montgomery, 6 October, 1777.

ABRAHAM PARSONS, Second Lieutenant in the 2d New Jersey regiment. Commissioned, 17 September, 1777. Taken in Gloucester County, 5 March, 1778.

HENRY BRUSTER, First Lieutenant in Col. Allison's New York regiment. No commission. Taken at Fort Clinton, 6 October, 1777.

BENJAMIN HOLSTER, Second Lieutenant in Col. Allison's New York regiment. No commission. Taken at Fort Clinton, 6 October, 1777.

OLIVER GLEAN, A. D. Q. Master General, Col. Hugh's New York service. Commissioned, 1 September, 1777. Taken at Fort Montgomery, 6 October, 1777.

ROBERT BRADFORD, Ensign in the 4th Connecticut regiment. Commissioned, 2 December, 1776. Taken at Norwalk, 15 March, 1777.

JOHN McCLAUGHRY, Ensign in Col. Dubois' New York regiment. Commissioned, 21 November, 1776. Taken at Fort Montgomery, 6 October, 1777.

THOMAS COVERLY, Ensign in Col. Matthew's Virginia regiment. Commissioned, 7 November, 1776. Taken at Germantown, 4 October, 1777.

A RETURN OF THE OFFICERS PRISONERS OF GRAVES END.

NATHANIEL CLEAVES, First Lieutenant in Col. Hutchison's Massachusetts regiment. Commissioned, 1 January, 1776. Taken at Fort Washington, 16 November, 1776.

DAVID POORE, Second Lieutenant in Col. Hutchison's Massachusetts regiment. Commissioned, 1 January, 1776. Taken at Fort Washington, 16 November, 1776.

GIBSON CLOUGH, Ensign in Col. Hutchison's Massachusetts regiment. Commissioned, 1 January, 1776. Taken at Fort Washington, 16 November, 1776.

THOMAS H. LUCKETT, First Lieutenant in Col. Rawling's Maryland regiment. Commissioned, 11 July, 1776. Taken at Fort Washington, 16 November, 1776.

SAMUEL FINLY, [of Virginia], First Lieutenant in Col. Rawling's regiment. Commissioned, 9 July, 1776. Taken at Fort Washington, 16 November, 1776.

NATHL. PENDALTON, [of Virginia], First Lieutenant in Col. Rawling's Maryland regiment. Commissioned, 28 July, 1776. Taken at Fort Washington, 16 November, 1776.

WILLIAM GEORGE, [of Virginia], First Lieutenant in Col. Rawling's

Maryland regiment. Commissioned, 17 July, 1776. Taken at Fort Washington, 16 November, 1776.

THOMAS WARMAN, [of Virginia], Second Lieutenant in Col. Rawling's regiment. Commissioned, 17 July, 1776. Taken at Fort Washington, 16 November, 1776.

JAMES LINGAN, Second Lieutenant in Col. Rawling's regiment. Commissioned, 12 July, 1776. Taken at Fort Washington, 16 November, 1776.

HENRY BIDINGER, [of Virginia], Third Lieutenant in Col. Rawling's regiment. Commissioned, 9 July, 1776. Taken at Fort Washington, 16 November, 1776.

REZIN DAVIS, Third Lieutenant in Col. Rawling's regiment. Commissioned, 11 July, 1776. Taken at Fort Washington, 16 November, 1776.

EDWARD SMITH, [of Virginia], Third Lieutenant in Col. Rawling's regiment. Commissioned, 17 July, 1776. Taken at Fort Washington, 16 November, 1776.

CHRISTIAN ORNDORFF, Second Lieutenant in Col. Griffith's Maryland regiment, Flying Camp. Commissioned, 18 July, 1776. Taken at Fort Washington, 16 November, 1776.

HENRY HARDMAN, Captain in Col. Griffith's Maryland regiment, Flying Camp. Commissioned, 19 July, 1776. Taken at Fort Washington, 16 November, 1776.

JOHN McELHATTEN, Captain in Col. Watts' Pennsylvania regiment, Flying Camp. Commissioned, 18 September, 1776. Taken at Fort Washington, 16 November, 1776.

THOMAS CAMPBELL, Captain in Col. Watts' Pennsylvania regiment, Flying Camp. Commissioned, 25 September, 1776. Taken at Fort Washington, 16 November, 1776.

WILLIAM McFARLANE, Captain in Col. Watts' Pennsylvania regiment, Flying Camp. Commissioned, 16 September, 1776. Taken at Fort Washington, 16 November, 1776.

JAMES McFARLANE, Third Lieutenant in Col. Watts' Pennsylvania regiment, Flying Camp. Commissioned, 8 July, 1776. Taken at Fort Washington, 16 November, 1776.

ANDREW ROBINSON, Second Lieutenant in Col. Swoope's Pennsylvania regiment, Flying Camp. Commissioned, 22 August, 1776. Taken at Fort Washington, 16 November, 1776.

JOHN VAUGHAN, Ensign in Col. Montgomery's Pennsylvania regiment, Flying Camp. Commissioned, 28 August, 1776. Taken at Fort Washington, 16 November, 1776.

WILLIAM SCOTT, Captain in Col. Clottz's Pennsylvania Regiment, Flying Camp. Commissioned, 16 September, 1776. Taken at Fort Washington, 16 November, 1776.

WILLIAM BEALL, 1st Lieut. in Col. Clottz's Pennsylvania regiment,

Flying Camp. Commissioned, 6 September, 1776. Taken at Fort Washington, 16 November, 1776.

JOSHUA BRAINARD, 2ª Lieut. in Col. Cook's Connecticut regiment State Troops. Commissioned, 2 December, 1776. Taken at Norwalk, 15 March, 1777.

EPHRAIM DOUGLASS, Quartermaster in Col. Brodhead's Pennsylvania regiment. Commissioned, 9 August, 1776. Taken at Bound Brook, 13 April, 1777.

WILLIAM FERGUSON, Lieut. in Col. Proctor's regiment of artillery, Pennsylvania. Commissioned, 5 October, 1776. Taken at Bound Brook, 13 April, 1777.

DAVID PARSONS, Captain in Col. Charles Webb's Connecticut regiment. Commissioned, 1 January, 1777. Taken near King's Bridge, 1 July, 1777.

JOHN CARLYLE, Captain in Col. Hazen's regiment. Commissioned, 3 November, 1776. Taken on Staten Island, 22 August, 1777.

RICHARD GRACE, 1ˢᵗ Lieut. in Col. Price's Maryland regiment. Commissioned, 10 April, 1777. Taken on Staten Island, 22 August, 1777.

HENRY LYLES, 1ˢᵗ Lieutenant in Col. Guest's [Gist] Maryland regiment. Taken on Staten Island, 22 August, 1777.

RIGNAL HILLERY, Ensign in Col. Stone's Maryland regiment. Commissioned, 10 April, 1777. Taken on Staten Island, 22 August, 1777.

JOHN LAVASHE, Ensign in Col. Price's Maryland regiment. Commissioned, 17 April, 1777. Taken on Staten Island, 22 August, 1777.

THOMAS ARMSTRONG, 1ˢᵗ Lieut. in Col. Arvin's Pennsylvania militia. Commissioned, 6 May, 1777. Taken near the White Horse, 16 September, 1777.

CHARLES CROXELL, 1ˢᵗ Lieut. in Col. Hartley's Maryland regiment. Commissioned, 5 February, 1777. Taken at Valley Forge, 20 September, 1777.

LEVIN JOINS, Major in Col. Mathews' Virginia regiment. Commissioned, 10 February, 1776. Taken at German Town, 4 October, 1777.

SMITH SNEAD, Capt. in Col. Mathews' Virginia regiment. Commissioned, 31 August, 1776. Taken at German Town, 4 October, 1777.

ROBERT WOODSON, 1ˢᵗ Lieut. in Colonel Mathews' Virginia regiment. Commissioned, 31 August, 1776. Taken at Germantown, 4 October, 1777.

CHARLES STOCKLEY, Ensign in Col. Mathews' Virginia regiment. Commissioned, 22 July, 1776. Taken at German Town, 4 October, 1777.

JOHN SCABROUGH, Ensign in Col. Mathews' Virginia regiment. Commissioned, 10 February, 1777. Taken at German Town, 4 October, 1777.

RUBEN FIELDS, 2ª Lieut. in Col. Bowman's Virginia regiment. Commissioned, 10 May, 1777. Taken at German Town, 4 October, 1777.

JOHN CLARK, 2ᵈ Lieut. in Col. Bowman's Virginia regiment. Taken at German Town, 4 October, 1777.

LUKE MARBURY, Col. Maryland militia. Commissioned, August, 1777. Taken at German Town, 4 October, 1777.

ABRAHAM LEGGETT, Ensign in Col. Duboyse's New York regiment. Commissioned, 21 November, 1776. Taken at Fort Montgomery, 6 October, 1777.

HENRY PAWLING, 1ˢᵗ Lieut. in Col. Duboyse's New York regiment. Commissioned, 21 November, 1776. Taken at Fort Montgomery, 6 October, 1777.

CORNELIUS SWARTWOUT, Capt.-Lieut. in Col. Lamb's New York artillery regiment. Commissioned, 1 January, 1777. Taken at Fort Montgomery, 6 October, 1777.

HENRY SWARTWOUT, Ensign in Col. Duboyse's New York regiment. Commissioned, 21 November, 1776. Taken at Fort Montgomery, 6 October, 1777.

EBENEZER WEST, Adjutant in Col. Ely's Connecticut regiment, State troops. Commissioned, 10 June, 1777. Taken in the Sound, 10 December, 1777.

JAMES ABBOT, Ensign in Col. Ely's Connecticut regiment, State troops. Commissioned, 10 June, 1777. Taken in the Sound, 10 December, 1777.

SANDS NILES, Ensign in Col. Ely's Connecticut regiment, State troops. Commissioned, 10 June, 1777. Taken in the Sound, 10 December, 1777.

WILLIAM DEMSY, Ensign in Col. Hannum's Pennsylvania militia regiment. Commissioned, — 1777. Taken at Gulph Mills, 11 December, 1777.

CHARLES CLARKE, 1ˢᵗ Lieut. in Col. Murray's Pennsylvania militia regiment. Commissioned, June, 1777. Taken at Gulph Mills, 11 December, 1777.

WILLIAM PRESTON, 2ᵈ Lieut. in the artificers of artillery, Pennsylvania militia. Commissioned, 11 November, 1777. Taken near Bustle Town, 14 February, 1778.

GEORGE WRIGHT, Major in Colonel Dean's regiment. Commissioned. He was taken from his own house, when not on duty, 14 February, 1778.

WILLIAM LAWRENCE, citizen. Taken, 14 February, 1778.

[1] JOHN W. ANNIS, citizen. Taken, 17 April, 1778.

[1] WILLIAM NEWMAN, Captain in Col. Bell's regiment of Pennsylvania militia. Commissioned, February, 1778. Taken near the Crooked Billet, 24 February, 1778.

[1] ROBERT FOSTER, Ensign in the 15ᵗʰ Virginia regiment. Commissioned, 16 April, 1777. Taken at Baron Hill Church, 24 April, 1778.

[1] JOHN WILLIAMS, citizen of Pennsylvania. Taken at Abington, 7 December, 1777.

[1] These names were added subsequent to the completion of the list.

LIST OF OFFICERS, PRISONERS OF WAR, BILLETED IN THE TOWN-
SHIP OF FLAT BUSH ON LONG ISLAND, 12 AUGUST, 1778.

ROBERT HODGSON, Major in the Delaware militia. Taken at his
house, 7 April —.

JAMES MCCLAGHERY, Lieut. Col. in the 2d regiment, New York
militia, Col. J. Clinton. Commissioned, September, 1775. Taken at
Fort Montgomery, 6 October, 1777.

JOHN RICHARDSON, 1st Lieut. in the 5th Pennsylvania regiment, Col.
Magaw. Commissioned, 5 January, 1776. Taken at Fort Washington,
16 November, 1776.

MATHEW KNOX, 1st Lieut. in the 3d Pennsylvania regiment, Col.
Lamb. Cadwalader. Taken at Fort Washington, 16 November, 1776.

JOHN LAWRENCE, 1st Lieut. in the 5th Pennsylvania regiment, Col. R.
Magaw. Taken at Fort Washington, 16 November, 1776.

ROBERT WILKIN, 1st Lieut. in the 5th Pennsylvania regiment, Col. R.
Magaw. Taken at Fort Washington, 16 November, 1776.

DANIEL BROADHEAD, 1st Lieut. in the 3d Pennsylvania regiment,
Col. Lamb. Cadwalader. Taken at Fort Washington, 16 November,
1776.

JOHN MORGAN, 1st Lieut. in the 5th Pennsylvania regiment, Col. R.
Magaw. Taken at Fort Washington, 16 November, 1776.

JOHN PRIESTLEY, 1st Lieut. in the 5th Pennsylvania regiment, Col. R.
Magaw. Taken at Fort Washington, 16 November, 1776.

CHARLES PHILE, 1st Lieut. in the 5th Pennsylvania regiment, Col. R.
Magaw. Taken at Fort Washington, 16 November, 1776.

JOHN HELM, 1st Lieut. in the 5th Pennsylvania regiment, Col. R.
Magaw. Taken at Fort Washington, 16 November, 1776.

WILLIAM TILTON, 1st Lieut. in the 3d Pennsylvania regiment, Col. L.
Cadwalader. Commissioned, 28 March —. Taken at Fort Washington,
16 November, 1776.

JOHN DUQUID, 1st Lieut. in the 3d Pennsylvania regiment, Col. L.
Cadwalader. Commissioned, 13 June —. Taken at Fort Washington,
16 November, 1776.

WILLIAM CRAWFORD, 2d Lieut. in the 5th Pennsylvania regiment,
Col. R. Magaw. Commissioned, 5 January, 1776. Taken at Fort Washington, 16 November, 1776.

THOMAS JENNY, 2d Lieut. in the 5th Pennsylvania regiment, Col. R.
Magaw. Taken at Fort Washington, 16 November, 1776.

JOHN FINLEY, 2d Lieut. in the 5th Pennsylvania regiment, Col. R.
Magaw. Taken at Fort Washington, 16 November, 1776.

WILLIAM STANLEY, 2d Lieut. in the 5th Pennsylvania regiment,
Col. R. Magaw. Taken at Fort Washington, 16 November, 1776.

JOHN RUDOLPH, 2d Lieut. in the 5th Pennsylvania regiment, Col. R.
Magaw. Taken at Fort Washington, 16 November, 1776.

ANDREW DOVER, 2ᵈ Lieut. in the 5th Pennsylvania regiment, Col. R. Magaw. Taken at Fort Washington, 16 November, 1776.

MATHIAS WIDEMAN, 1ˢᵗ Lieut. in Col. S. John Atley's [Atlee] State regiment of musketry. Commissioned, 6 April, 1776. Taken at Fort Washington, 16 November, 1776.

ROBERT CALDWELL, 1ˢᵗ Lieut. in Col. Atlee's regiment. Taken at Fort Washington, 16 November, 1776.

BERNARD WARD, 1ˢᵗ Lieut. in Col. Atlee's regiment. Taken at Fort Washington, 16 November, 1776.

JOHN DEAN, Captain in the 5th Maryland regiment, Col. William Richardson. Commissioned, 12 July, 1776. Taken at Fort Washington, 16 November, 1776.

ROBERT PATTON, 1ˢᵗ Lieut. in the 1ˢᵗ Pennsylvania Regiment, Flying Camp, Col. Michael Swope. Commissioned, 24 August, 1776. Taken at Fort Washington, 16 November, 1776.

JOHN CRAIG, 2ᵈ Lieut. in Col. William Baxter's Pennsylvania regiment, Flying Camp. Commissioned, 6 September, 1776. Taken at Fort Washington, 16 November, 1776.

MATHEW BENNETT, 2ᵈ Lieut. in Col. William Baxter's Pennsylvania regiment, Flying Camp. Commissioned, 19 September, 1776. Taken at Fort Washington, 16 November, 1776.

JOHN CARTER, Ensign in Col. William Baxter's Pennsylvania regiment, Flying Camp. Commissioned, 19 September, 1776. Taken at Fort Washington, 16 November, 1776.

THOMAS TANNER, 1ˢᵗ Lieut. in Col. Phil. B. Bradley's regiment, Connecticut State troops. Commissioned, 10 June, 1776. Taken at Fort Washington, 16 November, 1776.

BARNARD SMOCK, Captain in the 1ˢᵗ regiment New Jersey militia, Col. Nathᶦ Scudder. Taken at the Light House, 18 February, 1777.

JAMES HAMILTON, Captain in the 1ˢᵗ Pennsylvania regiment, Col. D. Chambers. Commissioned, 16 August, 1776. Taken near Brunswick, 24 March, 1777.

JOHN FLAHAVAN, Captain in the 1ˢᵗ New Jersey regiment, Col. Mattʰ Ogden. Commissioned, 27 December, 1776. Taken near Amboy, 20 April, 1777.

JAMES HERRON, Captain in "Congress' Own," Col. Hazen. Commissioned, 3 November, 1776. Taken on Staten Island, 22 August, 1777.

HENRY GODWIN, Captain in the 5th New York regiment, Col. Lewis Debois. Taken at Fort Montgomery, 6 October, 1777.

JAMES HUMPHREY, Captain in the 1ˢᵗ regiment of New York militia, Col. James Clinton. Commissioned, 18 May, 1776. Taken at Fort Montgomery, 6 October, 1777.

LEW AUGUSTUS D'UTRITCHT, Captain in Col. Armand's independent Pennsylvania regiment. Taken at Head of Elk, 1 September, 1777.

JAMES WHITLOCK, Lieut. in the 1st regiment, Pennsylvania militia, Col. Nath¹ Scudder. Taken at the Light House, 13 February, 1777.

CHARLES TURNBULL, Capt.-Lieut. in the 3^d Pennsylvania artillery, Col. Thomas Proctor. Commissioned, 20 March, 1777. Taken at Bound Brook, 13 April, 1777.

JAMES ANDERSON, 2^d Lieut. in "Congress' Own," Col. Wm. Hazen. Taken on Staten Island, 22 August, 1777.

ALEXANDER MCARTHUR, 2^d Lieut. in the 5th New York regiment, Col. Lewis Dubois. Commissioned, 21 November, 1776. Taken at Fort Montgomery, 6 October, 1777.

JOHN FURMAN, 2^d Lieut. in the 5th New York regiment, Col. Lewis Dubois. Taken at Fort Montgomery, 6 October, 1777.

JOHN HARPER, Brigade Major, from Pennsylvania. Commissioned, 12 July, 1777. Taken near Brandywine, 16 September, 1777.

JOHN WIDEMAN, Ensign in the German Pennsylvania regiment, Col. Baron Aren [Arendt]. Commissioned, 20 August, 1776. Taken near Brandywine, 16 September, 1777.

JONATHAN BREWER, Capt.-Lieut. in the third Pennsylvania regiment of Artillery, Col. Thos. Proctor. Taken at Germantown, 4 October, 1777.

GEORGE BLEWER, 2^d Lieut. in the 4th Pennsylvania regiment, Col. Lambert Cadwalader. Commissioned, 3 January, 1777. Taken at Germantown, 4 October, 1777.

THOMAS MARTIN, 2^d Lieut. in the 9th Virginia regiment, Col. Geo. Matthews. Taken at Germantown, 4 October, 1777.

JOHN ROBINS, Ensign in the 9th Virginia regiment, Col. Geo. Matthews. Taken at Germantown, 4 October, 1777.

CASPER GUYER, sub-Lieutenant of Philadelphia. Commissioned, 2 March, 1777. Taken in Philadelphia, 28 September, 1777.

JOHN HUNTER, 1st Lieut. in the 1st regiment of New York militia, Col. James Clinton. Commissioned, 31 January, 1777. Taken at Fort [Mont]gomery, 6 October, 1777.

THOMAS PARKER, 1st Lieut. in the 9th Virginia regiment, Col. Geo. Matthews. Commissioned, 30 July, 1776. Taken at Germantown, 4 October, 1777.

JOSEPH COX, Ensign in the 6th Pennsylvania regiment, Col. Rob' Magaw. Commissioned, 15 February, 1777. Taken at Newtown, 19 February, 1778.

BATEMAN LLOYD, 1st Lieut. in the 4th New Jersey regiment, Col. Eph" Martin. Commissioned, 1 January, 1777. Taken in New Jersey 26 March, 1778.

THOMAS HENDRY, Surgeon in the New Jersey militia, Col. Joseph Ellis. Commissioned, 2 April, 1777. Taken in Gloucester County, 10 May, 1778.

JAMES LEDDEN, Wagon master in Pennsylvania service, Continental regiment. Taken at Bristol, 17 April, 1778.

FRANCIS GRICE, Lieut. in Col. Mifflin's regiment of Pennsylvania militia. Commissioned, 5 June, 1775. Taken near Germantown, 25 September, 1777.

SILAS SNOW, 1st Lieut. in Delaware militia. Taken, 4 May, 1778, at his own house, Kent County, by Refugees.

A RETURN OF THE OFFICERS OF THE AMERICAN ARMY PRISONERS ON PAROLE IN FLATLANDS, AUG. 1778.

WILLIAM McKISSACK, Captain in Col. Baxter's Pennsylvania regiment. Commissioned, 8 August, 1776. Taken at Fort Washington, 16 November, 1776.

JACOB DRITT, Capt. in Col. Swope's Pennsylvania regiment. Commissioned, 23 August, 1776. Taken at Fort Washington, 16 November, 1776.

CONROD SNIDER, Captain in Col. Watts' Pennsylvania regiment. Commissioned, 7 September, 1776. Taken at Fort Washington, 16 November, 1776.

JOHN JAMISON, Captain in Col. Baxter's Pennsylvania regiment. Commissioned, 17 September, 1776. Taken at Fort Washington, 16 November, 1776.

NATHANIEL PORTER, Captain in Col. Freelanhouse's [Frelinghuysen] New Jersey regiment. Commissioned, 7 March, 1777. Taken near Quibbletown, 22 June, 1777.

JOHN P. SHOTT, Captain in the Independent Corps. Commissioned, 6 September, 1776. Taken at Short Hills, 26 June, 1777.

ROGER STAINER, Captain in the 2d Pennsylvania regiment. Commissioned, 1 January, 1777. Taken at Philadelphia, 26 September, 1777.

JOHN HAYS, Captain in the 9th Virginia regiment. Commissioned, 16 March, 1776. Taken at Germantown, 4 October, 1777.

ROBERT HIGANS, Captain in the 8th Virginia regiment. Commissioned, 9 March, 1777. Taken at Germantown, 4 October, 1777.

JAMES MOORE, Captain in Col. Hall's Delaware regiment. Commissioned, 2 December, 1776. Taken near Schuylkill, 20 January, 1778.

ROBERT SAMPLE, Captain in the 10th Pennsylvania regiment. Commissioned, 4 December, 1776. Taken at Germantown, 7 March, 1778.

JOHN HOLLIDAY, 1st Lieut. in Col. Watts' Pennsylvania regiment. Commissioned, 10 July, 1776. Taken at Fort Washington, 16 November, 1776.

ZACHARIAH SHUGART, 1st Lieut. in Col. Swope's Pennsylvania regiment. Commissioned, 22 August, 1776. Taken at Fort Washington, 16 November, 1776.

SAMUEL LINDSAY, 1st Lieut. in Col. Montgomery's Pennsylvania regiment. Commissioned, 6 September, 1776. Taken at Fort Washington, 16 November, 1776.

HEZEKIAH DAVIS, 1st Lieut. in Col. Montgomery's Pennsylvania regiment. Commissioned, 7 September, 1776. Taken at Fort Washington, 16 November, 1776.

JOSEPH MORRISON, 1st Lieut. in Col. McAllister's Pennsylvania regiment. Commissioned, 9 September, 1776. Taken at Fort Washington, 16 November, 1776.

GABRIEL BLAKENEY, 1st Lieut. in Col. Watts' Pennsylvania regiment. Commissioned, 11 September, 1776. Taken at Fort Washington 16 November, 1776.

JNO ERWIN, 1st Lieut. in Col. Baxter's Pennsylvania regiment. Commissioned, 17 September, 1776. Taken at Fort Washington, 16 November, 1776.

ROBERT BROWN, 1st Lieut. in Col. Baxter's Pennsylvania regiment. Commissioned, 18 September, 1776. Taken at Fort Washington, 16 November, 1776.

ERASTUS WOLCOTT, 1st Lieut. in Col. Webb's Connecticut regiment. Commissioned, 1 May, 1777. Taken at Marrinck [Mamaroneck], 1 July, 1777.

EBENEZER CARSON, 1st Lieut. in the 10th Pennsylvania regiment. Commissioned, 18 April, 1777. Taken at the Head of Elk, 1 September, 1777.

JOHN RILEY, 1st Lieut. in Col. Webb's Connecticut regiment. Commissioned, 1 January, 1777. Taken in the Sound, 10 December, 1777.

RUFUS LINCOLN, 1st Lieut. in Col. Bradford's Massachusetts regiment. Commissioned, 6 November, 1776. Taken near Schuylkill, 28 December, 1777.

SAMUEL ELDRED, 1st Lieut. in Col. Bailey's Massachusetts Regiment. Commissioned, 1 January, 1777. Taken near Darby, 28 December, 1777.

PETER CONROD, 1st Lieut. in Col. Stroud's Pennsylvania regiment. Commissioned, 1 May, 1777. Taken at Frankfort, 10 January, 1778.

JOHN HUTCHIN, 1st Lieut. in the 2d New Jersey regiment. Commissioned, 1 January, 1777. Taken at Cooper's Ferry, 4 April, 1778.

ASHER CARTER, 1st Lieut. in Col. McElvain's Pennsylvania regiment. Commissioned, 6 May, 1777. Taken at Bristol, 17 April, 1778.

GODFREY MYERS, 2d Lieut. in Col. Baxter's Pennsylvania regiment. Commissioned, 9 July, 1776. Taken at Fort Washington, 16 November, 1776.

THOMAS WYN, 2d Lieut. in Col. Montgomery's Pennsylvania regiment. Commissioned, 27 August, 1776. Taken at Fort Washington, 16 November, 1776.

JOHN CRAWFORD, 2d Lieut. in Col. Watts' Pennsylvania regiment. Commissioned, 7 September, 1776. Taken at Fort Washington, 16 November, 1776.

WILLIAM YOUNG, 2d Lieut. in Col. McAllister's Pennsylvania regiment.   Commissioned, 18 September, 1776.   Taken at Fort Washington, 16 November, 1776.

EPHRAIM HUNTER, 2ᵈ Lieut. in Col. Watts' Pennsylvania regiment. Commissioned, 29 September, 1776.   Taken at Fort Washington, 16 November, 1776.

ANDREW LEE, 2ᵈ Lieut. in "Congress's Own." Commissioned, 3 November, 1776.   Taken on Staten Island, 22 August, 1777.

JAMES WINCHESTER, 2ᵈ Lieut. in the 2ᵈ Maryland regiment.   Commissioned, 10 April, 1777.   Taken on Staten Island, 22 August, 1777.

PHILLIP HILL, 2ᵈ Lieut. in the 2ᵈ Maryland regiment.   Commissioned, 17 April, 1777.   Taken on Staten Island, 22 August, 1777.

SEVERN TECKLE, 2ᵈ Lieut. in the 9ᵗʰ Virginia regiment.   Commissioned, 4 June, 1776.   Taken at Germantown, 4 October, 1777.

EBENEZER MOTT, 2ᵈ Lieut. in Col. Dubois's New York regiment. Commissioned, 21 November, 1776.   Taken at Fort Montgomery, 6 October, 1777.

LIBBEUS DREW, 2ᵈ Lieut. in Col. Shepherd's Massachusetts regiment. Commissioned, 1 January, 1777.   Taken at Derby, 28 December, 1777.

ISAAC SHYMER, Ensign in Col. Baxter's Pennsylvania regiment. Commissioned, 9 July, 1776.   Taken at Fort Washington, 16 November, 1776.

JACOB MUMMEY, Ensign in Col. Baxter's Pennsylvania regiment. Commissioned, 9 July, 1776.   Taken at Fort Washington, 16 November, 1776.

EZEKIEL HOPKINS, Ensign in Col. Montgomery's Pennsylvania regiment.   Commissioned, 27 August, 1776.   Taken at Fort Washington, 16 November, 1776.

WILLIAM RICHEY, Ensign in Col. Baxter's Pennsylvania regiment. Commissioned, 6 September, 1776.   Taken at Fort Washington, 16 November, 1776.

SAMˡ McELHATTEN, Ensign in Col. Watts' Pennsylvania regiment. Commissioned, 25 September, 1776.   Taken at Fort Washington, 16 November, 1776.

THOMAS ROUSE, Ensign in the 2ᵈ Maryland regiment.   Commissioned, 17 April, 1777.   Taken on Staten Island, 22 August, 1777.

NATHANˡ DARBY, Ensign in the 9ᵗʰ Virginia regiment.   Commissioned, 14 August, 1776.   Taken at Germantown, 4 October, 1777.

JOHN GREEN, Ensign in Col. McElvain's Pennsylvania regiment. Commissioned, 6 May, 1777.   Taken at Bristol, 17 April, 1778.

JOHN JOHNSTON, Adjutant in Col. Baxter's Pennsylvania regiment. Commissioned, 10 July, 1776.   Taken at Fort Washington, 16 November, 1776.

N'CH CARPENTER, Qʳ Master of Col. Dubois's New York regiment. Commissioned, 21 November, 1776.   Taken at Fort Montgomery, 6 October, 1777.

LAWRENCE MANNING, Serg^t Major in "Congress's Own." Taken on Staten Island, 22 August, 1777.

CHARLES WILSON, Volunteer in Col. McAllister's Pennsylvania regiment. Taken at Fort Washington, 16 November, 1776.

ROB^T RANKIN, 1st Lieut. in Col. Taylor's Pennsylvania regiment. Commissioned, 6 May, 1777. Taken out of his house, 14 September, 1777.

CORNELIUS VANTASSEL, 2^d Lieut. in Col. Hammond's New York regiment. Commissioned, 1 June, 1776. Taken out of his house, 17 November, 1777.

BENJAMIN WALTON, 1st Lieut. in Col. McVaugh's Pennsylvania regiment. Commissioned, 12 May, 1777. Taken out of his house, 14 February, 1778.

JOHN BLAKE, 1st Lieut. in Col. McVaugh's Pennsylvania regiment. Commissioned, 12 May, 1777. Taken out of his house, 14 February, 1778.

JOHN OSBURN, 1st Lieut. in Col. Eyre's Pennsylvania regiment. Commissioned, 13 September, 1777. Taken out of his house, 14 February, 1778.

ANDREW BARNS, citizen of Pennsylvania. Taken out of his house, 27 February, 1778.

JOHN HOWSON, citizen of Pennsylvania. Taken out of his house, 1st April, 1778.

JOEL WESTCOTT, citizen, volunteer, of Pennsylvania. Taken out of his house, 25 April, 1778.

JAMES JONES, second. Citizen of Pennsylvania. Taken out of his house, 23 February, 1778.

———

JOHN KEMP, Lieut. on Sloop Sachem, Pennsylvania. Commissioned, 24 March, 1777. Taken at sea, 5 April, 1777.

Wm COTTRELL, midshipman, of Virginia.[1]

A RETURN OF OFFICERS PRISONERS AT NEW LOTS
11 AUGUST, 1778.

THOMAS HOBBY, Lieut. Col. of Bradley's regiment. Commissioned 10 June, 1776. Taken [at Fort Washington],[2] 16 November, 1776.

TARLTON WOODSON, Major in Hazen's regiment [Congress's Own]. Commissioned, 20 May, 1777. Taken [on Staten Island], 22 August, 1777.

PETER PARRET, Captain in Col. Knox's regiment. Commissioned, 1 January, 1776. Taken [at Fort Washington], 16 November, 1776.

[1] These last two names have been stricken out, presumably because marine prisoners were not included in the rules of a cartel for a general exchange.
[2] This list does not state the place of capture, and I have added it in brackets where identified.

JOHN COUCH, Captain in Col. Bradley's regiment. Commissioned, 19 June, 1776. Taken [at Fort Washington], 16 November, 1776.

SAMUEL KEELER, 2ᵈ Captain in Col. Bradley's regiment. Commissioned, 10 June, 1776 (tho : comis" 20ᵗʰ of same month). Taken [at Fort Washington], 16 November, 1776.

LEMUEL HOLMES, Captain in Col. Knowlton's regiment. Commissioned, 1 September, 1776. Taken [at Fort Washington], 16 November, 1776.

SAMUEL GILBERT, Captain in Col. Prescot's regiment. Commissioned, 1 January, 1776. Taken, 7 December, 1776.

JOHN POULSON, Captain in 9ᵗʰ Virginia regiment. Commissioned, 17 July, 1776. Taken, 4 October, 1777.

WILLIAM CLEVELAND, 1ˢᵗ Lieutenant in Parsons's regiment. Commissioned, 10 December, 1776. Taken 15 September, 1776 (*sic*).

NATHANIEL EDWARDS, 1ˢᵗ Lieut. in Col. Bradley's regiment. Commissioned, 10 June, 1776. Taken [at Fort Washington], 16 November, 1776.

JESSE COOK, 1ˢᵗ Lieut. in Col. Bradley's regiment. Commissioned, 10 June, 1776. Taken [at Fort Washington], 16 November, 1776.

JOHN BLACKLEACH, 1ˢᵗ Lieut. in Col. Bradley's regiment. Commissioned, 10 June, 1776. Taken [at Fort Washington], 16 November, 1776.

JOSEPH BLAKE, 2ᵈ Lieut. in Knox's artillery regiment. Commissioned, 1 January, 1776. Taken [at Fort Washington], 16 November, 1776.

JESSE GRANT, 2ᵈ Lieut. in Col. Charles Webb's regiment. Commissioned, 1 January, 1776. Taken [at Fort Washington], 16 November, 1776.

JOSEPH MARTIN, 1ˢᵗ Lieut. in Col. Baxter's regiment. Commissioned, 9 July, 1776. Taken [at Fort Washington], 16 November, 1776.

ABNER EVERETT, 3ᵈ Lieut. in Col. Baxter's regiment. Commissioned, 9 July, 1776. Taken [at Fort Washington], 16 November, 1776.

LIEUT. STRATTON, 1ˢᵗ Lieut. in Col. Serjeant's regiment. Commissioned, 1 January, 1776. Taken, 7 December, 1776.

JONᵀᴴ HOLMES, 2ᵈ Lieut. in Col. Martin's regiment. Commissioned, 28 November, 1776. Taken, near Trenton, 2 January, 1777.

THOMAS COOK, Lieut. in Ferman's militia. Commissioned, 12 October, 1775. Taken, at Light House, 13 February, 1777.

CHARLES SNEAD, 1ˢᵗ Lieut. in the 9th Virginia regiment. Commissioned, 5 January, 1777. Taken [at Germantown], 4 October, 1777.

JAMES MORRIS, 1ˢᵗ Lieut. in Col. Bradley's regiment. Commissioned, 1 January, 1777. Taken [at Germantown], 4 October, 1777.

THOMAS PAYNE, 2ᵈ Lieut. in the 9ᵗʰ Virginia. Commissioned, 4 January, 1777. Taken [at Germantown], 4 October, 1777.

JOHN MASSIE, Lieut. in the 26ᵗʰ regiment of Maryland militia. Commissioned, 24 April, 1775. Taken [at Germantown], 4 October, 1777.

(To be continued.)

HAMILTON.

BY A. BOYD HAMILTON, HARRISBURG, PENNSYLVANIA.

This history of those who carried the name of Hamilton from Scotland to Ireland in the tumultuous days from 1585 to 1650, shows how important and numerous it was, proving, also, its high social position.   To gather what I have condensed into this brief sketch has taken many years and the examination of volumes not easily accessible in libraries, public or private.   I hope my descendants, particularly those of our family name, will value and preserve it.   It is evidence of a respectable and influential ancestry.   I have endeavored to avoid traditional reminiscences, and have not alluded to them, unless I had reasonable proof of their truthfulness.

In 1585 the emigration of Scots from the Lowlands to Ulster, Ireland, commenced, and for forty years "came," as a diarist of the time expresses it, "like a flood."   When the miserable tribal wars of the north of Ireland were terminated, about the time of the accession of James I. of England, the conquered land "was a devastated waste."   Surveyors, lawyers, speculators, adventurers, and commissioners came from England, authorized to occupy a tract of country almost as uncivilized as our present Indian territory.   It was determined to reclaim this territory by allotting out the land to "Servitors," nearly all Scots.

From 1606–12 the government offered "allotments," upon certain conditions of improvement, to these Servitors, who generally were Scotch nobility and gentry.   As a rule, these parcels contained acreage of good land and an uncertain area of "black land," the former about one thousand acres, the latter frequently ten times as much, made up of "fewes or woods," hills and bogs.

It is stated that nearly ten thousand Scots came to Ulster in these years, under this form of ownership.   The most numerous and respectable of this immigration bore the name of Hamilton. In the history of this remarkable transaction it is most frequently mentioned, and acquired a very large share of the forfeited lands. The head of one branch was James Hamilton, Lord Abercorn; another Hamilton, Lord of Endervick; another John Hamilton, also an Abercorn; this last the most thrifty of all the lords and sirs of the name. He erected "Hamilton Bawn" or fort, and resided there. At his death, many years after, he left forty thousand acres of "good" and as many more of "black" land and "fewes or woods" to his very large family of eleven children. He carried no title, being addressed as Esquire. He was "one of the big men of Ulster." It is possible he came from Crickness, in Scotland, and had a brother, Sir Claude. Three sons out of seven, whose names were John, James, and Robert, have come down to our times. His daughters married into noble families. His main residence was near the Blackwater River. Most of the Hamilton name who came to America between 1680 and 1750 are of this descent. John Hamilton, of "Hamilton Bawn," I have every reason to suppose, from record and tradition, was father of Robert, who was father of another John, who was father of James, who was father of John Hamilton, born 1704, married Isabella Potter in January, 1735, came to America on the ship "Donegal," landing at New Castle, Delaware, September, 1741, where his wife died. In 1748 he married his second wife, Jane Allen.[1] She was born in

---

[1] Descent of JANE ALLEN HAMILTON.

Admiral Thomas Allen—1638 : '40.
|
Robert Allen.
|
Commodore Thomas, 1713—Jane, 1715—Eliza, 1720—Mary, 1725.
|
m. John Hamilton (1st) 1748.
|
Capt. John Hamilton (2d) *m.* Margaret Alexander.
|
Hugh Hamilton *m.* Rosanna Boyd.
|
A. Boyd Hamilton *m.* Catharine L. Naudain.

1715, in Chester County, died in 1791, and is buried at Harrisburg.

Their only son, John, born 1749, died at Harrisburg 1793, and is buried there. Among the numerous Johns of his descendants, he is known as Captain John Hamilton, "of Fermanagh," now in Juniata County. His son Hugh was my father.

From various sources,—papers in possession of the family, tradition, and my own extensive research,—the descent from John Hamilton, of "Hamilton Bawn," is as follows :

1. John, of the Bawn, born 1585, emigrated 1608–10, died 1660, aged seventy-five years.
2. Robert, his son, born 1616, died 1680, aged sixty-four years.
3. John, his son, born 1645, died 1695, aged fifty years.
4. James, his son, born 1670, died 1716, aged forty-six years.
5. John, his son, born 1704, died 1755, aged fifty-one years.
6. John, his son, born 1749, died 1793, aged forty-four years.
7. Hugh, his son, born 1785, died 1836, aged fifty-one years.

The Hamilton migration previously to 1620 consisted of the following heads of families :

Sir Claude, of Endervick.
John, " of the Bawn."
James, of Keckton.
George,—two of this name, cousins.
Robert, son of the Duke of Hamilton.
Sir Alexander.
John, Lord of Arran.
Francis, son of Claude.
Francis, "son of the Duke."
Gordon, Lord Aberdeen.
Margaret, of Litterkinney.
Eliza, of Cavan.
Frederick, son of George, 1619.
William.
Sir Archibald, of Edmeston, 1686.
James, ancestor of the present Duke of Abercorn.

Seventeen large families of this name, with servants and farm stock. Claude and the two Georges had, 1613, thirty-two houses, "many horses, 300 cows, with stock to match," and "2000 acres in process of improvement."

With this flood "by the name of Hamilton" came several bearing the name of Boyd, of the family of Kilmarnock, among them an Adam Boyd, whose son Adam, thirty years after, was a "Captain of horse, under King Charles I."

I have also ascertained that in 1733 the Rev. Baptist Boyd, who married John Hamilton and Isabella Potter, lived at Aghalow, or Agaloe, in county Tyrone, near the waters of the Foyle.

Rev. Mr. Boyd married John Potter to Sarah ———. Captain Potter was first sheriff of Cumberland County, and ancestor of the Potters, Greggs, and Curtins of Centre County.   John Hamilton 1st and John Potter were brothers-in-law, and came to America together.

Rev. Mr. Boyd also married Colonel Adam Reed, in 1734, to Catharine Wood.   They came to the "big bend of the Swatara" about 1740; Reed was the important man of this part of the Kittatinny Valley.   One of his daughters married John Harris, of Harris Ferry; another, Robert Whitehill, of Cumberland County.

Archibald Edmeston Hamilton, in 1636, married Jane, daughter of Archibald Hamilton.   This connection, or a remarkable similarity of names, is preserved in the family of John Hamilton 3d, of Juniata, a grandson of John Hamilton 1st and Jane Allen.   John 3d married an Edmeston. His son Hugh 2d a lady of the same race.

The family of Isabella Potter, who married John Hamilton, was an only daughter, Katharine Hamilton, who married, in 1760, Colonel James Chambers, of Franklin County. She was half-sister to John Hamilton 2d; died at "Ludlow Station," now Cincinnati, January 14, 1820, aged eighty-two years.   Had name Chambers : Sarah Bella, Ruhamah, Charlotte, Benjamin Chambers.

Sarah Bella Chambers married Andrew Dunlop, of Chambersburg; second, Archibald McAllister, of Fort Hunter, Dauphin County, Pennsylvania; first marriage issue name Dunlop.   No family by second marriage.

Ruhamah Chambers married Dr. Thomas Scott; issue name Scott.

Charlotte Chambers married Israel Ludlow; issue name Ludlow. Second, David Riske; issue name Riske.

Benjamin Chambers, an ensign when fifteen years of age, married ―――― Penn, of St. Louis. He resided, in 1827, near Saline, Missouri; issue four sons and two daughters. He died about 1835, aged seventy-five years, and I infer from a comparison of dates that he was the eldest child of General Chambers.

In 1874 the number of living grandchildren of General and Mrs. Hamilton-Chambers was seventeen, all residing west of Pennsylvania.

See "Hamilton Record," 1874.

―――――――

Jane Allen, second wife of John Hamilton, son of James, had an only child, John Hamilton, of Fermanagh, who married Margaret Alexander, daughter of Hon. Hugh Alexander, of Shearman Valley, December, 1772. Her descent, children and grandchildren:

1660. Thomas Alexander, Glasgow.
1700. John Alexander.
1724. Hugh Alexander.
1754. Margaret Alexander.
1785. Hugh Hamilton.
1808. A. Boyd Hamilton.

The children of John and Margaret Hamilton were:

Jane, who married General John Kean.
Martha, who married James Alricks, Esq.
John (or 3d), who married Francesca Blair Edmeston.
Hugh, who married Rosanna Boyd.
Margaret, who married Moses Maclean, Esq.
Catharine Allen, who married General Jacob Spangler, of York.

They had a family of eight children; two died young. Their daughter Jane had five, Martha seven, John nine, Hugh nine, Margaret three, Catharine six,—in all of the first and second generation, fifty-seven; an average age at death of about fifty years. The family of Jane became extinct in 1885.

Before entering into family details it is proper to preserve the following incident in the life of Captain John Hamilton to show how greatly he was respected when only twenty-five years of age, and how active and earnest he was before the Revolution in sustaining the efforts made to obtain independence.

Subscriptions "in aid of the suffering brethren in Boston" were made in Fermanagh Township, Cumberland County, Pennsylvania, in the year 1774, and forwarded to the "Boston committee" by Captain Hamilton. The farmers of the Juniata Valley appear to have opened their purses for the "pore of Boston" in a very cheerful and liberal manner. In money they were very poor, in patriotism and charity very rich. All that is known of the contributors of this particular section is the following, collected from the Hamilton papers: John Hamilton, Sylvester Moss, John Martin, William Stewart, James Riddell, Samuel Tennis, John Tennis, William Riddell, William Ray, Samuel Ramsey, Arthur Cunningham, Joseph Leech, James Williams, James McKim, James Crampton, John Kiplar, Michael Quigle, John Martin, James Gallagher, Charles Cunningham.

Most of these names are found upon the day-books of Mr. Hamilton, on the assessment rolls, and as soldiers under his command in 1776–78. The amount of money contributed by these gentlemen was about seven pounds Pennsylvania currency. The largest subscriptions were by John Hamilton and William Stewart, ten shillings each. A pound was $2.66.6 : 7*s.* 6*d.* to the pound.

I now present a sketch of the active life of Captain John Hamilton. The simple narration of his possessions in real and personal property is sufficient evidence of an intelligent and prosperous man who had great capacity for affairs. In his books of account the penmanship is uniform and clear, his orthography excellent. Indeed, his whole career can be traced with great exactness, including his military services, for the twenty years of his short life ; he was only forty-four years of age when he died. He was a pure and excellent gentleman, whose character was formed in the toilsome surroundings of a frontier residence, and has come to his descendants without a stain upon it. All persons with any pride love to know of their forefathers, and none more than those whose ancestors assisted in council or in arms to compact the elements which have given us our present system of personal and political freedom. The great landholder of Ulster was followed by worthy successors that seem to have inherited a passion for land from the Scot, the owner of so many acres of good and bad land, mead and moor, in Tyrone, Fermanagh, and Donegal Counties, of Ulster.

About 1754 John Hamilton 1st, of Chester County, purchased one hundred and fifty acres, with a saw-mill, in "Toboine," now Perry County, situated on Muddy Run, an affluent of Shearman Creek ; also a fulling-mill. He willed this to John Hamilton 2d, of Fermanagh. An equal share of his property was left to his other child, Katharine Hamilton, wife of General James Chambers. These were his only heirs.

In 1766 John 2d, but seventeen years of age, his guardian, or his mother, Jane Hamilton, purchased " about 210 acres in Toboine."

In 1768 the same parties purchased a mill and land on Cocalamus, "across the Juniata."

In 1769, when nearly twenty-one years of age, he purchased " a farm in Toboine," now Madison Township, Perry County,—the present Loysville,—of three hundred and fifty acres. Nicholas Loy purchased one hundred and forty-nine acres of this tract after his death.

In 1770 he purchased a distillery " on Cocalamus."

In 1771 he purchased five hundred acres in Juniata County, and erected a mansion-house, yet standing. He called it " Fermanagh," and its owner was thereafter known as John Hamilton, of " Fermanagh," to distinguish him from other John Hamiltons in Tuscarora Valley and Armagh Township. Here he had the greatest general store in all the region for thirty miles. From his account-books before me I learn how extensive and diversified his business was from 1771 to the time of his removal to Harrisburg in 1785—86. His grandson, Hugh 2d, is the present owner of part of this beautiful estate of "Fermanagh," and has his residence here. He has many other papers of my grandfather's estate.

In 1780 he purchased "Oakland," of two hundred acres, on Lost Creek, where he had previously erected a saw-mill, and as soon as possible after this purchase he built a grist-mill.

Hugh Alexander, the father-in-law of John Hamilton 2d, purchased, February 3, 1755, three hundred and forty-four acres of land in Toboine. At the death of Mr. Alexander, in February, 1778, Mr. Hamilton took it all, as well as the land of David Edmeston, adjoining, purchased in 1766, comprising three hundred acres. His plantation was supposed to be seven hundred acres. A survey after his death makes it six hundred and fifty-two acres, which fell to my father, Hugh Hamilton, of Harrisburg, as well as four hundred acres of David Edmeston,—in all, about eleven hundred acres.

In 1789 John Hamilton purchased the Galbraith land, one hundred and twenty-five acres, where the present State Hospital is erected; also one hundred and fifteen acres of what was left of "Penn's Manor of Paxton." This covered from the creek to the Susquehanna, comprising part of the Sixth and Seventh Wards of Harrisburg, and some land above in the present Susquehanna Township.

In 1785 he purchased Lot No. 21 of John Harris, on Front Street, west corner of Blackberry Alley, and in 1789, of John Carson, the lot southeast corner of Market Square and Market Street, erecting the first brick houses in the new town of Harrisburg. Among the family papers is the following, showing the valuation and apportionment of this estate :

"Memoranda of the appraisement of different tracts of

land in the counties of Mifflin, Cumberland, and Dauphin, belonging to the estate of John Hamilton, late of Harrisburg, deceased,—viz., 1793-94.

First—Alricks: Two tracts on Lost creek, Mifflin county, supposed to contain 188 acres, including a grist and saw mill now in the possession of James Alricks . . . £1,200

Second—John Hamilton: The old place, 'Fermanagh,' in the possession of William Wray, supposed to contain about 498 acres and allowance 2,300

Third—Alricks: A small improvement right near Thompson's Town, supposed to contain about 60 acres . . . 15

Fourth—Alricks: A tract on Cocalamus creek, including an old saw mill adjoining lands of David Boies and one Fry, supposed to contain about 270 acres and allowance, value in Mifflin 375

Value in Mifflin county . . £3,890

Fifth—H. Hamilton: A tract of land in Cumberland county, adjoining lands of Henry Cunningham and George Robinson, Esq., containing about 344½ acres and allowance . 1,722.10

Sixth—H. Hamilton: Two tracts of land in said county, surveyed in Rt. of John Hamilton and Hugh Alexander, adjoining the last mentioned tracts, containing in the whole about 805 acres and allowance 286

Seventh—H. Hamilton: An improved right in said county, adjoining lands of the Rev. Mr. Linn, supposed to contain about 54 acres, and said to be surveyed on a warrant . . 75

Eighth—H. Hamilton: A tract in said county, surveyed in right of D. Edmeston, adjoining H. Alexander on the southwest, and said to contain about 400 acres 150

Value in Cumberland county £2,233.10

Ninth—Kean: A tract of land in Dauphin county, adjoining lands of John Forster and others, on the east side of Paxton creek, containing 240 acres 3,720

Tenth—J. Hamilton: A lot of land on Susquehanna river, containing about 40 acres, neat measure 1,000

Eleventh—Kean: A three story brick house, corner of Second and Market streets 1,100

Twelfth—Kean: Another three story brick house, adjoining the latter 760

Thirteenth—J. Hamilton: A house and full lot of ground on the Bank corner of Blackberry alley 1,140

Value in Dauphin county . £7,720

Mifflin .	.	£8,890. 0. 0.
Cumberland .		2,238. 10. 0.
Dauphin	.	7,720. 0. 0.
		£18,843. 10. 0."

Personal property of all kinds, exclusive of slaves, £7000.
John, of Fermanagh, was taxed for a slave in 1775; in
1778 for two, no rate or amount given; in 1781 for

two, value	£23 or $62.00
1785, for 2 slaves, value	55 or 147.00
1810, for 8 " "	50
1813, for 8 " "	100 or 266.67
1817, for 3 " "	75
1822, for 8 " "	50

The last four rates upon this personalty disappeared after
1823, but some of these slaves resided with John 3d, of
Fermanagh, until 1830. One man of them became a prosperous farmer in Northern Ohio. I played with the young-
sters of this happy family in my early youth, and well
remember the fun we had.

MEXICAN WAR BATTLE-FLAGS PRESENTED TO THE HISTORICAL SOCIETY OF PENNSYLVANIA.

On the afternoon of April 18, 1893, the forty-sixth an-niversary of the battle of Cerro Gordo, the Mexican war veterans of the "Scott Legion," of Philadelphia, presented to the Historical Society of Pennsylvania the two flags given to the First and Second Regiments of Pennsylvania Volun-teers by General Scott, in the City of Mexico, for gallantry upon the battle-field. In addition to the officers and mem-bers of the Legion, who were accompanied by their families, there were present ex-Governor Andrew G. Curtin, Mayor Edwin S. Stuart, General William Farrar Smith, General Lewis Merrill, Dr. Edward Shippen, U.S.N., James S. Bid-dle, and descendants of General Robert Patterson. Letters of regret were received from Governor Robert E. Pattison, Professor Henry Coppée, General D. McM. Gregg, General W. W. H. Davis, Mr. P. S. P. Connor, and others.

The meeting being called to order by President Stillé of the Historical Society, he introduced Captain George L. Rilman, of the Legion, who said,—

Mr. President and Members of the Historical Society,—As Chairman of the Committee who were appointed to secure a perma-nent depository for our flags, where they would be preserved to future generations, I desire to make a few introductory remarks. In the autumn of 1846 the President of the United States called on the Governor of Pennsylvania for two regiments of volunteer infantry to serve for three years or the war. They were promptly organized and accepted. Strange though it may seem, we were allowed to depart for the seat of war with-out a stand of colors. While *en route* from New Orleans to Vera Cruz, Captain William F. Small, of Company C, First Regiment, caused to be made from such material as was found on board the ship, that crude representation of our State flag [pointing to the flag], which we carried on our march and in all the battles between Vera Cruz and the City of Mexico. Not long after the capture of the ancient capital of the Mon-tezumas, General Scott presented to us, as a token of his appreciation of our gallantry upon the battle-field, two beautiful flags, which we are to present you to-day.   They were made in Mexico.   Within these walls, where our old commander, General Patterson, lived and died, we think it most fitting that our flags, which we have so long cherished, should find their home.   And now, sirs, on behalf of the Scott Legion, I call on Comrade John Dolman to formally present them to you.

John Dolman, Esq., thereupon made the formal presentation in the following eloquent address :

MR. PRESIDENT OF THE HISTORICAL SOCIETY OF PENNSYLVANIA, —Forty-six years ago to-day, amid the thunder of artillery and the smoke and blood of battle, a small American army was storming the rocky heights of Cerro Gordo, defended, and bravely defended, by a much larger force of the flower of the Mexican army.

The American army was so small as to excite surprise, and at first the ridicule of other nations at venturing into a hostile country with so insignificant a force.

But it was an army the history of whose victorious progress from the Gulf to Mexico's capital reads like a tale out of the " Arabian Nights."

On the 15th day of September, 1847, a force of only about six thousand men, as victors, entered that capital, containing a population of about two hundred and fifty thousand, and whose supposed impregnable approaches were guarded by an army of about twenty-five thousand soldiers.

The details of that brilliant campaign are a part of our common school history, and perhaps the most fascinating part of it to the American youth.   The conquest of Mexico by Cortez, about which history has thrown such a halo of romantic admiration, was a dress parade in comparison.   Cortez led a trained band of mounted warriors, with fire-arms and clad in steel.   The bows and arrows and reed lances of the half-naked Aztecs offered them but slight resistance.   The American army fought every foot of ground from Vera Cruz to Mexico with a brave, well-armed force, inured to the climate, familiar with the country, and commanded by a famous military genius, Santa Anna, " *the one-legged Mephistopheles*," as he was called, yet never suffered a single defeat. Cortez and his followers left a track of devastation and ruin behind them wherever they passed.   The smoke of burned homes and the groans of tortured aborigines who would not disclose their hidden treasures ascended unto heaven.   The American army struck the people of Mexico with astonishment at rigidly respecting private property and paying full prices for all provisions and supplies used.

And as we recall one by one the names of those heroes who led that devoted band, their martial forms and well-loved features, indelibly stamped upon the hearts of those who followed them, rise up before our mental visions, and through the dim vista of nearly half a century call

up the memory of such strange and thrilling scenes as seem now like a far-off romantic dream of youth.

Riding at the head in chief command was the grand and magnificent Winfield Scott, like Saul, the leader of Israel, towering above the heads of all his army with his six feet four inches, and every inch a soldier.

It was in that City of Mexico, while our beautiful flag was floating in victory from its capitol, on the plaza in front of the site of the ancient halls of Montezuma, that General Winfield Scott with his own hands bestowed these two flags upon the First and Second Pennsylvania Regiments, as a token of his appreciation of their gallantry upon the field of battle.

These flags have been cherished and preserved as sacred relics by us, the survivors of the Mexican war, organized under the name of the "Scott Legion," ever since. We glory in them as reminders not only of the victories of the campaign, but as reminders to all the citizens of our Commonwealth of the only war of foreign invasion in the history of our country.

In some particulars the war with Mexico was unique. It is an old and true adage that war is costly and ruinous to both victor and vanquished. But the Mexican war was a great exception, and repaid its cost more than a hundred-fold. The territory ceded by Mexico to the United States at that time was greater than all of the original thirteen States. And what a territory it was! How blessed by nature in wealth of mines, wealth of soil, and wealth of climate! California, Utah, Arizona, Nevada, New Mexico, Colorado; San Francisco, the empress of the Pacific, sitting upon her throne of gold, encompassed with luscious fruits and yellow grain.

The whole cost of the Mexican war to the American government was about sixty million dollars. Between two and three thousand million dollars in gold and silver alone have been taken from the mines of that territory, and the port of San Francisco pays into the United States Treasury in customs duties the whole cost of the Mexican war every five years.

But sadness comes upon us naturally when we consider that most of those who participated in those trying scenes are gone,—gone to answer the great roll-call above, where the savage throat of war is forever silenced in the presence of the Prince of Peace. But few there be that remain, and they are fallen into the sere and yellow leaf. We feel that the time cannot be far distant when the last survivor shall pass away, and fully appreciating that fact, the Scott Legion of Philadelphia desires to resign the further care and custody of these precious relics into the hands of some public body, which, while to some extent representing our great Commonwealth, at the same time especially cares for whatever keeps the memory of her greatness fresh in the hearts of her children.

It was but natural that our choice should turn to you, the Historical Society of Pennsylvania, instituted as you are for that express purpose. Therefore we, the survivors of the Mexican war, beg you to accept and receive from our hands the future care and custody of these beautiful gifts from the hands of our country's military chief. These reminders of Pennsylvania's gallant part in a war, not for conquest, but in vindication of that great principle that "governments derive their just powers from the consent of the governed."

At the conclusion of Mr. Dolman's address President Stillé accepted the flags on behalf of the Historical Society, and said,—

SOLDIERS OF THE SCOTT LEGION!—In the name and on behalf of the Historical Society I accept the guardianship and care of these precious mementos of your patriotism and valor. In other countries when flags have done their duty, and the victory which they inspired has been won, they are suspended beneath the arches of some venerable cathedral, where as long as a shred of their glorious tatters remains they serve as an example to the living of all virtue, and as a memorial of the dead who have died in their defence. Here we have no "long-drawn aisles" in which to hang these emblems of your courage and devotion to your country, but we shall give them a home in a building long the residence of one of your foremost generals, and made still more fitting as a repository because here on the 13th of September anniversary (of the capture of the City of Mexico) for many years the most illustrious officers of the Mexican war met to recall the scenes of the past and to renew their fellowship.

The importance of the Mexican war in the general history of the country is not always understood. It seems to me that it ought to be recognized as the most far-reaching event in that history, except the war of the rebellion. It is a singular fact that twice at least in the history of the world its fate has been decided by battles in the valley of Mexico. As I stood on the tower of the cathedral of that city and overlooked the vast prospect lying before me, of unsurpassed grandeur and beauty, I could not help feeling that the capture of the City of Mexico by Cortez was the means by which Philip II. of Spain was supplied with the gold which enabled him to band together the Catholic powers of Europe and to equip that "Invincible Armada" which was to destroy the supremacy of England as a Protestant power. And so, when my imagination summoned before me General Scott and his heroic legions besieging that city, I thought less of their valor in their assaults on Chapultepec, on Molinos del Rey, on the city gates of San Cosme and Belem, transcendent as that valor was, than I did of the imperial domain which was added to our country by the victories of that little band ; of California and its gold ; of the whole face of the world and all the conditions of modern society changed by the discovery of the new Pactolus, a stream which was to fertilize this country and the world with a wealth of which Crœsus had never dreamed.

What can I say in the way of recognition and thankfulness for the discipline and bravery by which you were enabled to accomplish such vast results? I have explored every accessible portion of the hill of Chapultepec with increasing wonder, at a loss to understand how the bravest of the brave forced their way to the fortress on its summit. I have stood on the spot where the brave Twiggs met his death, wondering again why all his comrades did not meet the same fate as he. I have explored the deadly pass at Molinos del Rey, where more than four hundred of your comrades were slain. I have wandered through the streets of Puebla, and while my soul has been filled with glorious recollections of the defence of that place for more than a month against thousands of Mexicans by a garrison composed chiefly of five companies of the First Pennsylvania Regiment, I was, as I think I had reason to be, proud of being a Pennsylvanian.

Soldiers of the Mexican war! do not think your country is ungrateful or that it is forgetful of your prowess; believe me that as time goes on, and the vast benefits which you have conferred upon that country become more clearly understood, your trials and your labors will be more fully appreciated, and even if your names are forgotten, the deeds which you have done can never die. Your memory will be kept alive by that universal instinct of mankind which forces us to honor the brave, and by the gratitude which millions of hearts must feel for those by whose sufferings and by whose blood the blessings of the peaceful homes which they now enjoy were purchased.

Believe me, your countrymen do love, at least at times, something more than the gold your valor has secured to them in such abundance.

After the interesting ceremonies were closed the persons present viewed the flags, which had been repaired and appropriately draped and put in a walnut case.

COLONEL CHARLES READ.

BY J. GRANVILLE LEACH.

Among those distinguished in the colonial history of New Jersey was Colonel Charles Read, collector of the port of Burlington, mayor of that place, a justice of the Supreme Court, and sometime chief-justice of the Province, many years secretary to the Provincial Council, and a colonel in the service of New Jersey prior to the Revolution, and one of the founders of the American Philosophical Society.

Some writers have erroneously supposed him to be the Charles Read who, in July, 1776, was commissioned colonel of a battalion of the Flying Camp, in New Jersey, and in December following took British protection (see " Keith's Provincial Councillors" and " Appleton's Cyclopædia of American Biography"), which error the writer is now able to correct, having been privileged to read recently, through the kindness of Aaron Leaming, Esq., of Cape May, the manuscript journal of his great-grandfather, the Hon. Aaron Leaming, who was a contemporary of Colonel Read, and prominent in public life in New Jersey, long a member of the Assembly, and quite famed as a diarist. Under date November 14, 1775, his journal gives the following graphic character-picture, by which it is shown that Read died in 1774 :

" When I was in Burlington Jacob Read informed me that his father the Honourable Charles Read Esq'. died the 27ᵗʰ of December 1774 at Martinburg on Tar River 20 miles back of Bath town in North Carolina where he had kept a small shop of goods for some time.

" He was born in Philadelphia about 1718. He was the son of Charles Read a merchant and sometimes mayor of Philadelphia an active and ruling man by his wife Anne Bond.

" Charles had his education under Alexander Annard

who taught him the Latin, and he was near 20 when he left that school.

" About 1786 his father sent him to London where he was patronized by Sir Charles Wager one of the Lords of the admirality and said to be a relation.

" Sir Charles made him a midshipman on board the Penzance man of war of 20 guns, and his father made him remitances to support him in that rank. The Penzance sailed for the West Indies : But Charles not having been bred to sea, but used to the Philadelphia luxuries and tasted the pleasures of London that life did not suit him. Beside there was a war approaching and Charles had not been used to that Boisterous romantic honour that characterizes the seaman.

" About 1787 or 1788 Charles sold out and married the daughter of a rich planter on Antiagua. She was very much of a creole, not hansom, nor gentele but talked after the creole accent. Charles at that time passed for a rising genteel young fellow the son of a very rich merchant and eminent grandee in Philadelphia. But its probable that Charles' father might have trusted him with the secret of his affairs for his father died about the time of this marriage. Its said his estate was £7000 worse than ever with the world & Charles had very soon the intelligence. Its supposed he knew it before he married. Charles however kept all that a secret and soon came over with his bride to take possession of his supposed estate. When he came away his father-in-law ordered the negroes to rool him out 87 Hogsheads of rum and had many more consigned to him : So that he made his appearance in Philadelphia in quality of a rich marchant. He made the best use of all this. But determined to enter upon the state for which nature seemed to have designed him.

" About 1789 he bought the Clerk's office of Burlington of Peter Bard & moved to that town. Soon after the Collector's office of the Port of Burlington being vacant Sir Charles Wager gave him that with a sallary of £60 per annum.

"About 1740 he got the office of Clerk of the Circuits. This was given him by Robert Morris then Chief Justice.

"He now made his appearance in the world in his own proper character. He had more vices than virtues, he had many of both and those of the high rank. He was intriegueing to the highest degree. No man knew so well as he how to riggle himself into office nor keep it so long nor make so much of it.

"From 1747 to about 1771 he had the almost absolute rule of Governor, Council and Assembly in New Jersey except during the short ministration of Mr Boone who was Governor without a prime minister. I have known the Governor & Council to do things against their inclinations to please him and the Assembly have often done so. He seemed to be their leader. During that time he took the whole disposal of all offices. He little consulted the merits of the person he preferred; the sole object was whether it suited his party principles. His intrigues with women, tho' they employed a large share of his thought were not worth naming, they were rather the foibles than the vices in so large a character yet because I know he would never have pardoned the man that should attempt his story without making honourable mention of them I draw them into his shade. He was so vain of them that if he had penned this character they would have filled many pages.

"On the death of Mr Arch^d Home he procured the Deputy Secretary office in about 1743. He then commenced attorney at Law and had the best run of practice of any attorney in my time. He was sometimes 3^d and sometime 2^d chief justice of the Supreme Court. His greatest virtues were found among his vices. His offices furnished him with a constant flow of cash. This power and flow of cash enlarged his mind above himself. Instead of founding a fortune to his two sons as he ought to have done in those prosperous times, he ran upon schemes for the improvement of the country, witness his Fishery at Lamberton, his Iron Works and many other schemes which tho' virtuous in a very high degree in a man of great fortune, it ought to be treated with distrust with men of little estates. He was industrious in the most unremitting degree. No man planned a scheme so well as he nor executed them better. He loved the country better than his family. And knew no friend but the man that could serve him.

"He never embraced any of the sectaries; but always joined the Quakers in party except that it interfered with his politics and then he made them bow. They contributed largely towards his [rise] and he supported them, but it was with a high and prominent hand, taking to himself the mastery.

"His airs and action was much after the french manner, ever on the wing & fluttering never long fixed frequently courting, frequently whispering as if to make the person believe they were in his confidence a little too severe in enmity and not grateful for good offices high strung and selfish unwilling to forgive an injury not very faithful to his client's cause, a better judge than Lawyer. Upright as a Judge. A fine memory, understood the law well, spoke very well off hand but short and to the purpose, not capable of arranging and delivering a long train of Ideas, nor of replying and mending his first essay, either in speech or writing. Timorous almost to cowardice, whimsical to the borders of insanity, which he inherited maternally, and was sometimes perceived to be of unsettled mind especially for some years before his death.

"He was several years a member of the house for Burlington & Speaker and afterwards one of the Council which last however did not add much to his influence in council for he was Secretary here before and did most of the State business and of course did it in his own way, partly because the Governor and council were ignorant and partly from his" . . .

This interesting biography here abruptly closes, the remaining leaves of the valuable document having been worn away by the hand of time, and unfortunately so, since they no doubt would have revealed the cause which led a man of such high attainments and commanding influence to leave his favorable environment in Burlington to keep a "small shop of goods" in what was then but little more than a wilderness in North Carolina.

The Colonel Read of the Flying Camp who accepted the protection of the British was Charles Read, a son of the above, and in 1776 was chosen colonel of the second regiment raised in the county for the defence of the Province. He died November 20, 1788.

The elder colonel was the eldest son of Hon. Charles Read, who served in the offices of councilman, alderman, mayor of Philadelphia, justice of the peace, and sheriff of the county, trustee of the Loan Office, judge of the Admiralty, and provincial councillor of Pennsylvania, and the grandson of Charles Read, a member of the Colonial Assembly, and one of the first aldermen of the city under Penn's charter of 1701.

James Read, brother of the elder colonel, was a distinguished lawyer; the first prothonotary, register of wills, and clerk of the courts of Berks County; served in the General Assembly and Supreme Executive Council of Pennsylvania, and from 1771 to 1783 was register of the Admiralty.

Miss Read, who became the wife of Benjamin Franklin, was a relative of Hon. Charles Read, mayor of Philadelphia.

LETTER OF THOMAS MATHEWS TO GEORGE FOX, 1683.

[Thomas Mathews was a son of Richard Mathews, of Stoke Newington, in the county of Middlesex, England. He came to the Province of West Jersey with his sister Hannah (who in 1684 was married to Thomas Gardner, Jr., at Burlington), and settled on a tract of land near Woodbury Creek, which had been conveyed to him by his father. In 1684 Edward Byllynge appointed him his attorney to dispose of thirty shares of propriety of West Jersey, and in 1685 he was returned as one of the members of the Legislature from the Fourth Tenth. He died about 1702, and his landed estate passed to his sister. The letter which we print is addressed, "For George Fox in London or Elſe where. Leaue this at Frances Plumſteds Ironmonger at yᵉ Croſs hanſawes in the minneres [Minories] London." It is also endorsed, "Thoˢ Mathews Letter to G. F. 11 4ᵗʰ Mᵒ : 88. About Tenths in W. J. & diviſion of Lands &c."]

Weſt new Jarzey in America
Burlinton yᵉ 11ᵗʰ of yᵉ 4ᵗʰ mo 1683

Drare George

Hauing this oportunity by John Bartlit I wos willing to aquaint thee with ſom of yᵉ affers of this Prouince sopoiſing there will bee neede of thy help to moderate & ſettell things heare which are at preſent But unſtable in Relation to Common affares : I beeleive thou knowes heretofore how things haue Bin that thoˢ : oliue [Thomas Olive] & moſt of thoſe that Came with him mett with diſapointments bauing there Goods ſeaſed for Custom by new york Gouerment with other trubles which I had from his mouth that thay waire upon yᵉ point of quiting yᵉ place & Goe into ſom other Cuntry now ſince that Edward Byllyng with yᵉ aſiſtance of his friends hath Gott yᵉ dukes Confermation : yᵉ Grate doubte is heare amongſt them whather bee will nott Impoiſe himſelf Gouerners ouer ouer them Louking upon it that thay haue bought both Land & Gouerment this is yᵉ mind of moſt of them others of them ſay thay bought yᵉ Gouerment but of 2 tenthes that is yᵉ york & London tenth ſo that at this Rate wee ſhall haue variaty of Gouerments : this would

bee of an ill Confequance But oure Eye is to God: now
Samuell Jenings & thay Rule all y⁰ Cuntry & Clame y⁰
Gouerment of all hee is a man moſt Rafalute in whot hee
takes too & Immouable & his maxim is to fplit a hare in
Gouerning & keeps up y⁰ Lettere of y⁰ Law to its hight
which has acaifened fom Inconueniances in y⁰ adminiftera-
tion thereof—y⁰ Late afsemly begun y⁰ 10ᵗʰ of y⁰ 8ᵈ mo Laſt
& contenued with fom deffeculty by refon of y⁰ salem men
about 2 weeks: but fo it fell out that y⁰ Laſt day of y⁰ afsemly wos on a 7ᵗʰ day whereon thay had pafsed a unanimus
uote that no more propofitions peterions or other matters
fhould bee offerd or brought in but to finish and Conclude
whot thay had don or maid Rady y⁰ 2ᵈ day folloing but fee
how it happened william Pen that 7ᵗʰ day about twlue at
night with John Fenwick & 5 or 6 more Came from Philla-
delpha in fuch a night of Raine that I haue neuer or sell-
dom feene y⁰ Like y⁰ Refon wos fopofd to bee to Gatt heare
befoure all wos Ended: for hee wos detand till then with
buifsines about y⁰ Lord Balltemore who is a futtle man & to
this day Giues him y⁰ Goe by faing hee will talke with him
a twlue-month hence—thus on y⁰ 2ᵈ day things ware fott on
fott againe & wos maid a day of Conferance where many
queſstens waire put to y⁰ uote—humly propofed by w: P &
John Fenwick who know uery well how to tune there In-
ſtrument to fute y⁰ hearers) George I wos Greeud & ſtill
am without perfhalaty neuer man wos more minſt & Run
downe then E: B not beeing there to fpake for himfelf
& ould dirt throne upon him by w: P: in y⁰ face of y⁰
afemly & others to y⁰ truble of seauerall & himself Loft byte
ground for John Fenwicks Rediculos behauer its not worth
y⁰ menshining squefing of his hat of 40 times Referuing to
hisfelf his Lordfbip of Right in Gouerment & yett wos one
of y⁰ afsemly men—y⁰ matters propofd ware many as
whather y⁰ Gouerment wos not purchafed togather with y⁰
Land: whather y⁰ firſt Consefions ware not to ſtand Good:
& whather y⁰ truftees ware not ſtill oblegied to ſtand by y⁰
peeple to fee them fettled in there Rights with many other
all which ware Caried in y⁰ affermatiue & Concluded with

that ould ftory of nemenycontradecente [*nemine contradicente*]
& Recorded & fo to y° Choice of a gouerner for y° years In-
feuing which wos Samuell Jenings being one that fo Radely
Complyd with them: onely heare Lyes y° knack which I
fopofe thay did not well perceiue: which wos his Com-
mifhon from Edward Byllyng Rouled by them as oute of
date but yett uncald for out of his hand fo that hee may
yett faiue his Cradit & part of his truft in not throing that
up & thus in fted of an honeft Condefending Compliance
in y° fimplefsity of truth here is bending of wits to fett that
ould Refoner a work that can nether truft God nor man
As to y° Countrey proceedings about Land there way is this
from y° falls which is about 12 miles aboue burlinton to y°
fea is about a 150 miles this deuided into 10 parts are called
tenths ye upermoft downe to burlinton is y° yorkshire or
firft tenth from burlinton 12 miles Lower is y° London or 2ᵈ
tenth from thence 12 miles Lower is y° Irifh or 3ᵈ tenth &
fo dowward to y° Cape for this tract of Land in Euery 10ᵗʰ
there are commis apointed to Giue out warans to any that
brings there his deeds & names his tenth hee Goes to pick
& chufe where hee Likes baft thus thay hauing proceded
themfelues Cannot do Less then Giue y° fame Liberty to
others notwithftanding this will bee to y° damage of E: B
or thofe that fhall bye Laft of him fo after my ariuell I
fhewde to Samuell Jenings & y° Commisheners the Letter
of aturny Giuen mee by Edward Byllyng for y° taking up
of a Confiderable quantite of Land for himfelf Gowing
Lowry & others as John Hind a Gouldfmith &: c: then
affter fom time I Gott a warane of y° Clark of y° Prouince
& had it figned by fix of y° Commifhiners aforefaid who at
y° fame time had deliberated upon it & wos all fo approued
by Samuell Jenings.

Thus thinking myfelf furnifhed for y° performence of my
truft I proceded in y° fouth & difcouery of y° Cuntry Reuers
& Cricks aboue a hundred miles downe y° Grat Reuer into
y° bay & fo at fertain times for new [now] fiue months from
place to place with Extreme hardfhip & hard Laber day &
night fare from any hous or habitation a tafk that I did not

well fourefee but when once undertaken I had a feale to
performe it there are many Exalent Crick or Rather Reuer
that Runes far into yᵉ Cuntry sofefiant to Carry up fhips of
Confiderable burden in many of thefe are few or no Inhab-
itance but upon yᵉ Grate Reuer are many plantations &
houfes where prouifions are to bee had thus hauing trau-
erfhed much of yᵉ Cuntrey I touk up seauerall tracts of
Land & hauing marked there bounds Entered them in a
book for yᵉ ufes aforefaid now all feemd uery well but as
foune as yᵉ afsemly wos ouer Samuell Jenings with Tho
Budd & 2 or 8 more comifheners fent for mee in Grate haft
to Call in my warran & make uoide whot I had don hauing
nothing to Charge mee withall in any Eraguler proceedings
but fom new deuice Came in there minds that E : B : fhould
haue his Land all in one tenth & for that I might haue a new
warran but thay hauing taken up yᵉ baft tenths I faw it would
bee much to yᵉ prejudiges of Edward & others fo not Com-
plying therewith wee Reafoned yᵉ Cafe but to no porpos I
tould them I fhould make an apeele in this mater which is
here offered to thyfelf G : W : A : P : or others if thou fee
meete after this Samuell Jenings took a perteculer acount
of whot Land & where I had taken it up which did not
amount to a 20ᵗʰ part of whot my Letter of aturnye diricted :
but there wos fom Littell mifstrey in this thing in Relation
to Gouerment that E : B : might bee hedgd up in as littell
Compas & yᵉ feru[ants] are [?] Genaral wos forbidden to
sirue any for me[e] this seemd Grate unkindnes to a man
that had bin maid yᵉ firft Inftrument of fo Good a Cuntry
that when hee Comes has not fo much Land to fitt downe
on as fom of them haue bought for Lefe then yᵉ ualley of
5ᵗʰ now william biddell Thomas Gardiner & fom of yᵉ more
moderate ware againft fuch proceeding but yᵉ Grateft in
power would haue it foo——

thus wee are not heare without fom Exarcifes but yᵗ
wᶜʰ makes us amenes is yᵉ abounding Loue of God wᶜʰ
offten uifits oure foles & that is it that makes all places
Comfortable & Giues fatiffaction meetings are heary [*sic*]
uery Liuing that makes us flock togather & Glad when

wee feele y⁰ power of God to Rife; this wee hope will preferue us & fettell all Righte in his owne time fo my deare Loue is to thee with G : W : A : P : W : G : Stephen Crifp & others of y⁰ Anfhants of Gods hous [* * * * *torn here*] y⁰ Rememberance of you in this place doth [* * * *torn again*] times melt my fole in y⁰ Loue of God.
[*Signature torn off.*]

BIOGRAPHICAL SKETCH OF DR. JOHN GOTTLIEB MORRIS, SURGEON OF ARMAND'S FIRST PARTISAN LEGION.

CONTRIBUTED BY HIS SON, REV. JOHN G. MORRIS, D.D.

John Gottlieb Morris was born in the village of Redekin, near Magdeburg, Prussia, in March of 1754. He was baptized and confirmed in the Lutheran Church, and educated in the schools of his native province. Subsequently he studied " medicine and surgery," and was granted a diploma to practice. " After finishing my professional studies," he writes in his journal, " I came to this country late in 1776, and served the United States as an army surgeon, with general approbation." In 1777, after an examination by the State Board of Physicians, Dr. Morris was granted a certificate to serve as " surgeon in the Continental army," which was signed by Drs. William Shippen, William Brown, and other members of the board.

Congress, on the 10th of May, 1777, commissioned Armand, Marquis de la Rouerie, colonel, and authorized him to raise an independent corps, which became known as the First Partisan Legion, of which Dr. Morris was appointed surgeon's mate. He served with the legion while it was attached to the Northern department of the army, and also when it was sent to the South; and after the battle of Camden, in which he lost all his private papers, was promoted surgeon. After the surrender of Cornwallis at Yorktown, the legion remained in Virginia for some months, when it was ordered to York, Pennsylvania, where it was mustered out of service.

The following letter was written by General Armand to Dr. Morris :

" YORKTOWN, PENNSYLVANIA this 25ª Nov. 1783.
" SIR,

" At the instant the legion is disbanded it becomes my duty to give you my thanks for the attention, care, intelligence and propriety with which you conducted yourself in both capacity of second and first surgeon to the Partizan Legion under my command. I cannot be silent on the bravery which you evidenced on all occasions when you accompanied the legion to the enemy. I shall add that your conduct in general has merited & obtained the esteem and attachment of all the officers. I am happy in this opportunity to express myself these sentiments for you.

"I have the honour to be Dʳ Sir,

"Your most obeᵈᵗ hᵇˡᵉ Svt.

"ARMAND MQS. DE LA ROUERIE

"Mʀ MORRIS post surgeon to the

"first partizant Legiou."

To this letter Dr. Morris sent the following reply:

"YORKTOWN, PENNA. Nov. the 25th 1783.

"DEAR GENERAL,

"Language is wanting to express the Sentiments due to you, but excuse a heart full of Gratitude. I give you my humble thanks for your last expressions that you have been pleased with my Conduct in the time I have had the honor to serve in the first Partizan Legion under your command. I thank you likewise for your kindness you always shewed to me—and for the particular enquiries, your concern in the condition of the sick officers and soldiers which suffered either by wounds or sickness in the cause of their country, your solicitude to procure them every possible assistance and relief—cannot fail to excite the highest admiration of your goodness in my breast and the warmest gratitude in the heart of every officer and soldier.

"The knowledge of these circumstances is most agreeable to my feelings, it being the greatest ambition of my heart to receive your farewell expression that I have done my duty to your approbation and I assure you of my earnest wishes for your welfare and that you may enjoy complete happiness in every quarter of the world in which your lot may be cast. May Heaven prosper you and grant you all these blessings —these are the ardent wishes of

" Dear General your most faithful and most obedient humble servant

" JOHN MORRIS, M.D.

" GENERAL ARMAND,

" Marq. de la Rouerie."

From some mutilated fragments of Dr. Morris's journal of the march of the legion from Virginia to Pennsylvania we select the following:

March 8.—Reached Staunton, and quartered at Squire F——s.

July 21.—We had a grand ball.

July 28.—Raffanear [cornet of the Sixth Troop] was tried and broke. I presided at the Court Martial.

August 3.—Raffanear was restored.

August 18.—Seven men deserted—only three were recaptured.

August 25.—The three men had to run the gauntlet.

September 2.—Baron de Uechtritz [captain of the Sixth Troop] and Cornet Head [Richard Head, of the Second Troop] fought a duel and the Baron was wounded.

September 18.—The soldiers cause great disturbances among the people of Staunton.

October 9.—We arrived at Winchester; the inhabitants do not like us. Capt. Bedkin [Henry Bedkin, Second Troop] had a fight with some of them at the tavern.

October 28.—We gave a ball at the Burke House to the inhabitants, to induce them to give us winter quarters; they refused and disturbances ensued.

November 19.—I became acquainted with General Morgan.

December 11.—General Morgan and Muhlenberg visit us. We had a sham fight and a ball.

December 15.—Col. Armand and Major [George] Shaffner play and the Colonel lost heavily.

December 16.—I was sent with my saddle-bags full of money to Gen. Morgan, who is at at Col Nevill's, his son-in-law.

December 18.—Col Armand was challenged by Mr Sniker, a Virginia gentleman.

December 19.—Col. Armand refuses to fight and abuses Mr. Sniker.

December 22.—We arrived at Fredericktown. Col. Armand fights a duel with Mr. Sniker—his pistol went off only once. We have a ball at the tavern, my partner was Miss Schofe. Became acquainted with a number of Hessian officers.

December 25.—Reach Yorktown, and quarter at Snerly's; nobody would take me with my sick soldiers. Capt. Sharpe [Fifth Troop] and Lieut. Henry Reidel [Fourth Troop] fought a duel.

In 1788 Dr. Morris became a member of the Society of the Cincinnati, and received from Washington the following certificate :

" This certifies that John Morris Surgeon in the First Partizan Legion, being in virtue of his services in the American Army, Intitled to become a member of the Cincinnati and having signed the Institution and complied with the Regulation therein specified, is accordingly admitted a Member and is Intitled to all the Rights and Privileges of the said Society of the Cincinnati.

" Given under my hand and seal at Philadelphia this day of December 1788

" G. WASHINGTON."

" When the war ceased," continues the journal, " and peace was restored, my surgical services were no longer required, and I settled in York as a practising physician. My practice was extensive and by God's blessing successful, but in my later years, owing to nervous prostration, I could not serve those kind friends who had entrusted their lives and health to my professional skill, and made this announcement through the public paper, against which there were many strong protests."

In June of 1784, Dr. Morris was married to Barbara Myers, of York. He died in 1808.

LETTER OF REV. WILLIAM SMITH, D.D., TO JAMES WILSON, ESQ., ON ELECTIONS.

CONTRIBUTED BY ISRAEL W. MORRIS.

CHESTER, KENT COUNTY, MARYLAND, Jany. 19th, 1789.

DEAR SIR,—I congratulate you on the favourable Issue of the Election of *federal representatives* in Pennsylvania, & the Probability, amounting, (from what I have seen in the News Papers) almost to a certainty of the like favourable issue in Respect to Electors of a *President-general* &c. What is called the *Federal List* has a vast majority, both for Representatives & Electors on the Eastern Shore of this State; &, as I apprehend, far more than sufficient to set against the Majority in some of the populous counties of the Western Shore for the other List, called Antifederal, altho' in that List also, there are generally avowed federalists, & only two (Col. Mercer & Mr. Sterret) who are any way suspected; & they themselves say the suspicion is unjust & injurious, as they are earnest for an effective Government, upon the whole Plan of the New Constitution with a few Amendments to be made by Congress itself, in which they wish to be moderate, & have no Desire of Recurring to another *Convention*—But it is not probable that either of them will be elected, as the other Side were unwilling to trust any one, of whom they had the least suspicion. In 8 or 4 Days we shall have the Election declared by Proclamation.

We are apprehensive here of Difficulties, nevertheless, still remaining—especially respecting the Election of General Washington, some of which, as they have occurred to us here, I promised to state to you, as at the Head of the Pennsylvania Electors; altho' I doubt not everything of the kind has long since occurred to your own more sagacious & penetrating Understanding, anxious & active as you have been for an effective Government & a speedy operation of it.

Our first apprehension, respecting Pennsylva. is that, from the mode of election in each County by Districts, & it having taken more than five Weeks, before all the Returns at the former Election for Representatives were brought to Philada. to enable the Presdt. & Council to issue their Proclamation, the four Weeks allowed by the New Constitution, between the Day of choosing Electors & the Day of their Meeting at Reading, for the Choice of a President will not be sufficient; for how, in 4 Weeks (especially from beyond the Allegenny Mountains & some Sheriffs, perhaps in no great Disposition to be in Haste with their Returns) I say, how in 4 weeks, shall all these Returns be brought to Philada., more than 300 miles down; then a Proclamation to go 300 miles up again, & 3dly some of the Electors, after that, to come 300 miles down to Reading in all near 1000 miles backward & forward, at this season of the year, in 28 Days; besides the Time spent at the elections, & in Council, in numbering &c, and making out their Proclamation? No Doubt, you have thought of this, & have sent, or will immediately send, Expresses to the most distant Electors, viz, James O'Hara, Lawrence Keene, Alex. Graydon & David Greer, with Copies of the Returns from the Counties already come to Hand, which being compared by them with the Counties over Susquehannah or in their vicinity will enable them to judge of the Probability of their being among the 8 Highest on the Return for Electors; & altho' these accounts will not be *official*, yet they ought to be induced by their Zeal for Gen. Washington & the Federal Interest, to set out immediately so as to reach Reading by the time appointed, & to meet the official Account or Proclamation, if the executive Council (by Returns from all the Counties) should be enabled to publish it before that Time. But if all the Counties should not have made their Returns by 1t. Wednesday in February—Qu—What is to be done? Might not the Executive Council authenticate those Returns wch. may be made before the day of meeting at Reading? And if they appear an undoubted Majority (in Whatever manner the Defaulting Counties might have voted) might not the

Electors having such Majority (yourself & others) proceed to the Nomination directly on the Day appointed; or adjourn, de Die in Diem, till all the Returns come officially to Hand?

But another Difficulty appears to rise from the Constitution itself. The two highest in Votes having a Majority of all the Electors of the confederating eleven states, are to be President & Vice-president—Suppose then the Electors of even Nine States all agreed to have Gen. Washington President, & Mr. Adams, or any other V. Presdt. These nine States cannot say in their Nomination or vote Genl. W. Presdt; John Adams V. P., but must vote indiscriminately for both, & neither will be highest in Votes but perhaps have an equality. Suppose, then, but one other State, (say Virginia, or New York, or both) give but one or two Votes, still keeping the Name of Adams, but joining with it either a Clinton or a Henry, then those two States or any one of them, or a single capricious Vote of any one of them, can make Mr. Adams President.

We know there is one Way to secure this Business, by any Number of the eleven States, having a Majority of all the Electors, to agree, all of them, to nominate Gen. Washington, while some of them give some 8 or 10 Votes to some other Persons in the Room of Adams, so as to leave Him lower in Number than Gen. W. but yet higher than any other, if it is wished that he should be V. Presdt. But there ought to be some exchange of sentiments, & some previous Plan on this Head—among the 4 middle States of New Jersey, Pennsylvania, Delaware & Maryland—who are sufficient for this Work; but if Connecticut can be consulted, so much the better. Then suppose it agreed that Delaware vote for Mr. Jay with Gen. W. & Jersey some other or the same; Pennsylvania a few votes for the same or any other—And if you will on Receipt of this let me know what you think Maryland had best do, Mr. Wm. Tilghman of this Town, whose Name will stand highest among our Electors, desires you to be informed that he will do his utmost, in Concert with us for the fed. cause, & the

Election of the President whom we all wish should his Election be supposed in any Danger.

There is still another Evil, of a very threatening aspect —We no election at all, either of Representatives or Electors, is like to be obtained in N. Hampshire, & only in three Districts of Massachusets—If this be certain, it will be an Evil indeed—Yet I hope a Majority of the whole Eleven States will act as Electors, & a like Majority of the Representatives meet in Congress; a Majority being a Quorum, we trust they will be able to put the Government in Operation, & pass new Laws respecting " the Time & Mode of filling up their B [*torn*] by new Elections in the defaulting States, who have adopted the Constitution."

I hope Mr. Lewis, as the Scire Fac. agt. the University, was returnable to the Jany. Term has got the money to enable him to take up my Note to you lately in the Hands of Mr. Todd, agreeably to my Directions: I hope also to see you in Feb. at the Meeting of the Assembly. Pray write me a few lines in answer to such Parts of this Letter as require your Notice; & tho' you have no Doubt thought of & provided for every chance respecting the execution of the Government, you will still ascribe what I now write to the well meant Zeal of Yours,

                                                      WM. SMITH

I wish Time had allowed to transcribe this Letter fair, but I trust you will be able to spell out its Contents.

                                                      W. S.

P.S.—Direct by Post to me at Chester, Kent County, Maryland.

THE WASHINGTON ANCESTRY—A SUPPLEMENTARY NOTICE.

BY EDWARD D. NEILL, D.D., SAINT PAUL, MINNESOTA.

In an article on the Washington Ancestry which, in October, 1892, appeared in the MAGAZINE, it was mentioned that there was "no evidence that John Washington was before 1658 in Virginia."

Mr. W. G. Stanard, in the April number of the *William and Mary College Quarterly*, contributes extracts from the records of Westmoreland (Virginia) County, which show that as early as 1655 John Washington was major and Nathaniel Pope lieutenant-colonel of the military organization of that county.

It now appears probable that Washington came to Virginia from Barbadoes in 1654, with his first wife and two children.

Theodore Pargiter, in a letter dated London, August 2, 1654, mentions that his cousin John Washington is at Barbadoes.[1] From a deposition preserved in Westmoreland County records, John Washington, of Virginia, at this time was twenty-nine years old. The Stanard extracts show that in 1654 Edward Prescott, of Virginia, owned a vessel which came from Barbadoes to Virginia with a cargo. It is not improbable that John Washington and family arrived in that ship.

Waters, in his Washington Ancestry, published the following:

"February 1655, The Eighth day Lres of adcon yssued forth to John Washington the nrall, and lawful sone of Amphilis Washington late of Tring in the County of Hertford decd to adster the goods Chells and debtes of the said decd."

[1] New England Hist. Gen. Register, October, 1884.

Some time in 1656 the son must have visited England. This year Captain Edward Prescott, who was with a ship at the port of Dantzic, on the Vistula, wrote to Washington to come and be his assistant in sailing the vessel. He went, and when the ship left Elsinore, a port north of Copenhagen, "he took halfe watch in y* voyage to Virginia, and did assist as second man in sayleing y* vessel."[1]

After the vessel reached Virginia (before May, 1657), with consent of Prescott, Washington settled there. His first wife soon died, and before the middle of May, 1659, he was again married, to the widow Ann Brodhurst, the daughter of Nathaniel Pope, of Appomattox, contracted often to Mattox, in Westmoreland County.

Nathaniel and Francis Pope were among the earliest planters in Maryland, and their names as early as 1638 appear in the records of that Province. Nathaniel was accused of being in sympathy with the disaffected of Kent Island, and removed from Maryland. Francis remained, and in 1663 was sheriff of Charles County, and it is noteworthy that this year he received a grant of land from the proprietor of Maryland, on a portion of which stands the magnificent capitol at Washington, the city named in honor of a descendant of John Washington and his wife Ann, the daughter of Nathaniel Pope.

The Westmoreland records show that Lawrence did not come to Virginia until several years after his brother John. As late as 1660 he was a merchant at Luton. Stanard gives the following:

"Power of Attorney for Gabriel Reve of London, merchant, to Lawrence Washington of Luton, in County Bedford, merchant, to demand of the heirs of Nathaniel Pope late of Virginia, merchant deceased, all debts &c due the said Reve. Dated October 31st 1660; recorded in Westmoreland Co. Va. February 4th 1661"

In the article on "The Ancestry and Earlier Life of George Washington" (PENNSYLVANIA MAGAZINE, October,

[1] Westmoreland County Records.

1892) the writer mentioned that Washington dined with General Braddock at Williamsburg, and the authority was a work published in London by John Lewis Peyton, L.B., F.R.G.S., etc., with the title "Adventures of my Grandfather." The work was a romance, and worded so as to mislead. Mr. Peyton is still living and writing in Virginia, and his last fiction is "Tom Swindel." A good name. There are three books written by admirable story-tellers which careful historians should avoid: the "True Travels and Adventures of Captain John Smith, for a time Admiral of New England," "My Lady Pokahontas. A true relation of Virginia. Writ by Anas Todkill, Puritan and Pilgrim. Notes by John Esten Cooke," and the "Adventures of my Grandfather," by Peyton.

AMERICAN POLITICS DISCUSSED IN COMMERCIAL LETTERS, 1764–1766.

LONDON Septem^r 21, 1764.

DEAR COUSIN—

Politicks are at a stand at present and will I believe remain so till the meeting of Parliament; it is supposed then there will be a strong push between the majority and minority— there can be no judgement formed on which side the scale will turn. The Papers every day *lug* in an acct. of this great personage & t'other having joined the Minority, and that before the next meeting of Parliament the minority will be the Majority, are all without the least foundation and serve merely to fill up a vacant page.

The thing that at present engrosses the attention of the People, is the relief of the Palatines, which to the honor of the Nation they have amply done, as you will see by the Papers.

It is hoped that on the meeting of Parliament they will see into the Absurdity of some of the Acts Passed last Session with regard to America, and amend them,—it is surprising what little knowledge the Parliament & People in general have of us; one should think that the last war would have given them a thorough insight into every particular.

I am sorry things wear such a Gloomy face with us, Mr Allen I heard carry'd over orders from the Proprietors to relax in some Particular points which I hope will give satisfaction. The Ministry would be extreemly glad to have the Govern^t of Pennsylvania in the King, as they detest all Proprietary Govern^{ts}, thinking them inconsistent with the Perogative of the Crown. The Proprietors take great pains to keep in with the Court so that the Petition for the change of Government will not meet with success, and I believe it will be happy if it does not, as I am afraid were it to take Place we should be deprived of those darling Priviledges we at present enjoy. . . .

Your affectionate Cousin,

SAMUEL MEREDITH.

LONDON 24 Feby 1766.

ESTEEMED FR'D.

I have now to inform thee desiring thou wilt make it public for the general good, that yesterday morning about two o'clock after long Debates & sitting all Night the House of Commons divided on a Motion for the total Repeal of the Stamp Act; and 'twas carried for the Repeal by a Majority of 108 the Numbers being 275 for the Repeal & 167 against it: which has afforded great Joy to every true Lover of his Country here & I make no doubt will do the same in America, & I do heartily congratulate them thereon. Many have been very assiduous & zealous in bringing about this happy event, and among the rest our worthy Frd Benj⁎ Franklin Esq: has had no small hand, and richly deserves the Thanks of his Country.

I have very good Grounds also to conclude that the Repeal will also pass the House of Lords and become effectual; so I hope it may be productive of very happy Fruits in the Removal of every Appearance of Discord & in the Promotion of a happy Union & durable Peace and Tranquility between these and your Parts of the same King's Dominions, which I hope will become united by Representation. I am very respectfully thy ready

Fr'd to Serve

THO⁎ CROWLEY.

HALIFAX Feb⁎ 26ᵗʰ 1766.

GENTLEMEN

We had the Pleasure of your esteem'd Favour of the 14ᵗʰ December, inclosing your Memorial, setting forth the many oppressive & destructive Measures, lately imposed upon the Colonies in America, wherein we are fellow sufferers with you, & feel too sensibly the distressing Effects occasioned by such unsalutary Laws. Animated by these impending Dangers, can assure you we have been as active as our Situation would admit.

The first Step we took was, presenting a Memorial to the Lords of the Treasury in October Last, praying that the free Importation of Gold & Silver from the Spanish Main to the Colonies might be permitted, to this we reced a favourable Answer with a Copy of the Minutes of the Board of Treasury relative thereto, which gave us great Satisfaction, & we doubt not by this Time you feel the happy Effects of that Trade being open & free from the arbitrary Interuptions of our Men of War. Since then we have corresponded with the London Committee of North American Merchants, & with their Approbation sent up a Petition to the House of Commons, complaining of the great Decay of our Trade to North America, praying for a Repeal of the Stamp Act, & at same Time exerted our little Influence with some Members of the House to unite in the Repeal of this Act. We have now the Pleasure to give you Joy in the great Probability of this Happy Event. Last Friday, after debat⁴ 18 Hours on this Subject, between the Hours of 2 & 3 on Saturday Morning the Question was put, which the new Ministry carried it by a Majority of 108 in the House of Commons, it has turned out a political Point, & seems to be a Contest between the old & new Ministry to try their Strength. We hope the same Influence will be held in the House of Lords, & that we may soon enjoy the Happy Effects resulting from a Repeal of this oppressive Stamp Act. (Verte.)

When we can render our American Friends any good Services, they may rely on our steady Attachment to their Interest. I remain with a most sincere Regard to all the Gentlemen, for Mr H. Hamer & Self

Gentlemen

Your m° obed⁴ hble Serv⁴

CHRIST^R RAWSON.

RECORDS OF CHRIST CHURCH, PHILADELPHIA.
BAPTISMS, 1709–1760.

BY CHARLES R. HILDEBURN.

(Continued from p. 112.)

1751 Dec.	8	Pane Rebekkah d. James and Mary Dec. — 1751
1711 Dec.	23	Parham John s. Thomas 6 dys.
1718 Sept.	13	Margaret d. Thomas and Hannah ——
1734 Dec.	22	Thomas s. Thomas and Hannah 2 wks. 1 dy.
1721 Feb.	24	Parker Elizabeth d. Richard and Elizabeth Feb. 5 1721
1723 Aug.	23	Thomasin d. Richard and Elizabeth ——
1726 Sept.	2	Mary d. Richard and Elizabeth Aug. 8
1731 Sept.	11	Robert s. Richard and Elizabeth 2 wks.
1734 July	28	Frances s. Thomas and Mary 18 mos.
1735 June	5	Sarah d. Richard and Elizabeth 3 wks.
1735 Nov.	13	Richard s. Richard and Elizabeth Aug. 25 1732
1735 Nov.	13	Anne d. Richard and Elizabeth April 27 1729
1738 Nov.	28	Rebecca d. Richard and Elizabeth 2 wks.
1756 Mch.	7	William Adult
1757 April	24	Elizabeth Adult
1760 Feb.	20	Hannah d. George and Christian Oct. 23 1759
1760 Sept.	13	William s. James and Elizabeth Aug. 16 1760
1787 Aug.	20	Parkhouse Mary d. Richard and Mary 9 mos.
1759 Feb.	9	Parmer Mary d. John and Deborah Jan. 9 1759
1728 Mch.	8	Parry Catherine d. David and Mary 4 mos.
1730 June	24	Rowland s. David and Mary 7 wks. 1 dy.
1732 Oct.	18	John s. David and Mary 10 wks.
1734 Nov.	28	Margaret d. David and Mary 5 mos.
1760 Dec.	17	William s. John and Elizabeth Oct. 25 1758
1760 Dec.	17	Elizabeth d. John and Elizabeth Nov. 1 1759
1713 May	22	Parsons John s. John and Ann ——
1750 Oct.	24	Joseph s. Richard and Alice Oct. 6 1750
1720 Aug.	5	Paschal William s. William and Sarah
1726 July	21	Susannah d. William and Sarah ——
1744 May	24	William s. William and Sarah 22 mos. 1 dy.
1732 Oct.	20	Sarah d. William and Sarah 10 mos.
1722 Dec.	2	Patch Mary d. John and Mary 2 mos.
1754 Sept.	28	Patison Samuel s. Joseph and Anne Sept. 12 1754
1721 Dec.	25	Patten Thomas s. Pitchford and Frances ——
1711 June	18	Patterson James s. Robert and Sarah ——
1751 Dec.	29	Joseph s. Joseph and Anne Oct. 28 1750

1757 Mch.	1	Patton John s. Robert and Catherine Aug. 3 1755
1749 Dec.	27	Paul John s. William and Elizabeth Nov. 14 1788
1749 Dec.	27	Joseph s. William and Elizabeth June 24 1747
1749 Dec.	27	Sarah d. William and Elizabeth Oct. 25 1742
1749 Dec.	27	William s. William and Elizabeth Sept. 24 1749
1749 Dec.	27	Elizabeth wife of William
1740 Jan.	18	Pavy George s. George and Avis 1 yr. 4 mos. 5 dys.
1738 June	20	Paxton Thomas s. Alexander and Elizabeth 8 wks. 4 dys.
1742 July	4	Eliz⁴ d. Alexander and Eliz⁴ 4 mos. 7 dys.
1743 Jan.	30	Payne Mary d. James and Mary 9 dys.
1745 Jan.	27	Catherine d. James and Mary 2 dys.
1747 Aug.	20	James s. James and Mary Dec. — 1746
1748 Oct.	23	Elizabeth d. James and Mary Oct. 17 1748
1753 Oct.	30	Rachel d. Thomas and Mary Jan. 20 1753
1758 Oct.	25	Violet d. John and Elizabeth Oct. 23 1758
1712 Dec.	27	Peacock John s. George and Ann 9 yrs. 2 mos.
1736 Nov.	30	James s. Noah and Mary 2 dys.
1747 Sept.	17	Pear Martha d. John and Naomi Aug. 28 1746
1737 July	23	Pearce Hugh s. John and Mary 1 yr.
1715 July	1	Pearson Mary d. John and Anne 1 dy.
1720 Aug.	26	Peart Elizabeth d. Benjamin and Rachel ——
1723 Mch.	30	Mary d. Benjamin and Rachel 9 wks.
1730 Nov.	26	Thomas s. Benjamin and Rachel 8 mos.
1732 July	8	William s. William and Mary 8 dys.
1736 Nov.	17	Rachel d. Benjamin and Rachel 4 yrs. 4 mos.
1736 Nov.	17	William s. Benjamin and Rachel 1 yr.
1756 April	2	William s. Thomas and Elizabeth March 4 1756
1744 July	13	Peel Margaret d. John and Elizabeth 4 mos. 21 dys.
1746 Nov.	18	Sarah d. John and Elizabeth July 80 1746
1749 June	28	Rebekah d. James and Elizabeth May 16 1749
1740 Feb.	6	Pellitory Daniel s. Daniel and Mary 6 mos.
1738 July	80	Penrose Bartholomew s. Thomas and Sarah 1 yr.
1739 Dec.	19	Mary d. Thomas and Sarah 7 wks.
1741 Aug.	19	Joseph s. Bartholomew and Mary 2 yrs. 8 wks. 4 dys.
1741 Aug.	19	Margaret d. Bartholomew and Mary 6 mos. 3 dys.
1746 Sept.	7	Bartholomew s. Thomas and Sarah Sept. 6 1746
1752 Aug.	17	Jonathan s. Thomas and Sarah July 10 1752
1712 May	9	Pepper William s. William and Frances 2 wks.
1714 Feb.	14	Perry Charles s. John and Sarah 8 wks.
1730 Sept.	2	William s. Obadiah and Phœbe 1 wk. 2 dys.
1732 May	18	William s. Obadiah and Phœbe 2 mos.
1736 Aug.	14	Rachel d. Obadiah and Phœbe 8 mos.
1746 June	9	Christopher ——
1728 Dec.	7	Pert Bryan s. Benjamin and Rachel 2 yrs. 2 mos.
1729 May	9	Jane d. William and Mary 8 wks.

1738 Dec.   24 Pert Rachel wife Benjamin 46 yrs.
1758 Sept. 20 Peterkin David s. Thomas and Mary Aug. 31 1758
1733 Aug.   26 Peters Anne d. Simon and Mary 5 wks.
1734 May   19   Elizabeth d. Thomas and Alice 12 yrs. 9 mos.
1751 Mch.   10   Mary d. William and Mary Dec. 16 1750
1753 Jan.   22   Thomas s. William and Mary Aug. 1 1752
1747 Nov.   19 Peywell Susannah d. William and Mary Oct. 24 1747
1728 May   9 Pharoah Martha d. Samuel and Ann 2 wks.
1756 Aug.   16 Philip Thomas Short s. Samuel and Hannah Jan. 24
                    1756
1731 Nov.   11 Philips Elanora d. William and Mary 8 wks.
1711 Sept. 19 Phillips Rachel d. William 2 wks.
1715 April 29   Richard s. Richard 4 mos.
1730 Mch.   2   Richard s. John and Elizabeth 11 yrs.
1732 June   12   Charles s. John and Ann 4 mos.
1733 Nov.   13   Thomas s. William and Ann 6 dys.
1734 May   5   William s. William and Phœbe 6 wks.
1734 Dec.   20   Joseph s. William and Anne 5 dys.
1739 June   19   Susannah d. William and Anne 3 wks.
1739 Aug.   26   John s. John and Hannah 1 mo.
1741 April 19   James s. John and Ann 5 wks.
1741 Aug.   9   William s. John and Ann 9 mos. 7 dys.
1743 June   21   Martha Elizabeth d. George and Elizabeth 4 mos.
1750 June   25   John s. Thomas and Elizabeth Nov. 18 1748
1745 Mch.   18   Philpot Jane d. William and Jane 11 mos.
1731 Mch.   25 Phipps Thomas s. Thomas and Deborah 2 wks.
1736 Jan.   6   Etheldreda d. Thomas and Deborah 12 dys.
1737 Oct.   9   Thomas s. Thomas and Deborah 3 wks.
1737 Nov.   6   Margaret d. John and Anne 1 mo.
1741 Mch.   16   Stephen s. John and Deborah 1 yr. 4 mos.
1732 Oct.   29 Phips Thomas s. Thomas and Deborah 2 mos.
1734 Mch.   17   John s. Thomas and Deborah 1 dy.
1759 Feb.   25 Physick Henry White s. Edmund and Abigail Jan 3 1759
1732 Mch.   5 Pickle William s. Nathan and Rachel 1 mo.
1751 Nov.   17   Sarah d. John and Anne Nov. 5 1751
1717 June   4 Pierce Richard 17 yrs.
1717 Oct.   14   George s. Richard and Anne 14 yrs.
1735 April 13   Mary d. John and Mary 19 mos.
1738 Feb.   14   Elizabeth d. Edward and Frances 2 wks.
1739 Jan.   17   John s. John and Mary 5 dys.
1741 Feb.   10   Mary d. Richard and Mary 1 wk.
1739 Nov.   9 Pillar Hannah d. James and Frances 8 dys.
1744 Feb.   19 Pillow Mary d. James and Frances 11 dys.
1732 May   23 Pinckeney Rachel d. Caleb and Ann 1 mo.
1721 Oct.   15 Pini Margaret d. John and Elizabeth ——

1752 May	27	Pini Anne d. John and Elizabeth March 23 1752
1756 Feb.	28	John s. John and Isabella Dec. 9 1755
1735 Aug.	7	Piniard Margaret d. Joseph and Catherine 22 mos.
1735 Aug.	7	Ellinor d. Joseph and Catherine 2 wks.
1737 Aug.	7	Mathias s. Mathias and Rachel 5 mos.
1737 Aug.	7	Elinor d. Mathias and Rachel 1 mo.
1734 June	14	Pinkney —— 21 yrs. 3 mos.
1726 Nov.	25	Pinnard William s. James and Rachel ——
1729 Oct.	81	Pinyard Anne d. Mathias and Rachel 2 mos. 2 wks.
1739 April	25	Mary d. Richard and Anne 1 yr.
1739 Aug.	29	Catherine d. Joseph and Catherine 1 yr. 9 mos.
1739 Aug.	29	Mary d. Joseph and Catherine 1 mo.
1740 May	80	William s. Richard and Anne 2 mos.
1740 Aug.	11	Mercy d. Mathias and Rachel 4 mos. 2 wks.
1746 May	24	Mary d. Mathias and Rachel July 27 1742
1746 May	24	Mathias s. Mathias and Rachel Sept. 2 1744
1746 July	18	John s. Richard and Anne March 15 1745
1746 July	18	Susannah d. Richard and Anne April 7 1743
1748 Mch.	24	Anderson s. Richard and Anne March 5 1748
1750 Jan.	23	Anne d. Richard and Anne Jan. 23 1749
1745 May	28	Pitts Richard s. Richard and Mary Feb. 6 1741
1746 Feb.	23	Playstead Sarah d. Edward and Bridget Feb. 18 1745
1734 April	8	Plim George s. George and Frances 5 mos.
1735 Nov.	11	John s. George and Frances 12 wks.
1729 Nov.	28	Plimm William s. George and Frances 6 mos.
1727 Aug.	27	Plummer Joseph s. John and Eleanor 1 yr. 8 mos.
1748 Oct.	29	Plumsted Mary d. William and Margaret 4 mos. 5 dys.
1754 Sept.	4	William s. William and Mary Aug. 8 1754
1758 Nov.	4	Clement s. William and Mary Oct. 4 1758
1760 July	27	Ann d. William and Mary July 8 1760
1760 July	27	Catherine d. William and Mary July 8 1760
1746 Feb.	18	Plunket Mary d. Mary widow Nov. 17 1744
1748 Oct.	2	Elizabeth d. John and Mary Aug. 10 1748
1731 Nov.	21	Pocklington Ann d. William and Margaret 8 dys.
1734 May	7	William s. William and Margaret 9 dys.
1736 Mch.	7	John s. William and Margaret 5 wks.
1714 Oct.	15	Poland Sarah d. William and Katherine 8 wks.
1727 Aug.	9	Polegreen Susannah d. Thomas and Elizabeth June 8 1726
1721 Mch.	14	Polgreen Katherine d. Thomas and Elizabeth ——
1724 Mch.	27	James s. John and Elizabeth
1732 Aug.	1	Elizabeth d. Thomas and Elizabeth 1 yr.
1734 July	21	Thomas Buckley s. Thomas and Elizabeth 5 yrs. 3 mos.
1711 Oct.	24	Pollett Thomas s. William and Catherine 2 mos. 16 dys.
1755 Oct.	2	Pooley Charles s. Abel and Mary May 10 1752

1748 Dec.	26	Pope Hester d. John and Frinah Dec. 9 1748
1751 Dec.	28	John s. John and Ferreniah June 11 1751
1743 Aug.	14	Porter Mary d. Isaac and Hannah 14 yrs.
1738 May	29	Pote Epriam s. Thomas and Elizabeth 5 mos.
1740 Nov.	11	Elizabeth d. Thomas and Elizabeth 1 dy.
1740 Nov.	11	Thomas s. Thomas and Elizabeth 1 dy.
1743 Mch.	27	John s. Thomas and Elizabeth 4 dys.
1747 May	24	Letitia d. Thomas and Elizabeth Oct. 19 1746
1750 June	24	Potter Benjamin s. Larrance and Mary May 28 1750
1753 Dec.	26	Jane d. Edward and Mary Nov. 11 1753
1734 July	19	Potts Joseph s. Stephen and Anne 14 mos.
1736 Aug.	29	William Bickins s. Stephen and Anne 19 mos.
1737 Nov.	14	Sarah d. Stephen and Anne 11 mos.
1748 July	10	John Thomas s. Laurence and Mary Jan. 30 1748
1720 June	12	Poulson Sarah d. Charles and Sarah June 5
1748 Oct.	30	Powel —— s. John and Lucy ——
1752 Oct.	29	Margaret d. Evan and Dorothy May 12 1752
1735 Aug.	27	Powell William s. William and Elizabeth 1 mo.
1740 Jan.	27	William s. William and Elizabeth 1 mo.
1754 April	14	Power Susannah d. John and Anne March 21 1754
1759 Sept.	23	Elizabeth d. John and Elizabeth Sept. 11 1759
1759 Oct.	7	Elizabeth d. John and Agnes Sept. 10 1759
1744 Nov.	18	Powman Murcabous d. Michael and Aulass 19 dys.
1714 Oct.	28	Pratherow Anne d. Joseph and Mary 20 yrs.
1732 April	10	Pratt Hannah d. Henry and Rebecca 8 dys.
1735 Jan.	12	William s. Thomas and Anne 2 wks.
1740 Aug.	8	Mathew s. Henry and Rebecca 6 yrs.
1740 Aug.	8	Rebecca d. Henry and Rebecca 4 yrs.
1740 Aug.	3	Joseph s. Henry and Rebecca 1 yr. 6 mos.
1742 Jan.	3	Deborah d. Henry and Rebecca 10 wks. 4 dys.
1748 Dec.	15	Charles s. Henry and Rebecca 1 mo. 1 dy.
1752 Jan.	26	Deborah d. Henry and Rebecca April 7 1746
1715 June	19	Preston Samuel s. William and Mary 3 wks.
1717 June	23	Mary d. William and Margaret ——
1720 June	5	Margaret d. William and Margaret May 1
1721 Sept.	3	Margaret d. William and Hannah Aug. 24
1724 Feb.	24	Hannah d. William and ——
1739 Dec.	11	Hannah wife of William 38 yrs. 1 mo.
1743 Nov.	20	John s. Joseph and Elizabeth 5 wks. 4 dys.
1745 Mch.	14	Thomas Moor s. Joseph and Elizabeth 19 dys.
1710 Jan.	15	Price Catherine 21 yrs.
1710 Sept.	3	Margaret, born ye 3rd of March
1714 Feb.	13	Jonathan s. John and Ruth ——
1720 Aug.	1	Thomas s. Thomas and Elanor ——
1731 Sept.	26	Elizabeth d. John and Catherine 12 dys.

1732 Oct.	20	Price Thomas s. John and Rebecca 5 wks.	
1734 Feb.	21	Joseph s. John and Rebecca 3 mos.	
1737 Feb.	15	Mary d. John and Catherine 2 yrs.	
1737 Feb.	28	John s. John and Rebecca 18 mos.	
1738 Jan.	15	William s. John and Rebecca 9 mos.	
1738 Feb.	4	Benjamin s. John and Ruth 12 yrs.	
1738 Feb.	4	Mary wife Jonathan 22 yrs.	
1738 Feb.	4	Ruth d. John and Ruth 19 yrs.	
1738 Feb.	4	Elizabeth d. Jonathan and Mary 17 mos.	
1738 Oct.	22	Samuel s. John and Rebecca 5 wks.	
1744 Oct.	14	George s. Thomas and Deborah 17 dys.	
1746 Feb.	17	Anne d. Joseph and Hannah June 9 1745	
1746 Aug.	29	Elizabeth wife John	
1752 Oct.	11	Hannah d. William and Sarah August 26 1752	
1754 May	12	Catherine Adult	
1755 Oct.	4	Mary d. Jonathan and Mary Dec. 30 1748	
1755 Oct.	4	Susannah d. Jonathan and Mary March 3 1750	
1758 Sept.	20	Mary d. George and Elizabeth Aug. 18 1758	
1759 July	2	John s. William and Sarah April 7 1759	
1759 Oct.	2	Elizabeth d. Jenkin and —— Oct. 9 1758	
1760 Nov.	4	Elizabeth d. Jenkin and Martha 5 yrs. 9 mos.	
1744 Dec.	19	Prigg Hannah d. William and Sarah	
1728 Sept.	8	Pringle Samuel s. William and Rachel 1 wk.	
1731 July	11	John s. William and Mary 2 wks.	
1733 Feb.	25	Hannah d. William and Rachel 10 dys.	
1712 Feb.	24	Prise John s. John and Ruth 3 wks. 3 dys.	
1738 April	5	Prisgar Sarah d. Charles and Mary 8 mos.	
1742 Jan.	3	Pritchard Hannah 10 yrs. 1 mo. 6 dys.	
1715 May	1	Pugg Theodosia d. William and Mary 1 mo.	
1721 Sept.	21	Pugh Mary d. John and Hannah ——	
1730 Feb.	13	Margaret d. John and Hannah 3 wks. 4 dys.	
1734 June	9	Richard Sard d. John and Sarah 1 mo.	
1736 Nov.	3	Pullinge William s. George and Rose 5 dys.	
1738 June	27	Purdieu William s. William and Ann 2 wks.	
1741 Aug.	19	Purdue Sarah d. William and Ann 1 mo. 2 dys.	
1724 Mch.	30	Put Annie d. Nicolas and Rachel	
1720 Aug.	21	Putt John s. Nicolas and Rachel Aug. 13	
1721 Mch.	23	Elizabeth d. Nicolas and Rachel ——	
1726 Oct.	20	Pyewell John s. William and Deborah Oct 8	
1730 June	9	Elizabeth d. William and Deborah 1 yr.	
1736 Oct.	10	Deborah d. William and Mary Catherine 3 wks.	
1739 Mch.	8	William s. William and Mary Catherine 1 mo.	
1739 Mch.	8	John s. William and Mary Catherine 1 mo.	
1740 Sept.	17	Mary d. William and Mary Catherine 1 mo.	
1743 Nov.	28	Elizabeth d. William and Mary Catherine 20 dys.	

1746 Feb. 13 Pyewell Richard d. William and Mary Catherine Jan. 22
                  1745
1734 July 17 Quantrile Anne d. John and Penelope 22 mos.
1787 Aug. 14 Quantrill John s. John and Penelope 8 wks.
1748 Sept. 18 Quart Thomas s. Eward and Elinor Aug. 8 1748
1747 April 5 Quin Charles s. James and Mary March 25 1747
1752 Nov. 23   Mary d. James and Mary Oct 18 1752
1733 May   5 Quinion Isabella d. Phillip and Martha 6 wks.
1734 Feb.   8 Ramsey John s. Giles and Mary 17 dys.
1738 Jan. 15   Giles s. Giles and Mary 6 mos.
1738 Feb. 19   Henry s. Joseph and Ruth 2 wks.
1746 July 18   John s. Charles and Margaret Dec. 21 1741
1746 July 18   Phillip s. Charles and Margaret Nov. 25 1743
1746 July 18   Charles s. Charles and Margaret Dec. 23 1745
1747 Sept. 14   Margaret d. William and Catherine Sept 2 1747
1749 Jan. 22   John s. William and Catherine Dec. 31 1748
1749 July 15   Mary d. Charles and Margaret Dec. 1 1746
1753 June 18 Rankin John s. George and Elizabeth Feb. 16 1753
1714 Mch. 21 Ranton Rachel d. George and Elizabeth 3 wks.
1729 Nov. 18 Ratchford Robert s. Robert and Hannah ――――
1738 April 25 Ratcliff John s. John and Catherine 1 yr. 2 mos.
1740 Feb. 19   Joseph s. John and Catherine 2 yrs. 6 mos.
1741 Mch. 13   Joshua s. John and Catherine 5 wks.
1712 May   4 Raths John s. Josiah and Grace 7 yrs. 6 mos.
1730 April 1 Ratliff Anne d. John and Katherine 6 wks.
1735 April 5 Rawlinson Isaac s. Robert and Elizabeth 2 dys.
1754 Feb. 13 Raworth John s. William and Anne Aug. 19 1753
1721 Nov. 28 Raws Charles s. John and Dorothy Oct. 30
1744 Mch. 25 Rayl John s. George and Mary 5 yrs. 9 mos. 7 dys.
1744 Mch. 25   George s. George and Mary 2 mos. 10 dys.
1740 Feb.   5 Rea Anne wife of Thomas 28 yrs.
1711 Aug. 12 Read Mary d. John and Sarah 8 dys.
1717 Mch. 14   Thomas s. Charles and Ann 21 dys.
1720 Jan.   1   Mary d. Charles and Ann ――――
1721 Oct. 27   Robert s. Charles and Ann Oct. 4
1723 Feb. 15   Sarah d. Charles and Ann ――――
1726 Feb.   2   Thomas s. John and Elizabeth ――――
1728 June 28   John s. Charles and Elizabeth 1 mo.
1729 Nov. 28   Andrew s. Charles and Elizabeth 2 wks. 6 dys.
1737 Jan. 28   Mary d. Henry and Susannah 5 wks.
1739 May   18   Joseph s. Samuel and Dorothy 1 mo.
1742 Nov. 11   Samuel s. Samuel and Dorothy 8 wks. 5 dys.
1745 Jan. 21   William s. Samuel and Dorothy Dec. 26 1744
1749 July 11   Francis s. John and Martha May 15 1749
1748 Feb. 29 Reade Sarah d. James and Susannah Feb. 1 1748

1743 Feb. 26 Reddington Margaret d. John and Priscilla 5 yrs.
1760 Jan. 18 Redin Mary d. Lewis and Ann Aug. 4 1759
1721 Feb. 10 Redman Rebecca wife of Joseph March 3 1703
1728 Oct. 27   John 21 yrs.
1731 Mch. 29   Robert s. John and Sarah 3 wks. 2 dys.
1732 Mch. 29   William s. John and Sarah 3 wks. 1 dy.
1735 June 25   Jane d. Joseph and Mary 2 wks.
1736 Dec. 17   Rebecca d. John and Sarah 3 yrs.
1748 Sept. 1   Richard s. Joseph and Elizabeth 5 dys.
1745 Aug. 5   Sarah d. Joseph and Elizabeth July 8 1745
1748 Dec. 18   Elizabeth d. Joseph and Elizabeth Feb. 16 1747
1749 Jan. 18   Elizabeth d. John and Elizabeth Feb. 16 1747
1750 Jan. 21   Mary d. Joseph and Elizabeth Dec. 24 1749
1751 Dec. 8   Rebekkah d. Joseph and Elizabeth Nov. 8 1751
1752 Sept. 19   Sarah d. John and Mary Aug. 16 1752
1754 May 26   Joseph s. Joseph and Elizabeth April 25 1754
1754 July 15   Ann d. John and Mary June 11 1754
1757 May 22   John s. Joseph and Elizabeth April 17 1757
1759 Oct. 14   Thomas s. Joseph and Elizabeth Sept. 14 1759
1738 Jan. 29 Reece Charles s. John and Givin 1 mo.
1740 Mch. 23   William s. John and Gwenllian 5 dys.
1748 Oct. 11   Elinor d. Daniel and Hannah Sept. 11 1748
1712 Aug. 11 Reed John s. John and Sarah 10 wks. 5 dys.
1714 Sept. 8   Sarah d. John and Sarah 2 wks.
1714 Dec. 29   Anne wife Charles
1715 Feb. 20   Charles s. Charles and Anne 20 dys.
1715 May 11   Elizabeth d. Owen and Susan 3 wks.
1727 May 10   Israel s. Charles and Elizabeth 17 dys.
1740 Dec. 21   John s. Samuel and Dorothy 2 wks.
1751 April 17   Sarah d. John and Sarah Feb. 12 1750
1757 Sept. 20   Christopher s. David and Christiana Sept. 15 1757
1735 July 27 Rees Andrew s. John and Martha 14 wks.
1745 Sept. 13   David s. Daniel and Hannah Aug. 26 1745
1741 Mch. 11 Reeth Ann wife Lawrence 59 yrs.
1748 Aug. 13 Reiley Sarah d. John and Sarah June 16 1748
1752 May 6   John s. John and Mary April 10 1752
1754 Aug. 8 Reily Jane d. John and Mary June 7 1754
1756 Aug. 7   Samuel s. John and Mary July 5 1756
1787 Dec. 5 Remington John Bramley s. John and Margaret 7 wks. 3 dys
1784 Oct. 15 Renshaw Sarah d. William and Jane 2 mos.
1744 Mch. 12 Reyley Frances d. Hugh and Mary 7 mos. 23 dys.
1750 May 10   Robert s. John and Mary April 12 1750
1743 Nov. 6 Reyly Elizabeth d. John and Abigail Feb. 9 1743
1787 Jan. 17 Rhodes Mary d. Abraham and Ann 1 dy.
1781 Dec. 17 Rial John s. William and Elizabeth 1 mo.

1732 June 16 Riale Mary d. John and Rachel 9 mos.
1722 Dec. 23 Rice William s. John and Mary 8 mos.
1727 June 21   Emlen d. John and Mary 3 mos.
1732 Aug. 14   Emelin d. John and Mary 2 wks.
1732 Aug. 14   Helen d. John and Mary 2 wks.
1739 May 23   Joseph s. Laurence and Sarah 1 yr. 9 mos.
1750 April 11   Joseph s. Laurence and Sarah July 6 1741
1721 Oct. 15 Richards William s. William and Katherine ——
1733 Mch. 11   David s. John and Mary 8 yrs.
1733 Mch. 11   Susannah d. John and Mary 7 mos.
1733 June 24 Richardson Anne d. Joshua and Margaret 3 mos.
1734 Dec. 27   Phœbe d. Joshua and Margaret 3 mos.
1739 Sept. 2   Joseph s. Joshua and Margaret 4 mos.
1753 May 27   Jane d. Peter and Mary May 3 1753
1756 Nov. 4 Riché Lydia d. Thomas and Sarah Oct. 25 1752
1756 Nov. 4   Mary d. Thomas and Sarah Aug. 31 1755
1760 Aug. 1   Sarah d. Thomas and Sarah Aug. 31 1759
1730 July 5 Richey Rebecca d. David and Mary 5 mos. 17 dys.
1727 Nov. 10 Rickitts Mary d. Joseph and Mary 8 dys.
1731 April 5 Rider Elizabeth d. William and Sarah 3 wks.
1709 Sept. 8 Ridg Sarah d. Daniel and Martha
1742 Dec. 25 Ridge Martha d. John and Hannah 3 mos. 3 dys.
1746 Nov. 30   John s. John and Hannah July 31 1744
1746 Nov. 30   Peter s. John and Hannah Sept. 26 1746
1750 Oct. 21   Daniel s. John and Hannah Sept. 10 1748
1750 Oct. 21   Sarah d. John and Hannah Sept. 21 1750
1753 June 30   Hannah d. John and Hannah Nov. 30 1752
1731 Mch. 2 Ridley Thomas s. Steven and Elizabeth 6 mos.
1742 May 27 Rigby Ann d. Henry and Sarah 7 wks.
1743 July 6   Joseph s. Henry and Sarah 1 mo. 1 dy.
1746 Aug. 23   William s. Henry and Sarah June 18 1746
1749 Sept. 30   William s. Henry and Sarah Jan. 16 1747
1729 Dec. 15 Riggs Joshua s. James and Mary 10 wks.
1734 Aug. 14 Rightentown John s. John and Priscilla 2 wks.
1760 Mch. 6 Riley Thomas s. Edward and Catherine March 1 1760
1735 Nov. 30 Rimington Abraham s. John and Mary
1752 Nov. 30 Rine Anne d. Patrick and Margaret June 30 1752
1720 Nov. 18 Ring Rachel d. Samuel and Martha Nov. 4
1726 Nov. 20 Risdol John s. George and Ann ——
1729 May 25 Risdon Anne d. George and Anne 3 wks.
1752 Jan. 2 Risley Thomas s. Thomas and Elizabeth Dec. 21 1751
1757 April 20 Ritchie William s. William and Juliana March 20 1757
1742 May 27 Rivers Susanah d. Joseph and Mary 3 mos. 3 wks. 3 dys.
1744 Mch. 18   Shadlock s. John and Mary Oct. 25 1739
1744 Mch. 18   Sarah d. John and Mary Aug. 6 1743

1747 July	1	Rivers Mary d. Joseph and Mary Sept. 12 1746
1752 Oct.	5	Sarah d. James and Mary July 9 1752
1733 Sept.	23	Rix Benjamin s. Benjamin and Tales 7 dys.
1731 Mch.	4	Roat Catherine d. George and Mary 2 mos.
1738 July	5	Robbins Elizabeth d. Thomas and Susannah 1 yr. 3 mos.
1747 May	3	Roberson Alexander s. Alexander and Christian March 27 1747
1735 Jan.	12	Roberts Henry s. Henry and Anne 12 dys.
1735 Jan.	23	Rachel d. William and Anne 6 mos. 2 wks.
1736 Nov.	26	William s. William and Anne 13 wks.
1740 Aug.	8	Mary d. John and Susannah 2 wks.
1753 April	17	Elizabeth d. Robert and Mary Nov. 20 1752
1736 Sept.	19	Robertson Margaret Morrow d. Alexander and Sarah 19 mo.
1742 Nov.	21	Catherine d. Alexander and Sarah 2 mos. 19 dys.
1733 Aug.	16	Robins John s. Thomas and Susannah 4½ yrs.
1733 Aug.	16	Sarah d. Thomas and Susannah 1½ yrs.
1738 Sept.	7	Robinson Humphry s. John and Mary 1 mo.
1734 Oct.	24	Elizabeth d. John and Mary 17 dys.
1736 Feb.	14	Henry s. John and Mary 1 mo.
1737 June	26	Anne d. Budd and Rebecca 4 mos. 2 wks.
1738 Oct.	8	Mary d. Budd and Rebecca 3 wks.
1742 May	16	Edward s. Budd and Rebecca 3 wks. 3 dys.
1744 Nov.	20	Joseph s. Budd and Rebecca 21 mos.
1745 July	7	Sarah d. Thomas and Elizabeth Jan. 29 1738
1754 April	13	Elizabeth d. Francis and Elizabeth March 6 1754
1757 April	1	Thomas s. Francis and Elizabeth Jan. 9 1757
1759 Oct.	14	Richard s. Francis and Susannah Sept. 30 1759
1740 Aug.	17	Robison George s. Budd and Rebecca 3 wks. 4 dys.
1760 Nov.	30	Robotham George s. George and Mary Oct. 22 1760
1709 Aug.	20	Roch Mary d. Nicolas and Elizabeth 1 mo.
1711 May	4	John s. George and Penelope, born and baptised
1723 April	8	Rodrow Elizabeth d. John and Elizabeth
1723 April	8	Elizabeth wife John
1746 June	22	Roe Jane d. William and Anne April 30 1744
1720 July	27	Rogers Charles s. Charles and Sarah
1740 Jan.	24	Anne d. Richard and Anne Rebecca 2 wks.
1745 July	30	Nicolas s. Benjamin and Sophia Sept. 11 1744
1760 Jan.	13	Anne d. James and Mary Dec. 30 1759.
1731 April	19	Rolfe Mary d. Joseph and Mary 6 wks.
1710 Mch.	17	Rolph Josiah s. Josiah and Sarah 2 mos.
1716 May	23	Sarah d. John and Sarah 2 yrs. 2 mos.
1734 July	19	Romans James s. Mary 5 mos.
1736 July	15	Hannah d. Mary 14 mos.
1736 Oct.	6	Rome John s. Samuel and Mary 5 wks.
1721 Nov.	12	Rondo James s. James and Susannah ———

1723 Mch. 8 Rondo Jane d. James and Susannah ——
1746 Aug. 17 Rose John s. Peter and Mary Aug. 8 1746
1748 Jan. 10   Mary d. Peter and Mary Dec. 13 1747
1748 Aug. 2   Mary wife of Peter
1751 May 19   Peter s. Peter and Mary Oct. 10 1749
1754 Mch. 16   Peter Gardner s. Peter and Mary Jan. 12 1754
1754 Mch. 16   William s. Peter and Mary Jan. 12 1754
1760 June 10   Richard Gardner s. Peter and Mary Nov. 8 1757
1760 June 10   Jane d. Peter and Mary March 22 1760
1732 Aug. 20 Ross John s. Hugh and Sarah 6 wks.
1735 Feb. 5   Anne d. Hugh and Sarah 3 mos.
1738 Dec. 11   James s. Hugh and Sarah 1 mo.
1740 June 1   Elizabeth d. John and Elizabeth 1 mo.
1741 April 4   Mary d. Hugh and Sarah 1 mo.
1745 July 1   John Adult
1747 June 17   Margaret d. John and Elizabeth April 25 1747
1751 Dec. 15   Elizabeth d. Peter and Mary Nov. 23 1751
1758 Jan. 22 Rotholl John s. Richard and Elizabeth
1721 Jan. 6 Rothwell Mary d. Henry Dec. 5
1731 Feb. 24   Henry s. Henry and Elizabeth 4½ yrs.
1731 Feb. 24   Samuel s. Henry and Elizabeth 5 wks.
1725 Sept. 9 Rouse Emmanuel s. John and Dorothy ——
1727 Feb. 5   Thomas s. Thomas and Elinor 6 mos.
1755 July 14   Rebecca d. Charles and Patience Nov. 25 1753
1742 Feb. 17 Rowland John s. John and Christian 9 mos.
1760 July 21 Rowley Mary d. William and Joanna June 21 1760
1746 Oct. 12 Rowlinson Elizabeth wife of Robert
1723 Feb. 3 Royal Jane d. William and Mary
1712 Aug. 17 Royall Peiter s. Isaac and Frances 2 mos.
1731 Mch. 5 Rumble Mary d. Thomas and Mary 3 yrs. 2 mos.
1731 Mch. 5   Elizabeth d. Thomas and Mary 1 yr. 2 mos.
1758 Dec. 24 Rush James s. Jacob and Hannah Nov. 23 1758
1760 Dec. 20   Mary d. Jacob and Hannah Nov. 8 1760
1722 Aug. 5 Russel John s. Thomas and Mary ——
1722 Aug. 5   Mary d. Thomas and Mary ——
1728 Sept. 9 Russell Mary d. John and Sarah 1 yr. 7 mos.
1744 Nov. 8   Ann d. William and Sarah 1 mo. 4 dys.
1755 June 21   Rebecca d. James and Elizabeth ——
1730 Jan. 4 Rutter Catherine d. Thomas and Mary 3 wks.
1732 Jan. 30   Thomas s. Thomas and Catherine 2 wks.
1733 Dec. 2   Mary d. Thomas and Mary 2 wks.
1734 Nov. 17   Rebecca d. Thomas and Sarah 13 yrs.
1734 Nov. 17   Sarah d. Thomas and Sarah 10 yrs.
1735 Nov. 14   John 42 yrs.
1743 Mch. 5 Ryal Mary d. Samuel and Elizabeth 7 wks. 6 dys.

1746 April 13 Ryal Jane d. George and Mary Sept. 4 1745
1750 Jan.   9 Ryall Samuel s. Samuel Dec. 14 1749
1746 June   2 Ryals Sarah d. Samuel and Elizabeth June 6 1745
1715 Oct.   5 Ryell Rebecca d. Isaac and Frances 3 mos.
1742 June 24   Elizabeth d. Samuel and Elizabeth Feb. 12 1740
1742 Nov. 24 Sadler Sarah d. Alexander and Mary 3 wks.
1726 Dec. 26 Sage Edward s. John and Jane 3 wks.
1750 May 13 Saladee Elizabeth d. Maker and Mary Aug. 6 1749
1714 Sept. 21 Samms Triphany d. John and Mary ——
1715 May   1   William s. William and Catherine 11 mos.
1728 Sept. 16 Sample Mildred d. John and Catherine 2 yrs. 8 mos.
1728 Sept. 16   Catherine d. John and Catherine 4 mos.
1714 Sept. 26 Sanders Martha 19 yrs.
1754 April 7   Elizabeth d. William and Elizabeth Dec. 7 1753
1730 Oct. 11 Sands Rachel d. Thomas and Anne 5 mos.
1734 April 7 Sandwitch Sarah d. Henry and Mary 9 yrs.
1733 Sept. 30 Sapout Philip s. James and Sarah 1 dy.
1741 May   6 Saunders Mary d. John and Leah 8 wks. 3 dys.
1742 Nov. 14   John s. John and Leah 2 mos.
1744 June 29   Leah wife John ——
1753 Sept.   8   Thomas 23 yrs.
1754 Jan.   7   Anne Adult
1759 Oct.   9   John a foundling Aug. 16 1759
1789 Oct. 22 Savadge William s. William and Joanna 3 yrs. 3 mos.
1744 Oct. 25 Savage Samuel s. Joseph and Rebecca 1 mo. 1 dy.
1746 Aug. 31   John s. Joseph and Rebecca June 22 1746
1748 Sept. 19   Thomas s. Joseph and Rebecca July 20 1748
1752 Mch. 15   Joseph s. Joseph and Rebecca Nov. 22 1751
1714 Jan.   3 Sawell Edward ——
1759 July 25 Sayre Rachel d. John and Mary July 9 1759
1760 Aug. 28   John s. John and Mary Aug. 21 1760
1760 Oct.   5 Scanlin William Wallin s. William and Martha Sept. 9
                 1760
1742 May 20 Schlydhorn Henry William s. Henry and Eliz⁰ Oct. 13
                 1741
1748 Mch. 27 Schofield Sarah d. George and Rebeckah Oct. 20 1746
1740 Oct.   3 Schrack John s. Simon and Elizabeth 8 mos.
1744 June 20 Schrock Samuel s. Simon and Elizabeth 3 mos. 8 dys.
1744 June 20   Hannah d. Simon and Elizabeth March 5 1742
1748 April 13 Scot Mary d. John and Catherine April 1 1748
1742 Feb. 28 Scott Ann d. Robert and Catherine 2 yrs. 2 mos.
1756 May 28   Christopher s. Thomas and Ann April 2 1756
1758 June   5 Scotten Sarah Pilkerton d. Samuel and Anne May 10 1753
1752 Mch. 31 Scul Nicholas s. Joseph and Mary March 24 1752
1789 Aug. 26 Scull William s. Edward and Anne 2 mos.

1741 Mch.	5	Scull Rebecca d. Joseph and Mary 9 mos.
1743 Oct.	9	Edward s. Edward and Ann 3 mos. 9 dys.
1748 Mch.	10	Benjamin s. Joseph and Deborah Nov. 13 1744
1748 Mch.	10	William s. Joseph and Deborah, Feb 24 1748
1751 Feb.	25	Susannah d. Jasper and Mary Dec. 6 1750
1760 Aug.	28	Robert 33 yrs.
1758 Aug.	20	Seafield Thomas s. John and Hannah June 5 1755
1729 Nov.	9	Seal John s. Joseph and Ellenor 5 wks.
1746 Nov.	20	Searle Elizabeth d. John and Sarah Nov. 3 1746
1747 Jan.	2	Sarah wife of John
1751 May	18	Mary d. John and Mary Nov. 16 1750
1753 Jan.	20	Elizabeth d. John and Mary April 29 1752
1760 Aug.	25	Searson Sarah d. John and Mary Aug. 5 1760
1734 Jan.	18	Sedgrave William s. William and Mary 3 yrs. 10 dys.
1734 Jan.	13	Thomas s. William and Mary 2 yrs. 2 mos.
1734 Jan.	13	Sarah d. William and Mary 7 mos.
1743 Dec.	11	Sedley Sarah d. William and Ann 5 wks.
1731 April	1	Seeler William s. David and Mary 3 mos.
1733 July	5	Peter s. David and Mary 1 mo.
1740 Sept.	25	Seigell Catherine d. Jacob and Susannah 1 mo.
1735 Sept.	6	Selby Mary d. Evan and Catherine 8 wks.
1754 June	8	Sellers William Hamilton s. William and Ann March 25 1754
1722 Nov.	9	Sells John s. John and Ann ——
1734 July	18	Senck Mary d. George and Hannah 1 dy.
1756 July	3	Seth Charles s. James and Ann July 28 1747
1756 July	3	James s. James and Ann Oct. 25 1753
1756 July	3	Elizabeth d. James and Ann Nov. 30 1756 (*sic*)
1711 May	28	Sevons William s. Robert and Mary ——
1711 May	28	Jonathan s. Robert and Mary ——
1728 April	10	Sewell Hannah d. Richard and Hannah 2 wks.
1730 June	21	Thomas s. Richard and Hannah 4 mos. 2 wks.
1729 Mch.	10	Sewers Elizabeth d. James and Faith 11 dys.
1757 Mch.	1	Sexton Mary d. Thomas and Elizabeth Oct. 24 1756
1728 Nov.	17	Shackledon Sarah d. William and Mary 6 wks.
1729 Dec.	27	Shackleton Mary d. William and Mary 1 mo. 8 dys.
1731 Nov.	21	Ann d. William and Mary 6 wks.
1734 May	15	William s. William and Mary 6 wks.
1736 July	17	Sarah d. William and Mary 6 wks.
1739 Mch.	30	William s. William and Mary 8 dys.
1741 Aug.	13	Elizabeth d. William and Mary 11 mos. 2 dys.
1733 July	28	Shadock Isaac s. Isaac and Penelope 2 wks.
1747 Oct.	25	Shane Mary d. Dennis and Catherine ——
1741 Nov.	8	Sharkley Marcus s. Millins and Mary 3 mos. 3 dys.
1734 July	19	Sharp Mary d. Thomas and Rachel 5 wks.

1711 April	26	Sheards Mary d. Samuel and Sarah ——
1720 Feb.	28	Sheed Isabella Feb. 1
1721 July	19	Susannah d. George and Isabella June 24 1721
1722 Nov.	18	William s. George and Isabella ——
1726 Sept.	18	John s. George and Isabella Sept. 9
1728 Sept.	28	Elizabeth d. George and Isabella 3 wks. 6 dys.
1731 Sept.	5	Mary d. George and Isabella 14 dys.
1733 July	22	Reverdy s. George and Isabella 3 wks. 3 dys.
1735 Aug.	12	Elizabeth d. George and Isabella 12 dys.
1737 Sept.	8	Susannah d. George and Isabella 1 mo.
1748 June	5	Elizabeth d. William and Martha Dec. 26 1747
1758 April	2	Sarah d. William and Martha March 6 1758
1759 Dec.	15	Thomas s. William and Martha Sept. 16 1759
1739 Oct.	7	Sheepherd Robert s. Robert and Elizabeth 7 mos.
1725 Nov.	14	Shepherd John s. Thomas and Sarah
1726 Jan.	26	Elizabeth d. Robert and Annie Dec. 23
1726 Mch.	23	Elizabeth d. Robert and Annie ——
1727 Jan.	31	Robert s. Edward and Mary 1 dy.
1737 Mch.	20	Shepperd Isabella d. Robert and Elizabeth 5 mos.
1760 Dec.	2	Sherer Robert s. Henry and Mary Nov. 19 1760
1754 July	15	Sherlock Easter d. Simon and Jane Oct. 31 1752
1754 July	15	Simon s. Simon and Jane June 16 1754
1756 Dec.	22	James s. Simon and Jane June 3 1756
1736 Oct.	21	Sherly Margaret d. Lewis and Mary 4 mos.
1759 Mch.	19	Sheren William s. Joseph and Mary April 20 1758
1731 Aug.	8	Sherrard Laurence s. Francis and Jane 10 dys.
1732 Sept.	7	Rebecca d. Francis and Jane 1 mo.
1735 Jan.	1	Anne d. Francis and Jane 6 wks.
1738 June	25	Shewbert Robert s. John and Margaret 2 yrs.
1738 June	25	Philip s. John and Margaret 3 wks.
1736 Dec.	19	Shillingford Grace d. James and Priscilla 2 mos.
1759 Aug.	1	Robert s. Robert and Catherine June 9 1759
1759 Dec.	9	Thomas s. James and Mary Feb. 28 1759
1741 Oct.	12	Shillingsford Sarah d. James ——
1738 Mch.	25	Shillingsworth Mary d. James and Priscilla 10 yrs.
1747 Oct.	28	Shilts Mary d. Charles and Agnes Jan. 12 1747
1758 Aug.	19	Shine William s. John and Jane July 10 1752
1757 Oct.	23	Elizabeth d. John and Jane Sept. 6 1757
1737 Nov.	2	Shippen Catherine d. Joseph and Mary 1 mo.
1740 Mch.	19	Margaret d. Joseph and Mary 4 mos.
1741 Dec.	13	Catherine d. Joseph and Mary 1 mo. 13 dys.
1743 Nov.	16	Joseph s. Joseph and Mary 1 mo. 18 dys.
1745 Oct.	2	Mary d. Joseph and Mary April 4 1745
1747 Oct.	11	Abigail d. Joseph and Mary Dec. 12 1746
1749 Mch.	17	Ann d. Joseph and Mary Feb. 22 1749

1751 Dec.   15 Shippen Margaret d. Joseph and Mary Nov. 15 1751
1756 April 22   Elizabeth d. Edward and Margaret Sept. 15 1754
1756 April 22   Sarah d. Edward and Margaret Feb. 1 1756
1758 June   8   Mary d. Edward and Margaret Aug. 15 1757
1740 Feb.   17 Shocalier Mary d. Henry and Anne 2 wks.
1752 Jan.   26 Shoe Sarah d. John and Jane Jan. 17 1752
1736 May   31 Sholar David s. David and Mary 5 mos.
1710 Jan.   15 Shores Samuel 21 yrs.
1717 Oct.   4 Shot Mabel d. Samuel and Mary 10 mos.
1752 June   25 Shute William Adult
1754 Dec.   26   Thomas s. William and Elizabeth Dec. 3 1754
1756 Aug.   4   Mary d. William and Elizabeth July 4 1756
1758 June   4   Attwood s. William and Elizabeth April 11 1758
1760 Aug.   1   Elizabeth d. William and Elizabeth July 3 1760
1747 Aug.   7 Shuttle John s. Jacob and Anne July 6 1747
1743 Feb.   15 Sibbald Mary d. John and Rebecca 2 yrs.
1754 June   16   Rebecca d. John and Rebecca June 2 1754
1756 Sept.   6   David s. John and Rebecca Aug. 22 1756
1736 Nov.   15 Sigel Benjamin s. Jacob and Susannah 2 wks.
1738 July   9 Silas Elizabeth d. John and Elizabeth 3 yrs. 2 mos.
1740 July   10   Joseph s. Joseph and Margaret 2 mos.
1743 Oct.   31   Mary Adult
1743 Oct.   31   Martha Adult
1709 Oct.   27 Simcho George s. George and Elizabeth 7 mos.
1751 Aug.   13 Simes Sarah Woodrop d. Joseph and Anne Jan. 10 1750
1734 April   4 Simons William s. Richard and Margaret 10 wks.
1737 July   14   Stephens s. Wheldon and Anne 8 mos.
1740 April   8   John s. Wheldon and Anne 4 dys.
1741 Mch.   16   Leson s. Wheldon and Anne 1 yr. 4 mos.
1746 April 23   John s. Weldon and Anne March 17 1742
1746 April 23   Anne d. Wheldon and Anne March 19 1745
1757 Mch.   13 Simpson Ann d. Samuel and Ann March 8 1757
1758 April 13   Alexander s. Alexander and Sarah April 10 1758
1758 Oct.   6   Unis d. Samuel and Ann Sept. 22 1758
1758 Dec.   14 Sims Woodrop s. Joseph and Ann Nov. 13 1758
1754 Oct.   27 Simson John Sanders s. John and Mary Oct. 26 1754
1728 Aug.   15 Sinclair Mary d. Robert and Elizabeth 18 mos.
1753 Sept. 26   Barbary wife Joseph
1753 Sept. 26   Joseph s. Joseph and Barbary Nov. 20 1752
1754 Oct.   15 Sinkler Sarah d. Joseph and Barbary Sept. 21 1754
1749 Sept.   3 Siot Thomas s. John and Catherine Aug. 2 1749
1736 Nov.   1 Sippen William s. John and Elizabeth 8 wks.
1759 May   26 Sitgreaves William Deshon s. William and Susannah
                 April 22 1759
1742 June   24 Skinner John s. Edmund and Mary 10 dys.

1745 Mch. 15 Skinner Susannah d. Edmund and Mary 38 dys.
1749 Oct. 13   Mary d. Edward and —— Sept. 10 1749
1753 June 10   Abraham s. Abraham and Margaret June 6 1753
1755 Feb. 5   Thomas s. Abraham and Margaret Jan. 14 1755
1755 Oct. 17   Rachel d. Edmond and Mary Sept. 19 1755
1756 June 7   William s. William and Elizabeth May 3 1756
1757 Jan. 31   Isaac s. Thomas and Sarah Dec. 16 1756
1758 Sept. 17   Sarah d. Thomas and Sarah Aug. 28 1758
1745 Jan. 27 Skofield Stephen s. George and Rebecca 1 mo.
1745 July 1   Jane d. John and Hannah June 11 1745
1739 Dec. 10 Slack Henry s. William and Margaret 5 mos.
1741 Dec. 6   George s. William and Margaret 3 mos. 2 wks. 2 dys.
1710 April 24 Slube Rebecca d. William and Sarah 1 dy.
1755 June 4 Small William s. William and Mary May 19 1755
1756 Aug. 28   John s. William and Mary June 24 1756
1759 Mch. 19   Peter s. William and Mary Dec. 14 1758
1729 Jan. 11 Smallwood Sarah d. Thomas and Ann 1 yr. 8 mos.
1728 Nov. 17 Smart Rebecca d. James and Honner 7 mos.
1759 Feb. 27   Joseph s. John and Ann Dec. 27 1758
1742 Aug. 29 Smiley Elizabeth d. William and Mary 3 yrs. 11 mos. 18 dys.
1742 Aug. 29   Mary d. William and Mary 6 mos. 8 dys.
1746 Feb. 23   William s. William and Mary Feb. 26 1743
1746 Feb. 23   John s. William and Mary Jan. 17 1745
1710 Jan. 15 Smith Mary d. Samuel and Mary 21 yrs.
1710 May 22   Daniel an Indian ——
1713 Oct. 4   William s. John and Mary 3 wks.
1716 May 13   William s. Isaac and Susannah
1721 Mch. 11   Mary d. George and Ann 12 yrs.
1726 Oct. 19   Elizabeth d. William and Sarah 9 mos.
1726 Dec. 2   Katherine d. William and Mary Nov. 19
1726 Dec. 27   Mary d. Edward and Elizabeth 3 mos.
1728 Dec. 9   Nathaniel s. Christopher and Joanna 6 wks.
1729 Jan. 6   James s. Andrew and Susannah 4 mos. 2 wks.
1729 Feb. 28   Mary d. William and Mary 6 wks. 2 dys.
1729 Dec. 27   Elizabeth d. Edward and Elizabeth 8 mos.

(To be continued.)

NOTES AND QUERIES.

Notes.

To the Editor of the PENNSYLVANIA MAGAZINE OF HISTORY AND BIOGRAPHY.

I wish to give a word of advice to those of your readers who may be interested in preparing genealogical charts, to be careful in their research to prove the various lines of descent they may be hunting up by means of wills, church registers, and other reliable sources, before submitting the result to the printer's hands. An example of lack of thoroughness in research may be found in an account of Dr. Thomas Wynne, the early Philadelphia physician, who died in 1692. The article in question is on page 662 of Part II. for the year 1882 of the *Magazine of American History*. In it the writer states that Dr. Wynne was a son of Peter Wynne, of Leewood and the Tower, and that the latter was the fifth son of Sir John Wynn, of Gwydir; further, that he entered the Royal College of Surgeons, at London, and that he married Mary Bultall or Bulteel, daughter of Samuel Bultall, a younger son of James Bulteel, of Fleet, County Devon, by the latter's wife, Mary, daughter and sole heir of Courtney Crocker, of Lyneham, County Devon. Now, the Wynns of the Tower and those of Gwydir were distinct and separate families (see Lewis Dwnn's "Welsh Visitations"). Sir John Wynn, in his admirable "History of the Gwydir Family," does not mention having a son Peter. After a careful search through the books of both the Royal College of Surgeons as well as those of the Royal College of Physicians, the name of Thomas Wynne could not be found during the period mentioned,—1650 to 1660. James Bulteel, who married Mary, daughter of Courtney Crocker, and who is stated to have been the grandfather of Mary, the wife of Thomas Wynne, was an M. P. for Tavistock. He died 19th May, 1756, aged eighty, making the year of his birth 1676, some thirty years after the approximate time of the birth of Dr. Wynne's wife,—making her a wonderful freak, which at this *fin de siècle* realistic age would cause, if she were alive, thousands to come many miles to see a woman born before her grandfather. A member of the Bulteel family has kindly looked the matter up for me from his own family papers and from the church registers and Quaker Meeting records. Being myself a descendant of Dr. Wynne, I am anxious to have a correct account of his ancestry. This led me to investigate the statement made in the *Magazine of American History*, which, after considerable time, has brought the results mentioned.   HOWARD WILLIAMS LLOYD.

THE FAYETTE COUNTY HISTORICAL AND GENEALOGICAL SOCIETY has been organized at Uniontown, Pennsylvania, with the following officers: President, E. Baily Dawson; Vice-Presidents, Dr. Wm. H. Sturgeon, Dr. James B. Ewing; Secretary and Treasurer, Paoli S. Morrow; Corresponding Secretary, O. J. Sturgis; Trustees, Colonel John Collins, James A. Searight, Amos M. Jolliffe, Dr. H. B. Mathish, and Colonel Thomas B. Searight. The Society will be chartered, and the constitution provides that in case of dissolution its property shall go to the Historical

Society of Pennsylvania. The regular meetings will be on the last Thursday evenings of May and October, and the 22d of February.

Fayette County is rich in historical treasure, and the Society will aim to gather and preserve the rapidly-perishing records and traditions of the olden time. In Fayette County soil the bones of the brave but indiscreet General Braddock repose, and near by his grave is the site of Fort Necessity, where the youthful Washington first tried conclusions with the French and Indians; and a few miles farther west, on the mountain-side overlooking Uniontown, is the scene of the famous Dunbar's camp, now occupied by the Jumonville Soldiers' Orphans' School. Few counties in the State witnessed more stirring scenes in the ante-Revolutionary period than Fayette, and the new Historical Society has an inviting field for its operations.

O. J. STURGIS.

THE "COMO HOUSE."—On the right-hand side of the Bethlehem turnpike road, going north, and near the summit of the first rising ground beyond Chestnut Hill, stands an ancient two-story stone house, often spoken of as the "Como House," from the inscription cut upon the front wall, and which reads, or seems to read, "COMO 1743." There is, however, a point, not easily seen from the high-road, between the first O and the M, and the explanation of the mystery that has puzzled so many passers-by is, that CO stands for Christopher Ottinger, and MO for Mary Ottinger, wife of Christopher. So, at least, I am informed by the occupant of the house. T. S.

"WITH ALL MY WORLDLY GOODS I THEE ENDOW."—The Countess Dowager of Sunderland, writing to Mr. Sidney ("Times of Charles II."), under date of March 22, 1680, states, "He is not a very pleasant man—very few are; neither is he the very next for entertainment. One thing pleased: when he said 'With all my worldly goods I thee endow,' he put a purse upon the book with 200 guineas; everybody puts somewhat, but this the most I ever heard."

A CORRECTION IN THE REGISTER OF BAPTISMS, CHRIST CHURCH, PHILADELPHIA.—"Henry White Physick s. Edmund & Abigail Physick b. 3 January 1759; baptized 25 February 1759." (*Church Register*.)

"Philip Syng Physick, son of Edward [recto Edmund] & Abigail Physick, born 7 July, 1768, baptized 30 December 1770." (*Church Register*.)

"Henry White Physick, Born on Sunday the 26th November, 1758, at 10 minutes after 3 o'clock in the afternoon. Baptized on Sunday." (*From the Bible of Mr. Edmund Physick, the entry being in his own handwriting*.) From a comparison of these entries, I infer that the transcriber has erred in making that of Christ Church Register.

PHILIP SYNG PHYSICK CONNER.

WEDGEWOOD WARE, 1784.—Extracts from the diary of Samuel Shoemaker, written for his wife from London, January 9, 1784.

"After breakfast my Friend Majendie accompanied us to a House in Greek street where the noted Wedgewood has his collection of curious earthen Ware, in viewing of which we were quite lost in the infinite variety of this large and curious collection. After spending an hour in going thro' the different Rooms I was loth to depart without purchasing something and bought a small Tea Pott and milk Pott for thee, to which Majendie insisted on adding a Bowl & Plate which he desires thou wilt

accept of as a small Testimony of his remembrance & esteem. I also
bought a Tea Pott for Betsy and left orders to send them down to my
Lodgings today."
       Same, January 30, 1784.
       " R Alexander then accompanied me in a walk to Soho Square & we
call'd at Wedgewood's ware house to take another look at his Collection
and I was tempted to purchase three *small* oval Bass reliefs to send to
Benjamin."
       Letter, Mrs. Samuel Shoemaker to her husband, April 22, 1784.
       " The teapots bowl creampot are uncommon & very curious. I be-
lieve nothing of the kind has ever been sent over here ; they have
brought this kind of manufactory to great perfection indeed, & I wish
my best respects & thanks to our frd. Magendie for his curious Bowl &
plate. I shall value it for his sake. We thought the little creatures
should have been *cloathed."
       Letter, same to same, May 15, 1784.
       " The Bass reliefs I think are extreme curious, indeed inimitably well
executed & the Design pretty & if the little creatures on the teapots had
been a little dressed, if it had been only a thin mantle thrown over them,
we could have introduced them more freely into company without fear of
hurting any person's delicacy."

       THE VALUE OF SYSTEMATIC RESEARCH.—Assuming that people
would rather not have their property consumed by expensive lawsuits,
or wasted in the delays and uncertainties accompanying them, here is a
chapter of modern experience which seems to prove very clearly the
value of systematic genealogical research, and the orderly examination and statement by families as to who do and who do not belong to
them. If this family had known who their relatives were, by a care-
fully-kept record, they might have been spared these costly experiences.
       A despatch from Reading, Pennsylvania, April 12, 1893, says, " In
court here this morning, in the ejectment suit of Jacob Gehr and others
vs. David Sittler and others, a compulsory nonsuit was entered.
       " This bare statement conveys no important public information, but it
is probably the final act in one of the most interesting and romantic
chapters of litigation in Eastern Pennsylvania. When it was last before
the Supreme Court, Chief-Justice Paxson said that it developed some of
the most remarkable facts that had ever come before that body. It in-
volves a contest, covering sixteen years, for a farm of two hundred and
forty acres, in Maxatawney Township, this [Berks] county, for which
some twenty thousand dollars were offered a few years ago. In all, some
twenty lawyers were engaged in the case, and it is believed that the
greater portion of the value of the farm has been swallowed up in attorneys' fees. The facts are about these :
       " In 1875 Miss Kitty Gehr, an aged maiden lady, belonging to one of
the old families of Berks County, died in this city, and among other
property which she left was this farm. It descended to her through her
father, Jacob Gehr, to whom it was willed by his father, Baltzer Gehr,
one of the provincial judges of Berks, and well known in the early political history of this county. A branch of the family, residing in Kutztown, at Kitty Gehr's death put in a claim for the farm as the next of
kin, and at a hearing before arbitrators, the farm was awarded to them.
The next chapter in this famous case was enacted when Hannah Nicely,
an aged woman of Milton, came forward and established the fact that
she was the daughter of Frederick Yeager, whose sister had been married to Baltzer Gehr, and she, being one degree nearer than the Kutz-

town Gehrs, was awarded the farm, and the matter was looked upon as settled, when it developed that Frederick Yeager had another daughter, Maria Rothermel, who died in Shamokin, and her heirs brought suit against Hannah Nicely for one-half of the farm, and recovered. The contest for the farm was now looked upon as concluded. Mrs. Nicely and Mrs. Rothermel, sisters, then died, upward of ninety years of age, within a short time of each other, and their heirs were about to take possession of the farm. At this point another claimant turned up. About a dozen years ago several newspapers of Pennsylvania published the fact that Baltzer Gehr, an influential citizen of Crawford County, had just celebrated his one hundredth birthday anniversary, in which hundreds of people had participated.

" A copy of a paper containing this account fell into the hands of the attorneys of the Kutztown Gehrs, and they communicated with Baltzer Gehr, of Crawford County, who, after endless difficulty, clearly established the fact that he was the son of Joseph Gehr, whose existence up to this time was unknown, another brother of Baltzer Gehr, of Berks County, and, consequently, on an equal footing with the heirs of Mrs. Nicely and Mrs. Rothermel. Early records in Philadelphia, Germantown, Lancaster, Reading, Shamokin, Crawford County, and elsewhere were overhauled; inscriptions on tombstones in country church-yards introduced to show the genealogy of the Gehr family, old family records resurrected, and the affidavits of aged people who were too infirm to come to Reading to testify introduced. The case was tried several times in the Berks Court, and was on a number of occasions before the Supreme Court. The Crawford County centenarian died, but his heirs carried on the fight and won their third of the property. Therefore, the price realized for the farm will be divided into three parts between the heirs of Baltzer Gehr, of Crawford County, Mrs. Hannah Nicely, and Mrs. Maria Rothermel.

" A final contest was instituted by another branch of the Gehr family, and this is the case in which the nonsuit was entered to-day. David Sittler is tenant on the farm.

H. M. J.

ELIZABETH ESTAUGH'S RECOLLECTIONS.—The following is a copy of a letter from Elizabeth Estaugh, of Haddonfield, New Jersey, to John Smith, of Philadelphia, " Merchant," the son-in-law of James Logan. As the writer was an old woman when she wrote this, her memory carries us back to quite an early period of our Colonial history.

" HAD[—] ye 18th of m 1761.

" MUCH ESTEEM^D FR^D J : S :

" I've at Last put in practice what thou request^d to give ye an ac^{et} of what I could remember of valuable fr^{ds} in this part belonging to ye m^oly meeting of Newton viz

" Wm Cooper small Gift, but worthy examplery man, early convinced & much valued att home, belonged to Jordan's m^{tt}g.

" Tho Thackery a good minister did not travel much, but very serviceable about meetings hereaway, heart & house open to his friends.

" Tho Shackle small gift but worthy fr^d & wife a substantial fr^d meet^{er} kept many years att their house &c

" Tho Sharp, Clark & Overseer many years a zealious serviceable man Chester perticular m^tg

" John Adams acceptable minister

" Archabald Mickle & John Kaighn overseers together some years & was zeliously concern^d to discharge ye trust reposed to their care.

"Eliz͏ᵃ. Kay a good gift in y͏ᵉ Ministry visited fr͏ᵈˢ in Maryland &c England. Scotland & Ireland, well accepted.

"Eliz͏ᵃ Evins a very serviceable fr͏ᵈ whilst among us & much valued but concluded at Phila͏ᵈᵃ

"Sar͏ᵃ Roberts an innocent fr͏ᵈ & Gift in y͏ᵉ ministry, our fr͏ᵈ Han͏ᵃ Forster if y͏ᵉ has oppertunity can give a perticular acc͏ᵗ being I think her grandmother.

"Now my fr͏ᵈ these are w͏ᵗ I can remember of y͏ᵉ old names of fr͏ᵈˢ that are pretty much forgot being but few left that can remember em, yet by y͏ᵉ names when oppertunity offers among old folks, thou maiest be better furnish͏ᵈ.

"I hope & desire these lines will be reced in better health then they leave me, am so afflicted, w͏ᵗʰ my head, y͏ᵉ deeply affects & unquallifies me much, for writing. So I hope for a favourable construction on my rough performance, believing y͏ᵉ will not expose me, & conclude with an endeared Salutation of Love to thyself & Dear wife, w͏ᶜʰ is beyond what I can express, & bids you both Dearly farewell, farewell saith,

"Eliz͏ᴬ Estaugh."

The Gazette of the United States, Philadelphia, 1792.—The following extracts from *The Gazette of the United States* were handed to the editor of the Pennsylvania Magazine by the late Dr. James J. Levick, on the morning of the day on which he was attacked by his fatal illness, June 23 last. Dr. Levick was one of our esteemed contributors, and his historical and genealogical researches in connection with the early Welsh settlers in Pennsylvania are well known to our readers. At the meeting of the Council of the Society, June 26, an appropriate minute on his death was prepared and made of record.

"In looking over *The Gazette of the United States,* for the year 1792, I find the following notice:

"'*The Statue of Dr. Franklin* was, last Saturday, (April 7, 1792), fixed in its niche over the door in the new library on Fifth Street. François Lazzarini is the sculptor, and *Carrara* the name of the place where it was executed. If the intrinsic merit of this master-piece of art did not speak its value, the name of the artist, where he is known, would evince it. Here perhaps its price may give the best idea of its worth. We have heard, but not from such a quarter as positively to warrant the assertion, that it cost above 500 guineas.'

"Then follows a description of the statue now over the Hall of the Philadelphia Library on Locust Street, with which our citizens have long been familiar.

"'On Friday last the Governor of this State laid the corner-stone of *The President's House* on Ninth Street. The following inscription is on the stone :

This corner stone was laid
on the 10th day May 1792
The State of Pennsylvania out of debt
Thomas Mifflin, Governor.'

"*May* 16, 1797.

"James J. Levick."

Queries.

Lukens.—Who was the mother of John Lukens, surveyor-general of Pennsylvania? Was he a son of William Lukens, and was his father twice married? Data concerning his maternal ancestry is particularly desired. W. J. P.

SCHAUWECKER—LEAF—SNYDER—RITTER.—Genealogical data is requested of the following families:

Mary Barbara Schauwecker, of Germantown, who married the Rev. Johann Frederick Schmidt.

Catherine Leaf, who married Judge Frederick Smith, of Reading, Pennsylvania.

Anna R. Snyder, daughter of Jacob Schneider, of Reading, and Anna Ritter, of Oley Township, Berks County, Pennsylvania, and who married John Frederick Smith, of Reading, Pennsylvania.

MRS. W. HINCKLE SMITH.

2221 Trinity Place, Philadelphia.

HARDING—MEREDITH—TAYLOR—HOLME.—Information wanted of parentage and descendants of John Harding, member of the Provincial Assembly from Chester County in 1682, 1683, and 1685, and a justice of the peace in 1684. Also of Simon Meredith, member of the Provincial Assembly from Chester County in 1727. Also of Philip Taylor, member of the Provincial Assembly from Chester County in 1728, and county treasurer in 1724–26. Also of John Holme, justice of the peace, Philadelphia County, 1689.

THANKSGIVING SERMONS.—Was the Thanksgiving sermon of Rev. Samuel Stanhope Smith, Febuary 19, 1795, printed anywhere else than in Philadelphia? If so, where? How many editions?

The sermon by Rev. David Osgood, Febuary 19, 1795: was it printed in Philadelphia? I know of the Boston and Litchfield (Conn.) editions.

Hartford, Conn. W. D. L. L.

EDWARD DAVIES.—Information is desired of the ancestry of Hon. Edward Davies, a member of the Twenty-fifth and Twenty-sixth Congresses, from Lancaster County, Pennsylvania. He was a son of James Davies and Elizabeth Sullivan, who were married at Reading in 1777.

Washington, D.C. JULIA D. STRONG.

FAMILY OF DR. EDWARD JONES, OF MERION.—Can any one tell me the date and place of death and burial of Mary Jones, wife of Dr. Edward Jones, of Merion? In "The Friend," Vol. XXIX. p. 76. it states that she died 7th mo. 29th, 1726, and was buried at Merion. This must be a mistake, for Edward Jones, in his will dated "the Twenty Seventh day of the Third month in the year of our Lord one thousand seven hundred & thirty two," appoints "my wife Mary, my son-in-law John Cadwalader and sons Jonathan Edward & Evan afore said my Executors." This will was probated in 1738, and is No. 177 of that year, Register of Wills office, Philadelphia, Book N, 320.

The children of Dr. Edward Jones and Mary, his wife, daughter of Dr. Thomas Wynne, as named in his will, were Martha, Jonathan, Edward, Thomas, Evan, John, Elizabeth, and Mary. Can any one tell me whether Edward, Thomas, and John were married? If so, when, where, and to whom, and their issue?

Evan Jones was married twice: first, to Mary Stephenson, of New York; second to —— Mathews, daughter of Colonel Mathews, of Fort Albany, New York. Can any one tell me the given name of the second wife and names of her children? HOWARD WILLIAMS LLOYD.

MICKLE — WATTS — HUTCHINGS — BARCLAY.—Archibald Mickle, County Antrim, Ireland, arrived in Philadelphia Sixth month second day, 1682 (Philadelphia Meeting). He married, in same place, 1686, Sarah Watts. Her will, in 1718, mentions Abraham Carlisle and Joseph Cooper, her executors, as brothers-in-law. In the Woodbury Meeting records, 1709, there is a marriage, Joshua Lord to Isabella Watts. Can any one give me information of the Watts family?

Among marriages solemnized in open court at Salem, New Jersey, August 10, 1686, are those of John Allen to Mary Hutchings, daughter of Roger Hutchings; and on February 3, 1686, Hugh Hutchings to Mary Adams, daughter of John Adams. Information is wanted of the Hutchings family and connections.

Did not John Barclay, the brother of Robert, settle on lands of the latter in Monmouth County, New Jersey? Can any one give information of his descendants, or of early marriages in that family?

R. M. H.

DIARY OF AARON WRIGHT, A SOLDIER OF THE REVOLUTION.—In the *Historical Magazine and Notes and Queries concerning the Antiquities, History, and Biography of America,* for June, 1862, "J. B. R," of Washington, D.C., contributes extracts from the diary of Aaron White, a private in Captain Lowdon's company of Colonel William Thompson's Pennsylvania Rifle Battalion. The diary is said to comprise fifty-three pages, and to cover the period between June 29, 1775, and July 4, 1776. Information is desired of "J. B. R." as to the present owner of the diary, and whether it can be examined.

MRS. HARRY ROGERS.

1822 Spruce Street, Philadelphia.

JOHN STURGIS.—Information is requested as to the ancestry of John Sturgis, of Captain Josiah Harmer's company, First Pennsylvania Battalion, Colonel John Philip de Haas. After the Revolution he moved to Fayette County (1787), and settled near Uniontown. The history of his descendants is fully known, but that of his ancestry is not. It is believed that he came from New Jersey, and that his brothers were Nathan and Amos, one of whose grandsons was the late General Samuel Davis Sturgis of the United States army.

O. J. STURGIS.

Uniontown, Pennsylvania.

HOCKLEY GENEALOGY.—A genealogy of the Hockley and related families of Wescott, Story, and Rodgers is in preparation by Stevenson H. Walsh, 1806 Pine Street, Philadelphia. The name and address of any one who can furnish additional information of members of these families is requested.

DAMASCUS MILLS.—Was there ever a place called "Damascus Mills" within the limits of the State of Pennsylvania, or outside that State, but in the vicinity of Philadelphia? If so, where was it located and by what name is it known at present? ALICE COLE.
Centreville, Ia.

ARCHDEACON MOOR.—For purposes of annotation I am desirous of learning the Christian name of, and any other particulars concerning, Archdeacon Moor, of Queen's County, Ireland, who was probably the clergyman referred to in a letter from the Rev. Joseph Boyes, Dublin, September 22, 1707, to Ralph Thoresby. (Correspondence of R. Thoresby, London, 1832, Vol. II. p. 50.)

Boyes writes, " I have sent you enclosed a sheet against the Quakers. The queries were drawn up by a Conformist clergyman in the Queen's County (an Archdeacon and a very pious man). But he having left me an absolute power to model them as I pleased, I have almost entirely new moulded them, and they lay open, I think, a true scheme of the most refined Quakerism. The Quakers are alarmed by it, but have not yet answered them."

I presume that these are the queries printed at the end of Boyes's works, in two volumes, folio, London, 1728. T. S.

OTSEGO HALL.—I was present at a meeting of the Historical Society of Pennsylvania on the evening of the 9th November, 1857, when a paper was read by the Secretary (of which he afterwards kindly gave me a copy), and which began as follows:

" Richard Smith, the author of the journal of the proceedings of Congress herewith printed, was born at Burlington, N. J., on the 22ᵈ of March, 1736." According to the short sketch of his life which followed, he was admitted to the bar in both Pennsylvania and New Jersey, became Recorder of Burlington, Clerk of Assembly, and member of the Council of New Jersey, and " was a delegate from New Jersey both in the first and second Continental Congress convened at Philadelphia, the date of his withdrawal from which is shown by the following extract.

" ' New Jersey. Provincial Congress. Wednesday June 12, 1776. Richard Smith Esq., one of the Delegates for this Colony in the Continental Congress, asking leave to resign his seat there, on account of indisposition ; Ordered, That his resignation be accepted.' "

He was afterwards made Treasurer of the State. He died at Natchez, on the 17th September, 1803.

There is one statement in the paper that I would ask permission to make the subject of a query. It is said that " about the year 1790, Mr. Smith removed to his farm at SMITH HALL, Otsego County, New York, to which place he had long been attached, and which he continued to improve and cultivate till the year 1799, when he left it to reside with his son Richard Rodman Smith in Philadelphia."

It will be borne in mind that the material for this sketch was gathered from Mr. Smith's own papers, that had been lent for the purpose by a descendant. Compare with this the following, from " The Burlington Smiths," by R. Morris Smith, Philadelphia, 1877, p. 119.

" He (R. S.) had a country-seat called Bramham Hall, since destroyed by fire, and having, with other members of the Smith family, purchased a large tract of land on Otsego Lake, New York, he built thereon another fine hall. . . . (lately engraved in a biography of Fenimore Cooper), lived there some years, and called it ' Smith Hall.' The Smiths employed as their agent, to oversee their estates at Otsego, Judge Cooper, . . . who ultimately bought the property of them, and changed the name of the hall to ' Otsego Hall ;' and here his son, the celebrated novelist, James Fenimore Cooper, was born."

In my copy of the book there is a printed slip correcting the error as to Cooper's birthplace, which was at Burlington. But the statement that Smith built the hall remains unchanged.

Roundsbury's " Life of Cooper," in the " American Men of Letters" series, Boston, 1883, says, in substance (pp. 2, 3), that Cooper's father, who had come into possession of vast tracts of land along the headwaters of the Susquehanna, " laid out the plot of the village which bears his name," in 1788, and in 1799 had " completed the erection of a mansion which bore the name of Otsego Hall."

An unpublished letter from Mrs. George Dillwyn to her husband, written in 1790, says, " Burlington William Cooper . . . was just going to return to Otego [*sic*] where he had laid out a town on a tract of his own, raising large quantities of good sugar from maple trees. Burlington Richard Smith's son Dick had also been to Otego, & returned so well pleased with the country, as to conclude to settle there for a time & open store with Wm. Cooper."

My query is one that I think will suggest itself to any one that may have taken the trouble to read the foregoing : Who built Otsego Hall?

There is much that is interesting about the settlement of Otsego that has not yet been written. There were many purchasers from Burlington and Philadelphia, and many who had been solicited to become purchasers, but did not. Mrs. Dillwyn says in another letter,—this was in 1775,—" N. W. . . . has a new scheme of Osteago [*sic*] in view and goes next month to see & purchase lands. They are both very desirous of drawing thy inmates along with them—must have Bro^r D. A fig for ' posterity ' say I. If 50 acres can bound our desires, they may be found nearer home without the trouble of felling trees of an antediluvian growth, which w^d not answer to make pearl ash [Mrs. Dillwyn's husband was interested in this industry] after all."

In 1794 the New Jersey " Friends" who had gone to Otsego applied, as members, to the Monthly Meeting of Mount Holly for liberty to hold meetings. The application was referred to the Quarterly Meeting, which decided that " a Meeting being settled there would be, in the present weak state of Friends, improper," but advised the settlers " to apply for Certificates to the respective Monthly Meetings from whence they removed, to be directed to the Monthly Meeting nearest to their place of Residence," adding " the sooner this step is taken, the better it will be for the Individuals . . . concerned, . . . and the desire of seeing a Meeting established in that growing Settlement, will, by these means, be sooner gratified." This was addressed " To the Members of the Quarterly Meeting of Friends of Burlington, Settled within the Otego or Otsego Patent, in the State of New York."

T. S.

Replies.

COOPER FAMILY.—The " D. Cooper" referred to by " T. S." on page 467, Vol. XVI., No. 4, PENNA. MAG., was David Cooper, who lived near Woodbury, New Jersey. He was the son of John Cooper and Ann Clarke. John Cooper (born 9 mo. 22d, 1683 ; married 11 mo. 17th, 1711/12 ; died 9 mo. 22d, 1730) was the only son of William Cooper and Mary Bradway. William Cooper (born 9 mo. 26th, 1660 ; married 9 mo. 8th, 1682 ; died 4 mo., 1691) was the oldest son of William and Margaret Cooper, who settled in Burlington, New Jersey, in 1678, and in 1679 located a tract of three hundred acres at Pyne Point, now called Cooper's Point.

W. A. C.

CLAYPOLE PORTRAITS.—Your querist may be able to learn something of a portrait of one of this family from Colonel Joseph C. Clark, of Haverford, Pennsylvania. He was formerly of Mount Holly, New Jersey, and at his father's house I saw, many years ago, a portrait of the elder Mr. Joseph Clark's grandmother, who was a Claypole, of Burlington County, New Jersey. It was probably painted about the Revolutionary period,—a half-length in oil. Mr. Clark, Sr., possessed numerous other portraits, but they, with possibly an exception with other family relics, came, I think, from the Vandykes of New York, he having married Cornelia Vandyke for his second wife, great-granddaughter of Rodulphus Vandyke (or Vandyck), who died about the middle of the last century, and was buried in Trinity Church-yard, New York. He was a wealthy merchant.   X.

VALLEY FORGE (PENNA. MAG., Vol. VIII. p. 441; Vol. XV. p. 382). —The following extracts from a letter of Captain William Allen, of the Rhode Island Continental Line, informs us of the date of death of John Waterman, commissary of General Varnum's brigade. The troops of this brigade were encamped near the " Star redoubt," not far from which is still to be seen the solitary gravestone with its inscription, " J. W. 1778."

"CAMP VALLEY FORGE 24 April 1778.

" DEAR SIR

"Captain Tew and myself arrived safe to post the 22d inst. found the encampment in perfect tranquility, and the enemy peaceable in their quarters.   Am sorry to inform you that yesterday died of a short illness that worthy gentleman John Waterman Esqr. Commissary to our brigade. . . .

"Humble Servant
" WILLIAM ALLEN

" N.B.—Have returned your bill to Capt Olney as it would not pass in Pennsylvania.
" THEODORE FOSTER ESQ."

J. V. P. TURNER.

HOPE LODGE (PENNA. MAG., Vol. XVII. p. 121).—A respectable farmer, born at Hope Lodge, tells me that he has always understood that the house was built by one Roberts, who conveyed to Hope.   He is also familiar with the tradition of Amaryllis and the fateful speech, but with Roberts, not Hope, as the hero.   T. S.

DANIEL HUMPHREY, OF HAVERFORD.—Mr. Howard Williams Lloyd, in "Notes and Queries" (PENNA. MAG., Vol. XVII. p. 115), refers to the list of the children of Daniel Humphrey, on p. 471 of Dr. George Smith's "History of Delaware County," as " both incomplete and incorrect," and in proof of that statement cites the names of the children mentioned in their father's will as registered in Philadelphia in Will-Book E, p. 327.

It will be seen by reference to the introduction to Dr. Smith's book, that the brief biographical notices appended to it were based upon data gathered in preparation of the main work, and were neither expected nor intended to be complete.   In fact, the author expresses his regret that notices of many of the pioneer settlers had to be omitted entirely. The correctness of his list of the children of Daniel Humphrey, so far as it goes, has, however, been confirmed by subsequent research among the records of Haverford Monthly Meeting, made by the late Joseph W. George.   These records furnish the names, with dates of birth, of thirteen children of Daniel and Hannah Humphrey, two of whom—Thomas, born 20th of Fourth month, 1697, and Mary, born 10th of Twelfth month, 1704–05—are in Dr. Smith's list, but are not mentioned in the will above cited.   BENJAMIN H. SMITH.

Book Notices.

THE ILLUSTRATED ARCHÆOLOGIST.—We have received the first number of this new quarterly, edited by J. Romilly Allen, F.S.A. Scot. It is printed in good clear type, on toned paper, and copiously illustrated. The editor contributes "Sculptured Norman Capitals at Southwell Minster," and an interesting paper on the manufacture of flints, entitled "A Very Ancient Industry," by Edward Lovett; "Notes on Archæology and Kindred Subjects;" "Half an Hour in Grosvenor Museum, Chester," by G. W. Shrubsole, F.G.S., and other papers make up a valuable and attractive serial. Price 10s. 6d. per annum.

THE CLAYPOOLE FAMILY, a Genealogy of the American Claypooles, edited by Mrs. Paul Graff, is now ready for the subscribers.

The book is an octavo of about one hundred and seventy pages, and contains some autographs and a number of reproductions from family portraits, with full index and numerous notes. In addition to a chapter on the English Claypooles and the Wingfields, this volume includes a sketch of James Claypoole, the first emigrant, with a number of his letters to William Penn and others, sketches of his brothers, of the Bringhurst family, of the Hon. James Trimble, of Dr. James Trimble, of Bishop Hobart, of John Claypoole and his wife Elizabeth Ross, who is said to have made the first United States flag, of Timothy Matlack, of the Rev. John Gemmill, and other distinguished members of the family; also a copy of original grant of arms to the Claypooles. Price to subscribers, $5.00. Address Mrs. Paul Graff, 4040 Walnut Street, Philadelphia.

THROUGH COLONIAL DOORWAYS. By Anne Hollingsworth Wharton. Philadelphia, 1893. J. B. Lippincott Company. 237 pp.

The revival of interest in the Colonial and Revolutionary periods, with the natural curiosity to gain some insight into the social and domestic life of those days, has received an impetus through the organizations of Colonial Dames, Colonial Wars, Sons of the Revolution, and other kindred societies. Miss Wharton's book comprises sketches of the Meschianza, New York Balls and Receptions, the American Philosophical Society, the Wistar Parties, a Bundle of Old Love-Letters, and the Philadelphia Dancing Assemblies. Intelligence and judgment are displayed in the selection of these essays (some of which attracted considerable notice at the time of their serial publication), which give not mere history, but also the social history of those times, and they are presented with the usual literary grace for which the writer is well known. The artistic beauty of the book is deserving of especial notice; the original illustrations add to its attractiveness, and a comprehensive index to its value. We are therefore not surprised to learn that the second edition issued is well-nigh exhausted.

HISTORICAL SOCIETY OF PENNSYLVANIA.

The following are some of the Historical and Genealogical serials to be found on the tables in the Library:

FOREIGN.

Collections of the Powys-Land Club	London.
Gloucestershire Notes and Queries	London.
Miscellanea Genealogica et Heraldica . . .	London.
Northamptonshire Notes and Queries . . .	Northampton.
Notes and Queries	London.
Northern Notes and Queries	Edinburgh.
The East Anglican, or Notes and Queries on subjects connected with the Counties of Suffolk, Cambridge, Essex, and Norfolk.	Ipswich.
The Genealogist	London.
The Index Library	London.
The Western Antiquary or Note Book for Devon, Cornwall, and Somerset	Plymouth.
Yorkshire Notes and Queries: with Yorkshire Genealogist, Yorkshire Bibliographer, and Yorkshire Folk-Lore Journal	Bradford.

DOMESTIC.

American Journal of Numismatics and Bulletin of American Numismatic and Archæological Societies	Boston.
American Notes and Queries	Philadelphia.
Essex Institute Historical Collections . . .	Salem, Mass.
Magazine of American History	New York.
Magazine of Western History	Cleveland.
New York Genealogical and Biographical Record	New York.
Notes and Queries, Historical and Genealogical .	Harrisburg, Pa.
Proceedings and Collections of the Wyoming Historical and Geological Society	Wilkesbarre, Pa.
Proceedings of the Academy of Natural Sciences	Philadelphia.
Southern Historical Society Papers . . .	Richmond, Va.
The American Journal of Philology . . .	Baltimore, Md.
The American Catholic Historical Researches .	Philadelphia.
The Book Mart	Pittsburg, Pa.
The Cambrian	Cincinnati.
The Granite Monthly	New Hampshire.
The Historical Record, with Notes and Queries .	Wilkesbarre, Pa.
The Iowa Historical Record	Iowa City.
The Journal of the Military Service Institution .	New York.
The Library Journal	New York.
The Nation	New York.
The New England Historical and Genealogical Register	Boston.
The New England Magazine and Bay State Monthly .	Boston.
The Pennsylvanian	Philadelphia.
Rhode Island Magazine	Newport.

[Publishers of other serials will please forward prospectus.]

For Sale at 1300 Locust St., Phila. Price, 75 cts. per
Number, or $3 per year.

No. 67.

THE

PENNSYLVANIA

MAGAZINE

OF

HISTORY AND BIOGRAPHY.

PUBLISHED QUARTERLY.

No. 3 OF VOL. XVII.

October, 1893.

"I entertain an high idea of the utility of periodical publications: insomuch
that I could heartily desire copies of the Museum and Magazines, as well as
common Gazettes, might be spread through every city, town, and village in
America. I consider such easy vehicles of knowledge more happily calculated
than any other to preserve the liberty, stimulate the industry, and meliorate the
morals of an enlightened and free people."—*Washington to Mathew Carey,*
June 25, 1788.

PUBLISHED BY
THE HISTORICAL SOCIETY OF PENNSYLVANIA,
FOR SUBSCRIBERS.
PHILADELPHIA:
1893.

Entered at the Post-Office at Philadelphia as Second-class matter.

CONTENTS

BOUND VOLUMES OF THE MAGAZINE.

Copies of all the volumes of this MAGAZINE can be obtained at the Hall of the Historical Society, bound by Messrs. Pawson and Nicholson, in the very best manner, in the style known as Roxburgh, half cloth, uncut edges, gilt top, for $3.75 each and the postage. They will be furnished to subscribers in exchange for unbound numbers, in good condition, on the receipt of 75 cents per volume and the postage.

Address F. D. STONE, 1300 Locust St.

PRINTED BY J. B. LIPPINCOTT COMPANY.

THE

PENNSYLVANIA MAGAZINE

or

HISTORY AND BIOGRAPHY.

| Vol. XVII. | 1893. | No. 3. |

THE FOUNDING OF THE GERMAN CHURCHES OF PENNSYLVANIA.[1]

BY JOSEPH HENRY DUBBS, D.D.

A century ago the Germans of Pennsylvania were generally recognized as consisting of two widely-contrasted classes, which were popularly known as " church people" and " sect people." In more recent times this classification has been somewhat affected by the rise of new denominations; but in a general way it is still understood. There was nothing invidious or disrespectful in the use of these terms, and the ground of the distinction was very simple. The " church people" were those who in the Fatherland had belonged to the churches, as by law established : Lutheran, Reformed, or Roman Catholic. The Moravians were also recognized as " church people," because in a general way they agreed with the churches in doctrine, and preferred to be regarded as a missionary brotherhood rather than as a separate ecclesiastical organization. Concerning the Roman Catholics it need only be said that they were few

---

[1] An address delivered before the Historical Society of Pennsylvania, April 17, 1893.

in number and did not constitute an important element in the religious life of the province.   Indeed, in Philadelphia, no less than in Lancaster, Goshenhoppen, and Canawauga, they constituted a close community; and the successful establishment of these missions, in the face of ancient prejudices, was not the least of the achievements of the Jesuit order.

The distinction between the church and the "sect people" was broad and unmistakable.   The latter represented bodies which, in Europe, were not recognized by the government and had frequently been made the object of unrighteous persecution.   In some respects they were much more picturesque than the "church people," for it is always the unusual which attracts attention.   Though they differed widely among themselves, they could at a glance be recognized by their peculiar garments, said to have been a survival of the ordinary attire of the German peasantry of the sixteenth century, which had long been discarded by the "world's people."   The sects included all the minor bodies, such as Mennonites and Amish, "Brethren," or Dunkards, and Schwenkfelders, besides others which have passed away, leaving hardly a trace of their existence, such as Labadists, Gichtelians, "New Born," and Inspirationists.   Not all of them were disciples of Menno Simonis,[1] for the "Brethren," or Dunkards, though they adopted many Mennonite peculiarities, were founded by men who were born in the Reformed Church and were actually disciples of Jakob Boehme, the mystic of Görlitz; and not all of them were Anabaptists, for the Schwenkfelders did not baptize at all; but if we except a few sectarians who have now disappeared, all of these varying communities agreed in testifying against war and its attendant horrors, and it is not without reason, therefore, that they are sometimes called "the peace sects."

The early history of these sects is peculiarly fascinating on account of the peculiarities or, if you please, the oddi-

---

[1] Also written Simon, Simons, and Symons; pronounced *Seemons.*— Goebel, I., p. 191.

ties of their leaders. For this reason, perhaps, it has been more written about, especially in the form of popular articles, than the development of that peculiar Anglo-German life which characterizes the greater part of the State of Pennsylvania. It should, however, not be forgotten that the sects, after all, constitute but a small part of the German population of the State, and that in some counties they are almost unknown. That they were first in the field may in a general way be conceded, and it is not to be doubted that many Germans who belonged to the established churches at first preferred to settle in other provinces, because Pennsylvania was regarded as in a peculiar sense " the land of the sects ;" but it did not take long to exhaust the obscure fountains from which the sects were derived. In some instances, such as the Dunkards and Schwenkfelders, the whole sect emigrated to America, and in others the body was so depleted that it ceased to occupy an important place in the ecclesiastical history of Germany. Long before the middle of the last century the sects had come to be greatly in the minority; though as the important publishing houses of Christopher Saur and of the monks of Ephrata were in their hands, they exerted an influence greater than that to which their numbers might have justly entitled them. Whoever would understand the development of the German life of Pennsylvania must, therefore, make himself familiar with the history of the German evangelical churches. There are German churches besides these, but I venture to consider my theme in the popular sense, as it would have been understood by a German farmer a century ago. Even in this sense the subject is too broad to be properly treated in a single discourse, and I must crave your indulgence if I should say little or nothing concerning the Moravians, who have a splendid history of their own, and the Roman Catholics, whose extraordinary increase in numbers and influence is a source of constant astonishment. If I should, unfortunately, at any time appear to give undue prominence to the religious denomination with which I am personally connected, I hope the deficiency will rather be attributed to want of information than to any lack of disposition to do full justice to others.

The two so-called "evangelical" churches—the Lutheran and the Reformed—have since the days of the Reformation been the main channels of German religious life. To relate their history would be to tell the story of Protestantism in Germany and the world; to describe their peculiarities would be to enter on the field of theology, and to attempt to include in a single lecture what has been made the theme of thousands of volumes. The Lutheran Church—the church in a special sense of Martin Luther—certainly needs neither description nor eulogy. It included from the beginning the great body of German and Scandinavian Protestants; and even in this country it has prospered until it is known throughout the land. The Reformed Church, on the other hand, presents the curious anomaly of being "least known because it is best known." In history and doctrine it has been so closely allied to the forms of Protestantism with which England and Scotland are most familiar that it has frequently been identified with them. It is, in fact, the oldest of the series of national churches which derive their origin from the great religious movement in which Zwingli and Calvin were the most prominent leaders, and in its early history its most important centres were Zurich, Geneva, and Heidelberg. Some one has found in its history a certain analogy to the river Rhine, on whose banks so many of its members dwelt; deriving its origin from comparatively obscure sources in Switzerland, it gathered tributaries from France and Germany, while it flowed onward to refresh the plains of Holland.

The founding of the German Lutheran and Reformed churches in Pennsylvania was practically simultaneous, though the earliest records of the Lutheran Church antedate those of the Reformed Church by a few years, and are rather more complete and satisfactory. Both churches founded some of their earliest congregations in other colonies, particularly in New York, and both were in Pennsylvania preceded by Christians of other nationalities who professed a similar form of faith. The Swedish churches were Lutheran in doctrine, and their pastors freely co-operated with the German Lutheran missionaries. We are informed by Acrelius that in 1708 the Swedish pastors, Rudman, Björk, and Sandel, ordained in Wicacoa Church a student named Justus Falkner, who had been invited to take charge of " a congregation of Germans in Falkner's Swamp, in Philadelphia County, which received its name from him." [1] This, it appears, is the oldest German Lutheran congregation within the present territory of the United States.[2] In this way we may trace a connection between the German Lutherans and the Swedes who had preceded them. The dependence of the German Reformed churches on the Dutch churches of their own confession was even more complete. These churches were not numerous along the Delaware, though they had been early on the ground. Peter Minuit, the leader, in 1638, of the earliest Swedish colony, had been a deacon of the Reformed Church in the German city of Wesel,[3] and a Dutch Reformed church was founded at New Castle in 1642.[4] The Dutch Reformed congregations at Bensalem and Neshaminy, in Bucks County, were the earliest Reformed churches in Pennsylvania, and antedate all the German Lutheran congregations, except the one at Falkner's Swamp.[5] From the Bensalem record we learn that on the 4th of June, 1710, the Rev. Paulus Van Vleck organized a church at White Marsh. This may be regarded as a Dutch church, because it was founded by a Hollander; but as we find a German Reformed preacher settled there ten years later, it becomes probable that the church was organized in the interest of the Germans. In those days the national difference counted for nothing in ecclesiastical matters, and the relations of the Reformed people of Pennsylvania to the Dutch of New York and New Jersey were most

---

[1] " History of New Sweden," p. 214.
[2] " Halle Reports," Dr. C. W. Schaeffer's translation, p. 54.
[3] Kapp's " History of the Immigration," etc.
[4] Corwin's " Manual of the Reformed Dutch Church," p. 307.
[5] Dr. B. M. Schmucker, *Lutheran Church Review*, July, 1887.

intimate and fraternal.   Of the purely *German* Reformed churches it was once usual to assign priority to the congregation at Skippack, Montgomery County (now extinct), and to fix the date of its organization at 1726 or 1727; but it is now known that a Reformed church was built in Germantown in 1719, and that John Philip Boehm preached for the Reformed churches at Falkner's Swamp, White Marsh, and Skippack at least as early as 1720.   The first Reformed church of Philadelphia was founded in 1727, and its first pastor was George Michael Weiss.   The oldest consecutive church records are those of the church at New Goshenhoppen, Montgomery County.   They were begun in January, 1730, by the Rev. Johannes Heinricus Goetschius, who styles himself *Helvetico Tigurinus*, a native of Zurich in Switzerland. On the title-page he enumerates ten congregations as constituting his charge.   They are scattered through a region which is now occupied by at least a hundred Reformed ministers.

In a letter recently received from Dr. Herman Escher, city librarian, I am informed that it is stated in the MS. *Züricher Geschlechtsbuch*, that Moritz Goetschius, pastor at Saletz, about 1736 set sail for America.   According to a letter written by his son, he landed at Philadelphia, April 30, 1736, but fell dead immediately after he had stepped on shore.   The son was but seventeen years old at the time of his father's death, but at once began to preach in Pennsylvania, probably as an assistant to his relative, John Henry Goetschius.   These facts appear to be unknown in this country, and it affords me pleasure to announce them on this interesting occasion.

The late Dr. B. M. Schmucker says, in an article in the *Lutheran Church Review* for July, 1887, "Throughout the district between the Schuylkill and Delaware the Reformed congregations were formed somewhat earlier than the Lutheran congregations in their vicinity;" and for some time the allied churches of Philadelphia, Trappe, and Falkner's Swamp were the main seats of the German Lutheran Church in Pennsylvania.   The earliest existing congregational record of St. Michael's Lutheran Church, Philadelphia, was begun by the Rev. J. Caspar Stoever, in 1733; but its organized existence dates from the arrival of Muhlenberg, in 1742.[1] It might be added that the Reformed were at first decidedly in the majority; and, indeed, in a report presented to the Synod of South Holland, convened at Breda in 1730, it is stated that at that time "the Reformed holding to the old confession constituted more than one-half of the whole number [of Germans], being about fifteen thousand." It could not well be otherwise, for most of the early immigrants came from the region of the Rhine, and along the whole course of that river the Reformed was the leading church. As the great migration extended to other parts of Germany, the Lutherans in Pennsylvania rapidly increased in numbers, and long before the end of the century had become the larger body. Indeed, it must be confessed that the Reformed Church in many respects failed to employ its early opportunities for denominational advancement. It represented different nationalities, and included elements which even in Europe had never been completely harmonized. Of this character were the Huguenots who had lingered awhile in Germany, but had never been thoroughly Germanized. There were so many points of contact between the Reformed and the English churches, that where the latter were already in the field the former rarely attempted a separate organization. To their mind the English churches were Reformed also; and the government of the Presbyterians was recognized as in most respects like that with which they had been familiar in the Fatherland. Indeed, in 1743, before the Synods of Holland took charge of the Reformed churches of Pennsylvania, they addressed a letter to the Presbyterian Synod of Philadelphia, inquiring whether it would not be practicable to consolidate the Presbyterians, Dutch Reformed, and German Reformed into a single body; but national prejudices probably interfered, and the Presbyterians tacitly declined the union. Dr. Briggs, in his "American Presbyterianism," expresses his regret that this grand opportunity

---

[1] "Halle Reports," Reading edition, pp. 64 and 65.

was neglected; but perhaps it was better that the Reformed Church was left to work out its mission in its own way.

Whatever may have been the doctrinal position of the Lutheran and Reformed churches, it is certain that their social relations at the time of their first settlement in this country were most intimate. They had passed through the same mill, and the grist was very much alike. While it is manifestly impossible to relate on this occasion the history of these churches in Europe and America, it cannot be denied that their development was similar, and that in many places they came into the closest contact.

It has sometimes been said that the sects left their Fatherland on account of religious persecution, while the " church people" emigrated to America for no higher purpose than to improve their temporal condition. If such a statement is accepted at all, it must be done with many qualifications. No persecution was ever more atrocious than that which the Lutherans of Salzburg endured from 1728 to 1732, before they fled to America; and religious elements played an important part in the sufferings of the Reformed and Lutherans in the Palatinate. Historians tell us that by the terms of the treaty of Westphalia, in 1648, religious freedom had been granted to Protestants. This freedom was, however, more apparent than real; and such as it was it would never have been granted if it had not been expected—in accordance with the policy of Richelieu and Mazarin—to promote dissension, and thus to aid in the final dismemberment of Germany. The " three confessions"—Roman Catholic, Lutheran, and Reformed—were formally recognized; but there was a vast difference in the positions which they were severally made to occupy. By a secret article in the treaty, it is said, the imperial government pledged itself to maintain Roman Catholic worship wherever there were people who desired it, and it often happened that in villages which were prevailingly Protestant, a few Roman Catholics, on this pretence, secured permanent possession of the churches. Some of the princes made their peace with Rome, and the servile company of their flatterers was only too ready to follow their example. "The government," says Löher, "cared nothing for the people, and almost everywhere the party which happened to be in power oppressed dissenters. This state of things was worst in the Palatinate, where the electors had changed their religion four times in as many reigns. The whole country was expected to follow the example of its rulers, and whoever was unwilling to submit, could do no better than to take up his pilgrim's staff and leave his native land."

That under such circumstances religious persecution was a matter of frequent occurrence cannot be doubted, but after all it was but a single element in the prevailing misery of the Fatherland. Of this misery it is difficult at present to form a proper conception. It embraced all the relations of life, civil, social, and religious; and it seemed, says a writer of the period, "as if hope had left the earth forever."

In a general way it may be said that this misery was the result of the wars which went on unceasingly during the seventeenth and the earlier part of the eighteenth centuries. Many writers have derived the great Palatinate migration from the destructive raids of Turenne, in 1674 and 1675, and especially from the invasion of 1688–'89 which was the direct result of the violent sequestration by the French king of the hereditary estates of the Duchess Elizabeth Charlotte of Orleans, who had been a Palatinate princess. It may be said that as far as Pennsylvania is concerned these dates are too early; but it is true that in those dreadful days the German people, who had hitherto clung with peculiar attachment to their native soil, first began in large numbers to seek a refuge in distant lands. No country in modern times had been so dreadfully desolated. In one year Worms, Mainz, Speyer, Mannheim, Heidelberg, and many other cities and villages were either burned or utterly devastated. The castle of Heidelberg, the chief residence of the Electors of the Palatinate, was ruined, and its remains still stand as a memorial of that awful time. The barbarity of the invasion was unexampled in history. The French general, Melac, it is said, cut down all the vines on the hill-sides near

Heidelberg, thus depriving the people of their sole means of subsistence, and driving thousands from their humble homes in the dead of winter.   Many of them found a refuge in Switzerland and Holland, and multitudes died of starvation.   No wonder that, as a German friend once told me, the peasants of the Palatinate still call their dogs "Melac," but that the name is given only to curs of inferior degree.

In their profound misery the suffering people of the Rhine country might naturally have turned to their hereditary rulers for sympathy and relief, but all authorities agree in declaring that the German princes of this period had no conception of the responsibilities of their position.   They are described as, in general, a multitude of petty tyrants, without enough dignity or culture to render them respectable.   Prince Eugène said concerning them, " God forgive them, for they know not what they do; much less do they know what they want; and least of all, what they are."

Not the Palatinate only, but all the surrounding countries suffered intensely during this dreadful period.   " War," said Turenne, " is a terrible monster that must needs be fed," and all the Rhine provinces, Alsace, Upper Hesse, Baden-Durlach, and Würtemberg were swept by constant raids.   Switzerland was overcrowded with Huguenots and Palatines, and the poverty of the people became extreme.   Trade had found new channels, and the ships of Hamburg and Bremen lay rotting at their wharves.   The peace of Ryswick, in 1697, brought an interval of peace, but it continued only until the breaking out of the War of the Spanish Succession, in 1701.   Indeed, it is doubtful if the condition of the people was more tolerable during this interval of peace than it had been before.   The soldiers who robbed the land had at least been prodigal with their booty, and in this way some fragments had returned to their original owners; but now even this uncertain means of subsistence was taken away, though their merciless rulers did not hesitate to send out companies of soldiers to distrain the goods of a people who were already on the verge of starvation.[1]

[1] *Der Deutsche Pionier*, xiv. 271.

According to Christopher Saur, the great migration to America was due to an official invitation from the British government. " In 1704," he says, " after the Duke of Marlborough had defeated the French at the battle of Schellenberg (Blenheim), Queen Anne of England invited the suffering Palatines to find a home in America, and transported many thousands thither at her own expense." If the queen actually extended this invitation,—which is more than doubtful,—she probably soon discovered that she had been too generous, though she certainly pitied the sufferers and did all in her power for their relief. A sufficient reason for the migration was the fact that the misery of the Fatherland still continued and was even increasing. For several years the harvests failed, and the winter of 1709 was the severest that had ever been known. " It was so cold," says Löher, " that the birds froze in the air and the wild beasts in the forest." Then the people said one to another, " Let us go to America, and if we perish, we perish !"

It is not our purpose to relate the story of the emigration. It has often been told, and no one can doubt that, compared with the sufferings of the German emigrants on the way and in the forest, the trials of the Pilgrim Fathers in the preceding century were very gentle experiences. It is no wonder that the joyous dwellers by the Rhine became on the way a solemn people. The theme is one on which I would willingly linger, more particularly as it appears not to have received the attention which it properly deserves. The pictures which imagination presents may not be brilliant, but they are full of the heroism of patient endurance. For our present purpose it is enough to call attention to the fact, that in their greatest trials the German pioneers were sustained by a profound religious consciousness. Through all their sufferings they held firmly to their ancient confessions. Every father regarded it as his duty to have his children baptized, and as soon as they were able to learn, to see to it that they were prepared for confirmation and the Holy Communion. In the iron-bound chest of almost every German immigrant might have been found at least a Bible, a hymn-book, and a catechism.   Before their churches were established they were especially careful to cultivate religion in the home and in the school.   In my own family, I have often been informed, the house-father gathered the household for instruction on every Sunday afternoon, and I still have in my possession the great Palatinate catechism which every one in the family committed to memory, proof passages and all.   All this could not, however, supply the wants of public instruction, and we accordingly find that wherever Germans were settled in sufficient numbers they proceeded to found a church and a parochial school.   In some instances a good farm was set aside for the use of the school-master; and though the schools are now no longer strictly parochial, there are still a few teachers in ancient German settlements who enjoy glebe and stipend for playing the organ on Sunday.

In early days the school-master was a very important personage.   For many years ministers were few in number. Several companies of immigrants had, indeed, been accompanied by their pastors.   In 1708, Joshua von Kocherthal had led his "Palatine" congregation of Lutherans to the banks of the Hudson, and in 1709, John Frederick Hager was ordained in London for service among the "Reformed Palatines" in the same region.   Seventeen years later, it is said, George Michael Weiss, the earliest Reformed pastor in Philadelphia, was also the leader of a "colony;" but what were these among so many ?   The minister, I conceive, was in popular estimation a great personage, who, like a diocesan bishop, was almost constantly travelling, and who under the most favorable circumstances could not be expected to visit each of his congregations more frequently than once a month.   For this reason, in the best churches, the school-master became a kind of vicar, who in the absence of the pastor sometimes read sermons from an approved European collection.   Naturally enough, some of these teachers developed talent as public speakers and irregularly assumed the pastoral office.   Fortunately for both churches, there were from the beginning some congregations which declined to be served by unordained ministers; but it must be confessed that for many years there was great confusion. Much more objectionable than these *autodidacti*, as Muhlenberg called them, were bold pretenders who, unwilling to make their living by honest labor, assumed to be ministers until their wickedness found them out. Some of them claimed to be of noble descent, though I have not been able to learn that their titles secured them special consideration. In the records of the Lutheran churches of Berks County I have seen the name of Baron Adolf von Geresheim, who may have been a better man than I suppose; and in the Reformed Church the most wicked of all pretenders called himself Cyriacus Spangenberg von Reidemeister. Harbaugh tells a story of one of these fellows who entered the pulpit in a state of intoxication, announced the text, "Follow me!" and then fell reeling down the pulpit stairs. Then one of the elders arose and said, "No, brethren, we will not follow him," and the career of that evangelist was ended.

During this gloomy period sects arose which were mostly short-lived, but served to alienate many from the church of their fathers. From this cause the Reformed Church was, I think, the chief sufferer, and to illustrate my meaning I need but refer to the defection of John Peter Miller. In company with George M. Weiss and John B. Rieger, he had been sent to Pennsylvania by the Consistory of Heidelberg,—a brilliant young man who had just completed his course at the University. For four years he was pastor of the Reformed Church at Tulpehocken, but then fell under the influence of Conrad Beissel, "the Magus of the Conestoga," and in 1735 became a member of the monastic brotherhood at Ephrata, of which he was afterwards for many years the leading spirit.

The plan for promoting the unity of the German churches, which was in 1741 proposed by Henry Antes, and afterwards elaborated by Count Zinzendorf, was so grand in its conception, so exalted in its purposes, that we may regret that it did not prove more successful. Seven synods were held, at which a plan of union was formed which was to be known

as " The Congregation of God in the Spirit." This " congregation," as I have ventured to say on a previous occasion, " was founded in strict accordance with Zinzendorf's
theory of Tropes, according to which every one might retain
his denominational peculiarities, while at the same time he
stood in connection with a higher unity. There was no
intention of destroying the Lutherans, Reformed, or Mennonites, as religious denominations, but they were to be
united by the confederation of those who had reached the
highest grade of spiritual perception. Though the fact was
rather implied than expressed, the Moravians were the controlling power in the whole movement. Zinzendorf had no
idea of establishing a sect; but to him it appeared beautiful
that there should be within the church a community of elect
souls who would more and more withdraw themselves from
worldly affairs to live a life like that of the angels in
heaven." [1]

It seemed at first as if this well-meant movement might
prove successful. The " congregation" proceeded to ordain
ministers for service in the Lutheran and Reformed churches,
and in each church there was a little company of pious men
who labored in its interest. It soon, however, became
evident that the churches were not ready for the proposed
union, and in the end it led to controversies and conflicts.
When the Lutheran and Reformed churches were severally
consolidated, the men who had been most active in the
movement generally found a home in the Unity of the
Brethren, and the last vestiges of the " congregation" were
swept away.

It was now evident that the evangelical churches must be
established on the old historic lines, but progress was greatly
impeded by the extreme poverty of the people. They were
too poor to build churches or to support pastors. I do not
suppose that they were ever quite as poor as those settlers
in the province of New York, of whom Rupp relates that
nine of them clubbed together to buy an old horse to be

---

[1] " Historic Manual of the Reformed Church," p. 193.

used successively for agricultural purposes, but they all endured innumerable privations. A few had brought with them the means to purchase land; but the best land was covered by the heaviest timber, and it took many blows to fell the mighty monarchs of the forest. Others were in actual want, especially after the inauguration of the iniquitous system, even then called a "traffic in souls," by which poor people were persuaded to sail to America without paying their passage, and without fully understanding that they were to be sold as *Redemptioners*.

The German churches of Pennsylvania were sorely in need of help, and it was evident that it could not be secured on this side of the ocean. The country was still too young and too poor to engage in an extensive scheme of missionary activity. In 1730, Pastor George Michael Weiss and Elder Jacob Reiff went to Holland and Germany to collect money for the Reformed congregations of Philadelphia and Skippack, and in 1733, Daniel Weissiger, in company with Pastor John Christian Schultze and John Daniel Schöner, was sent to Germany by the United Lutheran congregations in Philadelphia, New Hanover, and New Providence to collect contributions for their brethren in Pennsylvania. The results in each case were unsatisfactory and unpleasant; but these missions, at any rate, directed attention to the condition of the American churches. Through the influence of such men as Ziegenhagen, court preacher in London, and Franke and his coadjutors at Halle, a bond of union was formed which continued unbroken for many years and greatly contributed to the prosperity of the American Lutheran Church. The Reformed would naturally have turned for aid to the Palatinate, but in its depressed condition the church of that country recommended them to the care of their brethren in Holland. The trust was accepted, and for more than sixty years the Reformed churches of Pennsylvania remained under the special care of the Classis of Amsterdam.

As a direct result of these arrangements two men were sent to America, each of whom may be regarded as, in a special sense, the organizer of his denomination. Henry Melchior Muhlenberg, who is often called "the patriarch of the Lutheran Church in America," reached Philadelphia in 1742. Though he claimed no higher dignity than that of a simple pastor, the sphere of his influence soon extended from New York to Georgia, and wherever he went he firmly laid the foundations of his church. It was chiefly through his influence that the German Lutheran ministerium of Pennsylvania was founded in 1748. By his voluminous correspondence he prevented the zeal of European friends from growing cold, and induced faithful pastors—Brunnholtz, Schaum, Kurtz, and others—to come to his aid in establishing the church. He might have been called, like Annoni of Basel, "the pastor after God's own heart;" and when at last he passed away, in the year of the adoption of our Federal Constitution, his name was honored throughout the land.

Michael Schlatter, who was sent to America in 1746, with the rank of Missionary Superintendent, to organize the Reformed churches, was less learned than Muhlenberg, but for zeal and energy he was perhaps unequalled. He was a native of Switzerland, but had lived long enough in Holland to become familiar with its language. Though he became pastor of churches in Philadelphia and Germantown immediately after his arrival, he made extensive missionary journeys, visiting the widely-scattered churches in Pennsylvania, New Jersey, Maryland, and Virginia. By rude bridle-paths he took his way from one settlement to another, enduring privations of which we can hardly form an adequate conception.

Wherever he preached he induced the people to promise to pay a specified amount for the support of a settled minister. In 1747 he succeeded in establishing a "cœtus," which differed from a synod only in the fact that its proceedings were subject to revision by the "fathers" in Holland. His visit to Europe in 1751 resulted in the collection of the sum of £12,000, which was invested for the benefit of the American churches, and on his return to this country in the following year he was accompanied by six young ministers, of whom Stoy and Otterbein afterwards became distinguished. The publication of Schlatter's "Appeal," which was translated into English by Rev. David Thomson, was the indirect cause of the organization of the "Society for the Promotion of the Knowledge of God among the Germans" and the establishment of the so-called German charity schools. In order to attract attention to this scheme in England, it is possible that the condition of the Germans was grossly exaggerated. They were not only represented as ignorant beyond comparison, but as fast becoming "like unto wood-born savages." It was even suggested that unless their children received an English education, they might finally join with the French and drive the English from the continent of America. The Lutherans, in 1754, and the Reformed, in 1756, adopted resolutions expressing their indignation at such insinuations. The charity schools proved an utter failure, and Schlatter, who had been persuaded to become their superintendent, was personally the chief sufferer. For some time the Lutheran and Reformed ministers sustained him, but the people were greatly excited and his influence was entirely destroyed. He subsequently became a chaplain in the British army, and was present at the siege of Louisburg. His later years were spent in retirement at Chestnut Hill, near Philadelphia, where he died in October, 1790. Schlatter's public ministry did not occupy a decade of years, but it was brilliant and fruitful. From the fund which he had collected, and which was invested in Holland, every member of the "cœtus," until 1793, received an annual stipend. The unexampled liberality of the Church of Holland must always be remembered with gratitude; but, after all, I cannot think that, after the first years, these benefactions were really needed. It would have been better if the whole amount had been devoted to the establishment of a literary and theological institution. As a guardian the Church of Holland was kind but stern. The "cœtus" was allowed no liberty of action; it was not even permitted to confer the rite of ordination. Every year its minutes, with minute accounts of each particular case, were sent to Holland, and sometimes years elapsed before a question could be definitely settled. As the synods of Holland declined to receive communications in German, the correspondence was conducted in Latin or Dutch, and, as one of the secretaries of the "coetus" says in an extant document, "it is difficult in writing to have to choose between a language which one has forgotten and another which one has never properly learned." In short, the whole arrangement was cumbrous in the extreme, and it is not surprising that some ministers preferred to labor independently. Among these the most eminent was the Rev. Dr. John Joachim Zubly, who exerted an extensive influence in Pennsylvania, though his field of labor was in the South. It will be remembered that he subsequently became a member of the Continental Congress.

The dependence of the Reformed churches on the synods of Holland continued through all the disturbances of the Revolution until 1793, when the correspondence was finally concluded, and the "coetus" became a synod. It is the centennial anniversary of the latter event which the Reformed Church of this country now proposes to celebrate.

There is an engraving which represents Muhlenberg and Schlatter embracing each other in German fashion. The interview which it depicts is historical, and there can be no doubt that these good men were intimate friends. The picture is, however, suggestive of the fraternal relations of the ministers of the two churches during the whole colonial period. On all important questions they stood together, and there were no denominational controversies between them which were worthy of the name. No doubt these relations were greatly influenced by the prevalence of Pietism[1] in both churches; for, as is well known, Muhlenberg and his coadjutors belonged to the school of Halle, and many of

---

[1] Pietism, a name applied to a movement in behalf of personal religion and the cultivation of a higher spiritual life, inaugurated by Philip Jacob Spener, of the Lutheran Church, in the latter part of the seventeenth century. The term is often made to include various forms of later mysticism, but it is here used in its original meaning.

the Reformed pioneers were Pietists of a very similar type. But apart from this similarity of sentiment, it could not well be otherwise than that, as educated men living in agricultural communities, the pastors of neighboring churches should seek each other's society and become intimately acquainted. There were always certain peculiarities of ritual and observance by which the religious services of the two churches could be distinguished; but it must be confessed that after the first generation more important distinctions became very obscure. The development of the "denominational consciousness" belongs to a later period. "Union" churches, which were occupied in common by both denominations, had hitherto been erected only in cases of necessity, but they now became numerous. Though they may have served an important purpose in their day, they are now regarded as an obstacle to progress. Under the best conditions, union churches are like houses occupied by several families; there are possible complications which might as well be avoided.

The German churches of Pennsylvania were fortunate in numbering among their pioneers a long series of highly-educated men who exerted an influence which extended far beyond the limits of their immediate denomination. The Lutheran Church was honored by the presence of scholars like Kunze and Helmuth, and scientists like Muhlenberg, the botanist, and Melsheimer, the entomologist; and in the history of the Reformed Church occur the names of such men as Daniel Gros, author of "Moral Philosophy," Otterbein, Weyberg, and Hendel. Otterbein, it will be remembered, in his later years founded religious societies after the Methodist pattern, from which sprang the denomination which is known as the United Brethren in Christ, though he personally, like Wesley, remained in connection with the church of his fathers.

It has been said that the Germans were too slow in accommodating themselves to new conditions, and their ministers have been especially blamed for not encouraging the use of the English language in the services of the church. The imputation may not be entirely undeserved; but, possibly, if we were familiar with all the circumstances, our judgment might not be severe. The language of a people is not to be changed in a day, and there is a natural presumption in favor of the speech of one's forefathers. That the change of language at a later date was the occasion of serious conflicts we are painfully aware; but I really do not think the pioneers were unduly prejudiced. Muhlenberg, who was an excellent linguist, preached in English every Sunday on his voyage to America, and unless Schlatter had made himself familiar with English he would hardly have been appointed a chaplain in the British army. Sometimes, it must be confessed, the pioneers employed a form of speech which was hardly " the king's English," except that it was of the kind which was spoken by the earlier Georges. There is a story, for which I cannot vouch, that in the days of the Revolution the pastor of the Reformed Church of Germantown occasionally preached in what he fondly supposed to be English. On one of these occasions a British officer found his way into the church, and remained to the end under the impression that the sermon was, as usual, delivered in German. At its conclusion he said to one of the elders that he never before knew that German was *so much like English;* he had understood nearly one-half of what the minister said.

It was the patriotic dream of the "founders" to establish in this country a cultured German community, with literary institutions that could not fail to command respect. We have no time to give an account of their earnest labors in this direction. Certainly the highest credit belongs to Drs. Kunze and Helmuth for the establishment of the German department of the University of Pennsylvania, which in its day did excellent service in the cause of higher education. From this " department" was, in 1787, derived Franklin College, at Lancaster, in whose interest the best German elements were for a time united. Without undervaluing the importance of the patronage of such distinguished men as Benjamin Franklin and Benjamin Rush, the chief honor for the establishment of that institution undoubtedly belongs to four German ministers: Helmuth,[1] Hendel,[2] Weyberg,[3] and H. E. Muhlenberg.[4] Why the institution which was founded under such brilliant auspices was not immediately more successful it might now be difficult to explain; but apart from the fact that the new institution had no endowment worth mentioning, and that there were from the beginning differences of opinion concerning policy and management, it must be evident to any one who has studied the subject that the expectations of its promoters were unduly exalted, and consequently could not fail to be disappointed. They did not fully realize the fact that the tree which they had planted must have time to grow, and that years must pass before they could expect to taste its fruits.

It has frequently been intimated that the early Germans

[1] Justus Heinrich Christian Helmuth was born May 16, 1745, in Brunswick, Germany; died in Philadelphia, February 5, 1825; came to America, 1769; pastor of Trinity Lutheran Church, Lancaster, 1769–1779; Zion's Church, Philadelphia, 1780–1820. He exerted an extensive influence in the Lutheran Church, and was an eminent author. Of his publications, his "Brief Account of the Yellow Fever in Philadelphia" (1793) is now best known.

[2] Wilhelm Hendel was a native of the Palatinate. He was sent to this country in 1762 by the synods of Holland, and was pastor of the following Reformed churches: Lancaster, 1765–1769; Tulpehocken, 1769–1782; Lancaster, the second time, 1782–1794; Philadelphia, 1794–1798. He was regarded as one of the best preachers of his time. Dr. Harbaugh calls him "the St. John of the Reformed Church." He died of yellow fever, September 29, 1798.

[3] Caspar Dietrich Weyberg was a native of Switzerland. He came to America as an ordained minister in 1762, and was pastor of the Reformed Church of Easton, Pennsylvania, 1763, and of the Race Street Reformed Church, Philadelphia, 1763–1790. He died in Philadelphia, September 26, 1790. During the Revolution he was imprisoned for his devotion to the American cause. He ranks among the foremost men in the early history of the German Reformed Church in this country.

[4] Gotthilf Heinrich Ernst Muhlenberg, the celebrated botanist, was the youngest son of the Rev. Henry Melchior Muhlenberg. He was born at New Providence, Pennsylvania, November 17, 1753; died at Lancaster, Pennsylvania, May 23, 1815. Studied at Halle, Germany; assistant minister in Philadelphia, 1774; pastor of Trinity Lutheran Church, Lancaster, Pennsylvania, 1780–1815. He was the first president of Franklin College.

were a rude and uncultured people, abhorring literature and science as proper works of the devil.   In the light of their history they could hardly be expected to devote much attention to the cultivation of the social graces, but that as a people they were exceptionally ignorant may be confidently denied.   That they were a reading people is abundantly proven by the extent of the German book-trade of Philadelphia during the last century.   Though not themselves learned, they had a traditional reverence for learning.   Their religious services were dignified and solemn.   The furniture of the church was not regarded as complete without an organ, and to its accompaniment they sang the grand old chorals of the Reformation.   In social life they were hospitable, and their honesty was even then proverbial.   In brief, I venture to say that the darkest period in the history of the German churches of Pennsylvania was not the earliest. It came with the inevitable transition from one language to another, when one was neglected and the other not fully acquired; when the learned pastors of the earlier period had passed away, and their places were supplied by men who had not enjoyed the same scholastic advantages.   This was the period when the most eminent men doubted whether the German churches, as such, could claim to have a mission in America.   It may be said to have extended through the first quarter of the present century.   It was in the year 1825 that the Lutheran and Reformed churches each established a theological seminary, and these have gradually been followed by a long series of literary and theological institutions.   Through trials and conflicts innumerable, through occasional periods of deep depression, the course of the churches has since then been upward and onward.   To tell the story of their progress and prosperity is not our present purpose.   That they have produced men eminent in church and state cannot be denied; that their presence has been felt in the literary and theological development of our country will be freely acknowledged; but their best work has been done in obscure places, and will not be known to men until it stands revealed in God's eternal light.

EXTRACTS FROM THE DIARY OF DANIEL FISHER, 1755.

CONTRIBUTED BY MRS. CONWAY ROBINSON HOWARD, RICHMOND, VA.

[The following extracts are from a journal which was found among the papers of my great-grandfather, Mr. George Fisher, of Richmond, Virginia. He was one of the prominent men of the city for many years, and had married Miss Betsey Ambler, a daughter of Mr. Jaquelin Ambler and Rebecca Burwell, "the beautiful Belinda" to whom Thomas Jefferson wrote poems and also acrostics in Greek. This journal was kept by Daniel Fisher between the years 1750 and 1755. He had come first to this country in 1720, but did not remain, and returned to London. In 1750 he returned, bringing his family and establishing himself first at Williamsburg, then the capital of the Colony, and afterwards at York.

Mr. Fisher made the trip from Williamsburg to Philadelphia on horseback, finding, according to his own account, every man's hand against him on the way. He went at the suggestion of the Honorable Mr. Nelson, then an influential man in the Virginia colony. I have only copied the account of his stay in Philadelphia of eleven weeks, and have virtually made no changes whatever in style or spelling. —C. R. H.]

I arrived at Philadelphia in the afternoon of May 22, 1755, the 10th day on horse back from Williamsburg, Va. I put up at the "Indian King," in the Market Street, kept by one Mr. John Biddle, a very civil courteous Quaker. This person and his wife, not one jot behind him in rational benevolence, or what may be very properly esteemed true politeness, confirmed in me the favorable opinion I had long entertained of their peaceable, inoffensive Society. For tho' this house is one of the greatest business in its way in the whole city, yet everything is transacted with the utmost regularity and decorum. There is a regular ordinary every Day, of the very best provisions and well dressed, at 12d a head, that is eight pence sterling, the best of liquors proportionately moderate; and the best use taken of horses. Yet there is one, old custom attends this house, which tho' agreeable to me, may not perhaps be so to all People.   For whom remains here after Eleven of the Clock in the Evening is very civilly acquainted with the time by a servant, and that after that hour, it is the invariable custom of the House to serve no more liquor that night to any Body, and this Custom I am told never is infringed.   And this I think is a true specimen of what every House of entertainment should be.

Having been ten days at this house, my courteous host placing himself in a Chair by me, desired I would walk into the next room and drink a dish of Tea with his wife.   "At first," says he, "thou appearest to us a Stranger, and what is very agreeable to us, a Sober one, for which reason we are apprehensive it may not be so pleasing to thee to continue in a Publick House, so hurried as ours sometimes is, tho' we do believe ours is not the worst of the sort.   If it is so, pray be free, and let us know, for my wife in that case, will very easily inquire out a private lodging for thee in some reputable, sober family, in the neighborhood; thee will be pleased to take notice, the desire of making things most easy and agreeable to thee, is the occasion of this motion; and if thee should like best to continue still with us or to dine only at the ordinary, then thee will be welcome; but before thee determinest, thee will consider thereupon."

I immediately replyed the thing required no consideration; for tho' his was the most agreeable Public House I had ever lived in, a private one, such as he proposed, would be more to my satisfaction; that I had myself, tho' without effect, made such enquiry, but should be now thankful if Mrs. Biddle would take the trouble upon her, which she Cheerfully accepted, recommending only to a very worthy family.

As my stay in Philadelphia was eleven weeks and my observation of what passed at the time somewhat particular, it was once my intention to have made them public as they would in my humble apprehension have tended towards a manifestation of the Quakers' integrity while they were a part of the Legislature, and by a recapitulation of a number of clear and incontrovertible Facts, have also exploded the Malicious, Calumnious falsehoods and absurdities Contained in two invidious Pamphlets, entituled " A Brief State," and " A Brief View of Pennsylvania," published in the years 1755 and 1756, but I shall suspend this design for the present, as I am given to hope this task will be more effectually executed ere long, by a far nobler hand.

Friday May 23, about 8 in the morning I walked down to Mr. Allin's,[1] who was not yet arrived from his Country House about eight miles out of Town, where, it seems he generally is all the Summer time. I called again at 10, when I met with and delivered him my letter from the Honble. W. Nelson, which when he had looked over he turned to me and said, he had a very great regard for the Gentleman who wrote that Letter, but did not perceive he had it in his power to do anything for me ; as to the Sugar Works and Distillery they were now in other hands, and he had little or no Interest in them, or indeed in anything else. He advised me to look about myself, and if I found any one inclined to employ me in any shape, on my applying to him, he would inform them of the character Mr. Nelson had given me. This I own, was a reception I was not prepared for ; yet mortified and confounded as I was I begged he would reflect, I was an utter Stranger in the place, to which I observed, he was Sensible. I had traveled merely at the instance and advice of the Honble. Mr. Nelson. That I was now so destitute of acquaintance, that I did not know where nor to whom to apply for a private Lodging, for want of which advantage, I shall be obliged, both horse and self, at a large expense, to continue at a Public Inn.

But this instead of exciting in him any feeling of my distress or anxiety, only increased his impatience to get rid of me, keeping me standing, and moving divers times towards the Door, as if he apprehended, that I did not

---

[1] Chief-Justice William Allen.

know the way.   However, at the third or fourth motion, I took the hint, walking out of the Room into the Passage, he very civilly keeping me company to the Street Door; but before we parted, I entreated to know whether I might have the liberty of waiting on him again.   When he had considered my case, and I might have the happiness of finding him more at leisure.   As to that, he said, he might generally be spoke with about 9 in the morning.   I went to my Inn very melancholy, but sat down in the afternoon and on paper stated my misfortunes and unhappy circumstances, with my views in taking this fatiguing Journey, and the next morning sent it to Mr. Allin to consider until Monday when I proposed waiting on him again.

Saturday, May 24, being the chief market day (Wednesday is the other), I took a view of it—good part of the town I had seen yesterday evening.   There seems to be a good supply of most kinds of Provisions and a vast concourse of People, Buyers as well as sellers.   Meat in the Shambles (some at least) of each sort, very good and might well vie with the best in the Leadenhall Market; Fish and Poultry, the market don't seem over well supplied with, tho' in the cool weather a fine sort of large Sea Pearch of about six pounds, called the Sheeps' Head, from its teeth resembling those of a sheep, are frequently brought from the Sea Coast, quite through the Province of New Jersey, not less than seventy miles, land carriage, and are sold for 18d. each.

Butter is quite plenty and very good at about 8d. a pound; vegetables plenty enough tho' not so many good or handsome Gardens about Philadelphia as one might expect, and with all my enquiry I could not find a Plant deserving the name of Cauliflower.   Nor did I ever see or hear of a good one either in Virginia or Maryland and the best in both of those places are raised in Autumn, even so late as November.   As there are such fine Rivers in Pennsylvania as well as in the other Provinces, their markets not abounding in Fish, I should attribute to their want of skill more than want of Fish, not but sometimes I have seen a good many Fish in the market.   Sturgeon in the Spring I observed in every River I have seen in America, and Ten or Twenty miles above Philadelphia on the Delaware, the curing of Sturgeon is become a Manufacture. The first Green Peas seen in this Market was this 24th of May, and they sold very dear. In Virginia, as before observed, I had them in plenty at Fraysers' Ferry on the 12th, and at Williamsburg I heard of their being at tables a fortnight, at the least, before that. Good milk at a Penny a Pint (or an English half-penny), as in London, is brought Morning and Evening to the People's doors and it generally stands all Day to be sold in the Market place. But to go on with my journal.

Sunday, May 25, Mr. Osborne leaving word he would call on me at Eleven this morning, I staid at home till Three, then went to the Lutheran Church, a neat Brick Building where there is a good organ to which I heard them sing Psalms, agreeably enough, tho' I was a Stranger to the Language (High Dutch). Then I walked about Two miles out of Town in the "Proprietors' Garden," but viewed first that of the late Governor James Hamilton, Esq., a small half mile short of the other. Mr. Hamilton's was much the largest, but not disposed with judgment, nor that I could find, did it contain anything that was curious, unless what is by some gazed at and spoke of, may be esteemed so, a few very ordinary statues. A shady walk of high trees leading from the further end of the Garden, looked well enough; but the Grass above knee high, thin and spoiling for the want of the Sythe, rendered it too troublesome to walk to the top.

The proprietors' tho' much smaller, was laid out with more judgment, tho' it seemed to have been pretty much neglected. A pretty pleasure garden, the trees of which now hardly visible, a small wilderness, and other shades, shows that the contriver was not without judgment; but what to me surpassed everything of the kind I had seen in America was a pretty bricked Green House, out of which was disposed (now) very properly in the Pleasure Garden a good many Orange, Lemon, and Citron Trees in great perfection loaded with abundance of Fruit and some of each sort seemingly then ripe.

The House here is but small, built of Brick, with a small Kitchen, etc, justly contrived rather for a small than a numerous Family. It is pleasantly situated on an eminence with a gradual descent—over a small Valley—to a handsome level Road cut through a wood, affording an agreeable vista of near Two miles. On the left hand the slope, descending from the house, is a neat little Park, tho' I am told there are no Deer in it. In coming home I went into a Tavern, called the "Centre House," as being seated in the very midst of the original plan of the first intended City; tho' at present this house is half a mile or more from the nearest building in the City. Here is a Bowling Green, and neat people seem to keep the House, but a strange Brute of a Landlord.

In the morning early, I should have observed, I walked to the Platform, the very fartherest part of the City on the south east, or down the River Delaware. The Platform by being uncovered appears much decayed and out of order. There are upwards of Fifty Guns lying about there, the carriages entirely ruined. The bores of some of the largest Guns are 7 or 8 inches in Diameter; but there is only Twenty-five Ports. The Channel seems there to lie on the further side the River, so that it is imagined a ship of any Burthen cannot come within a mile of the Fort.

Monday, May the 26th.—I went again this morning to wait on Mr. Allin as I had intimated in my Letter I purposed to do, but he not coming to Town that Day, and the Servants behaving somewhat Cherrlishly answering me very shortly when I civily inquired when their Master was expected, that they did not know, and having asked one among several whom I saw come from Mr. Allin's Door whether he was then come to Town, he civily said the servants had informed him Mr. Allin would not be in Town that Day, but was expected on Wednesday morning, from whence I concluded that was a secret I was not to be let into; yet as I was determined on seeing him I took my Horse after dinner and rode over to what is called his Country Seat, which I found about 8 or 9 miles distant on the top of a Hill at the further end of a village two miles in length, called German Town, from the number of German weavers and others settled there. The House was small, built of stone, as most of the Houses thereabouts there are; stands close to a large much frequented Road, which often occasions the Dust to be very troublesome. The spot, doubtless from its elevated situation, must be as healthy as any thereabouts, but to me it appeared very naked, much exposed to the sun and to bleak winds. A small Portico, facing the South East is a good contrivance and to my thinking the very best about the house.

My reception here was more gracious than I expected for he took me by the hand and invited me to seat myself in the Portico and asked me what I chose to drink. I preferred Small Beer, being almost choked with the Dust raised by the wagons, etc., I met on the Road, and a large Tankard of very good was brought me, after which he quickly let me know that it was not in his power to do anything for me, but informed me of Mr. Osborne's being in Town, and recommended my return with him again to Williamsburg, saying it would be a fine opportunity. I desired to continue somewhat longer, hoping he would not be offended at my calling on him sometimes to inquire whether something might not intervene in my favor, to which he politely replied he should always be glad to see me.

He afterwards walked me into his Garden, consisting of Edibles only, which seemed well manured and in as good order as a Garden upon a Hill could be. He pointed to a field of Clover adjoining the Garden, of, as I should guess, about eight acres, which He, and I too, considered as a fine improvement, tho' I should doubt its long continuance in the scorching heats and so high a situation; he staid me to drink tea with his lady, a daughter of the late Governor, Mr. Hamilton, which I did not know till I unluckily in relating (at their asking) my observations of what I had seen, gave the preference to the "Proprietors' garden" which I could perceive was not overpleasing, tho' they no otherwise manifested their dislike than after informing me of that circumstance by saying that the generality of People, who were Judges, thought Mr. Hamilton's garden greatly superior to the Proprietaries'.

After Tea I set out for Philadelphia, but perceiving my horse was ready bridled when called for and looked extremely thin and faint, I stopped at an inn in German Town to feed him and came to Philadelphia before it was dark.

Tuesday, the 27th, I spent chiefly in viewing the city and making some observations.

Wednesday, May 28.—I attended Mr. Allin again this morning and was with him in his parlor about fifteen minutes.   He again inquired if I did not purpose returning with Mr. Osborne.   I assured him I should not, tho' I observed it as my intention to write by him to Mr. Nelson, and begged to know whether I might give him any hopes of my appointment.   I waited on Mr. Allin again about 11, tho' to my apprehension my presence was far from being grateful to him. He inquired whether I had sent home my horse.   I said No, and then a silence ensued till a person relieved him, who I presume might have business with him, so in compassion to his visible uneasiness, I moved to depart, at which he seemed pleased, walking with me to the door.   I let him know at parting I would not trouble him again till the ensuing Wednesday, to which as usual, with his wonted politeness and serenity, he replied he should always be glad to see me. These two last days in May were, I think, the coldest, for the season, that I ever felt in my life, the young shoots of the common bushes in the Fields being cut off.   People say, too, it is the dryest time that they ever remember.

June 1 *and* 2 I spent very melancholy, hearing nothing from Colonel Hunter, whom I was cautious of teazing, till on the 3d I was informed he that morning set out to Virginia.   So whether he had any talk with Mr. Allin concerning me I never knew.   Thus circumstanced, in a kind of despair it entered my romantic head to Communicate my unhappy condition to Mr. Franklin, a gentleman in good esteem here and well known to the Philosophical World.   I without reserve laid the whole of my affairs before him, requesting his aid, if such a thing might be without inconvenience to Himself.   This in writing I sent to him June 4, early in the morning.   The same day I received a note by a servant under a wafer in these words :—

" Mr. Franklin's compliments to Mr. Fisher and desires the favor of his Company to drink Tea at 5 o'clock this afternoon."

I went at the time, and in my imagination met with a humane, kind reception.   He expressed concern for my afflictions and promised to assist me into some business provided it was in his power.   In returning from Mr. Franklin's, a Silversmith in the neighborhood of Mr. Franklin seeing me come out of that Gentleman's House, spoke to me as I was passing his door and invited me to sit down. This man's name was Soumien.   I had been several times in his company at my Inn and considered him as a very inquisitive person, craving a knowledge of other People's affairs, though noways concerning himself.   I accepted his offer of sitting at his door and he soon began to fish for my business with Mr. Franklin by asking whether I had any previous knowledge or acquaintance with him ; not obtaining as thorough information of all he wanted to know and knowing I wanted a private Lodging he made me an offer of his which I gladly accepted.   We agreed at Twelve shillings a week and I came thither the same evening.   The family consisted of himself, his Wife and a daughter of hers, a young woman about 13 years of age, a Negro man and two Negro wenches.   I was very well pleased to observe that his Family seemed to be acquainted with Mr. Franklin's.

June 5—Thursday.—As I was coming down from my chamber this afternoon a Gentlewoman was sitting on one of the lowest stairs, which were but narrow, and there not being room enough to pass, she arose up and threw herself upon the floor and sat there.   Mr. Soumien and his Wife greatly entreated her to arise and take a chair, but in vain ; she would keep her seat, and kept it, I think, the longer for their entreaty. This Gentlewoman, whom, though I had seen before, I did not know, appeared to be Mrs. Franklin. She assumed the airs of extraordinary Freedom and great Humility, Lamented heavily the misfortunes of those who are unhappily infected with a too tender or benevolent disposition, said she believed all the world claimed a privilege of troubling her Pappy (so she usually calls Mr. Franklin) with their calamities and distress, giving us a general history of many such wretches and their impertinent applications to him. Mr. Franklin's moral character is good, and he and Mrs. Franklin live irreproachably as man and wife.

Sunday, June 8.——About half an hour after 9 this morning I went to the Quakers' meeting on Society Hill. It proved a silent one, except one old man in the gallery who spoke about two minutes. What he said was not very edifying, nor had he the approbation of the Friends themselves, some of them in my hearing esteeming him a babbler. I dined to-day with Mr. Franklin and went afterward to the Dutch Churches. The Lutheran Church has an organ and a good performer. The Calvinist Church had none. Appearance of great devotion at both.

Thursday, the 12*th*.——This morning about 9 Mr. Franklin sent for me to copy a pretty long letter from General Braddock, acknowledging the care of the Pennsylvanians in sending provisions, etc., to the forces, Mr. Franklin in particular, and complaining of the neglect of the Governments of Virginia and Maryland especially, in speaking of which two colonies, he says: They had promised everything and had performed nothing; and of the Pennsylvanians, he said: They had promised nothing and had performed everything. That even the small supply he had received from the first two colonies were in general so decayed or damaged as to be of no use. And in a letter before this, of which I only saw a Copy, the General acknowledges he had been greatly imposed on in the character given him of the People of Pennsylvania, but that he would ere long take an opportunity of doing ample justice to the Ministry at Home. When I had finished several hasty Copies for which the post then waited, he desired I would breakfast with him the next morning and he would then give me more work.

June 13 and 14.—I was closely employed on several Copies of a Manuscript Treatise entitled, "Observations Concerning the Increase of Mankind, Peopling of Countrys, Etc."

From June 16 *to July* 10 : employed generally in writing or sorting of Papers at the Printing Office. I should observe that on St. John the Baptist Day (June 24) there was the Greatest Procession of Free Masons to the Church and their Lodge, in Second Street that was ever seen in America. No less than 160 being in the Procession in Gloves, Aprons, etc., attended by a band of Music. Mr. Allin, the Grand master, honoring them with his company, as did the Deputy Grand Master, Mr. Benjamin Franklin and his son, Mr. William Franklin, who walked as the next Chief Officer. A Sword-Bearer with a naked sword drawn headed the Procession. They dined together elegantly, as it is said at their hall upon Turtle, etc. Perceiving that I had nothing ever to hope or expect from Mr. Allin, I rarely went near him, unless twice for a supply of money. Mr. Nelson, in case of need, having given me a Bill of Credit for Twelve Pistoles.

Friday, July 18.—This afternoon about Three o'clock we were terribly alarmed by an express by way of Maryland from Colonel Innis, dated at Will's Creek or Fort Cumberland, July 11, giving an account that the Forces under General Braddock were entirely defeated by the French on the ninth, on the River Monongahela, the General, Lieutenant John St. Clair and a number of the officers killed, and all our fine Artillery taken. The Consternation of this City upon the occasion is hardly to be expressed. The next day we secured other accounts, less terrible, but none very authentic or particular, and on the twentieth some Indian Traders from the upper parts of the county, though not from the camp, brought still more flattering accounts, and reports were various, till Wednesday, July 23, when, about noon, arrived the following paragraph by the Lancaster Post, dated, Carlisle, 21st July, 1755 :—

"It is now reduced to a certainty that our army under

General Braddock, is defeated.   The General and Lieutenant John St. Clair dangerously wounded, about a Thousand men lost with the Train of Artillery and Baggage.   The remaining part of the Army, under Colonel Dunbar, have destroyed all their baggage except two six-pounders and Provisions necessary for their Retreat to Will's Creek, where I expect they are by this time."

This account was credited, and afterwards more particularly confirmed by Mr. Orme, aid-de-camp to the General. The Mob here upon this occasion were very unruly, assembling in great numbers, with an intention of demolishing the Mass House belonging to the Roman Catholics, wherein they were underhand excited and encouraged by some People of Higher Rank.   But the peaceable Quakers insisting that the Catholics as well as Christians of other denominations were settled upon the faith of the Constitution, or William Penn's Charter, and that the Government were bound to protect them so long at least, as they remained inoffensive and paid dutiful regard to the Establishment; the Magistrates met and with a good deal of difficulty prevailed with the Mob to desist.

Having as yet made no settled agreement with Mr. Franklin, I was not certain that he had any real occasion for my services, having Several Days together nothing for me to do.   I happened to have a very slender acquaintance with one Captain Coultas, who lived at the Upper Ferry on the River Schulkil, and who, it was generally believed, would be elected Sheriff of Philadelphia at the ensuing Election.   A Person of Sense and Character and to my apprehension of no less generosity and good nature.   To this Gentleman I wrote a few lines, importing that if the business he was entering upon required any such aid as it was in my power to administer, should be glad to serve him ; I apprehending the frequent auctions or sales which as Sheriff was necessarily concerned in might require such assistance.   In a Day or two after this, meeting with Captain Coultas at the Indian King he called me aside, acknowledged the receipt of my letter, said that it would not have a decent look to dispose of any part of an office which he was not then possessed of. Not, but he said, from the assurances of his Friends, he believed he could depend on it : But this he would assure me if it so happened, I might rely upon any act of friendship or kindness in his power to serve me.

Extremely pleased with the humanely rational generosity of this sensible man, I immediately flew to my friend, Mr. Franklin, with the news, that he might participate in my satisfaction, but was somewhat surprised that he did not consider what I had done in the same view with myself. He allowed Captain Coultas was a very worthy man, and would sincerely perform everything I was encouraged to expect or hope for, but could not apprehend that anything he could do for me would be worthy my acceptance; that he had himself thought of several ways of serving me, and has rejected them only because he esteemed them too mean. Particularly, he said, he could immediately put me into the academy, in the capacity of English School Master, a place of £60 a year, with some other advantages, but refrained mentioning it to me in hopes of having it soon in his power of doing better for me. I assured him with the utmost gratitude, the employ did not appear in so mean a light to me ; and the only reason I had for declining the favour, was the diffidence of my ability in doing justice to his recommendations, a thing which he said, he was not in the least apprehension of. However, presuming it gave him no offense, I craved his leave to decline the kind offer, and he declared himself very well satisfied.

Having informed him that I should prefer serving him as a clerk provided he had any occasion for me, on Monday morning, July 28, I received the following letter from him :—

" *Monday morning, July* 28—SIR :—Till our new building is finished, which I hope will be in two or three weeks, I have no room to accommodate a clerk. But it is my intention to have one, though my business is so small that I cannot afford to give more than I have always given, Viz. : Diet at my own Table, with Lodging and Washing and £25 per Annum.

"I could never think this worth offering to you but if you think fit to accept it, till something better shall fall in the way, you shall be very welcome to, &c.   B. Franklin."
"P. S.—It may commence from the time you first began to write for me, in which case I discharge your Board, etc., at Mr. Soumien's, or from the present time, and then I pay you for the writing done, or if you choose it, I will get you into the Charity School, as I mentioned before."

Without the least hesitation I gave the preference to his service and he let me know that it should not hinder his endeavors of serving me further.   Mr. Soumien had often informed me of great uneasiness and dissatisfaction in Mr. Franklin's family in a manner no way pleasing to me and which in truth I was unwilling to credit, but as Mrs. Franklin and I, of late, began to be Friendly and sociable, I discerned too great grounds for Mr. Soumien's Reflections, arising solely from turbulence and jealousy and pride of her disposition.   She suspecting Mr. Franklin for having too great an esteem for his son in prejudice of herself and daughter, a young woman of about 12 or 13 years of age, for whom it was visible Mr. Franklin had no less esteem than for his son.   Young Mr. Franklin, I have often seen pass to and from his father's apartment upon Business (for he does not eat, drink or sleep in the House) without least compliment between Mr. Franklin and him or any sort of notice taken of each other, till one Day as I was sitting with her in the passage when the young Gentleman came by she exclaimed to me (he not hearing) :—

"Mr. Fisher, there goes the greatest Villian upon Earth."

This greatly confounded and perplexed me, but did not hinder her from pursuing her Invectives in the foulest terms I ever heard from a Gentlewoman.   What to say or do I could not tell, till luckily a neighbor of her acquaintance coming in I made my escape.   I ever after industriously avoided being alone with her and she appeared no less cunning in seeking opportunities of beginning the subject again in so much that I foresaw a very unpromising situation. The respect due this young man, which his father always

paid him and which I was determined he should receive
from me, would not, I perceived clearly, be endured by a
woman of her violent spirit, and I began to wish my engagement had been with Captain Coultas.

In this situation I was when on August the 7th I received
a most Kind Letter from Mr. Walthoe informing me that
Mr. Mitchelson, the Person who rented his store, was
become a Bankrupt and that if I thought his House would
be of service to me, I should have the preference to any
Person whatever, and that I might rest assured of any other
friendly aid in his Power.   My family too he assured me
had now manifested an entire conformity to my will either
to embrace this opportunity and trying how far our friends
at York would assist us or if I was better pleased with the
prospect that Philadelphia afforded, they would remove
thither upon the first notice.   The uncertainty of my situation, my apprehensions of Mrs. Franklin's turbulent temper
together with reflecting upon what might be the Consequence of General Braddock's defeat brought me to a
resolution of seeing my Family and Mr. Walthoe at Williamsburg before I came to any certain determination of a
settlement; yet I showed Mr. Franklin my letter and craved
his opinion, who very readily came into mine, assuring me
that he would wait a considerable space for the result of our
conferences before he supplied himself with a clerk or the
School with a Master.   So I fixed upon Sunday the 10th for
setting out on my journey to Williamsburg.

Being not determined which road I should take (there
being several) Mr. Franklin said if I went the Upper he
would get me to take an order for a small matter of money
on Mr. Mercer in Virginia with whom he had had no settlement for nine years, upon which I told him I did not regard
a few miles of riding to serve him and he might depend
upon my making Mr. Mercer's in my way.

He gave me also Six Pistoles, asking if that was sufficient
for the trouble he had given me.   I told him it was.   The
Evening (Saturday) before I set out, I was with him till after
11 o'clock, when he pressed me to accept Ten Guineas more,

which I refused and I said that in case of accident from my horse failing or any other misfortune I had a Gold Watch in my pocket which would give me some credit. It was near Twelve when we parted with mutual good wishes.

Sunday, August 10, 1755, at five in the morning I left Philadelphia to return to Williamsburg.

THE LAST LETTER OF WASHINGTON.

In March of 1893 there was presented to THE FERDINAND J. DREER AUTOGRAPH COLLECTION of the Historical Society of Pennsylvania the last letter written by Washington before his death, at Mount Vernon, December 14, 1799. It is addressed to one of his stewards, James Anderson, and accompanying this sketch we give fac-similes of the letter and of the endorsement on the cover in which it was preserved. The letter reads as follows:

"MOUNT VERNON 13ᵗʰ Decʳ 1799

" MR ANDERSON

"I did not know that you were here yesterday morning until I had mounted my horse, otherwise I should have given you what I now send.

"As Mr Rawlins was going to the Union Farm, to lay off the Clover lots, I sent by him the Duplicate for that Farm to his brother—and as I was going to River Farm myself, I carried a copy for that Farm to Dowdal—Both of them have been directed to consider them attentively, & to be prepared to give you their ideas of the mode of arranging the Work when they are called upon.—

"Such a Pen as I saw yesterday at Union Farm, would, if the Cattle were kept in it one Week, destroy the whole of them.—

"— They would be infinitely more comfortable in this, or any other weather, in the open fields—Dogue run Farm Pen may be in the same condition—It did not occur to me as I passed through the yard of the Barn to look into it—

"I am Your friend &cʳ

"G WASHINGTON

" MR Jaˢ ANDERSON."

The history connected with this most valuable of Washington's letters, from the date of its writing until it came into the possession of the Historical Society, is set forth in the following letter of Arthur Appeltofft, addressed to Frederick D. Stone, Librarian of the Society:

" DEAR SIR,

" I will with pleasure give you an account of the Washington letter which you refer to.

" From letters which I have received from my aunt in Sweden I gather the following: In the spring of 1800 a Swedish sea-captain, then a young man, by the name of John Schall, visited Norfolk, Va., in his vessel. At this place Mr. James Anderson, the person to whom General Washington had written the letter, made Captain Schall a present of it. When he returned to his native land, where he was engaged to a lady (Eva Charlotta Wallin, *b.* 1771, *d.* 1844, in Gällared socken, Sweden), he left with her a writing portfolio containing letters, papers, etc. For some reason or other they were never married, and as John Schall never turned up, she kept the portfolio, which was found to contain this last letter of General Washington. At this lady's death it descended to her niece, Mrs. Charlotta Kuylenstjerna, *née* Bagge, of Sotanäs socken, Sweden. This Mrs. Kuylenstjerna, who died eight years ago at a good old age, gave this letter two years before her death to her daughter Anna, who is the mother of the Rev. Carl Adolf Carlsson, in Gällared socken, Sweden.

" About two years ago she made a present of it to her daughter-in-law, who is my aunt (my mother's sister), because, as she told her, ' you are so fond of everything that is antique.' Until then nobody had an idea of the real value of the letter. My aunt told her she would try to dispose of it to somebody in the United States, and sent it over to me about a year ago for that purpose. After several unsuccessful attempts to sell it, I finally turned it over to Mr. Henkels, manager of the autograph department of Messrs. Thomas Birch's Sons, to be sold at public auction, with what result you know.

" I am, sir,
" Very respectfully,
" ARTHUR APPELTOFFT."

JOURNAL OF MAJOR ISAAC ROACH, 1812–1824.

CONTRIBUTED BY MARY ROACH ARCHER.

(Continued from p. 158.)

We soon became great favorites with the natives, not only from their sympathy for us, but from the contrast between our behaviour to them and that of haughty John Bull of their own army, who always considers them as a conquered people, and several scales beneath him in society; and very unjustly so, for in all the good offices of society, they were their superiors. The Canadian retains all the simplicity of manners and habits of the early settlers.

The lands were granted by the kings of France in seigniories of several miles in extent to settlers of good families, and are yet held by their descendants; the peasantry holding small farms on lease by paying tithe rent, and their seignior owns mills at which they must have their grain ground and pay toll. Each one is compelled to give a portion to feed the curé and keep the church in repair, and to keep the highroads opposite to his or their bounds in good order, and to serve in the Militia when called on for defence; and this is all the burden placed on the Canadian. He pays no taxes, and the expenses of the country are borne by the British Government, costing them many pounds sterling per annum, and it is by this system only they have been able to retain possession of their provinces.

About three miles north of Beauport are the falls of Montmorency,—a beautiful perpendicular fall of about 240 feet in height. The stream is about of the same width. We were occasionally allowed to visit the falls, and tho' one finds none of the grandeur of Niagara, yet the falls and the neighboring scenery are beautiful. The mountains in the east, Isle D'Orleans in the west, Quebec to the south,—with the milky whiteness of the fall contrasted with the dark slate of its banks, together are very interesting. Below the falls the stream quietly enters the St. Lawrence opposite the south end of Isle D'Orleans. The stream may be ascended to within a few yards of the sheet of water, and stepping on some rocks one may stand so near that the spray soon wets the clothes, and if about noon or after, you appear encircled by a miniature rainbow of brilliant colors beautiful and interesting at all times, but yet more so when, by being placed in the centre of it, as if by magic one seems to ride on it, and the cataract of milky whiteness falling in all its grandeur at your feet.

It was on the seventh of July, 1813, we arrived at Quebec. I was told the snow had only disappeared from Beauport about three weeks—say the 15th of June, and by the 1st of September harvest began. I have seen very fine strawberries, peas, wheat, oats and corn, all ripe at once and on the 1st of October everything is cut and secured and winter again notifies its approach. Thus in three months Nature furnishes a supply (such as it is) for the year. Severe as is their winter, the Canadian looks with pleasure to its approach. His labor is over; his wants are few and provided for. He prepares his covering of fur, and mounting his cariol, (or light sleigh) and accompanied by his brunette, who has borne with him the heat and labor of the harvest, his spirited horse dashes off with him on a visit to a neighboring "habiton" sure of a kind reception, which is encouraged by the tenets of their religion, teaching them hospitality as an important duty. The stranger, rich or poor, is always sure of a kind reception from the Canadian, more especially from the kind and charitable curé of the village,—forming a striking contrast with surly John Bull, who bears the sway in Quebec.

On September 13, 1813, Major Taylor and twenty-four captains and subalterns were sent to Halifax, Nova Scotia. The general officers and the balance of us kept within hailing distance of "his Excellency," Sir George Prevost &c.

On the 12th of October we were told to prepare for a trip by water. It was at this time I had an opportunity to read the correspondence of the British and American agents for prisoners, accusing each other of their prisoners having taken up arms when paroled previous to being exchanged. The British allegation was unfounded, and I am satisfied not an instance occurred during the war of an American officer having violated his parole, tho' many were the violations of British pledges. A battalion of Royal Scots, taken in the transport ships Samuel and Sarah, tho' on parole were in the field under Sir George, and fighting, four months before they were exchanged. This, no doubt, was considered " coming old soldier over us," as was the pledge of the Governor General to General Scott to release me for Captain Fitzgerald of the 49th Infantry, who was sent in to Sir George, and immediately I was placed in close confinement, supposing from my being named as an act of friendship only, that my return was in some way important, and therefore the honor of the British Governor General was made pliable.

On the 29th of October, 1813, whilst sitting at dinner with General Winchester's mess, our quarters were surrounded by a troop of Cavalry, and Brigadier Major Dennis —a worthy officer whom I had met before—presented an order for the close confinement of 23 commissioned and 23 non-commissioned officers as hostages. This was afterwards explained by a general order of October 27th at Montreal, and which was produced by General Dearborn's having imprisoned some British non-commissioned officers and men as hostages for 23 Americans who were captured at Queenstown in 1812, and sent to England as being British subjects,—this producing the hostage question which occasioned more trouble and torment than half a dozen battles, and which when abandoned, proved of no advantage to either country—like most other quarrels national or private. As I had before determined, when John Bull placed a guard over me I should not be bound by my parole, when I was called into the General's private room and informed of my name being the second on the list of hostages, I immediately turned to Major Dennis and said—" Major, I am your prisoner, and from this moment released from my parole." For now I had to set my wits to work, and going thro' the dining-room to my chamber, I called my old friend Major Madison of Kentucky into my chamber, and said—" now I shall escape from prison if possible," and then took paper and hastily wrote a number of sentences having double meanings, by which I could correspond with him on my intended escape. For instance this phrase —" present my regards to General Winchester"—meant " I have determined to escape ;" " my friends Major V—— and Captain S—— are well," meant " they were to join me in the attempt ;" " present my respects to our kind friends in Beauport" meant " obtain a guide and a boat to cross the St. Lawrence ;" and other sentences I do not now remember. In a few minutes I copied this paper and handed it to the Major, who appeared alarmed at the idea of an attempt to escape from such a strong place as Quebec, but said he would do all in his power to aid me.

A soldier's trunk is soon packed, and in an hour I was ready to march ; but it occupied several hours to collect the officers through the village extending two miles, and it was near sunset before we reached our prison house, which was not the citadel of Cape Diamond as we expected, or any other part of the military defences,—but the common prison of the city :—as tho' insult was to be added to all the other evils of captivity. This prison was a new stone building on the south side of the city, between St. John's and the Port Louis Gates, and built on a declivity, on one side three stories high and on the other I believe five stories, and as we found when we intended to burrow our way out of it " it was built on a rock."

Major Van De Venter, Quarter Master General, Lieutenant Sydney Smith and myself had often conversed on the subject, and determined if practicable to make our escape, and after some time of cool reflection and survey of the strength of our prison house many obstacles presented themselves. The building was of stone and when we directed our servants to dig in the cellar to try the foundation it was a solid rock.

A strong guard was quartered a hundred yards on the left; five sentinels were posted at the prison; arms loaded day and night; and most of them much enraged against us,— for when we had been much annoyed by aggravating orders relative to looking out the dormer windows, and burning candles after 9 o'clock in the evening, some of our officers had amused themselves in throwing missiles from the windows at the sentinels.

The garrison in Quebec at this time was filled with the arrival every week of troops from the victorious army of Wellington in Spain, and without doubt the best soldiers in the world. As one regiment arrived a preceding one moved off to their army in the upper Canada, always having about 4000 men,—the local militia no doubt fearing a sudden attack from the United States.

After waiting a sufficient time for the notice of our imprisonment as hostages to reach Washington, and no measures being taken for our release, our trio determined to change their quarters. The officers were confined on the upper floor of the building, having the garrets paved with flagstones, in which we used to walk for exercise. The north wing was so high from the ground that it had been considered useless to defend the windows with iron bars as all the other rooms were. Whilst we were waiting to hear from Washington, I amused myself in taking the mainspring out of my watch, and having procured a small file I made a saw, with which in a few evenings' work, I cut off a bar in one of the windows in a lower room. This room was on the second floor, and by application to the Major, Ross Cuthbert (who married a daughter of Doctor Rush of Philadelphia), we were permitted to furnish this room for Major Van and myself to read in. I measured the room and purchased an ingrain carpet, double the size of the room, determined to use it in our escape. I now made saws for the officers in several other rooms, and the bars of their windows were cut also.

Major Van's plan of escape was to undermine the walls of the prison, which, when our servants attempted in the cellar, was found to be a "house built on a rock" as indeed is the whole city. Lieutenant Smith's plan was to bribe the guard, and escape by the front door. This was not attempted as the garrison was changed so often that it would be impracticable. My plan was urged as being least liable to suspicion, altho' attended with personal danger. Each advocated his own plan, and most of the day was thus occupied, whilst we were walking in the long attic rooms of our prison house.

Innumerable difficulties presented themselves to deter us. We were closely confined as hostages and under circumstances unprecedented in modern warfare. Our every look was watched by the enemy. We were surrounded by guards and sentinels, inside as well as outside the prison, and visited often during day and night by the commanding officer,—then by his aids; now by the Town Major "Rissleweller," again by the officer of the day, Sergeant of the Guard, Keepers, Turnkeys, &c. We were in a fortress second only to Gibraltar in strength, and at this time garrisoned by 4000 of Wellington's veteran troops,—the conquerors of the French army in Spain. Every precaution was taken to keep us secure. The city was strongly walled. At every gate was a guard, and as our prison was near St. Louis and St. John Gates, we could plainly hear of a quiet morning the challenge of the sentinel—"Who goes there?" and the answer "A friend," as the inhabitants passed from the city. We were in an enemy's country where not one in ten spoke English except in the towns. We were ignorant of the road, and when one adds the near approach of dreary winter (the thermometer is not often higher than 18 below zero at Quebec), I think it may be inferred our prospect was not very bright. On the other side when we turned our eyes to our present degraded situation, and the duty we owed our country to leave no exertions untried to escape; and I think we may add, a little malicious disposition in each of us, to annoy John Bull on all occasions;—the attempt was to be made.

As a conclusive argument in favor of my plan to go from

the roof of the building, I promised to make all the arrangements, tie all the knots, and then descend first myself. This was agreed to. Now came into operation my plan of corresponding with Major Madison at Beauport, and all my notes except one were sent thro' the hands of Major General Glasgow, Commanding, by which a boat was prepared to cross the St. Lawrence, and a guide was obtained to go with us, intending to take Craigs Road, which leads direct to the United States. Van De Venter said, if I could effect our escape from the garrison, he would get us out of the country, and to him was given the direction. Indeed my part of the drama was certainly the star if it succeeded, and if it did not we neither of us would have a " benefit"— unless it might be the benefit of clergy.

Our greatest difficulty was to avoid the sentinels, one of whom walked at night under the window that we were to descend from. But I was fixed on trying it. By dropping a thread with a piece of lead to the ground the height was found. My hip joint was three feet, and as we measured the number of yards we were likely to tumble, many jokes were exchanged; and it was concluded that as Smith was a sailor, and I a piece of one, if any tumbling was to be done, it must be by Van De Venter, that, as his name indicated, he could bear it best.

The almanac was consulted to avoid the moonlight, and Saturday evening fixed on, as on that evening many arrangements were required for supplies for Sunday, of food, books, clothing, &c., and we were locked up an hour later on that evening, say 9 o'clock, when the sentinel was removed from inside, and posted with the others outside. My washerwoman from Beauport, Mademoiselle Poullin, bro't me a note from the mess, begging me not to attempt what to them seemed a mad and visionary project, but says the good Madison, " I am ready to do all I can for you." My answer was in these words, " to prevent any mistake, we will be at your quarters, Beauport, at 9 o'clock on Saturday evening next." I gave the note to the woman, a few minutes afterwards informed my comrades, and went to work in earnest.   We had not only the enemy to deceive but our own friends, for if any of the others knew of our plan, it must produce confusion.   Our trunks and papers were arranged, each of us provided with a haversack filled with biscuit, cheese, loaf sugar, &c.   A letter was written to the Major thanking him for civilities received, and exonerating all his Majesty's subjects from having aided us.   We were yet in hopes of hearing of some arrangement of Government for our release, but none came.

On Saturday morning, November 27, 1813, we met each other with much anxiety, but went to work destroying our public papers, and leaving orders with our servants, who were now entrusted with our plan.   They were told to get the keys of the wing, as the attic was called, and to keep them till evening.   Our favorite carpet had been taken up the day before on pretence of cleaning our room, and hung up to the collar beams of the roof, and as often as I could, unobserved, had been ripping the seams, even whilst others were eating, and when I had to be on the look out the servants finished it.   Towards evening we became very sociable with the keeper of the prison, whom we had heretofore kept very distant from us, and as we began to try the effects of brandy, he became very obliging.

I had now double duty to do, for as the time approached, the other conspirators looked cool, tho' Van said " call me when you are ready."   Smith said :—" Roach, it won't do. Van De Venter thinks he ought to drop out of it.   We must be caught."   We were in the upper entry, and the moon appeared to me to be very lazy in retiring, and no anxious lover ever watched her with more interest than I at that moment.

The moon shone on the path of the sentinel, and must be down before I could lower the carpet from the roof.   In this moment of intense excitement the rattling of keys announced the keeper's approach, and we imagined we were discovered, for the first person he asked for was Sydney Smith, as he called the Lieutenant.   We came from our hiding places looking queer enough.   The keeper went with his Sergeant of the Guard into one of the rooms, and I asked what he wanted with Mr. Smith, for I was afraid to trust Smith to say a word. He had a letter for him only. Smith took the letter, but could not read it, and giving it to me said:—" Read it whilst Read (the keeper) and I take some grog,"—and mixing a real Man O' War's dose handed it to Read who swallowed it very kindly, and said to my servant Cornelius :—" Where are the keys of the wing?"   " O ! by Gosh !" says my fellow, scratching his pate, " I lef' 'em down stairs."   I affecting to be angry with him, said :— " How dare you take their keys or have anything to do with them ?"

Now for a jump. I gave Smith and Van a sign to be ready, and turning to Read, said :—" I want something out of our room below.   Light me down there before you lock up."   " Yes, sir !" and down we went.   At the room below I heard some one calling for water, and said :—" Read, you would not be so cruel as to keep those poor creatures all night without water !   Go and give them a bucket of water, and then I will be ready for you."   He was now pretty tolerably drunk, and off he went with his Sergeant, and as they descended the next flight of stone stairs, I closed my room and locked it, put the key in my pocket, ran up to the wing, where all was ready ; lashed the one end of our carpet to a rafter, threw the other end over the roof, and it was scarcely down before I was on it and wending, or rather, sliding my way to the earth.   Where the carpet was tied together sufficed for a momentary resting place.   On my alighting on the ground I was not a little alarmed to find the sentinel posted and walking near to me, when he turned again and walked a distance.   I now shook the carpet which was the signal of my being down, and next in order comes Sir Sydney Smith, and when down I pushed him behind me, and held the carpet before me, until the sentinel came up to within a few yards of us, and turned, without seeing us, to the opposite direction.   Now I can only account for our not being seen from the weather being cold, there was snow on the ground, and it was a very different climate from

VOL. XVII.—19

Spain, where these men had served.   The carpet was shaken again, and it shook as if it was loaded again, when, before my good friend, the Quarter Master General had reached the ground in safety, he came to the conclusion that as he had been descending so long he must be near the ground, and disdained holding on to the carpet for the last ten feet, and as he touched the ground his feet instantly flew off to make room for his weightier parts.   He said he was not much hurt, and we all started in an instant before our good friend the sentinel came back.   As it appeared afterwards, he had to walk a long distance to look at a storehouse.

Now, as we knew we must be missed in the prison in a few minutes, we pushed for St. John's Gate, and as it lay much below our prison, and not having been on the ground for one month, and the declivity being very steep, we had several falls before we reached St. John's Street.   I was ahead, and as I came near the sentinel at the gate, I walked very leisurely past him.   He challenged.   I answered, and the others followed close behind, and we walked thro' the several gates hung in the wall, until we reached the bridge over the ditch.   We had scarcely dared to breathe for the last fifteen minutes.   We now made off in fine style for Beauport by the St. Charles Bridge.   The road was frozen and rough.   Smith was no great traveller, and Van felt sore from his fall.   I therefore gained the bridge first, and taking out a shilling to pay our toll ran over the bridge to the north end where the gates were, which I found shut, and it occurred to me, if possible, to get thro' unobserved, as it might confuse our pursuers.   For we had not gained but a few hundred yards from the city, when we heard the alarm,—bugles and drums, and heavy rattling of the chained gates shutting and a great uproar,—and expected to be followed on the Beauport Road.   On examining the gates of the bridge, which were of oak shingling lath, I found them made close to the floor and roof, and that they were locked.   On going to the side which was a considerable height from the water, I found the lath fence extended over the water 8 or 10 feet; but jumping up on the bridge rail, and shaking the lath to try them, I swung hand over hand around the wing and landed on the ground t'other side of the fence before my friends came up, whom I hushed to be silent, and showed Smith the way round, and then Van De Venter. I now walked up to the toll-house and looking in the window, saw the gate keeper asleep in his chair before the fire. Away we went delighted with our ruse and with our success so far. We had gone near a mile when we heard the clattering of horses on the bridge. Not wishing to see company that evening, we jumped the fence and travelled thro' the meadow expecting every moment to hear the cavalry alongside of us. But see the effect of our Yankeeism. I was told afterwards by Dr. Clark who directed this troop, that as soon as they could get thro' the gates, he reined up his horse, and enquired who had gone thro' since dusk. The keeper, half awake, said "no one." "It is false," said the Doctor, "The American officers, Hostages, have escaped from prison, and they have gone thro'." For he was certain we would go to our friends at Beauport. The keeper, finding his veracity and his allegiance thus called in question, replied with an oath, that no one had passed thro' since dark; and my friend, the Doctor, called back his troop, and walked their horses to Garrison.

Doctor Clark had attended Doctor Rush's lectures in Philadelphia, and I had a good laugh at him, when I told him he did not study long enough with us to outwit a Philadelphian.

We now trotted along over hedges and ditches, and fearing every bush an officer, till panting and perspiring, we reached the gate in front of General Winchester's quarters, where we found a trusty negro, (Christie), Smith's servant, who had been left by Major Madison to look out for us, yet little dreaming that we would be at his quarters within fifteen minutes of the time I had promised. Not having the remotest expectation of our succeeding, General Winchester, Lewis and Madison had gone half a mile to sup with Colonel Zooch of the British army, and when the black (probably now nearly white) slipped into the room and whispered in Madison's ear " Captain Roach and Mr. Smith are at your quarters," Madison said he apologised to Colonel Zooch, and came to us in a few minutes. We now went into the barn, yet expecting to be pursued, and where we could converse freely with " old Kentuck," as we called the Major. The other gentlemen came home, but not wishing to implicate or get them into trouble, we would not see them. We remained in the barn until near 11 o'clock, preparing for another start. The good old Major bro't us two bottles of wine, " a barley loaf and a few small fishes," and we moved quietly down to the shore of the St. Lawrence, where the Quarter Master General, Van De Venter, intended crossing, and to whom was now given the command ; as he had promised if I would effect our escape from the Garrison of Quebec, he could get us out of the country, and his plan was to cross the St. Lawrence, gain Craig Road, which was open to the United States line, and thus avoid the suspicion of going towards the army,—which was very prudent.

On reaching the river shore, we found our guide, who was an old Canadian and apparently very timid, with an old log canoe, which he had hid under the ice, which now bordered the shore. But before we could embark, the noise made by a boat's crew in pursuit of us, compelled us to hide our boat, and ourselves with it among the shore ice. We are at length embarked in our frail gondola, yclept a log canoe, which from long use,—and abuse,—had been so broken at the bows, that when we three gallant knights, with our squire, essayed to move on the waters, it was evident we should not exhibit a large object for the enemy to fire at, for the water ran over the bows so fast that it was doubtful whether we were going over or under the water; and as in a canoe every one is obliged to sit flat on the bottom, we looked rather too flat with our bottom covered in freezing cold water; but tho' we were cooled, our ardor was not, and I being placed to steer, Van taking his hat to bail out the water. Smith and our guide, each with a paddle, we made our way from among the ice into the rapid St. Lawrence, which at this place is from 4 to 5 miles wide, and with strong arms and stout hearts, we made considerable progress.   We had proceeded a few hundred yards when we heard a great noise of men in a boat, doubtless in pursuit of us; and by their orders and counter orders, to row and to back-water, &c., which we were so near as to hear distinctly, we knew they were not sailors, and quietly keeping our little canoe head to tide, the enemy went blustering down the stream and we pursued our course.   In a few minutes the noise of oars again struck our watchful ears, and another pursuer came rushing down the tide, but we could easily avoid them by their noise; and after a very hard and fatigueing voyage, we gained the southern bank of the river, tho' carried down several miles below Point Levi by the strong current of ebb tide, and avoiding the guard boats.

When our boat reached the shore half full of water,—ourselves wet, and having sat in the cold water more than an hour,—and with the water splashed on us in paddling, frozen all over our clothes—we could with difficulty stand on our feet, especially Van whose fall from the prison now caused him much pain.   We found our provisions all destroyed by the water, one bottle of wine broken, and the prospect rather dreary.   But we kicked our canoe adrift, and with her we kicked care behind, and helping our wounded Major along we gained the high bank, and headed up the road toward Point Levi.   The Major now asked us to leave him near some house, and we might then travel much faster, as he could with difficulty get along, but we reminded him of promises made before we were placed in prison not to leave each other, and we were determined to escape or be taken together.

Our progress was slow indeed, and it was one o'clock A.M. when we reached a piece of woods back of Point Levi,—fatigued,—our clothes frozen on us,—our guide begging us to go into some farm house, or, as he said, we must perish. But our hearts were warm.   We were cheerful, and telling him to go to the Point, and ascertain what pursuit was making for us, and in the morning to bring us some bread, —we commended ourselves to the protection of our Heavenly Father, and scraping away a bed in the snow, which was now falling fast, we lay down, spoon fashion, placing our wounded comrade between Smith and myself. With no other covering than our frozen great coats and the snow, we actually slept soundly! until sunrise of a clear and cold Canadian Sabbath morning, November 28th; and with grateful hearts for preservation thro' the night, we commenced jumping to circulate our almost frozen blood, and when our guide returned, no doubt expecting to enjoy the benefit of emptying the pockets of three dead men, he found us as merry as could be, and he seriously declared no Canadian would have borne such exposure. He now begged us not to attempt to proceed, as he said all the militia of the country were ordered out in pursuit of us, and large rewards offered for us, and reminding us if he were taken with us his life would of course be forfeited. He said the ferry over which we must cross the Chaudière River was already occupied by a famous Captain of the Militia, &c.

Van De Venter said that if he could reach a farm house now in sight, and get his hip bathed, he would be ready to march, and we would be too much for the Captain of Militia when we reached the ferry. We now demolished a large loaf of brown or rather black bread our guide had bro't us, and instructing him to obtain the best information of the enemy he could get, and to meet us on the other side of the Chaudière ferry the next day, we dismissed him; and taking Van between us we moved for the farm house with a story—or lie, ready manufactured for the *maitre de maison*, and after much pain and exertion of the Major we reached the house. We found only a young girl, 10 or 12 years old, who was busied in preparing dinner for her parents, whom she said were gone to church. Van was now so ill as to be obliged to lie down on a bed, whilst Smith and myself thawed ourselves at the stove, and endeavored to dry our clothes. In drying my clothes I had opened my great coat, and the little girl, young as she was, noticed my uniform buttons on an inner coat. Now we had agreed to pass for merchants passing up the river, who had lost our boat in the night, and wanted to purchase horses to go up by land. And to gain any information only I was to understand or speak any French. Now the good man and his wife came home from church, and there was any quantity of bowing and scraping on finding his house thus occupied. But the Canadian never forgets his politeness and hospitality.

Our story—or lie—was soon told, and I went with Monsieur to the stable to chaffer for his horses, leaving Van and Smith in the house. The little girl, who it seems, had heard of our escape that morning, and not knowing that Van De Venter understood her, told her mother we were officers, for she had seen my buttons, and we might be the American officers; and Van crept out to tell me, and to "damn my buttons." But we were not daunted. The man had one horse and a grey mare, which, no doubt, was his wife's, for she protested against his selling her, until she got a sight of some guineas I held carelessly to her view, when the bargain was made. We took some dinner, and mounting Smith and Van on horseback, we moved off towards our piece of woods, where we again found our guide, much frightened, who told us the whole country was in arms in pursuit of us, and begged us to surrender, as if he were taken he must be executed, and begged us to allow him to return to his family. We again said everything to encourage him, and told him to go on before us, and we would follow him as soon as it became dark, as we had before arranged to meet him beyond the ferry. We now saw one of the young men from the farm house passing the wood in great haste toward Quebec, and we had reason to believe we were suspected by the people. He was most likely on his way to inform some one of our being there. The snow now fell very fast. We pushed off, our guide ahead, and then took the main road, intending, if possible, to cross the Chaudière and gain the Craig Road,—cut by Sir James Craig when Governor of Canada. Our guide was to give us notice, if he could do so, of the condition of the guard at the next ferry. In an hour or two we again met our Sancho, who trembling now told us we must give up, as at every house in which he had been, the inhabitants were looking out for us; and a troop had passed him towards the ferry where the guard was waiting for us. Thus at every step new difficulties met us; and we had also to encourage and spur on this timid Canadian.

We were now entering a village about three miles from the ferry, and telling our avant courrier to cross the ferry and keep a good lookout for us, he began to think us deranged, and repeating his *Pater Noster* he obeyed our direction. We were obliged to halt occasionally and proceed slowly, as in my haste to buy our horses, I had not discovered that one of them had no shoes on the hind feet and the frozen road not yet covered enough with snow, made him go lame. This village, like all others in Lower Canada, reached a long way on either side of the road, and we moved on cautiously looking for the road to the ferry until we must have gone five miles, and having passed the village and seeing a light at a distance from the main road and a path leading towards it, we turned into it, and soon found ourselves at a farm house near the river, and knocking we heard the usual " entre." Entering in the dark we asked for lodging and feed for our horses which was readily promised, when the *bonne homme*, striking a light, there was mutual surprise,—on his part at our appearance in dress so different from their own and from wet and dirt not very genteel, and our French none of the best. We were no less surprised to find ourselves in the midst of men women and children in bed in one large room *en masse*, and on enquiry we found ourselves on the bank of the river near the falls of Chaudière—and having passed the ferry we intended crossing five miles below. We supped on *soup meagre*, and lay down on the floor, adding three more to the grotesque assembly,—the women and children not appearing to notice our joining them. We were thankful for escaping the enemy so far, and promised ourselves a warm lodging by the stove, and very different from the previous night in the snow. Warm it was! for we were soon attacked by an army of fleas, and again we suffered and bled in the good cause, but we were determined to sleep, and it was not a little thing that could prevent us.

At daybreak we were up, when the "habiton" said he could put us over the river but the rapids were too strong for our horses, and they would be drowned. We insisted on making the attempt, and by showing some money, he agreed upon making the attempt. We found the river rapid and rocky, but narrow, and we crossed in a small boat towing over the horses, who seemed as much alarmed as the Canadians were. As for ourselves we had made up our minds to consider nothing impracticable until proven to be so. Having crossed the river, paid the host, and received his directions to gain the road, and with the "adieu" and "bon voyage" we left him. The Major mounted on the grey mare, and Smith and myself, taking it ride and tie with the small grey horse, which appeared to grow more lame for want of shoes. As soon as we emmerged from a piece of wood about 8 A.M., we passed in front of a farm house where the Militia appeared to be collecting to go in pursuit of us, but did not appear to notice us,—or perhaps did not like to attack us, as there were not more than twenty-five of them!

Presently we met an officer with a sword under his arm going to the muster. We now expected he would stop us and call to his men to secure us. But it is said one never loses by politeness. In this case we did not. I was walking by the horses and as soon as our officer came near us, I commenced with "salut! Bonjour. Il fait beautemp," &c., and passing on really convinced this "man of war" that we were too polite to be prisoners, by which mistake he lost some three or four hundred dollars reward, and promotion to be a Major of his Majesty's Militia. After turning to the right, as the man at the river told us, we were much pleased again to see our Monsieur Tonson, who putting up both hands and with some pious ejaculation at our having got

over the river, told us we were now on the highway back to
Quebec via that identical ferry we so much desired to avoid.

"Ah! Monsieur, attendez voila!" said he, "Here is Le
Major Francis De Le Marie de—something else—parading
his men to pursue you, and every man is under orders to
take you.   How impossible for you to proceed!"

"Courage!" we replied,—"Put us in the right road again;"
and agreeing on a rendezvous at night, away we went until
we came near a village, and thinking it not prudent to pass
another detachment of Militia in daylight, we turned our
horses into a wood to wait till evening, and here our guide
promised to meet us.   But the enemy were increasing so
fast, and the certain destruction consequent on his detection
drove him from us and we never saw him again.

After standing quiet a while we found a peasant was
hauling logs from this wood to build a house; and having
with him a small dog, every time he passed us this little
rascal would run in and come to a dead set at us.   And
thus did we three stand from 10 A.M. till 4 P.M., in the
snow, fearing to move sufficiently to circulate the blood, lest
we or our horses might be seen.   Poor Van De Venter was
much crippled from his fall at the prison, and Smith complained of his feet having been frozen in sleeping out the
first night, and I felt too cross to give either of them much
comfort, and we were almost frozen and very hungry.   Now
considering we were volunteers on this expedition we took
it very coolly and went ahead in spite of wind and weather.

At 4 P.M. it was growing dark, and as usual toward
evening the snow began to fall very fast.   We made another
move on the road, and at dusk entered the village without
meeting more than one or two *habitons*.   Now our *petit
Cheval* became quite lame, and I mounted him to urge him
whilst Smith and Van jogged along on the grey mare,—and
truly "the grey mare was now the best horse."

After much exertion to spur on my beast and finding I
made slow progress, I had to dismount and seizing a piece
of fence rail, drove him on before me, and it amused my
comrades to hear me imitating the natives in driving, which

was requisite to avoid suspicion; and tho' I made great noise, not one of the villagers came out; therefore my imitation must have been a good one. Now as a further proof of my true Canadian French,—on our return we lodged in this village with Major Verault, who said that when we had passed thro' the village he was changing his clothes, and had orders to go in pursuit. He heard me singing out "marche donc"—"marche tu"—and "le diable paresseux," &c., but did not imagine it was any other than some neighbor going home from work.

My lame horse was for stopping at every house we came to, and after getting thro' the village about 11 o'clock P.M. and not finding our guide, we turned off the road some distance to a light we observed, intending to purchase a small sleigh, or exchange our lame horse for one. We had now determined to pass ourselves for graziers going towards the United States to purchase cattle.

Knocking at the door, the farmer opened it and received us kindly, gave us some soup, and we told our story—or rather lies. Now they say liars should have good memories, and I had not, for when the man asked me if I knew the butcher in Quebec I said "no,"—and the man told the priest afterwards he then began to suspect we were not true men. For if we were graziers, we must know the principal butcher in Quebec, and he thought we must be the American officers who had escaped. However, he was cunning enough to keep his suspicions from us, lest perchance we might have put him and his son out of the way of informing. Long before daylight I called up the old man to renew our dealings of the preceding night for a sleigh or other vehicle. It was too near Winter, he would not sell his cariole, but he had a "*bien beau charette*"—a light cart—he would dispose of, and as soon as he said his prayers he sent his son with a lantern to the barn to show me the charette. I preferred the sleigh, but he would not sell it, and telling him as our horse was lame we would be obliged to take the cart, and paying him more than its value in addition to the lame horse, we hastily geared up the grey mare, and before it was light moved off at a rapid pace, and took the road up the bank of the Chaudière. We were yet on the lookout for our guide, and hoping to gain the wilderness, as we had every reason to think that some one who had seen us would aid in our pursuit, and to gain the mountains was our only safety, as there was no byeroad and our guide had said if we could reach the last house in this last settlement, kept by Monsieur Jean Jacques Charledeauluce, who was not only a good hunter and guide but very friendly to the Americans, and no doubt he would secrete us. And now we urged on our *grise*, worthy of—not a more respectable employment—but a more stylish equipage and not used to as severe driving as we were compelled to give her. Now I was the jehu, and to avoid suspicion, when we came near a house or met anyone—(we might have been tho't anything else but gallant officers,—from the preceding days of our march being much exposed and clothing abused and torn, we did not look too genteel, and I was seated in the bottom of the cart with a Canadian cap on,. and only wanted a short piece of pipe in my mouth to complete the figure; but using tobacco in any form was a practice I never could comply with)—whenever we approached a house or person, we drove slow until out of their view. Having as we supposed, travelled about 40 miles, at noon we found ourselves near the last of the settlements of St. Famine on the Chaudière, and on the route which Generals Arnold and Montgomery took in 1775 to attack Quebec, and where General Montgomery was killed.

With some assistance from a peasant we crossed the river to the house of Charledeauluce, who spoke English, and the first we had heard except that of our guide, since leaving our friends at Beauport. Our only hope now was to procure this man to guide us, as we almost despaired of again seeing our Sancho, whose neck was in too much danger to meet us after all the detachments of Militia he had passed,—for we had passed several of them ourselves. We told the hunter our story of expecting to meet some cattle near the lines of the United States, and wanted a guide to go with us. He said his brother was ill, and he must go for a physician. We used many arguments to persuade him to go direct into the woods with us, but without effect. We afterwards overheard him conversing with his brother, and found he suspected who we were. He then came and told us he was our friend, and would do all he dare for us; but he had already been imprisoned by the Mayor of Quebec for only bringing in some newspapers from the United States, and if he was now detected he would forfeit his property and perhaps his life. He promised if we were not pursued that night, he would procure an Indian to guide us, and as we could not proceed without one we had now to submit.

We were now at the foot of a mountain,—the country covered with snow,—the winter set in, and this the last house in Canada and sixty miles from an American settlement. Smith now found his feet so badly swollen and frozen, we had to cut his boots in pieces, and found large black spots of frost bite on his feet, and he could march no further. Van De Venter, tho' lame, was in good spirits, and willing to take to the woods; but as we had before refused to separate, we now refused to leave Smith, as he proposed. Indeed a beneficent Providence directed us otherwise, for our best friends in Canada all agreed if we had gone into the mountain, we must have perished with cold.

We were compelled to halt for the night, and we did all halt and hobble enough, but Charley gave Smith and Van something to bathe with, and cooked us an excellent supper of spare ribs, which we did not spare—tho' I never liked much to hear of spare ribs afterward—and we went to bed not much satisfied with the appearance of things.

A word here on the subject of exposure to frost. In crossing the river St. Lawrence, we had all been equally exposed, all equally wet, and all slept together in the snow. Previous to lying down, I persuaded Van to take off his boots, and doing the same, I tied both our feet close together in two silk handkerchiefs, having from a child dreaded frosted feet. Smith refused to take off his boots. Our feet were uninjured,—his badly frosted. My head and that of the Major's was covered with a cotton cap and hat, and yet both our heads were injured by frost, as well as Smith's, and I am convinced a silk covering would have been a great protection.

Thus far, in our attempt to escape, the fickle Goddess, Fortune, had been unusually kind, and led us with smiles, but coquette like, she now withdrew, to make our disappointment greater, and left us—perhaps thinking it too cold to go any further with us. I am sure we deserved better treatment at her hands, for never did any of her votaries more faithfully labor in her service, or court her smiles; than we three gallant knights. But turning from us, we were left to a fate which our daring and perseverance had not deserved.

About 4 A.M. December 1st, we heard the trampling of steeds, and soon found the house surrounded. I turned to Van, who was in bed with me, and asked him what he thought of our chance now. In a minute we heard them post sentinels at each window. The room door was opened, and about 20 armed men entered to make a desperate charge on us, and frightened our poor host very much. Smith slept in the next room, and we could not but laugh to hear the sailor abusing them in English, whilst they in French demanded his surrender, and not understanding a word each other said. They next charged on Van and myself, and in the name of His Majesty demanded our surrender, whilst their muskets were pointed at us over the shoulder of their officer. We told them not to be uneasy, that we did not feel disposed just then for a fight, especially as we were unarmed, and they ten to one in numbers,—tho' looking at the time, I really thought I could have managed three of them. For after we had surrendered, and were getting something to eat previous to our journey " bock agen," they begged their officers to tie us, supposing no doubt as we had escaped from the Regulars at Quebec, and given them such a chase, we must be dangerous fellows. Now as the country and climate presented so many difficulties to any further attempt at that time, we did not hesitate to assure the officer in command, Major Verault, that we would give him no further trouble to Quebec. And whilst under his charge, this gentleman treated us with every kindness, in opposition to the urgent desire of his men to tie us, who, poor fellows, did not know how much more secure our promise given to the officer made us.

About sunrise, sleigh and sled were in readiness, and surrounded by our guard, we began to retrograde towards Quebec. Our feelings were not to be envied. After so much daring, so much exposure and suffering, we thought we were entitled to better luck; yet such is the elasticity of the youthful mind,—and more so that of a soldier, who when he enters on the Military career, and his country demands from him his entire devotion, must make up his mind to take the smiles and frowns of War as they may chance to come,—and we were young, we had done what was our duty to attempt an escape, and having persevered to the utmost, we were now content, and when our eyes met occasionally on the road, could jest each other on our grotesque appearance. Smith was told he expected promotion soon, as he appeared to be making a chapeau of his hat by sleeping on it. Van was told he looked like his ancestor, Rip Van Winkle, just awakened. I was reminded I need not mind the *rips*, as I had enough of them in my clothes, tho' they might serve me till we reached Quebec, when Jack Ketch would be entitled to them. Now this was no joke, for we had been threatened with execution as hostages;—but my friend, Tom Randall, told a British Colonel,—"Just you hang us now, and it will be dear hanging to you." To return—we stopped at the house of Captain Chiquet of Militia, who had formerly commanded a vessel on Lake Erie and who spoke good English. The Captain told us when we passed within a hundred yards of his house in our charette, he held in his hand the order for our arrest, and was directing his Lieutenant to muster his Company, and supposing we were some of the civil authority, jogging along so leisurely, he commenced abusing our want of zeal in His

Majesty's service, little dreaming that we were the veritable men that he was displaying so much military skill in pursuit of.   Then Major Verault told him how I had made so much noise in passing his house, with my "marche donc" &c., and we had a good laugh.

We were soon joined by a Lt. Marinault of Quebec Embodied Militia in pursuit, and with orders, if retaken, to receive us from any detachment of Militia, and return with us to Quebec.   Lt. Marinault was very polite also, and that evening we reached the house of Major Verault, where we were entertained sumptuously, and rested all night, and on the next, left for Quebec where we arrived at 7 o'clock P.M., December 2nd, and went with Lt. Marinault, at our request, to the quarters of Major Muir of Embodied Militia, then on duty, whom Van was acquainted with,—a Scotch gentleman who always evinced much kindness to all of us.   The Major went with us to the prison, and gave orders that we should be treated with kindness; that we had only done our duty in endeavoring to escape.

On our return to Quebec we found the whole garrison in confusion.   A general order had been issued by the Commander in Chief, Sir George Prevost, severely reprimanding Major General Glasgow, Commanding, for permitting three prisoners of war, and hostages also, to escape from such a fortress as Quebec, garrisoned with 4000 of veteran troops, and the country full of Militia.   For the British as well as our friends thought we were clear.   On our return to prison, what a scene of confusion!   Our companions had been treated very badly, and more closely confined.   Yet they were almost in tears at seeing us again, and said they would rather suffer ten fold more than see us retaken.

The keeper of the prison, Sergeant of the Guard and sentinel in close confinement, the officer of the Guard under arrest, the officers of the garrison generally much censured, and even the Mayor of the city suspected of having aided in our escape, because he had been kind enough to let us buy a carpet for our room, or perhaps because he had married a Philadelphia lady (daughter of Dr. Rush), but

Mr. Ross Cuthbert soon repelled the base accusation, and frowned into silence these John Bulls, who were anxious to blame anyone but themselves, and not disposed to give us three Yankees the credit of outwitting them.   For they ever after scouted the idea of our having escaped from the roof of the prison.   Altho' we had written to the Mayor, when we left, to assure him of the innocence of those persons in charge of us, they told us that hanging a carpet from the roof was a Yankee *ruse de guerre* to cover our movements, and they continued to try, and to punish innocent soldiers for our escape.

We had been advertised as deserters from His Majesty's kind protection, and a large reward offered for us.   Our friends soon collected around us, and various and amusing were their expressions of regret.   They told us that when we escaped, we had not been gone more than ten minutes, when Read the keeper came up, and missing us began a search.   The brandy we had given him was operating, when a mischievous Midshipman, Monteith, who had suspected our movements, undertook to show Read in which room we were ; and led him occasionally against the edge of an iron door, until he ran down stairs, crying :—" Murder! Sergeant of the Guard,—Major Van De Venter,—Sydney Smith,"—&c.

The prison was soon filled with British officers.   The second in command, Colonel Parry of the 103rd Infantry, examined each of our companions, and heaped insult on those who dared to express their satisfaction at our escape, calling us by abusive names for daring to elude his vigilance. He confined two officers in the same dungeon with a murderer for defending us.   My servant was called up, and as he could give no information, the redoubtable Colonel of His Majesty's 103rd Foot pulled the poor fellow by the ear, where he had been wounded in battle until the blood ran down his neck.   This poor fellow's suffering distressed me much more than my own, and I sent a message to Colonel Parry by an officer, and tho' he was in Quebec some days after our return, he did not come near us.   Yet we were visited by many officers who expressed their sympathy for us.

VOL. XVII.—20

The next day after our return we three were separated from our comrades, and placed in separate rooms, with positive orders for no person to be allowed to visit, except the Aids of the Commanding General.   Even our good friends, the Catholic priests, were denied admittance to us.   But when my friend, the Rev. Mr. Mignault, was stopped at the threshold,—" What," said he,—" the minister of God forbidden to visit the sick and prisoner!   Open that door instantly, and let Sir George Prevost dare to prevent my entrance here again."   And he continued almost daily to visit us whilst we remained in prison.

The first night of our separation by order, I managed the Sergeant who had the keys,—for since our escape poor Read the keeper was a prisoner in his own castle, and the officers and men were more vigilant.   But I had always treated the Sergeant well; and every night, after all was quiet, my door was unlocked, and I spent most of the night with Van De Venter, and in a few days we had planned another escape.   The bars of our windows already sawed off, an entirely new mode of travel was marked out, and poor Smith was to be left behind.   He now appeared to be quite contented to while away his time between his violin, a walk of ten feet across his room, and his glass of grog,— and no doubt thinking, as most others placed in our situation have supposed, that having made so much exertion to escape, and been defeated, they had done enough.   But no, a soldier should be stimulated by defeat to renewed exertions, and to use increased vigilance, and Van and myself, trusting to Providence, were nearly ready to cut and run,— when down comes an order from Sir George Prevost in the field, to take those three troublesome officers out of prison, and place them on parole.

What a compliment to a Yankee officer, thus to acknowledge that his hostages were to be better secured by our word, than by the massive walls of his prison and fortress, and by the bristling bayonets of his Wellington veterans! Van De Venter and myself were not desirous again to risk our lives opposed to the attacks of our guards, or the intense severity of the winter (which was yet severe), but we never would have relaxed our exertions to escape from a loathsome prison. Van De Venter, Smith and myself were now (March 1814) paroled, after being closely confined five months, and removed to quarters in Port Louis Street, near the gate of that name, and in view of the grand parade ground. Here we found Generals Winchester Chandler and Winder, Colonel Wm. Lewis, Major Madison, and a dozen Captains, Lieutenants, and Sailing Masters, who, tho' not closely confined, were not allowed to go beyond the house and garden, and even this was a liberty that we who had been closely confined, estimated a great blessing. We had greater advantages of conversation and books; we could send into the city for anything we wanted, and had more frequent opportunities of hearing from our army and from home. A mess was established, and as I had evinced some ingenuity in doing without food, I was appointed caterer and major domo, and we lived very comfortably thro' the remainder of a long Canadian winter; my mind being about equally divided between my housekeeping duties, reading and reflection, and—looking at the girls, more especially at the daughter of Lord Jacob Mountain, Bishop of Quebec, whom I had selected for my Dulcina Del Toboso, and from my observation across the narrow street of Port Louis, I fancied the young lady was everything that that damsel should be. I further had reason to think the young lady knew of my profound devotion, and if like Sancho, in describing the manner of the lady's mounting, I did not see her vault on horseback in exactly the same style, I had evidence of her horsemanship, and tho' I lived all winter in regrets of having no means of introduction to this scion of the church, —when we removed the following summer to Beauport, I met her by entire accident in the road, and I almost feel tempted to carry out honest Sancho's description of his master's mistress. I never sought an introduction, but in the society of our estimable friends Colonel Salibury and family, we enjoyed much pleasure and seldom met with any of the English ladies. It may be readily seen our situation was far from being pleasant or even comfortable, altho' so far preferable to a prison house. We were mostly young men, who had cheerfully perilled our lives for the honor of our country, and felt very sensibly our being deprived of the opportunities of serving with our comrades in the field, but we cheered each other.

We amused ourselves in the various ways of riding, walking, fishing &c., occasionally getting up a cat fight to the utter horror of some half dozen spinsters of Beauport, who had prepared a remonstrance to the Governor General, to be presented by a committee of old maids, until they were induced to suspend this delegation by the good Colonel De Salibury showing them that—as the English officers were in the practice of cock fighting, it no doubt was the custom in the United States to fight cats; and it would seem hard to prevent their amusements,—advising Mamselle Le Blanc, who appeared on behalf of the cats, to endeavor to keep them at home, until the Americans should leave the village. I believe this cat question was greatly aggravated by the mischief of Tom Randall, who affected to sympathize very much with the tom cats, and in a feigned French hand wrote to Mamselle Le Blanc, condoling with her on the insult to her bel-chat, and urging her to revenge. Now this Mademoiselle Le Blanc was a very dignified lady of the *ancien régime*, and Van and myself took tea with her a few days after the battle of the tom cats, when the lady recounted to us minutely all the damage actual and supposed her poor cat had sustained, whilst puss sat at a distance laboring to wash off the effects of the battle, and evidently afraid to approach the tea table,—altho' Van and myself were in no manner concerned in this offence to the single ladies of Beauport.

Lt. Gregory of the Navy acted as Mischief Master General on those occasions, and he deserved Provost rank. Our mischief was not always harmless. It extended to practising on each other the burning of gunpowder, lest we might forget the use of it,—but no more on this subject.

After being prisoners a year, our time became very unpleasant, and our desire to be of use to our country increased. The British officers endeavored to keep from us all intelligence of a cheering nature, and gave us their own version of every battle fought. Our letters from home, if they contained any unfavorable opinions of John Bull, were not delivered to us. The capture and burning of Washington City was speedily handed to us; and on the same day that we were lamenting over the fallen honor of our country, some kind friend gave us the account of the defeat of the British at Baltimore and at Plattsburgh. What a glorious contrast was here! Thus were we agitated by hopes and fears until the close of the campaign of 1814. At length both Governments became heartily tired of the hostage question, and this war of words was ended by an exchange of prisoners on both sides; and after much ceremony and preparation, all the American officers, prisoners at Beauport, took their departure from Quebec for the United States in sleighs, December 14th, 1814, and arrived at Plattsburgh, New York, in a few days. We were here welcomed by our brother officers, and we received many attentions from Colonel Smith, Commanding, and brother of our companion in trouble, Lt. Sydney Smith, who was now at home. Remaining two days at Plattsburgh, we had an opportunity of examining the defences of the place, and when the rude and hastily built batteries were examined; the small number of guns placed in them; the want of men and ammunition and the totally unprepared condition of our army at that period to oppose the veterans of Britain; it was matter of utter astonishment how Sir George Prevost—with the best troops in the world, and in number fifty to one, having taken a position within gunshot on ground commanding the place, having attacked and partly carried the bridge over the Saranac, and the stream itself fordable,—yet when the British fleet was defeated, without a moment's delay retreated in utter confusion, to the dishonor of not only himself, but thousands of as gallant officers and men as ever lived. I subsequently met many officers who served with Sir George in that disgraceful campaign, and I verily believe better troops never lived than they were, and 14,000 strong.[1]

As to the battle of Lake Champlain, it was truly characteristic of the brave tars of both countries and was literally an affair of " hard knocks," in which McDonough fought until one side of his vessel was cut entirely out, then sprung his cable and turned the other side, which proved too hard for John Bull.

On leaving Plattsburgh, our detachment of officers crossed thro' the ice in a packet boat to Burlington, Vermont, and next day reached only Vergennes, and left next morning and arrived at Whitehall. Here we found several officers of the Navy with the remains of McDonough's fleet, which we went on board of in the evening, and left next morning, and on the second day, December 24th, 1814, arrived at Albany. Having travelled from Quebec all the distance, 350 miles, except 50 in sleighs, we were right glad to exchange for a good warm post coach, and the rattle of its wheels. We left for New York, and after an absence of nearly two years, I once again reached Philadelphia, and was heartily welcomed by my parents, and I felt thankful to the Almighty who had preserved me thro' many dangers and much suffering, and bro't me in safety to my home.

Our party of officers was diminished at every halt we made, but we did not separate without mutual kind feelings and professions of lasting friendships, which had formed in scenes of danger, and cemented by mutual suffering; and to this day those who live are yet endeared to each other.

Altho' I had suffered much and long, I knew it was for my country, and with youth and a yet unbroken constitution, and the solace of having at all times endeavored to do my duty, enabled me to push dull care away, and prepare myself for the next campaign, which was likely to be a severe one, as our country was becoming more disposed to support the Government, which had thus far carried on the war by the Democratic citizens alone, but now every one found it was requisite to defend his home and country.

[1] See " Thompson's History of the War."

On the other side the British had defeated and driven back the French, and every exertion was making to strike the Yankees a hard blow in 1815.

Our Government received their prisoners home with much kindness, and in a day or two after my arrival, I received a very affectionate congratulation from my friend General Scott, to welcome me home; and as he commanded the department, I was handed by his Inspector, General J. Hare Powell, at Baltimore, a furlough to remain quiet at home as long as I wished. The General knew that that would not be long. It was soon known that Lt. Col. Boerstler was to have a Court of Enquiry on his conduct, and I among others was summoned to Baltimore to give testimony. But the Court and everyone else thought the Colonel had suffered enough for his ignorance and folly, and therefore acquitted him.

I spent two or three weeks in Baltimore very pleasantly surrounded by military friends,—for General Scott (commanding a large department, including Pennsylvania, Delaware, Maryland and Virginia) had his headquarters here, and the patriotic citizens of Baltimore were devoted to their military friends. General Scott was preparing to go to the Canadian frontier in the Spring, and said I must join his staff as Assistant Adjutant General, with the rank of Major, for which he applied to the War Department to commission me. Immediately every preparation was making by both countries to prosecute the next campaign most vigorously.

It was now the middle of February, and we expected to move to the frontier. I had dined with General Scott, when he directed me not to wait for my commission, but to go on duty next morning as Assistant Adjutant General at headquarters. I was awakened about midnight with a great noise and shouting in the streets, and on enquiry found an express was passing thro' to Washington with the news of peace with Great Britain. This was undoubtedly blessed news for thousands of the inhabitants of both countries, but to many military men it was a sad disappointment, and to none more so than myself,—who retired at night a Captain of the line in full expectation of appearing next morning in General orders, as a Major on the staff of a favorite General; and in place of sending my first order to announce my promotion to the troops, I was directed to order—a salute to be fired at Fort McHenry for the news of peace. Alas! Alas! I thought I was most unfortunate that I should have no other chance of running my head in the way of an enemy's shot.

What an uproar and confusion now took place! In a few days came orders to stop recruiting; to recall all troops under marching orders; and officers and soldiers now thought they had nothing to do but go to sleep. No more expresses—no more videttes—no more patroling all night. And now we saw the merchant with animated face and brisk step, moving towards his former scene of operations; making a hasty visit to the Exchange; then with bundles of keys opening his ware-house and counting-room, which had for nearly three years been deserted. Then came on the fever of trade and speculation, with its mistakes and failures, &c.

To no one, I believe, was the news of the blessings of peace more heartily welcome than my aged parents; and I was not unmindful of my duty to them, and at the latter part of February, 1815, resumed my furlough and returned to Philadelphia.

Various were the opinions as to the fate of the army, but orders were soon issued to discharge all the officers of the Regiment from number 42 down to 10, reserving the men to fill up the remaining corps. A board of officers was convened at Washington, and the army reduced to 10000 men; and as my friend Scott was one of the board, I was retained and assigned to the Corps of Artillery. In June I received orders to take command of about 250 men at Judge Peters Farm near Fairmount, and in a few days I marched them to Fort Mifflin, filled up Major T. Biddle's company, then moved to Fort McHenry, filled up the garrison there, and finding that the Corps of Artillery was apportioned in two divisions, North and South, and all the old Captains claiming the North, I went on to Washington, and obtained an order to remain at Fort McHenry on duty, not wishing to go far from my parents. Colonel George Armistead who had defended Fort McHenry, going on a furlough, I was placed in command of this favorite garrison all summer and autumn, till by exposure I was attacked with intermittent fever, and the Colonel returning, I returned to Philadelphia to recruit men for the Colonel, great numbers of men having been discharged. Whilst on this duty in Philadelphia, my father was violently attacked, October, 1815, with paralysis of the entire left side; and it was a blessing that I was near to attend on him, as he continued sick and lame till his death nearly three years after. My dear mother's health was also failing very fast.

In the spring of 1816, Captain Boyle died at New York, and I was kept in the North division, and his company was ordered to join Major T. Biddle, and I obtained the company. I was this year stationed at Fort Mifflin, tho' I spent much of my time in the city, and enjoyed many advantages from having endeavored zealously to do my duty during the war. Every one I found willing to accommodate me,—the Government as well as my friends in the army. This year Major T. Biddle went on an exploring tour to the Rocky Mountains with Major Long, and I was several months in command of Fort Mifflin.

I had for some time wished to become settled in life and to get married, but the sickness of my parents prevented me; tho' many of my leisure hours were passed very pleasantly among my female friends, who received me very kindly after the hard rubs I had suffered during the war.

Early in 1817 my company was ordered to Fort Washington, a large new work being built on the Potomac River, nearly opposite Mount Vernon. Now for many reasons I disliked this change, for I had other attachments in Philadelphia than its being my home and that of my parents; and when this order came I found this attachment very personal, and I never obeyed a marching order more reluctantly. But I was now an experienced soldier and understood manœuvring, for in the three following years I was ordered away from Philadelphia about twenty times, but soon managed to get back. I marched my company to Fort Washington and reported to Colonel Roger Jones, Commanding, and in a few days I was allowed to return to Philadelphia to recruit, but I must confess I would rather have enlisted one female than one hundred soldiers. I now passed my time very happily, recruiting by day and courting by night, until the close of the year, when Colonel Jones applied to go into Virginia—recruiting too. I, poor fellow, had to move off to the Potomac, and spend a dreary winter, worse by far than a Canadian climate to me; for now I found that no other latitude than that of Philadelphia would suit my constitution.

In the spring of 1818, Colonel Jones returned, and I was allowed to return to Philadelphia to recruit, but in the summer had to return for a short time, and left Fort Washington again for Philadelphia in November, 1818. June 25, 1819, I left Philadelphia for Fort Washington to remove my company to Fort Columbus, New York Harbor; June 30th, embarked with my company on board Schooner Dash, and arrived at Fort Columbus July 8, 1819. July 11th, left New York for Philadelphia, and returned with some recruits. I omitted to mention the death of my mother in November, 1817, and that of my father in August, 1818,—both of them having been sick a long time; and I was now left alone in the world, having no near relatives. September 21, 1819, returned to Philadelphia, and on the 4th of October, 1819, was married to Mary, daughter of Joseph and Rebecca Huddell, and obtained leave of absence several times to come to Philadelphia, on account of the illness of Mr. Huddell, who was very old and much enfeebled. I find from my memorandums I passed very often between the cities, as Mrs. Roach could not leave her father, and in January, 1820, Mr. Huddell died at the 82nd year of his age. I now could not think of asking Mrs. Roach to leave her mother, who had but her two daughters left to her, having in a few years lost her husband and four children; and as I was in favor at head-quarters, I could be in Philadelphia every week almost, and I looked forward with delight when I should bring my beloved wife to garrison,—and a more delightful spot cannot be found in this country than Fort Columbus, Governor's Island, was at that time. The garrison consisted of four companies U. S. Artillery, and one of the Infantry, one company at Bedloe's Island, and one company at Ellis Island.

Thursday, June 19, 1820, I arrived at Fort Columbus with my beloved wife, where we were welcomed by all our military friends and families. I was now happy indeed, and the more so in finding Mrs. Roach soon became accustomed to garrison life—indeed all ladies do. Miss West of Philadelphia soon joined our family; then Mrs. R——'s sister; then her mother; and on July 18, 1820, another blessing was added in the birth of a son, and an uncommon fine child. But this perhaps made us too selfish, and the next year the Almighty removed from us this inestimable gift, and we were left childless.

The following winter of '20–'21, Mrs. Roach spent in Philadelphia with her mother; and in May, 1821, the army having undergone a third filtration and reorganization, I was ordered to the command of Fort Mifflin near Philadelphia, intended, no doubt, as a compliment to me, being near my home; but it was a sad reverse, as I believe our beloved child contracted a disease here which tended much to his death.

I remained in command of Fort Mifflin until December 21, 1823, when I received a furlough till April 1, 1824, at which time I resigned my commission in the army of the United States, having entered a Second Lieutenant in July, 1812, and retiring a Major,—zealously striving at all times to do my duty,—serving near twelve years without once having been tried or arrested, and never having once been censured by any commanding officer for the slightest neglect of duty,—having served two severe campaigns on the Niagara Frontier,—been twice wounded,—eighteen months a prisoner of war at Quebec,—and closely shut up in prison for five months of that period.

BRITISH AND AMERICAN PRISONERS OF WAR, 1778.

CONTRIBUTED BY WORTHINGTON C. FORD.

(Continued from p. 174.)

JOHN CUNNINGHAM, 1ˢᵗ Lieut. in Pennsylvania militia. Taken not far from Philadelphia, 16 September, 1777.

ABRA'M STOUT, 1ˢᵗ Lieut. in the 2ᵈ New Jersey regiment. Commissioned, 1 January, 1777. Taken at Cooper's Ferry, Jersey, 6 April, 1778.

HENRY MURFITS [Murfields], Lieut. in the Pennsylvania militia. Commissioned, 6 May, 1777. Taken at his own house, 19 February, 1778.

ROBERT WALKER, Lieut. in Col. Brewer's regiment. Commissioned, 6 November, 1776. Taken 15 miles from Philadelphia, 7 April, 1778.

JOHN HYAT, 2ᵈ Lieut. in Col. Hall's regiment. Commissioned, 5 April, 1777. Taken at his own house while on furlow, 25 April, 1778.

SAMˡ WHITING, 2ᵈ Lieut. in Col. Lamb's regiment. Taken, 10 December, 1777.

TIMOTHY TAYLOR, Ensign in Col. Bradley's regiment. Commissioned, 10 June, 1776. Taken [at Fort Washington], 16 November, 1776.

JOSEPH HULL, Ensign in Col. Bradley's regiment. Commissioned, 10 June, 1776. Taken [at Fort Washington], 16 November, 1776.

DANˡ KNOWLTON, Ensign in Col. Knowlton's regiment. Commissioned, 20 June, 1776. Taken [at Fort Washington], 16 November, 1776.

ELI BARNUM, Ensign in Col. Bradley's regiment. Commissioned, 1 July, 1776. Taken [at Fort Washington], 16 November, 1776.

THOˢ U. FOSDICK, Ensign in Col. Charles Webb's regiment. Commissioned, 10 July, 1776. Taken [at Fort Washington], 16 November, 1776.

JOHN THOMSON, Ensign in Morgan's militia. Commissioned, March, 1776. Taken near Princeton, 8 January, 1777.

JEREMIAH B. EELLS, Ensign in Col. Bradley's regiment. Commissioned, 10 June, 1776. Taken [at Norwalk], 15 March, 1777.

JOSEPH PAYNE, Ensign in the 9ᵗʰ Virginia regiment. Commissioned, 4 January, 1777. Taken, 4 October, 1777.

JONᵀᴴ SMITH, Ensign in the 8th Virginia regiment. Commissioned, 16 March, 1777. Taken, 4 October, 1777.

JACOB SOMERS, Ensign in the Pennsylvania militia. Taken at his own house, 1 May, 1778.

PETER PAUL, Ensign. Commissioned, 31 July, 1776. Taken, 16 November, 1776.

BENJ^A STORRS, Q^r Mas^r of Col. Durkee's regiment. Commissioned, 7 September, ——. Taken, 22 November, 1776.

ISAAC CRANE, Adjutant of Field's militia. Taken, 16 March, 1777.

JOHN RAY, Q^r Mast^r of militia. Taken, 24 February, 1778.

THOMAS KENNEDY, Volunteir. Taken, 22 April, 1777.

WILLIAM MILLS, citizen. Taken from his own house. Never bore a commission.

SAMUEL MILLS, Q^r Mas^r Sheldon's troop of cavalry. Taken, 15 December, 1777.

THOMAS MILLARD, 2^d Lieut. in Phila. militia. Commissioned, 1 May, 1777. Taken, 14 February, 1778.

AARON CHEW, 2^d Lieut. in Jersey militia. Taken, 19 June, 1778.

JOHN COZENS, Captain in Jersey militia. Taken, 9 March, 1778, at his house, New Jersey. No commission. Should be No. 36 if exchanged as a Captain.

—— GOODALL, Captain.

JOHN SWAN, Captain in Baylor's Dragoons. Taken, 28 Sept., ——, Jamen Town.

WILLIAM MARTIN, Lieut. in Proctor's artillery regiment. Commissioned, 1 April, 1777. Taken in New Jersey, 15 March, 1778.

SAMUEL McFARLAN, Lieut. of the Jersey militia. Taken in New Jersey, 28 March, 1778.

JOSEPH BRITTON, Lieut. in Gist's "additional" regiment. Commissioned, 6 February, 1777. Taken on Philips Heights, above King's Bridge, 16 September, 1778.

JAMES SIMS, Lieut. in the 1st Maryland regiment. Commissioned, 17 April, 1777. Taken on Philips Heights (was taken before Britton).

WILLIAM RODGERS, Lieut. in the 4th Virginia Continental. Commissioned, 28 September, 1776. Taken in English neighborhood, New Jersey, 23 September, 1778.

ROBERT RANDOLPH, Lieut. in Baylor's Dragoons. Taken in New Jersey, 28 September, 1778.

PEREGRINE FITZCHEW [Fitzhugh], Cornet in Baylor's Dragoons. Taken in New Jersey, 28 September, 1778.

THOMAS EVANS, surgeon's mate in Baylor's Dragoons. Taken in New Jersey, 28 September, 1778.

BALDWIN DADE, volunteer in Baylor's Dragoons. Taken in New Jersey, 28 September, 1778.

JOHN KELTEY, volunteer in Baylor's Dragoons. Taken in New Jersey, 28 September, 1778. (In the provost guard.)

ALEXANDER McCASKEY, D.C.G. of forage. Taken at Maroneck, 8 September, 1778.

MARK GARRETT, Com^y of forage. Taken at Maroneck, 8 September, 1778.

General Washington to Colonel Samuel B. Webb.

HEAD QUARTERS MIDDLE BROOK
25ᵗʰ Febʸ, 1779.

DEAR SIR:

Agreeable to my promise, when you were at Head Quarters, I have had a calculation made from the last returns of the Commissary of Prisoners, of the number of privates which upon the several propositions that have been made by the enemy, we should have to give them in a general exchange of our officers for officers and privates of the Convention Troops—By submitting this to Congress, if necessary, they will be the better able to decide on the propriety of adopting the measure solicited in the memorial which you have been appointed to present.

I am with great regard
Dear Sir
Your most obed Serᵗ.

COLONEL WEBB.   Gᵒ WASHINGTON.

[See table on opposite page.]

A LIST OF OFFICERS, PRISONERS TO THE BRITISH, NOT EXCHANGEABLE BY THE RULES AND ARTICLES OF WAR, TAKEN FROM THEIR DIFFERENT RETURNS.

Rank.	Names.	Remarks.
Lᵗ Colonel	John Smock	
Major	George Wright	
	Robert Hodson	
Captain	Edward Hertan	
	Jacob Covenhoven	
Lieutˢ	Francis Grier	
	Benjamin Walton	
	John Blake	Taken from the return of these on Parole, Long Island.
	John Ofburn	
	Henry Murfits	
	Silas Snow	
	Theophilus Little	
	Cornelius Van Tafsel	
	Thomas Millard	
	James James	
	Aron Chew	
Ensign	Jacob Summers	
Colonel	William Coates	
Lᵗ Colonel	Thomas Reynolds	
Major	Enoch Edwards	
Brg-Majʳ	Danˡ Hammel	Taken from the return of these at home on Parole.
Lieuᵗ	Jacob Bright	
Enfign	Andrew McMinn	
Comfsʸ Genˡ Musters	Gunning Bedford	

STATE OF THE AMERICAN OFFICERS WHO ARE PRISONERS TO THE BRITISH ARMY, 24TH NOVEMB, 1778.

	Confined in provost	Broke parole	At home on parole	On parole L. Island	
8	...	...	2	1	Brig. Generals.
18	...	1	8	4	Colonels.
14	...	1	7	6	Lieut Colonels.
14	...	2	6	6	Majors.
8	...	...	2	1	Maj's Brigade.
42	...	17	7	18	Captains.
6	...	1	...	4	Cap't Lieutenants.
177	2	48	11	116	Lieutenants.
84	1	7	6	21	Ensigns.
2	1	...	...	1	Cornets.
1	...	...	1	...	Dep. Adj't Gen'l.
2	...	...	...	2	Dep. Com. Gen. Forage.
1	...	...	...	1	A. D. Q. M. General.
1	...	...	...	1	A. D. C. Gen'l Forage.
1	...	1	...	...	Commissary.
1	...	...	...	1	Forage Master.
8	...	...	1	5	Adjutants.
4	...	1	...	8	Quarter Masters.
8	...	1	1	1	Surgeons.
1	...	...	1	...	Chaplains.
1	...	...	...	1	Sub: Lieut's County.
1	...	...	1	...	Commad. State Fleet.
4	...	3	1	...	Captains.
2	...	2	...	...	Mates Armed Vessels.
1	...	...	...	1	Cadets.
831	4	80	54	193	Total.

Commissioned Officers. · Staff. · Navy.

Rank.	Names.	Remarks.
Colonel	John Hannum	
Lt Col{l}	Persifer Frazier	
Major	William Williams	
	Benja Bowne	Taken from the return
Captain	Samuel Swift	of those who deserted
Lieut	Andrew Forrest	their Parole.
	Daniel Cressop	
	Joseph Blake	
Enfign	William Marrener	
Lieu	Joel Westcot	In Provost.
Comit	Thomas Kilty	

	Colonels.	Lt Colonels.	Majors.	Captains.	Lieutenants.	Enfigns.	Cornets.	Brig{r} Major.	Commy Genl Musters.	Total.
On Parole Long Island	...	1	2	2	11	1	...	...	...	17
On Parole at home	1	1	1	...	1	1	...	1	1	7
Deserted Parole......................	1	1	2	1	8	1	...	...	...	9
In Provost.............................	...	...	...	...	1	...	1	...	...	2
Total not Exchangeable	2	3	5	3	16	3	1	1	1	35

N.B.—Besides the above there are twenty Prisoners of different Ranks to be deducted from the Enemy's General return who have been either since exchanged, Came under the Navy Department or are Citizens. Those whose names are specified in this List, ought not to be accounted for, according to the Custom of War, as I am well acquainted with the Circumstances of their Capture & the manner in which they made their escape.

A LIST OF OFFICERS DUE FROM THE ENEMY THE 8 DAY OF DECEMBER ANNO 1778.

Rank.	Names.	Corps.	Remarks.
Major	Frederick Hundran	Long Isd Milit{a}	
	—— D'Marbaum	Dragoons	
Captain	R. Dawes ——	53d Regiment	
	Simon Lord ——	do do	
	John Beard	do do	

Rank.	Names.	Corps.	Remarks.
Captain	D. Guyun	L* Infantry	
	Dammies ——	ditto	
	Slagentuffle	Dragoons	
	John Barbarie	1ˢᵗ Jersey Volunt*	
Lieuᵗ	Thomas Hughs	53ᵈ Regimᵗ	
	Archibᵈ Gordon	do do,	
	John M. Brown	do do	
	Alexʳ Frazer	71ˢᵗ Regimᵗ	
	—— Meyer	Grenadiers	
	—— Beryhoff	ditto	
	—— Breva	Dragoons	
	—— Roachrodt	do	
	—— Roch	do	
	—— Nesbit	do	
Ensign	Chevalier Dentrofhe	62ᵈ Regmᵗ	
	Thomas Mann	Kings Loyˡ Amᵉ	
	Jemeriah Pemberton	ditto	
	—— Audra	Infantry	
	—— D Nacke	do	
	—— D. Ranzan	do	
Comit	—— Strutza	Dragoons	
Chaplain	—— Melikimer	ditto	
Judge Advoᵉ	—— Thomas	} Dragoons	
Surgeon	Verbroof		
Barrack Master	} Ifaac Bonnell		
Comfˢʸ	—— Fromaute		
Surgeon	—— Menza	} Hospitals	
Mate	—— Chew		
Surgeon	—— Seely		

	Majors.	Captains.	Lieutenants.	Ensigns.	Comits.	Commiffaries.	Quaʳ Masters.	Surgeons.	Mates.	Chaplains.	Cadets.	Barrᵏ Masters.	Judge Advoᵉ.	Rank Unknown.	Privates due us Prˢ Settleᵈ Novʳ 23ᵈ 78.	Servᵗˢ of British & German Officers.	Total.
With the Enemy.........	2	7	11	6	1	1	...	2	2	1	...	1	1	...	80	28	138
With us.......	...	6	9	3	...	1	1	...	...	...	3	...	...	6	800	...	829
Total	2	13	20	9	1	2	1	2	2	1	3	1	1	6	880	28	967

N.B.—There may probably be more Officers and Privates prisoners with us than are included in the above return, but having no regular reports from my Deputy's, I cannot exactly ascertain the number.

VOL. XVII.—21

STATE OF OFFICERS IN CAPTIVITY, EXCLUSIVE OF THOSE OF
THE CONVENTION TROOPS.[1]

	Brigadiers.	Colonels.	L. Colonels.	Majors.	Captains.	Lieutenants.	Enfigns.
American officers in Captivity per return N° 1	8	18	14	14	42	176	86
Officers included in the above whom we refuse to exchange as p lift N° 2	...	2	8	6	8	16	4
By the fame lift there appears to be 20 others not enumerated, who are not properly exchangeable, which may be proportioned thus	...	...	...	1	6	10	4
Officers, prifoners with us, who have been fent into the enemy for whom they have not returned others—and thofe ftill in our hands, exclufive of the Convention troops—as p Return—N° 3	...	...	...	2	18	20	10
Total to be deducted from the above	...	2	8	8	21	46	18
Ballance in favour of the enemy	8	11	11	6	21	180	18

From the above eftimate, it appears, that the ballance of
Prifoners, in officers, in favour of the enemy exclufive of the
troops of the Convention, and inferior ftaff officers who are
omitted as they do not materially affect the calculation—is

3 Brigadiers	21 Captains
11 Colonels	180 Lieutenants
11 L Colonels	18 Enfigns
6 Majors	

The ultimatum of the enemy's propofitions as mentioned
in private converfation was to exchange one half of our
officers for as many of theirs of the Convention troops and
the remainder in private men on this plan.

The number to be exchanged for privates will be

1 Brigadier	10 Captains
6 Colonels	65 Lieutenants
6 Lieutenant Colonels	9 Enfigns
8 Majors	

[1] This table is in the MS. of Alexander Hamilton.

The loweſt ratio that can be thought of between officers which is founded upon the number of grades in each commiſſion is—

a Colonel	as	6	Captain	as	3
Lieut. Colonel	as	5	Lieutenant	as	2
Major	as	4	Enſign	as	1

This was proposed by the American commiſſioners at German town; but not acceded to—The loweſt ratio to which the British Commiſſioners would conſent, was the following—

a Colonel	as	13	Capt	as	3
L Colonel	as	8	Lieu	as	2
Major	as	5	Enſ	as	1

The ratio ſettled in the cartel between the French and Engliſh in 59 was, in the infantry

German florins.

a Colonel	as..	600
Lieut Colonel	as..	300
Major	as..	120
Captain	as..	70
Lieutenant	as..	24
Enſign	as..	20
Private	as..	4

Reduced to numbers upon the principle of the two foregoing it would ſtand thus—

a Colonel	as..	30
L Colonel	as	15
Major	as..	6
Capt	as..	$3\frac{1}{2}$
L⁴	as	$1\frac{1}{2}$
Enſign	as..	1

The calculation on the firſt ratio will ſtand thus—

1 Brigadier ſay equal to	2 Colonels	@ 6.........	12
	6 Colonels	@ 6.........	36
	6 L Colᵃ	5.........	30
	3 Majors	4.........	12
	10 Captains	3	30
	65 Lieutenants	2.........130
	9 Enſigns	at........	9
			259

Five privates for an Enfign is as low an eftimate as can well be made. It is agreeable to the precedent of 59 before mentioned and would be infifted on, upon the credit of that precedent; not to fay, that to uphold the importance of a commiffion it cannot decently be valued lower.

Privates.

$$259 \ @ \ 5 \text{ will amount to } 1295$$

Calculating on the fecond ratio by the fame procefs the amount will be.. 1680

On the third ratio it will be............. 2350

N.B.—In the propofition lately made by the British Adjutant General through Mr. Loring to M[r] Beatty, it was propofed to fettle the equivalent of privates for officers, agreeable to the third plan.

The plan moft commonly held out by the enemy for the exchange of the Convention troops is to do it by whole corps. On this plan as thofe troops particularly the German are very thinly officered they would receive a much larger number of privates, than on the calculation here made for exchanging one half our officers for private men.

Thefe calculations could not be entirely accurate; but they are nearly fo; and will ferve to form a judgment upon. They if anything rather fall fhort of than exceed the truth.

DESCENDANTS OF JOHN RUSH.

[The following genealogy is taken from a chart presented to the Historical Society of Pennsylvania, in 1880, by Robert Bethell Browne, of Jeansville, Luzerne County, Pennsylvania, it being a copy of a record compiled by General James Irvine in the year 1800, and placed by him in the family Bible of his cousin, Frances Bethell, mother of R. B. Browne. A few additional notes are now added.—ED.]

1. JOHN RUSH commanded a troop of horse in Cromwell's army. At the close of the war he married Susanna Lucas, at Hortun, in Oxfordshire, June 8, 1648. He embraced the principles of the Quakers in 1660, and came to Pennsylvania in 1683, with seven children and several grandchildren, and settled at Byberry, thirteen miles from Philadelphia. In 1691 he and his whole family became Keithians, and in 1697 most of them became Baptists. He died at Byberry in May, 1699. His sword is in the possession of Jacob Rush, and his watch now belongs to General William Darke, of Virginia. He had issue (as appears by a record in his own handwriting now in possession of Dr. Benjamin Rush), viz. :

1. Elizabeth, *b.* June 16, 1649.
2. William, *b.* July 21, 1652.
3. Thomas, *b.* November 7, 1654 ; *d.* in London, 18th of Fourth month, 1676.
4. Susanna, *b.* December 26, 1656.
5. John, *b.* 1st of Third month, 1660.
6. Francis, *b.* 8th of Second month, 1662.
7. James, *b.* 21st of Seventh month, 1664 ; *d.* and was buried at Banbury, 24th of First month, 1671.
8. Joseph, *b.* 26th of Tenth month, 1666.
9. Edward, *b.* 27th of Ninth month, 1670.
10. Jane, b. 27th of Twelfth month, 1673–74.

2. ELIZABETH RUSH, eldest daughter of John and Susanna Rush, married Richard Collet, May 27, 1680, as appears by a certificate of a Quaker Meeting in London, now in the possession of Mary Peart. They came to Pennsylvania in

the same ship with William Penn in the year 1682, and settled in Byberry upon five hundred acres of land, two hundred of which are now owned by Captain Decator and one hundred by two of his great-grandchildren, Elizabeth Messer and Mary Peart. They lost their first child, aged two years, by the fall of a tree. They had afterwards the following issue :

11. John Collet.
12. Mary Collet.
18. Rachel Collet, *m.* Benjamin Peart.

3. WILLIAM RUSH, eldest son of John and Susanna Rush, married first in England and afterwards a second wife. [According to some authorities, the name of his first wife was Aurelia.] He died at Byberry in the year 1688, five years after his arrival in the country.

Issue by first wife :

14. Susanna, *m.* John Webster and [John?] Gilbert.
15. James, *m.* Rachel Peart ; *d.* 1727.
16. Elizabeth, *m.* Timothy Stephenson, by whom she had no issue.
    He afterwards married Rachel Rush, widow of his brother-in-law, James Rush, by consent of the Synod of New York. No issue.

By second wife :

17. Sarah (first called Aurelia), *m.* David Meredith.
18. William, *m.* 1711–12, Elizabeth Hodges.

5. SUSANNA RUSH, second daughter of John and Susanna Rush, married in England, John Hart, born at Whitney, in Oxfordshire, November 16, 1651. He was a member of the first Assembly called by William Penn in 1683. He was educated a Quaker, but became a Keithian in 1691 and a Baptist in 1697, being a preacher among each of these sects, and much respected for his piety. They had issue :

19. John Hart.
20. Joseph Hart.
21. Thomas Hart.
22. Josiah Hart.
28. Mary Hart.

These married into the Crispin, Miles, Paulin, and Dungan families, from whom have descended a numerous issue in Philadelphia and Bucks counties. John Hart was shot dead by accident in Virginia. His brother Thomas, who lived in Virginia, had nineteen children before he removed from thence to South Carolina, where many of the family are settled. [See, also, Hart Genealogy, by Davis, 1867.]

6. JOHN RUSH, third son of John and Susanna Rush, married and had issue:

24. John, *m.* ———.
25. Thomas, *m.* ———.

11. JANE RUSH, youngest daughter of John and Susanna Rush, married John Darke, son of Thomas Darke, and had issue:

26. John Darke, *b.* in 1698.
27. William Darke, *b.* in 1700; *m.* ———.
28. Joseph Darke, *b.* in 1702; *m.* ———.
29. Samuel Darke, *b.* in 1706; *m.* ———.
30. Mary Darke, *b.* in 1709; *m.* ———.

The other sons and daughters of John and Susanna Rush died single or childless, or if they had children, they died young.

14. RACHEL COLLET [3] (Elizabeth,[2] John[1]) married Benjamin Peart, youngest son of Bryan Peart. [The will of Bryan Peart, " of Throughfare to Duck Creek," is dated January 1, 1705–06; proven at New Castle, April 18, 1706. He mentions his daughters Anne Steather and Margaret as living in Maryland; his wife, Jane, and other children, William, Benjamin, Ralph, and Rachel. The will of Jane Peart, widow of Bryan Peart, " late of Haurskip, in Yorkshire, whitesmith," was dated April 28, 1708, and proven at Philadelphia, December 7, 1709. Children: Benjamin, Ralph, William, Ann, Margaret, and Rachel, and son-in-law, James Rush.] Benjamin and Rachel Peart had issue:

31. Thomas Peart, *m.* ——.
32. William Peart, who had seven children (not named).
33. Elizabeth Peart, *m.* twice.
34. Mary Peart (living in 1800), unmarried.
35. Bryan Peart, *m.* ——.

15. SUSANNA RUSH[3] (William,[2] John[1]) married first, John Webster, and secondly, —— Gilbert, by whom she had no issue. [John Gilbert, of Byberry, died intestate, and letters of administration were granted at New Castle, September 14, 1744, to Susanna Gilbert, his widow. He had property in New Castle County. Some authorities state that Susanna had children by both husbands.] By John Webster she had issue :

36. A son.
37. Phœbe Webster, who *m.* William Lockhart.

16. JAMES RUSH[3] (William,[2] John[1]) married Rachel Peart, the youngest daughter of Bryan Peart. He lived on a farm on Poquestion [Poquessing] Creek, where he died in 1727.
Issue :

38. John, *m.* Susan (Hall) Harvey.
39. William, had children, William and John.
40. Joseph.
41. James.
42. Thomas.
43. Rachel.
44. Ann, *m.* John Ashmead.
45. Elizabeth, *m.* Edward Cary.
46. Aurelia, *d.* young.

18. SARAH RUSH[3] (William,[2] John[1]) was called Aurelia till her marriage and baptism. She married David Meredith and lived to be about eighty-six years old, when she left upward of one hundred descendants. [They resided in Whiteland Township, Chester County, Pennsylvania, where David died in 1754.]

Issue :

47. Susanna Meredith, *m.* —— Hayes.
48. David Meredith, *m.* [Elinor] Garrett; [died, 1755].
49. Rebecca Meredith, *m.* John Jenkins.
50. William Meredith, *m.* [Margaret? daughter of Walter?] Lloyd.
51. Rachel Meredith, *m.* —— Connolly.
52. Joseph Meredith, went to Cape Fear and never returned.
53. John Meredith, *m.* —— Cloyd.
54. Mary Meredith, *m.* —— Bean [Bane].
55. Hannah Meredith, *m.* —— Guest.

There were several other children, who died young. One of them, a son, was lost and perished in the woods.

19. WILLIAM RUSH [3] (William,[2] John[1]) was married, March 1, 1711–12, to Elizabeth Hodges, at a Quaker Meeting held at the house of his brother, James Rush, in Byberry, as appears by a certificate now in possession of James Irvine. He died January 31, 1733, at Boston, in New England, and his widow in Philadelphia, April 15, 1755.

Issue :

56. Mary, *b.* February 9, 1712–13; *m.* George Irvine.
57. William, *b.* February 26, 1717–18; *m.* Esther Carlisle.
58. Joseph, *b.* January 8, 1719–20; *m.* Rebecca Lincoln.
59. Elizabeth, *b.* January 6, 1721–22; *d.* same day.
60. Elizabeth, *b.* February 12, 1722–23; *d.* December 8, 1754.
61. Francis, *b.* November 5, 1725; *d.* August 27, 1726.

25. JOHN RUSH [3] (John,[2] John[1]) married Sarah ——, and had issue :

62. William, *b.* February 26, 1703.
63. Mary, *b.* January 10, 1713; *m.* —— Norwood; had son, John.
64. John, *b.* April 11, 1717.
65. Joseph, *b.* August 19, 1722; *m.* and had issue.
66. Sarah, *b.* October 14, 1725.
67. Benjamin, *b.* September 5, 1730.

26. THOMAS RUSH [3] (John,[2] John[1]) married and had issue :

68. John, who married, but left no issue.
69. Thomas, *d.* young.
70. Mary, *m.* —— Crow; settled in Virginia.
71. Rebecca, *m.* J. English, and had issue.
72. Elizabeth, *d.* unmarried.
73. Esther, *d.* unmarried.

28. WILLIAM DARKE³ (Jane,² John¹), born in 1700; married and had issue:

74. John Darke.
75. Ann Darke, who *m.* and had issue: a son, who was drowned; Esther, who *m.* a Bembridge, and had a son Henry; and Rachel, who *d.* single.

29. JOSEPH DARKE³ (Jane,² John¹), born in 1702; married and had issue:

76. Jane Darke, *b.* May 9, 1734.
77. William (now General) Darke, *b.* May 6, 1736.
78. Mary Darke, *b.* June 13, 1738.
79. John Darke, *b.* March 10, 1741.
80. Joseph Darke, *b.* September 20, 1744.
81. Martha Darke, *b.* September 17, 1750.

30. SAMUEL DARKE³ (Jane,² John¹), born in 1706; married and had issue:

82. Sarah Darke.
83. Jane Darke.
84. Samuel Darke.
85. Mary Darke.
86. Lydia Darke.
87. Thomas Darke.
88. William Darke.

31. MARY DARKE³ (Jane,² John¹), born in 1709; married [name not given] and had issue:

89. Elizabeth, *b.* in 1734.
90. John, *d.* young.
91. Edward, *b.* in 1738.
92. Robert, *b.* in 1740; killed by the Indians; left seven children.
93. William, *b.* in 1742.

32. THOMAS PEART⁴ (Rachel,³ Elizabeth,² John¹) married and had issue:

94. William Peart.
95. Edmond Peart.
96. John Peart.

97. Thomas Peart.
98. Bryan Peart.
99. Rachel Peart.
100. Elizabeth Peart.
101. Rachel Peart.

34. ELIZABETH PEART⁴ (Rachel,³ Elizabeth,² John¹) married first, —— Millard, and secondly, —— Messer. She is now living, July 14, 1800, and is nearly eighty years of age.
Issue:

102. Mary Millard.
103. Elizabeth Millard.
104. Rachel Millard.
105. Mary Millard.
106. Jonathan Millard.
107. Thomas Millard, who *m.* and had twelve children.

108. Ann Messer.

36. BRYAN PEART⁴ (Rachel,³ Elizabeth,² John¹) married [(Swedes' Church record), November 30, 1752, Elizabeth Walton, born Third month 27, 1725, daughter of Benjamin and Rebecca Walton, of Byberry. He died December 27, 1757, and his widow married again (Christ Church record), August 17, 1760, Benjamin Gilbert, and they with their children were taken captives by the Indians in 1780. She died in Fallowfield Township, Chester County, Eighth month 5, 1810]. Bryan Peart left three children:

109. Benjamin [*b.* 1753; *d.* 1840; *m.* Elizabeth Jones].
110. Rebecca [*b.* 1754].
111. Thomas [*b.* 1756; *d.* 1831; *m.* Mary Roberts].

39. JOHN RUSH⁴ (James,³ William,² John¹) married Susan Harvey, formerly Hall, daughter of Joseph Hall, of Tacony.
Issue:

112. James, *d.* single, at sea.
113. Rachel, *m.* Angus Boyce, by whom she had a son, Malcolm Boyce; and by a second husband, J. Montgomery [Rev. Joseph. See "A Sketch of the Life of the Rev. Joseph Montgomery," by John Montgomery Forster, Harrisburg, 1879], had a son John. She died in 1798.

114. Rebecca, *m.* [June 11, 1761] Thomas Stamper, and had issue: Joseph and Susanna Stamper. She died of the yellow fever in 1793.
115. Benjamin (M.D.), *m.* Julia Stockton.
116. Jacob, *m.* M. Rench.
117. Stephenson, *d.* young.
118. John, *d.* young.

45. ANN RUSH [4] (James,[3] William,[2] John [1]) married John Ashmead, and had issue:

119. William Ashmead, *m.* ——.
120. John Ashmead, *m.* Mary Mifflin.
121. Rachel Ashmead, *m.* J[ames] Hood.
122. Benjamin Ashmead.

By second husband [Samuel Potts]:

123. James Potts [*b.* June 17, 1752; *d.* July 28, 1822; *m.* Sarah Wessell. See "Sketch of Major James Potts," by Thomas Maxwell Potts, Canonsburg, Pennsylvania, 1877].

46. ELIZABETH RUSH [4] (James,[3] William,[2] John [1]) married Edward Cary, and had issue:

124. Elizabeth Cary.
125. Jesse Cary.
126. Ezra Cary.
127. Ann Cary, *m.* —— Gouge.
128. Rachel Cary.
129. Sarah Cary.

50. REBECCA MEREDITH [4] (Sarah,[3] William,[2] John [1]) married John Jenkins, and had issue:

130. David Jenkins, *m.* and had seven children.
131. Margaret Jenkins, *d.* young.
132. John Jenkins, *m.* —— Douglas, and had eight children.
133. Isaac Jenkins, *d.* single.
134. George Jenkins, *m.* and had one child.
135. William Jenkins, *m.* and had two children.
136. Jenkin Jenkins, *d.* young.
137. Rebecca Jenkins, *m.* and had six children.
138. Joseph Jenkins, *m.* —— Morgan, and had thirteen children.
139. Benjamin Jenkins, *d.* young.

57. MARY RUSH⁴ (William,³ William,² John¹) married (May 24, 1733) George Irvine, who died October 2, 1740. She died January 5, 1766.

Issue:

140. Elizabeth Irvine, *d*. March 2, 1801 [aged sixty-seven].
141. James Irvine (General), *d*. [Philadelphia, March 28, 1819, aged eighty-four].
142. Susanna Irvine, *d*. young.
143. Mary Irvine, *d*. single.

58. WILLIAM RUSH⁴ (William,³ William,² John¹), born February 26, 1717–18; married Esther Carlisle.

Issue:

144. John, *b*. November 9, 1742; *d*. young.
145. Joseph, *b*. May 8, 1745; *d*. young.
146. William, *b*. October 13, 1746; *d*. young.
147. John, *b*. November 10, 1748; *d*. young.
148. Elizabeth, *b*. December 8, 1750; *m*. R. Bethell.
149. Hanna, *b*. and *d*. same day.

William Rush married second wife, Frances Decowe, and died November 30, 1791.

Issue by last wife:

150. Abraham, *d*. young.
151. Francis, *d*. young.
152. Joseph, *b*. August 20, 1761; *m*. S. Massey, of South Carolina.
153. Sarah, *m*. Joseph Kerr.

59. JOSEPH RUSH⁴ (William,³ William,² John¹), born January 3, 1719–20; married first [September 19, 1750, Christ Church record], Rebecca Lincoln [probably daughter of Abraham Lincoln, of Springfield Township (now), Delaware County, Pennsylvania].

Issue:

154. Elizabeth, *m*. William Allen.
155. William, *m*. Martha Wallace.
156. Mary, *m*. Joseph Tatem.
157. Abraham, *d*. young.

By second wife, Elizabeth Hilton :

158. Catharine, *m.* John Cochran.
159. Joseph, *d.* single.
160. Susanna.
161. George, *d.* young.
162. Esther, *d.* young.
163. Rebecca, *d.* young.
164. Benjamin, *m.* Deborah Jones.
165. Esther, *m.* John Loughrey.
166. Sarah.
167. James Irvine.

116. BENJAMIN RUSH [5] (John,[4] James,[3] William,[2] John [1]) [the celebrated physician, signer of the Declaration of Independence, etc., born near Poquessing Creek, 1741] married Julia Stockton. [He died in Philadelphia, 1813.]
Issue :

168. John.
169. Emila.
170. Richard.
171. Susanna.
172. Elizabeth.
173. Mary.
174. James.
175. William.
176. Benjamin.
177. Benjamin.
178. Julia.
179. Samuel.

117. JACOB RUSH [5] (John,[4] James,[3] William,[2] John [1]) married M. Rench, and had issue :

180. Rebecca.
181. Sarah.
182. Mary.
183. Louisa.
184. Harriet.

120. WILLIAM ASHMEAD [5] (Ann,[4] James,[3] William,[2] John [1]) married and had issue :

185. John Ashmead.
186. Thomas Ashmead.
187. William Ashmead.
188. James Ashmead.
189. Mary Ashmead.
190. Ann Ashmead.

121. JOHN ASHMEAD [5] (Ann,[4] James,[3] William,[2] John [1]) married Mary Mifflin, and had issue :

191. John Ashmead.
192. Benjamin Ashmead.
193. Ann Ashmead.
194. Joseph Ashmead.
195. William Ashmead.
196. Mary Ashmead.
197. Eliza Ashmead.

122. RACHEL ASHMEAD [5] (Ann,[4] James,[3] William,[2] John [1]) married, 1768, James Hood [son of Thomas and Rebecca Hood, of the Northern Liberties, Philadelphia].
Issue :

198. Mary Hood [*m.* August 11, 1792, Samuel Boys, and had fourteen children].
199. James A. [*d.* unmarried about 1806].

149. ELIZABETH RUSH [5] (William,[4] William,[3] William,[2] John [1]), born December 8, 1750; married R. Bethell.
Issue :

200. William Bethell.
201. Robert Bethell.
202. Frances Bethell [*b.* June 21, 1783; *d.* April 29, 1855].

CORRESPONDENCE OF THE CHILDREN OF CHRISTOPHER MARSHALL.

[The following letters from and to the children of Christopher Marshall, the diarist, have been kindly intrusted to me for publication. According to the information furnished me, Mr. Marshall left his home in England, early in the last century, in consequence of a second marriage contracted by his father, leaving behind him a sister, Isabella. At this time he was about eighteen years of age. He was twice married. There was no issue of the second marriage. His children were Benjamin, born 1737; Christopher, born 1740; Isabella, born 1741; and Charles, born 1742. Benjamin married, on the 22d day of the Tenth month, 1761, Sarah, daughter of Joseph Lynn, "late of the Northern Liberties, . . . deceased." The marriage took place "at Friends' Meeting-house, Second and Market Streets." In the certificate of marriage, Benjamin is described as "of the City of Philadelphia, . . . Tinn plate Worker." The illness referred to in the correspondence proved fatal, and he died January 29, 1778. Christopher married Ann (surname not given). Isabella died unmarried. Charles married Patience Parrish. Upon the entry of General Howe, Christopher Marshall, Senior, left Philadelphia, and remained with the "Government," at Lancaster, during the British occupancy. At the same time his three sons, with their families, removed to the country, Benjamin's home being at or near the fork of the road between Plymouth and Valley Forge, in Providence Township, whence some of the letters are dated. The Providence from which the account of Bunker Hill was sent was, of course, Providence in New England. Benjamin was often at army head-quarters, and nursed many sick officers at his own house. It was here that he contracted a fever and died.—T. S.]

Jabez Bowen to Messrs. Benjamin Marshall and Brothers, merchants, Philadelphia.

(Endorsed) "The within Letter is Examined p^r John Jinckes, one of the Genl Com'tee of Correspondence."

"PROVIDENCE June 20 1775

"MY FRIENDS,

"After informing you of my safe Arrival and finding my Family in Health, I give you the News from the Army as authentick as possible. Fryday night last Co^l Putnam took post at Bunkers Hill, and hove up trenches sufficient to cover Three hundred Men, in the Morning preparations were made by the Kings Troops to Dislodge our people, they fired the Town of Charlestown in divers places and under cover of the Smoke, marched up and attacked our people with a Body of 5000 Men, (our Men on the hill consisted of about 2000). They attacked with spirit Three times and were Repulsed with great loss on their side, but (unfortunate for us) just as they were wheeling off the Third time some of our people in the left cry'd out that their Powder was all gone, which being heard by the Regulars they wheeled up and charged our people with their Bayonets, on which they were ordered to Retreat. They marched off as fast as possible from the ground till they were out of gun shott and then formed. They were not persued at all, but in the mean Time six Men of War and four floating Batteries were brot up and kept a Constant fire on the Causeway that leads on to Charlestown, which prevented the Troops that were orderd to assist our people on the Hill, joyning of them, however Putnam and his Men run the gauntlett, but not without the loss of several Killed, and many Wounded by the Fire of the Ships &c. They have now Intrenched themselves on Pleasant Hill within Cannon shott of the Hill that the Regulars now possess. Our Loss in the action amounts to 60 Killed and Missing and about 100 Wounded. Doct^r Warren was wounded on the Hill, and fell and is supposed to be Dead, (tho' I this moment hear that he is alive and a prisoner I cant say that I Believe it.) Co^l Gardner of Cambridge is Wounded in the Groin I hope not mortally, it is impossible to tell the loss on the other side, neighther do we know who commanded the attack. On the same night that Putnam took post on Bunkers Hill another party broke ground on Dorchester Hill, we expect to hear an attack on them soon. We suppose that Roxbury was set on Fire last night and part or the whole of it Burnt down from the great light that was seen that way last Night. We lost six field pieces on Bunkers Hill. Our People are in high Spiritts, and seem earnest to be led on to some action to signalize themselves anew. Gen¹ Ward gave it as his opinion before our people took post on Bunkers Hill that it could not be made tenable, and that he tho't it not best to make an Intrenchment on it.

"Our Government have ordered Two Cruizers to be equiped and sent out to protect our Trade. They have Retaken Lindsays packett in sight of the Men of War, which Wallis had fitted as a Tender. The Men of War have taken Mr. Gibbs Brigg Loaded with Flour. They have put all the Flour on Board of the Men of War, for fear that the Brigg should be Retaken and unloaded as several Vessells from the West indies was, a few Days agone. The Sloop has not yet arrived that has my Goods on Board she stands a great Chance to fall into their Hands. Thus I have given you all the News that our Country affords. You will give my Respects of the good Women your Wives. I have put off writing till the last Moment to give you the Freshest Intelligence. I remain your Friend &c.—in great haste.

"JABEZ BOWEN."

Benjamin Marshall to his father, at Lancaster, Pennsylvania.

"PHILADᴬ Aug. 3 1777

"HONOURED & MUCH ESTEEMED FATHER

"I have been in Town but once before this since thee went away at which time Charles wrote thee & I desired him to Enform thee I shᵈ have wrote but was obliged to attend the Navy Board & Board of War to know abᵗ their sending down a fleet to clear the Cape May Channell & went out next morning early. . . . I am well pleased to hear that thou art so fully satisfied with the place . . . hope by this time you are pretty well settled & got things to your mind for indeed fitting & altering places & Removing is attended with much trouble & I have often thought that it was too much for thee to undertake but well knowing that Mother would ease thee as much as in her power & indeed am afraid she will overdo the matter & fatigue herself too much, I wish it may not hurt her. I assure thee y^r Absence is very fully felt by us for whenever we come to Town it seems so odd. Especially as we all our life time have lived so near together. . . . The kind advice contained in thy Letter we received with pleasure as coming from a Father ever mindfull of his Children's Welfare both here & hereafter. . . . We have had frequent allarms this severall days concerning the Enemys fleet consisting of between 2 & 300 Sail being off our Capes & sometimes said to be in but they have again disapeard & have heard nothing of them these 2 days, it was fully expected they w^d have come here. G. Washington's Army March'd & are now Encamped about Germantown, the Falls &c & every preparation was making to receive them, the Troops in high Spiritts & eagerly wishing for Action, as it was hoped our people, had the Enemy attempted, would have given a good acc^t of them, but we are every hour in Expectation of hearing something from them. About 40 Large Ships sail'd from N. York lately with Sick & wounded Soldiers for England. No particular news from the Northward, the Enemy not having made any advances. Gen. Arnold & Gates are I hear orderd up there & Gen. Schuyler & St. Clair to be brought to Court Martiall which I hope will satisfy the people where the fault (if any) lay.

" The Court of France have orderd Packquets to saill every Month for America with dispatches to Congress, they are very fast Sailing Vessells & are each to bring 80 Ton of Goods, one of which is arrived & brings very favourable acct^s some of which are to be published in 2 or 3 days. They have offer'd to Lend the Continent any Sum of Money on Loan & thereby Establish our Currency, to supply us with Goods on their own Risque, great Quantities are now coming to Congress, amongst which is 50 or 60,000 stand of Arms, great Q^y of Blankitts, Cloathing & other Goods, & that the people in generall there heartily wish us Success.

" Dean & Doc^r Franklin wrote to Lord Stormont at Paris complaining of the Ill Usage our people received in England, he answered them that the Ambassador of the King his

Master received no Letters from Rebells except to implore his Mercy.

" A French nobleman, Son in Law to the Duke de Noailes, one of the first Families in France, is arrived in this City by the way of South Carolina (with severall Gentlemen) in a Vessell at his own Expence & Risque, & its said has made a present of some Brass Cannon, Musquets & Military Stores to the Contin¹ Army there, the Congress have made him a Major Generall tho' not to have any Brigade neither will he receive any pay or pension but bear the whole Expences himself, only to have Liberty to be with Gen. Washington in every Engagement, a noble Instance of Honour. . . .

" Paull Fooks has been very Bad & his Life despaired of, but is now much better . . . thy ever dutiful & affectionate Son whilst

" Benj. Marshall.

" P.S.—Thou'll see by the writing that I intended to have copied this over & corrected it, but as its too late & R. Fleming going very early I hope thee will be able to Read it & therefore Excuse my transcribing it."

Benjamin Marshall to his wife.   This letter is addressed " Benjamin Marshall at Newton Hall."

" Philad. Sep. 12 1777

" My dear Sally,

" Yesterday morning between 8 & 9 O'Clock a report of Cannon was heard which continued till near 11 O'Clock & afterward begun to slacken ab' 12 a Letter from the Gen¹ informing that the Enemy were advancing that his men were in good Spirits & hoped to give a good acc' since which no acc' till this morning about 4 o'clock.   Express from the Gen¹ enforming that during the Heavy firing at Chads Ford on Brandywine, a Large Body of the Enemy went round & cross'd a Ford ab' 6 miles higher up where we had 2 Battalions who received them with a heavy fire but the Enemy ab' 5000 rushed on with fixt Bayonetts; so that our people

were obliged to give way before the Gen¹ could gett to support them, the remainder then attackt Waynes & Maxwells
Brigades & after a heavy fire gott accross the Ford. Our
whole Army then retreated, and when the acc⁴ came away
were ab⁴ 2 mile from the Enemy. Gen. Washington was
at Chester ab⁴ 2 O'Clock this morning & orderd the Army
to Form behind them. Our Loss of men said to be ab⁴ 50,
the Enemy considerable by their forcing the Creeck—the
French Nobleman wounded in the Leg. Coll. White of the
Light Horse wounded. Gen. (I forgett) shot thro' the hand,
Coll. Stone & L⁴ Coll. Smith of Maryland killed. Cap⁴ For-
rest of Artillery wounded, & some others names not ment⁴.
We allso lost several pieces of Cannon. Expect to hear
more particulars presently. Yesterday they hauled a number of large Cannon to the ferry on Sculkill & this morning
some very heavy ones goes to the Swedes Ford, great number of shovells, spades, picks, Wheel Barrows &c were allso
sent in order to throw up Breast works; the Militia are
all to turn out this morning as Volunteers, they having mett
yesterday afternoon for that purpose. Gen. Livingston goes
to Jersey in order to gett out their militia, this matter prevents any Business being done as all the Shops are ordered
to be shutt up, & we cannot yet do any thing with our Salt,
only Congress have engaged to take it at their risque. I
cant say when shall come up as I cannot leave here till I
hear how things is like to be, tho' hope to be up to Morrow.
My Dear Love to the Children & all ffr⁴ˢ & am with sincere
affection thine whilst

" BENJ. MARSHALL.

" N.B.—The Frd⁴ & other prisoners were sent away yesterday afternoon from the Masons Lodge."

Charles Marshall to his father, at Lancaster, Pennsylvania.

" PROVIDENCE January 19ᵗʰ 1778

" DEAR FATHER
" Thine pʳ Jacob Baker came safe to hand last fifth Day
about noon accompanied by Dr. Phile whose Presence was

very agreable as his Wife and Children had come out of Philadᵃ & were at my House anxiously wishing for his Arrival. . . . I wish yᵗ Opertunities from us to Lancaster were more frequent yᵗ we might oftener inform you the Situation of our Families (as since the Army has removed across the Skuilkill we do not meet with so many Opertunities). . . . I perceive by thine that thou wast apprized of Brother Benjamin's being sick . . . I just now heard from him by Dr. Morgan who attends him, he saw him this afternoon & says yᵗ (he) is very poorly & thinks his Disorder will turn to be nervous, however I refer thee to Dr. Phile who can inform thee more particularly he having seen him. Patience has been in Philadᵃ twice, her main Inducement the first Time was to try to gett her Sister Betsy Phile out but when she was in Town she found further Business as the very Day after her Arrival she understood that the English intended to take Possession of the Things yᵗ were in our back Store up Vidells Alley which untill then they had not touched, so yᵗ she had to use all the Influence she could to try to save them & the Officer in my House (who intended to sieze them) promised that if she produced a List of what was in the Store & affirm to it, she might have them upon which she came up to us & we made out a List as well as we could and she went down the Second Time but tho' she stayed Several Days in Town she had but once an opertunity of seeing him, & altho she had nearly a Promise of having the Things yet when the List was given him he required Some Time to consider of it & as Patience chose to come out with her Sister she has not yet obtained an Answer tho the Officer told her that she need not wait as he could inform her Brother who will wait on him for his Answer, however I think it is necessary yᵗ she should go down again to know the Fate of the Things. . . . The Officer yᵗ first lived in my House when he removed took part of our Furniture with him also part of Bro Chrisᵃ Furniture is also taken out of his House which Patience has also to see after tho the Officer has promised her to deliver hers back, & upon the whole Patience has been used with good manners by them or rather full as well as could expect. . . . Thy affectionate Son

" Charles Marshall.

" Almost 11 O'Clock at night."

Christopher Marshall, Jr., to his father, at Lancaster, Pennsylvania.

" January 28ᵗʰ 1778

" Dear Father

" I am now at Brother Benny's & have been up with him these two last nights past to attend him in his Illness, which I have been anxious to communicate to thee from time to time . . . but as the Army is in Quarters on the other Side of Sckuylkill, Oppertunities do not present here so frequent as formerly, neither do I meet with any at my own habitation, being in that Respect a private place, and from head Quarters there may be Oppertunities, but the Passage over the River has been obstructed by floating Ice, otherwise believe I should have gone over & might have forwarded a few Lines from thence—however I now write but know not how it will be conveyed to lett thee know that the different Branches of our Families are all well in Health at present, except our dear Brother Benjamin, who still continues very ill, thou wast before appriz'd by Letters from Charles & Self as well as personally by Dr. Phyle who saw him, of the Situation he was in. . . . Dr. Morgan & Hutchinson who attended him declare it to be the Putrid Fever . . . on the whole from many Circumstances think he is something better, but know not how to flatter ourselves with his Recovery. . . . Sister Sally . . . almost constantly with him . . . her Bodily fatigue is much lessened by having Aunt Lydia Darragh here who heard dismal accounts of Sickness amongst us induced her to come out of Town, so yᵗ its great Ease to all our minds to have her here, as thou knows she's so tender hearted, skillfull & willing to do any thing about a Sick person. We should have been pleased to have heard from thee pʳ return of Rees's Waggon, but suppose he came off sooner than thou expected, if thou hast wrote pʳ Kolb's Waggon or any other Oppertunity, they have not come to our hands, the last we rec⁴ was pᵗ Jac : Baker who came in Coʸ with Dr. Phyle.

" Brother Charles & Patience lodged here last night . . . she has been to Town in hopes of getting many of our articles returned, those in our back Store she has got leave to remove, as the English Army want the Store . . . had she apply'd when one Col. Maxwell was in her House believe she would have mett with little Difficulty, but as he's removed there's another Officer in his place not so oblidging which requires much prudence to know how to act with him. . . . Thy affectionate Son

" CHRISTOPHER MARSHALL JUNᴿ.

" N.B.—We rec⁴ several Letters from England which had lain in the Post Office in Town, but they were Old Dates & had been first Examined ; there was one for thee but they would not deliver it.

" 2 O'Clock P.M."

Charles Marshall to his father (written on back of the foregoing).

" January 29ᵗʰ 1778 ½ past 4 O'Clock P.M.

" Annexed is what Broʳ Chrisʳ wrote thee yesterday. . . . Betwixt 10 & 11 o'clock at night . . . instead of his appearing better . . . we were surprized to find yᵗ he was considerably worse . . . so yᵗ we called up Sister Sally (whom we had a little before perswaded to go to Bed) & sent for Bro Chris & Sister Betsy who had gone over to David Rittenhouse's to lodge . . . we think he cannot survive over this night . . . we have now sent Jacob Baker on purpose to convey this Letter. We should be greatly pleased to see thee here, but on accoᵗ of the badness of the Weather & Roads cannot promise ourselves that Satisfaction. . . . Sister Sally tho considerably afflicted on this most trying & affecting Occasion, has nevertheless I think behaved with becoming Fortitude & endeavours to be resigned & to submitt to the Will of Providence, which owing to the unsettled State of the Times & her peculiar Situation, (she being very lusty & expecting to lay in some Time in March) makes it a more trying Dispensation to her as well as to thee & us. . . . Thy Loving & affectionate Son

" CHARLES MARSHALL."

Charles Marshall to his father, at Lancaster, Pennsylvania.

" PROVIDENCE February 5ᵗʰ 1778

" RESPECTED FATHER

" Thy several favours pʳ Gen. De Kalbs Waggon, Will Armstrong & Jacob Baker all came safe to hand, the last I did not receive untill yesterday afternoon as Baker was detained from crossing Skuilkill the night before by the water being high. Patience and I were at Sister Sally's when he came there . . . we could not but sympathyze with thee for the Loss we have all sustained . . . especially as being at such a great distance yᵗ thou couldst not have the opertunity of being with thy dear Son during his Sickness. . . . I sincerely wish that our aged Father may be supported under this Tryal. . . .

" As our Broʳ Benjaᵃ dyed without settling his affairs Sister Sally is desirous yᵗ we (Broʳ Chris & self) should have the Settlement thereof which indeed we are very willing & desirous to undertake & assist therein all that we can, but as we presume we cannot act, & thou canst, we therefore think it will be best for thee to administer to his Estate, but at same time we can be assistant in doing all the Business, for which Reason we are desirous that thou wouldst come down that we might consult with thee on the Occasion. . . . I am sorry thou shouldst have to undertake such a Journey at this Season of the Year but as matters are situated I think it cannot well be avoided & therefore we shall postpone doing anything material untill thou comes down or we hear further from thee, perhaps it would be best to try to gett an easy Creature & come on Horseback rather than in the Chair as the Roads are so heavy, & tho' it will not suit either of us at present to leave our Homes to come up all the way to Lancaster yet if thou can send us word where

& when to meet thee on the Road, one of us might if the Roads are not too bad meet thee with a Carriage. . . . I hope this may find thee & Mother in the Enjoyment of Health. . . .

> " Thy Loving Son
> " CHARLES MARSHALL.

" I have herewith sent 2 News Papers yᵗ I rec'd from Philad yesterday & I desire by every Opertunity thou wouldst send me down the Lancaster News Paper & I will endeavour to send thee up the Philad Papers as often as possible.

" Please to purchase & send me 2 of Dunlaps Almanacks with the Articles of Confederation in. I have not Time at present to write about Patiences being in Philad, only she says she was at Jnᵒ Lynns & they were all well there as well as most of our friends in general, Uncle Hallowell & Family desired particularly to be remembered to you, as also Stephen & Mary Collins & Rob Parrish.

" ½ past 11 O'Clock at night.

" I forgot to mention that our dear Brother was buryed last Seventh Day at Plymouth Meeting Yard as Sister Sally proposes yᵗ if she is so happy as to gett to Philadᵃ again to have him removed there."

Charles Marshall to his father, at Lancaster, Pennsylvania.

> " PHILADᴬ December 1ᵗ 1781

" ESTEEMED FATHER

" Brother Christopher wrote to thee a few Days past advising thee of the Safe Delivery of Sister Betsy of a Daughter, . . . now I have to convey to thee the awfull Tidings of her Departure, she having expired yesterday about 20 minutes past 12 O'Clock. . . . I have often to view our present Separation with Concern shouldst thou be taken ill. . . . I therefore request thee to reconsider our Separation in this Light & if thou canst find freedom to remove to thy old Habitation, be assured it will afford great Satisfaction &

Pleasure to all of thy Dear Offspring as well as to many of thy other Friends. . . .

> " Thy affectionate Son
> " CHARLES MARSHALL.

" Please to inform Widow Kuhn y' I had her Things packed up Several Days, & I expected y' Bowsman might have called again to have informed us that his Waggon was come. . . .

" The Child seems bravely & has a good breast of Milk so that we have hopes it may do well."

LETTER OF SILAS DEANE TO HIS BROTHER SIMEON DEANE,[1] FROM PHILADELPHIA, 1779.

PHILADELPHIA, July 27th, 1779.

DEAR BROTHER :

I sent you a Dict[y], by Mons : De Francy, which doubt not you have received, but untill I have Lett[rs] from you acknowledging it will make no Use of it. We are here in the greatest possible Anarchy & Confusion.   On Saturday Night the House of M[r] Humphreys a respectable Citizen, & as True, & brave a Whig, as any in this State was forced by the Rabble, excited, & led on, by Two of the Committee, He was from Home, but returned, just after they had entered in search of him.   They had knocked down, and Wounded his Sister a Young Lady in the House, and were retiring just as He made his Way thro. them into his House ; He armed himself, and stood on his defence, whilst they insulted, and Abused him, and to intimidate Him, led up a File of Soldiers armed, but He bravely defied them all Unitedly, and without any Assistance from the Authority of the City or his Neighbors, dispersed them.   This daring outrage, tho. not the greatest that has been committed here, has alarmed the Citizens, & yesterday there was a Town Meeting, at which the Committee found themselves greatly embarrass'd and were severely censured ; M[r] R Morriss was acquitted of every Charge, and greatly applauded, this indeed looks favorable, but the Meeting stands adjourned until this Morning, & the proceedings of this Day, will shew what will probably be the Event, the Contest is between the Respectable Citizens, of Fortune & Character, opposed to the Constitution of this State, and People in lower Circumstances, & Reputation, headed by Leaders well qualified for their Business, & supposed to be secretly supported, by the

---

[1] From "Correspondence and Journals of Samuel Blachley Webb," edited by Worthington C. Ford.

Pres⁺ & Council   However Things may End, It may at this Instant be truely said, there are few unhappier Cities, on the Globe than Philadᵃ, the reverse of its Name, is its present Character, which I hope will not be its situation for any Time.

It is a Melancholy Reflection to Think, that whilst Our Common Enemy, is Wasting Our Sea Coasts, & laying Our fairest, & most peaceable Towns, in Ashes, We are quarrelling among Ourselves, and can scarcely be constrained from plunging Our Swords in each others Bosoms.   Fairfield, Norwalk, & the Country between them, are Plundered, & burnt to almost the last House by the Enemy, N Haven was Plundered, & the Stores on the Wharf burned, and many Houses in E Haven, the individual Acts of Barbarity You must suppose many, & Atrocious, they are so, almost beyond description, or Example   The Enemy have evacuated the State ;   The Surprise of their Garrison at Stoney Point was a most gallant Affair And conducted in some degree, to make them retire from Connecticut.   Lord Cornwallis is arrived at New York with some Recruits, & it is given out that Admˡ Arbuthnot may be daily expected with a large Reinforcement   I doubt it, though Our Friends in France, write positively, on the subject.   He must have sailed in May, which induces Me to think his Destination changed, & that his being bound to America was given Out rather as a blind. I send you inclosed Two Lettʳˢ from Mʳ Limozin which I opened, impatient for News from France, from whence I received Nothing by Letter.   pray write Me Your situation and What You have Suffered, also how the Land Office goes on.   I send you part of Two Papers by which you will see how Payne [Thomas Paine] is handled, there are Two more still severer but I have them not by Me at this Time.   The Verses merit preserving.

Our Brother B. D. is gone to Boston, he has been successful in Privateering lately, in the Mars particularly.

I am my Dʳ Brother most Affectionately

Yours

S. Deane.

28th I miss'd the Post of yesterday, & will now add briefly, the transactions of the Day.   At Nine oClock Two or Three Hundred Men of the lower Orders of the People armed with large Staves or Bludgeons with Drum & Fife entered the State House Yard, and Stationed themselves Near The Hustings, soon after a large Number of Citizens of the first Character entered.   A few Resolutions passed, when Genl Cadwallader offering to Speak the Phalanx prepared for the purpose raised such a Noise that He could not be heard, the Chairman call'd to Order and put the Question if He should be heard, a very great Majority declared for the hearing of him.   But the Moment He began, He was interrupted by the same party, with their Shouts, striking, & cracking of their Sticks against each other &c, on this He with His Friends amounting to near Three fourths present, to prevent the most fatal as well as disgraceful Consequences retired in a Body to the College where they formed a Meeting & went on with their Business, & appointing a Comm. to protest against the proceedings of the other party, they came to several Resolutions and Adjourned   The party left in the State House yard also went on, & passed a Number of Resolutions, such as might be expected from them, & then broke up.   Thus The Two Parties are pitted against each other, each making Proselytes as fast as possible, against another Tryal of their Forces meantime the Minister has taken up the Insult offered to Mr Holker, & thro. him, to his Most Christian Majesty by the late Committee in a perious Stile, & demanded satisfaction; This will I hope bring some of these Leaders to their Senses, but some of them I have no doubt have their Views, & their Interest so strongly & deeply fixed in promoting Anarchy & Confusion, That Nothing will call them off the desperate Course they are pursuing, some of them I doubt not are well paid for all This by the Enemy; and sure I am, the Enemy is now gaining more, by this kind of Campaign, than by any other they can devise or plan.   I am now seriously intent on leaving the City as soon as possible, without any further reference to Congress, for I see no probability of their waking from the Lethargy they are in, and Attending to Business of the utmost importance, in a regular and decisive Manner.   The Report is that Lord Cornwallis and the Fleet are arrived, but Acc^{ts} of the Troops uncertain, some say Five Thousand some More, if they are really arrived I expect a large detachment of them will be employed in Maneuvring, with Genl Washington, & in destroying Our Coasts   Or that their Fleet and a principal part of their Army will strike on some part Eastward, perhaps Attempt Boston   whether I shall go Northward or Southward first is uncertain, but I shall leave the Continent the Moment I can do it with probable Safety, of Arriving, in the first Neutral, or Friendly Port, pray let Me know what Bromfield & Roach are doing, their Conduct is very surprising and they do not write Us one Word.   I am ever my Dear Brother

Most Affectionately

Yours &c

S. DEANE.

RECORDS OF CHRIST CHURCH, PHILADELPHIA.
BAPTISMS, 1709–1760.

BY CHARLES R. HILDEBURN.

(Continued from p. 229.)

1730 Oct.	12	Smith Jonas s. Morris and Anne 4 dys.
1730 Oct.	12	Jacob s. Morris and Anne 4 dys.
1730 Nov.	1	Andrew s. Andrew and Elizabeth 6 mos.
1731 May	19	William s. William and Mary 2 mos. 8 wks.
1732 Sept.	4	Mary d. John and Mary 1 yr.
1732 Dec.	8	Martha d. Andrew and Elizabeth 2 wks.
1734 Mch.	31	John s. Morris and Anne 3 wks.
1734 Mch.	31	Anne d. Morris and Anne 3 wks.
1734 July	27	George s. Jonas and Mary 3 wks.
1734 Aug.	12	Anne d. John and Mary 11 mos.
1735 Aug.	17	Edward s. George and Elizabeth 6 mos.
1735 Sept.	3	David s. Andrew and Elizabeth 6 mos.
1735 Sept.	26	John s. John and Mary 5 dys.
1735 Oct.	5	Mary d. Morris and Anne 5 wks.
1735 Dec.	25	Noah s. George and Elizabeth 6 mos.
1736 Oct.	24	John s. William and Mary 3 yrs. 11 mos.
1736 Oct.	24	Thomas s. William and Mary 1 mo.
1736 Dec.	20	Alexander s. Edward and Elizabeth 6 yrs. 9 mos.
1736 Dec.	20	Hannah d. Edward and Elizabeth 1 yr. 5 mos.
1737 Oct.	5	Seamore s. Morris and Anne 2 mos.
1738 May	5	Joseph s. John and Christian 5 dys.
1739 Dec.	5	Mary d. John and Mellina 1 yr. 11 mos.
1740 April	10	Margaret d. John and Elizabeth 2 yrs. 6 mos.
1740 July	12	Joseph s. John and Emillia 5 mos.
1740 Nov.	2	Mary d. William and Isabella 1 wk. 4 dys.
1741 Sept.	13	Rachel d. Daniel and Dorothy 11 mos.
1741 Oct.	7	Eliza d. James and Mary 3 mos.
1742 May	19	Hannah d. John and Amelia 3 mos. 19 dys.
1743 July	31	Elizabeth d. Thomas and Mary 11 dys.
1744 Oct.	14	Samuel s. Thomas and Elizabeth 16 dys.
1745 June	2	James s. William and Rebecca June 18 1743
1745 June	2	George s. William and Rebecca May 5 1745
1746 Mch.	7	Anne d. John and Amelia March 5 1745
1746 Sept.	28	Anne d. Thomas and Mary July 22 1746
1747 April	10	Joseph s. James and Mary March 26 1747

1747 July 24 Smith Mary d. William and Susannah Feb. 13 1747
1748 Nov. 25   George s. George and Catherine Oct. 21 1748
1748 Dec. 4   Joseph s. Jeptha and Dinah Nov. 7 1748
1749 Aug. 27   Anne d. William and Jemima July 16 1749
1750 Nov. 11   William s. William and Jemima Oct. 1 1750
1752 May 28   Matthew s. William and Jemima April 9 1752
1752 Oct. 5   Robert s. Christopher and Susannah June 28 1752
1754 July 3   Anne d. Jacob and Mary April 1 1754
1754 Oct. 27   Anne d. James and Martha Oct. 13 1754
1755 Jan. 26   Martha d. Charles and Martha Nov. 30 1754
1755 Dec. 24   Thomas s. Richard and Mary Dec. 17 1755
1759 Oct. 13   William Moore s. Revd William and Rebecca
1760 Nov. 4   William s. Samuel and Jane March 18 1755
1760 Nov. 4   Ann d. Samuel and Jane Jan. 14 1760
1736 Aug. 24 Smithers Sophia d. Richard and Elizabeth 16 yrs.
1717 July 9 Smout Eltony[1] s. Silvanus and Elinor 1 yr.
1727 Aug. 24 Sneed Elizabeth d. William and Elizabeth 9 mos.
1726 Jan. 12 Snowden Margaret d. Margaret
1746 May 30 Sober Mary
1735 Dec. 25 Soutt John d. Edward and Mary 6 mos.
1714 Feb. 9 Sowers John s. John and Mary 2 mos.
1741 Oct. 7 Spafford Ann d. John and Ann 3 mos. 3 wks. 4 dys.
1739 Feb. 25 Spaford William s. John and Anne 5 dys.
1759 May 26 Sparks Margaret d. James and Mary May 3 1759
1745 Nov. 22 Spelman Catherine Gordon d. Elizabeth wife John
1727 Sept. 10 Spencer Daniel s. John and Mary 2 wks.
1730 Mch. 18   Thomas s. Thomas and Margaret 7 mos.
1732 Mch. 15   John s. John and Mary 6 yrs. 6 mos.
1732 Mch. 15   Mary d. John and Mary 2 mos. 5 dys.
1734 July 3   James s. John and Mary 7 mos.
1737 Jan. 1   Sarah d. John and Mary 9 mos.
1738 Sept. 2   Richard s. John and Mary 2 mos.
1744 Mch. 12   George s. George and Florinda 1 dy.
1759 Dec. 5   Sarah d. Daniel and Elizabeth Jan. 4 1758
1759 Dec. 5   Daniel s. Daniel and Elizabeth Dec. 29 1757
1726 Dec. 25 Spirer John s. Abraham and Sarah 7 mos.
1728 Feb. 2   James s. Abraham and Sarah 4 mos. 1 dy.
1733 Oct. 3 Springer Deborah d. Benjamin and Anne 4 mos.
1735 June 6 Sprogle John Lodwick s. John Henry and Joanna Christianna 3½ yrs.
1735 June 6   Samuel Christian s. John Henry and Joanna Christianna 5 mos.
1750 Aug. 10 Spurgeon Laurence Anderson s. William and Hannah July 12 1750
1737 May 24 Squires Mary d. John and Sarah 2 wks.

1734 May   19 Stainman Jacob s. Daniel and Mary 6 wks.
1726 June   22 Stamper John s. John and Hannah ——
1729 June   8   Mary d. John and Hannah 3 wks.
1732 Jan.   8   Joseph s. John and Hannah 1 mo.
1736 June   5   John s. Thomas and Dinah 18 mos.
1787 Mch.   2   Thomas s. Thomas and Diana 3 mos.
1756 Oct.   7   Hannah d. Joseph and Sarah July 29 1756
1760 Dec.   21   John s. John and Hannah June 8 1758
1729 Nov.   2 Stanhope Richard s. Thomas and Mary 1 mo. 1 wk.
1733 Mch.   25   William s. Thomas and Mary 9 mos.
1727 Dec.   22 Stanley Eleanor d. Luke and Mary 1 wk.
1734 July   28   Mary d. Thomas and Elizabeth 1 mo.
1734 Dec.   25   Thomas s. James and Sarah 4 wks.
1755 Dec.   3 Stanling Walter s. Walter and Dorothy June 24 1755
1716 June   10 Stapleford Eliza d. Thomas and Mary 2 wks.
1727 Aug.   22   Rebecca d. Thomas and Mary Jan. 9 1720
1731 Mch.   8 Stapler Richard s. Richard and Elizabeth 1 yr. 5 mos.
1751 Oct.   18 Stedman Margaret d. Alexander and Elizabeth May 24
                   1750
1752 Oct.   23   John s. Alexander and Elizabeth March 27 1752
1754 April   7   Charles s. Alexander and Elizabeth Dec. 22 1753
1760 May   7   Elizabeth d. Alexander and Elizabeth April 19 1760
1736 May   24 Steel Sarah d. Jacob and Thomasine 3 wks.
1760 May   1   Jane d. William and Elizabeth April 18 1760
1753 Aug.   27 Stephenson Margaret d. James and Mary July 31 1753
1734 Mch.   17 Stevens Robert s. Richard and Dorothy 3 wks.
1751 Jan.   2   Mary d. John and Elizabeth Nov. 10 1750
1752 June   22   John s. John and Elizabeth April 21 1752
1749 Nov.   13 Stevenson Edward s. James and Mary Oct. 22 1749
1756 Oct.   7   John Rumley s. James and Mary Sept. 6 1756
1733 July   1 Steward James s. Peter and Mary 2 mos. 8 dys.
1751 Dec.   26   Hannah d. John and Anne Nov. 13 1751
1753 July   24   John s. George and Ann July 15 1753
1739 Aug.   16 Stewart Sarah d. James and Priscilla Aug. 3 1739
1759 July   25   James s. James and Anne July 9 1759
1735 Dec.   21 Stiles Ellinor d. William and Susannah 5 wks.
1738 Feb.   19   Margaret d. William and Susannah 3 wks.
1751 Oct.   6   Henry s. Henry and Elizabeth Feb. 4 1750
1754 Mch.   20   John s. Henry and Elizabeth Feb. 21 1754
1757 April 20   Elizabeth d. Henry and Elizabeth April 3 1757
1726 Oct.   9 Stilly George s. Peter and Sarah Oct. 2
1731 Nov.   21   Peter s. Peter and Sarah 14 wks.
1733 Oct.   20   Elizabeth d. Peter and Sarah 1 mo.
1736 Mch.   28   William s. Peter and Sarah 12 dys.
1756 Mch.   11 Stocker Anne d. Anthony and Margaret Jan. 3 1756

1758 Jan.	1	Stocker Mary d. Anthony and Margaret Dec. 18 1757
1758 Aug.	30	George s. John and Rebecca Aug. 8 1757
1760 Mch.	2	James s. John and Rebecca Feb. 21 1760
1760 June	2	John Clements s. Anthony and Margaret Feb. 19 1760
1742 Jan.	24	Stockes Ann d. John and Mary 1 mo.
1729 Dec.	14	Stokes Robert s. Stephen and Mary 8 dys.
1731 Dec.	19	Stoks Mary d. Stephen and Mary 11 wks.
1735 Dec.	24	Stone William s. William and Hannah 5 mos.
1738 Aug.	3	John s. William and Hannah 3 mos. 2 wks.
1741 June	25	Millenicent d. William and Hannah 6 mos.[21 dys.
1743 Oct.	19	William s. William and Hannah 5 wks. 6 dys.
1747 May	20	Edward s. William and Hannah June 11 1745
1752 Oct.	19	Thomas s. William —— March 30 1752
1721 July	5	Store Samuel s. Nathaniel and Sarah June 10 1721
1729 Nov.	80	Stork Sarah Adult.
1711 Dec.	15	Story Patience d. Enoch and Sarah 3 wks. 5 dys.
1714 Sept.	18	Enoch s. Enoch and Sarah ——
1717 Aug.	10	Sarah d. Enoch 2 wks.
1726 Nov.	4	John s. Thomas and Mary Oct. 26
1726 Nov.	4	Diana d. Thomas and Mary Oct. 26
1746 April	11	Stout Anne d. Cornelius and Rebecca Oct. 12 1745
1750 May	8	Hannah d. Cornelius and Rebecca March 10 1747
1750 May	8	Joseph s. Cornelius and Rebecca May 9 1748
1750 Dec.	5	Margaret d. Cornelius and Rebecca Nov. 16 1750
1752 Nov.	19	Cornelius s. Cornelius and Rebecca Oct. 22 1752
1754 Sept.	8	Rebecca d. Cornelius and Rebecca Aug. 8 1754
1727 Mch.	15	Stow John s. Charles and Rebecca 3 wks.
1729 Feb.	23	Martha d. Charles and Rebecca 1 mo.
1731 Sept.	30	Lazerus s. Charles and Rebecca 3 wks.
1732 Nov.	3	Thomasin d. William and Hannah 5 wks.
1747 Sept.	11	Street Mary d. Benjamin and Elizabeth Jan. 6 1747
1751 May	11	Joseph s. Benjamin and Elizabeth March 27 1751
1715 May	1	Streeter Benjamin s. James and Sarah 8 dys.
1756 Sept.	27	Streetson Martha d. Francis and Mary Nov. 27 1753
1756 Sept.	27	Elizabeth d. Francis and Mary May 27 1754
1758 July	4	Stretson Mary d. Francis and Mary May 6 1757
1760 Sept.	3	Strettell John s. Amos and Hannah May 29 1760
1755 Sept.	4	Strettle Robert s. Amos and Hannah Dec. 17 1753
1755 Sept.	4	Ann d. Amos and Hannah Jan. 12 1755
1758 Nov.	14	Frances d. Amos and Hannah Oct. 14 1758
1757 Nov.	4	Strickland Joseph s. John and Margaret Aug. 14 1757
1759 May	20	William s. John and Mary Jan. 31 1759
1733 Aug.	30	Strong Abraham s. Abraham and Dorothy 1 mo.
1710 April	2	Stroud Ann
1710 April	2	Ann 23 yrs.

1733 Nov. 25 Stroup Catherine d. Peter and Barbary 2 dys.
1752 July 19 Sturgeon Susannah d. Rev. William and Hannah June 18 1752
1755 May 21   Ann d. William and Hannah April 9 1755
1756 July 18   Robert Anderson s. William and Hannah June 18 1755
1726 Feb. 1 Sturges Jane d. Joseph and Jane 8 wks.
1729 Mch. 4   Cornelius s. Joseph and Jane 8 mos.
1737 Jan. 23   George s. Joseph and Jane 7 mos.
1737 Jan. 23   Mary d. Joseph and Jane 6 yrs.
1738 June 1   Joseph s. Joseph and Jane 3 mos.
1738 June 1   Susannah d. Joseph and Jane 3 mos.
1759 Feb. 26 Style Henry s. Henry and Elizabeth Nov. 7 1758
1717 Aug. 27 Styles Mary d. Robert and Sarah 8 mos.
1760 Sept. 11   Mary d. Henry and Elizabeth April 26 1760
1720 Sept. 4 Suber John s. John Peter and Magdalen ——
1742 Mch. 17 Sullavil Sarah d. Luke and Abigail 4 yrs. 5 mos. 16 dys.
1731 Aug. 29 Sundergill Elizabeth d. Christopher and Elizabeth 1 yr.
1725 Oct. 1 Surnneck Richard s. John and Mary Sept. 19
1728 Aug. 27 Sutton Sarah d. Henry and Anne 5 mos.
1740 June 29   John s. John and Mary 4 mos.
1758 Sept. 18   Ann d. William and Sarah May 11 1758
1738 Sept. 28 Swan Anne d. Richard and Anne 9 dys.
1740 Jan. 21   Richard s. Richard and Anne 3 wks.
1745 Dec. 27   Sarah d. Richard and Anne Dec. 6 1745
1756 June 14 Sweetapple Elizabeth d. Edward and Mary Aug. 17 1748
1750 Aug. 25 Swift John White s. John and Magdalen ——
1752 April 22   Alice d. John and Magdalen Feb. 20 1750
1752 April 22   Joseph s. John and Magdalen Feb. 9 1752
1756 May 5   Jacob s. John and Magdalen May 16 1755
1760 Jan. 23   Charles s. John and Magdalen Aug. 26 1757
1760 Jan. 23   Mary d. John and Magdalen Sept. 14 1759
1760 Feb. 10   Eleanor d. Joseph and Margaret Jan. 6 1760
1749 May 8 Sybald David s. John and Rebecca Jan. 27 1749
1746 June 16 Sybbald Jennet d. John and Rebecca June 3 1746
1751 April 28   John s. John and Rebecca April 3 1750
1736 Sept. 17 Sybil Peter s. Jacob and Mary 1 wk.
1710 Sept. 1 Sykes John s. James and Mary
1713 Aug. 3   Susannah d. James and Mary
1745 April 27 Symes Elizabeth d. Joseph and Anne March 29 1745
1745 Dec. 29   Anthony s. Zachariah and Elizabeth Sept. 28 1745
1748 Oct. 27   Anne d. Joseph and Anne Sept. 27 1748
1714 July 27 Symons Deborah d. Stephen and Mary 6 yrs.
1714 July 27   Mary d. Stephen and Mary 3 yrs.
1714 July 27   Werdon s. Stephen and Mary ——
1732 April 16 Syng Abigail d. Philip and Elizabeth 17 mos.

1732 April 18 Syng Elizabeth wife of Philip 18 yrs.
1734 Jan.　27　　Philip s. Philip and Elizabeth 6 wks.
1734 Sept.　29　　Mary d. Daniel and Mary 5 dys.
1735 June　8　　John s. Philip and Elizabeth 7 wks. 4 dys.
1737 July　17　　Philip s. John and Deborah 1 mo.
1743 Jan.　24　　Hester d. Philip and Elizabeth July 28 1736
1743 Jan.　24　　Elizabeth d. Philip and Elizabeth Feb. 20 1739
1743 Jan.　24　　Martha d. Philip and Elizabeth April 5 1741
1743 Jan.　24　　Isaiah s. Philip and Elizabeth Jan. 2 1742
1749 Feb.　21　　Joseph s. Philip and Elizabeth Oct. 10 1745
1749 Feb.　21　　Ann d. Philip and Elizabeth Sept. 11 1747
1755 May　24　　Hannah d. Philip and Elizabeth Oct. 18 1749
1755 May　24　　Ann d. Philip and Elizabeth March 20 1751
1755 May　24　　Mary d. Philip and Elizabeth May 15 1752
1748 Mch.　20　Taber John Adult
1720 Nov.　20　Tabiner John s. James and Martha Oct. 20
1736 Nov.　29　Tacklebury Mary d. Robert and Mary 18 mos.
1720 Nov.　9　Talbot Margaret d. Benjamin and Susannah ——
1722 April　13　　Edmund s. Benjamin and Susannah ——
1740 Oct.　19　Tanton Mary d. Randall and Quin 3 mos.
1749 Sept.　10　Tate Elizabeth d. Andrew and Susannah Aug. 19 1749
1752 May　6　　Anne d. William and Susannah April 10 1752
1760 May　7　　John s. Andrew and Susannah March 14 1760
1722 Sept.　14　Taverner Elizabeth d. James and Martha 3 wks.
1716 July　8　Taylor William s. Robert and Jane 10 dys.
1721 Mch.　18　　Edward s. Robert and Jane Feb. 17
1722 July　6　　Mary d. John and Katherine ——
1723 July　6　　Mary d. John and Katherine
1727 April　24　　Isaac s. Benjamin and Amable 2 wks.
1730 Aug.　14　　Jeremiah s. Benjamin and Aimable 11 dys.
1731 Nov.　7　　Thomas s. Benjamin and Martha 5 wks.
1732 Dec.　21　　Mary d. Thomas and Elizabeth 2 mos.
1733 Oct.　28　　Sarah d. Henry and Elizabeth 4 mos. 2 wks.
1733 Nov.　4　　Joseph s. Alexander and Elizabeth 4 mos. 2 wks.
1733 Dec.　29　　Isabella d. Abraham and Philadelphia 1 mo.
1734 May　7　　Anne d. Benjamin and Martha 7 dys.
1734 Oct.　8　　Edward s. Thomas and Elizabeth 6 wks. 4 dys.
1735 Aug.　24　　John s. Abraham and Philadelphia 2 wks.
1736 June　11　　Henry d. Henry and Elizabeth 5 wks.
1747 Oct.　14　　Jane d. Abraham and Philadelphia Aug. 17 1747
1747 Dec.　10　　Mary d. Daniel and Letitia Aug. 11 1747
1751 Aug.　30　　Benjamin s. William and Martha Dec. 18 1742
1751 Aug.　30　　Samuel s. William and Martha Nov. 2 1744
1751 Aug.　30　　Charles s. William and Martha Nov. 23 1746
1753 Jan.　28　　Thomas s. Thomas and Mary Dec. 22 1752

1753 May   7 Taylor Martha wife of William
1753 May   7   William s. William and Martha May 22 1752
1756 April 22   Katherine d. —— and Mary March 28 1756
1757 Mch. 13   Robert s. John and Mary Feb. 11 1757
1758 July 13   Elizabeth d. Henry and Mary March 15 1758
1758 July 13   Sarah d. Henry and Mary March 15 1758
1758 Oct. 18   John s. John and Mary Sept. 21 1758
1759 Aug. 31   Elizabeth d. Richard and Mary Aug. 12 1759
1759 Dec. 15   Mary d. Henry and Mary Oct. 30 1759
1733 Nov. 25 Teals Henry s. Richard and Mary 8 wks.
1731 June   7 Tennant John s. Moses and Rachel 11 mos.
1735 Aug. 21   Sarah d. Moses and Rachel 10 mos. 10 dys.
1739 May   17   Susannah d. Moses and Rachel 2 yrs. 3 mos.
1744 Sept. 8 Tesley Peter s. Samuel and Mary 7 dys.
1753 June 18 Tew David s. Edward and Hariot April 17 1753
1730 April 8 Thein Elizabeth d. John and Celia 8 wks.
1710 Jan. 15 Thomas Sarah 17 yrs.
1711 June 26   John s. John and Patient 1 wk.
1720 Nov. 27   Margaret d. Edward and Catherine 7 yrs.
1728 Dec. 18   Jane d. Rees and Gwenllian 1 mo.
1730 Jan. 14   Samuel s. Evan and Mary 9 mos.
1730 Nov.   8   Mark s. John and Mary 18 mos.
1731 July 25   Nathan s. Owen and Catherine 1 mo. 3 dys.
1732 Nov. 22   James s. James and Anne 15 mos.
1734 April 30   Sarah d. Anne 14 mos.
1737 Mch.   4   Anne d. William and Anne 1 yr.
1737 Dec.   4   Sarah d. Evan and Margaret 9 dys.
1739 April 7   John s. John and Jane 1 wk.
1740 Sept. 8   Evan s. Evan and Margaret 8 wks.
1745 July 24   Margaret d. Hon. George, Governor, and Elizabeth
                       July 18 1745
1746 June 20   Benjamin d. Benjamin and Elizabeth 11 mos.
1736 Dec. 26 Thompson Hugh s. John and Catherine 7 mos.
1737 July 20   Elizabeth d. Edward Rogers and Elizabeth 3 yrs.
1739 July 10   George s. John and Catherine 14 mos.
1746 Mch.   2   Anne d. James and Anne Jan. 11 1745
1747 Dec. 25   James s. James Steel and Martha Dec. 4 1747
1748 Sept. 25   Elizabeth d. Slane and Elizabeth July 4 1748
1750 May   27   Anne d. John and Martha May 4 1750
1752 Jan.   8   James s. James and Jane Oct. 7 1751
1752 Aug. 16   William s. John and Martha July 10 1752
1754 Jan. 20   John s. John and Martha Dec. 6 1753
1755 July 27   Martha d. John and Martha June 28 1755
1757 Feb.   8   William s. William and Hannah Jan. 18 1757
1734 Jan. 27 Thomson John s. Thomas and Hannah 3 wks.

1740 Nov. 17 Thomson Edward s. John and Catherine 7 wks.
1720 Jan. 15 Thorn Robert s. Roger and Mercy ——
1728 June 12   Mary d. Roger and Sarah 15 mos.
1741 Sept. 13 Thornhill Jane 25 yrs. 8 mos. 8 dys.
1742 Aug. 13   Joseph s. John and Jane June 28 1742
1744 June 24   John s. Thomas and Elizabeth 7 dys.
1744 Aug. 5   Mary d. John and Jane 27 dys.
1747 Mch. 8   Richard s. John and Jane Feb. 2 1747
1750 Aug. 24   John s. John and Jane July 22 1750
1717 Dec. 27 Thorp Thomas s. John and Mary 9 dys.
1716 July 6 Thorpe Elizabeth d. John and Mary ——
1728 July 17 Thrift James s. Joseph 3 mos.
1751 Sept. 13 Thwates Thomas s. Joseph and Agnes March 5 1751
1715 June 1 Tiebling Elizabeth d. Mary 1 yr.
1713 Oct. 21 Tiely Samuel s. Nathaniel 1 mo.
1720 Oct. 6 Tiley Elizabeth d. Nathaniel and Ann March 24 1716
1720 Oct. 6   James s. Nathaniel and Ann Dec. 15 1718
1720 Oct. 6   Josiah s. Nathaniel and Ann Sept. 25 1720
1729 Aug. 1   Elizabeth d. John and Mary 10 wks.
1720 Nov. 29 Till John s. John and Brightly Aug. 3
1722 Jan. 14   Hannah d. John and Brightly Jan. 1
1729 April 17   Thomas s. John and Brightly 1 yr. 10 mos.
1729 Sept. 24   William s. John and Bretty 5 yrs. 1 mo.
1729 Sept. 24   Thomas s. John and Bretty 7 mos. 3 wks.
1729 Sept. 24   Rebecca d. John and Bretty 4 yrs. 6 mos. 3 dys.
1730 April 23   Elizabeth d. John and Bretty 20 dys.
1732 Sept. 15   Elizabeth d. John and Brightweed 8 mos.
1738 Oct. 27   Thomas s. John and Britty 4 yrs. 11 mos.
1738 Oct. 27   Joseph s. John and Britty 2 yrs. 6 mos.
1751 Feb. 9   Anne d. William and Demaris Oct. 10 1750
1758 June 30   George s. William and Demaris Dec. 22 1752
1760 Sept. 7   Mary d. William and Demaris Feb. 5 1760
1737 June 20 Tilla John s. John and Elizabeth 2 wks.
1738 Dec. 20   George s. John and Elizabeth 1 mo.
1710 Dec. 10 Tilly John ——
1732 Aug. 2 Timothy John s. Lewis and Elizabeth 3 wks.
1733 Dec. 21   Michael s. Lewis and Elizabeth 12 dys.
1754 Dec. 26 Tinley Mary d. John and Elizabeth Nov. 2 1754
1756 Dec. 22 Todman Amorah d. Thomas and Amorah Dec. 20 1756
1735 Mch. 13 Tombs John s. Robert and Mary 5 mos. 2 wks.
1733 Jan. 17 Tomms Elizabeth d. Robert and Mary 8 mos.
1738 Mch. 13   Sarah d. Robert and Mary 4 mos.
1726 Oct. 9 Toms Mary d. Robert and Mary Sept. 12
1729 Dec. 26   Martha d. Robert and Mary 1 yr.
1735 Aug. 31 Tonge Abraham Bickley s. John and Mary 2 yrs.

1746 June 14 Tool Thomas s. Daniel and Dorothy Jan. 15 1745
1746 June 18   Dorothy wife Daniel
1735 June 19 Topp Thomas s. Joseph and Anne 10 dys.
1737 Feb. 28   Anne d. Joseph and Anne 5 wks.
1741 April 19 Topplift Richard s. Richard and Ann 10 mos.
1734 Dec. 17 Towers Mary d. William and Ann 6 mos.
1738 May 29   Isaac s. William and Ann 3 mos. 2 wks.
1741 Aug. 26   James s. William and Ann 10 mos. 1 dy.
1745 June 14   William s. William and Ann Feb. 15 1744
1750 June 28   William s. John and Margaret May 24 1750
1752 Aug. 5   Benjamin s. John and Margaret Oct. 10 1752 (*sic*)
1760 Dec. 21   Rebecca d. Robert and Rebecca Aug. 28 1760
1759 Oct. 14 Town Joseph s. Thomas and Elizabeth April 28 1759
1727 April 9 Townsend Samuel s. Thomas and Margaret 3 mos. 8 wks.
1727 May 17   Lawrence s. Richard and Ann 2 yrs. 1 mo.
1728 May 1   Mary d. Richard and Ann 2 wks.
1787 Jan. 6   John s. John and Mary 2 mos.
1717 June 4 Toy Nicolas s. Frederick and Bridget 5 mos.
1738 July 26 Tremble John s. William and Mary 4 dys.
1711 June 1 Trent Thomas s. William and Mary 2ⁿᵈ wife born and
                baptised
1713 Sept. 13 Tress Margaret d. Thomas and Mary ——
1717 Aug. 14   Thomas s. Thomas and Elizabeth Born ye 6ᵗʰ
1720 Jan. 31   Rebecca d. Thomas
1722 July 18   Ann d. Thomas and Elizabeth
1745 June 26   Thomas s. Hugh and Hannah
1745 Dec. 8   Thomas s. Hugh and Hannah Feb. 4 1744
1748 April 10 Tribbet Mary d. Simon and Elizabeth Feb. 27 1748
1750 June 10   Simon s. Simon and Elizabeth May 18 1750
1740 Aug. 10 Trimble William s. William and Mary 2 wks.
1744 Jan. 26   Mary d. William and Mary 15 dys.
1712 Mch. 13 Trisse Hugh s. Thomas and Mary 8 dys.
1716 July 28   Mary d. Thomas and Mary 8 dys.
1715 April 28 Trope Susan d. John and Susan 7 mos.
1727 July 16 Truston Elizabeth d. Thomas and Anne 7 mos.
1736 May 16 Tuffe Elizabeth d. Robert and Sarah 8 mos.
1735 Dec. 28 Tunnicliff Isaac s. Isaac and Anne 6 mos.
1734 June 19   Elizabeth d. Isaac and Anne 8 dys.
1730 Sept. 25 Turner Mary d. Peter and Hannah 2 yrs.
1730 Nov. 22   Sarah d. Anthony and Sarah 20 wks.
1732 April 3   Samuel s. Peter and Hannah 2 dys.
1735 Oct. 6   Peter s. Peter and Sarah 19 mos.
1736 May 20   Simon s. Anthony and Sarah 14 mos. 3 wks.
1736 Oct. 24   James s. Peter and Hannah 2½ yrs.
1739 May 6   Martha d. Edward and Rebecca 8 wks. 1 dy.

1740 Nov. 10 Turner Mary d. Edward and Rebecca 1 yr.
1742 May 2 Lucy d. Edward and Rebecca 1 mo.
1745 April 14 Sarah d. Edward and Rebecca 5 wks.
1747 April 5 Rebecca d. Edward and Mary March 2 1747
1749 Jan. 15 John s. John and Mary Dec. 31 1748
1749 May 21 John s. Edward and Rebecca April 17 1749
1750 Dec. 28 Anne d. John and Dorothy Feb. 4 1749
1754 April 20 Hannah d. Edward and Hannah Oct. 6 1744
1754 April 20 William s. Edward and Hannah April 21 1747
1754 April 20 John s. Edward and Hannah Oct. 8 1753
1755 June 3 Sarah d. Richard and Sarah April 30 1755
1757 July 28 Mary d. Morris and Sarah April 20 1757
1760 Feb. 25 William 23 yrs. 3 mos.
1723 Jan. 1 Turton William s. Thomas and Lucy
1732 April 19 Tuthill John s. Christopher and Susannah 7 wks.
1740 Jan. 18 Unger George s. Wolf and Anna Maria 3 dys.
1742 June 27 Ungerer John Nicolas s. John and Margaret 13 dys.
1742 Mch. 2 Unkree George Henry s. John Woolf and Ann Mary 6 dys.
1726 Feb. 20 Upham Moses s. Aaron and Elizabeth ——
1727 Dec. 24 Ann d. Aaron and Elizabeth 3 wks. 3 dys.
1731 May 20 Upton Mary d. Aaron and Elizabeth 4 mos.
1755 Feb. 26 Usher Ann d. Abraham and Rose Feb. 5 1755
1757 May 10 Rose d. Abraham and Rose April 12 1757
1760 June 20 John s. Abraham and Rose May 8 1760
1740 June 19 Vagle James s. George and Margaret 9 wks.
1745 Aug. 22 Vanderspeigle Henry s. William and Margaret Aug. 7 1745
1747 Nov. 5 Marian d. William and Margaret July 26 1747
1749 Jan. 1 Anne d. William and Margaret Nov. 10 1748
1750 Mch. 28 Abraham William s. William and Margaret Feb. 15 1749
1751 Sept. 2 Margaret Van Veghter d. William and Margaret July 22 1751
1753 June 30 Margaret Van Veghton d. William and Margaret April 2 1753
1736 Aug. 28 Vane Susannah d. John and Ann 7 mos.
1743 May 20 Vangerel Benjamin s. John and Sarah 6 mos. 2 wks. 3 dys.
1758 Mch. 8 Vann John s. James and Mary March 15 1758 (*sic*)
1758 Mch. 8 Vannot John s. Isaac and Susannah March 16 1758 (*sic*)
1755 Nov. 12 Vanost Isaac s. Isaac and —— Oct. 7 1755
1741 June 8 Varney Elizabeth d. Henry and Elizabeth 11 dys.
1738 April 13 Vernell Thomas s. John and Jane 18 mos.
1749 Feb. 6 Voto Sarah d. Paul Isaac and Sarah Feb. 5 1747
1713 May 12 Voyer Ann d. Peter and Judith 2 wks.
1716 Sept. 20 Mary d. Peter and Mary ——
1710 Feb. 5 Wade Ruth wife of William 21 yrs.

1710 Feb.   5 Wade Mary d. William and Ruth 1 yr.
1710 June 24   Catherine d. William and Ruth 2 wks.
1756 June 27 Wag John s. John and Mary May 31 1756
1741 Dec. 26 Wager Peter s. Peter and Margaret 4 yrs. 3 mos.
1741 Dec. 26   Mary d. Peter and Margaret 1 yr. 8 mos.
1759 Mch.   4   Mary d. Thomas and Mary Feb. 4 1759
1759 June 25 Wagg Jonathan s. John and Mary Feb. 27 1759
1734 Sept. 30 Waine Sarah d. Edward and Mary 8 mos.
1759 Oct. 14   Elizabeth d. Abraham and Mary Dec. 21 1753
1759 Oct. 14   Abraham s. Abraham and Mary Dec. 31 1755
1759 Oct. 14   Jacob s. Abraham and Mary May 3 1758
1710 Jan. 11 Waire Rebekah d. Lydia 1 yr.
1750 Dec. 28 Wakefield Elizabeth d. John and Elizabeth Dec. 4 1746
1742 July   5 Waldecker Conrat s. Conrat and Margaret 3 wks.
1744 Aug. 26 Waldron Thomas s. Edward and Sarah 6 mos.
1735 April 20 Waley Elizabeth d. Alexander and Mary 5 dys.
1735 April 20   Alexander s. Alexander and Mary 5 dys.
1711 Oct. 15 Walker Jane d. Richard and Christian 2 wks. 4 dys.
1720 Sept. 11   John s. David and Mary
1726 July 24   William s. David and Sarah ——
1728 Aug. 29   Mary d. Morris and Sarah 2 mos.
1732 Nov. 18   Susannah d. John and Elinor 10 wks.
1742 June 30 Wall Nathaniell s. Gurney and Martha 8 dys.
1760 May   10   Elizabeth d. Gurney and Margaret March 17 1760
1747 Aug.   3 Walters William s. William and Martha May 22 1747
1720 July   7 Wanless John s. William and Elizabeth May 24
1721 Dec.   3   Sarah d. William and Elizabeth P. B.
1723 Nov. 26   —— d. William and Elizabeth
1727 Sept. 20   William s. William and Elizabeth 2 wks.
1722 Feb. 22 Ward Edward s. Ralph and ——
1741 April 17   Mary d. Thomas and Ruth 10 wks.
1714 April 4 Warford Nathaniel s. Jeffrey and Jane 10 yrs.
1744 Oct.   8 Warmer Martha d. Thomas and Mary 14 dys.
1744 Oct.   8   Hannah d. Thomas and Mary 14 dys.
1731 Oct. 20 Warner William s. Jacob and Charity 5 wks.
1711 July 24 Warren Jacob s. Jacob and Mary 1 yr. 5 mos.
1721 Aug. 17   John s. John and Ann
1723 Jan. 25   Robert s. John and Mary from Bohemia Landing
1731 May   8   Sarah d. John and Anne 8½ yrs.
1731 May   8   Anne d. John and Anne 7 yrs.
1731 May   8   Bartholomew s. John and Anne 5 yrs. 4 mos.
1731 May   8   Hannah d. John and Anne 3 mos.
1750 May   27 Was Catherine d. John July 4 1748
1727 Jan.   4 Wassell John s. John and Ann 8 dys.
1739 Jan. 14   Catherine d. Luke and Ann 3 wks. 3 dys.

1748 Aug. 24 Waterby Richard s. Robert and Susannah June 25 1748
1728 Nov. 15 Waterfield James s. John and Elizabeth 2 wks.
1733 July 23 Waters Joseph s. Joseph and Anne 1 dy.
1733 July 23 John s. Joseph and Anne 1 dy.
1743 July 15 James s. William and Martha 12 dys.
1720 Jan. 17 Watkins Thomas s. Evan and Hester ——
1720 Aug. 2   John s. Thomas and Mary
1721 Aug. 6   Hester d. Evan and Hester July 7
1751 Mch. 14 Wats James s. Charles and Margaret Feb. 24 1750
1728 Jan. 10 Watson Rebecca d. Joseph and Frances 3 mos.
1733 Dec. 16 Elizabeth d. George and Mary 1 mo.
1735 Oct. 26 James s. George and Mary 21 dys.
1737 May   8   Mary d. George and Mary 1 mo.
1759 July 2   John s. Samuel and Mary June 16 1759
1759 Sept. 23 Patrick s. James and Christian July 10 1759
1760 Jan. 7   Watt John s. James and Martha Nov. 27 1759
1738 April 24 Watts John s. Samuel and Elanor 6 mos.
1744 Jan. 22 Wattson Samuel s. Luke and Ann 14 yrs. 7 mos. 5 dys.
1744 Jan. 22 Jane d. Luke and Ann 10 yrs. 11 mos. 3 wks.
1744 Jan. 22 Luke s. Luke and Ann 9 yrs. 10 mos. 3 wks.
1744 Jan. 22 Rebecca d. Luke and Ann 8 yrs. 1 mo. 13 dys.
1744 Jan. 22 Adam s. Luke and Ann ——
1729 Jan. 28 Way Elizabeth d. John and Mary 3 mos. 3 wks.
1752 June 12 Wayman Mary d. Edward and Rebecca March 10 1722
1731 Jan. 2   Wayne William s. Jacob and Elizabeth 4 dys.
1731 Mch. 30 William s. Edward and Mary 4 mos.
1733 June 23 Jacob s. Jacob and Elizabeth 10 dys.
1734 July 8   Abraham s. Jacob and Elizabeth 6 mos.
1733 Feb. 2   Webb Elizabeth d. Thomas and Margaret 6 wks.
1735 Aug. 3   Thomas s. Thomas and Margaret 3 wks.
1738 Oct. 15 Webber John s. Robert and Catherine 2 mos.
1732 June 27 Weed Mary d. Robert and Hannah 15 mos.
1720 Aug. 7   Weldon Grace d. John and Mary ——
1722 April 22 —— d. John and Grace ——
1726 Dec. 5   Rebecca d. Jonathan and Mary Oct. 6 1724
1726 Dec. 20 Mary d. John and Mary Oct. 1 1724
1727 Oct. 25 Grace d. John and Mary 9 mos.
1736 Aug. 24 Margaret d. John and Mary 1 yr.
1724 Feb. 27 Wells Mildred d. Henry and Mary 9 dys.
1726 Feb. 9   Henry s. Thomas and Mary ——
1732 June 5   George s. George and Jeoshabe 2 dys.
1743 Mch. 13 Cowley s. Thomas and Sarah 3 wks. 6 dys.
1744 Jan. 15 Mary d. George and Jane 10 dys.
1746 Sept. 7   William s. Thomas and Sarah July 27 1746
1748 April 3   Mary d. Thomas and Sarah Dec. 13 1747

1749 Oct.   29 Wells Sarah d. Thomas and Sarah Oct. 29 1749
1753 May   22   Hannah d. Thomas and Sarah Nov. 4 1751
1756 Mch.   11   Jehoshabe d. George and Lydia Jan. 3 1756
1747 June   14 Wendrige Mary d. John and Martha May 10 1747
1729 Nov.   5 Weasel Edward s. John and Ann 4 mos.
1728 July   14 West William s. William and Ellenor 2 wks.
1730 June   14   Thomas s. William and Ellenor 3 mos. 15 dys.
1733 Mch.   25   Charles s. William and Abigail 5 mos.
1734 Sept. 29   Mary d. Richard and Elizabeth 2 wks.
1735 Oct.   19   Jacob s. William and Abigail 3 mos. 4 dys.
1737 Nov.   21   Elizabeth d. Richard and Elizabeth 9 wks.
1759 June   7   Susannah d. Thomas and Susannah March 4 1759
1739 July   14 Westfield Richard s. John and Anne 1 mo.
1729 Dec.   30 Weston Martha d. Perregrine and Mary 5 mos.
1743 Jan.   2 Whalen William s. William and Mary 1 wk.
1732 Sept.   3 Wheldon Calon s. John and Mary 1 yr. 9 mos.
1734 June   30   John s. John and Mary 13 mos.
1741 Oct.   4   William s. John and Mary 3 yrs. 6 mos. 2 dys.
1744 Jan.   15   Mary d. William and Mary 10 wks. 6 dys.
1715 June   28 Whillingham William s. William and Mary 10 mos.
1748 Oct.   2 Whilton Mary d. James and Sarah Sept. 3 1746
1748 Oct.   2   Elizabeth d. James and Sarah Sept. 26 1748
1721 July   7 White Robert s. Robert and Jane Jan. 29 1721
1727 Oct.   8   Thomas s. Robert and Jane 3 wks.
1730 May   17   Elizabeth d. Joseph and Mary 5 mos.
1730 Aug.   3   Elizabeth d. Robert and Jane 1 yr.
1734 July   26   Anne d. Robert and Jane 3 yrs. 3 mos.
1734 July   26   Mary d. Robert and Mary 7 mos.
1734 July   28   Elizabeth d. John and Susannah 7 wks.
1737 April 20   Jane d. John and Jane 6 wks.
1739 Dec.   24   John s. John and Jane 2 yrs. 1 mo.
1739 Dec.   24   Martha d. John and Jane 5 wks.
1741 Nov.   19   Elizabeth d. James and Mary 3 mos.
1742 Mch.   14   Susannah d. John and Jane 1 mo. 3 dys.
1742 July   9   Sarah d. Townsend and Anne 2 mos.
1744 Jan.   8   Rebecca d. John and Jane 1 mo.
1747 Dec.   28   Townsend s. Townsend and Anne Feb. — 1747
1748 May   25   William s. Thomas and Esther March 24 1748
1749 May   10   Mary d. Thomas and Hester April 2 1749
1749 Aug.   11   Anne d. Townsend and Anne April 3 1749
1750 Oct.   29   John s. Townsend and Anne July 30 1750
1753 July   25   Isabella d. Townsend and Anne June 26 1753
1754 Sept. 28   Thomas s. James and Sarah Sept. 18 1754
1755 July   27   Martha d. John and Elizabeth July 6 1755
1757 May   10   John s. John and Elizabeth April 15 1757

1759 May   13 White Mary d. William and Elizabeth March 2 1759
1759 Aug.   1   David s. John and Jane Jan. 11 1757
1759 Aug.   1   John s. John and Jane July 30 1759
1759 Aug.   11   Sarah d. James and Jane Jan. 22 1758
1759 Aug.   11   Elizabeth d. James and Jane April 23 1759
1759 Oct.   10   Anne d. Townsend and Anne July 15 1759
1786 Dec.   6 Whitebread Hannah d. William and Mary 2 wks.
1738 Jan.   6   William s. William and Mary 7 mos.
1739 Sept.   10   Mary d. William and Mary 1 mo.
1741 Mch.   29   George s. William and Mary 2 mos. 2 dys.
1743 May   15   Ann d. William and Mary 1 mo.
1741 Mch.   29 Whitehead Elizabeth d. Robert and Jane 6 wks.
1749 July   29   Mary d. Robert and Hannah June 1 1749
1758 April   16   William s. Robert and Hannah Feb. 24 1758
1743 July   3 Whiteley Mary d. Anthony and Mary 11 mos. 25 dys.
1749 May   29   Abigail wife of Anthony
1755 Aug.   30 Whitelock Sarah d. Thomas and Ann Aug. 2 1755
1759 Oct.   8   Thomas s. Thomas and Ann June 10 1759
1760 Aug.   15   Thomas s. Thomas and Ann 9 wks.
1745 June   16 Whitepain John s. Jachariah and Sarah Jan. 16 1743
1752 Aug.   17   Anne d. Jachariah and Sarah April 27 1748
1752 Aug.   17   William s. Jachariah and Sarah July 4 1751
1751 June   2 Whitesides Rebekkah d. James and Margary May 16 1735
1757 Sept.   20 Whitlock Elizabeth d. Thomas and Ann July 24 1757
1743 June   5 Whiton Mary d. James and Sarah 10 mos. 2 wks.
1744 June   3 Whitton James s. James and Sarah 3 mos. 23 dys.
1759 April   6 Whyte Mary d. Robert and Jane Jan. 12 1759.
1742 Nov.   24 Wicklow David s. David and Frances 3 wks. 1 dy.
1758 Aug.   23 Wigmore James s. Daniel and Frances July 1 1758
1738 Dec.   6 Wilcocks Thomas s. John and Elizabeth 2 wks.
1740 April   23 Wilcox John s. John and Elizabeth 2 wks.
1744 April   4   Elizabeth d. John and Elizabeth 5 wks. 1 dy.
1746 Mch.   12   Benjamin s. John and Elizabeth Feb. 5 1745
1736 Nov.   21 Wilieff John s. Rodolph and Mary 2 wks.
1721 Oct.   27 Wilkinson Ann d. Anthony and Elizabeth 4 yrs.
1728 July   31   Elizabeth d. Anthony and Elizabeth 2 yrs. 2 mos.
1728 July   31   Rebecca d. Anthony and Elizabeth 2 wks.
1731 April   29   Margaret d. Anthony and Elizabeth 2 wks.
1731 Nov.   17   Ann d. Gabriel and Sarah 2 wks.
1734 July   7   Gabriel s. Gabriel and Sarah 16 yrs.
1734 Oct.   21   Sarah d. Gabriel and Sarah 1 mo.
1735 Feb.   22   Anthony s. Anthony and Elizabeth 1 wk.
1737 Jan.   24   Rebecca d. Gabriel and Sarah 2 mos.
1738 Sept.   2   Mary d. Gabriel and Sarah 1 mo.
1740 Jan.   27   Anne d. John and Jane 2 wks.

1740 Nov.	2	Wilkinson Gabriel s. Gabriel and Sarah 5 mos. 7 dys.
1741 April	19	Elizabeth d. John and Jane 2 wks. 2 dys.
1742 Mch.	28	John s. Brian and Hester 1 wk.
1746 Mch.	19	Elizabeth d. Brian and Hester Feb. 17 1745
1748 Nov.	6	Mary d. Brian and Hester Sept. 18 1748
1751 April	21	Anthony s. Brian and Hester March 25 1750
1753 Sept.	19	Rebekkah d. Brian and Hester Aug. 22 1753
1755 June	10	Elizabeth d. Jeremiah and Elizabeth Jan. 18 1755
1756 April	28	John s. John and Mary March 8 1756
1758 June	4	Hester d. Brian and Hester May 17 1758
1759 May	23	Eleanor d. John and Mary May 4 1759
1727 Sept.	15	Willard Thomas s. Benjamin and Sarah 6 wks.
1727 Nov.	17	Arthur s. John and Margaret 3 mos.
1730 June	16	Ann d. Benjamin and Sarah 1 mo.
1748 Sept.	25	Willdecker Fanny d. Conrade and Margret Aug. 15 1748
1736 Jan.	28	Willett George s. Peter and Ruth 6 dys.
1710 Feb.	3	Williams Peeter s. John and Mary 2 wks.
1710 Feb.	3	Georg and Joseph s. John and Annie born and baptised
1714 April	10	Samuel s. John and Mary 2 yrs. 6 mos.
1715 April	10	Phœbe d. John and Mary 4 dys.
1717 Dec.	27	Annie d. Hannah 9 dys.
1720 Feb.	21	Rachel d. Nicolas and Hannah ——
1723 June	18	John s. John and Sarah P.B.
1726 July	31	Jane d. John and Mary ——
1726 Oct.	14	John s. Charles and Mary Sept. 29
1728 July	5	Mary d. Charles and Mary 11 wks.
1728 Dec.	17	James s. William and Catherine 1 yr.
1730 Sept.	19	Nicolas s. Nicolas and Rachel 11 mos.
1731 Oct.	1	Charles s. Charles and Mary 22 mos.
1731 Oct.	1	George s. Charles and Mary 11 dys.
1733 Nov.	19	William s. Charles and Mary 3 wks.
1734 July	23	Edward s. Edward and Jane 10 mos.
1736 Sept.	4	Susannah d. Thomas and Rebecca 10 dys.
1736 Sept.	4	Deborah d. Thomas and Rebecca 10 dys.
1738 Feb.	8	Benjamin s. Charles and Mary 2 wks.
1738 June	9	John s. Edward and Jane 8 mos.
1738 Sept.	3	Charles s. Adam and Hester 2 dys.
1739 Feb.	14	Sarah d. Thomas and Rebecca 4 mos. 2 wks.
1739 Feb.	14	Elizabeth d. Thomas and Rebecca 4 mos. 2 wks.
1739 April	23	Sarah d. Elizabeth 3 mos.
1739 July	18	Rachel d. Adam and Hester 1 dy.
1739 July	30	Anne d. John and Anne 8 dys.
1740 June	3	Elizabeth d. Charles and Mary 10 wks.
1741 June	24	John s. Adam and Hester 5 mos.
1744 Feb.	24	William s. Thomas and Rebecca 27 dys.

1744 Dec.   18 Williams Samuel s. Edward and Jane 3 mos.
1745 May   26   Elizabeth d. Adam and Sarah Oct. 4 1744
1745 June   24   Mark s. Phillip Dec. 25 1729
1746 Mch.   23   Mary d. Thomas and Rebecca Dec. 4 1745
1748 May   15   Hannah d. Morris and Lettice May 11 1737
1748 June   12   Thomas s. Thomas and Rebecca May 8 1748
1749 June   25   William s. Thomas and Rebecca May 1 1749
1754 Feb.   8   Robert s. James and Deborah Jan. 16 1754
1755 June   12   Mary d. William and Susannah Jan. 17 1755
1756 Feb.   3   Elizabeth d. William and Elizabeth Jan. 24 1755
1756 Nov.   17   James s. John and Sarah Sept. 8 1756
1757 July   26   John s. Charles and Rachel Oct. 22 175—
1757 Oct.   6   Samuel s. Thomas and Rebecca Aug. 10 1757
1757 Oct.   18   William s. Samuel and Sarah July 17 1757
1758 Jan.   20   Joseph s. John and Sarah Oct. 8 1757
1758 Oct.   4   Silvanus s. William and Susannah Sept. 2 1758
1759 Aug.   31   Catherine d. John and Sarah Sept. 12 1758
1760 Oct.   20   James s. Phillip and Rachel Oct. 16 1760
1783 Dec.   22 Williamson Elizabeth d. Henry and Lydia 10 dys.
1785 July   10   William s. Henry and Lydia 6 dys.
1787 April 11   John s. Henry and Lydia 12 dys.
1788 Dec.   27   Thomas s. William and Sarah 2 yrs.
1739 Feb.   2   Henry s. Henry and Lydia 2 wks. 5 dys.
1741 April 27   Martha d. Henry and Lydia 3 wks. 5 dys.
1723 Aug.   10 Williard John s. John and Mary ——
1782 Nov.   12   Isaac 28 yrs.
1783 June   20   Rebecca d. Joseph and Margaret 2 wks.
1783 Sept.   8   Benjamin s. Benjamin and Sarah 5 yrs. 3 wks.
1783 Sept.   3   Samuel s. Benjamin and Sarah 2 yrs. 1 mo.
1783 Sept.   3   Sarah d. Benjamin and Sarah 4 mos. 1 wk.
1736 Jan.   7   James s. Benjamin and Sarah 1 yr.
1736 Nov.   2   Mary d. Richard and Dina 2 yrs. 3 mos.
1782 Mch.   14 Willing Thomas s. Charles and Anne 12 wks.
1733 Aug.   9   Anne d. Charles and Anne 3 wks. 5 dys.
1785 Aug.   18   Dorothy d. Charles and Anne 15 dys.
1788 July   6   Anne wife of Charles 28 yrs.
1788 July   6   Charles s. Charles and Anne 5 wks.
1741 Aug.   4   Mary d. Charles and Anne 10 mos. 8 dys.
1743 Sept. 15   Elizabeth d. Charles and Anne 7 mos. 5 dys.
1745 Oct.   4   Richard s. Charles and Anne Jan. 2 1744
1749 Nov.   9   Joseph s. Charles and Anne Oct. 13 1749
1751 Feb.   9   James s. Charles and Sarah Feb. 9 1750
1758 Feb.   14   Margaret d. Charles and Sarah ——
1713 Aug.   24 Willis Thomas s. Richard and Elizabeth 3 wks.
1739 June   24   Thomas s. Thomas and Sarah 3 wks.

1732 Aug.	15	Willmott John Reed s. James and Frances 15 mos.
1751 Nov.	26	Wills Joseph s. Joseph and Margret Oct. 1 1751
1744 Feb.	4	Willson Martha d. John and Mary 3 yrs. 10 mos.
1744 Feb.	4	Mary d. John and Mary 20 dys.
1731 Nov.	21	Willy Anne d. Alexander and Mary 2 wks.
1715 Sept.	1	Wilson Bethia d. John and Mary 2 wks.
1718 Feb.	12	Mary d. John and Mary Born 26 Jan.
1735 Aug.	14	Mary d. Abraham and Mary 5 wks.
1737 June	26	Abraham s. Abram and Mary 3 mos. 2 wks.
1753 Nov.	28	Anne d. David and Mary Aug. 10 1753
1746 April	23	Wincles Frances d. John and Susannah Feb. 7 1745
1745 May	29	Winkle Elizabeth d. John and Susannah Dec. 13 1744
1720 Oct.	16	Winstarley William s. James and Mary Sept. 17
1736 May	8	Winter Michael s. Michael and Sarah 2 yrs. 2 mos.
1733 Sept.	30	Winton Hannah d. William and Mary 8 mos.
1746 Aug.	8	Wipton William s. Jachariah and Sarah Jan. 28 1745
1736 Jan.	25	Wiser David s. Daniel Wooldrick and Elonor 1 mo.
1737 Nov.	13	Wisinger Eve d. Daniel and Mary Barbara 8 dys.
1757 Feb.	3	Witbey James s. John and Mary Oct. 24 1756
1711 Sept.	1	Wivell Edward s. William and Mary ——
1712 Aug.	17	Mary d. William and Mary 2 dys.
1739 Oct.	8	Wizengar Maria Catherine d. Daniel and Mary 3 wks.
1760 April	24	Wondsly Margaret d. Emanuel and Jane March 1 1760
1732 Dec.	12	Wood George s. John and Mary 3 wks.
1784 July	8	Elizabeth d. Daniel and Mary 2 mos.
1736 Sept.	5	Samuel s. Daniel and Mary 2 mos.
1737 Feb.	1	John s. John and Mary 11 mos.
1737 Oct.	15	Elizabeth d. John and Hannah 3 mos.
1737 Nov.	21	Elizabeth d. John and Hannah 4 mos.
1746 Aug.	8	Mary d. John and Elizabeth Feb. 4 1737
1746 Aug.	8	Elizabeth d. John and Elizabeth Jan. 1 1743
1752 May	20	Catherine d. John and Anne April 17 1752
1754 Feb.	1	William s. Robert and Mary July 1 1753
1754 May	7	George s. George and Anne March 6 1754
1756 July	23	Margaret d. Joseph and Mary April 25 1751
1756 July	23	Mary d. Joseph and Mary Aug. 1 1753
1756 July	23	William s. Joseph and Mary June 4 1756
1731 April	9	Woodfield Samuel s. Thomas and Mary 3 wks.
1733 Jan.	20	Mary d. Thomas and Mary 2 wks. 4 dys.
1746 May	25	Joseph s. Thomas and Mary July 10 1744
1723 Nov.	15	Woodrop Ann d. Alexander and Ann ——
1726 Jan.	26	Elizabeth d. Alexander and Ann ——
1731 April	11	Hannah d. Alexander and —— 16 dys.
1784 June	1	Francis Alexander s. Alexander and Ann 12 dys.
1737 May	13	Sarah d. Alexander and Anne 6 mos.

1721 Dec. 15 Woodros William s. Alexander and Ann Nov. 20
1740 Jan. 11 Woods Lucy d. Peter and Margaret 6 wks.
1731 Nov. 24 Woolard John s. John and Margaret 1 yr. 2 wks.
1743 Mch. 9 Worrel Demas s. Isaiah and Rachel 5 wks.
1745 June 26 Rachel d. Isaiah and Rachel May 23 1745
1739 Sept. 18 Worrell Timothy s. Isaac and Rachel 1 dy.
1740 Sept. 21 Jaecheus s. Isaac and Rachel 1 mo.
1735 Aug. 20 Wort Anna Maria Magdalena d. Conradus and Anne 3 dys.
1753 Sept. 26 Wosedale Mary d. William and Mary Sept. 20 1753
1727 May 31 Wostle Robert s. Phillip and Mary 6 wks.
1731 Mch. 18 Wrath Mary d. William and Sarah 2 yrs. 5 mos.
1731 Mch. 18 Rachel d. Thomas and Sarah 6 dys.
1732 Sept. 16 Sarah d. William and Sarah 3 wks.
1734 Oct. 5 William s. William and Sarah 1 mo.
1736 Aug. 29 Leah d. William and Sarah 1 dy.
1738 July 18 Robert s. William and Sarah 8 dys.
1748 May 1 Wriggins William s. William and Mary Feb. 14 1748
1726 Oct. 15 Wright Moses s. Moses and Susannah July 15
1730 July 7 William s. Elisha and Mary 2 wks.
1734 Dec. 29 Anne d. William and Deborah 7 dys.
1745 Dec. 8 John s. John and Jane Dec. 9 1740
1752 July 12 Matthew s. William and Onner July 7 1752
1760 Oct. 26 William s. John and Mary 6 wks.
1735 Aug. 6 Wyatt Sarah d. Edward and Mary 1 mo.
1737 Sept. 11 Dorothy d. Edward and Mary 3 wks.
1737 April 10 Yeaton Elizabeth d. Randall and Jane 1 yr.
1741 Feb. 24 James s. Randall and Jane 1 yr.
1737 Feb. 7 Yeats Sarah d. John and Elizabeth 5 yrs. 10 mos.
1754 Feb. 21 John s. John and Elizabeth Aug. 17 1743
1754 Feb. 21 Joseph s. John and Elizabeth April 9 1745
1739 Sept. 26 Yehton Elizabeth d. Randall and Jane 2 wks. 3 dys.
1728 Dec. 15 Yeomans Elizabeth d. John and Margaret 2 yrs. 1 mo.
1728 Dec. 20 Joseph s. John and Margaret 7 mos. 3 wks.
1738 Jan. 9 Yetton James s. Randal and Jane 4 dys.
1737 Dec. 18 Yong William s. John and Anne 7 wks.
1750 Oct. 18 York Martha d. Thomas and Mary June 11 1747
1750 Oct. 18 Margret d. Thomas and Mary March 22 1749
1751 June 19 David s. Thomas and Mary May 23 1751
1755 April 24 Mary d. Thomas and Mary March 26 1755
1757 July 19 Elinor d. Thomas and Mary June 24 1757
1712 Mch. 16 Young Elizabeth d. John and Catherine 8 dys.
1725 Oct. 29 Elizabeth d. Henry and Judith ——
1725 Nov. 19 James s. William and Joanna 1 yr. 7 mos.
1725 Nov. 19 Elizabeth d. William and Joanna 10 wks.

1727 Nov.	10	Young Mary d. William and Elizabeth 6 wks.
1780 Feb.	2	Joannah d. William and Joannah 3 wks. 2 dys.
1739 Mch.	14	Thomas s. John and Anne 1 mo.
1740 June	18	John s. John and Anne 7 mos.
1742 Dec.	22	Charles s. John and Anne 2 mos. 4 dys.
1745 April	22	Samuel s. John and Anne April 18 1744.
1745 Oct.	7	Louisa d. John and Anne Sept. 5 1745
1747 June	21	Anne d. John and Anne April 28 1747
1749 May	21	Rebecca d. John and Anne Nov. 22 1748
1751 April	20	Charles s. John and Anne March 20 1750
1752 Oct.	25	James s. John and Anne Sept. 16 1752
1754 Aug.	7	Edward s. Thomas and Ann April 11 1754
1754 Nov.	17	Thomas Grame s. James and Jane Oct. 22 1754.
1756 Dec.	8	Ann d. James and Ann Nov. 5 1756
1757 Feb.	1	Lucy d. John and Anna July 12 1756
1757 Dec.	2	John s. John and Jane Nov. 6 1757
1759 Oct.	8	Frances d. John and Anne Aug. 15 1759
1760 Aug.	28	Elizabeth d. Elizabeth Aug. 27 1759
1728 Aug.	25	Yowell Sarah d. Andrew and Elizabeth 2 mos.
1788 Feb.	12	Zefferance Abigail d. John and Elizabeth 3 mos.
1742 May	13	Zetfrance Mary d. John and Elizabeth 5 dys.
1714 Oct.	15	Zodong Hannah d. Peter and Ann 1 yr. 10 mos.

NOTES AND QUERIES.

Notes.

WHARTON'S STOREHOUSES OCCUPIED BY THE BRITISH COMMISSARY DEPARTMENT, 1777–78.

" This is to certifie to Daniel Wier Esq. Commissary General &c., that on the 21st December last I took possession of Mr. Thomas Wharton's Sen' Stores at Carpenter's Wharf consisting of two detached Buildings. The one on the North Side having Six Rooms on the Ground floor, with as many on the first floor beside the same number of Garretts for Bread &c & on the South Side I had four Rooms, which I turned into two Stores ; and that I have occupied them for his Majesty's use untill this day, Intending totally to clear them and deliver up the Keys tomorrow.
" Philadelphia 30 May 1778

" A KNICHT
Commiss'.

" To DANIEL WIER,
" Commissary General &c."

LAMBERTS OF NEW JERSEY.—The following records are taken from an old sheet of paper loaned to the contributor:

Abigail Lambert, Born May 2ᵈ 1742,
Mary Lambert, Born April 14, 1744,
Sarah Lambert, Born febʳʸ 11ᵗʰ 1746,
Elizabeth Lambert, Born October 8 1749,
John Lambert, Born April 30 1752.

H.

FROM A LETTER FROM JOHN WOOLMAN TO ABRAHAM FARRINGTON.

" MOUNT HOLLY 1ᵈᵃ 10ᵐᵒ 1757

" . . . After raising 1000 men in this province by a draft of the Militia to go out on an Emergency, was fresh orders in our County to draft 8 times yᵗ number to hold yᵐselves in readiness to march at any time when called upon. In this Second draft several young men of our Society were chosen. On the day appointed to meet the Captain in our Town, several of our young men not less than 4 or 5, came and acquainted him in Substance as follows that for Conscience Sake they could not fight nor hire any one to go in their Stead, and that they should not go out of his way. They were all dismist at that time, with orders to remain in readiness, and soon after came accounts from the General, that they were not likely to want them this time. It was a day of deep Tryal to the young men, yet the Effect it appeared to have on their minds was such, that I thought I saw the kindness of providence in it. . . . In the first draft I know not of any of our young men in our town being drafted, but in some places they were, and such who stood True to their principles though they were taken away and nearly tryed I have not heard that the officers were Inclineing to Severity. . . .
" Our Late Governor Died about 3 weeks past, and John Reading at present succeeds in yᵉ administration." . . .

EXTRACT FROM A MANUSCRIPT LETTER FROM JOSEPH BRINGHURST TO JOHN MORTON.

"BRISTOL, PA., 10th of 7th mo. 1794.

"I went over to Burlington yesterday forenoon and on my way down to the boat, returning, I stopped at the house of Richard or Thos. Gardner, mention'd in our ancient records; a man was sitting at the door, whose name is Gardner, a great great Grandson of its first proprietor; on expressing a curiosity to go into the house, he civilly invited me to walk in, and shewed me the room in which the first yearly meeting of Friends for Pennsylvania & New Jersey was held, in the year 1682, or thereabouts, according to our record, tho' Jno. Gough in 1683, says it had been held at Burlington for the past four years. However it was, the number that attended must have been small, for I don't think the room is as large as thy front parlour, and the present possessor thinks it has remained without alteration since the house was built. It is a frame house, and I think (tho' it bears the marks of antiquity) has stood the test of time tolerably well."

At the date of the letter, Bringhurst was stopping in Bristol for the benefit of his health, using the "cold bath" and drinking the "mineral water."

THE WELSH TRACT.—It is well known that the first purchasers of Pennsylvania lands were frequently only trustees or agents of some "company," who, as individuals, could not afford to secure the land they required in large enough tracts to insure good locations. Whether or not these trustees or agents were occasionally speculators and profited by the transaction, either through the advance prices paid for very choice lots, or from a commission paid by Penn or his agents on these sales, does not always appear, but that in some instances they were prompted by a desire to help their countrymen and frequently their kinsmen, as well as to assist in establishing a permanent and entirely safe retreat for those oppressed on account of their religious or political opinions, is very evident, and especially is apparent in the circumstances connected with the founding of that Cymric plantation in Pennsylvania known as the "Welsh Barony," or more usually the "Great Welsh Tract." Some of the first purchasers for the Welsh Quakers and the acres of land patented were—

Richard Davies, Welspoole, Montgomery . . .	5000	acres.
Edward Prichard (ap Richard)	2500	"
Charles Lloyd, Dalobrom, and Margaret Davies . .	5000	"
John ap John, Rhuabon, Denbigh, and Dr. Thomas Wynne, Flintshire	5000	"
Lewis David, Llandewy Velfrey, Pembroke . . .	3000	"
John Bevan, Treverig, Glamorgan . . .	2000	"
John Thomas, Llaethgwm, and Dr. Edward Jones, Bala	5000	"
Richard Thomas, Whitford Garne	5000	"

A large part of these tracts were surveyed in Merion, Haverford, or Radnor. The price paid for each five thousand acres was one hundred pounds.

The conveyances from these patentees to proposed settlers were executed usually in Wales, and as the place of residence and occupation or profession of each grantee is impartially set forth, the list should be of great interest as showing the class of settlers composing this portion of the colony, and will no doubt be useful to the genealogist in determining definitely from what parish a settler came.

These deeds were recorded in Pennsylvania :

Conveyances from Richard Davies, dated 19/20 June, 30/31 July, 1682.
Richard Miles, Llanvihangel Velgyen Parish, Merioneth, weaver.
John Evans, Nantmell Parish, Radnor, gentleman.
James Price, Mothvery Parish, Carmarthen, gentleman.
Richard Humphrey, Llan Glynin, Merioneth, gentleman.
Margaret James, Newchurch Parish, Radnor, spinster.
Roger Hughes, Llanishangell Rhydrython, Radnor, gentleman.
David Meredith, Llanlister, Radnor, weaver.
Ellis Maurice, Dolgynecha, Merioneth, gentleman.
Lewis Owen, Gwanas, Merioneth, gentleman.
Richard Conn, Langunllo Parish, Radnor, glover.
Rowland Owen, Gwanas, Merioneth, gentleman.
Thomas Jones, Glascombe, Radnor, gentleman.
Richard Cooke, Langunllo, Radnor, glover.
Edward Owen, "late of Dolserey," Merioneth, gentleman.
John Lloyd, Dissart Parish, Radnor, glover.
John Roberts, Llangian Parish, Caernarvon, gentleman.
Edward Jones, St. Harmon Parish, Radnor, gentleman.
Evan John William, Llangylynin, Merioneth, gentleman.
Evan ap William, Llanwchreth, Merioneth, gentleman.
David Evans, Llanwchreth, Merioneth, gentleman.
Ellis Jones, Nantmell Parish, Radnor, weaver.
Rowland Ellis, Bryn-Mawr, Merioneth, gentleman.
Evan Oliver, Glascombe Parish, Radnor, gentleman.

Conveyances from Lewis David, dated May, 1682.
William Howell, Castlebigch, Pembroke, yeoman.
Henry Lewis, Narbarth Parish, Pembroke, yeoman.
Rees Rotheroe, Lanwenog Parish, Cardigan, yeoman.
Evan Thomas, Lanykeaven, Pembroke, yeoman.

Conveyances from John ap John and Dr. Thomas Wynne, 1682–1687.
John Roberts, Pennycklowd, Denbigh, yeoman.
Isaac Wheeldon, Lancoost, glover.
Owen Fouke, Bettws y Coed, Carnarvon, tanner.
Thomas Taylor.
Richard Davids.
Owen Parry, Dynhunllo issa, Denbigh, yeoman.
Trial Rider, Wrexham, flax-dresser.
Mary *Fouk*.
Howell James, Radnor, Pennsylvania.
Philip James, Philadelphia.

Conveyances from John ap Thomas and Dr. Edward Jones, dated 1 April and 18 March, 1682, all of Merioneth.
*Hugh Roberts, Ciltalgarth Township, yeoman.
Robert David, Gwern Evel Ismynydd, yeoman.
Evan Rees, Penmaen, grocer.
John Edwards, Nanlleidiog, yeoman.
Edward Owen, "late of Doleysere," gentleman.
William ap Edward, Ueneldri, yeoman.
*Edward Rees, Ciltalgarth, yeoman.
William Jones, Bettws, yeoman.
Thomas ap Richard, Nantlleidiog, yeoman.

Rees John William, Llanglynin, yeoman.
Thomas Lloyd, Llangouer, yeoman.
Cadwallader Morgan, Gwernefee, yeoman.
John Watkins, Gwernefee, batchiler.
Hugh John Nantlleidiog, yeoman.
Gainor Robert, Ciltalgarth, spinster.

Conveyances from Charles Lloyd and Margaret Davies, dated 1683, all
    grantees of Montgomeryshire.
  *Thomas Morris, Marchnant Issa, yeoman.
  Thomas Jones, Llanwthin Parish.
  Edward Thomas, Llanwthin Parish.
  Margaret Thomas, Garthlwlch, widow.
  *John Humphrey, of Llanwthin, yeoman, 312½ acres; dated 24 April,
    1683. Witnesses: Thomas Lloyd, Richard Davies, Richard Owen,
    Amos Davies, Rowland Ellis, David Davies, Solomon Jones.

A few of these grantees did not come to Pennsylvania, but changed
their minds and sold out their lands to others. Among other such conveyances is one from Lewis Owen and Rowland Owen, of Gwanas, and
Ellis Morris, of Dolgunucha, to Thomas Ellis, of Isoregenan, "in said
county,"—*i.e.*, Merioneth,—gentleman, dated June 30, 1683, for all of
their Pennsylvania land, the witnesses being Richard Davies, Morris
Ellis, Owen Lewis, Evan Harry, John Humphrey.

The John Humphrey here mentioned was identical with John Humphrey, of "Llanwthin," or Llanwddyn, who was brother to Owen Humphrey, of Llwyn-du, Merionethshire, and brother-in-law to Richard
Humphrey, whose sister Jane he married. It should be mentioned here
that some of those called here yeomen are elsewhere described as gentlemen. Such cases as have come especially under the notice of the writer
are marked thus *.   T. A. GLENN.

LETTER OF THOMAS JEFFERSON, 1806.—We are indebted to Dr. William L. Shoemaker for a copy of the following letter:

                               "MONTICELLO, July 26, 06.

"SIR:
"I find my mill considerably less advanced than was expected. She
will not be ready by a month or two as soon as had been promised. I
would advise therefore that your son should not come on till further
notice from me, which you shall certainly receive in due time.

"The drought here is beyond every thing known in the history of this
country. I pass five rivers from the Potomac to this place; not one of
which passes as much water as will turn a mill. I have known the river
on which mine is, intimately, for 50 years. There never was a time
before when it had less than 4 times its present current of water. After
taking off what now turns my tollmill, there is not more left in the
stream than would turn another. It's navigation is entirely over, nor,
with even seasonable weather, can it be expected to be so recruited as
to afford navigation till mid-winter. Both merchants & millers refuse
to receive wheat, which will therefore all lie on the farmer's hands till
the river is replenished. Our hope is that as nothing like this was ever
seen before, so it will never be seen again. I salute you with esteem &
respect.
                                    "TH. JEFFERSON.

"Mr. Shoemaker."

" DAVID BARCLAY of Cheapside where he resided above 70 Years, died at Bush-hill near Enfield in 3 mo : 1769—with that universal Reputation for laudable Industry, strict Probity, unaffected Benevolence & Liberality which will perpetuate his mem' with Honour & Respect to the latest Posterity.   He had the singular Honour of receiving under his Roof three successive Kings on their Accession to the Throne when they favoured the City with their Royal Presence.

" GEORGE DILLWYN."

ESLER-DIEFENDORFF RECORDS.—" Henry Esler born in Zurich Switzerland, emigrated to North America in the year 1758 died 1770.   Mary Frey Esler his wife died in Frankford Pa 1792.   Anna Maria Esler Diefendorff daughter of Henry and Mary Esler was born in Frankford Pa. in 1763 died in Portsmouth Va. in the year 1807.   Barbara Esler Folkroth born in Fd Pa. 1766.   Died in Frankford Pennsylvania—July 19 1848.

" James Potts Died in Wilmington Delaware Sep. 28, 1860.   Elizabeth E. Diefendorff Potts obit June 9 1866.   Jacob Diefendorff born in Germany in 1677, obit 1781.   George Diefendorff his son born in Germany in 1709 obit 1815.   John Hendree Diefendorff son of Geo Diefendorff born in the State of New York Montgomery County in $\left\{\begin{array}{l} 1745 \\ \text{obit 1802.} \end{array}\right.$ Anne M. E. Diefendorff wife of John H. Diefendorff born 1763 obit 1807.

" In the War of the Spanish Succession the Lower Palatinate in Germany was ravaged by the French and laid waste by fire and sword. Thousands of the terrified inhabitants, reduced to poverty, fled for protection to the camp of the Duke of Marlborough who with Prince Eugène commanded the allied Army.   In 1709 Queen Anne learning the condition of these suffering people sent a fleet to Rotterdam and conveyed seven thousand of them to England.   Three Thousand of them were assisted to Emigrate to America.   Most of them settled in Pennsylvania and North Carolina—a few in the State of New York. Among the latter, was—one ancestor John Jacob Diefendorff who with his wife and five sons settled in Montgomery County New York in Danube township about seven miles from fort Plain where he died at the advanced age of one hundred and four in the year—1781.

" His sons were, Rudolph who perished at Sea.   George who lived on the farm of his Grandson Peter Garlock—Died 1815.

" Third son John Jacob whose descendants are settled about three miles from Fort Plain.

" Henry who was killed in the battle of Oriska August 5 1777—Settled near Fort Plain."

HOW TOWNSHIPS IN NEW JERSEY WERE CONSTITUTED.—Dr. Henry Race, of Pittstown, New Jersey, writes to the *Hunterdon Republican :* " For several years we were desirous of knowing by what authority and at what date the several colonial townships were constituted.   The histories of New Jersey are silent on the subject and the colonial laws give no information about it.   We recently found the solution to the problem in one of the books of deeds and concessions in the colonial record office.   The townships were constituted by patents issued by the governor in the name and under the authority of the British sovereign.

" The following is the patent for the township of Amwell :

" ' Anne by the Grace of God of England Scotland France and Ireland Queen Defender of the Faith &c., to all to whom these Presents may come or may concern GREETING Know Ye that we of our special grace our certain knowledge and meer motion have granted and by these presents do grant for us our heirs and successors to the men and inhabitants and their successors inhabiting above the uppermost bounds of that tract of land commonly known by the name of the thirty thousand acres in the County of Burlington in the Western Division of our Province of New Jersey on the Eastern Shore of the Delaware River Beginning at the line of the land commonly known by the name of the thirty thousand acres and thence running as high as the upper end of Panamsung from thence with a northeast course to the land of partition between the Eastern and Western Division of the Province aforesaid; so along the partition line to the line of thirty acres; thence running along the line of the thirty thousand acres to the River Delaware where first began. To be and remain in a perpetual township or community in word and deed To be called and known by the the name of the Township of Amwell and we further grant to the said inhabitants of the Township aforesaid and their successors to Chuse Anealy a Constable Overseer of the Poor and Overseer of the Highways for the Township aforesaid and to enjoy all the privileges rights liberties and Immunities that any other Township in our said Province do or may of right enjoy and the said Inhabitants are hereby constituted and appointed a Township by the name aforesaid. To have and enjoy the privileges aforesaid to them and their successors forever. In Testimony Whereof we have caused these our letters to be made patents Witness our right trusty and right well beloved cousen Edward Viscount Cornbury or Captaine General and Governor in Chief in and over our Provinces of New Jersey New York and all the territories and tracts of land dependent thereon in America and Vice Admiral of the same &c this Eighth day of June in the Seventh year of our reign Anno Dom. 1708 J. Bass Secretary.'

"The 'Act for dividing and ascertaining the Boundaries of all the Counties,' passed Jan. 21, 1709–10, includes, in the description of Burlington County, the territory 'along the Line of Partition, (between West and East Jersey,) by *Maidenhead* and *Hopewell*, to the northernmost and uttermost Bounds of the township of *Amwell;*' and the Act for erecting Hunterdon County, March 11, 1713–14, includes 'all and singular the Lands and upper Parts of the Western Division of the Province.' This shows, without uncertainty, that the township of Amwell comprised originally all of West Jersey above the line of Hopewell Township, which was also a boundary of Dr. Daniel Coxe's thirty-thousand-acre tract.

"Amwell Township was patented June 8, 1708; Readington, called 'Reading,' July 15, 1730, and Kingwood and Bethlehem have not yet been found. The patents for many townships have never been found and perhaps were never recorded."

LYNN—MARSHALL.—Joseph Lynn Senyore was born the 14th of June in the year of our Lord 1691.

Joseph Lynn Senyore was married the 25th of December in the year of our Lord 1712—

Joseph Lyn Juner was born the 22nd day of Aprell in the morning betwixt 8 or 9 of the clock in ye year of our Lord 1716.

John Lyn was born the 17th of September at half an hour after 11 at night in the year of our Lord 1718.

Elizabeth Lyn was born ye 13th of June at 26 minutes after 9 in the Morning in the year of our Lord 1720, and the Second day of the week.

Martha Lyn was born the 29th of May at 50 minutes after Eleven in the morning and in the year of our Lord 1722.

Esther Lyn was born the 19th of February at 35 minutes after one in the morning and in the morning and in the year of our Lord 1724.

Susanah Lyn was born ye 20th of September between two and three in the morning and in the year of our Lord 1725.

The Second Susanah Lyn was born the 18th of December between two and three in the morning and in the year of our Lord 1726.

Seth Lyn was born the 29th of September 3/4 after eleven at night and dyed the 27th of November following.

Martha Lyn wife of —— departed this Life 16th of August 1736 at 8 Oclock in the evening.

Joseph Lyn Senr was married to his Wife Sarah the 25th of May 1737.

Jeremiah Lyn was born the 22nd of February about 4 of the Clock in the morning, in the year 1738.

Sarah Lyn was born the 8th of October about half an hour after 6 in the Evening in the year 1739.

Hannah Lynn was born the 8th of August about 4 of the Clock in the morning in the year 174—.

Joseph Lynn Senr departed this life October ye 12th 1742, aged 51 years and 3 month, 28 days.

Sarah Lynn wife of Joseph Lynn departed this life ye 4th of June 1759 at 6 in the morning, aged 52 years 11 months and 28 days.

Hannah Lynn departed this life ye 11th of January 1760 aged 18 years 4 months and 22 days at half an hour after 3 afternoon and Sixth day of the week.

Sarah Marshall was born December 11th 1762.

"SPRING CHICKENS AND ASPARAGUS" AT THE CITY TAVERN, PHIL-ADELPHIA, 1789.—For the following extracts from a letter of Joseph Barrell to his friend Major Samuel B. Webb, we are indebted to Mr. Worthington C. Ford, Brooklyn, New York :

"PHIL., 18th May, 1789.

"DEAR SAM :

"Had it not been for the fear of laughter I certainly should have re-turn'd to New York last evening. When I had been taught to expect a bowling green road and most excellent Inns, judge my surprize to find the roads so deep & cut to pieces that the wheels sunk to Hubbs almost every trip; so that with all our dilligence we could not get but forty seven Miles & nothing to eat but what would poison the Devil. All the way from New York to Prince Town to say nothing of the Ferrys (which are Infamous & extravagent) the roads are Intollerable, and altho' in the general pretty level, yet there are hills wch would be respectable even in the Neighbourhood of Horse Neck. From Prince Town to Trenton, they are not so bad. From Trenton to Phil., they are delightful and the County the whole way charming in Prospect. We road 50 miles to day & were in Town before 5 o'Clock, but then We were in the Carriage at 5 in the morning. I've Orderd Chickens & Asparagus for Supper, for upon my first entrance into this City Tavern I saw fifty Chickens, big enough, and crying, come toast me, and I always love to attend to every call that is agreeable to me. I am not determined, but expect to be with you by Wednesday next at furthest, perhaps Monday, but this depends on Circumstances. * * *

"Jo BARRELL."

LETTER OF HANNAH PEMBERTON TO HER SISTER SARAH PEMBERTON.
" DR SISTER :

> "The Muse inspires, from *Bolton-farm* [1] I write,
> Whose varied prospects please th' admiring sight,
> There at a distance, on a rising ground,
> Stands beauteous Clifton [2] wth each charm around,
> Here *Roxborough Manor* [3] elegantly gay,
> With smiling neatness owns the master's sway ;
> Whose plenteous gardens rich with fruits appear,
> The peach all lucious, & delightful pear,
> The cantelope with yellow verdure shines,
> And cooling Mellons deck the circling vines ;
> Oft have I here some pleasing moments past,
> And shared with pleasure in the sweet repast.
>
> * * * * * * *
>
> Here lives *Benvolio* with his Anna blest,
> Whose gentle minds with ev'ry virtue dress'd,
> These charms unite & elegantly blend
> The fond companion with the chearful friend,
> Ne'er shall remembrance banish from its view
> The kind attention I've received from you.
> Come then, my Sister, taste these much lov'd joys,
> That dwell not in the city's busy noise.
>
> * * * * * * *
>
> There strange Commotions fill each anxious breast,
> While hope & fear deprive the Soul of rest ;
>
> * * * * * *
>
> . . . the drum's unpleasing sound,
> Its cruel mandate thro' the streets resound
> To rouse the Soldier from the sweets of life
>
> * * * * * *
>
> To where rude war now holds his dismal reign.
>
> * * * * * *
>
> Oft shall remembrance represent the scene
> I've past at Bolton, tranquil & serene.
>
> " CLEORA."

INCIDENTS OF THE SUMMER OF 1783.—The following extracts are copied from a letter of Margaret Morris to her daughter Deborah Morris :

" PHILADA. 7 mo. 1783.

" . . . I have been very thoughtful about you, my Dear Children, fearing the hot weather w^d make you sick, there have died 26 persons of the heat since 5th day, as we were informed, & yesterday the Cryer went about wth a Bell by order of the Magistrates, desireing People who lived near the Pumps to prevent Persons from Drinking much cold water when hot. As thy Aunt Patty & myself went up to B^r W^s in the even^g, the day before yesterday, we met 4 men carrying a Corpse on a Board & I stopt & asked if they were going to Bury it without a Coffin, & they told me he was a young man that had just dropt down dead after drinking a draft of cold water—the same evening another young man, a Journey Man of Jo^s Rakestraw's died, after being part of the day at

[1] Samuel Rhoads's country-seat.
[2] Formerly Benjamin Chew's country-seat.
[3] Henry Hill's country-seat.

work in the Vault of Wm West's Brew house. Yesterday morning, old Saml Garrick eat his Breakfast, & at seven o'clock in the evening he was Buried, but it was supposed to be an Apoplectick fitt that took him off, & the extreme heat of the day made it necessary to bury him the same night. I mention these things as Cautions to you, my dear Girls, not to drink when you are too hot, & not to alarm you." . . .

DOCTOR CHARLES MOORE.—"From our Monthly Meeting held at Philadelphia the 28th of the 8th mo. 1748.

"To the Monthly Meeting of Friends at Edinburgh or Elsewhere.

"Reciting the application for our Certificate on behalf of Charles Moore, 'who intends for your parts wth a design of Improving himself in the Practice of Physic,' & certifying that he is ' Religiously disposed . . . a diligent Attender of our Meetings for Worship & . . . clear from Marriage Engagements.' " . . . Signed by Abel James, William Logan, William Callender, Jonath. Mifflin, Charles Norris, John Warner, George Mifflin, and others.

SOME FAYETTE COUNTY SETTLERS.—Morgan Jones, great-grand-father of the late Horatio Gates Jones, Esq., was a brother of Robert and Benjamin Jones, who came from Delaware to Western Pennsylvania about 1770. They settled first in Greene County, on Whitely Creek, a tributary of the Monongahela River. The records of the Goshen Baptist Church at that place, as far back as 1781, show Robert and Benjamin Jones to have been members then, having been associated with Rev. John Corbley, the famous Baptist preacher whose wife and children were massacred by the Indians as they were on their way to the Goshen Church, on Sunday morning, May 10, 1782.

In 1794 and '95 Robert and Benjamin Jones built Springhill Furnace, in Southern Fayette County, near Cheat River, one of the first iron furnaces erected west of the mountains, whose remains are still standing. In 1799 they leased the furnace to Jesse Evans, who had married Robert's daughter Mary. Young Evans had come to Fayette from Chester County, whither his father, Abner Evans, had immigrated from Wales in 1755. One of Jesse's brothers, George Evans, was the father of Abner Evans 2d, who died at Pottstown, Pennsylvania, aged ninety-one years. Jesse's sister, Mary Evans, had married Jeremiah Evans (not a kinsman), also of Chester County, and their son Lewis Evans also came to Fayette County, and in 1801 married Rachel, another daughter of Robert Jones. Lewis Evans, who was Jesse's nephew, thus became his brother-in-law. His descendants are numerous and prominent in Fayette and Greene counties, as are also Jesse's. The latter's son, Colonel Samuel Evans, who died a few years ago at the age of eighty-eight, served in the Legislature from Fayette in 1827. Jesse's daughter Eliza became by marriage the mother of the late Hon. Alpheus Evans Wilson, who was president judge of the Fayette-Greene judicial district from 1874 to 1884. Her daughter, the late Mrs. Hon. John K. Ewing, of Uniontown, was the mother of Hon. Nathaniel Ewing, present judge of the Fayette County courts.

Robert and Benjamin Jones had a sister named Rachel also, and she married Captain William Brice of the Revolutionary army. Robert's only son was John, and he married Mary, daughter of William and Rachel (Jones) Brice, and his own cousin. They had many children, one of whom, Robert Jones, was the father of Sophia Jones, who married Frederick Burdette, and thus became the mother of Robert Jones ("Bob") Burdette, now of Bryn-Mawr, but who was born at Greensboro' on the

Monongahela River, near where his ancestor, Robert Jones, sleeps, in the old Goshen Baptist Church cemetery, Garrard's Fort, Greene County. Of the above family of Brices is United States Senator Calvin S. Brice, of Ohio, and John Jones Brice, Commander in the United States navy, at Chicago. The Brices were prominent families in Harrison and Marion Counties, now West Virginia. They are connected by marriage with the Wilsons, one of the best-known representatives of whom was Colonel Ben. Wilson, of Lord Dunmore's War, who was the father of twenty-nine children by two wives, Ann Ruddle and Phœbe Davison. Ex-Congressman Ben. Wilson, of Clarksburg, West Virginia, is a descendant.

THE CENTENNIAL OF ST. PAUL'S PROTESTANT EPISCOPAL CHURCH, BLOOMSBURG, COLUMBIA COUNTY, PENNSYLVANIA, was celebrated on May 28, 1893.

This parish was organized, probably, as early as the year 1790, and was known as St. Paul's, Fishing Creek. On the 11th of September, 1795, Mr. Joseph Long, for the consideration of five shillings, agreed to convey to the parish the acre of land which is now occupied by the church property, and in the agreement for the same it is described as "the ground on which the church now stands," so that in 1795 and before that time an Episcopal church building stood in the enclosure where the present one is erected. In 1793 Mr. Elisha Barton was the deputy from this parish to the Ninth Diocesan Convention as "from St. Paul's Church, Fishing Creek township." In that convention, held in Christ Church, Philadelphia, on May 28, 1793, the parish was admitted into union with the Convention of the Diocese of Pennsylvania.

The Rev. Caleb Hopkins was the first rector of this parish. He also had charge of St. Gabriel's, Sugarloaf, and Christ Church, Derry.

A pencilled memorandum on a fly-leaf of the oldest existing record of St. Paul's Church says, "Mr. Hopkins was here in 1794 or 1795, then left and was recalled in 1806." He seems to have remained in charge until 1818. In 1827 the log church gave place to a frame structure, which remained for about ten years. In 1837 a brick church was erected on the spot where the rectory now stands, and in that was placed in the following year the first church-bell ever heard in the town.

The brick building of 1837 continued in use until 1868, when the congregation resolved to begin the construction of a new edifice. The corner-stone of this, the fourth building, was laid on September 11, 1868, and the church was finished, with the exception of the tower, early in 1870, and was consecrated on June 28, 1881, by the Rt. Rev. Dr. Howe.

Returning to the succession of rectors, we find that after the Rev. Mr. Hopkins left the parish, in 1818, lay readers maintained the services until, in December, 1824, Mr. William Eldred, from England, who had been acting as a lay reader here from the 10th of May, 1823, was ordained deacon by Bishop White, and continued in charge of the parish for a year or more. Rev. James De Pui, 1828–32; Benjamin Hutchins, 1832–33; George C. Drake, 1833–42; William H. Bournes, 1842–44; Samuel T. Lord, 1845–46; A. A. Marple, 1846–48; Joel Rudderow, 1848–53; Henry Tullidge, D.D., 1853–57; A. M. Weily, 1859–60; J. A. Russell, 1860–62; Thomas H. Cullen, 1863–76; John Hewitt, 1876–77; Louis Zahner, 1877–86; and in December of the latter year, the present rector, William C. Leverett.

JOHN G. FREEZE.

Queries.

RIDGWAY FAMILY: AFFILIATION WITH THE MAIN LINE DESIRED.— The writer is acquainted with the various outline genealogies of the Ridgway family, as given by Major E. M. Woodward, and the fragmentary account by Mr. Edwin Salter, as well as an unpublished manuscript pedigree by the late Gideon Delaplaine Scull which gave the descent of the *Scully, Ridgway,* and other families from the Delaplaines and De Bellangé families as far as could be ascertained. That there were *several intermarriages* between these old Huguenot names De la Plaine and De Bellangé (now Delaplaine and Bellangee) and the Ridgways is certain, and that this branch, who bear unmistakable traces in personal appearance to their French ancestry, came down from one of these is equally positive. It may also be as well to state that the writer is acquainted with Mr. Thomas Shourd's sketch of the Bellangés, and with the MS. pedigree by the late John Bellangee Cox, and the account of the Ridgway family in the "Proceedings of the Surveyors' Association of West New Jersey," p. 262 *et seq.* (the most complete). The duplication of names is very confusing, and the number of Johns in the Ridgway family misleading. The Bible record of one family is here given in the earnest hope that some one will make the affiliation with the earlier members. It will be seen that the birth or parents' names of the first John here mentioned is not given, but we believe him to have been living at or near Mount Holly, New Jersey, from, say, 1761 (when it is reasonable to suppose he was at least twenty-one) until his death in 1809. This family were members of the Society of Friends.

Children of Postrema Shinn and John Ridgway, Mount Holly, New Jersey.

Births.

	Day.	Month.	Year.
Thomas	17	8	1761
John	20	12	1762
William	6	11	1765
Aquilla	16	10	1767 [1]
Anna	24	9	1769 [2]
De la plaine	9	10	1772
Mary	24	11	1774 [3]
Martha	5	8	1777
Thomas Shinn	4	11	1779
Elizabeth	21	7	1782
Edmund	13	2	1785 [4]

Deaths.

	Day.	Month.	Year.
John	4	3	1809
Postrema	23	9	1831 [1813]
Thomas	14	9	1761
Aquilla		9	1799
Edmund	15	9	1805
Thomas Shinn	1	4	1857

The notes to the above, excepting that signed with my initials, are from the records of Mount Holly Meeting, for which I am indebted to the courtesy of Mr. Barclay White, whose extracts I am inclined to be-

[1] Married Martha Lippincott.
[2] Married William Hudson Burr.
[3] T. S. Ridgway married Mary Joy, daughter of Captain Daniel Joy of the Revolutionary army in Pennsylvania, an inspector or prover of cannon. He died in Philadelphia in 1784. What connection was he, if any, of the New England family? Further information desired.—W. J. P.
[4] *Edward* in Meeting Records.

lieve more correct as regards the dates; names are always a matter of usage. Mr. Thomas S. Ridgway left a daughter Postrema, who died recently at an advanced age. "Postreme" is given in the Meeting Records instead of "Postrema," "Edward" instead of "Edmund," and Mrs. John Ridgway's death as the 22d instead of 23d. From the same records Mr. White obtained the following, which may interest some of your readers; it shows that Postreme Ridgway was the youngest child of "Thomas Shinn and Martha Earl who were married in 1718." Their children were as follows :

Susannah Atkinson Shinn	born	3 mo.	10, 1721
Martha Shinn	"	1 mo.	22, 1722/3
Thomas "	"	6 mo.	7, 1725
Mary "	"	10 mo.	23, 1727
Elizabeth "	"	7 mo.	20, 1733
Earl "	"	10 mo.	27, 1736 [1]
Gamaliel "	"	5 mo.	10, 1738
Aquilla "	"	1 mo.	8, 1739-40
Postreme "	"	1 mo.	5, 1744

Some of the children of Thomas Shinn Ridgway, who died in Gloucester, New Jersey, in 1857, are still living, and their traditional recollections are given below in hopes that some of the other descendants may have preserved a more ancient record. It is said that Mr. Thomas S. Ridgway had two uncles named Delaplaine living in Germantown. This is quite likely, but I believe there were other Delaplaine and perhaps Bellangé marriages at a much earlier date in the main line of descent. The Delaplaine intermarriages, it will be seen, took place in or before 1772, which theory is based on the date of the birth of Delaplaine Ridgway. The writer is acquainted with the references to the Delaplaines in the PENNSYLVANIA MAGAZINE, who were in Germantown as early as 1684.

Anna Ridgway married William Hudson Burr, associate judge, Mount Holly.

Mary married Daniel Knight, of Philadelphia ; of this line is Daniel Ridgway Knight, the well-known artist.

Martha married Aaron Boker, of New York and Philadelphia, who lived also in Mount Holly. The late George H. Boker was of this line by a second marriage.

Elizabeth married Robert Evans, of the Great Valley, Chester County, Pennsylvania, and left descendants.

William married Elizabeth Wilson ; their daughter was Eliza Ridgway, wife of Thomas Silliman, then a widower with several children. Their only child, Henry Silliman, married Miss Buck ; they had two children, Charles and Harriet.

De la Plaine married three times ; his last wife was a Miss Reed, of Mount Holly.

It is also said that Thomas Shinn Ridgway was a *first* cousin of Jacob Ridgway, of Philadelphia, the father of the well-known Mrs. Rush ; but as Jacob Ridgway was also himself the son of a John Ridgway, this must be an error.

The probabilities seem to be that the John Ridgway, of Mount Holly, was third in descent from the first settler, Richard Ridgway.

The John Ridgway, a Friend, of Little Egg Harbor, New Jersey, an elder of that meeting, who died there 21st of Fifth month, 1774, having been born in Burlington County in 1705, could not have been the father of the John, of Mount Holly, according to Woodward, who gives a list of

[1] Married Rebecca Monrow.

his children, and states that the junior John died in 1845, aged ninety years, and also mentions his marriage to Elizabeth Wright, who died in 1843, and gives a list of their children.

The *Philadelphia Repository* for December 3, 1803, p. 391, contains the following lines "On the Marriage of Mr. Thomas Ridgway to Miss Mary Joy." Signed R. L.

> "Happiest of mortals can thy bliss e'er cloy
> When in possession of the charmer *Joy;*
> Doubtless thy cup of bliss was full before,
> But to it, *Joy* must now run o'er.
>
> "PHILA., Nov. 18th."

In the same newspaper, July 2, 1803, p. 215, "25 [June] at Mount Holly (Jer.) Mr. Dillaplain Ridgway of this city to the amiable Miss Dolly Read of Mount Holly." Since writing the foregoing I have examined all the Delaplaine wills in the Philadelphia office to 1809 : Joshua Delaplaine, proved 1788, and Anna Delaplaine, widow, 1791, and a letter to Mrs. Rush on the Ridgway pedigree, written by a Mr. James Ridgway in 1855, and containing various data collected by a Thomas Ridgway, of 353 Arch Street, Philadelphia, the same date, the youngest son of John Ridgway and Elizabeth Wright, mentioned above. It gives no light on the Mount Holly Ridgways. These MS. letters are in the Ridgway Library.

WILLIAM JOHN POTTS.

Camden, N.J.

BOUDE.—1. Are there any descendants of Joseph and Elizabeth (Baldwin) Boude living? 2. Are there any descendants of John and Gertrude Boude living? 3. List of names of children of Thomas and Sarah Boude requested. 4. Did Henrietta Boude, who married Richard Sewell, August 30, 1733, leave descendants? 5. Did Elizabeth, daughter of Thomas and Sarah Boude, who married, November 14, 1745, John Nigely, leave descendants?

EMMA ST. C. WHITNEY.

Pottsville, Penna.

HARRIS.—I have recently bought a fine eighteenth-century edition of the works of Nathaniel Lardner, containing the autograph of Theophilus Harris. The Philadelphia directories show that he lived at 208 S. Front Street and at 212 Chestnut Street between 1806 and 1817. Can any one tell me more about him? A. J. E.

HARRISON.—Information is desired regarding the antecedents of George Harrison, Navy Agent at Philadelphia during the war of 1812.

O. O. P.

Allegheny, Penna.

Replies.

HARRISON.—Refer to "Descendants of Colonel Thomas White, of Maryland." By Thomas H. Montgomery, p. 162 *et seq.*

Book Notices.

HISTORY OF THE AMERICAN EPISCOPAL CHURCH FROM THE PLANT-
ING OF THE COLONIES TO THE END OF THE CIVIL WAR. By Rev.
Samuel D. McConnell, D.D. New York: Thomas Whittaker.
392 pp.

The fourth edition of this valuable work of historical interest, revised
and enlarged by its author, has been issued by his publisher.

THE VIRGINIA MAGAZINE OF HISTORY AND BIOGRAPHY. Vol. I., No.
1, July, 1893. 112 pp. Richmond, Virginia. Price, $5.00 per annum.

We have received the first number of this new quarterly published by
the Virginia Historical Society, the editor in charge being Philip A.
Bruce, Esq. It is well printed on good paper, and contains the " Diary
of Captain John Davis, of the First Pennsylvania Line, in the Brigade
of General Wayne," " Letters of William Fitzhugh," " Proclamations of
Nathaniel Bacon," " List of Officers, Sailors, and Marines of the Virginia
Navy in the American Revolution," " Abstracts of Virginia Land
Patents," and other papers of interest and value. There is much valuable
material relating to the history of Virginia, now hid away or forgotten in
county offices, as well as family papers, which should be printed, and we
believe that the Society, through its Magazine, will be the medium of
development, and enlarge the scope of the good work it has already
accomplished. We bespeak for this new serial the liberal support of all
who are interested in history and biography.

1815–1832. JOSEPH BONAPARTE EN AMÉRIQUE. Par Georges Bertin,
accompagné d'un Portrait d'après une Gravure de M. Rodolphe
Piquet, Paris, Libraire de la Nouvelle Revue, 18 Boulevard Mont-
martre, 1893. (Droits de traduction et de reproduction réservés.)
12mo. Pp. xv–422. Prix, 3 francs 50 centimes.

Dedicated to Admiral Macauley, with much of its information derived from the papers of the Hopkinson, Biddle, and Ingersoll families,
the subject of this book is of particular interest to Philadelphians. The
frontispiece is a portrait unknown here, strongly Bonaparte, and yet with
an individuality of its own. One can understand how there still lingers at
Bordentown an almost affectionate and respectful memory of the original, after viewing this agreeable face. Marion Crawford, in his charming article in the May number of *The Century*, " Joseph Bonaparte in
Bordentown," has left little to be desired as a notice of this work. Scholarly, the result of much research among the living, from rare books,
newspapers, original MSS. and unpublished autograph letters, with a
graceful style, M. Bertin has well arranged the whole history of Joseph
Bonaparte in America, tracing him step by step from 1815 to 1832, illus-
trating his actions often by his own letters. Of value also are the side-
lights thrown on the distinguished company of exiled foreigners who
gathered around the ex-king and the eminent Americans who tendered
him their respect and friendship. An interesting list, with values, in
Joseph's own handwriting, of his famous collection of paintings, a
detailed brief of title of the Point Breeze estate, with a good index,
complete this interesting memoir. P.

[... to be found in the ... of the Library ...]

FOREIGN

Collections of the Powys-Land Club	London
Gloucestershire Notes and Queries	London
Miscellanea Genealogica et Heraldica	London
Northamptonshire Notes and Queries	Northampton
Notes and Queries	London
Northern Notes and Queries	Edinburgh
The East Anglican, or Notes and Queries on subjects connected with the Counties of Suffolk, Cambridge, Essex, and Norfolk	Ipswich
The Genealogist	London
The Index Library	London
The Western Antiquary or Note Book for Devon, Cornwall, and Somerset	Plymouth
Yorkshire Notes and Queries: with Yorkshire Genealogist, Yorkshire Bibliographer, and Yorkshire Folk-Lore Journal	Bradford

DOMESTIC.

American Journal of Numismatics and Bulletin of American Numismatic and Archæological Societies	Boston.
American Notes and Queries	Philadelphia.
Essex Institute Historical Collections	Salem, Mass.
Magazine of American History	New York.
Magazine of Western History	Cleveland.
New York Genealogical and Biographical Record	New York.
Notes and Queries, Historical and Genealogical	Harrisburg, Pa.
Proceedings and Collections of the Wyoming Historical and Geological Society	Wilkesbarre, Pa.
Proceedings of the Academy of Natural Sciences	Philadelphia.
Southern Historical Society Papers	Richmond, Va.
The American Journal of Philology	Baltimore, Md.
The American Catholic Historical Researches	Philadelphia.
The Book Mart	Pittsburg, Pa.
The Cambrian	Cincinnati.
The Granite Monthly	New Hampshire.
The Historical Record, with Notes and Queries	Wilkesbarre, Pa.
The Iowa Historical Record	Iowa City.
The Journal of the Military Service Institution	New York.
The Library Journal	New York.
The Nation	New York.
The New England Historical and Genealogical Register	Boston.
The New England Magazine and Bay State Monthly	Boston.
The Pennsylvanian	Philadelphia.
The Rhode Island Magazine	Newport.

[Publishers of other serials will please forward prospectus.]

Pennsylvania and the Federal Co...

EDITED BY

Prof. JOHN B. McMASTER and FREDERICK...

Published for the Subscribers by The Historical Soci...

Price, $5.00.

Address, FREDERICK D. STONE, Secretary of the Committee, 1300...

The New York Genealogical and Bi...
Record for 1893.

DEVOTED TO THE INTERESTS OF AMERICAN G...
AND BIOGRAPHY.

ISSUED QUARTERLY, AT TWO DOLLARS PER...

PUBLICATION COMMITTEE.

The Society has a few complete sets of the Record on...
the twenty-two volumes, well bound in cloth, $66.00. Sub...
in advance, should be sent to WILLIAM P. KETCHAM...
West Forty-fourth Street, New York.

For Sale at 1300 Locust St., Phila.   Price, 75 cts. per
Number, or $3 per year.

No. 68.

THE

PENNSYLVANIA

MAGAZINE

OF

HISTORY AND BIOGRAPHY.

PUBLISHED QUARTERLY.

No. 4 OF VOL. XVII.

January, 1894.

"I entertain an high idea of the utility of periodical publications; insomuch
that I could heartily desire copies of the Museum and Magazines, as well as
common Gazettes, might be spread through every city, town, and village in
America.   I consider such easy vehicles of knowledge more happily calculated
than any other to preserve the liberty, stimulate the industry, and meliorate the
morals of an enlightened and free people."—*Washington to Mathew Carey,*
June 25, 1788.

PUBLISHED BY
THE HISTORICAL SOCIETY OF PENNSYLVANIA,
FOR SUBSCRIBERS.
PHILADELPHIA:
1894.

CONTENTS.

BOUND VOLUMES OF THE MAGAZINE.

PRINTED BY J. B. LIPPINCOTT COMPANY.

THE

PENNSYLVANIA MAGAZINE

OF

HISTORY AND BIOGRAPHY.

| VOL. XVII. | 1893. | No. 4. |

THE EARLY WELSH QUAKERS AND THEIR EMIGRATION TO PENNSYLVANIA.[1]

BY DR. JAMES J. LEVICK.

If in the Divine economy chance is an unknown factor, it must have been something more than a mere human impulse which, in the year 1653, led one Morgan Floyd, a priest of Wrexham, to send two of his congregation to the north of England "to trie the Quakers" and to bring back an account of them. What came of this mission is thus told by George Fox : "When these triers came down among us the power of the Lord overcame them and they were both of them convinced of the truth. So they stayed some time with us and then returned into Wales, where afterwards one of them departed from his convincement, but the other, whose name was John ap John, abode in the truth, and received a gift in the ministry to which he continued faithful."[2] From this mission of Morgan Floyd and this conversion of John ap John may be traced a chain of events with which are closely

[1] Read before the Historical Society of Pennsylvania, March 13, 1893.
[2] "A Journal or Historical Account of the Life, Travels, Sufferings, and Christian Experiences of George Fox." London, 1694, p. 123.

linked the settlement of Eastern Pennsylvania, the conservative character of her people, and a history almost unique in its character. Who was this Morgan Floyd, priest of Wrexham, and who this John ap John, the apostle of Quakerism in Wales, it is one of the objects of this paper to consider. Rightly to understand this subject we must examine the character of the Welsh people, their early history and their national peculiarities. Whatever opinions may exist concerning original sin and the natural depravity of man, there can be no doubt that for generations the Welsh people have been congenitally disposed to piety. Nor can this fact excite surprise. Moral attributes of character may be the subject of inheritance as well as physical traits, and the ancient Britons were a religious people in their earliest history. Long before the Roman invasion they had in their Druids and bards the teachers of a religion which, though not free from error, had as its basis great truths analogous to those of the Christian religion. The fundamental objects and principles of this Druidical system were the search after truth and a rigid adherence to justice and peace. The bards themselves never bore arms, they recognized one Supreme Being, and their religion called for a severe and inflexible morality; so much so, indeed, that an early writer has said that "it comprehended all the leading principles that tend to spread liberty, peace, and happiness among mankind, and was no more inimical to Christianity than the religion of Noah, Job, or Abraham." [1]

Hence the Britons were prompt, even so early as the first century of our era, to accept the Christian religion, which they retained in a simple Druidical form until the fifth century, when the Roman Catholic form of Christianity was introduced among the Welsh people.

Very early in the Church history of Wales we find differences of opinion between the Britons and the Romans. To think for himself in matters religious and political is, in his opinion, the Welshman's birthright, and the germ of dis-

[1] "The Welsh Non-Conformist Memorial," by the Rev. William Richards, LL.D. London, 1820.

sent from the Established Church, whether that of the Roman Catholic hierarchy or the Anglican Church, has never died out in Wales.

It showed itself early, most conspicuously in the person of John Penry, a man born in Brecknockshire, educated both at Oxford and Cambridge, who suffered death for conscience' sake three centuries ago,—May 29, 1593.

The blood of the martyrs is the seed of the Church, and a long line of Non-Conformist ministers came up, as it were, from Penry's ashes.

One Wroth, rector of Llanfaches, in Merionethshire, an Oxford graduate, formed a dissenters' church so early as 1639. Other Oxford graduates followed in his footsteps, prominent among whom were William Erbury and Walter Craddock, vicar and curate of St. Mary's, Cardiff. Driven from their charge by the Bishop of Llandaff and by Archbishop Laud, they went about the country as itinerant preachers. At the breaking out of the civil war, Craddock and his adherents were driven out of Wales by the violence of the cavalier and high-church party, but returned there after the close of the war and went vigorously to work in the cause of Christ. Their preaching was successful. Walter Craddock lived for some time at Wrexham. Here Morgan Lloyd, as we shall now call him, was at this time at school. Here he heard the preaching of Walter Craddock, the effect of which influenced his whole subsequent life. Morgan Lloyd was of good family, and was born in Merionethshire on an estate long belonging to his family, called Cynfal, or Cymfael. His mother appears to have been a religious, thoughtful woman inclined to Puritanism. Thus trained, we cannot wonder that the fervent preaching of Walter Craddock affected her boy. During the civil war Morgan Lloyd was in Cromwell's army, probably as chaplain. Wherever he went he preached. So, says Palmer,[1] "people in authority as well in England as in Wales came to be aware of his power and his promise." Up to the time of

[1] "A History of the Older Non-Conformists of Wrexham and its Neighborhood," by Alfred Neobald Palmer, F.C.S., etc. Wrexham, 1888.

parliamentary government the officiating clergy of the Established Church in Wales, it is said, were generally unfit for their stations; many of them were extremely ignorant; not understanding the Welsh language, they rarely preached; of some, indeed, it is said they were scandalous livers. On February 22, 1649-50, an act was passed for the better propagating of the gospel in Wales and for ejecting scandalous ministers and school-masters. Among those appointed as "triers" and to supply ministers as they should adjudge best for the advancement of the gospel were Walter Craddock, Vavasor Powell, and Morgan Lloyd.

Finding it difficult to secure suitable men among these English (but non-Welsh-speaking) ordained clergymen, they had recourse to the encouragement, promotion, and appointment of lay preachers who were intelligent, pious men from the different churches or who had good gifts for public speaking, thus preparing, though unconsciously, the way for a religious body who, respecting the ministry, have ever held, in the words of a Celtic poet, that

> "There is a consecration not of man,
> Nor given by laid-on hands, nor acted rite."

Hence arose in Wales those husbandmen and artisans often mentioned as among the Welsh ministers. This, it will be remembered, was so early as 1650, some years before George Fox had visited Wales. When the authority of Cromwell was established, Morgan Lloyd was placed in charge of the great parish church of Wrexham,[1] of which he remained the vicar for many years. Later in life, either voluntarily or because his religious views did not fully accord with those of his parishioners, there is reason to believe he gave up his vicarage and became the minister of the Congregational Church of Wrexham. Morgan Lloyd was not only a great preacher, but he was also an author and a poet. His book best known is entitled "The Three Birds, a Mystery for

---

[1] This parish church of Wrexham has for Americans an especial interest, as here repose the remains of Elihu Yale, the founder of Yale College.

some to understand and others to deride, being a Discourse between the Eagle, the Dove, and the Raven." In the conversation which ensues between the three birds, the dove stands for God's people (*i.e.*, the Puritan portion of them), the raven for the godless, while the eagle, who directs the conversation, is Oliver Cromwell. The dove is really the exponent of Morgan Lloyd's own religious views.[1] There is much in his words which reminds us of George Fox's "great exercise" in the vale of Beavor, and a remarkable similarity may be noticed between the views of Morgan Lloyd and those of the early Friends; so much so, indeed, that Palmer writes, "Lloyd's doctrine of quietism was so closely allied to the doctrine of the indwelling spirit as preached by George Fox, that he naturally took an interest in the latter, befriending his friends and remonstrating with Richard Baxter for denouncing the Quakers." He died June 3, 1659, aged forty years, and was buried in what for many years has been known as the Dissenters' Burying-Ground of Wrexham. Last summer I visited this graveyard. The sidewalk of the street in Wrexham has recently been widened, and as I trod it my friend Palmer told me I was standing over the dust of Morgan Lloyd. Much as he was loved and honored by his congregation, he was bitterly hated by others, and it is on record that after the restoration of the monarchy a soldier sought out Morgan Lloyd's grave and in great rage and malice thrust down his sword into it as far as he could.

So much for the priest of Wrexham who sent two of his men to try the Quakers and bring back an account of them, both of whom became converts to the faith of Fox and his friends, one of whom received a part in the ministry, to which he remained faithful. If Morgan Lloyd was indirectly the cause, this man, John ap John, was the direct agent, under Providence, in bringing about the changes which resulted in the settlement so largely by Welsh emigrants of the Township of Merion and the vicinity of Phila-

---

[1] See "A History of the Older Non-Conformists of Wrexham and its Neighborhood," by Alfred Neobald Palmer, F.C.S., etc. Wrexham, 1888.

delphia. But of this man, the apostle of Quakerism in Wales, there has been a degree of ignorance which is surprising. So far as I could discover, when I began this investigation there had been nothing known of him in Pennsylvania other than what is noted in the journal of George Fox and of Richard Davies, of Cloddeau cochion. All knowledge of his later years seemed to be lost, and at a time when " testimonies" and memorials of deceased Friends were so general, no such record of this man appears. Did he fall away from his faith in his later years, as his companion had so early done, or did he join the followers of Fox who came to the New World? If so, how is it that we have no record of his home, and how is it that no man knows his sepulchre ?

Impressed by this strange and anomalous ignorance, I devoted a considerable part of last summer to an investigation of the subject, which happily led to results of a gratifying character. For the success of these investigations I am largely indebted to Alfred Neobald Palmer, of Wrexham, North Wales, a gentleman well known in Wales and in Great Britain as an authority in archæological and historical matters, and whose histories of the parish church of Wrexham and of the early Non-Conformists of Wrexham, etc., are especially interesting.[1] Under his guidance I visited Plas Ifa, the home (as he assured me) of John ap John, who I learned, like Morgan Lloyd, belonged to a good Welsh family, —a yeoman living on his ancestral estate. Plas Ifa is near the vale of Llangollen, not far from Ruabon, into which parish it is quite probable that the estate extended. Though a yeoman, he was evidently an evangelical preacher. George Fox says of him in his Journal, that John ap John had once been a preacher in Beaumaris. It is probable he was one of the lay preachers selected by Morgan Lloyd and his asso-

---

[1] I wish also here to acknowledge the aid kindly given me, in my local investigations, by Evan Powell, Esq., of Llanidloes ; by Robert Jones, late rector of the parish church at Bala ; by Edward Griffith, Esq., J.P., of Dolgelly ; by John E. Southall, Esq., of Newport, Monmouth ; and by William Norris, Esq., of Coalbrookdale, England.

ciates, to the former of whom he had been known from his childhood.

The old house, Plas Ifa, is nearly gone and a new one has been built on the original site. The place has evidently been the home of a well-to-do country gentleman. In the garden were bits of carved timber taken from the old house, and in one room of the house one of the rafters showed more of this carved work, which my friend Palmer said was not of later date than the fifteenth century. At the lower end of the lawn in front of the house was formerly the Friends' burying-ground, but in digging the canal of Ellsmere, and later in constructing the railway between Chester and Dolgelly, this graveyard was obliterated. The view from Plas Ifa in John ap John's time must have been beautiful : it certainly is so now. Before it is the beautiful vale of Llangollen, the Berwyn mountains on one side, near by the dancing waters of the Dee, while between these are highly-cultivated fields of grass and grain with well-trimmed hedges intervening, making the whole look like one vast highly-cultivated garden. There was everything to tempt to rest and ease here; but as Fox has said of John ap John, the power of the Lord was upon him, and he had received a gift in the ministry, to which he remained faithful. And so from this peaceful home he went forth on his apostolic mission. First he went to his own personal friends and neighbors, the men of Wrexham, Ruabon, Corwen, Llangollen, Bala, and Dolgelly,—to your ancestors and to mine. They knew the integrity of the man, and the Power which had melted his heart, under his preaching, melted theirs. In the year 1657 Fox passed into Wales, beginning at Cardiff and Swansea, and going so far north as Beaumaris. In this journey he had as his companion John ap John, a companion in every way helpful to him,—helpful as speaking the Welsh language, to which, as they do now, so then, the Welsh people loyally adhered, helpful as a fearless servant of the same Divine Master.

At first they were kindly received. Justices of the peace, the high sheriff of the county, the mayor of Tenby, the gentry of the county, all heard them, if not with entire approval, with at least some show of Christian courtesy. At Dolgelly, writes Fox, " many people accompanied us to the inn, rejoiced in the truth that had been declared to them, and as we went forth from the town they lifted up their hands and blessed the Lord for our coming." And so, from one end to the other of Wales, George Fox and John ap John travelled, as Fox writes, " sounding the day of the Lord, until very weary with travelling so hard up and down in Wales we came to a place within six miles of Wrexham, where we met with many Friends and had a glorious meeting." This place was doubtless Plas Ifa, and the meeting-house that which lately has been swept away in building the railway and canal of which I have already spoken. Everywhere in Wales the effects of this visit were seen. Wales was soon alive with Quakers. The whole country was indeed ripe for such a harvest. The independence of thought of which I have spoken as a trait of the Britons from the days of the Druids, the simplicity of religious truth, as taught by these early Britons, confirmed by Penry and his successors, the glimmerings of a truth now shining in full brightness,—all had prepared the mind of the Welsh people for just such teaching as was that of Fox and of John ap John in this memorable visit, and I repeat it, Wales was soon alive with Quakers. Montgomeryshire gave to this faith Charles and Thomas Lloyd, of Dolobran, and Richard Davies, of Cloddeau cochion. Pembroke gave Henry Lewis, Richard Hayes, Thomas Ellis. Dolgelly gave Rowland Ellis, Robert and Jane Owen. Bala and its vicinity, John ap Thomas, Cadwalader ap Thomas, Edward Jones, Hugh Roberts, John Roberts, Robert Vaughan, David ap John, William ap Edward, and others. Flintshire, Thomas Wynne. Glamorganshire, John Bevan and others. Of these men I shall have occasion to speak later.

What manner of men were these who thus so promptly accepted the faith preached by George Fox and John ap John? Happily, this question can be readily answered. Still in Wales, especially in North Wales, their homes remain, retaining their old names though their former owners have long since passed away from them. Happily, too, by a law of their religious Society, certificates as to their character and standing were furnished the heads of every family removing to the New World. These "certificates" are individual or family biographies, and in these days when details of ancestry are so eagerly studied I know no reading so interesting, so instructive, so satisfactory as that which may be found in the minute-books of Radnor, Haverford, and Merion Meetings.

Like John ap John, those I have named, most of whom subsequently crossed the sea and founded the colony of Pennsylvania, were of good old Welsh families, yeomen, freeholders, well-educated men. Some of them were cadets of ancient houses; more than one had been at Oxford. With the history of Charles and Thomas Lloyd, the latter Penn's chosen governor, the members of this Historical Society are familiar. In an unbroken line their family history is traced to the sixth century or earlier.

Dolobran still remains, with its oaken stairs and wainscoted walls, to tell of the luxurious home in which these early Quakers had been reared.

The family of Henry Lewis, of Trewern, near Narberth, has for centuries held a good position in Pembrokeshire, and the last of the family in Wales, who has lately died, was widely known for his philanthropy.

John ap Thomas, gentleman, of Llaithgwm, of whom I have spoken before this Society on another occasion, and whose house may still be seen a few miles from Bala, and his brother, Cadwalader ap Thomas (the father of John Cadwalader), were seventeenth in descent from Marchweithian, of one of the princely tribes of North Wales and Lord of Isallet. Lleweni, the home of Marchweithian, who lived in the tenth century, is but a few miles from Denbigh, and is now the heritage of the Saulsbury family, who are also descendants of Marchweithian.

Robert Vaughan, whose name appears among these early Friends, bore a name yet honored in Wales, and his home,

Hendri Mawr, a mile or two beyond the town of Bala, still shows its owner to have been a man of wealth, if not of rank. A long and noble avenue of trees leads to the house, parts of which have been traced to the fifth century. Hendri Mawr is the Briton's name for the great summer home (or residence), and the name itself is one of great antiquity. The home of Hugh Roberts, another of those early converts to Quakerism, was Ciltalgarth, " the corner at the end of the hill." The old house is now gone, but a newer house on the old site commands one of the most beautiful views in Merionethshire. Near by Hendri Mawr, lying between it and Llaithgwm, was and still is Coed y Foel, the then home of Edward Foulke, who, though not so early a Friend, later became one, and who was the friend and associate of the men I have named, and who, as he has himself told us, was fourteenth in descent from Ririd Flaidd, Lord of Penllyn. Two miles from Bala is Rhyridog, the home in the fifth century of his ancestor Ririd Flaidd, a recumbent effigy of one of whose family may be found in the old church of Llanychlin.

Six miles beyond Bala is Dolgelly, where, as Fox has told us, he was so kindly received. Here at Dolscrau, a mile and a half from the town, lived Robert and Jane Owen, the former a justice of the peace and belonging to one of the most influential families in North Wales. He was fifth in descent from Baron Lewis Owen, whose parents came of the royal tribes of Wales. Baron Owen was himself Chancellor of North Wales, and after filling many public offices was cruelly murdered by a band of outlaws in the year 1555.[1] Jane, the wife of Robert Owen, was daughter of Robert Vaughan, of Hengwert and Nannau, one of the oldest families in North Wales. Near by, living at ease in his ancestral home, Bryn-Mawr, was Rowland Ellis (a yeoman descended from a prince of Powys), whose home has given us a name so familiar to us that we may pause for a moment to describe it. It was then, as it is now, a comfortable stone house; the floors are of stone, and it was built by Rees Lewis, grandfather of Rowland Ellis, A.D. 1617, as an inscription on

[1] See *The British Friend*, November 2, 1891.

one of the rafters tells. To the right of the house are the
remains of an ancient garden which has seen better days. Its
walls are gone, but there are traces of old paths, while ancient box- and venerable yew-trees tell of what has been.
The view of the valley, the river running through it, and in
the distance Cader Idris with its adjacent range of hills, and
on the opposite side another long range of hills, the whole
looking not unlike some of the prettiest parts of Scotland,
all make Bryn-Mawr well worthy of a visit.

These were all men of good social standing in the communities in which they lived, and were among the first to
accept the faith preached by George Fox and John ap John.

A well-known statesman, ex-Secretary Bayard, has lately
said it was well for the development of our nation that its
founders belonged rather to the three hundred of Leonidas
than to the four hundred of McAllister. This is doubtless
true; Spartan courage and fearless patriotism are important
factors in the founding of a new and a permanent government; but I have yet to learn that there is any incompati-
bility between such courage and patriotism and that culture,
education, systematic habits of thought which generations
of good social life develop. And I may go so far as to
say that I believe much of the quiet, dignified, conservative
character of Philadelphia is due to the good old blood of
these her first Welsh settlers.

What was this faith thus preached by Fox and John ap
John which took such early and deep root in the hearts of
these Welsh people?

I enter on this part of my essay with, I trust, a just appreciation of the gravity, shall I not say the responsibility of
the subject? For myself I am satisfied with the faith held
by Fox, as all my fathers were; but I have long since
learned that in things spiritual, as in things temporal, the
food which is most grateful and, as I think, most helpful to
me may not be equally so to my fellows; that from differences
of constitution, temperament, education, taste, even the way
of serving the same food may be attractive to one and repel-
lent to another. Happily, He to whom we owe our daily

bread has so ordained it that the ultimate constituents of our food are much the same, however varied it may be in its externals, and that as it is eaten with gladness and single-ness of heart it may alike promote the growth, health, and strength of the individual. I say this because it would grieve me greatly if in what follows I should seem to arro-gate to myself the position of teacher when I wish to act simply as a truthful historian.

George Fox tersely declares his faith in these words : " I saw that Christ died for all men and was a propitiation for all men and had enlightened all men and women by his Divine and saving Light." These are two inseparable halves of one great proposition, and George Fox did not separate them. The first, that Christ died for all men and was a propitiation for all men, accorded with the general sentiment of the English Church. Much as men then and since have endeavored to show that Fox preached the second half of this proposition to the exclusion or the belittling of the first, such a charge is utterly disproved by his own words spoken again and again before his accusers and left on record in his autobiography. I do not propose to offer any words of my own in support of this statement, but shall content myself with quoting George Fox's own declaration of faith, prepared by himself and two of his friends, printed and issued under his immediate supervision at Barbadoes in the year 1671 ; and that there may be no doubt of its correct-ness, I shall quote it from the first edition of Fox's Journal, printed in the year 1694, under the immediate supervision of William Penn and other prominent Friends.[1] The fact that George Fox's faith has been so strangely misunderstood by some and so grossly misrepresented by others must be my apology for giving the quotation in full. Says Fox, " Whereas many scandalous Lies and Slanders have been cast upon us to render us odious, as that we do deny God and Christ Jesus and the scriptures of Truth. This is to in-form you that all our Books and Declarations which for these many years have been published to the world do clearly

[1] Journal, etc., of George Fox (*op. cit.*), p. 358.

testify the contrary. Yet notwithstanding for your satisfaction we do now plainly and sincerely declare That we do Own and Believe in God, the only Wise, Omnipotent and Everlasting God, who is Creator of all things both in Heaven and on Earth and the Preserver of all that He hath made; who is God over all blessed forevermore! And we do Own and Believe in Jesus Christ his beloved and only begotten Son, in whom he is well pleased; who was conceived by the Holy Ghost and born of the Virgin Mary, in whom we have Redemption through his Blood, even the forgiveness of Sins. Who is the Express Image of the invisible God, the First-born of every Creature by whom were all things created that are in Heaven and that are in Earth visible and invisible whether they be Thrones or Dominions or Principalities or Powers, All things were created by Him. And we do Own and Believe that he was made a sacrifice for sin who knew no sin, neither was guile found in his mouth. And that he was crucified for us in the Flesh without the Gates of Jerusalem and that He was buried and Rose again the third day by the power of his Father for our justification. And we do Believe that he ascended up into Heaven and now sitteth at the right hand of God. This Jesus who was the Foundation of the Holy Prophets and Apostles is our Foundation and we do believe that there is no other Foundation to be laid, but that which is laid even Christ Jesus who we believe tasted Death for every Man and shed his Blood for all Men and who is the propitiation for our Sins and not for ours only but also for the sins of the whole world. According as John the Baptist testified of him when he said Behold the Lamb of God that taketh away the sins of the world: John 1: 29. We believe that He alone is our Redeemer and Saviour even the Captain of our Salvation. . . . And he is our Mediator that makes Peace and Reconciliation between God offended and us offending, he being the Oath of God, the New Covenant of Light, Life, Grace and Peace, the Author and Finisher of our Faith. Now this Lord Jesus Christ, the Heavenly man, the Emanuel, God with us we all own and believe in; him whom the High Priest raged against and put to death; the same whom Judas betrayed for Thirty pieces of Silver, which the priest gave him as a reward for his Treason, who also gave large money to the Soldiers to broach a horrible lie,—namely, that his Disciples came and stole him away by Night whilst they slept. And after he was Risen from the dead the History of Acts of the Apostles sets forth how the chief Priests and Elders persecuted the Disciples of this Jesus for preaching Christ and his Resurrection. This, we say, is that Lord Jesus Christ whom we own to be our Life and Salvation.''

Accepting this, then, as the exposition of his faith on the important subject of which it treats, and we cannot do otherwise, it does not, of itself, place George Fox before the world as a reformer in the Christian Church.

For this we must turn to the second half of the proposition : '' I saw that Christ died for all men and was a propitiation for all men *and had enlightened all men and women by his Divine and saving Light.*'' To preach this Divine Light as in the heart of all was the especial service of George Fox. By this his position among the great reformers of the Christian Church becomes a positive and clearly-defined one.

We hear much nowadays in this connection the words '' The Inner Light,'' and so great an authority as the historian Bancroft has said, '' the Quaker has but one word, the Inner Light;'' but he wisely adds, '' it is the voice of God in the soul.'' Other men claiming to be historians, but with much less knowledge of history, have adopted his earlier words, forgetting his later ones, and have ventured to speak slightingly, if not sneeringly, of the Inner Light.

For myself, I have never been quite content that these especial words, '' The Inner Light,'' should be accepted as the Shibboleth of the Quaker. I turn in vain over the many hundred pages of Fox's Journal, of Penn's select works, and look in vain through Barclay's Apology to find these very words, '' The Inner Light.'' And so I do not hesitate to say that neither Fox, Penn, nor Barclay applied to the Divine Teacher the words '' The Inner Light.'' For an inner light would be a light born from within, evolved out of man's own inner consciousness, taking its coloring from his social or educational environment,—a varying and an unsteady flame, and apt to prove an uncertain, if not an unsafe, guide.

George Fox did not preach such a light. But what he did preach everywhere, on all fitting occasions, as the Light, the Companion, the Guide, the Teacher, the Comforter of man, was the *Light of Christ* in the heart. He accepted in all its fulness for them, for himself, and for all Christians the words spoken by their Divine Master to his sorrowing disciples, " If I go away I will pray the Father, and he shall give you another Comforter, that he may abide with you for ever; even the Spirit of truth, whom ye know; for he dwelleth with you, and shall be in you." On this promise the distinctive faith and preaching of George Fox were founded.

Said William Penn, " That which the people called Quakers lay down as a main fundamental in Religion is that God, through Christ, hath placed a Principle in every man to inform him of his duty; and to enable him to do it; and that those who live up to this Principle are the people of God; and that those who live in dishonour to it are not God's people whatever name they may bear or profession they may make of religion. This is their ancient, first and standing testimony, with this they began and this they bore and do bear to the world." (Penn's " Christian Quaker.") Elsewhere Penn calls this principle " The Light of Christ within man."

It was the conviction that this Divine Light was needed and yet was sufficient for every duty in life that led these early Friends to dispense with external forms of worship which were then and are now highly valued by so many Christians. But in dispensing with these they did not for a moment propose to dispense with the spiritual service, the spiritual communion, the spiritual baptism they are supposed to typify. Nay, because, it may be, of the very omission of these outward forms to which many of them had been accustomed, they pressed the more upon the people the necessity of that change of heart without which these outward rites are acknowledged to be unavailing.

Thus, William Penn says of the early preachers among the Quakers, "They were changed men themselves before they went about to change others," and George Fox, in an epistle to the early believers, writes, " Let all your religious meetings be held in the power of God. Mind the Light— we are nothing—Christ is all."

Happily, nowadays we hear this doctrine of the immanence of the Holy Spirit preached elsewhere than among the descendants of the early Quakers. But the important fact to bear in mind is that in Fox's time, in Great Britain, though less so in Wales, the nature of spiritual religion seemed largely lost sight of. Lest I should be thought a prejudiced and therefore an unreliable authority on this subject, I prefer to quote the words of a distinguished author in the Church of England, Canon George Herbert Courteis, who, in his Bampton Lectures, delivered at Oxford in the year 1871, after speaking of "the majestic truth" (as he calls it) "preached by Fox," but claiming that it was what the Anglican Church had long believed, adds, " but it must be confessed it was not in Fox's time, nay, it is not *now* brought out in its full force and significance." A little later the same writer says of the religious Society of Friends, " It has been able to infuse the spirit and sense of George Fox's teaching into the very veins, as it were, of the modern world." And in concluding his lecture, Canon Courteis, though telling where, in his opinion, George Fox fell short in his con ception of the whole gospel, adds, " I fear not to say that within the Church of England, no less than among the Dissenting communities, this doctrine of the Holy Ghost and of this indwelling light had been far too little heard, and especially was this the case in or before Fox's time, and, therefore, that no small debt of gratitude is due to one who first (even amid some error and extravagance) recovered for us the true prominence of the third great section of the Nicene Creed."

Another authority in the Anglican Church, Canon Westcott, now Bishop of Durham, in a series of discourses delivered in Westminster Abbey, says of Fox and his companions, "The Quakers seem to me to express with greatest force the new thought of the Reformation, the thought of individuality;" and after many kind words respecting Fox's distinctive views, he says, "If Fox's message was met by fierce denunciations of technical theologians, it was welcomed as indeed a gospel by many who had not heard the like before. It opened once again the prospect of that universal kingdom to which Isaiah looked. It gave back to mankind the idea of a Divine Fatherhood commensurate with the Divine Love. We may think that many of the details on which Fox laid stress were trivial, but in spite of every infirmity of disposition, he was able to shape a character in those who followed him which, for independence, for truthfulness, for vigor, for courage, and for purity, is unsurpassed in the records of Christian endeavor." [1]

I have given these extracts because an American writer on Church history has recently said of these same early Friends that "after passing through a riotous and dangerous phase they became the negatively good folk their few surviving descendants still are. They had earned and compelled that curious, half-contemptuous, good-will which is still accorded them!" Such is not the estimate placed on these early Quakers by the Bampton lecturer and by the Lord Bishop of Durham.

This, then, was the faith held by George Fox, preached by John ap John; the faith in which our Welsh ancestors and the founder of this great Commonwealth lived, and in which and for which they were willing to die. Because they believed this Light to be the Light of Christ, the gift of His Holy Spirit, His promised Comforter, it became to them the supreme law of their being, as it was the supreme joy of their hearts. For this faith in the Divine Presence within them was no dim, misty dream, but a positive, I had almost said a tangible, reality. It influenced every thought and

---

[1] "Special Aspects of Christianity," by Brooke Foss Westcott, D.D., etc. London, 1888, p. 119 *et seq.*

every act of their lives. And with this faith there came such a sense of Divine companionship as made for them hard things easy, bitter things sweet. What to them the solitude of the dungeon, if its darkness was illumined by this Divine Light? What to them the perils of the deep, if He who walked the sea of Galilee and calmed its waves was with them in the ship? And so it heightened every joy, it lightened every sorrow, gave them strength in weakness, life where death seemed else inevitable.

And soon they had need for all this help, for though at first Fox and his coadjutors were kindly received in Wales, yet when it was found how great was the number of his followers; how that not only the common people heard them gladly, but that men of position in the Church and of influence in the community became converts and zealous workers in their cause; how that the services of the Church were neglected, its tithes unpaid, a free gospel preached everywhere, and the doctrine openly taught that the priesthood was reserved for no privileged class, but that all true Christians might be, should be, priests unto God; how that the One Divine Mediator had forever rendered unnecessary any human mediator between God and man; how that worship to be availing must be in spirit; then it was that those in authority took alarm and brought to bear, seemingly with crushing force, all the authority of Church and State on these offenders. On the table before me is an original order bearing date May 20, 1675, addressed to the high and petty constables of Merioneth, ordering the arrest of twenty-eight men and women (whose names are there given) who had " met at a house called Llyny Branar under colour or pretense of religion not according to the litargie and practice of the Church of England, contrarie to the Act of Parliament, instituted to prevent and suppress seditious conventicles." Next to this on the table is an original record of the sufferings of Friends for non-payment of tithes, made at the time. Next to this is a writ committing to the common jail, at Dolgelly, Cadwalader ap Thomas ap Hugh, Robert Owen, Hugh Roberts, John David, and others. Other papers of like character are preserved, brought to Pennsylvania by the family of John ap Thomas, who, though a Friend, was high constable at that time.

Forbidden to meet in public places, these Welsh Friends built houses on their own estates or continuous with their own homes. In the old town of Salzburg, in the very cleft of the rocks, are still shown the traveller the excavations in which early Christians were wont to meet to worship in secret when they dared not do so openly.

Often have I been reminded of these when viewing the little, cheerless, comfortless, cell-like rooms in which these Welsh Quakers were compelled to meet, and rarely has my heart been so deeply touched as it was last summer, when, driving a few miles beyond Dolgelly, my companion stopped before a dense piece of woods and said, "Here it was that Robert Owen, Rowland Ellis, and the Friends of Dolgelly were accustomed to hold their religious meetings when they dared not meet under any roof."

I do not propose to-night to go over the sickening details of this history. It is the old, old story of good men persecuted by men some of whom aimed to be good men also, but who had failed to learn the lesson or to profit by the rebuke given to his over-zealous disciples by their Divine Master : "other sheep I have, which are not of this fold"— "he that is not against us is for us."

Old friends and neighbors became alienated, and never is the bitterness of strife more intense than when a man's foes are they of his own household. For ten years, it is said, Charles Lloyd was a prisoner in the smoky jail of Welshpool, within a few miles of his home at Dolobran. For five years Robert Owen was a prisoner at Dolgelly, within two miles of his home at Dolscrau, which he was not allowed to visit, and this, too, although he had himself been a justice of the peace, his wife's sister married to the rector of the parish church of Dolgelly, and his brother-in-law high sheriff of the county. Well may we say of religion, as of liberty, "what crimes have been committed in thy name !"

It was not until after the fiercest storm of persecution had somewhat subsided that the thought of a New World seems to have taken hold of the people of Wales.

Does it ever occur to us how slight at first and gradual in its development this thought of leaving the old home and its associations must have been? How the consent of one member of the family after another must be gained, what ties of natural affection had to be severed, what courage—almost superhuman—was required for such a radical change in their life? John Bevan, the ancestor of two of the most useful officers of our Historical Society, has left us the record of his motives in coming to the New World. John Bevan, as the memorial respecting him tells us, was well descended, and was left by his father a considerable estate; but the rest of the children, four in number, being unprovided for, he therefore, when he came of age (his sister being dead before), portioned all his brothers and gave them a helpful subsistence in the world. He thus writes of his emigration to America: "Some time before the year 1683 we had heard that our esteemed friend William Penn had a patent from King Charles the Second for that Province in America called Pennsylvania, and my wife had a great inclination to go thither and thought it might be a good place to train up children amongst sober people and to prevent the corruption of them here, by the loose behaviour of the youths and the bad example of too many of those of riper years; she acquainted me therewith, but I then thought it not likely to take effect for several reasons. But as I was sensible her aim was an upright one, on account of our children I was willing to weigh the matter in a true balance; and I can truly say my way was made easy and clear to go thither beyond my expectation, and it was the Lord's great mercy to preserve us over the great deep to our desired port. And what hardships we met at the beginning of our settlement the Lord was our helper and support to go through." I wish to avoid personalities, but I cannot help saying that to this upright aim of Barbara Bevan for her children our Historical Society owes one of its most valued vice-presidents and the bench of Philadelphia one of her purest and wisest of judges.

What was thought by his friends and neighbors of this decision of John Bevan and his wife to come to Pennsylvania is thus stated in the minutes of the Meeting at Trevereg, Glamorganshire, South Wales, "10th of ye 7 mo. in ye year 1683."

"We whose names are under written doe hereby sertifie unto all whom it may concern the great loss we and others have sustained in the removal of our deare friends John ap Bevan and Barbarah his wife, both belonging to this Meeting, with their tender family to Pennsylvania.

"The precious truth was much in their eyes and this alone moved their hearts and wrought upon their sperits in order to their removal hence. And no earthly things whatsoever, having left behind them a very considerable estate surpassing many in their outward abode here with us, without any encumbrances in the least whatever thereupon.

"And further we do certifie that we accounted them as Pillers to this Meeting! [and] accounted as nursing father and nursing mother in this place to some weake and young amongst us severally. Blessings from above with peace and everlasting rest continually surround them within their dwelling forevermore."

Such was the "send-off" given two hundred and ten years ago to John and Barbara Bevan.

What was the invitation given by William Penn at this time and earlier to these Welsh Friends and others who were considering this important subject of a removal to the New World? What were the inducements he held out, what the advantages to be gained by such a removal? In the settlements of New Jersey, and especially of Pennsylvania, he had invested largely of his pecuniary means; his reputation as a successful leader was at stake; failure meant disgrace abroad and ruin at home. What inducements, I repeat, were held out by him, what temptations of ease, what hopes of sudden wealth which have proved such potent factors in the settlement of our distant lands? Hear what he says : "In whomsoever a desire is to be concerned in this intended plantation *such should weigh the thing before the Lord and not rashly con-clude on any such remove,* and that they do not offer violence to the tender love of their kindred and relations, but soberly and conscientiously endeavour to obtain their good wills, the unity of Friends where they live, that whether they go or stay it may be of good favour before the Lord from whom alone can all heavenly and earthly blessings come.   This am I, William Penn, moved of the Lord to write unto you, lest any bring a temptation upon themselves or others, and in offending the Lord slay their own peace.   Blessed are they that can see and behold Him their leader their orderer, their conductor and preserver in staying or going.   Whose is the earth and fulness thereof and the cattle upon a thou-sand hills!''

Is there elsewhere in all history such a record?   Men of Pennsylvania, can we ever too highly honor the name or too fondly cherish the memory of our Founder?

And to this Western world they came, in several instances preceding the Proprietor, in whose good ship, '' The Wel-come,'' there were, besides William Penn and his friend and physician, Dr. Thomas Wynne, comparatively few Welsh-men.   Here is the original subscription list of John ap Thomas, Edward Jones, Hugh Roberts, and others, in all seventeen families, showing what sum of money every Friend in Penllyn '' hath layed out to buy land in Pennsylvania, and what quantities of acres of land each is to have, and w't sum of Quit Rent falls upon every one.''   In a late number of our PENNSYLVANIA MAGAZINE, and in the number about to be issued, will be found the names of about fifty families pur-chasers of land in the Welsh Tract.   Among these are the names of Thomas Wynne and our old friend John ap John, who are there recorded as having together purchased five thousand acres, doubtless for themselves and others.

But my researches last summer showed that, though per-haps at one time contemplating a removal, John ap John did not come to Pennsylvania.   This is confirmed by the paper I now hold in my hand, which has recently come into my possession, and which is an exemplification of record of release of William Penn, Esq., to John ap John *et al.* By this it appears that " on the 15th day of September in the year of our Lord 1681 William Penn granted to John ap John of the Parish of Ruabon in the County of Denbigh, Yeoman, and to Thomas Wynne of Caerwys, county of Flint, Chirurgeon, in consideration of the sum of one hundred pounds Sterling moneys, 5000 acres of land." In this paper also " John ap John of his part 2500 acres there have been sold two thousand acres, reserving for himself 500 acres," and by this copy of another paper I find the remaining five hundred disposed of. So that John ap John did not cross the sea as so many of his faith did, but died at the house of his son-in-law, John Miller, of Whitehugh, England, on the 16th day of the ninth month, 1697, as has been but recently learned by a careful examination of the papers at Devonshire House Meeting,[1] where in the return from Staffordshire of answers to the queries for 1698, " What Public Friends deceased this year?" it is answered, " none save our antient Friend John ap John," whose death is recorded as above and his interment at Basford, a hamlet adjoining Whitehugh. In the year 1712, Friends in North Wales were desired by the Yearly Meeting to collect books and manuscripts relating to the services of " our ancient and faithful friend John ap John," and to send them up to the second day's Meeting. If this was done, no record of it can be found now. It may be that with characteristic humility he had left a request that no such records should be preserved. No stone marks his resting-place, and I know not, other than that of this evening, any public tribute has been paid to his memory. And yet had this messenger sent by Morgan Floyd to try the Quakers fallen away from his convincement, as did his companion, who can tell how different it might have been in Wales and in Pennsylvania? Who can say that any of us who are of Welsh ancestry would be here to night?

How the voyage across the sea was conducted, we have their own account. Here is a letter written by Edward Jones, which I have once before brought before this Society,

[1] By Isaac Sharp, Jr., of Friends' Institute, London.

dated "Skool Kill River ye 26th of 6th mo., 1682," in which he writes "we were eleven weeks before we made the land. It was not for want of art, but contrary winds." Think of it, we who would groan over a voyage of eleven days on the "New York" or the "Etruria." Here in this old Bible, their companion on the voyage, this record tells us how a widowed mother, Katharine Robert Thomas, who had left a most comfortable home at Llaithgwm, saw two loving daughters in the bloom of their womanhood, one after the other, laid away in the silent deep.

This letter tells how the voyagers on their ship were captured by privateers and carried to the West Indies; and what a history is that given us by Richard Townsend of his voyage on "The Welcome" in company with the Proprietor, whom I claim as of Welsh ancestry! Townsend writes of William Penn, "His singular care was manifested in contributing to the necessities of many who were sick with the small-pox then on board, of which company about thirty died." What a picture does even this slight sketch give us of the character of Penn! In the midst of this loathsome pestilence, with all the painful responsibilities resting upon him as the leader of the emigration, we see him going from bed to bed, animating the sick, comforting the dying, and by his singular care in every way relieving the necessities of his fellow-passengers. Amid all these depressing influences the faith of the founder of Pennsylvania never failed him. To him the words of the Psalmist were a reality: "The Lord is my refuge and my fortress: my God; in Him will I trust. Surely he shall deliver me from the snare of the fowler, and from the noisome pestilence." [1]

In the old Massachusetts town of Plymouth, held sacred by the people of New England, are carefully preserved in their Memorial Hall everything belonging to the "Mayflower." The walls are covered with pictures representing the departure of the Pilgrims, their religious services, and their arrival at Plymouth.

[1] See article by the writer on "'The Welcome,'" *Public Ledger*, Philadelphia, October 23, 1876.

It has not been our habit in Pennsylvania to paint pictures or to build monuments, but where could better material be found for these than in this sketch of the Founder given by Townsend, and in this record of the sailing of one of the ships given by Thomas Story :

" Everything needful for our voyage and journey being ready, on the 10th day of the 9th month, in the evening, we went on board, near Deptford, in the river Thames, accompanied by several of our dear friends and brethren, viz., John Field, John Butcher, . . . and many others ; and soon after came to us William Penn, Joseph Wyeth, and some more.

" And being together in the great cabin, the good presence of the Lord commanded deep and inward silence before Him, and the Comforter of the just brake in upon us by his irresistible power, and greatly tendered us together in his heavenly love, whereby we were melted into many tears. Glorious was this appearance, to the humbling of us all, and the admiration of some there who did not understand it. And in this condition we remained for a considerable season, and then William Penn was concerned in prayer ' for the good and preservation of all, and more especially for us then about to leave them; with thanksgiving also for all the favors of God, and for that holy and precious enjoyment as an addition to his many former blessings.' And when he had finished, the Lord repeated his own holy embraces of Divine, soul-melting love upon the silent, weeping assembly, to the full confirmation of us more immediately concerned, and further evidence to the brethren, of the truth of our calling.

" In this love unfeigned, and tender condition of soul, we bade each other farewell to our mutual satisfaction, for the same powerful love of truth that made us loth to depart from our friends and brethren of our own native land, drawing us to remote parts of the world, and remaining in our hearts, gives courage and strength also to leave all and follow the Lord, even wheresoever He will.

" We looked after them so long as we could see them, not

with minds to go backwards or hearts with any desire now to return, but in the comfort of Divine love, which neither distance of place nor number of years shall ever be able to obstruct or deface, as we keep true to the Lord in our-selves." [1]

Of what happened to the Welsh emigrants after their arrival here I need say but little. The words of John Bevan briefly indicate some of the hardships they had to endure and other histories tell us more. Not the least among their trials was the apostasy of one of their religious Society, George Keith, who seems to have been animated with especial hatred of the Welsh Friends, as is particularly noted in the memorial respecting Governor Thomas Lloyd. Long before William Penn came to America, George Keith had been an honored member of the religious Society of Friends, and had travelled with Penn in his religious visits on the Continent. It was because he was not a stranger, but their own familiar friend, that made his defection so hard to bear, and which gave to the controversy that bitterness which is so apt to exist when one's foes are they of his own house-hold.

Another trouble occurred later in the attempt to deprive these early settlers of the especial privileges promised them by William Penn before they left Wales, in what was known as the Welsh Tract, a sort of barony growing out of the desire of these early settlers, so characteristic of the Welsh, to be settled near each other, having their own laws, man-aging their own municipal affairs, speaking their own British language.

The warrant for the survey of this Welsh Tract may yet be found in the Surveyor-General's office at Harrisburg, and a copy of it in "The History of Delaware County," by Dr. George Smith. The Welsh Tract included forty thousand acres lying chiefly in Merion, Radnor, Haverford, including a part of the whole of Goshen. In the absence of William Penn this distinct barony was broken in on by the running

---

[1] "Journal of the Life of Thomas Story." Newcastle-upon-Tyne, A.D. 1747, p. 121.

of a division between Philadelphia and Chester Counties through the Welsh Tract, separating the Welsh settlements of Radnor and Haverford from those of Merion; this, and later an oppressive form of collecting quit-rents, caused great dissatisfaction among the Welsh; and notwithstanding "the pathetic appeal" of Griffith Owen, that "the descendants of the Ancient Britons might be allowed to have their bounds and limits by themselves, within which all causes, quarrels, crimes, and disputes might be tryed and wholly determined by officers, magistrates and juries of our language," the Welsh Tract was thrown open for settlement to others besides these descendants of the ancient Britons, though the number who availed themselves of the opportunity was not large. (Smith's "History," p. 177.)

I have said that these early Welsh Friends were men of education or, to use a modern word much in vogue, were men of culture. That I may not be thought to have made this statement at random, I desire to call the attention of this audience to papers on the table before them, where original letters written by them may be seen, the orthography and penmanship of which are such as only can be found among men of education. The minutes of Merion Meeting in the first ten or more years of the settlement prove the same, and the memorial respecting Thomas Lloyd, prepared by Haverford Monthly Meeting, whether as a loving tribute to an honored fellow-member or as a work of literary merit, may challenge comparison with anything of the kind in our day.

It is an interesting fact which I have noted elsewhere, that for twenty-five years the only physicians of Philadelphia and its vicinity were Welshmen. It is also a fact of which as Welshmen we are proud, that the physician of George Washington, Dr. John Jones, was the great-grandson of Dr. Thomas Wynne, who was himself the physician of William Penn; so that the Founder of our State and "the Father of his country" owed their lives, humanly speaking, to the care and skill of Welsh physicians. Had this skill and care failed the one amid the pestilence on "The Welcome" or the other in the perils of the Revolution, who can tell what the fate of our Commonwealth and our country had been?

And now, as I see before me this evening among the members of this Historical Society the descendants of Thomas Lloyd, of John ap Thomas, of Cadwalader ap Thomas, of John David, of Henry Lewis, of John Roberts, of Hugh Roberts, of Thomas Wynne, of Edward Jones, of William ap Edward, of Rowland Ellis, of Robert Owen, of John Bevan, of Edward Foulke, of Robert Cadwalader, of Rees Thomas, of Ellis Pugh, and others, and know that not only are they useful members of the Historical Society, but are also useful members of the community in which they live; know, too, that the lines have fallen to them in pleasant places and that they have here a goodly heritage, I think that they owe—SONS OF THE FOUNDERS, I think that we all owe—a debt of gratitude to one Morgan Lloyd, a priest of Wrexham, who sent two of his men to the north of England to try the Quakers and bring back an account of them. SONS OF THE FOUNDERS, I think we owe a debt of gratitude to that messenger, John ap John, who abode in the truth and received a gift in the ministry, to which he remained faithful, and who in the exercise of that ministry wrought such results as have so closely bound his life to our lives. SONS OF THE FOUNDERS, I think we owe a debt of gratitude to those brave men and gentle women who gave up their own homes, braved the perils of the deep, endured the hardships of a new and untried world, not for themselves, but for those who were to come after them,—for you and for me.

And so to-night, with feeble hand it may be, but with a heart full of filial love and gratitude, I have endeavored to lift the veil of two centuries which separates us from them, and in this simply colloquial way to tell you of their names, their homes, and their daily life.

I need not tell you, members of the Historical Society, that truth and justice were both the foundation and the bulwark of the homes they builded here; that the virtues of the people were their palaces and towers. Centuries ago he who was both the bard and the king of Israel commanded his people to walk about their Zion, and go around about her, to tell the towers thereof; to mark well her bulwarks, to consider her palaces, that they might tell it to the generation following.   Happy will it be for us if, having done this aright, we may take up what remains of the Psalmist's words, and in all humility but in all sincerity can say, " For this God of our fathers is our God for ever and ever : he will be our guide even unto death."

THE CAMP BY THE OLD GULPH MILL.

BY WILLIAM S. BAKER.

[An address delivered before the Pennsylvania Society of Sons of the Revolution, June 19, 1898, on the occasion of dedicating the memorial stone marking the site of the encampment of the Continental army at the old Gulph Mill, in December, 1777.]

In the closing scenes of the eventful campaign of 1777, the encampment of the Continental army near the old Gulph Mill [1] is an interesting feature. The army remained on these grounds from December 13 to December 19, and it is curious to note that this fact has been passed over by most historians, or, if alluded to at all, spoken of in very brief mention.

As a part of the story of the march to Valley Forge, it is well worthy of remembrance, and the permanent memorial which has been so generously presented to the Society by Mr. Joseph E. Gillingham, erected on ground courteously tendered by Mr. Henderson Supplee, the owner of the mill, has been fitly located. [2]

[1] The Gulph Mill, erected in 1747, is situated in Upper Merion Township, Montgomery County, Pennsylvania, at the intersection of the Gulph Road with the Gulph Creek, which empties into the Schuylkill at West Conshohocken. It is about a mile and a half west of the river and six miles southeast of Valley Forge. What is understood as the Gulph is where the creek passes through the Gulph Hill, and to effect a passage has cleft it to the base.

[2] The memorial consists of a large boulder, nine feet in height, taken from the adjacent hill and erected upon a substantial foundation. It is located at the intersection of Montgomery Avenue with the Gulph Road, about one hundred yards southeast of the mill. The entire cost of construction was defrayed by Joseph E. Gillingham, of Philadelphia, a friend of the Society. The stone, which weighs about twenty tons, bears the following inscription: "GULPH MILLS. THE MAIN CONTINENTAL ARMY COMMANDED BY GENERAL GEORGE WASHINGTON ENCAMPED IN

If, in presenting some facts concerning this encampment, and the movements of the army which led to it, I am unable to throw around the subject any of the " pride, pomp, and circumstance of glorious war," I would beg you to consider that the month of December, 1777, was one of the gloomiest periods of the struggle for independence.

Brandywine and Germantown had been fought and lost; Congress was a fugitive from its capital, and the capital in the hands of the enemy; the currency was rapidly depreciating; supplies were rotting on the roads for lack of transportation; the commissariat in the direst confusion, and the army in the utmost straits.   It was stern reality, not a chapter of romance.

After the battle of Germantown (October 4, 1777) the Continental army fell back to the Perkiomen Creek, at Pennybacker's Mills, now Schwenksville, Montgomery County, the ground of a previous encampment.[1]   Notwithstanding this lengthened march of some twenty miles,[2]—I suppose we may as well call it a retreat,—the troops do not seem to have been badly demoralized, as there exists good evidence to the contrary.   The writer of a letter from this encampment to the *Continental Journal,* of Boston, under date of the 6th, and published in that paper of the 30th, states that " all the men were in good spirits and seem to grow fonder of fighting the more they have of it;" and again, General Knox, in writing to Artemas Ward on the

THIS IMMEDIATE VICINITY FROM DECEMBER 13 TO DECEMBER 19 1777 BEFORE GOING INTO WINTER QUARTERS AT VALLEY FORGE. ERECTED BY THE PENNSYLVANIA SOCIETY OF SONS OF THE REVOLUTION 1892. THIS MEMORIAL TO THE SOLDIERS OF THE REVOLUTION STANDS ON GROUND PRESENTED BY HENDERSON SUPPLEE OWNER OF THE GULPH MILL ERECTED IN 1747."

[1] From September 26 to September 29, 1777.

[2] " After the army were all retreating, I expected they would have returned to their last encampment, about twelve or thirteen miles from the enemy at Germantown; but the retreat was continued upwards of twenty miles; so that all those men, who retired so far, this day marched upwards of thirty miles without rest, besides being up all the preceding night without sleep.   This step appeared to me not of such pressing necessity."—*Pickering's Journal.*

7th, uses the following language : "Our men are in the highest spirits, and ardently desire another trial. I know of no ill consequences that can follow the late action ; on the contrary, we have gained considerable experience, and our army have a certain proof that the British troops are vulnerable."

While the army was resting at Pennybacker's Mills a considerable re-enforcement from Virginia was received, and on the morning of the 8th a move was made into Towamencin Township, the camping ground being in the vicinity of the Mennonite meeting-house (near Kulpsville), in the burial-ground of which rest the remains of General Francis Nash, of North Carolina, and other officers mortally wounded at Germantown.

It was at this encampment that Washington received a letter from the Rev. Jacob Duché, of Philadelphia (who had forsaken the patriot cause), which has assumed much greater historical importance than it is entitled to. In this letter the reverend gentleman, after censuring the motives of Congress and those of the leaders in the cause of freedom, urged the commander-in-chief to "represent to Congress the indispensable necessity of rescinding the hasty and ill-advised Declaration of Independency."

Washington transmitted the letter to Congress, with this remark : "To this ridiculous, illiberal performance, I made a short reply, by desiring the bearer of it [Mrs. Ferguson, of Graeme Park] if she should hereafter by any accident meet with Mr. Duché, to tell him I should have returned it unopened if I had had any idea of the contents."

Here the army was again re-enforced by some troops from Peekskill, under General Varnum, of Rhode Island, and on the 16th a further move was made to the southward, near "Methacton Hill," in Worcester Township, the point from which the army had started on the evening of October 3 to attack the enemy at Germantown. While here, the cheering news of the defeat and surrender of General Burgoyne was received, and the general order issued in reference to it directed the chaplains of the army to prepare discourses suited to the occasion.

On the 19th of October the British army entirely evacuated Germantown and retired nearer to Philadelphia, their new line of intrenchments extending from the upper ferry on the Schuylkill, at Callowhill Street, to Kensington on the Delaware.[1]

On the 21st the army moved lower down into Whitpaine Township, within fifteen miles of the city. It was from this encampment that the following general order was issued on the 25th, announcing the successful defence of Fort Mercer on the Delaware by Colonel Christopher Greene, of Rhode Island :

"The Gen[l] again congratulates the Troops on the success of our arms. On Wednesday last [October 22] a Body of about 1200 Hessians under the command of Count Donop made an attack on Fort Mercer at Red Bank, and after an action of 40 Minutes were repulsed with great loss. Count Donop himself is wounded and taken prisoner together with his Brigade Major and about 100 other officers and soldiers, and about 100 were left on the Fields, and as they carried off many of their wounded their whole loss is probably at least 400—our loss was trifling, the killed and wounded amounting only to about 32."

Count Donop died from his wounds three days after the battle. His last words, "I die the victim of my ambition and of the avarice of my sovereign," are painfully suggestive.

The gallant defender of Red Bank, Christopher Greene, while on duty at Croton River (May 13, 1781), was basely murdered by a band of Westchester County Tories.

On November 2 the march was made to Whitemarsh Township, twelve miles from the city, the encampment at this place being formed of two commanding hills, whose front and flanks were additionally secured by a strong advanced post, the right wing resting upon the Wissahickon

---

[1] At the time of the battle of Germantown the British army was encamped upon the general line of School-House Lane and Church Lane, crossing the town at the centre. The extreme left was at the mouth of the Wissahickon, and the right near Branchtown, on the Old York Road. These lines were retained until the movement of October 19.

and the left upon Sandy Run.   A redoubt known as Fort
Washington, on the right of the lines, is still well preserved.   Near this spot a memorial stone was erected by
the Society two years ago.[1]

Here news was received of the evacuation of Fort Mifflin
on the night of the 15th, followed by that of Fort Mercer
on the 19th.   The loss of these forts ended the defence of
the Delaware, and the obstructions in the river being removed, the enemy had full possession of Philadelphia.

Winter was now rapidly approaching, and it became
necessary to determine whether any attempt should be
made to recover possession of the city.   Accordingly a
council of the general officers was called to meet at head-
quarters[2] on the evening of the 24th of November, to consider the expediency of an attack on the enemy's lines, the
arrival of some troops from the Northern army and the
absence of a large body of British under Lord Cornwallis,
in New Jersey, being considered favorable circumstances.

The council adjourned without coming to a decision, and
the commander-in-chief, despatching a special messenger to
General Greene, who was watching the movements of Cornwallis in New Jersey, required of the other officers their
written opinions.   On comparing them, eleven were found
against making the attack (Greene, Sullivan, Knox, De
Kalb, Smallwood, Maxwell, Poor, Paterson, Irvine, Du-
portail, and Armstrong) and four only (Stirling, Wayne,
Scott, and Woodford) in its favor.

---

[1] The stone, a neat granite slab, stands on the southeasterly side of
the Bethlehem Turnpike Road, about thirteen miles north of Philadel-
phia.   It bears the following inscription : "ABOUT 700 FEET SOUTH OF
THIS STONE IS AN AMERICAN REDOUBT AND THE SITE OF HOWE'S
THREATENED ATTACK DEC. 6, 1777.   FROM HERE WASHINGTON'S
ARMY MARCHED TO VALLEY FORGE.   ERECTED IN 1891 BY THE
PENNSYLVANIA SOCIETY OF SONS OF THE REVOLUTION."

[2] The Whitemarsh head-quarters are still standing, about half a mile
east from Camp Hill Station on the North Pennsylvania Railroad.
The house, built of stone, is two and a half stories in height, eighty feet
front, and twenty-seven feet in depth.   Camp Hill, on which part of the
left wing of the army was posted, is directly in the rear of the house.

The letter of General Wayne, advising the attack, is so characteristic of the enterprise and dash of the man that we quote it entire. It is dated " Camp at White Marsh, 25th November, 1777.

" After the most Dispassionate & Deliberate Consideration of the Question your Excellency was pleased to put to the Council of Gen¹ Officers last evening—I am solemnly and clearly of Opinion; that the Credit of the Army under your Command—the safety of the Country—the Honor of the American Arms—the Approach of Winter that must in a few days force you from the field, and above all the Depreciation of the Currency of these States, point out the Immediate necessity of giving the enemy Battle.

" Could they possibly be drawn from their lines it is a measure devoutly to be wished—but if that can not be effected It is my Opinion that your Excellency should march tomorrow morning and take post with this Army at the upper end of Germantown, and from thence Immediately detach a working party to throw up some Redoubts under the Direction of your Engineers—this Intelligence will reach the Enemy—they will Conclude that you Intend to make good your winter-quarters there—and however Desirous they may be to dislodge you—they can't attempt it until they withdraw their Troops from the Jersey—this cannot be done in the course of a night.

" By this manœuvre you will be within striking distance—the Enemy will be Deceived by your working Party—and luled into security—your Troops will be fresh and ready to move that Night so as to arrive at the Enemies lines before daylight on this day morning—agreeable to the proposed plan of Attack—the outlines of which are good and may be Improved to Advantage and Crowned with Success.¹

¹ The plan of Lord Stirling and those in favor of the attack was, that it should be at different points, the main body to attack the lines to the north of the city, while Greene, embarking his men in boats at Dunk's Ferry (below Bristol), and passing down the Delaware, and Potter, with a body of Continentals and militia on the Schuylkill, should attack the eastern and western fronts.

" It has been objected by some Gentlemen that the attack is hazardous—that if we prevail it will be attended with great loss.   I agree with the Gentlemen in their position.

" But however hazardous the attempt and altho some loss is Certain—yet it is my Opinion that you will not be in a worse Situation—nor your arms in less Credit if you should meet with a misfortune than if you were to remain Inactive.

" The eyes of all the World are fixed upon you—the Junction of the Northern Army gives the Country and Congress some expectations that vigorous efforts will be made to Dislodge the Enemy and Oblige them to seek for Winter quarters in a less hostile place than Phil'a.

" It's not in our power to command Success—but it is in our power to produce a Conviction to the World that we deserve it."[1]

On the morning of the 25th a careful examination of the defences on the north of the city was made by the commander-in-chief in person.   The results of this reconnoissance, taken from the west bank of the Schuylkill, is best exhibited in the following extract from a letter written on the 26th by John Laurens to his father Henry Laurens, President of Congress:

" Our Commander-in-chief wishing ardently to gratify the public expectation by making an attack upon the enemy—yet preferring at the same time a loss of popularity to engaging in an enterprise which he could not justify to his own conscience and the more respectable part of his constituents, went yesterday to view the works.   A clear sunshine favoured our observations: we saw redoubts of a very respectable profit, faced with plank, formidably fraised, and the intervals between them closed with an abattis unusually strong.   General du Portail declared that in such works with five thousand men he would bid defiance to any force that should be brought against him."

All intentions of making an attack were then abandoned,

---

[1] " 'Tis not in mortals to command success,
    But we'll do more, Sempronius; we'll deserve it."
        CATO, Act I. Scene II.

and the question of winter-quarters for the army came up for consideration. On this point the views of the general officers were widely separated, some inclining to Reading, others to Lancaster and Wilmington.[1] It is said that Washington himself made the decision in favor of Valley Forge.

On the evening of December 4, General Howe, with nearly all his army, marched out from Philadelphia, with the boasted purpose of driving the rebels beyond the mountains. His advance arrived at Chestnut Hill about daylight the following morning, in front of and a short distance from the right wing of the Americans. General James Irvine, with six hundred men from the Pennsylvania militia, was ordered to move against them. A smart skirmish ensued, resulting in the retreat of the militia, leaving the general wounded in the hands of the British.

On the 7th the enemy moved to Edge Hill, on the American left, when their advanced and flanking parties were attacked by Colonel Daniel Morgan and his riflemen, and also by the Maryland militia, under Colonel Mordecai Gist. A sharp contest occurred, and the parties first attacked were driven in; but Washington, being unwilling to come to an engagement in the open field, declined re-enforcements, and Gist and Morgan were compelled to give way.

The enemy continued manœuvring the entire day of Sunday, the 7th, in the course of which Washington, expecting at any moment an attack, "rode through every brigade of his army, delivering in person his orders respecting the manner of receiving the enemy, exhorting his troops to rely principally on the bayonet, and encouraging them by the

[1] "If you can with any convenience let me see you to-day. I would be thankful for it. I am about fixing the winter cantonments of this army, and find so many and so capital objections to each mode proposed, that I am exceedingly embarrassed, not only by the advice given me, but in my own judgment, and should be very glad of your sentiments on the subject, without loss of time. In hopes of seeing you, I shall only add that from Reading to Lancaster inclusively, is the general sentiment, whilst Wilmington and its vicinity has powerful advocates."— *Washington to Joseph Reed*, December 2, 1777.

steady firmness of his countenance, as well as by his words, to a vigorous performance of their duty."[1]

The dispositions of the evening indicated an intention to attack on the ensuing morning; but Howe was afraid to assail Washington, and, failing in all attempts to draw him out, gave up the design, and on the afternoon of Monday, the 8th, changed front, and by two or three routes marched back to the city, burning a number of houses by the way.

"Washington, on receiving intelligence of Howe's retreat, said: 'Better would it have been for Sir William Howe to have fought without victory than thus to declare his inability.'"[2]

This virtually closed the campaign of 1777, and early on the morning of Thursday, the 11th of December, the army of eleven thousand men, many of them unfit for duty, set out for winter-quarters,[3] moving up the Skippack Road to the Broad-Axe Tavern, and from thence five miles westward to the Schuylkill, the intention being for the main body to cross at Matson's Ford, now Conshohocken, where a bridge had already been laid. It was also arranged that a portion of the troops should cross the river at Swede's Ford, some three miles higher up the stream.

When the first division and a part of the second had passed over the bridge at Matson's Ford, a body of British, three thousand strong, under Lord Cornwallis, was discovered stationed on the high ground on both sides of the road leading from the river and along the Gulph Creek. This forced the return of those who had crossed, and, after rendering the bridge impassable, the army was ordered to

---

[1] Marshall's "Washington," Vol. III. p. 319.

[2] Lee's "Memoirs," Vol. I. p. 45.

[3] *"December* 11.—At 3 A.M. we struck tents, passed White Marsh Church, and on to the upper bridge over the Schuylkill, when the enemy having crossed at the Middle Ferry [Market Street], attacked a party of Militia under Gen. Potter. The loss was inconsiderable on both sides. We then turned W.N.W. and proceeded thro' Hickorytown and encamped near Swedes Ford."—*Diary of Lieutenant James McMichael,* PENNSYLVANIA MAGAZINE, Vol. XVI. p. 156.

Swede's Ford, now Norristown, where it encamped for the night. The British, who were on a foraging expedition, were met in their advance by General James Potter, with part of the Pennsylvania militia, who behaved with bravery and gave them every possible opposition till he was obliged to retreat from superior numbers.

General Potter's report of his opposition to this raid, made to Thomas Wharton, President of the Supreme Executive Council of Pennsylvania, if not very good English, is certainly quite graphic:

"Last Thursday [December 11] the enemy march out of the City with a desine to Furridge; but it was Nesseserey to drive me out of the way; my advanced picquet fired on them at the Bridge [Market Street]; another party of one Hundred attacted them at the Black Hors.[1] I was encamped on Charles Thomson's place,[2] where I staeconed two Regments who attacted the enemy with viger. On the next Hill, I staeconed three Regments, letting the first line know, that when they were over powered, the must Retreat and form behind the sacond line, and in that manner we formed and Retreated for four miles; and on every Hill we disputed the matter with them. My people Behaved well, espealy three Regements, Commanded by the Col[.] Chambers, Murrey and Leacey. His Excellencey Returned us thanks in public orders;[3] — But the cumplement would have Been mutch more substantale had the Valant Generil Solovan [Sullivan] Covered my Retreat with two Devissions of the Army, he had in my Reare; the front of them was

[1] The Black Horse Tavern was on the old Lancaster Road, about five miles northwest of Philadelphia.

[2] Charles Thomson, Secretary of Congress. The Thomson place, known as "Harriton," was on the Old Gulph Road, about twelve miles from Philadelphia and three miles from the Gulph Mill. The mansion-house is still standing.

[3] "The Commander-in-Chief, with great pleasure, expresses his approbation of the behavior of the Pennsylvania Militia yesterday, under General Potter, on the vigorous opposition they made to a body of the enemy on the other side of the Schuylkill."—*Orderly-Book*, December 12, 1777.

about one half mile in my Rear, but he gave orders for them to Retreat and join the army who were on the other side of the Schuylkill, about one mile and a Half from me; thus the enemy Got leave to plunder the Countrey, which they have dun without parsiality or favour to any, leaving none of the Nessecereys of life Behind them that the conveniantly could Carry or destroy . . . His Excellancey was not with the Army when this unlucky neglact hapned; the army was on there march, and he had not come from his Quarters at Whit marsh."[1]

Lord Cornwallis returned to Philadelphia the following day.

Want of provisions[2] prevented any movement of the troops until the evening of the 12th, when at sunset the march was commenced, some crossing the river on a bridge of wagons at the ford and others at a raft bridge below. Early on the morning of the 13th of December the army arrived at the Gulph,[3] the depressing aspect of which prompted the Connecticut surgeon, Albigence Waldo, to record in his journal entry of that day that the place was well named, "for this Gulph seems well adapted by its situation to keep us from the pleasure and enjoyments of this world, or being conversant with any body in it."[4]

During the whole course of the war but few marches may be compared with this, short as it was, for hardship, privation, and almost despair. Yet, half starved, half naked

---

[1] *Pennsylvania Archives*, Vol. VI. p. 97.

[2] "The next morning [December 12] the want of provisions—I could weep tears of blood when I say it—the want of provisions render'd it impossible to march till the evening of that day."—*John Laurens to Henry Laurens*, December 23, 1777.

[3] "*December* 12.—At 6 P.M. we marched to the bridge [made of wagons], which we crossed in Indian file, and at 3 A.M. encamped near the Gulph, where we remained without tents or blankets in the midst of a severe snow storm."—*Diary of Lieutenant James McMichael.*

[4] Albigence Waldo was a regimental surgeon in the brigade of General Jedediah Huntington, of Connecticut. His diary from November 10, 1777, to January 15, 1778, from which we quote, is published in the fifth volume of the *Historical Magazine.*

as they were, their footsteps leaving tracks of blood,[1] the *Soldiers* of the Revolution bore up against all, and the *Sons* of the Revolution, in honoring their memories by the simple services of to-day, honor themselves.

It was cold, stormy weather, beginning with snow on the night of the 12th and ending with rain on the 16th, when for the first time the tents were pitched[2] and some little degree of comfort secured for the men, whose miserable condition is described by Dr. Waldo : " There comes a soldier—His bare feet are seen thro' his worn out shoes—his legs nearly naked from the tatter'd remains of an only pair of stockings—his Breeches not sufficient to cover his Nakedness—his shirt hanging in strings—his hair dishevell'd—his face meagre—his whole appearance pictures a person forsaken & discouraged."

Dismal as were the days, unpromising as was the future, we find the commander-in-chief still hopeful, still courageous, as he issues his order to the army on the 17th, wherein, after expressing his thanks to the officers and soldiers for the fortitude and patience with which they had sustained the fatigue of the campaign, he adds, " Although in some instances we unfortunately failed ; yet upon the whole Heaven hath smiled upon our arms and crowned them with signal success; and we may upon the best grounds conclude, that, by a spirited continuance of the measures necessary for our defence, we shall finally obtain the end of our warfare, Independence, Liberty and Peace."

Brave words, well worthy of such a commander and such soldiers.

While some of the letters written by Washington during

---

[1] " *December* 14.—It is amazing to see the spirit of the soldiers when destitute of shoes and stockings marching cold nights and mornings, leaving blood in their foot-steps ! yet notwithstanding, the fighting disposition of the soldiers is great."—*Letter from the army, Continental Journal,* January 15, 1778.

[2] " *December* 16*th.*—Cold Rainy Day — Baggage ordered over the Gulph, of our Division, which were to march at Ten—but the baggage was order'd back and for the first time since we have been here the Tents were pitch'd to keep the men more comfortable."—*Diary of Albigence Waldo.*

this encampment are dated "Head Quarters Gulf Mill," others again are from "Near the Gulph," and one to the Board of War is dated "Head Quarters Gulf Creek, 14 Dec. 1777." In the absence of any positive information on the subject, and with the knowledge that the mill merely marked the locality, it is, therefore, impossible to name with any accuracy the premises occupied by the commander-in-chief as head-quarters. The army was posted on the high grounds on both sides of the Gulph, and the tradition which points to a house which stood about one mile north of the mill and beyond the creek may be entitled to some consideration. It was at the time the residence of Lieutenant-Colonel Isaac Hughes, of the Pennsylvania militia. The house, a substantial stone building, was taken down some years ago.

An entry in the orderly-book of General Muhlenberg, directing "The Guards to Parade at the Gulph Mill at 3 o'clock" on the afternoon of December 13, is thought by some to indicate that head-quarters were in the immediate vicinity of the mill. If such is the case, the house which stands on the opposite side of the road may be entitled to the distinction. This house, considerably increased in size and importance, is now owned and occupied by Henderson Supplee, the proprietor of the Gulph Mill.

Apart from the usual routine of an army at rest, the incidents connected with this encampment which are known to us are few. We are told that on one occasion a party of the enemy, to the number of forty-five, was surprised and made prisoners,[1] but beyond this there is little to note. When the army lay at Valley Forge, however, the Gulph was an important post, and a characteristic anecdote of Aaron Burr in connection with it, related by his biographer, Matthew L. Davis, is of sufficient interest to repeat.[2]

---

[1] "*December* 17.—We have been for several days past posted on the mountains near the gulph mill, and yesterday a party of the enemy, to the number of forty five were surprised and made prisoners."—*Letter from the army, Continental Journal,* January 22, 1778.

[2] Colonel Burr joined the main army at Whitemarsh in November. He was at this time in the twenty-second year of his age.

It appears from this story that the militia stationed to guard the pass at the Gulph were continually sending false alarms to camp, which obliged the officers to get the troops under arms and frequently to keep them on the alert during the whole night. These alarms, it was soon found, arose from the want of a proper system of observation and from a general looseness of discipline in the corps. General McDougall, who well knew the quality of Colonel Burr as a soldier, recommended the commander-in-chief to give him the command of the post.

This was done, which resulted in the introduction of a system of such rigorous discipline that mutiny was threatened and the death of the colonel resolved upon. This came to the knowledge of Burr, and on the evening decided upon (every cartridge having been previously drawn from the muskets) the detachment was ordered to parade. When in line, one of the men stepped from the ranks and levelled his musket at him, whereupon Burr raised his sword and struck the arm of the mutineer above the elbow, nearly severing it from his body. In a few minutes the corps was dismissed, the arm of the mutineer was next day amputated, and no more was heard of the mutiny.

General Wayne, in writing from this encampment to a friend, requesting him to apply to Congress in his behalf for a short leave of absence, gives as his reasons ill health, a continued service of twenty-three months, and a desire to attend to his private affairs. Three very good pleas for such an indulgence, it being the first, as he says, that he had ever asked. The letter, dated "Camp at the Gulf 19th Decr. 1777," reads thus:

"After strugling with a stubron cold for months with a pain in my breast occasioned by a fall at Germantown—the Caitiff has taken post in my Lungs and throat—and unless I am permitted to change my Ground I dread the Consequence. I have not Interest sufficient with His Excellency to Obtain leave of Absence long enough to effect a Radical cure. My physicians advise me to go to some Inland town or place when I can be properly attended and procure a suitable Regimen. I have now been on constant duty for 23 months, sixteen of which I served in Canada and Ticonderoga, the Remainder with his Excellency during which period I have never had one single moment's respite. My private Interest is in a suffering Condition, all the amts of Money's Recd and Expenditures since then remain unsettled—so that if any misfortune should happen me—there is no person who could liquidate them.

"These considerations together with my state of Health induces me to request you to lay my case before Congress and endeavour to obtain leave of Absence for me for five or six weeks. I am confident that when they reflect on the length of time I have served them together with the hard duty I have underwent they will not hesitate to grant me this Indulgence it being the first I ever asked."

It does not appear that the leave of absence was obtained; at all events, we know that Wayne was still on duty at Lancaster and York in January, looking to a supply of clothing for the Pennsylvania troops.

On the 18th of December, a day set apart by Congress for thanksgiving and prayer, the troops remained in their quarters, and the chaplains performed service with their several corps and brigades. On this day, in general orders, the commander-in-chief gave explicit directions for constructing the huts for winter-quarters.

Although it has generally been stated that the establishment of winter-quarters at Valley Forge was fully decided upon at Whitemarsh, yet it seems that even when the army lay on these hills the matter was still under consideration. Timothy Pickering, in a letter to Mrs. Pickering, under date of December 13, wrote, "The great difficulty is to fix a proper station for winter quarters. Nothing else prevents our going into them . . . it is a point not absolutely determined." And, two days later, John Laurens, writing to the President of Congress, says, "The army cross'd the Schuylkill on the 13th and has remained encamped on the heights on this side. Our truly republican general has declared to his officers that he will set the example of passing the winter in a hut himself. The precise position is not yet fixed upon in which our huts are to be constructed; it will probably be determined to day; it must be in such a situation as to admit of a bridge of communication over the Schuylkill for the protection of the country we have just left.''

This uncertainty, which does not seem to have been removed until the 17th of the month, will account for the lengthened period of the encampment at the Gulph, and it may not be too much to say that in all probability this locality was also taken into consideration.

At ten o'clock on Friday morning, December 19, the army marched from hence to Valley Forge, six miles to the northward.[1]

We are standing on historic soil. Yonder hills, one hundred and sixteen years ago, witnessed the privations and sufferings of a band of heroes,—the soldiers of the Revolution. The old Gulph Mill, its walls grim and gray with age, still guards the spot, a faithful sentinel. Here have passed and repassed men whose names are history itself, whose deeds are a cherished inheritance. Washington, modest as virtuous; Greene, wise as brave; Knox, gallant as true; Lafayette, the friend of America; Sullivan, Stirling, De Kalb, Muhlenberg, Maxwell, Huntington, and Wayne! Anthony Wayne! Pennsylvania's soldier and patriot.

These grounds were the threshold to Valley Forge, and the story of that winter—a story of endurance, forbearance, and patriotism which will never grow old—had its beginning here, at the six days' encampment by the old Gulph Mill.

The memorial which we dedicate to-day in remembrance of this encampment—rough, unchiselled, nature's monument —is a fit emblem of the dreary days of December, 1777.

[1] The movements of the army which have been traced in this paper were entirely in what was then Philadelphia County, now (since 1784) Montgomery County, Pennsylvania, the townships or districts mentioned being the same as at present.

THE OLD IRON FORGE—"VALLEY FORGE."

BY HOWARD M. JENKINS.

The encampment of the American army at Valley Forge has invested the place with a permanent interest which makes every authentic detail in relation to it worthy of attention. I have therefore collected some data referring to the earliest buildings of importance which stood on the encampment grounds. These include:

1. The iron forge from which the place has derived its name. It was called Mountjoy Forge by its first owners, though commonly known, later, as Valley Forge, and was built by a partnership composed of Stephen Evans, Daniel Walker, and Joseph Williams, between December, 1742, and April, 1751. It stood on the lower (east) side of Valley Creek, in what is now Montgomery County, and was burned by the British in September, 1777.

2. A saw-mill on Valley Creek, which was built between 1751 and 1757.

3. A grist-mill on Valley Creek, built by John Potts in 1758 or 1759, and burned down in the spring of 1843.

4. The head-quarters mansion, built also, it is presumed, by John Potts, perhaps in 1758 or 1759, in connection with the work on the grist-mill, and now standing, carefully preserved by the Valley Forge Memorial Association.

5. The larger mansion-house, now known as the "Washington Inn," built before the Revolution, probably by some of the Potts family, and used by the American army during the encampment.

The most interesting and important of all these, of course, is the head-quarters mansion. Its history, no doubt, will in time be minutely traced by some one. In the present paper I have given most attention to the two points of (1) the location and (2) the history of the old forge, which doubtless is next in interest to the head-quarters mansion. To determine the question whether this forge stood on the lower (Montgomery County) side of Valley Creek or on the upper (Chester County) side, I have made examination of conveyances of land recorded in the office of the Recorder of Deeds, in Philadelphia. These researches, though not exhaustive (as I was not making a brief of title), are conclusive, as will be seen below, of the fact that the original forge stood on the lower side of Valley Creek, in Philadelphia (now Montgomery) County. Indeed, the evidence of this is so entirely clear and so readily accessible that it seems somewhat surprising that a question should ever have arisen concerning it.

THE EARLIEST CONVEYANCES.

Upon searching the records of deeds, I found a conveyance, of which the following memoranda give the essential points:

Release, December 13, 1742, Stephen Evans and Daniel Walker, both of Tredyffrin township, Chester county, yeomen, to Isaac Walker of the same township, yeoman, for 175 acres of land, the tract being bounded and described as follows:

"Beginning at a small gum by the Valley Creek, thence north 84 degrees east, by part of the same land, 72 perches, to a Spanish oak; thence north 16 degrees east, by the Widow Edwards's land, 222 perches to a Spanish oak, by the river Schuylkill; thence up the several courses of the said river 228 perches, to the mouth of Valley Creek, thence up the several courses of the same creek, 214 perches to the place of beginning, containing 175 acres."

This description, it is obvious, is that of the tract of land at the confluence of Valley Creek with the Schuylkill River, —on the east side of the creek and south side of the river, —it being the ground on which the Washington head-quarters building now stands, and including a considerable part of the encampment site.

Having fixed the place, we may with interest inquire how

these grantors of 1742, Stephen Evans and Daniel Walker, farmers in Tredyffrin, acquired their title. The recital of this in this conveyance is quite extended. First it recites the grant by William Penn to his daughter, Letitia Penn, October 24, 1701, of the "Manor of Mount Joy," supposed to contain seven thousand eight hundred acres, at a yearly rent of one beaver skin. From her the several conveyances down to Evans and Walker had been as follows:

1. Letitia (Penn) and her husband William Aubrey, July 10, 1730, to Sir Archibald Grant, "of that part of Great Britain called Scotland," the conveyance being for the whole Manor of Mount Joy, excepting such parts as had actually been sold and conveyed by the Aubreys.

2. December 10, 1735, deed to William Wilkinson, by Sir Archibald Grant, for the whole property, as conveyed to him.

3. An "indenture of release tripartite," June 22, 1736, the three parties to it being (a) William Wilkinson, of the parish of St. James, in the liberty of Westminster, and county of Middlesex, England, surviving assignee of the real and personal estate of John Thompson, late of London, merchant, against whom a commission of bankruptcy had been awarded; (b) the said John Thompson; and (c) William Penn,[1] "called of Kingston Bowrey, in the County of Sussex, Esq.,"—it being a conveyance by Wilkinson and Thompson to William Penn of "All that the aforesaid Manor of Mount Joy," etc.

4. William Penn, by a deed or letter of attorney, February 16, 1740–41, constituted James Logan, of Stenton, and William Logan, of Philadelphia, merchant, his attorneys, and they,—

5. Conveyed, February 1, 1741–42, to Stephen Evans and Daniel Walker 175 acres, (it being the same property which Evans and Walker now conveyed to Isaac Walker.)

OWNERSHIP OF EVANS, WALKER, AND WILLIAMS.

The tract of one hundred and seventy-five acres was thus fixed by this conveyance in the hands of Isaac Walker on December 13, 1742. This was evidently only a step precedent to an arrangement for a new ownership by three persons, and probably the improvement of the property. Five days afterwards, December 18, 1742, Isaac Walker and Sarah, his wife, reconveyed the tract (with precisely the same metes

[1] This was the grandson of William Penn the Founder, being the son of William Penn, Jr.

and bounds, and the same extended recitation of title) to Stephen Evans and Daniel Walker (from whom Isaac had just received it), and Joseph Williams, of Lower Merion, miller.

Joseph Williams, as stated in the deed, was a resident of Lower Merion, and a miller by occupation. (I find that, April 11, 1738, he and his wife Sarah executed a mortgage of their farm in Lower Merion—two hundred acres—to Hugh Jones, for two hundred pounds, and paid it off in 1750.) Without inquiring concerning him very particularly, it may be reasonably inferred that, being a miller, he was interested in utilizing the water-power of Valley Creek, upon which, from the description, no mills had yet been erected,—at this place, at least.

In the *Pennsylvania Gazette*, April 4, 1751, there appears this advertisement:

TO BE SOLD.

The third part of Mountjoy Forge, Situate in Upper Merion, on the river Schuylkill, by the great road, leading from Philadelphia, to the French-creek iron-works, 20 miles from Philadelphia, and not so far distant from 3 furnaces; the said works are in good repair, with one third of the utensils to be sold; also one hundred and twenty acres of land belonging thereto. For title and terms inquire of Daniel Walker, living near the said premises.

The advertisement, it will be observed, fixes the forge as being " situate in Upper Merion" Township, that being the lower (east) side of Valley Creek, in what is now Montgomery County. It also shows that the forge had been built in the interval between December, 1742, and April, 1751.

Why Daniel Walker desired to sell his one-third is not explained, nor is it important. Six months later it seems that his two partners were inclined to sell their shares also, for on September 26, 1751, this advertisement appears in the *Pennsylvania Gazette:*

PHILADELPHIA, September 26, 1751.

ON the feventh day of the Eighth Month, commonly called October, will be fold by auction, or publick vendue, by the fubfcribers, two thirds of about 375 acres of land, joining and near the mouth of Valley Creek and Schuylkill, most of it unclear'd; with two thirds of a forge or iron-works with the said land; also two thirds of a faw-mill on the said premises. The faid forge and faw-mill ftand in a very convenient place for custom and timber; and both ftand close by a publick road leading to Philadelphia. Any perfon or perfons inclining to purchafe the above premifes, by applying to the fubfcribers, may know the terms of fale before, or at the day of fale. The title is indifputable. STEPHEN EVANS, JOSEPH WILLIAMS.

CONVEYANCES TO JOHN POTTS.

What resulted from these advertisements, if anything, I have not developed, but the property was ultimately sold to John Potts. There is on record a deed, made March 12, 1757, by the executors of Stephen Evans, conveying his one-third of the forge property to John Potts. The grantors in this deed are described as " Mary Stephens, of the Township of Tredyffrin, in the county of Chester, [etc.], and Abijah Stephens, both of the said township, yeomen," " they, the said Mary, Abijah, and [a blank in the record] being the executors named in the last will and testament of Stephen Evans, late of the same township, deceased," etc. The deed recites the death of Stephen Evans, and that he left a will dated February 21, 1754. It says that he had become in his lifetime the owner in fee of an undivided one-third part of " a certain Iron Forge, saw-mill, and three tracts or parcels of land, one of the said tracts, on part whereof the said Iron Forge and saw-mill are erected, being situate in the said county of Philadelphia, part of the Manor of Mountjoy," etc. The metes and bounds of this tract being given, they prove to be precisely the same as in the deeds of 1742, above described, and the content remains one hundred and seventy-five acres. The conveyance by

Isaac and Sarah Walker to Evans, Walker, and Williams, December 18, 1742, is recited.

The language above will be observed,—"one of the said tracts, on part whereof the said Iron Forge and saw-mill are erected, being situate in the said county of Philadelphia, part of the Manor of Mountjoy." Besides confirming the statement of the advertisement of Daniel Walker as to the location of the forge on the Philadelphia side of Valley Creek, it also shows that there was now a saw-mill on the property, which, as it was not mentioned in the advertisement in 1751, had presumably been erected meantime.

The grantee, in this deed of 1757, "John Potts, of the Manor of Douglass, in the county of Philadelphia, Esquire," was the distinguished iron-master (the son of Thomas Potts, one of the pioneers of iron-making in Pennsylvania), born at Germantown in 1710, died at Pottsgrove in 1768. Details concerning him and his varied activities are extremely interesting, but need not be given here. Mrs. James, in her admirable "Memorial of the Potts Family" (Cambridge, Massachusetts, 1874), has worthily presented them. He was already largely engaged in the iron industry, and he and his sons continued to be for many years concerned in the ownership of the property at Valley Forge; so much so, indeed, that it has been a common supposition that the forge was established by some of them, which, as has been shown, was not the case.

The other two tracts, in which John Potts was now buying a one-third interest from the Evans executors, were very probably woodland, intended to furnish fuel to the forge. One of them lay on the upper side of Valley Creek, but did not extend to the river. It included one hundred acres, and was "situate in Charles Town, in the county of Chester, part of the manor of Bilton, beginning at a white oak near Valley Creek, thence south 80 degrees west by vacant land, 136 perches to a heap of stones, near a small marked chestnut, thence north 15 degrees west, by land late of John Jones, 166 perches to a post by the side of Philadelphia road, thence north 86 degrees east, by the said road 64 perches to a white oak saplin, thence south 82 degrees east by the said road 31 perches to a sugar tree, standing by the side of the Valley Creek, and thence up the several courses of the said creek, and on the same, 208 perches to the place of beginning" (being the same which John Jones and Jane, his wife, December 16, 1742, conveyed to Stephen Evans, Daniel Walker, and Joseph Williams). The third tract, also in Charlestown (one hundred and one acres), had also been bought of John and Jane Jones, December 18, 1742. It was not on Valley Creek.

This deed to John Potts by the executors of Stephen Evans also mentions that on Tract No. 2 there had been a reservation to John Parry of a water right on Valley Creek, " of erecting *a dam or ware*" across it at such place as he should think best " for watering his adjacent meadow ground," and to dig earth and gravel at or near the bank of the creek, to make the dam, and that this right had been conveyed to Stephen Evans by John Parry's executors in 1741. The conveyance now made to John Potts is for the undivided one-third in all three of the tracts. The pur-chase-money is two hundred pounds, sixteen shillings, lawful money of Pennsylvania. The conveyance included " All and every the messuages, tenements, houses, outhouses, buildings, improvements, Forges, Iron works, Tools, uten-sils, materials, stock, mines, minerals, ore-quarries, mill dams, mill races, [etc.] unto the said Iron Forge, saw-mill, and 3 Tracts of Land belonging."

By what conveyance John Potts acquired the other two-thirds interest in the property which had belonged to Daniel Walker and Joseph Williams, and which they advertised for sale in September, 1751, I have not ascertained. He may have bought it previously. At any rate, he became, about 1757, the owner of the entire property.

CONVEYANCES TO JOHN POTTS'S SONS.

The next document of which I took notes is a deed by John Potts, Esq., of Pottsgrove, and Ruth, his wife, March 24, 1768, to John Potts, Jr. (his son), of East Nantmeal

Township, Chester County, iron-master.   The consideration is three thousand five hundred pounds.   It conveys

"All that Iron Forge, called or known by the name of Mountjoy Forge, saw-mill and grist-mill, and three tracts or parcels of land . . . Together with all the working tools, bellows, hammers, anvils, gears, utensils, and implements to the said iron-works and mills respectively belonging or therewith used."

Then, the following day, March 25, 1768, there is another deed, in which John Potts, Jr., of East Nantmeal, iron-master, and Margaret, his wife, are grantors, conveying to John Potts, Sen., for five hundred pounds,—

"A certain messuage or tenement, grist-mill, saw-mill, and a small piece of land thereunto belonging, situate in Upper Merion township, in the said county of Philadelphia, beginning at a post on the east side of Valley Creek, where the Great Road leading to the City of Philadelphia crosses the said creek, thence by the said road south 80 degrees east 18 perches, thence by the said John Potts, Jr.'s land, north 11 degrees East, 8 perches, north 80 degrees west 5 perches, north 11 degrees east 10 perches, East 40 perches, and north 11 degrees east [blank] perches to the River Schuylkill, thence up the same river, by the several courses thereof to the north side of the said Valley Creek, thence up the said Creek to the place of beginning, containing [blank] acres and [blank] perches of land." "Also one other piece or parcel of land, supposed to contain about 40 acres, situate between the aforesaid great road and a road leading to the plantation of a certain David Stephen.   Also the free right and liberty of the mill race in the channel it runs now through the said John Potts, Jr.'s other land, and sufficient freeboard on both sides of the said race to come to the dam belonging to the said mills," etc.   It being part of the 175 acres "called the Forge Tract," conveyed by John Potts, Sen., to John Potts, Jr., the day before.

Endorsed on the back of this deed, the same date (March 25, 1768), is a conveyance of this property by John Potts, Sen., and wife, to Joseph Potts for five shillings. (Joseph was another son of John, Sen., and brother of the younger John.   See details below.)   From the description of the metes and bounds it is obvious that it includes the land in the corner formed by Valley Creek and the Schuylkill, and therefore the " messuage or tenement" built upon it may have been the present head-quarters mansion.

May 10, 1768, John Potts, Jr., still of East Nantmeal, iron-master, conveyed the whole one hundred and seventy-five acres to Joseph Potts, of the city of Philadelphia, merchant (the brother just named). It is described: "All that Iron Forge, called or known by the name of the Mount Joy Forge, saw-mill, & grist-mill, and 3 tracts or parcels of land, thereunto belonging, one of them whereon the said forge and mills stand situate in Upper Merion Township, in the county of Philadelphia, it being part of the reputed manor of Mount Joy."

These conveyances therefore lodged the whole of the one hundred and seventy-five acres in the possession of Joseph Potts.

DESCRIPTIONS IN JOHN POTTS'S WILL.

John Potts, Sen., died at his home (Pottsgrove, now Potts-town) June 6, 1768, a few weeks after the execution of the deeds described above. He had made his will about a year before (April 24, 1767), and in it had made disposition of his Valley Forge properties in the clauses which are given below, and which, though they became void as to these properties by his sale of them in his lifetime, I insert here because they afford some additional descriptive details:

"Whereas I stand seized of a certain Grist Mill in the County of Philadelphia, known by the name of the Valley Mill, & of a small piece of ground thereunto belonging bounded & described as follows, Viz. beginning at the Valley Creek, where the Great road crosses it thence along the same road towards Philadelphia by the Gardens to the fence of the field on the North side of the said road fence along the said fence to the barn-yard, thence along the fence between the garden & said barn-yard to the road leading to Schuylkill, thence along the same road to the other side of the barn-yard next Schuylkill, & thence up the barn-yard fence through the field to the middle of the old orchard in the Hollow, thence by a straight line to Schuylkill, thence up Schuylkill to the mouth of the Valley Creek to the place of beginning, And whereas I have also a tract of land, supposed to contain about 40 acres situate & lying between the Great Road leading from the Valley Creek to Philadelphia & a road leading to the plantations of a certain David Stephens, & whereas I have also reserved & am entitled unto for me my heirs & assigns forever the free use & benefit of the water running to the said mill with full liberty of cleansing & repairing the Race, &

amending & keeping in repair the dam at all times when necessary, It is my will & I do hereby order and direct my Executor hereafter named within a convenient time after my decease to make sale of the said Mill & Lands with the privileges above mentioned & all & singular other the Hereditaments & appurtenances whatsoever thereunto belonging.

"Whereas I have agreed & bargained with my sons Samuel & John for the sale of all my estate interest & title of in & to Warwick furnace & the lands, ores, hereditaments & appurtenances thereunto belonging, in the County of Chester, & of all my estate interest & title of in & to the Valley Forge, with the lands, hereditaments & appurtenances thereto belonging, (the Valley Mill & the lands & privileges hereinbefore mentioned only excepted), in the Counties of Philadelphia & Chester, for the sum of four thousand five hundred pounds, which said sum of money should have been paid to me the 1st day of April, A.D. 1765, with interest from that time: It is my will & I do give & devise for the consideration afs^d unto my Sons Samuel & John & unto their heirs & assigns forever, all my estate, title, interest, property, claim & demand whatsoever of into & out of the said Furnace forge, land, hereditaments, & appurtenances thereunto respectively belonging, (except as before excepted), they paying the residue of the said four thousand five hundred pounds with the interest as afs^d."

It may be repeated, in order to guard against misunderstanding, that the above clauses of John Potts's will became void, so far as the Valley Forge property was concerned, by the conveyances which he made of it to his sons in his lifetime. I cite them mainly because of the additional descriptive details which they furnish.

JOHN POTTS'S SONS AND VALLEY FORGE.

As we have seen, the whole Valley Forge tract east of Valley Creek—the one hundred and seventy-five acres on which the forge, the mills, and other buildings stood—became the property of Joseph Potts in May, 1768. It may be best, at this point, to speak more distinctly as to the several sons of John Potts, Sen., who were at this time, or thereafter, connected with the Valley Forge property. John Potts, Sen., and his wife Ruth (Savage), of Pottsgrove, had thirteen children, of whom eleven married and founded families. Those who need be mentioned are:

1. Thomas, of Pottsgrove, "Colonel Thomas" of Revolutionary times, member of the Assembly, born 1735, died 1785. General Washington

was several times his guest at his mansion at Pottsgrove (originally built by John Potts, Sen.), and Mrs. James says, "it was here, doubtless, that Washington formed the plan to winter his army at Valley Forge on the property of Thomas's brothers."

2. Samuel, of Pottsgrove, member of the Colonial Assembly, born 1736, died 1793. He was interested in the conduct of the iron-works at Valley Forge, with his brother John, in 1765.

3. John, the Judge and "Loyalist," born 1738. He was interested with Samuel in the Valley Forge works for a time, and, as we have seen, received the property from his father and conveyed it to Joseph in 1768.

4. David, merchant in Philadelphia, born 1741, died at Valley Forge, 1798. He owned the large mansion (now Washington Inn) at the time of the encampment, and was engaged, with his brother Joseph and their cousin Thomas Hockley, in carrying on the Valley Forge works in 1767 and later.

5. Joseph, of Philadelphia, born 1742, died near Frankford (Philadelphia), 1804. He acquired the whole of the Valley Forge property, 1768, and was of the firm of Potts, Hockley & Potts, conducting the forge in 1767 and later.

6. Isaac, of Valley Forge, owner of the head-quarters mansion and of the grist-mill at the time of the encampment, born 1750, died at Cheltenham, 1803. (It was he who saw Washington on his knees, at prayer, in the woods at Valley Forge.)

It thus appears that five of the brothers (Samuel, John, David, Joseph, and Isaac) were some time owners of the Valley Forge property, or interested in business upon it. John's interest, however, was brief; it began in 1765, and ceased entirely in 1768, when he sold to Joseph. Isaac's interest in the iron-works operations was after the Revolution, and then related to the new forge. It remains, therefore, that Samuel, David, and Joseph were those mainly concerned in operating the old forge.

Before the death of John Potts, the elder, he had arranged (as appears by his will) with his sons Samuel and John, at least as early as 1765, for them to take and carry on the forge. The purchase-money, the will says, was to have been paid April 1, 1765, and the agreement may have taken effect even earlier than that. Mrs. James mentions an old inventory of personal property made by Samuel and John when they took possession, amounting to twelve hundred and fourteen pounds, six shillings, and nine pence, but she does not give any date with it.

Samuel and John may have conducted the forge, then, from 1765 to 1767. In that year the firm of Potts, Hockley & Potts began to manage it,—Joseph and David Potts, and their cousin, Thomas Hockley. Mrs. James gives an "Inventory taken at Mountjoy Forge, June 12, 1767, by Potts, Hockley & Potts." How long they continued is not ascertained. The next year, 1768, the ownership of the property passed to Joseph, as has been stated above, by the deeds from his father and his brother John.

THE VARIOUS BUILDINGS.

Of the old forge Mrs. James (writing about 1874) says,—

"The site of this old forge, which was burned by the British more than two months before the American army encamped there, is now covered by water, and is at the foot of Mount Joy, and more than half a mile above the Valley mill. The new dam, which was built lower down the creek after the Revolution, and which . . . had been long contemplated, raised the water-level and covered the foundation. The new works, erected soon after the close of the war, were built near where the present factory stands."

Mrs. James gives copies of accounts with John Potts, Sen., in 1759, showing that the grist-mill was built that year (or, as appears from the dates, more probably in 1758), being almost immediately after he purchased of the Stephen Evans executors, and she adds this statement:

"I am inclined to think that the building of the house, afterwards Washington's head-quarters, is included in this account, and that both [it and the grist-mill] were erected at the same time."

If this surmise is correct, the head-quarters mansion dates from 1758 or 1759. It has already been stated that there was a "messuage or tenement" here when John Potts, Sen., conveyed to Joseph, in 1768. As it will be an important point for the historian of the head-quarters to fix its age precisely, I leave this point without further comment. Isaac Potts, it seems, had bought part of the one hundred and seventy-five acres from Joseph by 1773, for an agreement between them in that year, cited by Mrs. James, shows that he (Isaac) then owned the grist-mill and Joseph the forge. When the war movements of 1777 drew near the place, Isaac was living in the head-quarters mansion, and the larger one (Washington Inn) was used as a summer residence by David Potts, whose home was in Philadelphia. Mrs. James says,—

"His family resided there [V. F.] during the summer, in the large house, situated on the Great Road, above Washington's head-quarters. When the army occupied Valley Forge, this stone house was taken for the officers' rendezvous and a bakery. I have never seen any engraving of this building, which is now [probably 1874] much disfigured by fanciful iron balconies and railings painted yellow, but an antique wall of dressed stone still surrounds it, enclosing many fine old trees. It was probably the first mansion erected on the estate. . . . The large ovens for baking the army bread were built in the cellar of the house, and were taken out only a few years ago."[1]

Mrs. James does not give any very definite evidence that this mansion-house was built earlier than the head-quarters, though it may have been. If the latter was built, as previously suggested, at the same time with the grist-mill, in 1758 or 1759, the greater age of the "Inn" mansion would be doubtful. Mrs. James points out the passage in the will of John Potts, Sen., 1768, where the line of the lot of ground attached to the grist-mill passes "up the barn-yard fence" to the "middle of the old orchard in the Hollow," etc., these descriptions apparently referring to the surroundings of the "Inn" mansion, but this was several years after the date already suggested for the erection of the head-quarters.

The grist-mill was the place of the exciting episode, shortly after the battle at Brandywine, when Alexander Hamilton, then a lieutenant-colonel, accompanied by Captain

[1] Letter of the Board of War to President Wharton, August 30, 1777:

"Sir.—There is a large quantity of Flour spoiling for Want of baking. It lies at Valley Forge; I am directed to request of you that you with the Council will be pleased to order Furloughs to be given to six Bakers out of the Militia, for the purpose of baking the Flour into hard biscuit. Col. Dewees will receive your order and endeavor to find out the Bakers.

"RICH. PETERS Sec."

Lee ("Light-horse Harry"), came in haste, with a small party from the latter's troop, to destroy the stores of grain and flour, and, being hotly pressed by the British, barely escaped. (The account will be found cited in Day's "Historical Collections," though it is slightly confused and cannot be altogether accurate; and Lossing also gives it, more concisely.) This mill was carried on by Isaac Potts "until near the close of the century." It was burned down in the spring of 1848 by a spark from a locomotive on the railroad. Mrs. Ogden, cited by Mrs. James (p. 219), says,—

"It stood near the railroad, and was much larger than the mill my father built higher up the race the next year, now [1868] used as a paper-mill. The old mill had very massive timbers used in its building, which were unharmed by time, and I heard say the burrs were the best in the country; they were all destroyed by the fire. . . . If the house [the head-quarters] is as old as the mill, it has stood the storms of over a century well. There are the same doors and window-shutters (as well as sash) as when the house was built."

EXTRACTS FROM THE DIARY OF MRS. ANN WARDER.

CONTRIBUTED BY MISS SARAH CADBURY.

[Ann Warder, *née* Head, of England, was the wife of John, a son of Jeremiah and Mary Warder, of Philadelphia, who, in 1776, was settled in London as a shipping merchant, with a branch house in Philadelphia. After a lapse of ten years business called him to return to his native city for a visit, when he was accompanied by his wife and eldest son, Jeremiah, and, as it proved, the expected return to England for residence was never accomplished. From the time of her leaving home Mrs. Warder maintained a lively correspondence with her family, and during the first three years (1786–1789) she kept a diary detailing the social, domestic, and religious life of Friends in and near Philadelphia. From the stand-point of a foreigner many of their habits and customs impressed her as new and original and were noted for the edification of her only sister, Elizabeth. During the first year of their sojourn in Philadelphia they were the guests of her husband's widowed mother, whose house, on Third Street, opposite to Church Alley, was a centre of hospitality. At this time Mrs. Warder was about twenty-eight years of age, with attractive manners, sprightly disposition, and a fair share of beauty. Her husband died in 1828, and she one year later.]

1786.

6 mo. 6th.—[Bristol.[1]] At dinner a violent shower detained us long, but the good horses and no stopping soon carried us the twenty miles [to Philadelphia] where mother [Mrs. Warder] Aunt Hooten (who had not been out of bed for a twelve month) her husband, cousin John Hooten, the four Parkers and sister Emlen were impatiently awaiting our arrival, which they were not at all apprised of 'till I got up stairs, when it would not be in my power to do justice to all the professed joy and affection shown me. It was one hour and a half before my dearest arrived owing to the fatigue

[1] We omit the records of the voyage to New York and the few days spent in that city and vicinity, and take up the narrative at Bristol, the last stop made before reaching Philadelphia.

of the poor cattle. My arrival had prepared dear mother for the pleasure she had so much anticipated—think then of her delight to see one who was always the darling, after ten years absence. The evening was spent with the family, sister Emlen, Billy and Sally Morris, and J. Fry. Uncle Head welcomed our arrival—my dear father's image without a wig and less vivacity. Nancy Emlen called but would not stop 'till John arrived. She is a sweet innocent, but never I think beautiful, and her dress did not appear so singular then as I had had represented; candle light made some things which were brown appear white—her mind appears to be a perfect symmetry of heavenly love.

6 mo. 7th.—I rested well in mother's best bed the room large and house spacious. Below are the shop and counting house in front; one large and one small parlor back, a delightful entry from the street to the yard. Up stairs is a good drawing room and three large chambers, with the same size cool passage, and in the best sitting room is Johnny's picture, which is an excellent likeness. After breakfast I hastily prepared to receive company which came in such numbers that I should have been quite tired out did not one frequently make their appearance whom I had before seen. We dined at mother's with only our own family, which fills a long table. I have mentioned those present except some of the younger branches—Lydia Parker, Nancy Webb, Sophia Mayberry (is here to receive her education), Nelly Parker, sixteen, (Dr. Foulke is said to court her), a pretty, sweet behaved girl. Becky is a dear little creature, about Sophia's age,—they have fine hair and wear no caps, but handkerchiefs close up to their throats with a frill around the neck, in which dress much inconsistency appears to me. At tea we had a good round party of cousins, but I am informed that not half have been here, most on the Head side.

6 mo. 8th.—Nancy Emlen called on her way to meeting; I was not dressed or believe I should have gone though several had appointed to call. The house as yesterday kept filling and emptying. Nancy returned and stayed to dinner and 'till late in the evening.   I was ready to envy her situation except the dress, which my poor mind must go through severe conflicts to submit to—all brown except her cap, which was coarse muslin without either border or strings. Her cousin Samuel who has been several times our visitant sat a good bit with us this afternoon.   Supped at home Doctor Foulke and Jacky Fry with us—the latter not so forward in his matrimonial journey as I hoped—believe it is little more than a joke at present.

6 mo. 9th.—A crowded house began at 10 o'clock.   Sometimes the recollection of you would make me ready to burst out with laughter, such new scenes are presented.   Many in their own carriages have honored me with their company —Friends and others.   Such a general use of fans my eyes never beheld, you scarcely see a woman without one, and in Winter I am told they visit with them as a plaything.   Its impossible to attempt any description of all these at once, but as it is expected I should return all the visits each day, I hope that I may be as particular as thou wish.   The close of evening presented a clear'd house, so we set out for the first time to Uncle Hooten's,—his wife a sister of mother Warder's.   On our return found two of Dr. Foulke's sisters, the youngest a very pretty girl, which I at present think a rarity for those who are thought so here.   I dare not mention it for fear of being thought envious or having too high an opinion of my own dear country.   The family supped alone except dear Sister Emlen, whom I feel a singular love and pity for—with such a husband and so large a family.

6 mo. 11th.—In the forenoon went to Market Street Meeting which I think is full double the size of Gracechurch street.   It has five doors, one each side the minister's gallery, near which I sit though much courted by beckoners to come under it, which I refused, though not without feeling some pleasure, as sister Hannah had given me a very different account of their Friends.   We dined at dear uncle John Head's, for whom my heart is always filled with pleasure at seeing which happens pretty frequent, as the greatest sociability subsist in this place.   He has by his first wife a daughter married, with a large family. His second wife left him with three children. Uncle has not so much vivacity as our beloved parent in full health used to possess, and is now sixty two. At six went again to meeting, the day being so warm it was omitted in the afternoon. Returned home to supper when we met Brother and Sister Vaux with their only two children. The mode of dressing children here is not so becoming as with us, and I have scarcely seen a white frock since my arrival; their colored ones are very inferior to what we use, which with blue and yellow skirts and their necks entirely covered to preserve them, complete a dress very inconsistent with the mothers' appearance when from home, for not a woman has visited me but what was elegant enough for any bride. Indeed we could almost persuade ourselves that was the case from so much saluting—which is a practice here considerably out of use. A young girl esteems it an insult for a man to offer any such thing—the strictest delicacy subsists, beyond what I ever expected to find, particularly as they are more and much earlier exposed to men's company. Our family with the addition of my beloved friend Nancy Emlen supped together. She wore today a dark snuff colored Tabereen, but looked old and so awkward made that if her person was not so agreeable it would be disgusting—I mean the dress. She is not so handsome as Becky Gurney, but has all her sweetness of countenance with a taller and more agreeable person.

6 mo. 12th.—Breakfasted at home comfortably, but it would be more so if the family were more attentive to the summons. I arose at six o'clock and scrambled hard 'till ten, unpacking and setting my clothes to rights, which only arrived on seventh day evening. The certainty of company after that time obliged me to be ready for dining at brother Jerry's—such attention I had no idea was ever paid to strangers. Mother, Sister Vaux, and ourselves composed the party—at tea Sister Morris and little Fanny Vaux joined us. In the evening we took a nice walk, which gave me a clearer idea of the town, that it is in my opinion as far superior to New York as Westminster to the city. The regularity of the streets and buildings with their entire plainness I much admire, scarce a house but the color resembles our Mark Lane Hall painting.

6 mo. 13th.—The forenoon as usual engaged with company. The family dined at Billy Morris's. We had a very genteel dinner, indeed I think from my present observation that people here are more superb in their entertainments than with us. Provisions of every kind are cheaper, but the greatest luxury is the abundance of fruit. We have pineapples, strawberries, cherries, peas. We remained the evening 'till twelve o'clock, which doings we have been guilty of every night—supping late and chatting after; sometimes a walk after dark, which is much the practice here owing to the extreme heat of the day. I dread the increase about two months hence.

6 mo. 14th.—In the afternoon, the weather being cool, Johnny, sister Vaux and myself in a phaeton, and Billy Prichard and Sally Parker in a chair, took a ride of ten miles along the banks of the Schuylkill, with which I was much pleased. Several friends called in during the evening, which I find is occasioned by the intense heat of the Summer—they walk most after dark and sit much on their porches, which as a *mother* I think expose girls too early to the acquaintance of men.

6 mo. 16th.—Drank tea at Uncle Roberts, brother Jerry's first wife was his daughter; Richard Vaux also married another; she is destitute of beauty but an agreeable woman.

6 mo. 18th.—Being engaged to dine at Thomas Eddy's was induced to attend the meeting nearest their house, which being esteemed a cool one proved a double inducement. I dread the heat most where a number of people are gathered together. It was a pretty house called the Hill or Pine Street Meeting, not near so large as Market Street Meeting, but many friends were there who I knew from their attention in calling upon me. After tea returned home where we found Billy Parker and Harry Capper sitting at the door. At supper Dr. Foulke and Jacky Fry joined us.   People talk about Sally Parker and him.   Girls run so thick and lads so thin that if two are seen together several times people will talk.   We can't find any body in particular to joke Jerry and Dick about, they are attentive to all when thrown in their way, but engaged to none. Jerry says that in Winter the girls look so blooming by a good fire that he is induced to think about matrimony, and almost determined if they can stand the next Summer. Then the sultry heat discovers such poor relaxed, unhealthy constitutions that his resolutions vanish—they both talk of English wives in which more health, spirits and beauty are to be found than here.   I told him our husbands are obliged to exceed theirs in obedience.   He says that a good curtain lecture sometimes from a wife who would render herself at others lively and agreeable to him and his friends would be more bearable than lumps of dead or inanimate flesh.   I have threatened the destruction of their pig tails before I will consent to introduce them as my nephews in our country, which they both acknowledge will be cheerfully resigned.

6 mo. 19th.——We early prepared for a country excursion —Johnny, myself, brother Jerry and sister Hannah, Lydia Parker, and Nelly, with Sally Moore, in a wagon.   Sally Parker followed in a chair with a young widower, Jerry and Dick in another.   We had a pleasant ride of four miles, and the novelty of the conveyance diverted me much.   We met a considerable number, who with us, had received an invitation to partake of a fine turtle lunch given by Magnus Miller and George Emlen, a brother of Caleb's.   His wife is the most English looking woman I have seen here.   They keep their carriage but have little pride.   Two of her sisters were also present, the youngest a pretty girl.   We dined under an awning in the garden, and the day being beautiful, it was very pleasant.   The sweetness of the evening urged us to enjoy the country 'till it began to close when we prepared to return.   Our horses were so high spirited that I proposed to walk over a wooden bridge we had first to pass, the noise from which I feared would add to their desire to be moving, however, Jerry was not willing and I never wish to look singular particularly in imaginary fears. Yet a few minutes led me to think I should have been better off following my own inclination. A woman meeting us her horse took fright and ran around several times striking ours which with the general screams amongst us at her danger frightened our spirited beasts when they began to rear and back that we feared we would be overturned into the water. The woman was soon thrown, but mercifully not into the stream, which would have prevented the possibility of our saving her. Brother Jerry was using every endeavor to restore her and I jumped out and ran back to my companions and met my husband, who was frightened at my condition. However the landlord of the Inn ran to the poor creature and brought back word that she was intoxicated and did not appear hurt. We were told that she was of a reputable family in the neighborhood but gave herself up entirely to the horrid practice and had met with similar misfortunes before. Hannah undertook to correct us for being so frightened and she preached the whole way home upon our folly which I answered in silence and was sorry the rest did not do the same. The noise of the back seat rattling from nobody being on it drowned her voice, and she begged somebody to move there, but I would not let them, as it was much more uneasy than the other seats.

6 mo. 20th.—After supper we set off for a walk—Jerry Parker ran into Jacky Fry's store and Sally who is just my sister mischievous and myself followed him, when finding the master from home we had no better fun than turning out his cupboard, laid a coat for a table cloth and decorated it with all we could find except his tea and sugar, which with five spoons we hid to trouble him for breakfast, he keeping bachelor's hall.

6 mo. 21st.—After a great hunt in vain Jacky came over and threatened hard if his materials for breakfast were not produced, so we were obliged to confess. Dined with Nicholas Waln's wife (he is in New England with John Townsend) and the company consisted of Sammy Emlen and Nancy, Thomas Colley, Thomas Fisher and wife, Friend Beveridge and wife, Jesse Waln and wife, and a brother and sister of that name. We had a truly comfortable and agreeable visit. Friend Waln is a woman whose acquaintance will enrich any body, she is lively and sprightly, but much of the Friend and gentlewoman, and nothing in her dress or house or conduct bespeaks that gaiety we had been told in England she possessed. J. Townsend sent a letter to her by me asking for our intimate acquaintance and her earnest desire for which flatters me.

6 mo. 22d.—Went to weekday meeting at Market Street; after which shopping for white leather mitts—called in twenty stores before we succeeded. We dined at Miers Fisher's with Jerry, Dick, Lydia, Sally Parker, brother and sister Warder, Billy Rawle and wife, and a fine girl called their perfection of America, but she being dressed fantastical to the greatest degree and painted like a doll, destroyed every pretention to beauty to my view. She was a remarkable sensible woman, but too well knew it and was wonderfully affected. Miers Fisher and wife are truly agreeable, observing the strictest gentility with the Quaker. Sammy with an old maid sister called upon us after tea on purpose to see me and he also took care of me home, which is thought such a favor for him.

6 mo. 24th.—Old John ——'s wife and daughter, sister Hannah and her sister drank tea with us—so much stuff as usual when the former is present upon dress and gentility as made me almost cross, and I told her it seemed her first, last and only concern, that I never met any body who thought so much of that nonsense in my life before. It is a pity, for her great vanity and foolish conversation renders her company much less pleasing than it would otherwise be.

6 mo. 25th.—Went to Market street meeting morning and evening, the violent heat preventing my expecting to profit in the least by going in the afternoon; indeed without the frequent use of fans we must be melted down. Our meetings were large, particularly in the evening, when Thomas Colley and many other public Friends were present. One woman Friend appeared in supplication and whilst she was speaking Betsy Roberts (Nancy Vaux's sister) walked into the gallery and knelt down, and as soon as the first had finished, began very loud. Last first day evening there were three followed each other in that manner, and I could not help being struck with their appearance both having drab silk gowns and black pasteboard bonnets on ; brown is thought gayer, so much for custom. To see an old man stand up with a mulberry coat, nankeen waistcoat and breeches with white stockings, would look singular in England. My cap is the admiration of plain and gay, and had I that which I wore some years ago many would have asked for the pattern. They all wear a round one the border drawn close to the face without a pleat piece, some plain others quilled with narrow ribbon puffed—a consistency is wanted, their bonnets are more Friendly and gowns less so.

7 mo. 2d.—I summoned resolution to go out for the first time [since news of death of her child] to meeting this forenoon, which seemed a favored one. In the afternoon got a little nap to fit me for meeting in the evening. I rejoiced in attending, partly on account of a minister whom I thought exceeded most I ever heard and my mind from affliction seemed humbled, which no doubt was contributed by the comfort of his testimony which was long and eloquent. After meeting Charles Eddy's mother pitied my distress and begged me to sit a little 'till the Friends had dispersed, when another friend came up to me too and requested to speak with me a few minutes. When we retired I found her business what I little expected. She had been told of my getting a whalebone bonnet and the idea of my being persuaded to alter in dress had much distressed her and she begged I would be cautious. I told her I had not the most distant idea there was any difference in their plainness provided the pattern did not vary, but my mind was too much agitated then. However, I afterwards determined rather than give any one pain I would save the one which was really made to take home instead of getting another, that had been my intention, for in neatness of work they much exceed ours.

7th mo. 3d.——This day I accomplished more needlework than almost altogether since my arrival, for with one engagement or another I could scarce get more done than making caps and mending stockings, and that with some difficulty. My husband had a mind for a thin napping gown for coolness, so after dinner I began one and with a little help finished by evening. For my own part I have made no alteration in my dress on account of the weather, though sometimes I have felt a good deal oppressed, yet resolution would not let me wear short gowns, which are common here.

7th mo. 5.——About six this morning we departed to meet our companions Sammy and Hetty Fisher at the house where we dined on the turtle, where we also met two of their sisters in a phaeton driven by Sammy Emlen, who will drive with us a few miles. At Darby we breakfasted and then proceeded sixteen miles further to another village where we dined. The roads in many places were dreadful and upon the whole did not come up to my expectations. About twelve miles further on we perceived Robert Valentine in a farm yard which induced us to turn in——he was glad to see us. His habitation is humble and lonely, although on a high road. We retired to bed at 9 o'clock.

7th mo. 6th.——The night proved tempestuous, and the threatening morning prevented our going to meeting, for which we were rather glad as the men did not return until five in the evening owing to the bad roads. After dinner their nearest neighbor called [J. Baldwin, about half a mile distant] and pressed us to go over there. Johnny, Sammy Fisher and myself returned with him to tea. I could scarce help laughing at his curious questions about London and thou can'st not conceive how he admired me for my speech and appearance, the latter so different to what he expected an Englishwoman made. "Is it possible," said he, "thou should be so much of a Friend and come from London." We returned home in the evening after viewing all their curiosities, among which a milk house with a stream of fresh cold water running through it, in which every thing is kept fresh and cool.

7th mo. 7th.—After breakfast took leave of our worthy friend, rode about four miles 'till we arrived at a habitation which plainly indicated the innocent simplicity of the owner, Cadwalader Jones. We roamed about his plantation at will, and I could not help supposing that everything grew spontaneous. The hedges are all fruit trees of various kinds—apples, mulberries, with grape vines, raspberries, and many other things which succeed each other. The house was truly neat, but as usual undecorated by paint. We had a good dinner, but what is more a hearty welcome. After I had a short nap we departed to tea at Thomas Lightfoot's, where we met again that comfortable salutation in every countenance, a hearty welcome from Thomas, and I felt much at home. We supped and retired early according to the custom of the country. The house is large and rendered much more neat by a little white paint. During the troubles, the Americans made it an hospital, when the family were restricted to one room—the Doctors and officers occupied the others, the poor men were laid in the barn and stables where many died. Out of respect to Friend Lightfoot they would not bury them on his land, but the next neighbor's.

7 mo. 8th.—We rested well in a clean, white bed, and before breakfast we walked through a grove where the American officers used in fine weather to dine in. We resumed our journey early, but the way being thought bad and difficult to find our good host accompanied us through woods and little used paths never frequented by such a carriage as ours. At length we arrived safe at our looked for haven, Pottstown, after driving through a river as broad but not so deep as the Thames. Our oldest sister lives here, who we have not yet seen. When the chaise drove up brother Thomas Mayberry was sitting at the back door pulling on his boots to go out, and little imagining who we were, called he was coming. However, Johnny and myself stepped up to him, and it was long before believing it was us, and in confirmation of his joy he ran to sister, and soon called us to follow him. After the first pleasure of meeting was a little over, she left to provide for our dinner and I to changing my clothes, and I soon felt comfortable after an hot and dirty ride, and set to work making up a cap, mending my shoes and turning my bonnet.

7th mo. 9th.—It being First Day two Friends called on their way to Meeting which is a little distance off. It is very small, not more than twenty Friends, whose zeal did not keep them more than an hour.

7th mo. 10th.—The forenoon being warm I sat with my needle contemplating the place, which though quite a village appears to me more dull, than those who live entirely on their own delightful farms. Brother and sister are exceedingly kind—he is a little fat, short, good tempered, cheerful man; she has the great personal resemblance of the family and seems a sincere hearted woman. We rode to tea, at Friend Rutter's, where was much genteel neatness displayed. Company arriving from Philadelphia we took leave early and walked home by the banks of the river Schuylkill, which was rurally delightful.

7th mo. 11th.—After breakfast we set out with brother and sister to Vaux Hill, which after a pleasant ride we reached before noon, and were received with much joy by our brother and sister, also Richard Vaux and wife with little Molly Warder who is on a visit there. The situation is delightful, much cleared land about the house, with a distant view of the woods and river. We roamed through a sweet wood to a mill dam where we found a man fishing. I was induced to try my success and caught several cat-fish, which we feasted on at supper.

7th mo. 12th.—Early after breakfast Richard Vaux and Molly Warder set off, for we could not persuade them to wait until after dinner. The day was sultry and close, and about three o'clock we started for Philadelphia. We had a delightful ride to within 7 miles of the city by six o'clock when we stopped for tea and to bait our poor horse, and at 7 o'clock resumed our journey and reached home in safety

and were received by visible joy on every face.   Having a
headache from the heat and fatigue we retired early to bed.

7 mo. 16th.—My spirits somewhat depressed this forenoon,
which were rather increased by mother telling me that
Sister Morris and Emlen thought I rather slighted them by
my few visits, and conscious that every moment of my time
seemed too much engaged with such trifles, I could not
help weeping which did me good.   We went to Bank
Meeting, which was a favored one, where William Savery
long addressed us in such a lively manner I scarce ever
heard; indeed he is a wonderful man and though wrong to
follow preachers I would like to more frequently attend his
meetings.

7 mo. 17th.—Dear Uncle Head called this morning with
whom I had much private conversation respecting Nelly
[Parker] and the Doctor [Foulke], my husband having previously given him our sentiments about the matter.   This
afternoon the whole family drank tea with Sister Morris, so I
now feel at liberty to begin afresh with visiting more distant
connections—the idea of being obliged to without giving
offense, proves to me a burden in such very warm weather.

7 mo. 19th.—This afternoon we put in execution a ride
which had been proposed some days with Abijah Davis,
who drove his wife's niece Sally Gilpin in a chair, Sally
Davis and Tommy Fisher's wife went with Sammy Emlen
in his phaeton, Johnny, Jerry and myself in Uncle Head's
chaise, Lydia and Nelly Parker with Jacky Head and Sally
with Jacky Fry to a rural situation which they call Harrow-
gate, where there is shower baths and a water similar to
ours of the same name, so nauseous tasted that I must be
very sick to submit to drink it.   We all had a comfortable
dish of tea and after a pleasant ride returned home.

7 mo. 20th.—Went to meeting with Nelly and my dear
Nancy Emlen, who called as she frequently does to sit with
me, and her presence commands a love and respect I can
scarcely describe.   After meeting we called upon several
Friends who I am obliged to visit contrary to my inclination
on account of the weather.

7 mo. *22d.*—The intelligence of the death of Robert Valentine at first was rather a shock to me, and I felt a particular inclination to attend his funeral, though Johnny could not accompany me. I walked to Uncle Head's whose daughter Sukey, Billy Sansom and cousin John proposed setting out after dinner. I then walked to my fellow travelers before and found Hessy not able, but Sammy [Fisher] willing to take me, which rejoiced me, because he has a steady horse and knows the road. I returned to dine and about three o'clock we set out and got to Darby so near tea time that our cousin Parker insisted on our stopping, after which we set forward again, and learning that the friend with whom we expected to spend the night was too near, led us to fix on the Paoli Tavern which we reached at half past nine. After a good dish of coffee we retired to bed and I early to sleep, but my companion Sukey Head did not get much as she imagined mice were in the room.

7 mo. 23d.—At four o'clock we were aroused and got up just as day was breaking. We had twelve miles to go which we accomplished before seven. Billy and Sukey went to the burial house, but Sammy and I concluded to stop at Joshua Baldwin's, where I dressed for meeting and got breakfast, and then walked over to the house. We sat in the room with the corpse, whose features looked just as when alive— he was laid in one of his own shirts with a sheet first put into the coffin, which looked much more natural and comfortable than our woolen except his having no cap on, that I never remember seeing before. Afterwards we walked to Friend Baldwin's where we got our chaise and departed for the meeting [Uwchlan] two miles distant. We concluded to leave the multitude, not less I believe than five hundred and mostly on horseback, and take another route. I never saw the like, full half appeared to be women who are here very shiftable if they have a good creature,—which is what all in this part of the country call horses,—they ride by themselves with a safeguard which when done with is tied to the saddle and the horse hooked to a rail, standing all meeting time almost as still as their riders sit. The carry-

ing of the corpse I did not like, as it was only corded on to
a thing like the bottom part of a single horse chaise, which
is the general mode here when the distance is too far for
shoulder [carriers] except that a box in the shape of a coffin
is fixed and the corpse slipped in.   The burying ground ad-
joined the meeting house and dear Robert with solemnity
was interred, and after standing a few minutes at the grave,
we all went in.   I walked towards the upper end but seeing
no room returned and sat within five benches of the door,
which my friend Thomas Lightfoot seeing came out of the
gallery and handed me up to the top.   I reluctantly walked
with him, and though room was made I felt so conscious
of being higher than I ought to be, entirely among the
cloth hats, that I beg'd to return with the excuse that I
would be cooler.   We had a very long but comfortable
meeting, and several Friends spoke, but we were so disturbed by a troublesome man that he was led away by four
Friends, but he made such a noise that we heard him for a
long time.   When meeting was over he came again into
the yard and held forth among us 'till all were dispersed.
We dined at Cadwalader Jones's where were three Friends
besides ourselves.   At nine o'clock we retired as I was
rather tired from getting up so early.

7th mo. 24th.—Arose about seven o'clock and after a very
comfortable breakfast left our esteemed friends.   We dined
at cousin Mendenhall's, and then set out for Darby which
we reached by tea time, continuing on homewards where I
found my dearly beloved was walking the street with an
impatient hope for our arrival.   He with the rest of the
family were just returned from the interment of Uncle
Roberts who died on first day morning.

7th mo. 25th.—Our cousin Sukey Trotter is the youngest
daughter of uncle Hooten and has so great a personal resemblance to Nancy Capper that I delight to look at her.
She is married to a butcher, (a profession Friends follow
here), who is remarkably short, fat and a good tempered
looking man and everything about the house so plainly
indicated a happy connection that I felt truly comforted.

While out visiting met William Savery the Friend with whose ministry I am afraid of being too much captivated with, standing at his door, and after a short conversation was convinced he was a man whose conduct consisted with his profession. Called a few minutes at Uncle Hooten's, when Billy Trotter and Hannah went to supper with us, as also sister Emlen whose husband has been away several weeks and it might be happy if he would never come home again, though perhaps she don't think so.

7th mo. 26th.—Lydia Parker accompanied my husband and self to dinner at Samuel Pleasants, who with his wife appears a worthy Friend, but very genteel, have a large family of children, their oldest daughter reckoned the most genteel girl in the city, which I really think she deserves. Two of friend Pleasant's sisters were there, both widows, and each had their daughters Molly Rhoads and Sally Pemberton, and though the former is esteemed something extraordinary, I think she will bear no comparison with either of her cousins. We had a pleasant entertainment, which I find customary with all I have at present visited— carried to a greater excess than with us.

7th mo. 29th.—We dined today at sister Morris's and had a favorite dish of which I have not before tasted since my arrival (a nice little pig); we also had for the first time a good watermelon, (about which the natives of this country talk much about), and which in hot weather tastes like sweetened snow.

8th mo. 2d.—Prepared for a grand visit to John Clifford's, a brother of Tommy and his wife a sister of Billy Rawle, (who are here esteemed by some the Superior Male and Female for understanding in the city). We were invited for three o'clock and about that time when starting I perceived a coach coming (it having rained hard) and expressed a wish it might be for us, and so truly it proved. On our arrival we were ushered by John Clifford up stairs to a smart drawing room (not very common here) where was his wife, his own sister, Edward Shoemaker, Billy and Sally Rawle, Polly and Debby Foulke and Isaac Wharton. John Clifford is a stout, good tempered looking man; his wife a little woman but a great talker, has much affectation in her manners which is disagreeable at first acquaintance and she has the reputation for wearing the breeches, but whether deserved or not I cannot tell.   But one thing I observed, it was necessary that somebody should take the petticoat.   Tommy and Johnny's sister is a good tempered happy looking creature and I understand Elliston Perot had a mind for her but she refused him on account of not being in the Society.   He is now about coming in and being married to a sister of Billy Sansom's.   Isaac Wharton is an old bachelor, but thinking of a change in that despicable state, with Peggy Rawle, a sister to Billy.   We sat in expectation of the good summons, some of us being hungry, above an hour, when we were called to a dinner much resembling what we have had several times before—chickens, ducks, mock Turtle, Ham, with plenty of vegetables—after which the cloth was cleared, followed by pastry of various sorts and a Floating Island for the middle of the table, and fruits.   At the end Dr. Foulke joined the men when we left them to enjoy their pipes and own talk 'till tea was served one hour later at 8 o'clock.   We left in the coach at nine o'clock.

8th mo. 5th.—Went to Dr. Bass's with cousin Lydia Parker and my Jerry, Sally, Nelly and Sophia Mayberry, where we met a hearty welcome and I much delighted, as the place reminded me more of England than any I have seen.   The house looked neat and genteel, light and airy, a gravel walk led up to it and a pretty garden laid out with taste, which is unusual here—We had a comfortable dish of Tea on the lawn and afterwards walked to a thicket to gather Blackberries which are far superior to ours.   I would like to roam over the place did I not get into my head the fear of snakes, which though very rare so near to the city I cannot help apprehending.   There was a woods here early in the war, but the large trees were all cut down.

8th mo. 8th.—After meeting went to Aunt Emlen's to drink tea and while there was called to see a black's burial, who is reputed to have conducted himself with great reputation and was a man of some consequence. Six men walked first, then the corpse was carried by four of the most agreeable looking negroes I ever saw, being well dressed and appeared to be like men of property. Next followed fifty women, in couples, then one hundred and sixty men, then ninety-six more women, and about forty of our Friends brought up the rear, which would look very singular with us, but is common here for them to attend all church buryings. Before we could get there the parson's services were ended, when he stepped back a little to make room for our ministers two of whom appeared. William Savery was as usual delightful, which many of them acknowledged with a loud Amen, and one exclaimed "Amen! saith my soul with thankfulness for such a sermon." Few of our clergymen would admire this, but here they think nothing of it so they have the first preference and get the pay.

8th mo. 11th.—Mother, Tommy and Becky, Johnny and me with our dear boy dined at Morris's in honor of my wedding day [10th inst. the date], that she much wished spent there. We had an English dinner, fish, roast beef, plum pudding and pies, all very good, which indeed everything is always here, for Billy is provider and I call him a little of an epicure. At three o'clock we ate a fine watermelon. Drank tea with friend Gilpin.

8th mo. 12th.—Lydia Parker accompanied me to old friend Eddy's, who was much pleased to see us. Two grand daughters met us named Marshall, the oldest engaged to Dr. Casper Wister, who they are daily expecting from England. She appears a very amiable girl. I was much pleased with a softness and delicacy in her manners, without any affectation.

[From Eighth month 16th to Eighth month 23d the diarist and her husband, Sally Emlen, Tommy Fisher, George Emlen, Sally Fisher, son and daughter, and Sally Gilpin were visiting Bethlehem, Easton, Nazareth, Christian Spring, Reading, and Pottsgrove. At the latter place Mrs. Warder remained with the Mayberry family, spent a week with the Vaux family, and returned to Philadelphia Ninth month 17th.]

(To be continued.)

PENNSYLVANIA POLITICS EARLY IN THIS CENTURY.

BY WILLIAM M. MEIGS.

The election of Thomas McKean as governor of Pennsylvania in 1799 was an event of far-reaching importance. The recent hurricane of Federalist sentiment, which the conduct of the French government had brought about, seemed to be neutralized, and the Republican party swept[1] into the control of the second State of the Union with a majority of over nine thousand votes. This triumph was another milestone, and a most important one, in the onward march of the democratic element to the control of public affairs. The ancient aristocracy, which had controlled the affairs of the State until the overthrow of Dickinson and the moderates in 1776, may have been a wise and a mild aristocracy, but it was not in accord with what was destined to be the spirit of American government, and, as this spirit grew and felt its power, the old system had to go down before it.

McKean himself, it is quite true, was by no means a Democrat of the new type. On the contrary, his associations were far more with the hereditary element; but, none the less, his following was mainly Democratic, while the bulk of those belonging to the high social circles supported his opponent, Ross. Of all those who contributed to McKean's success, none was so important as William Duane, the editor of the *Aurora*. The power he exercised for some years on Pennsylvania politics and on the politics of the country was very great. McKean's election was

---

[1] Graydon ("Memoirs," etc., pp. 357, 358) writes that the Federalists were cunningly induced by the Republicans to pass a direct-tax law, under the representation that the people should know what they are paying. "This tax on real property," he adds, "was the fatal blow to Federalism in Pennsylvania."

probably, indeed, due to him, and Mr. Jefferson always recognized that the success of the Republicans in 1800 was largely due to the same cause.   William Duane was born in New York State, of Irish parentage, lived a short time in Philadelphia and then in Clonmel, Ireland, and at nineteen years of age married against his mother's wishes, and was thrown entirely upon his own resources.   Living for a time by various trades, he finally drifted to Calcutta, established a newspaper, and apparently accumulated a small estate.   He had not been there long before he was in a serious conflict with the government, owing to his espousal of the cause of some soldiers in a dispute they got into with the authorities.   Thus his tendency to side with the poorer classes was early shown, and it had the most serious consequences to him : his property was confiscated, while he was seized in a most infamous manner one evening by a band of sepoys acting under the orders of the governor, while he was on his way to a dinner to which he had been invited by that official.   He was immediately hurried on board a ship and carried off to England, where he spent some years in vain efforts to secure restitution, and again engaged himself in newspaper affairs, but finally drifted to Philadelphia and became editor of the *Aurora*.[1]   Such a wandering and changeful life could not but make a permanent impression on his character, and it is no doubt true that he was overbearing and violent, factious, most scurrilous and insolent, no respecter of character or position, and not very scrupulous as to the fairness of the methods he used ; but it should never be forgotten that he had been the sufferer from more than one disgraceful instance of gross wrong perpetrated on him by members of the very class who plumed themselves on their superiority and their high honor.   A life of Duane would show him almost incessantly engaged in wrangles of all kinds,—an unceasing and bitter abuse of his opponents, which is only to be compared to their abuse of him ; several

[1] See sketch of him in Simpson's "Eminent Philadelphians ;" McMaster's "History of the United States," Vol. II., pp. 439, 440; Appleton's "Dictionary of National Biography," under his name.

personal encounters, in one at least of which he was shame-
lessly beaten by a number of men ; and numerous libel suits
brought by, and still more against, him, and resulting generally unfavorably to him.   There is no reason to doubt that
he was a real democrat and always felt a true love for and
confidence in the mass of the people.

Such was, in a few words, the man who carried the State
of Pennsylvania into the Republican fold in 1799, under the
eyes of John Adams and his administration, in the very seat
of the federal government.   It is not to be wondered at that
he felt [1] he had strong claims on the party when Mr. Jefferson was elected ; [2] and we accordingly find that the new
President was hardly in office before Duane and the Pennsylvania Republicans were hot-foot after the offices.   Mr.
Adams has printed parts of a curious paper which Duane
sent to Gallatin, with a list of the clerks in federal offices
and their salaries, and a few words indicative of Duane's
opinion of the incumbents. [3]   It is needless to say that he
wanted them all turned out.   Here was a very serious and
difficult question for the administration.   For the first time
in the history of the government there had been a change,
and a most complete one, in its political character, and the
vast army which had succeeded was pressing for the offices.
Nor must it be forgotten that the preceding administration
had been in a high degree proscriptive ; so much so, indeed,
that the Republicans in Pennsylvania called that period the
" Reign of Terror." [4]   It was under these circumstances, and

[1] See *Democratic Press*, August 17, 1810.

[2] The vote of Pennsylvania in 1800 had to be divided and sixteen
votes cast for Jefferson and fifteen for Adams.   This was because there
was no law for a popular election for electors, and the federal Senate
would agree to no other law.

[3] Adams's " Life of Gallatin," p. 277.   " Nothingarian," " Nincum-
poop," " Democratic executioner," " three execrable aristocrats," and
" hell-hot" are among the pithy terms which Duane applies to the
clerks he refers to in this paper.

[4] See " Republican Address of 1802," printed in pamphlet and in
Aurora of September 27, 1802.   This address (referring to the period in
question) said, " Every citizen who did not implicitly adopt it [the

with party spirit at white heat,[1] that the first change in the politics of our federal government occurred; and, much as Mr. Jefferson was then and has since been criticised, candid examination must admit that he followed a very mild course in making removals. Certainly this was the case in Pennsylvania, where, although Duane's sway was almost absolute for several years, his urgency was so resisted as nearly to make a breach[2] with him. It was in his mind in 1803 openly to attack Gallatin and Madison upon the subject,[3] but the plan was not then carried out.

In his own State the influence of Duane and the *Aurora* was enormous, and I have found no evidence even of opposition to his control of the party until 1802. Dr. Michael Leib was then and for some years the rock on which the split occurred. He was a very close friend of Duane and extremely active in all political affairs, and seems to have

creed of Federalism] was exposed to persecution and proscription. His character, his person, and his house were alike doomed to insult and violence. . . . Thus pursued by the zealots of party and unprotected by the hand of power, the halls of justice seemed likewise to deny him a sanctuary; for every minister of justice was a federalist. . . . Nay, the law itself assumed the form of a weapon made for the federalists alone to wield; by whose magic, riots might be converted into rebellion, flattery became the test of political truth, and freedom of opinion was condemned as sedition."

[1] Those who have not studied the period have no idea of the state of party feeling during the end of the last and beginning of this century. Probably the cause is largely to be found in the one side's support and the other's unspeakable detestation of the French Revolution. But there were also tremendous changes going on in this country. The hottest campaigns of modern times are tame indeed by comparison, and it may well be doubted whether passions boiled any harder during the civil war.

[2] Mr. Adams ("Life of Gallatin," p. 439; see 313) rather criticises Jefferson for not breaking with Duane, and apparently does not appreciate the difference between his case and that of Burr. Mr. Jefferson was too good a politician voluntarily to break with Duane, who was the most potent factor in the party in his State. See Mr. Jefferson's statesman-like letter of August 14, 1801, to the rather unpractical Gallatin, printed in Adams's "Life of Gallatin," pp. 280, 281.

[3] See Adams's "Life of Gallatin," p. 311.

been a man of violent methods, who would brook no criticism; he had, moreover, been involved for years with members of the Penrose family in a suit growing out of alleged
dishonest practices.[1]   In this year he was nominated for
Congress.   In September the discontented met "at the
house of Martin Ludic, sign of the Rising Sun, Germantown
Road."   But the *Aurora* heard of this "conclave," published the notice of their intended second meeting, and
then got its people to go there in such force[2] as to control
the meeting absolutely and pass resolutions endorsing Leib
and the whole ticket.   The result was that Dr. Leib was
easily elected, though he ran about one hundred votes behind.[3]   Samuel Macferran, Nathan Jones, and C. B. Penrose were prominent[4] in this first revolt; but Alexander J.
Dallas,[5] who was in a few years to be the leader and chief
spirit of the opposition, was one of the Republican State
Committee of Correspondence.

In 1803 the restlessness under Duane had evidently
grown. The *Portfolio* of July 2 of that year says that his
influence on the Republicans was visibly decreasing, and
that several chiefs of the party had expressed indignation
at him and ridiculed the idea of his perpetual "dictator-
ship."   In the county elections the discontented element
again made a contest, principally on the sheriff, but the
result was that the regular candidate (John Barker) was
elected[6] without much difficulty. So complete had been
the defeat of the Federalists that they only nominated candidates for some of the offices. The year before they had
only cast 17,125 votes for Ross for governor, against 47,567
for McKean.

During these years, too, there was a rising spirit of dissatis-

---

[1] *Freeman's Journal*, June 18, 1804. See the *Aurora's* explanation of
these charges in end of May and on June 18, 1804.
[2] See *Aurora*, September 15, 21, 22, 23, 24, 1802.
[3] *Ibid.*, October 15 and 16, 1802.
[4] *Ibid.*, September 21, 1802.
[5] *Ibid.*, September 16, 1802.
[6] *Ibid.*, October 13, 1803.

faction with the judicial establishment of the State, which may be traced for a number of years. No doubt part of the feeling on this subject was unfounded and the changes advocated in many instances visionary, but that there was a real basis for discontent cannot be doubted. The feelings of the public were greatly excited, and the papers teemed with letters reviling the lawyers, advocating the abolition of the common law, and complaining of the delays, the costs,[1] the loss of good causes through technicalities, and many other things. A pamphlet,[2] under the suggestive title of "Sampson against the Philistines," was published in 1805, in which the whole subject was treated by some one who was not ignorant of the law, and the lawyers very roughly handled. In 1809, Richard Rush[3] wrote a pamphlet in defence of the common law and against its abolition. The Republicans complained, too, that the judicial establishment was altogether federal. "Every minister of justice," said their address of 1802, "was a federalist. The officer who prosecuted, the judge who presided, the marshal who summoned the jury, and the jury who tried the case, were all—all federalists." The State juries were also summoned at this time by selection by an individual, and not by lot; and Duane's failure to recover a verdict for his beating by J. B. McKean and others is probably to be attributed to this cause.[4] It should also not be forgotten

[1] One case was much talked of (see official statement, printed in *Democratic Press*, August 16, 1808), where the costs amounted to £365 16s. 8d. in a suit brought to recover £40 in 1776.

[2] "Sampson against the Philistines or the Reformation of Law Suits; and Justice made cheap, speedy, and brought home to every man's door, agreeably to the principles of the ancient trial by jury, before the same was innovated by judges and lawyers, compiled for the use of the honest citizens of the U. S. to whom it is dedicated. The Second edition. A large allowance made to those who purchase a number of copies. Philadelphia. Printed by B. Graves for Wm. Duane. 1805."

[3] A copy of this pamphlet, among the papers of Charles J. Ingersoll, has written on it, " by Richard Rush." It is doubtless the pamphlet referred to by Rush in a letter to his brother James, dated May 27, 1810. Manuscript in Philadelphia Library.

[4] Duane was said by his enemies to dread courts and juries much as a

that several shameful instances of misconduct on the bench
are known.   Addison was impeached and removed from
office for scandalous bullying of a brother judge; nor was
he the only judge who disgraced his office by manners more
suited to the prize-ring.[1]   It is not unusual to brush aside
all this phase of our history as a time when many "hay-seed
notions were abroad;" but history does not deserve to be
treated so superficially.   It is quite true that many men of
poor education were among the leaders, and that they proposed many impracticable and absurd measures; but it is
equally true that the other side adhered with a fatuous
blindness to the dead and senseless traditions of the past.
The lawyers, bred to precedent, clung to mere forms which
had long since lost their purpose and become meaningless
jargons, while the elderly men held fast to what was old,
merely because it was old, and cried aloud that the bonds
of society were being undone when any change whatsoever
was proposed.   But changes were undoubtedly needed:
they are always needed in the development of mankind, and
particularly so after so great a change as the Revolution.
The delays in trials at that time were very great, and it was
apparently not infrequently six or seven years[2] before a
case could be terminated.   This was, therefore, one point
specially calling for change, and the reformers wanted to
introduce for the purpose the system of compulsory arbitration[3] for the trial of causes by arbitrators outside of court.
Several laws were passed upon the subject and vetoed by
McKean, but it finally found its way on to the statute-book.

child does fire (see *Freeman's Journal,* March 22, 1805); and it is well
known that verdicts were repeatedly recovered against him.

[1] See, *e.g.,* McMaster's "History of the United States," Vol. III. p. 154.

[2] *Freeman's Journal,* October 6, 1807.   The opposition claimed that
this grew out of the refusal of the Republicans to make any increase in
the number of the judges of the Supreme Court.   See also, on delays
generally, *Aurora,* January and February, 1804; *Freeman's Journal,* July
20, 1805; *Democratic Press,* March 16, 1809.

[3] This subject was discussed *pro* and *con* by R. M. Patterson and
George Andrews and the vice-provost at the University commencement
in 1804.   See *Aurora,* June 25, 1804.

Another law much agitated was the Hundred-Dollar Act,[1] by which justices were given jurisdiction of suits involving less than one hundred dollars. The system of arbitration has been an utter failure, and so has the Hundred-Dollar Act in the large cities, whatever has been the case in the country districts. But if these laws were failures, others remain still on the statute-book as instances of wise and beneficial legislation. Numerous acts simplifying practice and modifying old rules of law were passed in this period, but the subject is too technical for the general reader.[2] The efforts to simplify judicial procedure, which were so characteristic of the movement, anticipated by many years the like tendency of legislation which is now to be found in all Anglo-Saxon countries. And the question of modifying imprisonment for debt was also discussed,[3] and the law upon the subject ameliorated in 1808, thus again anticipating a later tendency.

Addison was found guilty upon his impeachment in January, 1803, and early the same year a petition was presented to the Legislature for the impeachment of Judges Shippen, Yeates, and Smith, of the Supreme Court, for their conduct

---

[1] Simon Snyder was very active in effecting the passage of this act. Armor's " Governors of Pennsylvania," pp. 809, 810.

[2] For the benefit of any lawyer reader I will mention here the following: Act of March 81, 1812, § 1 (5 Sm. 895), abolishing survivorship in joint tenancy; Act of March 11, 1809, § 6 (5 Sm. 17), regulating appeals to the Supreme Court; Act of March 21, 1806, § 6 (4 Sm. 829), facilitating amendments; Acts of March 21, 1806, § 12 (4 Sm. 832), and of April 13, 1807, § 1 (4 Sm. 476), establishing our present method of ejectment; Act of April 18, 1807, § 4 (4 Sm. 477), providing that death of parties shall not abate an ejectment; Act of March 21, 1814, § 1 (6 Sm. 111), providing that verdicts shall not be set aside for defect in jury process; Act of February 24, 1806, § 28 (4 Sm. 278), providing that prothonotaries shall enter judgment on instruments with a confession of judgment, without the intervention of an attorney. All these laws still remain on the statute-book. I have not endeavored to find the multitude of others which were doubtless passed and have been since substituted by laws of a later date. The District Court of Philadelphia also owed its establishment to this period (Act of March 30, 1811).

[3] *Democratic Press*, December 9, 1808.

in the Passmore case, and this proceeding was a powerful factor in the disrupting of the Republican party.   Many of the leaders no doubt felt that this was going too far, and shuddered at the dangers ahead.   Mr. Dallas refused to be of the prosecuting counsel, and represented the defence in conjunction with Jared Ingersoll.

Meanwhile, the election of 1804 came on, and again there was an effort to break down the Duane-Leib power.   Early in this campaign the opponents of Duane secured the very important aid of a newspaper in the *Freeman's Journal*, edited by William McCorkle.   This paper and the *Aurora* were soon abusing each other vigorously.   The *Aurora* tried to fasten on the *Journal* the title of " Third-Party paper," while McCorkle replied that Duane was the real Third-Party man, called him a Jacobin, and maintained[1] that he had assumed all the errors of absolutism, proscription, and Robespierreism.

Again, this year, a principal cause of quarrel was the nomination of Dr. Leib for Congress.   He was selected in the county of Philadelphia in pursuance of notices of a " county" meeting, while the *Journal* advertised " district" meetings, at which William Penrose was selected by the county to run as one of the three members of Congress from the district.[2]   Dr. Leib was again successful,[3] but by a much smaller majority than other persons on the ticket.   In this contest Tench Coxe was a leader of the forces arrayed against Dr. Leib, and was most vehemently abused in the *Aurora.*

In the November election of this year the Federalists

---

[1] *Freeman's Journal*, May 16 and 22, 1804.

[2] At this time the Congressional district, which was composed of the city of Philadelphia, the county of Philadelphia, and the county of Delaware, elected three members to Congress by general ticket; one of these candidates was selected by each of the three subdivisions of the district.

[3] *Aurora*, October 11, 1804.   In factional fights in those days the papers printed notices before the election of the places where the tickets of their faction might be found on election-day.   See *Freeman's Journal*, October 9, 1804; October 8, 1807.

cast only 1179 votes for President, against 22,103 of the Republicans, and there was not[1] even any generally recognized Federal electoral ticket in the field. But causes were at work[2] which were soon to disintegrate for a time this overwhelming majority. In the first place, there was very great dissatisfaction with McKean, and the Duane faction appears[3] to have had it in mind in 1804 (if not sooner) to get rid of him at the next election. Not only was he overbearing and possessed of a very hot and intractable temper, but his distribution of patronage had of course been unsatisfactory to the *Aurora*, and there is no doubt that he had exhibited a great deal of nepotism. He was, moreover, opposed to many of the law reforms agitated, and had used the veto power with great frequency; he had treated some members of the Legislature with marked disrespect, and called them "clodpoles," or "clodhoppers;"[4] and he was opposed to the impeachment of the judges. When these latter were acquitted,[5] on January 28, 1805, Duane and his clique began at once to carry things in such a high-handed fashion as other members of the party could not endure. Abuse and proscription were incessant, and many members were expelled from the Tammany Society,[6] of which Dr.

---

[1] *Poulson's Daily Advertiser*, October 24, 1804.

[2] On October 16, 1804, Dallas wrote to Gallatin, "Thank Heaven, our election is over! The violence of Duane has produced a fatal division. He seems determined to destroy the Republican standing and usefulness of every man who does not bend to his will. He has attacked me as the author of an address which I never saw till it was in the press. He menaces the governor. You have already felt his lash. And I think there is reason for Mr. Jefferson himself to apprehend that the spirit of Callender survives."—Adams's "Life of Gallatin," p. 326.

[3] *Freeman's Journal*, October 3, 1804; and see October 29. The Address of the Constitutional Republicans of 1805 charged that "the malcontents had actually calculated the chances in favor of another candidate" in 1802.

[4] *Ibid.*, May 30, June 1 and 7, 1805.

[5] The vote was thirteen for conviction and eleven for acquittal; a two-thirds vote was necessary.—*Aurora*, January 30, 1805.

[6] The *Freeman's Journal* of April 10, 1805, has an account of this "War in the Wigwam," or Tammany Society. It says that most of the mem-

Leib was Grand Sachem, for daring to oppose some of the political plans of Duane and Leib. On February 28 the *Aurora* came out with its call for a convention to alter the constitution, and " Sampson against the Philistines" urged the same plan. A society of " Friends of the People" was also soon organized in the same interest. The opponents of Duane were now genuinely alarmed,[1] and at once began to take steps looking to the union of all men of any party who were opposed to the convention. A correspondent of the *Journal* of February 28 wrote, " Let the firm and decided friends of the constitution and laws, and not anarchy —of liberty and not licentiousness— . . . give an effectual opposition to this wild, this mad scheme of Duane's, and we believe likewise of Leib's. Remember, that if this scheme of Duane's takes place, all is lost—He will then reign the uncontrolled sovereign of Pennsylvania, no longer afraid of judges and juries." Those who thus united for a specific purpose presumably comprehended nearly all the Federalists, and with them went a very large following of the moderate Republicans. The name of " Third Party," which had had such terrors for the earlier seceders from the party,— apparently because Burr's followers in New York were so called,—did not frighten them, and one writer in the *Journal* accepted the name fully, explaining that " the *tertium quid* is something which is thrown into a composition in pharmacy, to correct the qualities of two other ingredients, *and to change a poison into a medicine.* It is in this point of view

bers of Tammany had been in the Democratic Society in 1795, but the harmony of this latter body was destroyed, and it was broken up by some resolution in the matter of the whiskey insurrection. " The Tammany Society was next formed by an active citizen of Philadelphia, in pursuance of a dispensation from the Tammany Society of New York." The article continues that Leib was admitted with difficulty, but finally secured control and got himself elected Grand Sachem. See also *ibid.* for February and March, 1805.

[1] The *Freeman's Journal* of May 28, 1805, announces positively that " the Revolutionary faction in Pennsylvania intend to overturn the government of the United States, if they can accomplish the destruction of our State government."

that I call myself a Tertius Quis, and what I write a Tertium Quid, if you please, thrown in to correct errors. There is no small necessity at this time for such interference. *It depends on a third party whether we have liberty or despotism.*"

The name which the new party gave itself was "Constitutional Republican," and in March propositions were published for forming "The Society of Constitutional Republicans." The parent society was organized at Philadelphia at a meeting on March 23, at which Mr. Dallas read the memorial, and Peter Muhlenberg was elected president and Mathew Carey secretary. Muhlenberg was soon succeeded [1] by George Logan, and Mathew Carey by Samuel Wetherill, Jr. Israel Israel was vice-president, and Blair McClenachan, Jonathan B. Smith, and Isaac Worrell were prominent members; [2] but the controlling spirit of the whole movement was Alexander J. Dallas. Steps were immediately taken to secure signatures to a petition to the Legislature against a convention, and on June 12 an address was issued which had been written by Mr. Dallas. [3]

Meanwhile the legislative nominating caucus at Lancaster had met and broken up in confusion, some members urging the support of McKean, while others placed Simon Snyder in nomination. The *Freeman's Journal* ridiculed Simon Snyder — a Pennsylvania "Dutchman" — as "Governor Log," and one very good authority [4] intimates that he was by no means the real choice of the *Aurora*, and even that that paper did not give him a hearty support. The campaign was extremely animated, the Constitutionalists making every effort to secure the support of the young men and of the expelled members of the Tammany Society. [5] They

[1] The *Democratic Press* of September 24, 1807, intimates that Leib had induced Muhlenberg to resign, in the hope of being taken up by the regulars as their candidate for governor.

[2] *Freeman's Journal*, November 26, 1805.

[3] Printed in G. M. Dallas's "Life of A. J. Dallas," p. 211 *et seq.*

[4] "Recollections of John Binns," p. 192.

[5] "All those members of the Tammany Society held in Race Street, who were accused or expelled without a hearing or trial, for exercising the free right of suffrage at an election in October last in opposition to

issued twenty-five thousand copies of their address through the whole State, and also translated it into German.   Numerous branch societies were, moreover, formed in different counties, and the opponents of the convention secured more signatures to their petition against that body than the *Aurora* and its allies could get in favor of it.   On the other side strenuous efforts were made, too, and it should be mentioned that in this campaign John Binns came into great prominence as a very warm supporter of the convention and of Snyder, in the *Republican Argus*, which he edited at Northumberland.   Nor should the "Quid Mirror" be forgotten here, a most scandalous and outrageous libel of leading Quid characters, which was surreptitiously circulated just before the election and the next year reprinted.

The result of this desperate political contest is well known.   McKean was re-elected by a majority of over five thousand votes, and the project of a convention was abandoned.   Right after the election, McKean brought libel suits [1] against Duane, Leib, Matthew Lawler, Thomas Leiper, and Jacob Mitchell, and the incumbents of numerous offices were removed and their places given to what the *Aurora* called [2] Mr. Dallas's " circle of hungry expectants." In April preceding the *Freeman's Journal* [3] had been given the publishing of the laws.

But, great as the victory of the Constitutionalists had been, they had no permanent bond of union, and they fell apart [4] almost at once.   A special election was held in Philadelphia in the end of November, to fill a vacancy in the Legislature, and, though strenuous efforts were made again to present a united front, they were entirely unavailing. The Federalists held a meeting of their own, and the Con-

the Congressional Sachem of that Society are invited" to become members of the Constitutional Republican Society.—*Freeman's Journal*, June 17, 1805.

[1] *Freeman's Journal*, November 6, 1805.
[2] *Aurora*, November 16, 1805.
[3] *Freeman's Journal*, April 25, 1805.
[4] *Ibid.*, November 19, 21, 23, 25, 26, 30, and December 6, 1805.

stitutionalists, or "Friends to the Constitution," called one of theirs, while the "Constitutional Republicans" insisted upon acting only with those who were friendly to the federal as well as the State administration. The consequence was that the party which had so lately been successful had several nominees in the field, and John Dorsey [1] (the *Aurora* candidate) was elected. On the 12th of December the Society of Constitutional Republicans resolved [2] "that this Society having attained the object for which it was instituted, be now dissolved." Thus went out of existence an organization which had accomplished a great work. It had for the first time broken the absolute power of the *Aurora*, and had so crushed the scheme of a constitutional convention that it was no longer heard of, except when its opponents occasionally asserted that the project was still brewing, and its once friends denied any further thought of it. Three years later, when Simon Snyder was again the candidate for governor, it was announced [3] authoritatively that he was against a convention. It is a great mistake, however, to suppose that the question of a convention was the only one involved in the contest. The desire to defeat McKean was quite as strong; and it showed itself again in 1807, when he was impeached [4] under the lead of Simon Snyder. It seems [5] that at the time the Constitutional Republican Society went out of existence the Constitutionalists had a majority in both branches of the Legislature.

Again, in 1806, a contest was made against the control of Duane, but the Third-Party men had not yet found the means of accomplishing their object. The day of their de-

---

[1] *Freeman's Journal,* November 30, 1805.

[2] *Ibid.,* December 13, 1805.

[3] *Democratic Press,* August 3, 1808.

[4] *Ibid.,* April 6, 1807. The impeachment was based on several grounds, some relating to patronage, some to high-handed proceedings in a disputed election, and one charging him with having endeavored to induce Duane to stop his personal suit against J. B. McKean if the governor would stop the suits of the Commonwealth against Duane.

[5] *Freeman's Journal,* December 5, 1805.

liverance, however, was near at hand.   The name of John
Binns has already been mentioned, and from 1807 he was for
many years a leading factor in politics in Philadelphia.   He
was born in Ireland, of humble parentage, and, like Duane,
was repeatedly in trouble with the English authorities from
1790 to 1801, when he came out to America and settled at
Northumberland.   Here he soon drifted into politics, and
established the *Republican Argus*, which shortly became one
of the prominent Republican papers of the State.   He was
evidently a bold and determined man, of very strong will,
and he wielded a severe pen.   Though far less scurrilous and
abusive than Duane, he could at times be very severe upon
an opponent, and he had, moreover, a strong power of drawing men to him.   At Northumberland he had become a close
friend of Simon Snyder, and was much in favor of nominating him again for governor in 1808.[1]   He says[2] that in
January, 1807, a friend in Philadelphia wrote him, urging him
to move to that city and establish a Democratic paper.   He
sounded members of the Quid party, and found them quite
willing to support Snyder for governor; but they could not
do so under the lead of the *Aurora*, which had so long been
abusing them unmercifully.   It was probably then arranged
that Binns should move to Philadelphia and establish a new
Republican paper there, under which the anti-Duane people
might return to the regular Republican fold.   This purpose
was accomplished early in 1807, and Binns was well received[3]
by all branches of the party.   The first number of the new
paper—the *Democratic*[4] *Press*—was issued March 27.   On

[1] The facts regarding Binns are taken from his "Recollections." He was
not a member of any church until he joined the United Brethren in 1812.
[2] *Democratic Press*, March 27, 1810.   See also Binns's "Recollections," pp. 192, 193.
[3] *Aurora*, February 18, 1807.
[4] Binns was advised by Duane not to use the word "Democratic" in
his paper's title, and later took much satisfaction in having started the
first paper anywhere published under that name ("Recollections," p.
197).   He thinks that the title of his paper led to the change of the party
name to "Democratic" (*ibid.*, p. 253).   The change was a very gradual
one, and would be difficult to trace.

May 15, Binns delivered the "Long Talk"[1] before the Tammany Society, and congratulated that body on having been "purged of all that was foul and unsocial in it" by the turning out of the Third-Party men. But he little knew then that before the end of September of that year he himself was destined to be purged[2] out of the same society for like reasons. In the same month of September, too, the *Aurora* announced[3] that, as the *Press* had taken up the proscription of the most useful political characters, "and probably was predestined by its original founders to become, under the mask of an odious and despicable hypocrisy, the successor of McCorkle . . . the editor of the *Aurora*, as a public centinel, deems it to be his duty to withdraw . . . those expressions of confidence &c., &c." Opposition to Dr. Leib was the political sin here referred to. Soon after Binns's arrival in Philadelphia he seems to have had a clash of some kind[4] with the doctor, and on August 26 he had come out openly against him as the cause of many of the dissensions among the Republicans. At this election Dr. Leib was running for the Assembly and Duane was nominated for the Senate, and a bitter campaign was waged. Duane tried to fix on his opponents the new name of "Quadroons," and spoke of their union as "The Fourth Coalition,—Federalists—Quids —and Quadroons." So hot were the dissensions that the Federalist ticket was largely successful. Leib was elected to the Assembly with the other Republicans, but by a smaller majority than they, while Duane was badly beaten for the Senate. The *Aurora* groaned[5] aloud at this "first federal

---

[1] This address was very laudatory of America, and sums up the author's political views as follows: "In truth, there are but two names in our language which designate the principles and views of the two parties. I mean the words *democrats* and *aristocrats*—the friends of the rights of the *many*—and the advocates of a *privileged few*." On this occasion Binns gave a volunteer toast to Simon Snyder.—*Democratic Press*, May 15, 1807.

[2] *Aurora*, October 3, 1807 ; *Democratic Press*, October 8, 1807.

[3] *Aurora*, September 4, 1807.

[4] See *Democratic Press*, March 27, 1810 ; see also June 4, 1807.

[5] *Aurora*, October 15 and 17, 1807.

triumph" since Jefferson's election, and the *Press* found [1] the cause of the evil in the multitude of voters who went to the polls to vote against Duane and then voted the whole opposition ticket.   In December a special election to fill a vacancy in the Assembly was held and the Republican candidate again defeated.   In this election there is evidence that Binns already had the upper hand in the party.   From the very first his paper had been highly successful.   Intending originally to publish it but twice a week, he started it with three numbers a week, and soon published it daily. Its circulation seems to have increased rapidly, while, at least in a few years, the *Aurora* began to lose subscribers.[2]

But what principally secured the power of Binns was no doubt the election of Snyder as governor in 1808.   Duane and Leib were probably strongly opposed to Snyder, but they could not stem the tide, and had to yield.   During the campaign Binns was very adroit in bringing back to the party the Constitutional Republicans; they were not abused and dragooned, but led gradually.   Thus, on August 13 a meeting was held, at the Rising Sun Tavern, of Constitutional Republicans who were opposed to Ross and in favor of Madison and Clinton, at which resolutions were passed to this effect, and also a resolution that the *Freeman's Journal* " can no longer be considered as speaking the language of the constitutional party."   Later, letters and leaders argued that Spayd was not really in the contest, and that the question was whether to vote for a Federalist or for Snyder.   Finally, on August 24, a second meeting at the Rising Sun passed distinct resolutions for Snyder.   Thus the seceders of 1805 were fully reunited with the party, with the *Democratic Press* at their head, while McCorkle was cast aside.   When the election occurred, Snyder was elected by a majority of over twenty-four thousand votes, and there was a good majority for him both in the city and county of Philadelphia.   The counties of Delaware, Chester, Bucks, Lancaster, Luzerne, and Adams alone gave majorities

---

[1] *Democratic Press*, October 16, 1807.
[2] *Ibid.*, February 8, March 27, 1810.

for Ross.   Leib was again elected to the Assembly, but had only 3512 votes, while the others on the same ticket had from 4300 to 4400.   The Federalist cause was so poorly cared for that there was doubt whether they had an electoral ticket in the field or not.   Late in October, however, the *Press* announced that there was one, in order that " there may be no lolling on the pillow of security, that no man may be taken by surprise."   It is worthy of observation that the *Press* was accused[1] of owing its maintenance to *French* gold, and at least the *Aurora*[2] found *British* gold in the pockets of the Federalists, while Ross was attacked in the papers and in a pamphlet during the campaign for his alleged harsh treatment of one Jane Marie in a lawsuit conducted against her by him.

Dr. Leib was elected to the United States Senate early in 1809, but the new governor's course was by no means pleasing to Duane.   The *Press* defended him, while the *Aurora* criticised his conduct in the Olmsted case,[3] and, indeed, in everything, and soon was distinctly in the opposition.   In August it threatened to impeach him, and in October announced[4] that he should never be governor again.   Binns called the *Aurora* and its supporters " The Philadelphia Junto," while they called themselves " Democrats of the Old School," and soon fell into acting with the Federalists, as the Quids had done in their day.   To touch for a moment on a broader point, it is probable that Binns was already in favor of war with England.   At a meeting in the State-House yard, in the end of January, resolutions were passed[5] with a decidedly warlike ring, though they

[1] This was charged in McCorkle's paper, and led to a suit against him by Binns.—*Democratic Press*, August 9, 1808.

[2] *Aurora*, October 15, 1808.

[3] This famous case and the governor's conduct in it were much discussed by the latter's friends and opponents.   Doubtless, Graydon (" Memoirs," p. 325) refers to it when he writes of "the actual war-measures of Governor Snyder against President Madison."

[4] Quoted in *Democratic Press*, October 5, 1811.   See also *ibid.*, August 21, 1809, and June 4, 1810.

[5] *Democratic Press*, January 24 and 31, 1809.

pledged their support to the administration measures for the enforcement of the embargo.

In Philadelphia a great question was and for some years had been between the advocates of a single county meeting for the county and of district meetings. Binns's friends maintained that "Leib, Duane & Co." would call one county meeting for the whole county, at which it was impossible for there to be any real representation of the districts at a distance, while they held district meetings, at which conferees were appointed. In 1809 this dispute was very warm. A stormy "county" meeting was held, at which Dr. Leib was chairman, and "some of the Junto were roughly handled and their blood shed."[1] But the other faction declined to be bound by this, on the grounds that "district" meetings were the only fair method, and that the call for the county meeting had publicly announced[2] that "Quids, Quadroons, Apostates, Hypocrites, and Conspirators should be driven from the ground, because their touch was pollution." At the election the "district" ticket was generally successful this year; and in 1810 the power of Duane seemed still more on the wane,[3] the *Press* announcing with great triumph that "Michael Leib's dictation is at an end" and that "The *Old School*[4] have not carried a single candidate they put in nomination." The Legislature had, moreover,

---

[1] *Democratic Press*, September 7, 1809.

[2] *Ibid.*, September 29, 1809.

[3] *Ibid.*, August 14, October 10, 11, and 13, 1810. One of the means employed by Binns was the establishment of new "Democratic Societies."—*Democratic Press*, May 10, 1810.

[4] Binns says ("Recollections," p. 310) that the strength of this faction lay mainly in the Northern Liberties. The divisions of parties in those days were nearly as numerous as in Continental European countries. Richard Rush, in 1812, counted six distinct parties in Pennsylvania: "1. The Anglo-federalists; 2. the federalists; 3. the McKean party; 4. the Duane or Leib party not only quite distinct from but bitterly hating the McKean; 5. those who are of no party at all; 6. the great state democratic party, or Snyder party, as it is sometimes called. The last is very small in the city, but taking the range of the State, it outweighs, by 30,000 votes at the least, all the others put together."—*Manuscript Letter to Dr. Rush, in the Philadelphia Library.*

apparently passed quite away from the control of Duane and
Leib, so that their power was gone, though they remained
still for a long time a disturbing element in the politics of
Philadelphia. They were charged [1] with having established
the *Pennsylvania Democrat*, some time in 1809, for the purpose of opposing Snyder, but the paper did not live but
about a year.

In 1811, again, the factional troubles were on foot in
Philadelphia, and the Federalists were largely successful,
though Snyder was overwhelmingly re-elected. The Federalists had been in doubt about making any nomination
against him, and their votes were divided between William
Tilghman, Richard Folwell, and others. In 1812, Binns
seems to have been far in the lead, owing probably to the
war enthusiasm. On May 20 strong resolutions in favor of
war were passed by a large meeting in the State-House
yard, at which Charles J. Ingersoll read the address. The
proceedings were published at length in the *Press*, but did
not appear in the *Aurora*, because (it was said) the copy was
first taken to Binns, " and Col. Duane would have the copy
first or not at all." [2] In the autumn of this year the Democrats were generally successful; but in 1814,[3] though Snyder was elected for his third term by some twenty thousand
over Wayne, and though the State Legislature was strongly
Democratic, yet the Federalists were largely successful in

[1] *Democratic Press*, November 28, 1810.
[2] *United States Gazette*, May 23, 1812.
[3] It was during the session of 1813–14, and while the nomination was
near at hand, that Snyder vetoed the Forty Banks Bill. The bill was
passed over his veto; but he had certainly exhibited great political courage in vetoing at such a time a measure so strongly supported. In 1810
banks had been much discussed upon the question of rechartering the
United States Bank, and Mr. Carey wrote a series of letters to the *Democratic Press*, advocating the recharter.—"Autobiography of Mathew
Carey," in a series of letters written in 1834–35 to the *New England
Magazine*, p. 53; and see *Democratic Press*, October and November, 1810.
Carey calls this question the "apple of discord." The question had also
been warmly discussed in 1804 (see, *e.g.*, *Aurora* of January and Feb-
ruary), during the efforts for and against a charter for the Philadelphia
Bank.

Philadelphia.[1]   Doubtless, this was partly due to the recent
alarms of the war and the burning of Washington; but
during all these years of factional trouble Philadelphia had
been the focus of the dissensions.[2]   In the city, too, more of
the feelings of the past survived, and prominent men were
long unconscious of the changes which had occurred.   In
1808 the nomination of the "Pennsylvania Dutchman" Snyder against the cultivated Ross had merely excited ridicule,
and the Federalists were absolutely confident of victory.[3]
And in 1812, after war was declared, Dr. Rush wrote [4] his
son Richard that he was *suspected* by the *citizens* of Philadelphia of writing for Binns's paper, and that a reference to
him by Bronson (editor of the *United States Gazette*) had
"spread a gloom over the whole family."   It is very plain
that in the doctor's mind the "citizens" meant a few prominent families, and that he was deeply distressed that his
son should be looked upon by these as guilty of what they
thought hardly less than a crime against society.

In February of 1814 a rumor was started in Harrisburg
that Michael Leib was to be appointed postmaster at Philadelphia, and Granger did make the appointment.   But he
little foresaw the consequences of the step.   A terrible storm
arose at once.   He was called upon by the Congressional
delegation; bills were introduced to inquire into the administration of his office and to take away his patronage; he
had to come out with explanations of his reasons; and soon
a petition, signed by over two-thirds of the Legislature, was
sent to the President praying for his removal; and, finally,
within a month of his appointment of Leib, the President
dismissed [5] Granger and appointed Return J. Meigs, Jr.,

[1] *Democratic Press*, November 3 and 17, 1814.
[2] *Ibid.*, October 9, 1811.
[3] On July 24, 1812, Richard Rush wrote his father upon the purblind-
ness of the Philadelphia Federalists, and reminded him that in 1808 the
betting in Philadelphia had not been as to the result, but as to the size
of the Federalists' majority.—*Manuscript in the Philadelphia Library.*
See also Binns's "Recollections," pp. 210, 211.
[4] Manuscript Letters of Richard Rush, in the Philadelphia Library.
[5] *Democratic Press*, February 14, 16, 19, 25, March 3, 10, 1814.

then governor of Ohio, in his place.   This new postmaster removed Leib[1] before long, and the latter seems then to disappear from the political field.

We have thus seen Duane supreme in power for a time, but wielding his power in such a way as to antagonize large numbers of his party.   These, by uniting temporarily with the Federalists, broke his prestige in 1805 and prevented the realization of his plans.   Later, under the lead of Binns, Duane was in a few years distinctly shorn of his power. Himself defeated as a candidate before the people in 1807, and with his devoted friend Leib always a point of attack and yearly running less well as a candidate, his final overthrow is probably to be attributed to the election of Snyder as governor in 1808.   Snyder was a close friend of Binns, and of course his election was a most powerful aid to the latter in his contest with Duane.   It has been seen that Duane was soon after in opposition to the State administration and driven to act with the Federalists during most of the nine years of Snyder's three terms of office.   Nor did he fare much better under his successor, Findlay, in 1817, nor apparently under Hiester in 1820, whom he had helped to nominate.   Indeed, I do not think that Duane succeeded at any time after Snyder's election in gaining any considerable measure of control, though the battles between him and his opponents were very bitter and a source of great injury to their party for a number of years.   In 1817 he again urged[2] the calling of a convention, and tried to make an issue upon the question, but in 1822 he finally gave up his paper and went to South America.

[1] Leib's history is but little known, though he played a leading part in the State for years.   He had voted in the United States Senate in favor of the declaration of war, on its final passage, but the *Press* accused him of voting eleven times against the administration on this question.— *Press,* June 6, 1814; and see Hildreth's "History of the United States," Vol. VI. p. 305.   Richard Rush also wrote to his father from Washington, on June 13, 1812, "Dr. Leib it is announced is opposed to war!! and against England!!!! a measure he has been labouring for fifteen years."—*Manuscript Letter in the Philadelphia Library.*

[2] *Aurora,* January 8, 1817.

—

Binns, to whom his defeat was undoubtedly in the main due, was in turn a great power for some years. This was, probably, especially the case under Snyder, as he quarrelled with Findlay soon after the latter's election, and helped to defeat him and elect Hiester; but Binns, too, was shorn of his power in a few years. In the almost entirely personal politics that followed the era of good feeling, he took sides against Jackson and opposed him most bitterly. He issued the famous coffin handbills in 1828, and excited so much opposition thereby that his house was mobbed and he escaped by the roof. He deplores in his "Recollections" the results of these steps which drove him out of his party, and he thinks he ought to have had sufficient political sagacity to avoid such an error. He also thinks that after Jackson's nomination in 1828 he might have ceased his opposition had there not been overtures made to him by General Eaton, which he took as an offer of a bribe. He was appointed an alderman by Governor Hiester in 1822, and in 1829 the publication of the *Press* was stopped.

That very acrid writer, whose custom it was to distil his hatred and jealousy of all his contemporaries into a Diary, wrote[1] as follows of Pennsylvania politics of this period, and the picture is not without value, after liberal deduction is made for the bile and distemper of a disappointed mental dyspeptic: "Pennsylvania has been for about twenty years governed by two newspapers in succession; one, the *Aurora,* edited by Duane, an Irishman, and the other, the *Democratic Press,* edited by John Binns, an Englishman. Duane had been expelled from British India for sedition, and Binns had been tried in England for high treason. They are both men of considerable talents and profligate principles, always for sale to the highest bidder, and always insupportable burdens, by their insatiable rapacity, to the parties they support. With the triumph of Jefferson in 1801, Duane, who had contributed to it, came in for his share, and more than his share, of emolument and patronage. With his printing

[1] Quoted from J. Q. Adams's "Diary," Vol. V. p. 112, in Adams's "Life of Gallatin," p. 442.

establishment at Philadelphia he connected one in this city; obtained by extortion almost the whole of the public printing, but, being prodigal and reckless, never could emerge from poverty, and, always wanting more, soon encroached upon the powers of indulgence to his cravings which the heads of Departments possessed, and quarrelled both with Mr. Madison and Mr. Gallatin for staying his hand from public plunder. In Pennsylvania, too, he contributed to bring in McKean, and then labored for years to run him down; contributed to bring in Snyder, and soon turned against him. Binns in the mean time had come, after his trial, as a fugitive from England, and had commenced editor of a newspaper. . . . Snyder, assailed by Duane, was defended by Binns, who turned the battery against him, and finally ran down the *Aurora* so that it lost all influence upon public affairs.''

During the period of the contests between Duane and Binns some important changes in political methods occurred. The old way of nominating [1] for governor (as also for President) is well known to have been by legislative caucus, but in the nomination for governor in 1808 the system was varied by the Pennsylvania Republicans, and in the discussions which attended this change is undoubtedly to be found the germ of our system of State and National nominating conventions. On August 29, 1807,[2] the Republicans of Delaware County met and passed resolutions referring to the fact that under the legislative caucus system those coun-

[1] The practice in making nominations in the city seems to have been as follows: A meeting was called, and at this a committee chosen ''to withdraw for the purpose of reporting to the meeting a suitable ticket for members of assembly, and for the select and common councils of the city to be supported at the ensuing election . . . and to confer with the delegates from the counties of Philadelphia and Delaware, in the selection of suitable persons to fill the offices of senator, sheriff and county commissioner,'' or whatever office extending over those counties, as well as the city, was to be elected. This committee withdrew and soon reported a ticket, which was then submitted to the general meeting for its approval. See *Freeman's Journal*, September 15, 1807.

[2] *Aurora*, September 4, 1807.

ties which had not members of their party in the Legislature
were without a voice in the nomination, and then proceeded
to recommend that "each county make choice of as many
persons as they send representatives to the assembly, to meet
at some central part of the state and there to nominate such
person as a majority of the republicans may think most eligible to fill the office of governor." William Anderson was
chairman and William Lewis, Jr., secretary of this meeting.
A few weeks later, at a like meeting in Philadelphia,[1] resolutions were passed approving the plan proposed by Delaware County, and the details of the plan were more developed. It was suggested that the convention should meet
every third year, some months before the election for governor, and that no one should be eligible to the convention
who at the time held office under the governor or who failed
to pledge himself not to hold any such office for the next
three years. It seems likely to me that this was a move by
the Duane element of the party in the hope of defeating
Snyder for the nomination. The members of the Legislature were plainly in favor of Snyder, and this plan would
have submitted the question to a new set of men, and gave,
moreover, the opportunity later to add leaders such as Duane
and Thomas Leiper to the body which made the nomination.
But the innovation proposed met at first with scant favor.
Not only did county after county declare strongly in favor
of Snyder, but they also expressed their entire approval of
the caucus system, and Berks, Centre, Clearfield, Cumberland, Mifflin, and Crawford added express disapprovals[2] of
the proposed plan, on the ground of the "trouble and expense" and the danger of party division and schism. On
January 6[3] the legislative caucus called upon the counties
not represented by Democrats to send delegates, in proportion to the number of their representatives, to meet at Lancaster jointly with the legislative caucus and make a nomi-

---

[1] *Aurora*, September 23, 1807.

[2] *Democratic Press*, November 24, December 9, 1807; January 14, 25,
1808.

[3] *Aurora*, January 11, 1808.

nation, and the same was advised [1] by a meeting in Erie County. On February 10 this proposed modification of the plan first proposed was approved [2] in Philadelphia, and on March 7 the convention [3] thus composed of the party members of the Legislature and of delegates from the counties not having party members met at Lancaster and unanimously nominated Snyder and an unpledged set of electors.[4] Again, three years later, the new plan was adhered to, and in February, 1811, a convention,[5] composed of the "Democratic Republican Members of the Legislature and the Delegates from the city and several counties not represented in the Legislature by Republican members," met at Lancaster and unanimously renominated Snyder. Chester County, which was entirely represented by Republicans, had instructed [6] its members to vote for Snyder.

In 1814, however, the new plan was abandoned for the time, and the legislative caucus again made the nomination, but meetings of Republican delegates in all the counties endorsed [7] the nomination. There was no opposition to Snyder, and the nomination went to him almost by default. But in 1817, Snyder not being eligible for a fourth term, the question of the mode of nominating was much discussed, and the *Aurora* advocated a separate convention, from which office-holders should be excluded. The party leaders did not apparently want this, and some call was made in 1816

[1] *Democratic Press*, February 6, 1808.
[2] *Ibid.*, February 11, 1808.
[3] *Aurora*, March 10, 1808.
[4] The electors so chosen were well understood to be in favor of Clinton for the Presidency, and it seems plain that he was the choice of both Duane and Binns, and of the regular Pennsylvania Republicans generally. The supporters of McKean, on the other hand, had nominated Spayd and a set of electors pledged to Madison. The caucus nomination of Madison had been criticised in the *Press*, and seventeen members of Congress had signed a protest against it.—*Democratic Press*, March 7 and 9, 1808, and see February 10. See Hildreth's "History of the United States," Vol. VI. p. 68.
[5] *Democratic Press*, December 26, 1810, and February 21, 1811.
[6] *Ibid.*, February 14, 1811.
[7] *Ibid.*, October 10, 1814.

upon the Presidential electors to recommend a method. They expressed doubt of the possibility of getting the necessary number of citizens to serve in a convention without pay, and advised[1] that the people should send delegates or appoint their members of Assembly, as they pleased. A convention was accordingly called in this way, for the sole purpose of nominating a candidate for governor, which met at Harrisburg on March 4, 1817, and nominated Findlay. In this body all the counties of the State but two or three of the most remote were represented. Sixty-nine members out of one hundred and thirteen were not members of the Legislature, but delegates specially chosen for the particular purpose.[2] These proceedings, however, by no means satisfied the other element of the party, which maintained that such a body was merely a mongrel caucus, and would inevitably be dragooned by the office-holders. In 1816 this faction also had held a convention—apparently not very largely attended—at Carlisle, and had nominated an independent and unpledged set of electors, in accordance, as they said, with the intent of the constitution. The members of this body passed strong resolutions against the legislative caucus, and advised[3] that a separate convention should meet in Carlisle in June, 1817, and nominate a candidate for governor. Such a convention, with representatives from fourteen counties, met[4] accordingly at Carlisle on March 4, 1817, and nominated Joseph Hiester; but Findlay was elected.

In 1820 there were three conventions, at one of which Findlay was renominated,[5] at another Hiester, and at a third no nomination was made. At this last, which was called by Republicans opposed to Findlay, Binns was very active, and

[1] *Aurora*, January 1 and 2, 1817. See also Mathew Carey's "Olive Branch," tenth edition, improved. Philadelphia: M. Carey & Sons, 1811, pp. 461, 462.

[2] *Aurora*, March 11, 1817; Carey's "Olive Branch," as cited.

[3] *Ibid.*, September 24, October 9 and 12, 1816.

[4] *Ibid.*, March 10, 1817.

[5] *Ibid.*, March 8 and 10, 1820. Jared Ingersoll was among those proposed to this convention for the nomination. The other points are from Binns's "Recollections," p. 209, but he is clearly in error as to dates.

induced the body to adjourn without making a nomination, on the ground that only in this way could they defeat Findlay. As has been said, Binns had early quarrelled with Findlay. The canvass resulted in Hiester's election by a small majority.

Thus it seems that a most important piece of political machinery, and an improvement of much moment, has grown out of the not very inspiring wrangles of some Philadelphia politicians. The legislative caucus must have been a very bad, and probably dangerous, system. Mr. Carey, in his "Olive Branch,"[1] stated and described some of its evils in regard to Presidential nominations, and advocated, in 1816, what he says Mr. Binns had proposed,—the adoption of the Pennsylvania plan to the then near Presidential canvass. Some years and some Presidential terms, however, passed before it was adopted. In New York[2] the legislative caucus made the gubernatorial nomination as late as 1824, but this was the last year of the caucus system; and, indeed, that same year the "People's Party" held a separate nominating convention. It is stated[3] that, as early as 1792, Clinton had received his nomination from a general meeting, "composed, as was alleged, of gentlemen from various parts of the State," followed by meetings in each county. But this was very unlike the modern method of nominating conventions, and was, moreover, entirely abandoned at an early date for the legislative caucus system, which survived there for many years. Indeed, in that State,[4] as late as 1811, even the nominations for the State Senate had been made by caucus of the members of the Assembly from each senatorial district. In Massachusetts[5]

[1] Pp. 439–452, 461, 462.
[2] Hammond's "Political History of New York," Vol. II. p. 156.
[3] Lalor's "Cyclopædia of Political Science, etc., in the United States," *sub* Party Government in the United States.
[4] Hammond's "Political History of New York," Vol. I. pp. 294, 295.
[5] I am indebted to Professor John Fiske for my information as to Massachusetts. The question has not, however, been much studied there, he informs me. See also Lalor, as above. Schouler ("History of the United States," Vol. II. p. 170) states that in Massachusetts traces

the caucus system seems to have been abandoned between
1823 and 1828, and it is curious to observe that the evolu-
tion of the new system there went through a process similar
to that in Pennsylvania, though so much later.   In 1823
delegates from towns not represented in the Legislature by
Republicans were added to the legislative caucus of Republicans, and five years later the Jackson Republicans are said
to have had the convention plan fully organized.   In Connecticut and New Jersey [1] nominations for Congress were
made by a sort of preliminary election, held under statutory
directions.

are to be found about 1808 of a practice similar to that introduced into
Pennsylvania in that year, but he gives no authority, and it does not seem
likely that the plan should have been introduced in 1808 and then have
lain dormant until as late as 1823.   I regret very much that his statement
has come under my notice too late for me to be able to ascertain his
authority and thus settle the matter.

[1] Carey's " Olive Branch," p. 451.

ORATION DELIVERED AT THE INVITATION OF THE CITY OF CHICAGO AND OF THE WORLD'S FAIR COMMISSION, ON THE FOURTH DAY OF JULY, 1893, IN JACKSON PARK, CHICAGO.

BY HAMPTON L. CARSON.

MR. PRESIDENT; COMMISSIONERS OF THE WORLD'S FAIR; MR. MAYOR; CITIZENS OF CHICAGO; FELLOW-COUNTRYMEN:

In response to your gracious invitation that a son of the city of the Declaration of Independence should give utterance to the sentiments appropriate to the celebration of the greatest of our national anniversaries, in the most marvellous city of modern times in the rapidity of her growth and the dazzling character of her achievements, I am here to bid you exclaim : All Hail! thou Fourth Day of July, 1893, All Hail!

To mortal eyes no scene like this has ever been vouchsafed. We are in the presence of the august representatives of our National and State sovereignties; of municipal governments and civic enterprises; of officers of the Army and Navy; of statesmen, civilians, artisans, and laborers; of honored potentates of foreign lands; of the subjects of five Continents and the Islands of the Sea,—all happily participating in this imposing display of the arts of peace, industry, commerce, labor, learning, science, literature, and religion; attesting the harmony to be derived from a common devotion to international unity, to a belief in the brotherhood of Man, and the beauty of liberty according to law.

The time, the place, the occasion, and the landscape are unique. This is the Columbian year; this is the anniversary of an immortal declaration of human rights; this is the city of Chicago; this is the World's Fair. The Old Liberty Bell is here; the New Liberty Bell is here; the American people are here; the nations of the earth are here. In ten thousand years of recorded history when was there ever such a conjunction of events? In all the unnumbered years to come, what probability is there that it will ever be repeated? National grandeur and State pride are in conjunction with international friendship. What political horoscope can equal this? The unclouded heavens, the boundless prairie, the teeming metropolis, the unvexed bosom of a vast inland sea, you viking ship and caravels, and yonder palaces of art, resting tranquilly on their shadows in the wave,—all are in harmony with the occasion.

This celebration is in truth a swelling epic; it is a psalm of thanksgiving; it is patriotism incarnate; it is both an inspiration and a prophecy! It recalls the past and its heroic struggles; it attests the present with its miracles of achievement; it foretells the infinite possibilities of the future. Its lessons are physical, intellectual, and moral. It confutes scepticism as to Republican institutions. It surpasses the wildest dreams of the most far-sighted of the fathers of the Republic; it satisfies the most ardent of the patriots of to-day; it arouses the loftiest hopes of the transcendent destiny of America.

The world has contemplated with awe the making of consuls and dictators, the crowning of kings, the proclamation of emperors; but in describing the scenes of to-day, and the triumphal march of this morning, the modern Plutarch will commemorate a far different spectacle from that witnessed by him who wrote two thousand years ago. No Paulus Æmilius, crowned with Delphic laurel, nor ambitious Pompey, decked with the spoils of plundered provinces, appeared in that procession. No wailing victims of the fate of war were there to grace in captive bonds the conqueror's chariot wheels; no bullocks were led out to slaughter; no savage games were thrown open to the people, where tigers, famished into madness, tore the flesh of men but little less ferocious than themselves; but the *Io Triumphe* of the American people rang out above the heads of the marching squadrons as they wound their glittering length through your great highways, to bow in reverence at the shrine of the Constitution, of liberty, of order, and of law. Not on the Field of the Cloth of Gold, the Champ de Mars, nor even in Trafalgar Square; not in Venice, in her days of glory, nor yet in the Crescent City by the Golden Horn, was ever witnessed such a convocation of mankind. All classes and conditions of persons, of all sects and creeds, of all nationalities, of all ranks and stations, are here met in vast concourse, controlled not by bayonets, but by civil authority, to testify their allegiance to the Constitution and to the flag of the United States, and, in the expressive eloquence of their tumultuous applause, to assert the truth of their belief that in that Constitution there was granted to man the noblest and the freest chart of government that either ancient or modern times can boast.

Such is the day and such is the meaning of these impressive ceremonies. Difficult as it is to realize at this hour the exact circumstances of the occasion which led to the adoption, in the city of Philadelphia, of that Declaration of human rights which is among the most admired of the world's political productions, and for which men waited in vain six thousand years, it is proper that I should advert in a general way to scenes which are dear to the memory of Americans, and which can never be forgotten while patriotism exists. The history of the Liberty Bell, which is so conspicuous an object in the Pennsylvania State Building, is intimately associated with those events.

The old State-House in Philadelphia stands upon the holiest spot on American earth. There, on the south side of Chestnut Street, beneath the shelter of majestic elms, protected against the ravages of time and the rage for modern improvement, a quaint yet simple structure of plain brick and wood, erected in the year 1732 for the purpose of furnishing a place of meeting for the State government of Pennsylvania, stands the birthplace of our nationality. In 1751, the Speaker of the Provincial Assembly wrote to his friend

Robert Charles, of London, as follows: "*The Assembly having ordered us to procure a bell from England to be purchased for their use, we take the liberty to apply ourselves to thee to get us a good bell of about two thousand pounds weight, the cost of which we presume may amount to one hundred pounds sterling, or, perhaps, with the charges, something more. Let the bell be cast by the best workmen, and examined carefully before it is shipped, with the following words well shaped in large letters around it, viz. : 'By order of the Assembly of the Province of Pennsylvania for the State House in the City of Philadelphia, 1752,' and underneath, ' Proclaim liberty throughout all the land to all the inhabitants thereof.' Levit. xxv. 10.*"

The bell arrived at the end of August, 1752, but upon being tested, the superintendent had the mortification to find that it was cracked by a stroke of the clapper, without any other violence. "Two ingenious workmen," then in Philadelphia, undertook to recast it, meeting with success; but as it was found to contain too much copper, it was once again recast. From this time forward for nearly one hundred years it was rung upon all extraordinary and unusual occasions, proclaiming either joy or sorrow, peace or war.

I need not dwell with particularity upon the oppression and the wrongs which led to the assembling of the Continental Congress within the walls of the State-House in 1776. The tale is known of all men. Suffice it to say that on the 7th of June, Richard Henry Lee, of Virginia, introduced his famous Resolution: "That these united colonies are, and of right ought to be, free and independent States; that they are absolved from all allegiance to the British Crown, and that all political connection between them and the State of Great Britain is, and ought to be, totally dissolved."

A memorable debate arose. For nearly a month was the great question agitated. The 1st of July arrived. Nine colonies were there to vote affirmatively, and ten, should Cæsar Rodney arrive from Delaware before the vote was called. Two of the colonies were still adverse, and one had declined to take part, as the subject of independence was outside of their instructions. Lee, the mover of the Resolution, was absent in Virginia. Jefferson, although a power with his pen, was no speaker on the floor. Chase, the Boanerges of Maryland, was away, while John Dickinson, the author of the "Farmer's Letters," was prominent in his opposition. Even James Wilson and Robert Morris counselled delay. Then it was that John Adams became "the pillar" and "the Colossus" of the party of independence, supported by George Wythe, of Virginia, and Dr. Witherspoon, of New Jersey. On the evening of the 1st, Adams wrote to Chase that the debate had taken up the day, while Jefferson wrote that it had lasted nine hours without refreshment and without pause. The critical hour had come. The vote was taken in Committee of the Whole. Massachusetts, New Hampshire, Connecticut, Rhode Island, New Jersey, Maryland, Virginia, North Carolina, and Georgia voted for the Resolution; Pennsylvania and South Carolina voted against it; Delaware was evenly divided, and New York, at the request of her delegation, was allowed to withdraw. The second day arrived. The debate was resumed. Abraham Clark wrote, "The Declaration is now under debate. The panic which has seized the army has not yet reached the Senate. In a few hours it will be determined whether we are to be a nation of free men or a race of slaves." The lion-hearted Adams renewed his efforts. Edward Rutledge, of South Carolina, requested that the vote of his State should be changed. Pennsylvania, taking advantage of the absence of Dickinson and Morris, reversed her adverse vote. Rodney arrived by express, and thus enabled Delaware to cast her vote for the Resolution. The deed was done. The bond which bound the colonies to the throne was sundered, and on the 2d of July, 1776, America, *attollens humeris famam et fata nepotum*, bearing up her glory and the destiny of her descendants, advanced with majestic steps to assume her station among the sovereigns of the world.

It is a common error to suppose that the vote upon the Resolution was taken upon the fourth instead of the second of July. The facts were as I have stated. It was upon the

Fourth that the Declaration was adopted of the reasons which had driven the colonies to this irrevocable step. The preparation of this important document had been consigned to a special committee, of which Mr. Jefferson was the organ, and the manner in which he discharged his task—with burning eloquence and terse philosophy—has caused the "Declaration" to supplant the "Resolution" in the affections and memory of mankind, and to mark the Fourth of July as a national holiday.

It is a common error, also, to suppose that the Declaration was signed on this day. The only signatures attached were those of John Hancock and Charles Thomson, the President and the Secretary of Congress. It was not until the 15th that instructions were given to the clerk to prepare the Declaration for signature, and on the second day of August, duly engrossed on parchment, it was brought into the chamber of Congress and placed upon the President's table for the signature of the individual members. All those actually present on that day affixed their names, and some were thus included who had had no share either in debating or voting upon the document.

The truths of history are more important than its fictions, and the part played in the great drama by the Old Bell must now be stated. Its voice was silent on the Fourth of July, 1776, for Congress then sat with closed doors and in secret session; but when it had been ascertained that the sentiments of the people were in accord with what the Congress had done, and that New York had signified her intention to concur, then was the word "unanimous" inserted in the published broadsides, and on the 8th of July the Declaration was read for the first time to the people by John Nixon, in the State-House Square, while the bell rang forth its joyous notes of jubilee and verified the prophecy of its inscription.

It was the tolling of a bell at the Sicilian Vespers which proclaimed the massacre of eight thousand French in a plot to free Sicily from Charles of Anjou; it was the tolling of a bell in the palace of Catherine de Médicis which ushered in the slaughter of one hundred thousand Huguenots upon the night of St. Bartholomew's Day; it was the iron tongue of Roland in the proud city of the Brewer of Ghent which shrieked to Flanders of famine, fire, and blood, and roused the Netherlands to resist the atrocities of Alva and the inquisitors of Philip II.; but never yet in human history did bell or tocsin ever sound upon occasion so momentous to mankind as did this holy and precious relic of our heroic age. Forever honored be thy name, O Isaac Norris, Speaker of the Assembly of the Province of Pennsylvania, who, in plainest Quaker speech, and under a potent moving of the Spirit, wast led to direct that there should be inscribed upon the crest: "And ye shall hallow the fiftieth year, and proclaim liberty throughout all the land unto all the inhabitants thereof: it shall be a jubilee unto thee"—words which shook the brightest jewels from the British crown and gave a continent to liberty. Inscrutable Providence! mysterious are Thy ways, and hidden are Thy purposes, for in Thy hands the modest men of peace become as potent instruments of destruction as they who forge the thunderbolts of war.

The subsequent history of the Bell is briefly told. In 1777, when the British occupied Philadelphia, it was removed for safety to Allentown, Pennsylvania, and after the battle of Monmouth was restored to its place in the State-House, ringing upon all occasions of national rejoicing or of woe. It welcomed to our shores, in 1824, the generous Lafayette, the companion of Washington, who had spilled his blood like water by the great chieftain's side upon the field of Brandywine, and had risked fortune, fame, position, and influence in defence of American liberty. Surely it is not the least pathetic incident in our national story that on the 8th of July, 1885, it tolled in sorrow for the death of John Marshall, and then was mute forever. The earthly voices of this harbinger of liberty and of the great Chief-Justice died away together. But according to an immutable physical and moral law, the tones of the one will never cease to vibrate, attuning the souls and hearts of men to harmonies divine, while the imperishable judgments of the

other have built up a Nation which "our hearts hold price-
less; above all things, rich and rare; dearer than health
and beauty, brighter than all the order of the stars."

The institutions established by our fathers we hold in
trust for all mankind.   It was the Pilgrim of Massachusetts,
the Dutchman of New York, the Quaker of Pennsylvania,
the Swede of Delaware, the Catholic of Maryland, the Cavalier of Virginia, and the Edict-of-Nantes man of South
Carolina who united in building up the interests and in
contributing to the greatness and the unexampled progress
of this magnificent country.   The blood of England, of
Holland, and of France, wrung drop by drop by the agony
of three frightful persecutions, was mingled by the hand of
Providence in the alembic of America, to be distilled by
the fierce fires of the Revolution into the most precious
elixir of the ages.   It is the glory of this era that we can
stand here to-day and exclaim that we are not men of Massachusetts, nor men of Pennsylvania, nor men of Illinois, but
that we are Americans in the broadest, the truest, and the
best sense of that word; that we recognize no throne, no
union of Church and State, no domination of class or creed.

American liberty is composite in its character and rich in
its material.   Its sources, like the fountains of our Father
of Waters, among the hills, are to be sought among the
everlasting truths of mankind.   All ages and all countries
have contributed to the result.   The American Revolution
forms but a single chapter in the volume of human fate.
From the pure fountains of Greece before choked with dead
leaves from the fallen tree of civilization; from the rude
strength poured by barbaric transfusion into the veins of
dying Rome; from the Institutes of Gaius and the Pandects
of Justinian; from the laws of Alfred and the Magna Charta
of King John; from the daring prows of the Norsemen
and the sons of Rollo the Rover; from the precepts of
Holy Writ and the teaching of Him who was nailed to the
cross on Calvary; from the courage of a Genoese and the
liberality and religious fervor of a Spanish queen; from the
enterprise of Portugal and the devoted labors of the French

Jesuits; from the scaffolds of Russell and Sidney and of Egmont and Horn; from the blood of martyrs and the visions of prophets; from the unexampled struggle of eighty years of the Netherlands for liberty, as well as from the revolution which dethroned a James; from the tongue of Henry, the pen of Jefferson, the sword of Washington, and the sagacity of Franklin; from the discipline of Steuben, the death of Pulaski and De Kalb, and the generous alliance of the French; from the Constitution of the United States; from the bloody sweat of France and the struggles of Germany, Poland, Hungary, and Italy for constitutional monarchy; from the arguments of Webster and the judgments of Marshall; from the throes of civil war and the failure of secession; from the Emancipation Proclamation and the enfranchisement of a dusky race; from the lips of the living in all lands and in all forms of speech; from the bright examples and deathless memories of the dead—from all these, as from ten thousand living streams, the lordly current, upon which floats our Ship of State, so richly freighted with the rights of men, broadens as it flows through the centuries, past tombs of kings, and graves of priests, and mounds of buried shackles, and the charred heaps of human auction blocks, and the gray stones of perished institutions, out into the boundless ocean of the Future. Upon the shores of that illimitable sea stands the Temple of eternal Truth; not buried in the earth, made hollow by the sepulchres of her witnesses, but rising in the majesty of primeval granite, the dome supported by majestic pillars embedded in the graves of martyrs.

And Thou, great Bell! cast from the chains of liberators and the copper pennies of the children of our public schools, from sacred relics contributed by pious and patriotic hands, baptized by copious libations poured out upon the altar of a common country by grateful hearts, and consecrated by the prayers of the American people, take up the note of prophecy and of jubilee rung out by your older sister in 1776, and in your journey round the globe proclaim from mountain top and valley, across winding river and expansive

sea, those tones which shall make thrones topple and des-
pots tremble in their sleep, until all peoples and all nationalities, from turbaned Turks and Slavic peasants to distant
islanders and the children of the Sun, shall join in the
swelling chorus, and the darkest regions of the earth shall
be illumed by the heaven-born light of Civil and Religious
Liberty!

COLONEL THOMAS BUTLER AND GENERAL WILKINSON'S "ROUNDHEAD ORDER."

General James Wilkinson, commanding the army of the United States, on the 30th of April, 1801, issued an order prescribing the mode of wearing the hair for both officers and privates, and also the fashion of cap, in which everything like ornament was severely disregarded. It was for a long time known in the army as the "Roundhead Order." The real object of the order was the abolishment of the "queue," or "pigtail" as it was more vulgarly styled then, and from time almost immemorial in fashion. Gentlemen in service, of the old school and of fixed habits, resented the innovation, and many officers positively refused to obey the order. Among these was Colonel Thomas Butler, of the Second Infantry. He was of that noted family of brothers—the "five Butler brothers of Pennsylvania"— who figure so prominently in our military annals, many of whose descendants are yet living, and with a just pride cherish their memory and fame.

He (born in 1754) was a captain in the Revolution, and was wounded in the battle of Monmouth; was in St. Clair's defeat, and there twice wounded. The gallant officer asserted his right to wear his hair as he pleased, and refused to obey General Wilkinson's order, denouncing it as impertinent, arbitrary, and illegal. He was arrested, court-martialled and sentenced to be reprimanded. This done, he resumed the command of his regiment (then stationed in Louisiana), but continued to defy the order.

A second time he was placed in arrest and court-martialled; but the story of his contumacy is best told in a series of letters addressed by him to General Andrew Jackson, a connection by marriage, from which we make the following extracts:

QUARTERS 10 MILES FROM ORLEANS,
Octr 15ᵗʰ 1804.

I arrived at this place a few days since after a journey the most fatiguing I ever experienced.   The distress of Orleans is great indeed.   The Yellow Fever rages with uncommon virulence. . . . The troops are encamped eight miles from town.   I have deemed it prudent to take up my quarters detached from either place, nor do I mean to enter the city until after the first frosts, which may be soon expected.

Having received no letter since my arrival from the General [Wilkinson] I can give you very little information relative to his determination to enforce the order for cropping the hair.   From every thing I can learn, his determination is to arrest me; a few posts will decide the business, and you shall be duly informed of the whole as soon as possible thereafter. . . .

Octo 25 1804.

The following I have extracted from a letter of General Wilkinson to the Officers and command at Orleans, dated the 17ᵗʰ of June : " The general order respecting Colonel Butler has received the cordial approbation of our superiors, though some of his partisans, equally ignorant and zealous, have made a feeble attempt to combat *principles which cannot be shaken.*   The destination of this officer seems, as yet undecided.   The Secretary of War had arrested his progress at Tennessee, but I shall, I believe, repeat the order for his descent of the Mississippi."

Also in a letter from the General to the commandant at Orleans I find the following paragraph, which I also state for your perusal : " August 31, 1804, Colo. Butler has signified to me, by letter dated the 8ᵗʰ ult., his intention to proceed to New Orleans to take the command agreably to my orders, and to prevent trouble, perplexity, and further injury to the service.   I hope he will *leave his tail behind him.*"

Unless the President & heads of departments have advocated the conduct of the General, (which I can hardley suppose,) the foregoing can be considered in no higher point of view than the bombast of the General arising from chagrin.

I have assumed command of the troops in Lower Louisiana and shall proceed in the duties appertaining thereto, independent of any considerations except that of duty; and, until I receive the General's answer to my letter of the 24th of August, wherein I gave him to understand that I should not conform to the order of 30th April 1801. As soon as I receive his answer you may rely on receiving the whole in detail. If the General has received the countenance of the President of the United States, and of the heads of departments, an arrest will be the consequence.

If that should not be the case, it will pass off in a puff, and he will be convinced that I do not copy his example in always leaving *my tail behind me.* . . .

CITY OF ORLEANS, Novr. 20th 1804.

DEAR SIR: Last evening I was arrested by the General in the manner following:

"HEADQUARTERS, FREDERICKTOWN,
"MARYLAND, Octr. 10th 1804.

"SIR: Your letter of the 24th of August has come to hand. Like that of the 5th of June which you addressed to the Secretary of War, it will receive all the consideration to which it is entitled. On the receipt of this you are to consider yourself in arrest, and will conform your conduct accordingly.

[Signed] "JAMES WILKINSON."

Thus, my worthy friend, you see that I am still persecuted. I have only a moment just to state the case. By next mail probably he may deign to let me know the charge, which you shall be immediately furnished with, when I shall have to call on my friends for their assistance to have the case stated to the President, as I presume the avenues to the President are shut against me as the communication which I sent him before I left Tennessee, as you advised, has not been answered. Surely the President will not tamely look on and see an officer borne down in this way, by oppressive journeyings; if so, then have I faithfully served my country for nothing.

NEW ORLEANS, Decr 17, 1804.

I had the honor and pleasure of receiving your esteemed favor of the 16th ulto.

Your kind attention and that of my friends in Tennessee, merits my sincere acknowledgments. I am extreamely anxious to have a letter from the Hon'ble Dr. Dickson,[1] as he will have an opportunity of discovering whether this act of the General's is countenanced by the Executive, or heads of Departments, which I can hardly suppose.

I had written on the 28th ulto to the Secretary of War, requesting a speedy trial. Should he not answer my letter, I shall really conclude that my case is prejudged and settled beforehand. . . .

My mind is superior to all kind of distress, but that of tender ties. I have met with marked attention from the Governor. I have not suffered my usual prudence to abandon me. I know the maliciousness of that man [Wilkinson]. His object would be to collect something to tack to his "cropping" charge.

Decr 31st 1804.

You will observe by the enclosure the state of my case, and that the General is determined to harass and oppress me until his malignant disposition is satisfied. I should feel but little uneasiness under his persecution had I not reason to suppose that he was countenanced in it by men in office. For the honor of my country, as well as of human nature, I hope I may be deceived in this idea. Be that as it may, General, I am sensible that power can only oppress for a time; principle must ultimately rise superior to tyranny.

I have frequently written to my friends at Washington and have not had a line from that quarter since the meeting of Congress, and from the shortness of its session any enemy will gain his object by keeping back my trial until the session is over. If the General is countenanced in this persecution it is with a design to force me out of the service; a short time will develope the business.

[1] Then a representative in Congress from Tennessee.

As the General means to raise his second charge on the sentiments expressed in my letter to him of the 24th August last, I will transcribe it for your perusal :

"NASHVILLE, Aug 24 1804.

"SIR : By last mail I received a duplicate of your letter of the 9th ulto . . . informed me that mine of June 5th to the Honorable Secretary of War had already been submitted to you and contents noted.

"The subject matter of that letter required an open and decisive answer; as I had therein announced my determination not to conform to the first part of the order of the 1st of February 1804 (so far as related to cropping the hair), and had the order been correctly recited in your letter of July 9, I should have reiterated in mine of the 6th inst. my determination not to conform to the first part of that order, having ever considered the order of April 30th 1801 as an arbitrary infraction of my natural rights, and a non-compliance on my part not cognizable by the articles of war. A correct recitation of that order would have drawn forth my refusal to conform to the first part, and enabled you to have taken such measures to enforce obedience as you might have deemed expedient; and probably have saved me the fatigues of a journey of which I complained to the Hon'ble Secretary of War as vexatious.

"Notwithstanding the obstacles which I perceive in my way, yet I flatter myself that I shall in due time surmount them all, therefore permit me to inform you, sir, that I shall commence my journey to the City of Orleans by land (the only alternative left me) on Tuesday the 28th inst., and in order that a decision may be obtained as to the legality of that order, it becomes necessary for me to inform you that I shall not conform the cut of my hair to the General Order of April 30th, 1801."

The foregoing was my answer to the General. I am not afraid of my ability to defend myself on this or on any other charge he may prefer, provided I have an intelligent Court.

ORLEANS, Jan 28th 1805.

The last mail having been cut open on the road to this place, has caused the failure of this day's post, and I have cause to believe that sundry letters to me from the City of Washington had been taken out. I received one from Dr. Dickson, wherein he observes that a resolution then lay on the table to enquire into the state of the military, the object of which was to keep up the General Staff.

I am extremely anxious to hear from Washington, but shall have to pass over one other anxious week.

506 Col. Butler and Gen. Wilkinson's " Roundhead Order."

The Hon'ble Secretary will not deign to answer one of my letters. I have little doubt that he is my enemy, and if the address of the General has not had its influence in the mind of the President, the other will not affect me much. Do, my worthy friend, give me all the information in your power from time to time. Be assured I am too proud to sink under this persecution, and a day of retribution must come round, and that before long.

FORT ADAMS Apl 17 1805.

Last evening I received the charges as exhibited by the General, which I shall state for your information; they are as follows:

" HEAD QUARTERS, WASHINGTON,
" February 11th, 1805.

"SIR: The following are the transgressions for which you are arrested, and must hold yourself in readiness to answer to a military tribunal:

"Charge 1st: Wilful, obstinate and continued disobedience of the general order of the 30th of April 1801, for regulating the cut of the hair, and also disobedience of the orders of the 1st of February 1804. Specification: By refusing to conform the cut of your hair to the General Order of the 30th of April 1801 as directed in the order of the 1st of February 1804, and contumaciously resisting the authority of the order after you had been tried by a general Court Martial, found guilty of the disobedience of the General Order of the 30th of April, 1801, and sentenced to be reprimanded in general orders.

"Charge 2nd: *Mutinous conduct.* Specification: By appearing publicly in command of the troops, at the City of New Orleans, with your hair *queued*, in direct and open violation of the general order of the 30th of April 1801, and of the 1st of February, 1804, thereby giving an example of disrespect and contempt to the orders and authority of the commanding General, tending to dissever the bonds of military subordination, to impair the force of those obligations by which military men are bound to obedience, and to excite a spirit of sedition and mutiny in the Army of the United States."

These are the charges to which I am to plead on the 10th of May, at the City of Orleans, to which place I shall proceed in a few days.

On the 25th of last February I requested permission of the Hon'ble Secretary of War to return to Tennessee as soon as my trial should close, but, from the treatment I have received, I have little expectation to obtain that privilege, as he has not answered a single letter addressed to him on my present case. Therefore the presumption is strong that I shall be ordered to remain until the General may think proper to return the proceedings. The 15ᵗʰ of October was the date of my arrest, and to say that the Court will convene on the 10ᵗʰ of May (which I doubt) will be a lapse of seven months. If the Secretary of War had been friendly towards me he would not have suffered me to remain so long in arrest without a trial. But do not be uneasy. I shall adhere to my old principles, *the laws of my country*, but should their protection be withheld by design, I shall defend myself. . . .

Orleans June 9ᵗʰ 1805.

I awaited with great impatience the arrival of this day's mail, in hope to ascertain when my court would convene, but without effect. I believe the order for convening the Court on the 10ᵗʰ of May was merely to amuse.

I am now persuaded that the President of the Court and the members from the upper posts are not to leave their stations until the General descends the river to *school them*, as there is not the smallest information of their being on the river.

I have no doubt but it would be a blessing were the climate and disease of the city to take me out of the way. I could not have supposed the President would have looked on and seen me treated in the manner that I have been; nor has the Secretary of War answered my letters soliciting his permission to visit Tennessee when my trial is closed.

I have no doubt of a wish existing to put me out of service—but I am determined not to go, and unless the protection of the laws of my country are withheld, I shall protect myself.

Orleans July 8, 1805.

You will no doubt expect to hear from me. You must know that under every disadvantage I named a President and put myself on trial on arrival of as many officers as would compose the Court, determining to have a trial, resting the case on the illegality of the orders.

What the fate may be is hard to say. Every stratagem has been used to gain a verdict against me, but before an intelligent Court I should have nothing to fear. My defense placed the whole subject matter in so clear a point of view, that let the decision be as it may my friends will, I am sure, approbate my conduct and principles.

This day, Mr. Brown, Judge Advocate, replied to my defense; to-morrow I give in a rejoinder, which will close the business. You shall as soon as possible have a copy of my defense. I mean to leave the city on Wednesday for a farm which my nephew has just purchased on the Coast about seven leagues from this place, where I presume I shall have to remain until the General may think proper to return the proceedings, as the Secretary of War has not deigned to answer my applications to visit Tennessee when the Court was over.

ORLEANS July 15ᵗʰ 1805.

I have now the honor to forward for your perusal a copy of my defense which I will thank you to confide to a few friends as it might be considered improper to let it pass to the world until the proceedings had passed to the proper department for approval. The points on which I founded my defense are generally stated and with an intelligent Court must have secured a verdict in my favor. But this I have no hopes of receiving, for if I have any knowledge of countenances I think I discovered a fixed determination in a majority of the Court to legalize the order in the face of a positive act of Congress and a precedent set by an order by the Marquis de la Fayette, and a decision of the Secretary of the Navy in the case of Dr. William Rogers, proves incontestably that an illegal order may be resisted.

I should not have consented to go to trial under the unfavorable circumstances that I was obliged to do, had I seen any possible mode of gaining a fair trial; as the General had nominated every member, and kept back those whom he doubted of. He even put two of my former court on the present. But I can not express to you the base intrigue to gain a verdict against me; and although I can not speak positively as to the decision, yet I have no expectation that it is otherwise than as I have stated.

I have not time to say half what I wish to say to you, nor would it be prudent. The Court would not receive as testimony the extract from the President's letter you sent me, nor would I be permitted to prove the illegal orders as cited in my defense. But, sir, as soon as the decision is known, I shall advise with you on the proper steps to be taken to procure redress, as I never will submit to so degrading an act where the laws should secure me.

SUMMER RESIDENCE, EIGHT LEAGUES FROM ORLEANS,
Aug 26ᵗʰ 1805.

. . . You request me if possible to give you a feature of the decision of the Court in my trial. This I hinted at in my last, but it is impossible to give a correct idea as to what the sentence will be, and it will be some time yet before the decision is fully known. However, Sir, I do not expect to be disappointed as to the result, as I thought I could discover that the General had established so decided an influence over a majority of the Court, and my only object in putting myself on trial under such degrading and unfavorable circumstances was to have it in my power (with the assistance of my friends) to lay a statement of my case before Congress at their next session; as I well knew if I declined coming to trial under every disadvantage imposed upon me by the General that he would procrastinate it and throw the blame on myself, and by that means defeat my object.

These were my reasons, Sir, for going to trial under every possible disadvantage, and if a majority of the Court has decided against me their decision is founded on the letter of the order, and consequently absurd!

Thence arises the necessity of laying the subject before Congress at their next session; who will no doubt not only conceive it a duty to inquire into the lawfulness of the general order of 30ᵗʰ April 1801, but also into the arbitrary persecution with which I have been goaded for upwards of two years. But I have this pleasing reflection, General, that I am certain every independent and virtuous American will spurn with contempt such baseness, and view it as calculated to destroy the principles and cut asunder the sinews of our Government.

Shall we never assume a National character? Are we to be eternally loaded with the arbitrary customs of Europe? Is it not evident that the principles on which our Government is founded, the rules and regulations as established by law for the government of the army as well as custom in the Revolutionary war, are all with me on this occasion? Nor do I doubt of having the approbation of all my fellow citizens who have the future welfare of the country at heart, as respects my conduct in this case.

I ask, General, must not the cause be radically wrong whose mover reduced to the pitiful necessity of artfully introducing long and labored communications from the disciples of Marshall Saxe, in order to bewilder the Court, and prevent an investigation of the lawfulness of the general order of the 30th of April 1801 on which the charges against me were based? Has not one of them (whom the General styles to the last army commanded by General Washington) told us in the language of despotism: "His inferiors have nothing left to their discretion—they *must obey*." Yes they must obey what the articles of War call "lawful commands." And I will here venture to observe that there never was, and I hope there never will be a Senate of the United States that would, by and with their advice and consent, place any man at the head of the American Army avowing such principles. Now, sir, let these gentlemen, who were so alert in mounting their war horses at the sound of the General's trumpet, lay their hands on their breasts and say, was it either lawful or honorable to give an opinion whilst a trial was pending?

But do you believe, or even suppose, Sir, that Americans would submit to shave their heads and wear *black* or *gray* lamb-skin caps, as Marshall Saxe recommended? Let those who admire and subscribe to the vagaries of Saxe answer that question. They will doubtless tell us that he has been considered a great man; but let them have it so, as they will have to acknowledge at the same time that he was visionary; fond of display and little in many things.

I would here ask the General and the admirers of Saxe what would be the fate of a General in the Prussian Service who would have dared by an order to crop off the queues of the troops under his command and substitute the Marshal's lamb-skin cap in opposition to the established regulations of his King? It would not require the second sight of a North Briton to discover what the fate of that General would be under Old Fritz. And shall a General in the American Army assert with impunity such a power, in open violation of the laws and established regulations? I shall never bring myself to believe that the legitimate authority of our country will suffer so dangerous a precedent to be established in the United States.

I shall close this letter with one other remark on the conduct of the General in putting into action his plans in order to gain his point. A few weeks previous to the commencement of my trial, he wrote to the commanding officer at New Orleans: "You will be pleased to say to the gentlemen of the corps that the President of the United States, without any public expression, has thought proper to adopt our fashion of the hair by cropping." Now, Sir, I can not believe or even suppose that the President of the United States would stoop to such an expedient in order to obtain a verdict against me! But if he has parted with his locks, and authorized the General to use his name for the purpose before mentioned, it would astonish me indeed, and for the honour of my country I hope and trust that it is not the case. Should it unfortunately be so, it would establish this position, that the President was sensible of the illegality of the order of the 30th of April 1801, and that by cropping his hair, and adding his weight to that of the General's it might probably reconcile the army and prevent the National Legislature from investigating the illegality of the order and of the General's conduct towards me. I fear that

I have tried your patience with the length of this letter, but as it may be of some importance to the interests of our country to throw as much light as possible on a subject founded in tyranny, I shall from time to time take the liberty of stating to you such matters as have occurred through the course of this unprecedented persecution.

Within a fortnight after the date of this letter (September 7, 1805) Colonel Butler lay dead of yellow fever. He realized the "blessing of being taken away by the climate and disease" of the country, of which he spoke in his letter of June 9, previous. The result of the court-martial which had given him so great trouble and anxiety has never transpired.

NOTES AND QUERIES.

Notes.

DEATH OF REV. EDWARD D. NEILL, D.D.—We regret to record the death of the Rev. Edward Duffield Neill, D.D., of Saint Paul, Minnesota, which took place on September 26, 1893. He was a son of Henry Neill, M.D., and was born in Philadelphia, August 9, 1823. After passing through the Sophomore class of the University of Pennsylvania, he entered Amherst College, and in 1842 received the degree of B.A. He also passed one year at Andover Theological Seminary, and in 1848 was ordained a minister of the Presbyterian Church. His first field of labor was in Illinois, and from thence he went to Minnesota, in which State most of his active and useful life was passed. He was conspicuously identified with the founding of the State University, the public school system, and Macalister College. During the Civil War, Dr. Neill became chaplain of the First Minnesota Regiment, and was subsequently appointed one of the private secretaries of President Lincoln. For two years he represented the United States as consul at Dublin, Ireland. After his return home he entered the ministry of the Reformed Episcopal Church. Dr. Neill was a cultivated, scholarly gentleman and an industrious and careful student of the history of the Northwest and of the earlier phases of that of the old thirteen colonies, and his contributions to the PENNSYLVANIA MAGAZINE will be remembered by our readers.

A WASHINGTON ORDER.—The following order of General Washington to Captain Caleb Gibbs, of his body-guard, was recently found in an old secretary in the Cooper mansion at Cooper's Point, Camden County, New Jersey:

"HEADQUARTERS, VALLEY FORGE,
"March 9, 1778.

"CAPTAIN CALEB GIBBS.

"SIR: Send Lieutenant Livingstone and fifty men to Morristown as an escort to Messrs. Cooper, Clymer and Potts as far as West Chester, and with the inclosed order for the transfer to his command at West Chester of the recruits, horses and wagons awaiting there an escort to headquarters.

"GEORGE WASHINGTON,
"*Commander-in-Chief.*"

RELICS FROM AN INDIAN MOUND NEAR BRADDOCK, PA.—The Hon. W. G. Hawkins, Jr., of Pittsburgh, Pa., kindly sent us relics (human bones and copper and shell ornaments) excavated from a mound on his farm near Braddock, Pa. "The mound," he writes, "was located on the first plateau above the Monongahela River, nearly on a level with Hawkins Station, about thirty feet in diameter at the base and five feet in height. About thirty years ago there was an elm-tree growing on the apex, but this shortly afterwards died and the stump showed about one hundred rings. In opening the mound we had a trench about three feet in width dug through its centre, and found the relics on a level with the

VOL. XVII.—33

surface surrounding the mound. The bones were of two persons, apparently of short stature, lying side by side in troughs made of two rows of flat stones, placed at right angles to each other, with one edge touching. Most of the bones crumbled into dust on being exposed to the air. The skulls were of unusual thickness. The mound was constructed of clay.''

GENERAL ARTHUR ST. CLAIR IN ACCOUNT WITH RICHARD AND WILLIAM BUTLER.—In an old day-book of Richard and William Butler, dating from the year 1766, the following account against Major-General Arthur St. Clair is entered, and, among others, Ephraim Blaine, Jacob Bousman, James Chambers, William Christy, Robert Callender, John Connoly, George Croghan, James Elliot, Daniel Elliot, William Elliot, Matthew Elliot, Peter Elrod, Joseph Erwin, John Gibson, William Grimes, Thomas Girty, John Kimberly, George M°Cully, Alexander M°Kee, John Ormsby, Ralph Naylor, and some Indians.

Dr. Maj^r Genl A^r St Clair (Public acc^t).

		£	s.	d.
1776	to the ferriage of 84 Men at Dunning's Creek, Juniatta, Pine ford & Susquehannagh	2	19	4
	to the carriage of My Company^s Baggage from Fort Pitt to Philadelphia	45	0	0
	to the Inlisting of 85 Men @ 10/ ℔ Man	42	10	0
	to the Bounty of 85 who found their own Riffles	212	10	0
	to the Porterage of the Regimental from the Barracks to the Vessell	0	18	0
	to Cash for Repairing the Mens Riffles	17	8	0
	to Cash Paid for a Drum for my Comp^y	8	0	0
	to Extra Expences of My Company^s subsistance from the Dates of Inlistments to the time they Drew Retions	142	15	6
	to Cash Paid 23 Men who found their own Blankets @ 15/ ℔ man	17	5	0
July	to the amount of My Comp^{ys} Half pay for the Months of Ap^l May, June & July as ℔ Pay Roll	529	0	0
23	to Cash Paid your self 46 Dollars	17	5	0
28	to Cash ℔ your order in favour of Ensign Hoffner	10	10	0
29	to Cash ℔ your self 60 Dollars	22	10	0
"	to ditto Paid Doct^r Hogan ℔ your order	14	12	6
	to Cash Paid Co^l Wood Being the ballance of pay as Maj^r	10	10	0
1777	to the Bounty of 30 Men @ 7/10 ℔ man	225	0	0
Ap^l 20	to Cash returned to you	205	2	6
		£1518	16	9

Contra Cr.

1776	By Cash Rec^d by the hand of Richard Butler	£135	0	0
	By Cash p^r Captⁿ Thomas Butler	31	10	0
	By Cash p^r Self at Biddles	189	0	0
	By Cash p^r y^r Self at the Barracks	81	0	0
	By the Ballance of Captⁿ Huffnagles acc^t	195	3	6
	By Cash p^r Self 144 Dollars	54	0	0
	By Cash p^r Ensⁿ M°Millan at Shippensburgh	9	15	0
	By Cash p^r Self 72 Dollars	27	0	0
	By Cash Rec^d for Recruiting my Comp^y at Ticonderoga	675	0	0

Queries.

COMMANDERS OF THE ARMY OF THE UNITED STATES.—The following list is submitted that any errors in it may be detected and corrected.　　　　J. H. M.

Commanders of the Army of the United States.

General George Washington, Virginia, June 17, 1775.
Major-General Henry Knox, Massachusetts, December 23, 1783.
Captain and Brevet Major John Doughty,[1] June 20, 1784.
Lieutenant-Colonel and Brevet Brigadier-General Josiah Harmar, Pennsylvania, September 29, 1789.
Major-General Arthur St. Clair, Pennsylvania, March 4, 1791.
Major-General Anthony Wayne, Pennsylvania, March 5, 1792.
Brigadier-General James Wilkinson, Maryland, December 15, 1796.
Lieutenant-General George Washington, Virginia, July 3, 1798.
Major-General Alexander Hamilton, New York, December 15, 1799.
Brigadier-General James Wilkinson, Maryland, March 5, 1802.
Major-General Henry Dearborn, Massachusetts, January 27, 1812.
Major-General Jacob Brown, Pennsylvania, January 24, 1814.
Major-General Alexander McComb, Michigan, May 24, 1828.
Major-General Winfield Scott, Virginia, June 25, 1841. To be Lieutenant-General by Brevet, March 20, 1847.
Major-General George Brinton McClellan, Pennsylvania, November 1, 1861.
Major-General Henry Wager Halleck, New York, July 11, 1862.
Lieutenant-General Ulysses Simpson Grant, Ohio, March 27, 1864. To be General of the Army, July 25, 1866.
General William Tecumseh Sherman, Ohio, March 4, 1869.
Lieutenant-General Philip Henry Sheridan, Ohio, November 1, 1883. To be General of the Army, June 1, 1888.
Major-General John McAllister Schofield, New York, August 13, 1888.

BARROWS.—I am a descendant of John Barrows, who came to Salem, Massachusetts, in 1637, and have been informed that a descendant of the name residing in Philadelphia has a genealogy of the family in England, with the coat of arms. The address or correspondence is requested.
　　　　MISS NELLIE BARROWS.
102 Elm Street, Montpelier, Vermont.

DESCENDANTS OF THE SIGNERS OF THE DECLARATION OF INDEPENDENCE.—The undersigned, who is compiling a work upon "The Signers of the Declaration of Independence and their Descendants," is very anxious to obtain the following data, relative to certain descendants of Robert Morris: 1. Date and place of death of Robert Morris, eldest son of the "Signer." 2. Also of "Signer's" fourth son, Charles Morris. 3. Date of marriage of Mary White Morris, daughter of Robert Morris (son of the "Signer"), to Paul Hamilton Wilkins (in March, 1827). 4. Date of second marriage of eldest daughter of Robert Morris (son of the "Signer") to John Cosgrove. 5. Date and place of death of Benjamin Shoemaker Morris, son of Robert Morris (son of the "Signer"), who died in infancy. 6. Date and place of birth of Sally Kane, daughter

[1] The senior captain of artillery commanding the Second Continental Artillery, now Light Battery F, Fourth Regiment of United States Artillery.

of Colonel John and Sybil (Kent) Kane, who married Thomas Morris, second son of the "Signer." 7. Dates and places of birth of Robert Kane Morris, Henry W. Morris, Harriet Morris, Emily Morris, Archibald Morris, William Morris, William White Morris, and Charles Frederick Morris, children of Thomas Morris and grandchildren of the "Signer." 8. Dates and places of death of Robert Kane Morris, Archibald Morris, and William Morris (not the latter's brother, William *White* Morris, who died November 5, 1865), three of the children of said Thomas Morris. 9. Middle name of Henry W. Morris, second son of said Thomas Morris. 10. Also place of death (September 13, 1847, in Mexico) of Charles Frederick Morris, youngest son of said Thomas Morris. 11. Dates and places of death of [Robert] Morris Nixon, Henry Nixon, and David Walker Nixon, children of Henry and Maria (Morris) Nixon, and grandchildren of the "Signer."

I will be very greatly obliged for any one or more of the data indicated above.   FRANK WILLING LEACH.
254 South Twenty-third Street, Philadelphia.

FORMAN, OR FOREMAN.—Information is desired concerning Ezekiel Forman (or Foreman), who left four children,—Samuel, Mary, Sarah, and Richard. The family belonged to Haverford Township, Delaware County, Pennsylvania. Ezekiel's brother John married Amy Britton. John was born in 1747; died in 1814.

Any reader of the MAGAZINE having knowledge of the ancestry of Ezekiel, or of his relationship to the New Jersey Formans, will confer a favor by communicating with

FRANCIS H. WILLIAMS.

JOHN GALBRAITH.—Information is desired as to the parentage of John Galbraith, who died in Donegal Township, Lancaster County, in 1769. In his will, on file at Lancaster, he mentions his wife Darechos, his daughters Elizabeth Spear, Mary Cook, Janett Work, and Barbera Allison, and his grandson, Galbraith Patterson.
Chestnut Hill, Philadelphia.   EDMUND H. BELL.

"HISTORY OF THE FOREST, ST. GEORGE'S, AND OLD DRAWGER'S CHURCHES, OF NEW CASTLE COUNTY, DELAWARE."—Can any of your readers give me information of a book or pamphlet entitled "History of the Forest, St. George's, and Old Drawger's Churches, of New Castle County, Delaware," by the Rev. Thomas Read, D.D.?
JAMES H. ELLIOT.
Tusculum, Wilmington, Delaware.

Replies.

RIDGWAY.—Family records of births are sometimes found in unusual places. On several occasions I have seen them in frames hung upon the wall of the reception-room, and in one case painted on the side of the barn, the latter being probably a duplicate copy.

In my library is a book of nearly one thousand pages, printed in 1679, entitled "The Testimony of Truth Exalted by the collected labours of that worthy man, good scribe and faithful minister of Jesus Christ, Samuel Fisher, who died a prisoner for the Testimony of Jesus and Word of God, Anno 1665."

In said book is the following record of a Ridgway family:

Lott Ridgway was born August the 9. 1718, at nine o'clock at night, son of Josiah Ridgway and Sarah his wife.

Lott Ridgway departed this life December the 30. 1784, aged 66 yrs, 4 mos and 3 weeks.

The Time of Birth & Names of the Severall Children Born unto Lot Ridgway by Susanna his Wife.

    I. Samuel Ridgway, Born about 5 in the morning, First day of the Week Feb^{ry} 10. 1751.

   II. Caleb Ridgway, July 29 : 1752, about 10 in the morning.

  III. Barzillai Ridgway, Born May 21 :: about 2 in the afternoon 1754.

  IV. Hephzibah Ridgway, Born November 20, 1755, about 5 at Night.

   V. Lott Ridgway, Born May 24 about Nine aClock at Night 1757.

  VI. Daniell Ridgway. Born December 4th 1758, about 4 in the morn.

 VII. Beaula Ridgway, Born the 4th day of ye week, May the 28th, about break of day 1760.

VIII. Richard Ridgway, Born October 2ond about midnight 1762, on 6th day of the week.

  IX. Freedom Ridgway. Born December 18th on ye 1st day of ye week, in ye evening 1763.

   X. Susannah Ridgway Born July 18th on ye 6th day of ye week in ye morning 1765.

Mount Holly, New Jersey.   Barclay White.

Notes to above.—Hepzibah Ridgway married —— Tonkin (probably Edward). Beulah Ridgway married Jacob Lamb ; second wife ; no issue. Susannah Ridgway married John Dobbins, Sen., of Mount Holly.

                                              B. W.

Book Notices.

History of Slavery in Connecticut. By Bernard C. Steiner, Ph.D. Johns Hopkins University Studies in Historical and Political Science. 84 pp.

Few questions have been more interesting to the American people than slavery, and the number of works which have appeared upon the subject has been proportional to the interest aroused. The author divides his history into two periods,—the first, from 1636 to 1774, embracing Indian slavery, colonial legislation on slavery, trials concerning slaves, and their social condition in colonial times ; the second period, extending from 1774 to 1861, is marked by the diminution and extinction of slavery, closing with the acceptance of the Fifteenth Amendment in 1869.

Early Sketches of George Washington, reprinted with Biographical and Bibliographical Notes. By William S. Baker. Philadelphia, 1894. 150 pp. J. B. Lippincott Co.

The earliest sketch of Washington which aspires to the dignity of a biography was that of Thomas Condie, published in 1798 in the *Philadelphia Monthly Magazine.* Prior to this date a number of sketches or notices of more or less interest had appeared in various forms of publication ; these Mr. Baker has reprinted in chronological sequence, giving a strict rendering of each without comment or correction, but adding valuable and interesting biographical and bibliographical notes. The description of the personal appearance of Washington, written in 1760 by Captain George Mercer, of Virginia, to a friend in Europe, is a very appropriate introduction to the series. A reproduction of Charles Willson Peale's original study for his three-quarters-length portrait, painted at Mount Vernon in May of 1772, adds interest to this excellent work.

THE ANCESTRY OF BENJAMIN HARRISON, PRESIDENT OF THE UNITED STATES OF AMERICA, 1889–1893, IN CHART FORM, SHOWING ALSO THE DESCENDANTS OF WILLIAM HENRY HARRISON, PRESIDENT OF THE UNITED STATES OF AMERICA IN 1841, AND NOTES ON FAMILIES RELATED. By Charles P. Keith. Philadelphia, 1893. 96 pp.

Few contemporary lives are as much studied as those culminating or suggested to culminate in the White House; and, as the ancestry of any man is a fact, important or otherwise, in his history, it is supposed that, while genealogists will value any work showing how far in each line, male and female, the ancestors of a living American can be traced, other people will be interested in such data concerning a President. The parental line of ex-President Benjamin Harrison is unique from its standing anterior to the Revolutionary War and its service during it and since. Moreover, while it is rare in this young country to find, even among the Presidents, any person both of whose great-grandfathers were Americans, he descends from many families known to have been here nearly two hundred years before his birth. The related families comprise the Armistead, Bacon, Bassett, Bedell, Burwell, Cary, Irwin, McDowell, Ramsey, Symmes, and Tuthill. The book is beautifully printed and bound by the J. B. Lippincott Co.

SCULL AND HEAP'S MAP OF PHILADELPHIA, 1750. Mr. Benjamin R. Boggs has very kindly presented to the Society a fac-simile reprint of "Scull and Heap's Map of Philadelphia and Parts Adjacent in 1750." Mr. Boggs, as a student of the early history of Philadelphia, became interested in this map, and, having found it to be so very rare, decided to have a fac-simile reprint made. Lobach's reprint of 1850 is also very difficult to obtain.

DEATH OF VICE-PRESIDENT GEORGE DE B. KEIM, ESQ.

We regret to announce the death of George de Benneville Keim, Esq., which took place on Monday morning, December 18, 1893. Mr. Keim was elected a member of the Historical Society in 1853, and at the date of his death was a Vice-President and Trustee of the Endowment Fund.

DEATH OF PROFESSOR OSWALD SEIDENSTICKER.

We open our forms to announce the death of another officer of the Historical Society. Professor Oswald Seidensticker, of the University of Pennsylvania, and for twenty years a member of the Council of the Society, departed this life on January 10, 1894.

MEETINGS OF THE HISTORICAL SOCIETY OF PENNSYLVANIA, 1893.

A stated meeting of the Society was held January 9, 1893, Vice-President Charles J. Stillé in the chair.

Thomas H. Dudley, Esq., was introduced and read a paper on "The Three Critical Periods in our Diplomatic Relations with England during the Late War," at the conclusion of which a vote of thanks was tendered.

A stated meeting was held March 13, 1893, President Charles J. Stillé presiding.

Librarian Frederick D. Stone announced that during the coming spring a series of lectures on Pennsylvania colonial history would be delivered before the Society, after which the President introduced Dr. James J. Levick, who accordingly read a paper on "The Early Welsh Quakers and their Emigration to Pennsylvania." A vote of thanks was passed.

A number of important additions to the collections of the Society were reported by the Secretary, among them an original portrait from life of General Philip H. Sheridan, by T. Buchanan Read, presented by Mr. E. T. Snow. From this portrait the head of Sheridan in the famous "Sheridan's Ride" was painted.

An original letter, dated Head-quarters Falls Township, 9th December, 1776, from Washington to Colonel Irwin, presented by Theodore Cooper, New York.

A manuscript map exhibiting the dimensions of the Weccacoe tract of land, divided among the heirs of Swen, Oele, and Andreas Swenson, old Swedish settlers, presented by Philip F. Snyder.

On motion, thanks were returned to the donors.

Nominations for officers of the Society to be voted for at the next stated meeting being in order, Franklin Platt, Esq., nominated the following :

President.
Charles J. Stillé.

Honorary Vice-Presidents.

Craig Biddle,   Ferdinand J. Dreer.

Vice-Presidents (to serve for three years).

Isaac Craig,   Henry Charles Lea.

Corresponding Secretary.
Gregory B. Keen.

Recording Secretary.
Hampton L. Carson.

Treasurer.
J. Edward Carpenter.

Members of Council (to serve four years).

James T. Mitchell,   William S. Baker,
Charles Hare Hutchinson.
And for the unexpired term of Charles J. Stillé,
William Brooke Rawle.

No other nominations being made, the chair appointed tellers to conduct the election on May 1.

A special meeting of the Society was held April 3, Vice-President Hon. Samuel W. Pennypacker in the chair.

President Charles J. Stillé read the second of the series of papers upon Pennsylvania colonial history, his subject being "The Social Changes caused by the Pennsylvania Constitution of 1776."

On motion, the thanks of the Society were tendered to President Stillé for his valuable and interesting paper.

A special meeting of the Society was held April 17, President Charles J. Stillé presiding.

The Rev. Joseph Henry Dubbs, D.D., read the third of the series of papers on Pennsylvania colonial history, his subject being "The Founding of the German Churches of Pennsylvania."

A vote of thanks was tendered.

The annual meeting of the Society was held May 1, President Charles J. Stillé presiding.

The Rev. Robert Ellis Thompson, on being introduced, read the fourth of the series of papers on Pennsylvania colonial history, his subject being "Civilization, Latin and Teuton, in America."

A vote of thanks was tendered to Rev. Dr. Thompson.

The annual report of the Council for the past year was read by its Secretary, Professor Gregory B. Keen.

The tellers appointed to conduct the annual election reported that the gentlemen nominated at the last stated meeting had been unanimously elected.

Dr. James J. Levick announced the deaths of Vice-President Horatio Gates Jones and Thomas H. Dudley, Esq.

A portrait of ex-Governor John F. Hartranft, by Matthew Wilson, was presented to the Society by Mr. Charles E. Smith.

A special meeting of the Society was held May 15, Vice-President Hon. Samuel W. Pennypacker in the chair.

Librarian Frederick D. Stone read the fifth of the series of historical papers, his subject being "The Revolution in Pennsylvania : a Social Picture."

On motion, a vote of thanks was tendered.

A stated meeting of the Society was held November 13, President Charles J. Stillé presiding.

The Rev. C. Ellis Stevens, on being introduced, read a paper entitled " From what Historical Sources came our National Constitution ?"

On motion, a vote of thanks was tendered to Rev. Dr. Stevens.

The Secretary announced the following contributions to the Society :

From Hon. M. Russell Thayer, two letters of George Washington Parke Custis, in which the writer expresses his opinion on the subject of the relative value of the various portraits of Washington.

From Professor Fairman Rogers, a manuscript " Map of the Highlands in the State of New York, Done for His Excellency Gen¹ Washington by Robert Erskine F.R.S.G. of the Army.   July, 1779."

The thanks of the Society were tendered to Judge Thayer and Professor Rogers for their respective gifts.

OFFICERS

OF

THE HISTORICAL SOCIETY OF PENNSYLVANIA.

PRESIDENT.

CHARLES J. STILLÉ.

HONORARY VICE-PRESIDENTS.

CRAIG BIDDLE,   FERDINAND J. DREER.

VICE-PRESIDENTS.

SAMUEL W. PENNYPACKER,   ISAAC CRAIG,
WILLIAM S. BAKER,   HENRY C. LEA.

CORRESPONDING SECRETARY.

GREGORY B. KEEN.

RECORDING SECRETARY.

HAMPTON L. CARSON.

TREASURER.

J. EDWARD CARPENTER.

LIBRARIAN.

FREDERICK D. STONE.

ASSISTANT LIBRARIAN.

JOHN W. JORDAN.

COUNCIL.

JAMES T. MITCHELL,   CHARLES HARE HUTCHINSON,
WILLIAM S. BAKER,   SAMUEL W. PENNYPACKER,
JOHN C. BROWNE,   CHARLES ROBERTS,
EDWIN T. EISENBREY,   OSWALD SEIDENSTICKER,
GEORGE HARRISON FISHER,   WILLIAM BROOKE RAWLE,
JOHN B. GEST,   WILLIAM G. THOMAS.

EXTRACTS FROM THE REPORT OF THE FINANCE COMMITTEE TO THE COUNCIL.

Statement of Finances, December 31, 1892.

DR.

The Treasurer and Trustees charge themselves with the following:

To Real Estate	$181,701 41
To Investments	82,913 67
To Cash	6,947 54

CR.

The Treasurer and Trustees claim credit for:

General Fund, Capital Invested . . .	$5,500 00
" " Loan Account to Real Estate	5,500 00
" " Cash, Interest Account . .	106 36
Binding Fund, Capital Invested . . .	5,800 00
" " Cash, Interest Account . .	165 68
Library Fund, Capital Invested . . .	16,000 00
" " Cash, Interest Account . .	127 72
Publication Fund, Capital Invested . .	32,111 78
" " " Uninvested . .	3,652 97
" " Cash, Interest Account .	1,821 44
Endowment Fund, Capital Invested . .	24,001 89
" " Cash, Capital Account .	445 03
Investments of Real Estate	126,201 41
Balance Donation for Harleian Publications	58 00
" in hands of Treasurer, Real Estate Account	193 42
Church Records Fund	100 00
Sundries	276 97
	$221,562 62 $221,562 62

General Fund.

Receipts: Cash on hand, January 1, 1892	. . . .	$292 55
Annual Dues, 1892	. . . .	6,520 00
Interest and Dividends .	. . . .	816 45
Trustees Endowment Fund .	. . . .	1,067 50
Donations . . .	. . . .	294 50
		$8,991 00
Disbursements: General Expenses and Taxes for 1892	.	8,884 64
Balance in hands of Treasurer	. . . .	$106 36

Binding Fund.

Receipts: Cash on hand, January 1, 1892	. . . .	$121 15
Interest and Dividends .	. . . .	386 00
		$507 15
Disbursements for Binding, 1892 .	. . . .	341 52
Balance in hands of Trustees .	. . . .	$165 63

Library Fund.

Receipts: Cash on hand, January 1, 1892	. . . .	$267 05
Interest, Dividends, and Sales	. . .	860 75
		$1,127 80
Disbursements: Books purchased in 1892	. . . .	1,000 08
Balance in hands of Trustees .	. . . .	$127 72

Publication Fund.

Receipts: Cash on hand, January 1, 1892	. . . .	$1,891 17
Interest, Dividends, and Rents	. . .	2,067 91
Subscriptions to Magazine, etc.	. . .	969 60
		$4,928 68
Disbursements for 1892 .	. . . .	3,107 24
Balance in hands of Trustees .	. . .	$1,821 44

Endowment Fund.

Receipts: Interest and Dividends .	. . .	$1,067 50
Disbursements: Paid to Treasurer of General Fund	.	1,067 50

Church Records Fund.

Cash on hand, January 1, 1892	. . . .	$100 00

INDEX.

(Family surnames of value in genealogical research are printed in SMALL CAPITALS; names of places in *italics*.)

(527)

HISTORICAL SOCIETY OF PEN...

The following are some of the Historical and Genea...
serials to be found on the tables in the Library:

FOREIGN.

Collections of the Powys-Land Club	London.
Gloucestershire Notes and Queries	London.
Miscellanea Genealogica et Heraldica	London.
Northamptonshire Notes and Queries	Northampton.
Notes and Queries	London.
Northern Notes and Queries	Edinburgh.
The East Anglican, or Notes and Queries on subjects connected with the Counties of Suffolk, Cambridge, Essex, and Norfolk.	Ipswich.
The Genealogist	London.
The Index Library	London.
The Western Antiquary or Note Book for Devon, Cornwall, and Somerset	Plymouth.
Yorkshire Notes and Queries: with Yorkshire Genealogist, Yorkshire Bibliographer, and Yorkshire Folk-Lore Journal	Bradford.

DOMESTIC.

American Journal of Numismatics and Bulletin of American Numismatic and Archæological Societies	Boston.
American Notes and Queries	Philadelphia.
Essex Institute Historical Collections	Salem, Mass.
Magazine of American History	New York.
Magazine of Western History	Cleveland.
New York Genealogical and Biographical Record	New York.
Notes and Queries, Historical and Genealogical	Harrisburg, Pa.
Proceedings and Collections of the Wyoming Historical and Geological Society	Wilkesbarre, Pa.
Proceedings of the Academy of Natural Sciences	Philadelphia.
Southern Historical Society Papers	Richmond, Va.
The American Journal of Philology	Baltimore, Md.
The American Catholic Historical Researches	Philadelphia.
The Book Mart	Pittsburg, Pa.
The Cambrian	Cincinnati.
The Granite Monthly	New Hampshire.
The Historical Record, with Notes and Queries	Wilkesbarre, Pa.
The Iowa Historical Record	Iowa City.
The Journal of the Military Service Institution	New York.
The Library Journal	New York.
The Nation	New York.
The New England Historical and Genealogical Register	Boston.
The New England Magazine and Bay State Monthly	Boston.
The Pennsylvanian	Philadelphia.
The Rhode Island Magazine	Newport.

[Publishers of other serials will please forward prospectus.]

This book should be returned to the Library on or before the last date stamped below.

A fine is incurred by retaining it beyond the specified time.

Please return promptly.

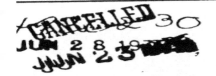

CPSIA information can be obtained
at www.ICGtesting.com
Printed in the USA
BVHW082208110819
555624BV00020B/3018/P